W9-BVQ-816

THE ARCHAEOLOGY OF CANTERBURY
NEW SERIES

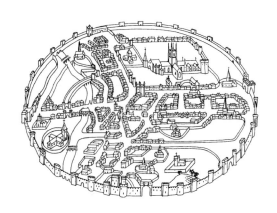

THE ARCHAEOLOGY OF CANTERBURY

New Series

VOLUME V

THE ROMAN WATERMILLS AND SETTLEMENT AT ICKHAM, KENT

by

Paul Bennett, Ian Riddler and Christopher Sparey-Green

with

Christopher Young

Malcolm Lyne, Quita Mould and Robert Spain

and

Barry Ager, Joanna Bird, Richard Brickstock, John Casey, Peter Clark, Hilary Cool, Brenda Dickinson, Louise Harrison, Colin Haselgrove, Martin Henig, Don Mackreth, Maeve Palmer, Adrienne Powell, John Shepherd, David Sherlock, Sasha Smith, David Starley, Adrian Tribe, Penelope Walton Rogers, David Williams, Andrew Wilson, Tania Wilson and Susan Youngs

Published by Canterbury Archaeological Trust Ltd
2010

Produced by Canterbury Archaeological Trust Ltd
Printed in Great Britain by Lanes (South East) Ltd

This publication was funded by English Heritage

ISBN 978-1-870545-19-8
British Library Cataloguing-in-Publication Data
A catalogue record for this book is available from the British Library

DEDICATED
to
JIM BRADSHAW

1919–2001

CONTENTS

Foreword xi
List of figures xiii
List of plates xvii
List of tables xix
Acknowledgements xxi

PART 1: INTRODUCTION (Paul Bennett and Christopher Sparey-Green)
Topography and geology 5
Previous archaeological work in the area 8
The excavations 10
The site archive 12
Structure of the report 13

PART 2: THE SITE (Paul Bennett, Robert Spain and Christopher Sparey-Green)
Introduction (Paul Bennett) 15
Prehistoric and early Roman periods (Christopher Sparey-Green)
    The northern quarry 1972–3 15
    The main quarry 1973–4 16
The later Roman settlement (Christopher Sparey-Green)
    Introduction 18
    The northern quarry 1972–3 20
    The main quarry 1973–4 20
    The Roman watermills (Robert Spain with Christopher Sparey-Green and Andrew Wilson) 42
    Roman burials 68
Post-Roman period (Christopher Sparey-Green)
    Late Roman and early Anglo-Saxon periods 70
    Medieval and post-medieval periods 71

PART 3: THE COINAGE AND CERAMICS (Ian Riddler and Malcolm Lyne)
Introduction (Ian Riddler) 73
The Coins
    Iron Age coins (Colin Haselgrove) 73
    Roman coins (Richard Brickstock and John Casey) 74
The pottery (Malcolm Lyne)
    Introduction 84
    Methodology 84

Fabrics 84
The assemblages 93
Miscellaneous sherds..119
The pot from Burial B 119
The Oxfordshire wares 120
The amphorae (David Williams and Malcolm Lyne)..120
Samian and Argonne wares (Joanna Bird with Brenda Dickinson) 121
The changing pattern of pottery supply 132
The ceramic evidence for specialist activities 138

PART 4: THE SMALL FINDS (Quita Mould and Ian Riddler)
Introduction (Ian Riddler)..141
Military equipment (Quita Mould) 142
Weaponry...142
Armour 144
D-shaped buckles 145
Helmets..145
Military fittings..148
Late Roman belt- and strap-fittings and other equipment (Ian Riddler, Barry Ager and
Quita Mould) 152
Objects of personal adornment and dress (Quita Mould) 167
Brooches (Don Mackreth)..167
Ear-rings 177
Miscellaneous jewellery 177
Pins (Quita Mould, Ian Riddler, Adrian Tribe and Susan Youngs) 178
Glass beads (H E M Cool)..188
Pendants (Martin Henig) 190
Bracelets (Quita Mould and Ian Riddler)...196
Finger rings (Martin Henig) 203
Personalia (Quita Mould)...206
Hobnails and cleats..206
Leather shoes 207
Toilet implements 212
Combs (Ian Riddler)..213
Objects with possible religious significance (Quita Mould)..215
Bells...215
Mount 215
Figurine (Peter Clark)...215
Circular tank fragment...217
Weights and measures (Quita Mould)...218
Steelyard..218
Lead weights..219
Measuring instruments 220
Written communication (Ian Riddler)..220
Styli 220
Household implements (Quita Mould) 223
Knives..223
Hones (Ian Riddler) 227
Locks and keys...228

Domestic implements (Quita Mould) 232
    Lighting 232
    Cooking utensils 232
    Frying pans 232
    Ladles 232
    Strainers 235
    Pestles and rubbing stone (Tania Wilson) 235
    Spoons (David Sherlock) 235
    Vessels 241
    Buckets and handles 248
    Box fittings 249
    Other fixtures and fittings 249
    Querns (Ian Riddler) 251
Agricultural implements (Quita Mould) 255
    Shears 255
    Harvesting tools 257
    Hooked blades 257
    Spud 258
Fishing equipment (Quita Mould) 258
    Netting needle 258
    Boathook 258
    Lead alloy weights 258
Transport (Quita Mould) 258
    Spurs 260
    Hipposandals 260
    Horseshoes 262
    Bridle-bits 262
    Curb-bits 262
    Cart fittings 262
Structural fittings (Quita Mould) 262
    Collars 262
    Window grilles and glass (Quita Mould, John Shepherd and Sasha Smith) 264
    Nailed bindings 264
    Hinges 264
    Split-spiked loops and staples 264
    Ring-headed pins 264
    Wall hooks, joiners' dogs and cleats 264
    Timber nails 265
    Lead alloy structural fittings 265
    Ceramic building material (Louise Harrison) 265
    Miscellaneous metalwork 276
Crafts and industries (Quita Mould) 276
    Millstones (Ian Riddler and Robert Spain) 277
    The bearing blocks (Robert Spain) 285
    Metal-working 289
    Non-ferrous metal-working 291
    Wood-working 293
    Leather-working 293
    Textile manufacture 295

Flax processing (Penelope Walton Rogers)..297
Modelling tools...298
Miscellaneous craft tools...298
Metal-working debris 298
Bone and antler waste (Ian Riddler)..301

PART 5: THE SMALL FINDS: SPATIAL DISTRIBUTION AND CHRONOLOGY
(Quita Mould and Ian Riddler)
Early Roman small finds...303
Material ascribed to areas of the site...304
Early Anglo-Saxon settlement 307

PART 6: THE ENVIRONMENTAL MATERIAL
Animal bone (Maeve Palmer and Adrienne Powell) 311
Representation of the main domestic animals...312
Other species 314
Ageing and sexing...315
Butchery..316
Pathology..317
Measurements...318
Discussion 318
Human bone (Ian Riddler) 318

PART 7: ICKHAM AND EAST KENT IN THE LATE ROMAN PERIOD (Paul Bennett)
Introduction...321
The evolution of the Ickham settlement
Pre-Roman occupation 322
Early Roman occupation 322
The third-century settlement 323
The fourth-century settlement 323
The post-Roman settlement 325
East Kent rivers..326
The Roman road system of east Kent 328
The Richborough to Canterbury road and settlement in the in the Little Stour valley 331
The Little Stour 335
Discussion: the Ickham site in its wider context..335

PART 8: SUMMARY (Christopher Sparey-Green)
Summary...347
Résumé...347
Zusammenfassung..348

APPENDIX I: LEATHER OBJECTS AND SCRAP (Quita Mould)..351
APPENDIX II: A ROMAN IRON HAMMER HEAD (Robert Spain)..353

BIBLIOGRAPHY 355
INDEX...367

FOREWORD

Writing a foreword for the report of an excavation in which I was involved three decades ago gives rise to any number of feelings. The first is gratitude – to those who involved me in one of the most interesting sites on which I have worked as well as to those who worked there with me, and to the Canterbury Archaeological Trust for finally galvanising everyone to do the work necessary to bring the results to publication. The second is regret that some of the prime movers for the rescue of the site have not lived long enough to see its publication. There are also fond memories of the excavation itself. It has also been salutary to realise the extent to which approaches to what used to be known as rescue archaeology have changed, and also the transformation of our understanding of the late Roman period and the Kent area to the extent that virtually all the hypotheses put forward by me after the excavation have now been disproved.

Ickham was dug long before the days of developer-funded archaeology under the auspices of PPG16 and in the early days of organised archaeological units. Even by the standards of those days the response was less than adequate for a site of this importance, particularly by comparison to what was even then happening in the Thames valley. At a time when the gravel terraces of the Middle and Upper Thames were being systematically surveyed, leading to the allocation of resources for major excavations, this was not possible, for a number of reasons, on the southern shore of the Thames estuary.

Instead the site had to be salvaged from in front of the quarry drag-lines. The pit was roughly rectangular and the gravel was extracted in strips working away from the river. The topsoil was removed from each strip of the quarry a little in advance of quarrying by the kindness of the quarry company. Jim Bradshaw's volunteers then recorded what they could before extraction of gravel from each strip began in earnest. Even so, much of the main quarry was seen only fleetingly with many of the finds being recovered from the spoil heaps, and sections recorded from boats floating on the water in the flooded gravel pit. It was fortunate that a wide margin of land was left on the south-western edge of the quarry since it was here that remains of three watermills were subsequently excavated.

I should at this point stress how much the Ickham site owes to the late Jim Bradshaw. If it had not been for his persistence in salvaging the site in appalling conditions, it would have been lost without knowledge and without record. Much of what we know results from the rescue work carried out by Jim and a small band of volunteers. It was his efforts and persistence which persuaded the forerunner of English Heritage, the Directorate of Ancient Monuments and Historic Buildings of the then Department of the Environment, to fund a short period of excavation under my direction in the summer of 1976 and to provide some further resources subsequently. Jim could have regarded me as the cuckoo in the nest. Instead he welcomed me in and gave me all the help that he could and shared with me all he knew about the site. It is very fitting that this volume should be dedicated to his memory and a matter of deep regret that he did not live to see publication completed.

In our short planned intervention, it was only possible to record the features in a couple of the strips of the quarry before the gravel was extracted, and to dig the land on its south-western margin. This, as noted above, contained probably three watermills, part of which had been dug already. Up-stream of this area everything lay under private woodland and down-stream there lay only the gaping maw of the quarry. At the time, these structures were a major advance in knowledge of mill structures while the water channels and associated features produced a range of artefacts remarkable both in their range, the state of their preservation, and in their quantity.

Cleary much was lost from the Ickham site. That can only be a matter of regret. Nonetheless much was recovered and much can be learnt from the evidence. Much of the speculation at the time of excavation that the site might be an imperial *fabrica* or otherwise military in its character must now be discounted. Nevertheless it is clear that Ickham was a major complex in its landscape carrying out a number of activities on an industrial scale. More work needs to be done in the future to place it properly in its immediate and wider landscape. More needs to be done, too, to assess the spread and role of this type of rural industrial complex in late Roman Britain.

This report provides the basis for doing so. The Canterbury Archaeological Trust, through diligent and patient effort, and working closely with the original excavators have managed to produce a coherent account of the site's development and use. The finds reports, including those on the ceramics, will form a major corpus of material for those working on the late Roman period. This volume finally places in the public domain what can be said about this riverside complex with its corn mills and other industry. Overall the report demonstrates how much can still be learnt from this site. It will be a source for future work for many years and a fitting tribute to the memory of Jim Bradshaw.

Christopher Young
Head of World Heritage and International Policy
English Heritage

March 2007

LIST OF FIGURES

Fig 1	Roman Kent	5
Fig 2	Map of north-east Kent	6
Fig 3	Detail plan of the Wickhambreax and Wingham area	7
Fig 4	General plan showing all features including the line of the Roman road, palaeochannel (shaded) and mills together with working areas. Inset detail Mill 1	11
Fig 5	Part of general plan showing phased features	17
Fig 6	Ditch sections, F301–F305 and F309	18
Fig 7	Trial trench through Road Section 1	19
Fig 8	Oblique sections (2 and 3) through Roman road	22
Fig 9	Road section 4	22
Fig 10	Detail plan showing Areas 1 and 6	23
Fig 11	Sections J, C and B	27
Fig 12	Sections G and D with key to sections	30
Fig 13	Plan of Pit 19	31
Fig 14	Section through Pit 19	31
Fig 15	Plan of Well 701	34
Fig 16	Section through Well 701	34
Fig 17	Plan of feature 335, Area 4	35
Fig 18	Detail plan of Channel C showing Mills 2 and 3 with pits 107 and 115	37
Fig 19	Detail plan of Mill 4	38
Fig 20	Detail plan showing Area 4 extension	40
Fig 21	Section through pit 414 and palaeochannel	41
Fig 22	Reconstruction view and plan of Mill 1	46
Fig 23	Reconstruction view of Mill 2	51
Fig 24	Reconstructed plan of Mill 3	52
Fig 25	Reconstructed plan of Mill 2	53
Fig 26	Distribution of Roman watermill sites and stray finds of powered millstones of Roman date in Britain.	64
Fig 27	Plan of inhumation burial B	68
Fig 28	Plan of inhumation burial A	68
Fig 29	All coins	75
Fig 30	Comparison between provisional and complete coin totals (2891 and 4373 legible coins, respectively)	75
Fig 31	Coins: Areas 10 and 14 by coin dates	75
Fig 32	Coins: Areas 10 and 14	75
Fig 33	Coins: all coins except Areas 10 and 14	76

Fig 34   Coins: Area 1 76
Fig 35   Coins: Area 4 77
Fig 36   Coins: 'Hut' 77
Fig 37   Coins: contexts 407 and 408..78
Fig 38   Coins: Area 2 78
Fig 39   Coins: Area 3 79
Fig 40   Coins: Area 5 79
Fig 41   Coins: excavated finds (Areas 1, 6 and 7)...80
Fig 42   Coins: metal-detected finds (Areas 2–5) 80
Fig 43   Actual number of coins and expected number in comparison to Richborough 81
Fig 44   Actual number of coins and expected number in comparison to Canterbury 81
Fig 45   Fourth-century coins. Actual number of coins and expected numbers in comparison to
          Richborough and Canterbury 82
Fig 46   Coarse and fine wares, Nos 1–17 86
Fig 47   Coarse and fine wares, Nos 18–36 90
Fig 48   Coarse and finewares, Nos 37–59 94
Fig 49   Coarse and finewares, Nos 60–79 98
Fig 50   Coarse and finewares, Nos 80–95 102
Fig 51   Coarse and finewares, Nos 96–116 106
Fig 52   Coarse and finewares, Nos 117–147 108
Fig 53   Coarse and finewares, Nos 148–162 114
Fig 54   Coarse and finewares, Nos 163–185 116
Fig 55   Coarse ware, No 186 119
Fig 56   Argonne ware, Nos 1–3 123
Fig 57   Argonne ware, Nos 4–6 124
Fig 58   Argonne ware, Nos 7–10 125
Fig 59   Argonne ware, Nos 11–13 126
Fig 60   Argonne ware, No 13..127
Fig 61   Argonne ware, Nos 14–15 130
Fig 62   Map showing potterysupply to Mill 1, *c* AD150–300 from British sources 133
Fig 63   Map showing pottery supply to Mill 1, *c* AD 150–300 from continental sources 134
Fig 64   Map showing pottery supply to Ickham, *c* AD 370–400+ from British sources............136
Fig 65   Map showing pottery supply to Ickham, *c* AD 370–400+ from continental sources......137
Fig 66   Weaponry..143
Fig 67   D-shaped buckles..144
Fig 68   Possible plume-holder (30) and decorative sheet appliqués...146
Fig 69   First-century harness fittings 149
Fig 70   Second- and third-century military fittings..150
Fig 71   Late Roman belt- and strap-fittings 160
Fig 72   Late Roman belt- and strap-fittings 161
Fig 73   Late Roman belt- and strap-fittings 162
Fig 74   Late Roman belt- and strap-fittings 163
Fig 75   Openwork fitting..166
Fig 76   Copper alloy sheath 167
Fig 77   Brooches 170
Fig 78   Brooches, ear-rings and jewellery fastening (209)...174
Fig 79   Metal hair pins...180
Fig 80   Copper alloy dress pin...182
Fig 81   Beads 189

Fig 82   Composition of pendants by XRF analysis 195
Fig 83   Copper alloy bracelets 198
Fig 84   Copper alloy bracelets 199
Fig 85   Bone or antler bracelets 202
Fig 86   Finger rings 204
Fig 87   Roman shoes: nailing patterns 208
Fig 88   Roman shoes: constructional details 210
Fig 89   Toilet implements (Nos 548 and 550) and comb fragments 214
Fig 90   Wooden figurine 216
Fig 91   Weights and measures 219
Fig 92   Styli 222
Fig 93   Knives and bone handle 224
Fig 94   Strap, lock fittings, mechanisms and latchlifters 229
Fig 95   Keys 231
Fig 96   Domestic implements 233
Fig 97   Domestic implements 234
Fig 98   Domestic implements 235
Fig 99   Spoons 237
Fig 100   Spoons and pewter vessels 238
Fig 101   Domestic implements 241
Fig 102   Glass vessels 244
Fig 103   Bucket and box fittings 249
Fig 104   Quernstones 250
Fig 105   Quernstone 254
Fig 106   Agricultural implements, possible boathook and fishing weights 256
Fig 107   Transport: horse bits and cart fittings 259
Fig 108   Cart fittings 260
Fig 109   Structural fittings 263
Fig 110   Roman tile: flue tile types 269
Fig 111   Roman tile: voussoir types 271
Fig 112   Roman tile: roof tile flange and cutaway types 273
Fig 113   Roman tile: signature marks 274
Fig 114   Millstone and whetstones 278
Fig 115   Millstones 282
Fig 116   Millstones 284
Fig 117   Millstones 286
Fig 118   Use and degradation of stones 288
Fig 119   Metal-working tools 290
Fig 120   Smithing (1254–6) and wood-working tools 292
Fig 121   Leather-working tools and textile implements 294
Fig 122   Textile-working, flax-working and modelling tools 296
Fig 123   Location of archaeological features visible as cropmarks close to Wickhambreaux 333

LIST OF PLATES

Pl I   Aerial view of Ickham and Wickhambreaux showing the line of the Roman road and the course of an old river channel prior to gravel extraction..1

Pl II   View south-west towards Wickhambreaux, summer 1973...2

Pl III   View north-east towards Wenderton Hoath, summer 1974 3

Pl IV   General view of Site 1 with Site 6 in the foreground, looking north-west across the valley of the Little Stour..4

Pl V   Aerial view showing fields south-west of Wickhambreaux with double and single ring-ditches...9

Pl VI   Aerial photograph of the main quarry during rescue excavation on 8th June 1974..........10

Pl VII   Work in progress in ?Area 3, Spring 1974 13

Pl VIII   Roman road section, ?Area 1..21

Pl IX   General view of Pit 333 showing plank lining and loose plank lying diagonally across lower fill...32

Pl X   Detail of Pit 333 showing a plank lying diagonally across the plank floor.......................33

Pl XI   Well 701 from the south-west showing part of the timber lining and surrounding brushwood 35

Pl XII   Detail of animal bones and flints within the timber structure 335 36

Pl XIII   General view of structure 335 36

Pl XIV   Area 1 as exposed in topsoil stripping Autumn 1973...47

Pl XV   The remains of Mill 1, as exposed in July 1974...48

Pl XVI   The same area of Mill 1 as Pl XV seen from the east 49

Pl XVII   The timber structure of Mill 2 looking north-west...50

Pl XVIII   General view of Site 6 looking north-west, with the main timber of Mill 4 in Channel D in the foreground 58

Pl XIX   Burial B looking north-east 68

Pl XX   Group of folded pewter vessels buried beneath stones, feature (802) or (902).................69

Pl XXI   Lead alloy pendants 191

Pl XXII   Lead alloy pendants 192

Pl XXIII   Lead alloy pendant no 282 194

Pl XXIV   Lead alloy pendant no 283 194

Pl XV   Detail of pole-axed ox skull 316

Pl XXVI   Slight earthworks of Roman road, boundary ditches and enclosures north-west of the road, east of Wickhambreaux 332

Pl XXVII   Air photograph of promontory site north-west of Ickham 334

Pl XXVIII   Hammer no 1233 353

Pl XXIX   Hammer no 1233, detail 353

LIST OF TABLES

Table 1   Period divisions used in the report for Roman coinage 74

Table 2   Ceramics from Context 1005 97

Table 3   Ceramics from Ditch 302 100

Table 4   Ceramics from Area 4, Layers 2–5, Pit 414 101

Table 5   Ceramics from Contexts 107 and 115 104

Table 6   Ceramics from Contexts 407.1 and 408 111

Table 7   Ceramics from Area 4, extension 113

Table 8   Ceramics from Context 333 115

Table 9   Ceramics from Well 701 118

Table 10   Oxfordshire industry products by vessel types 120

Table 11   Area 2 all contexts 121

Table 12   Area 4 all contexts 121

Table 13   The distribution of Argonne Wares 122

Table 14   Ceramic forms from third-century sites 139

Table 15   Ceramic forms from post AD 370 assemblages 139

Table 16   Military equipment 147

Table 17   First-century military material 149

Table 18   Second- and third-century military material 153

Table 19   Late Roman belt- and strap-fittings and other items 169

Table 20   Roman brooches 177

Table 21   Ear-rings 177

Table 22   Chain fragments 178

Table 23   Metal hair pins 179

Table 24   Investigative analysis of selected metal pins 186

Table 25   Bone pin 187

Table 26   Glass beads 190

Table 27   Lead alloy pendants 196

Table 28   Copper alloy bracelets 200

Table 29   Bone or antler bracelets 203

Table 30   Finger rings 206

Table 31   Hobnails 206

Table 32   Cleats 206

Table 33   Shoes of nailed construction 212

Table 34   Toilet implements 213

Table 35   Objects with possible religious significance 218

Table 36   Lead weights 219

Table 37   Concordance of stylus typologies 221

Table 38   Styli..221
Table 39   Knives...226
Table 40   Hones...228
Table 41   Locks and keys 230
Table 42   Domestic equipment and cooking utensils..236
Table 43   Spoons 239
Table 44   Spoons: qualitative analysis results 240
Table 45   Metal vessels 243
Table 46   Glass vessels...247
Table 47   Bucket fittings and handles...249
Table 48   Querns..252
Table 49   Agricultural implements...257
Table 50   Items relating to transport..261
Table 51   Iron nails by type and location 265
Table 52   Structural metalwork and glass 267
Table 53   Quantification of tiles by type and fabric 268
Table 54   Fabrics present in flue/voussoir types...272
Table 55   Roofing tile flange and cutaway types 272
Table 56   Signature marks 275
Table 57   Miscellaneous metal objects...275
Table 58   Millstones and bearing blocks 280
Table 59   Millstones and querns: slope of grinding surfaces 285
Table 60   Hammers..289
Table 61   Tongs 289
Table 62   Chisels and other implements with bevel-edged blades......................291
Table 63   Punches...291
Table 64   Wood-working tools 293
Table 65   Leather-working tools...295
Table 66   Textile-working implements..297
Table 67   Modelling tools...298
Table 68   Unfinished objects of copper alloy 298
Table 69   Early Roman objects from Ickham...304
Table 70   Early Anglo-Saxon objects from Ickham 308
Table 71   Number of identified specimens (NISP)...311
Table 72   Distribution of gnawing damage 312
Table 73   Distribution of butchery marks...312
Table 74   Loose teeth as a percentage of loose teeth and jaws 312
Table 75   Minimum number of elements for the main species 312
Table 76   Dog measurements mandibular...312
Table 77   Tooth wear in cattle and sheep 313
Table 78   Cattle fusion data...313
Table 79   Sheep fusion data...313
Table 80   Horse fusion data...313
Table 81   Measurements of cattle bones 314
Table 82   Withers heights..315
Table 83   Measurements of sheep bones 315
Table 84   Measurements of horse bones 317

ACKNOWLEDGEMENTS

A great number of individuals gave their time, expertise and enthusiasm, firstly to the work on site at Ickham in the 1970s and then during the report's long journey to publication. Sadly some of them are no longer with us to see the fruits of their labour, or to pass on their own thanks to friends and colleagues. The absence of Jim Bradshaw is particularly poignant at this time, but we know that he wished the following individuals who assisted in the salvage excavations from 1972–5 to be thanked: Alan Bruce, Kenneth Elks, Dr Gerrit Reizebos, John and Audrey Hamon, the late Fred Wall and Phylis Wall, Geoffrey and Annette Roberts, Philip Dunn, John Gower, Richard Cross, Damian Hone, Nigel Macpherson-Grant and John and Susan Scrivens.

Christopher Young would like most warmly to thank Clive Anderson, Katherine Kemp and Caroline Simpson who made his part of the excavation actually happen through their work on site, Mark Bowden and Jeany Poulsen for attempting to bring order into the archive after the excavation, and Freda Berisford for her invaluable work on the finds during and after the excavation. Like everybody else he owes an enormous debt to Jim Bradshaw who was the first to realise the importance of the site and, through his persistence and enthusiasm, saved so much information from it. He is also most grateful to the Canterbury Archaeological Trust for their efforts over the years to bring it successfully to publication.

Andrew Wilson would like to thank the Leverhulme Trust for the award of a Philip Leverhulme Prize which funded a period of research leave during part of which his contribution was written. Robert Spain extends his grateful thanks for the comments and advice given by Dr John Landels, Dr Michael Lewis and especially Dr David Sim in his study of the 'enigmatic' hammer. Susan Youngs would like to acknowledge the generously shared research of Ragnall Ó Floinn and help from Fraser Hunter, Richard Jones and Ralph Jackson. Thanks are extended to Cheryl Smith of the Museum of London for her helpful discussions on the pewter material. Quita Mould would also like to thank Jacqui Watson, English Heritage, for her work on minerally preserved organics and Adrian Tribe for his investigative analysis of many of the metal finds. Malcolm Lyne would like to thank Didier Bayard, Kay Hartley and Françoise Vallet for their comments on the Roman pottery.

The initial efforts to collate the archive and kick-start the publication process were undertaken by Maggy Taylor, Keith Parfitt and Barry Corke between 1994 and 1997. Peter Clark master-minded the production of an initial application for funding to English Heritage and with Ian Riddler guided the assessment process to the reporting stage.

We owe a considerable debt of gratitude to all the authors of assessment and publication reports, not only for their important contributions to the volume, but for their extreme patience in waiting for this volume to be completed and published. The final stage of publication was project-managed by Jane Elder who also prepared the volume for print with Mark Duncan. Drawings published here were made by Peter Atkinson, Dominique Bacon, Barry Corke, Will Foster, Beverley Leader, Kate Morton and Robert Spain. Sheila Rowntree drew the spoons. Photographs of the finds were made by Andrew Savage.

Finally we would like to thank English Heritage not only for their financial support, but also for the help and encouragement of their officers, particularly Peter Kendall, Dave Fellows and the late Sarah Jennings.

PART 1: INTRODUCTION

Paul Bennett and Christopher Sparey-Green

Between 1972 and 1975 part of a Roman roadside settlement was recorded in advance of quarrying in the valley of the Little Stour near Seaton in the parish of Ickham and Well (TR 231 590, Fig 3) some 8km east of Canterbury and 9km west of Richborough. Crossing the area was a Roman road extending roughly west-south-west to east-north-east flanked by settlement remains (Fig 4). On the southern side of the road, was a relict watercourse, visible in aerial photographs (Pl I) and the sites of perhaps four watermills of Roman date. North of the road line were traces of enclosures and

Pl I. View of Ickham and Wickhambreaux showing the line of the Roman road and course of an old river channel prior to gravel extraction. Copyright reserved. Image supplied by Bluesky International Ltd.

1

Pl II. View south-west towards Wickhambreaux, summer 1973, showing in the foreground, the earlier northern gravel working and, beyond, the cropmark of the Roman road on the main site prior to commencement of quarrying in the autumn.

other settlement remains. During the course of a salvage excavation the mills and a sample of the ditches, pits and other features were recorded while a large and varied assemblage of Roman artefacts, mostly of fourth-century date, was recovered.

Although the area had long been known for Roman finds, the site itself had not been studied in any detail. Plans for a major campaign of gravel extraction at Ickham had been noted in the local press by Dr Frank Jenkins, a local amateur archaeologist, and then president of the Canterbury Archaeological Society. In the early spring of 1972 when quarrying activities commenced west of the Wingham river and some way north-east of the present site, Jenkins arranged for a low level watching brief to be maintained by a member of the society. This provided the first hints that archaeological remains did survive in the flood plain at a point south of the junction of the Wingham river with the main channel of the Little Stour; a section of the road and traces of occupation

were recorded in the area of the silt lagoon and the northern quarry. In this report these early finds during 1972 and 1973 will be referred to as the 'northern quarry'.

Later, during July 1973, Jim Bradshaw, then a supervisor for the Forestry Commission and a local amateur archaeologist, undertook a watching brief of this northern quarry and recorded a section of the road cut for him by the gravel company (Fig 7, road section 1). Bradshaw also noted a linear bank extending west-south-west across the water meadows close to the Little Stour (Pl II). This he recognised as the line of the Roman road towards Wickhambreaux, continuing into an area threatened by the extension of the gravel workings. This area, here referred to as the 'main quarry', was subject to limited trenching prior to the stripping of topsoil, two trenches confirming the road line (Fig 9, road sections 2 and 3).

Jim Bradshaw, experienced in the identification of archaeological field monuments and with many discoveries

Pl III. View north-east towards Wenderton Hoath, summer 1974, showing the main quarry in the foreground with the earlier quarry beyond. Mill 1 may have lain in the area of darker soil close to the water's edge.

to his credit, recognised the importance of his find and after discussion with Frank Jenkins, agreed that the quarry workings should be regularly monitored and an excavation mounted to examine the road and adjacent features in more detail. With the consent of the quarry owners a site was chosen against the south-west boundary of the quarry, beyond the end of the first strip cleared of overburden (Area 1). Jenkins was unable to take part in the investigations because of work commitments, and Bradshaw, with members of the Ashford and District Archaeological Society and other volunteers, commenced investigations in late summer 1973, dividing their time between the maintenance of an intermittent watching brief in the active quarry and a minor excavation at the south-west corner of the workings.

As work continued under Bradshaw's direction during the winter of 1973 and the spring of 1974 the richness of the site quickly became apparent, with numerous features being recorded in the faces of the first strip of the quarry,

while a large assemblage of Roman coins and metal artefacts was retrieved. The most significant feature was a wooden structure, at first thought to be a sunken-featured hut, but later recognised as the well-preserved remains of a Roman mill channel and the foundations of the mill buildings (Channel C, containing Mills 2 and 3) (Pl IV). Identification of this structure was aided by the recognition during the expansion of the quarry in June 1974 of a better preserved mill, the subject of a detailed study by Robert Spain (Mill 1; Spain 1984a). Under the circumstances of discovery it proved difficult to retrieve and store the timbers and none survived for study. The state of the quarry at this point is illustrated in Pl III.

The quantity and quality of the finds being recovered from the quarry, particularly metal finds, led Bradshaw to enlist the support of a number of metal detectorists. The use of metal detectors on archaeological sites time was then almost unheard of at a time when their general

Pl IV. General view of Site 1 with Site 6 in the foreground, looking north-west across the valley of the Little Stour. Channel C and the timbers of Mills 2 and 3 are visible in the middle distance.

'hobby' use was already becoming a controversial issue in archaeological debate. The pace of extraction and the lack of experienced manpower meant that the site could only be sample excavated and even then the conditions prevailing at the time of excavation militated against the total recovery of all artefacts. The use of metal detectors was therefore inspired in that it allowed for the recovery of metal finds across those parts of the site where only inspection could take place and the increased recovery of finds, particularly coins (pp 76–8), where excavation did take place.

The combined discoveries prompted Jim Bradshaw to appeal for help from the then Department of the Environment. Following the exposure and identification of Mill 1 in the early summer of 1974, a professional team, directed by Christopher Young, mounted a short formal excavation (Pl IV) to record the initial structures before destruction (Young 1975; 1981). During this exercise, a further mill (here termed

Mill 4) was discovered (Pl XVII) though at the time this was thought to be a by-pass channel containing a sluice gate for Mills 2 and 3.

In addition to the mills there were many cut features, mostly ditches or pits, but little structural evidence, although ceramic building material and structural fittings were retrieved from the site. The quarry contractors reported to the excavators that a large masonry building was destroyed during quarrying, and although this was not seen by an archaeologist the remains were probably located in the initial northern quarry where Bradshaw noted building remains (*see* p 20). Observation continued until early spring 1975.

Although the importance of the site was recognised at the time, little integrated post-excavation study was carried out for nearly twenty years. During this period, some work was undertaken on the finds assemblages and site archive, and many catalogues and partial studies of the material

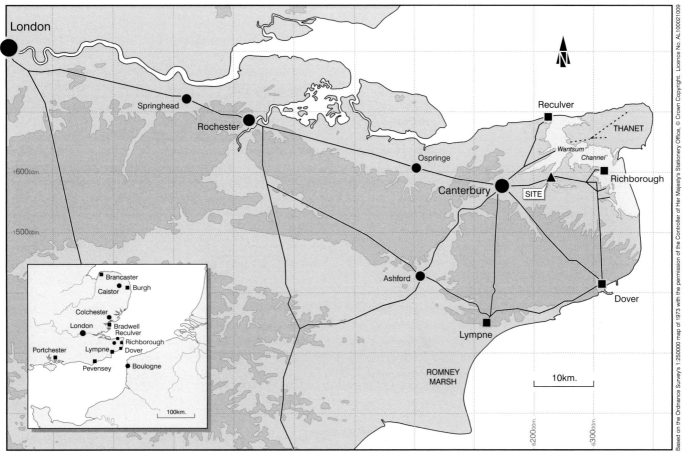

Fig 1. Roman Kent showing the site location, Roman road system and land over 60m with (inset) south-east England, English Channel and the French coast. Scale 1:625,000.

were prepared. A programme of post-excavation work by Keith Parfitt and Barry Corke, managed by Peter Clark, commenced in 1994 and, after a comprehensive study of the records and production of a base plan of the site, a draft report was produced (Clark 1997). The present report represents an expansion of this, developed from discussion of the results with a wide range of experts and further examination of the more intractable records. In particular, examination of photographs, correspondence and the sometimes fragmentary records has allowed the chronology of the archaeological operations to be refined and more certainty to be attached to the records and location of some features.

The present document therefore represents the collaborative effort of many specialists and the staff of the Canterbury Archaeological Trust, wholly funded by English Heritage. The report itself is an exercise in reconstructive archaeology, based on the existing archive of a site of national importance, but recorded under the most difficult of conditions, largely by volunteers, with few resources at their disposal.

Topography and geology

The site lay on the valley floor of the Little (or Lesser) Stour river that flows down the dip-slope of the North Downs (Fig 2) close to the hamlet of Seaton on the edge of the parish of Ickham and Well and about 1.3km to the north-east of the parish church. Situated adjacent to the south-eastern side of the present canalised course of the Little Stour, the excavated area was some 500 metres up-stream from the confluence with the Wingham river. The present course of the Little Stour was cut in the nineteenth century, replacing earlier channels of the river, one of which is marked by the modern parish boundary

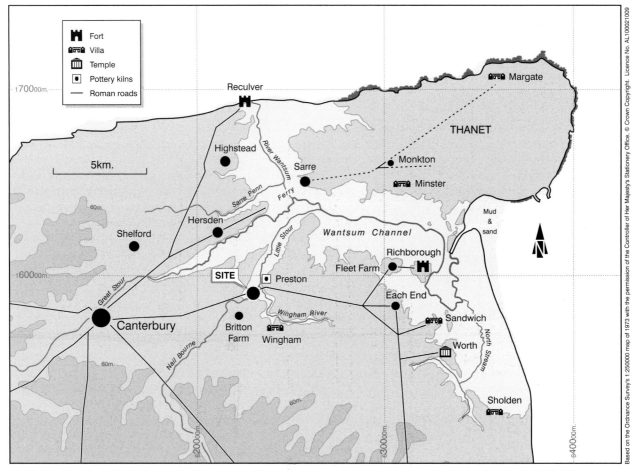

Fig 2. Map of north-east Kent showing the Stour estuary, Wantsum sea channel, principal sites and the site location. Scale 1:200,000.

some distance to the north-west, following the course of 'Blackhole Dyke' (Fig 3). The excavated site stands at an elevation of about 3m above Ordnance Datum. The subsoil here is primarily a flint river gravel, with some slightly higher areas of natural brickearth that represent extensions from the rising ground to the south.

The Little Stour originally emptied into the Wantsum channel which in Roman times separated the Isle of Thanet from mainland Kent (Figs 1 and 2), providing an inland waterway connecting the Thames estuary with the English Channel. The port of Richborough lay at its southern end. Today, the Little Stour joins with the Great Stour some 5km to the north-east of the Ickham site and flows through drained marshland which now represents the silted course of the ancient Wantsum. Passing below Richborough, the river enters the sea north of Sandwich. The Stour estuary and its attendant rivers were tidal and in the Roman period the Little

Stour tidal limit may have extended almost as far inland as the present site. Whilst it seems unlikely that the site could have been reached up-stream from the Wantsum channel, against the flow of the current, by even shallow draught boats, the reverse may not have applied. It may have been possible, even likely, for small boats to have followed the current down-stream into the Wantsum channel, the estuary and the port facilities at Richborough some 9km to the east.

Land communications in the Roman period were also good, the site lying against the route from Canterbury to Richborough, one of the most important road routes in the province. The exact route of this road was lost, perhaps as a consequence of changes in the Wantsum channel and the Stour river system feeding into it during the post-Roman period. A major road certainly passed through this site from Canterbury to cross the Wingham river and link with the important industrial site at Preston to the north, but the exact line of the road eastward to Richborough is, however, a matter of debate (pp 331–5).

Over the greater part of the site the natural gravel was sealed by a layer of up to 1m of clay, probably a waterlogged and altered brickearth, the majority of archaeological features

cut into this subsoil. The fills of features and the overlying deposits consisted of dark peaty soils containing varying amounts of archaeological material, frequently interleaved with lenses of gravel. Detailed descriptions of soils and the inter-relationships of intersecting features were often

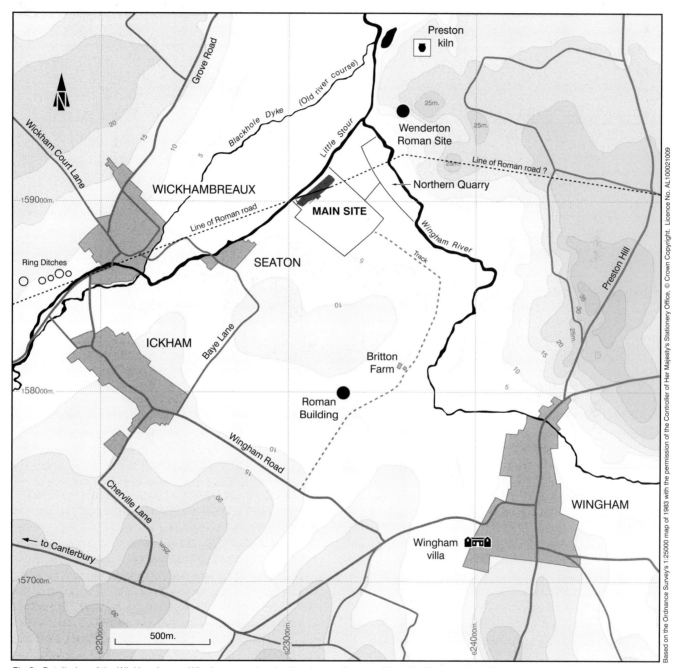

Fig 3. Detail plan of the Wickhambreaux-Wingham area showing the site, confluence of the Little Stour and the Wingham river and Roman roads. Scale 1:20,000.

impossible to discern and not recorded. In particular, some doubt arises as to the nature of the extensive layers of peaty soil and thin spreads of gravel, some of these possibly anthropogenic, others being depositions by water action in post-Roman watercourses.

A limited study had previously been undertaken of the peats higher up the Wingham valley, close to the present village, where observation of a sewer trench provided evidence for extensive peat deposits post-dating a Neolithic pit (Greenfield 1960; Godwin and Willis 1960, 68–9 quoted by F D Smith in litt, nd). The deposits are described as firstly, 'a fine detritus organic mud with fine sand' and secondly, 'a coarse detritus mud of reed swamp from valley fen deposit'. Two radiocarbon dates were obtained for these deposits, the former soil dating to 3105 ± 110 BP, the latter to 2340 ± 130 BP. Godwin and Willis concluded from this that from about 1600 BC to Roman times the chalk here was deforested with arable land and pasture. Evidence for brackish water at the base of the deposit showed that the sea had reached its present height at or before 1600 BC.

Smith concluded from his own observations on a visit to the present site that the presence of peat deposits below the Roman road confirmed the development of peat here in the late prehistoric period. He also felt that shells in some of the ditches indicated that there had been a tidal connection with the Wantsum at the time of infilling which would have brought brackish water with shells to the ditches. He concluded that peat had also been deposited naturally in the Roman period, this process continuing after that time, at least in the vicinity of the Little Stour. That the road had been visible as a cambered ridge of peat he ascribed to the road being laid on compacted peat, the peat deposits to either side being softer and able to shrink preferentially as peaty soils developed subsequently across the whole site.

The other major source of information about the early environment and the topography of the site is a limited number of air photographs which show the site prior to the commencement of quarrying. Those taken of the pasture areas in time of drought show the parched line of the Roman road in the area of the main site adjoined on the south by the darker mark of a sinuous and braided river course running through the site and apparently coinciding with the extensive gravel and peat deposits observed in Areas 1 and 6, 3, 4 and 4 extension (Pl I). In addition, it is possible that a different photograph taken in oblique sunlight shows that this water course was still visible as a slight earthwork hollow.[1]

Previous archaeological work in the area

A number of archaeological sites are known in the immediate area indicating settlement of all periods but, in particular, proving an extensive pattern of Roman settlement within the Ickham and Wingham area (Fig 3). The distribution of sites will only be summarised here, a fuller list of finds to 1960 has been published by Ogilvie (1977). It should perhaps be noted that many sites in the area, identified by Jim Bradshaw as a result of fieldwalking and air photography, were reported to the Ordnance Survey at the time and are now incorporated in both the National and the Kent Sites and Monuments Records.

For the prehistoric period, observation of two pipelines in the Wingham area showed the presence of Neolithic occupation close to the village, while a watching brief on a water main from Preston and passing to the east of Wingham, showed occupation from the Neolithic to Iron Age on the high ground north-east of the present site (Greenfield 1960; Ogilvie 1977).

Within the Ickham and Wingham area there is evidence for two substantial Roman masonry structures. Some 2km to the south-east, on the outskirts of Wingham, the remains of a fine bath-house, set on the south side of a large courtyard with an aisled barn on the north and another (unexcavated) building on the west, clearly relates to a major villa complex (Dowker 1882; 1883; Jenkins 1965; 1966; 1968; 1984). Rather less well known are the remains of the Ickham 'villa' situated 'half a mile east of Ickham Church', near to Britton Farm (Taylor 1932, 119). Discovered by agricultural operations in the late nineteenth century, the remains included substantial concrete footings, associated with painted wall plaster, Roman pottery and a quern. Trenching by Bradshaw in 1975 located the probable site of this building some distance to the east of the spot marked by the Ordnance Survey and about 1km south of the gravel pits. Subsequent metal detector finds from the site included lead seals suggesting long distance trading or official links with the area during the early to mid fourth century (Still 1994).

To the north of the Wingham river, at Dearston Farm, Preston, an important pottery kiln was found in 1872, close to an extensive cremation cemetery (Jessup and Taylor 1932, 163). At Wenderton, James Ogilvie examined an area on the north bank, opposite the northern quarry and 100m north-east of the Ickham site (Tomlinson 1961). This revealed an area of Romano-British occupation and the line of a road,

---

1.   AP 106G/UK 1829, 5.11.1946, frame 4157.

Pl V. Fields south-west of Wickhambreaux showing double and single ring-ditches from a prehistoric or Anglo-Saxon cemetery. The double ditch on the western side of the Roman road may be visible in the bottom right corner of the field nearest the modern wood. Wickhambreaux church lies on the right. © Crown copyright. NMR.

possibly the continuation of the excavated road heading to the Preston site or to Richborough.

The issue of the Roman road alignments passing through the area has been discussed without recognising a definitive alignment other than to support the Margary line as 'the most plausible' (Panton 1994, 15). As already noted, changes in the tidal regime may have caused re-alignment of the road in the post-Roman period; the issue of the road system in the area is discussed below (pp 331–5).

Most recently, observation of drainage operations higher up the Little Stour valley has allowed the identification of a Roman enclosure system on the flood plain (Sparey-Green 2005). The features on this site are both similar to the ditch system north of the road line on the present site and are also part of a system that extends further south, up the valley beyond Littlebourne.

Several early Anglo-Saxon cemeteries are associated with the villages in the area, the most significant being close to Wingham and Wickhambreaux (Dowker 1887; Meaney 1964, 140–1). At the latter site a hilltop cemetery is associated with a cropmark complex on a linear trackway along the ridge, possibly another minor Roman road. Cremation urns have been reported from Ickham village while circular cropmarks close to the line of the Roman road to the south-west of Wickhambreaux (Pl V) may also be significant and suggest a roadside cemetery in that area (*see* p 332). Excavation within the village of Ickham has recently identified settlement remains of the early medieval period, providing some insight into the origin and early organisation of this, one of the nearest successor settlements to the present site (Linklater and Sparey-Green 2004).

Pl VI. The main quarry during rescue excavation on 8th June 1974. The excavations on Area 6 are to the left, near the wood. The site of Mill 1 is probably the dark patch on the quarry edge, centre right. Photograph: Jim Bradshaw.

The excavations (Fig 4)

Emergency recording and salvage excavations were rapidly conducted ahead of the commercial operations, the degree of recording undertaken being largely dictated by the time available. As noted above, some initial observations were made in the northern quarry, close to the Wingham river and it also appears that one section of the road was recorded in that area prior to quarrying.

In the main quarry, to the south, two sections appear to have been cut across the road prior to quarrying, one in the north-east part of the field (Fig 8, Section 3) and the second in the south-west, close to the Little Stour (Fig 8, Section 2). As the quarry progressed the site was recorded by areas, reflecting the sequence of observation as each strip was cut from south-west to north-east, starting near the present river and progressing

eastwards. The quarry was operated by removing the topsoil in strips approximately 20 to 30m wide and then wet-digging the gravel with a drag-line. Opportunities for archaeological work were thus limited, but a significant amount of information was recorded, often from the examination of quarry sections (using a boat) or the areas stripped of topsoil by drag-line. Annotation of original site drawings shows that often up to 0.8m of topsoil and the upper fill of features was observed to have been removed by the drag-line before recording was possible. The areas recorded are shown on Fig 4. Areas 1–3 denote the three main bands of extraction observed in sequence during 1973 and 1974, the other areas were zones of detailed archaeological activity.

Within Area 1 Jim Bradshaw commenced work at the south-western end of the quarry. This initial excavation yielded the remains of a timber structure, thought to be a

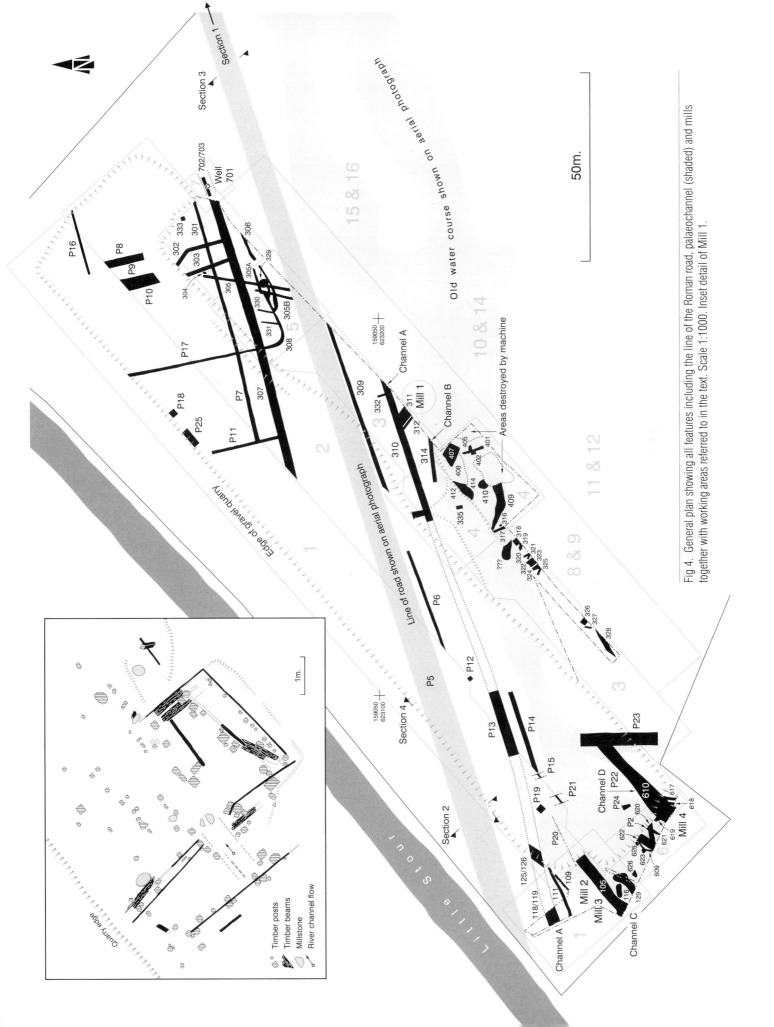

Fig 4. General plan showing all features including the line of the Roman road, palaeochannel (shaded) and mills together with working areas referred to in the text. Scale 1:1000. Inset detail of Mill 1.

building (designated at the time as 'the hut'), but which was later identified as a mill during more formal excavations by Christopher Young (Fig 4, inset). The area was extended to the north to include watching brief evidence obtained during gravel extraction. Here little was recorded in the initial stripping, but features recorded in the section allow parts of the ditch system and the road line to be identified.

Observation of Area 2 allowed recording of road metallings and a series of ditches as well as sections of possible mill channels.

Area 3 encompasses the river channel on the south, further sections of mill channel, the road and side drains and an enclosure system north of the road. In this area, the third major strip by drag-line, it seems that much recording was carried out after the stripping of topsoil and prior to gravel extraction. Areas 4 and 5 denote specific locations within Area 3 which were the subject of detailed investigation by Bradshaw and Young. A plan of this area cannot be exactly located, but appears to record important channels and timber structures at two points within the strip extending west towards Area 6.

Area 6, located at the south-western end of Areas 1 and 2, was also the subject of more formal excavation by Christopher Young. Within this area detailed recording of mill channels C and D was possible, as well as of the overlying riverine and superficial deposits.

Area 7 was a limited exposure east of Area 5 which provided evidence for a ditch and well on the north side of the road.

Areas 8, 9 and 11–13 have not been identified, but probably lay south-east of Area 3.

Areas 10 and 14 relate to Mill 1 excavated by Jim Bradshaw and Robert Spain. The precise location was not recorded on plan, but it was marked by Jim Bradshaw on an air photograph (Pl VI). Other records indicate the mill to have lain near the centre of Area 3 on its south-eastern edge, immediately east of Channel B and close to the northern edge of the major river channel.

Areas 15 and 16 are mentioned in the site records, but these have not been located. They probably lay on the eastern side of the quarry.

The main focus of formal excavation lay in Area 1, later extended to the south-east as Area 6. These two areas were contiguous, although partially separated by a baulk. The north-eastern limit of excavation was formed by the irregular edge of the quarry, the total area excavated measuring approximately 50m east–west and up to 22m north–south. Within the limits of the whole quarry, features were recorded over an area about 220 by 70m.

The site archive

The site was recorded by a number of different people at different times, with few resources, little time and often in appalling conditions (Pl VII). There was no overall strategy for recording, nor indeed any clear vision of the post-excavation methodology to be employed or the analytical destiny of the site records. It was a true 'rescue' or 'salvage' dig, not untypical of many others undertaken during the early 1970s.

The stratigraphic records, therefore, are incomplete, inconsistent and often lack precise information about the spatial location of particular features. The overall site plan (Fig 4) is the result of an intensive study of these records; although there are many unanswered questions, there seems little potential for further refining our understanding of site stratification.

Some 234 contexts were recorded in the stratigraphic archive. These were described in site notebooks, supplemented by twenty-six site plans and sections (prepared in various scales using both metric and imperial measurements), and various sketches and drawings in the notebooks. Many features and deposits that appear in plan or section were not assigned numbers. Six excavation areas are recorded: 1, 3, 4, 6, 7 and 9. Partial records of Area 2 exist but none are present in the archive for 5 and 8. Areas 10 and 14 represent Mill 1 by reference to the finds assemblage (Brickstock and Casey, pp 82–3; Lyne, pp 96–9); Area 5 appears to have lain close by. Photographic records comprise sixty-five colour transparencies and 114 monochrome exposures.

Most stratigraphic units from Areas 1, 4, 6, 7 and 9 were originally recorded in a site notebook, and subsequently transferred to DOE Context Record Sheets. Very little information about the wider stratigraphic sequence is recorded, but numerous sections of individual features exist. Recording of negative features is generally limited to basic identifications or characterisation as 'post-hole', 'pit' or other more specific and perhaps subjective term. Many contexts were not given unique numbers, but identified on a section drawing, so that for instance pit 10 may have five fills, numbered 1–5. These have been identified by using the feature number as a prefix to the layer number, ie layer 2 from ditch 309 is referred to as context 309.2. These are usually numbered from the bottom up, so that (for example) 309.2 was overlain by 309.3. In addition, many finds were not assigned to context numbers, but rather to locations denoted by subjective and interpretative terms such as the 'hut', or 'hut west end', or to Areas. The former is problematic and has had to be replaced by an alternative designation

Pl VII. Work in progress in ?Area 3, Spring 1974, looking north-east.

as 'Channel C' or 'feature 105' since this structure was certainly not a hut and can safely be re-interpreted as a mill channel. Most features without numbers in the site archive have been numbered, separately identified by the prefix 'P', but there remain some records identified at a late stage of the post-excavation process for which context numbers were not assigned. Not all finds could be related to a context or feature.

All of these primary records, together with various report drafts, correspondence, the pottery and the small finds are deposited with Canterbury Museums.

Structure of the report

Part 2 presents a description and brief discussion of the major categories of features and structures, including the watermills, by period and area. There then follows a description of Roman burials recovered from the site and a discussion of late Roman and early Anglo-Saxon deposits and features. Throughout the chapter dating evidence from the finds assemblage is included where appropriate.

Part 3 reviews the large numbers of coins and ceramics and describes ceramic assemblages. The discussion of each ceramic assemblage includes a summary of related significant finds and therefore provides a useful overview of material recovered from key features.

Part 4 comprises a catalogue of the remaining finds assemblage arranged by functional category and Part 5 discusses the assemblages and outlines the evidence for early Anglo-Saxon occupation. Part 6 presents a consideration of human and animal bone retrieved from the site.

Part 7 provides a concluding discussion of the Ickham site, placing the discoveries in a local and regional context and reviewing the implications of them to our understanding of late Roman east Kent.

PART 2: THE SITE

Paul Bennett, Robert Spain and Christopher Sparey-Green

Introduction

Paul Bennett

This part of the report is arranged chronologically, the features within each period described by category. The main structures and features are followed by minor or poorly preserved or recorded features, the latter presented by area. The chronological sequence is based on relationships between major features and the datable finds recovered. Over much of the site, detailed descriptions of features are lacking and uncertainty also remains about the location and interrelationship of some features.

The greater part of the following description covers parts of Areas 1–7 and 10 for which the most detailed records exist. In particular, details have been given of an enclosure system in Areas 2, 5 and 7, channels feeding the mills in Areas 1, 3 and 6, a feature complex in Area 4 (extension) while a full account has also been given of Mills 1–4 in Areas 1, 6, 10 and 14. The road line has been described with the aid of several sections, but these were sometimes diagonal cuts visible in the quarry face, the cross-sections across the projected line having only been approximately fixed. Other features for which exact contexts were not recorded have been included where they are of intrinsic interest; in Areas 8, 9 and 11–16 no records were available. Levels relative to Ordnance Datum were not taken and it has consequently not been possible to determine the fall of the various mill channels with any accuracy.

Prehistoric and early Roman periods

Christopher Sparey-Green

During the observation of the initial northern quarry in 1972 and the digging of the main quarry in 1973–4 a number of features were identified that underlay the line of what was later shown to be a Roman road and could thus be dated to the prehistoric or earliest Roman period. There were also a few scatters of finds or features which could more certainly be identified as of prehistoric origin.

The northern quarry 1972–3

The nature of the earliest activity on the site must remain imprecise but scatters of worked flint of presumed prehistoric date were recorded, principally in two locations near the Wingham river. A concentration of patinated and unpatinated flints was reported centred at TR 2345 5904 and others were seen along a ditch to the south-east, centred at TR 2361 5884. None of this material was available for detailed study. Extensive areas of peat were recorded in these workings centred at TR 234 591 and, although no study of the deposits was carried out, previous work in the general vicinity has shown that formation of the main peat horizon occurred in the late Bronze Age (above, p 8). Observation of the workings in this quarry and on the main quarry to the south showed that similar deposits had also formed in the Roman and post-Roman periods.

A single crouched burial (Burial A) was recorded at a point probably in the area of the northern quarry close to the line of the Wingham river (*see* p 69, Fig 28). No dating evidence was associated with this tightly trussed inhumation so a prehistoric date is only a presumption based on the layout of the skeleton. The burial lay on the line of a section of curving ditch approximately 1m wide and a few centimetres deep. An extended inhumation lay nearby (Burial B, Fig 27, *see* p 69). The area had been heavily truncated by the removal of overburden but may have formed part of an enclosure 10m in diameter surrounded by an intermittent ditch.

The cutting of a section of the Roman road (see below) at some point along its line in this quarry revealed no definite features beneath it other than some possible stake- or root-holes which were presumed to be part of its substructure (Fig 7, Section 1). Timber structures observed in the same area were presumed to be associated with occupation in the Roman period.

The main quarry 1973–4

Within the main quarried area there were no records of prehistoric features but there is a report of two cremation burials observed being destroyed by the drag-line, the features were identified solely by observation of the cremation vessels falling into the water-filled quarry.

Within the limits of the quarry two sections were cut at a slightly oblique angle to the road line prior to the commencement of the quarrying operation in 1973 (Figs 8–9, Sections 2–4). These sections were presumably set to cross the line of the road as previously observed and photographed from the north-east (Pl II). One was set in the south-west corner of the field close to the line of the River Stour (Fig 8, Section 2; TR 2305 5900), the other 200m to the north-east at the opposite end of the field (Fig 8, Section 3; TR 2325 5910). Both sections revealed features beneath the metalling. Details of the road surfaces and any associated roadside features are given below (below pp 21–4).

In Section 2 a V-cut ditch in the clay subsoil measured 1m wide by 0.4m deep and was apparently filled with the same peaty soil that underlay the metalling. Both this soil and the metalling had slumped into this feature which lay somewhere close to the centre of the road. The northern edge sealed or extended over the site of a hearth. This was a shallow, bowl-shaped feature, 1.4m wide and 0.3m deep and adjoined a ditch also overlapped by the road edge. It is possible that the hearth was the feature underlying the gravel metalling which produced pottery with a *terminus post quem* of *c* AD 70 (Assemblage 1, *see* p 95). The more northerly

Section 3 identified a ditch of U-shape profile 0.6m wide and 0.2m deep bounded by low banks on either side, apparently close to the centre line of the road.

Section 4 (Fig 9), recorded against the north-western side of the first quarry strip (Area 1) cut later in 1973, shows a diagonal section of the road in a position approximately 30m to the east of Section 2 at TR 2308 5903. At this point a hollow extended the full width of the metalling, the profile stepped, suggesting two adjacent features or a recut. The shallower feature on the south side was approximately 5m wide and 0.4m deep but the deeper northern cut was 4.5m wide and up to 0.9m deep with steeply sloping sides. Pottery and occupation material was recorded from this deeper feature but no details are available. Section 5, 45m to the east, identified the road which here overlay a slight hollow on the southern side of Area 1.

Within the main quarry the earliest features appeared to have been a series of linear features which, on their alignment and stratigraphic relationship, pre-dated the main enclosure system and Roman road (Fig 4; Fig 5). The most significant features were a number of drainage ditches approaching the road line from the north at an angle and apparently continuing up to and beneath its northern edge (Areas 3 and 5; 305, 305B, 330 and 331). Whether the features continued beneath the primary metalled surface is not recorded but, in Area 5, they were sealed by a spread of metalling on the northern side of the road. The most detailed records derive from a point where the metallings were cut by a later complex of features (305A, 308, 329 and 306) (Fig 5). A further group of features (704, 706–9 and 714) was recorded to have had a similar relationship to the road to the north-east but few details of these survive. These boundaries presumably related to a field system or settlement of early Roman date preceding the road.

The principal of these was ditch (305) which, at its southern end appeared to run beneath the northern edge of the metalling of the road and to terminate 22.5m to the north in a rounded end. This feature was about 0.7m wide and 0.5m deep, with steeply sloping sides and a flat base (Fig 6). The basal fill was a thin layer of dark grey silty clay (305.3) covered by up to 0.25m of orange-brown sandy clay and dark brown clay (305.2) over which was a dark grey-brown clay silt (305.1).

Immediately adjacent to the north terminal of 305 was a second feature (304, Figs 5 and 6). The extent of this was uncertain, since it was traced accurately for only 0.65m but may have been part of a linear feature continuing the alignment of 305. The feature had been heavily truncated, its remaining cross-section measuring

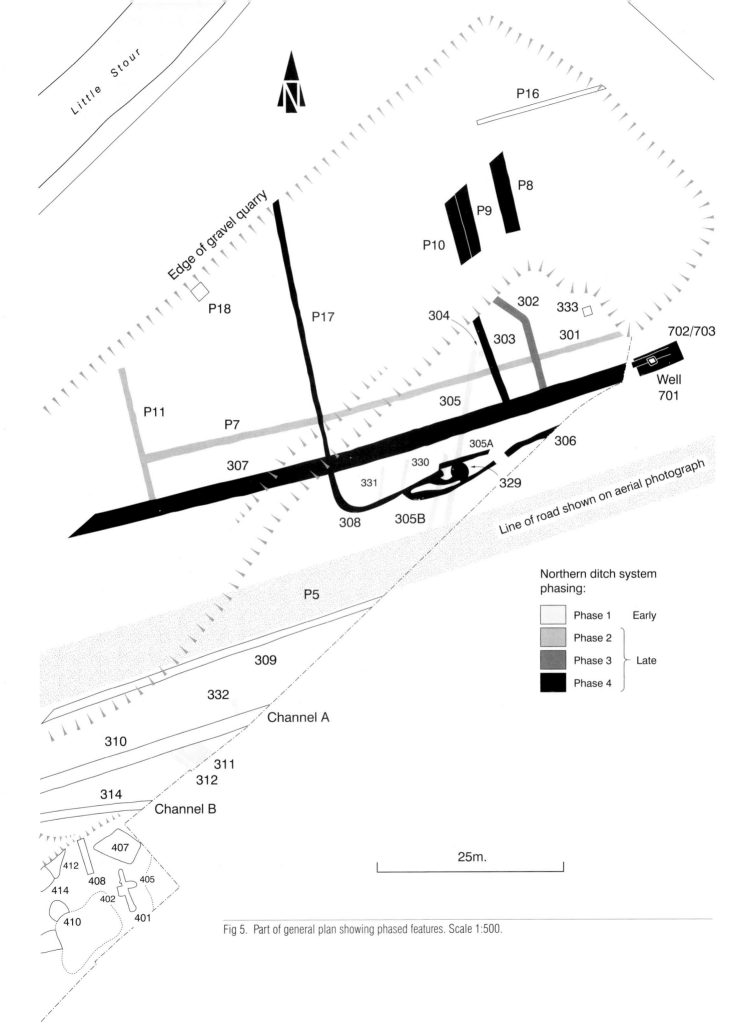

Little Stour

N

Edge of gravel quarry

P18

P17

P16

P8

P9

P10

304

302

333

303

301

702/703

305

Well
701

P11

P7

306

307

305A

330

P5

331

329

308

305B

Line of road shown on aerial photograph

Northern ditch system
phasing:

Phase 1   Early
Phase 2
Phase 3   } Late
Phase 4

309

332

Channel A

310

311
312

314

Channel B

407

412

408   405

414   402

410   401

25m.

Fig 5. Part of general plan showing phased features. Scale 1:500.

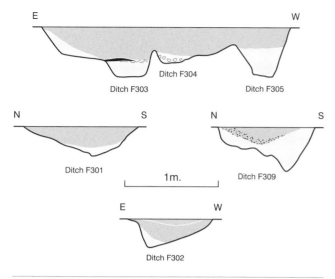

Fig 6. Ditch sections, F301–F305 and F309. Scale 1:40.

0.8m wide and 0.19m deep, with steep sides and irregular base. The ditch was filled with dark brown clay with large flints (304.2), which covered part of a leather boot in the base at one point. Above this was a dark grey-brown clay silt (304.1) which is shown in section as the same as (305.1) and the upper fill of 303.

Parallel to 305 and 2.5m west of it was another ditch (305B), traced for at least 10m up to the northern edge of the road and possibly continuing beneath it. The ditch, approximately 0.6m wide and up to 0.4m deep, was recorded as of stepped profile, suggesting that it had been recut at least once. Two short parallel lengths of ditch (330 and 331) to the south-west were set 2.5m apart and traced for only 5m These were approximately 0.3m and 0.5m wide, respectively, the depth and fill were not recorded. At their south end they terminated at ditch 308 but their exact relationship with the latter is not recorded; they are shown as draining to the south and possibly channelled water into ditch 308, their line not continuing towards the road. The alignment of both ditch 330 and 331 however, may indicate that they belong to the early set of features and therefore probably pre-date ditch 308.

On the south side of the road, in Area 3, a group of three features (311, 312 and 332) were recorded as predating 310 (Channel A), a linear channel set parallel to the road's south edge. The first two features were traced for only 4m between this feature and the then existing southern edge of the stripped ground surface. Their full extent is unknown but they were not observed to the west near the road while, to the east, they would have extended into the main watercourse

and an area for which no records survive. Ditch 311 was approximately 2m wide and on the south adjoined feature 312 which was only 0.55m wide. No details of the depth or fill are available. The third ditch (332) was traced in plan for 1.65m from the northern edge of 310 as a cut 0.45m wide, the depth or fill not recorded. Its relationship to this section of Channel A was unclear but was presumed to be earlier. This feature was not observed to the north, near the line of ditch 309 and the road.

Other features to the north-east in Area 7 were described as pre-dating the road but no site records survive detailing their relationship with the road so these are included in the general description of the site (p 42).

The later Roman settlement

Christopher Sparey-Green

Introduction

As noted in Part 1, before the commencement of gravel digging, observation by a series of field workers had identified archaeological sites near the confluence of the Wingham river with the Little Stour and on the hill to the north-east at Wenderton. The line of an ancient road through the valley of the Little Stour and across the course of the Wingham river had been identified as well as evidence of Roman and medieval settlement (Fig 3).

The road was first recorded at several points to the north near the Wingham river in the area of Wenderton where Dr Ogilvie in 1958 had traced a buried road on the north-east bank and had noted that metalling and timber work was visible in both banks of the river associated with Roman occupation (TR 236 592) (J D Ogilvie in litt, July 1973; Tomlinson 1961, liii). Observation of dredging in 1971 showed a concentration of Roman material and the presence of timbers set in the blue clay subsoil in the area north-west of a cattle bridge (TR 2352 5920), close to the projected line of the road identified in the gravel workings (J D Ogilvie *op cit*). South of this, in the area of the Horse Marsh, adjacent to the south-west bank of the river, a great depth of soft silt was identified by auguring. As a result of his excavations Dr Ogilvie considered that a Roman building of some importance lay on the east bank, this served by the road and connected with the Preston kiln site to the north and the site possibly of a terminal for river traffic.

Prior to gravel extraction in the area south-west of these early investigations the line of the road was recorded on a

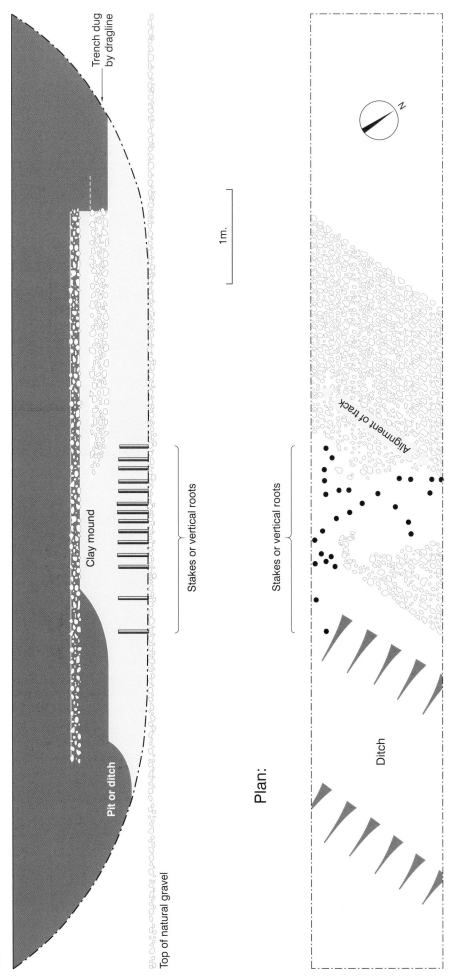

Section:

SE / NW

Trench dug by dragline

Clay mound

Pit or ditch

Stakes or vertical roots

Top of natural gravel

1 m.

Plan:

N

Alignment of track

Stakes or vertical roots

Ditch

Fig 7. Trial trench through Road Section 1. Scale 1:40.

series of air photographs taken between 1946 and 1972. The line of the road south-west of the Wingham river is recorded on a photograph of 1972, the pale line of the metalled surface visible in the pasture between TR 2328 5912 and TR 2336 5914.[2] At a slightly later date in 1973 photographs were taken from ground level in the northern quarry area, confirming the continuation of the mark in the meadow grass through the area to the south-west, the next intended area for quarrying (Pl II). It was this observation that alerted local fieldworkers to the potential of the main quarry and led to the main investigations in 1973–4 (*see* p 3).

In this area of the meadows the continuation of the road south-west as it approached the line of the Little Stour is also clearly visible on pre-existing air photographs (TR 2305 5902 to 2330 5912).[3] The line of the road here is visible on the north side of a sinuous and irregular dark outline which can be recognized as an early river channel and an important feature for the history of the later phases of the Roman and post-Roman river system. One air photograph taken in raking sunlight suggested it was still a slight earthwork in the period before the quarrying. These photographs also show that in the northern quarry area the line of an abandoned light railway had crossed the course of the road at TR 2342 5916, heading north-west; some features here may have been disturbed by its construction but the majority of the site and the structures described here would not have been affected.

The course of the road south-west towards Wickhambreaux, on the opposite bank of the present Little Stour has been noted previously (Panton 1994; Sparey-Green 2005) and is further discussed below (pp 331–5).

The northern quarry 1972–3

The road line and settlement remains

Early in the process of gravel digging on the south bank in 1972 and 1973, remains of occupation and the line of the road were recorded. At three points structures were recorded close to the road line, the first, of an unspecified nature, at a point on the east of the quarry, closest to the river (TR 2345 5917). To the south-west, observation at TR 2342 5916 and TR 2341 5915 identified pointed stakes and horizontal timbers which may have been supports for the road. A diagonal section of the road was obtained in a trial trench

in July 1973 although the exact position is not recorded. This drawing (Fig 7, Section 1) and an accompanying letter record that the natural gravel here was sealed by 0.5m of clay which had been raised with spoil from the flanking ditch to form a low agger 'retained by vertical pegs of wood laid in rows … Over this was placed a network of thin branches and flint metalling'.[4] The drawing differs slightly, showing a low mound of clay on the southern edge of a layer of tightly packed gravel 0.2m thick, this metalling sealing a mass of rushes on the south side and extending at least 2.8m north, its edge here not clearly defined. South of the surface and 0.8m from its edge was a ditch at least 2.1m wide and 0.6m deep, the section showing it was of a shallow, rounded profile, possibly recut. Sealing the surface was a thin band of clay 0.1m thick above which was an ill-defined spread of mixed peat and gravel 0.1m thick. This was sealed beneath 0.6m of peaty topsoil and extended for at least 1.5m over the road ditch on the south, perhaps as metalling spread by plough action.

Little opportunity was given for detailed recording of features within this area but a spread of flint and tile at TR 2343 5913 suggested the site of a Roman building south of the road line and close to the ancient course of the Wingham river. There are no details of the type of tile or brick but the location of a masonry building near the main water source might suggest a bath building. Such a building may also have been the source of the scattered brick and flue tile found redeposited in, for instance, pit 414 (layers 3 and 4) in Area 4 of the southern quarry site.

The main quarry 1973–4

The road line

As already noted, four cross-sections of the road (P5) were recorded over a distance of approximately 200m within the limits of the quarry. Two sections (Fig 8, Sections 2 and 3) were cut at an oblique angle to the road line at either end of the field, prior to the commencement of the quarrying operation. A photograph of a road surface is probably a view of Section 2 or Section 4 looking west (Pl VIII). At a later stage, after the cutting of the first quarry strip, two more diagonal sections were recorded (Area 2). One of these is illustrated here (Fig 9, Section 4). In each case only

2.   Air photograph HSL UK 72 84, 2406H, 6259 of 13 July 1972.
3.   Air photographs 106G/UK1449, 4062-3, CPE/UK1829 4157 and HSL KENT 67 16, 6637 of 17 July 1967.
4.   J Bradshaw in litt, I D Margary 14 July 1973.

Pl VIII. Roman road section, ?Area 1, looking north-west, with the Little Stour beyond.

a single phase of metalling was noted, the surface mostly without appreciable camber and not founded on any obvious raised ground or agger. Scatters of gravel to either side were identified as plough disturbance which would imply that the upper surface had been truncated. There is, however, some evidence for contemporary gravel surfaces co-terminus with Roman features, particularly on the north side of the road (below, p 24).

Starting with the most south-westerly section (Fig 8, Section 2: TR 2305 5900), this revealed the road to be at least 7m wide, only the western edge being identified. The metalling consisted of approximately 0.15m of gravel laid on up to 0.2m of peaty soil over the natural clay. The metalling had slumped into an earlier ditch and hearth cut into this subsoil.

The next diagonal section of the quarry face (Fig 9, Section 4), centred at a point approximately 15m eastwards, showed that the road surface was up to 0.3m thick, and, allowing for the angle of the section to the road axis, suggested a width of approximately 9m. The southern edge

overlay 0.25m of peaty soil, the northern side up to 1m of soil, filling an earlier feature.

On the opposite face of the quarry strip in Area 2 a metalled surface up to 0.45m thick was revealed similar to that in Section 4. The metalling, which overlay 0.3m of peaty soil, was traced for 27m along the section, suggesting a corrected width of approximately 10m.

Finally, on the north-eastern side of the field, at some point beyond Area 7 (Fig 8, Section 3: TR 2325 5910), an oblique section revealed at least 9m of metalling, without any margin identified on either side. The gravel metalling was up to 0.2m thick, sealing 0.3m of peaty soil over the clay natural.

Roadside features

Several features were identified on alignments close to the edges of the metalled surface, some of these probably serving as roadside ditches, others more likely to be associated with the enclosure system north of the road or the artificial watercourse

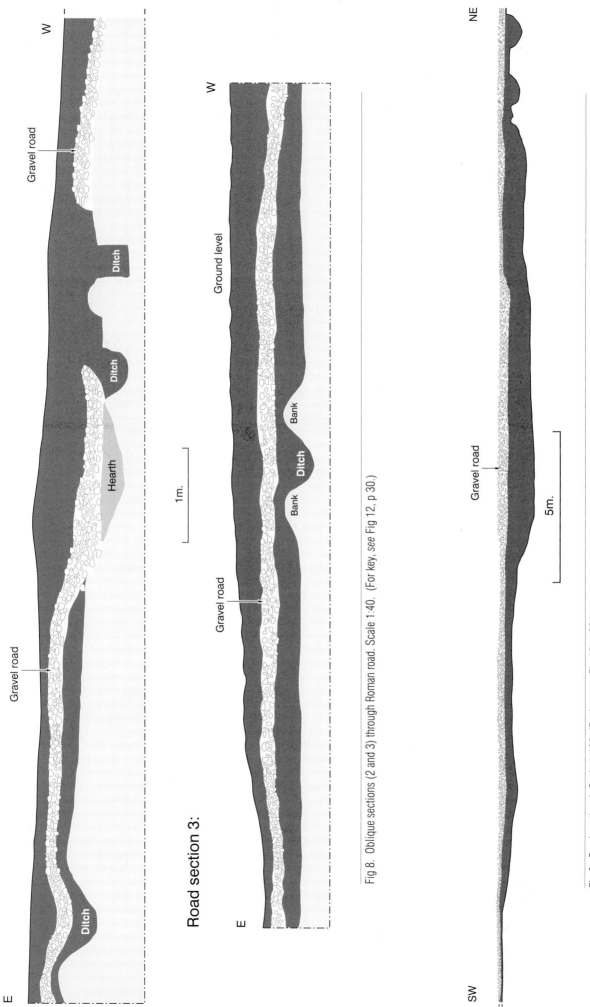

Road section 2:

E

W

Gravel road

Gravel road

Ditch

Hearth

Ditch

Ditch

Road section 3:

E

W

Gravel road

Ground level

Bank

Ditch

Bank

Gravel road

1m.

Fig 8. Oblique sections (2 and 3) through Roman road. Scale 1:40. (For key, see Fig 12, p 30.)

SW

NE

Gravel road

5m.

Fig 9. Road section 4. Scale 1:125. (For key, see Fig 12, p 30.)

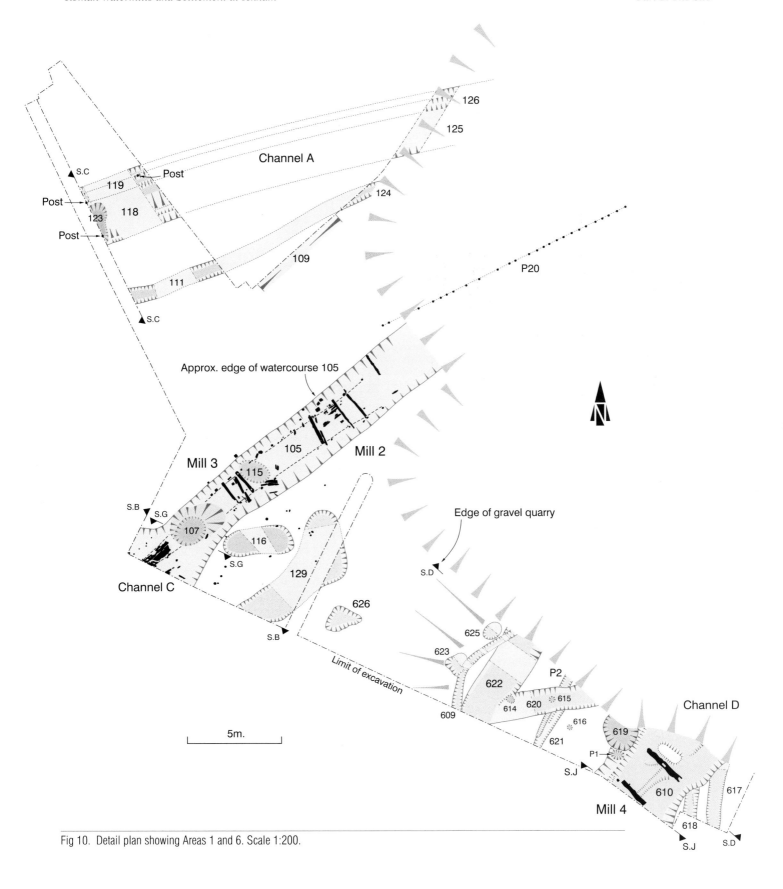

Fig 10. Detail plan showing Areas 1 and 6. Scale 1:200.

connected with the mills; these latter two groups of features are described below. Two, or possibly three, features can be identified as roadside ditches, on account of their profile, location and position close to the road. At the western end of the road features 119/126/P6/309 and 111/124 lay south of it while, on the north side, two un-numbered ditches in Sections 2 and 4 may have defined that side. To the east, ditches 307/702/703 continued the approximate line of the latter. Areas of gravel, particularly on the north side, between these features and the road margin may have been additional metallings or widenings of the road.

The most convincing roadside ditch was the narrow ditch (309 and P6) traced for a distance of some 90m along the south side of the metalled surface in Areas 1 and 3. Where sectioned in Area 3, near the centre of the site, the ditch was between 0.75–0.9m wide, and approximately 0.45m deep, with a steeply sloping side on the south and a more irregular profile towards the road, suggesting two or three successive recuts (Fig 6). The base fill was of four successive deposits of pale brown clay (309.4) and yellow clay (309.3), sealed by lenses of black ashy gravel (309.2), lying at an angle, suggesting they were derived from the northern edge of the road. The uppermost fill was a black ashy silt (309.1). The ditch fills yielded a small assemblage of late fourth-century pottery (Assemblage 17, p 109). P6 was of similar profile but on an alignment diverging southward from the road edge.

At the western end of Area 1 this alignment may be continued by a narrow ditch (119) set 7m from the road edge (Fig 10, plan; Fig 11, Section C). This ditch was 0.6m wide and 0.4m deep with steep sides and a flat base, the fill a black silt (119.1). As with 309, a marked step on the northern side suggested it had been recut, prior to its truncation by a wider channel (118, *see* p 26). Another similar feature (111), set approximately parallel to this and 5m to the east, may also have served as a roadside ditch. This was 0.9m wide and 0.35m deep with sloping sides and a flat base. The fill consisted of dark grey silt with some small flints and gravel in the base. The fill produced pottery comprising four sherds of late Iron Age date but also one of the third or fourth century (Assemblage 2, p 95).

Continuations of both 111 and 119 were recorded approximately 10m to the east where features 124 and 126, respectively, correspond in profile and alignment. The features here were cut tangentially, distorting the recorded

profiles, but ditch 126 was 0.7m deep while 124 was 0.3m deep. Ditch 126 was filled with silty brickearth mixed with lenses of gravel and dark silt (126.1), fills which would accord with it having filled with eroded road surface. While the latter feature, as already noted, could continue as P6 and 309, 111/124 was not traced in the quarrying further east. Feature P14, some 25m distant, might continue its line but its alignment equally suggested it was a continuation of Channel C (below p 29).

To the north of the road, sections 2 and 4 at the south-western end of the site suggest that two linear features could be traced along the northern edge of the metalling for a distance of at least 18m (Figs 8 and 9).[5] That closest to the road line was a U-shaped cut 0.6m wide and 0.3m deep, the fill described as peaty. In both these sections the metalling overlapped the ditch fill but this may be from the spreading of the gravel. To the west and 0.8m from this was another cut which, in Section 2, was 0.35m wide and 0.4m deep, with vertical sides and a flat base. Section 4 showed a similar sized cut but with rounded base, the fill unspecified but sealed by a thin layer of gravel, possibly plough spread. These roadside features were not observed to the east in Sections 3 and 5 but it should be noted that feature 307/702/703, although further out from the road edge, was broadly similar in profile and size and could represent a continuation of this roadside ditch (*see* below, p 25). The feature is however at some distance from the road edge and may have been cut to define a field or enclosure boundary.

If the features on either side of the road were sections of continuous ditches flanking a strip 15m wide then it would appear that their alignment was not strictly parallel to that of the axis of the recorded road. The alignment of the southern ditch would have lain progressively closer to the road edge the further east, the northern ditch mirroring this as it drew away from the edge the further eastward it was traced. The mis-alignment of ditches and recorded surface might also explain the identification of a ditch beneath the road surface recorded in Section 4, east of the main site, this a continuation of the southern ditch but there sealed by the metalling. The misalignment of road metalling and ditches might suggest the former is later in date and a replacement for an earlier surface laid between the ditches. In this respect a coin from the metalling dated to the mid second century may be significant, the coin relating to a later remetalling of an earlier major road line.

---

5. These features appear on drawings for which no context details exist other than annotations to the site drawings providing information on their fill and location within the quarry.

Enclosure system north of the road

To the north of the road was a series of ditches set roughly parallel to, or at right angles to, the line of the road (Fig 5). There was little dating evidence from these features and considerable doubt as to the inter-relationship of some features, observation of which was often curtailed by the nature of the quarrying operations. A group of features on the north side of the road, and apparently extending beneath it, have already been described (Phase 1 on Fig 5; *see* above, p 18). These were, in turn, cut by at least two and probably three phases of enclosure ditch defining areas adjoining the road.

The earliest feature group appeared to define the western and southern side of an enclosure. This enclosure was represented by ditches P7/301 and P11, the former located some 18m from, and parallel to, the road edge, the latter set at right angles to its western end and continuing towards the road. The relationship of P11 to 307 was uncertain; the plans suggested it terminated at, and therefore linked with, this much later feature.

Ditch P7/301 was traced for 62m and was 1.2m wide and 0.3m deep with sloping sides and a rounded base (Fig 6). The drain contained a primary fill of black greasy silt with large flint cobbles (301.1), sealed by a grey-brown silty clay flecked with ash (301.2) but yielded no datable finds. Ditch (P11) was traced for a length of some 18m and consisted of a U-profile ditch approximately 1.5m wide and 0.75m deep filled with peaty soil.

The second phase comprises ditches P17, 305A, 306 and 308 and the pit 329. The first of these ditches formed the western side, the others the south-west corner and a series of irregular ditch cuts along the roadside. The pit or hollow 329 may have formed in the entrance from the road. A northern limit to the enclosure may be indicated by a ditch (P16) aligned parallel to the road and 45m distant but no link between this and P17, or return towards the road, was recorded. It is possible that the angled ditch 302 could represent the eastern side linking with 306 since, like P17, it was recorded as cutting 301 and cut by 307.

The sequence of features on the roadside is not clear but the presence of a double lobed and recut terminal to ditch 308, adjoining areas of metalling, suggests that this may, at one stage, have been the western side of an entrance into the enclosure. In its earliest form ditch 308 was 0.75m wide and 0.5m deep, the rounded profile recut once. The later lobed terminal was 0.9m wide and 0.5m deep with steep sides and flat base. Its fill was recorded as a homogenous 'greasy, ashy fill'. The

shallow hollow (329) measured 2 by 3m and 0.4m deep, its base apparently lined with a 'pebble floor' 0.02m thick. The original section drawing describes the fill as a homogeneous 'greasy, ashy fill' (L-1), containing a coin of which no record survives. Its position suggested it might have been an erosion hollow in the entrance, formed by animal traffic and later metalled.

At a later date two ditches, 305A and 306, appear to have replaced and extended the line of 308, blocking the putative entrance. The former was 0.5m deep and of unknown depth or profile. 306 was a similar width and 0.55m deep with a steep-sided, almost V-cut profile, a step on one side suggesting a recut.

Ditch 302 was traced for 8.5m. The ditch was cut 1m wide and 0.3m deep with steeply sloping sides and a rounded sump. At its northern end the ditch turned to the north-west. Its primary fill was a dark brown clay (302.3) overlain by grey brown clay with flecks of ash (302.2) sealed by an ashy silt (302.1). Ditch 302 yielded a substantial corpus of pottery (Assemblage 9, pp 99–100) and a number of metal finds, including a copper alloy pin, an iron chain, and an iron chisel. The lowest fills yielded material of the mid second century, a range of late Roman pottery in the upper fill suggesting the ditch remained open and was only finally filled in the mid fourth century. If indeed associated with 305A and 306 this would establish this phase in the mid to late second century AD, and suggest P7/301 should be placed earlier, perhaps in the first or early second century.

The final phase of enclosure was represented by ditch 307/702/703 running parallel to the road and by 303 returning to the north at right angles to its line. The former length of ditch lay some 12m north of the road edge and was traced for 77m across Areas 2 and 3 (Fig 5). There is no record of the ditch extending across the initial quarry strip into the north-western face of the quarry, but to the east the recut line of 307 continued for a further 8m by a two phase ditch 702 and 703; beyond that point any continuation was destroyed in the quarry. At two points the relationship of this ditch to other features was recorded on plan, ditch 307 shown as cutting not only 302 but P17/308. At its more westerly exposure, feature 307 was 2.1m wide and up to 0.8m deep, its profile suggesting three recuts. The two principal cuts were of rounded V-shaped profile 0.7 and 0.8m deep with slight ledges 0.2 and 0.3m deep on each side. The multiple profile suggests the recutting of the ditch, in a similar way to ditch 309 on the south, but the homogeneous peaty soil did not allow the sequence to be established although the shallower cuts were perhaps replaced by the successively deeper ditches.

From the limited investigation of ditch 702 and 703, where cut by feature 701 (below, pp 32–3 and Fig 15 and 16), it would appear that the primary phase (703) was 1.75m wide and 0.45m deep, the fill a dark green-yellow silt (703.1). Ditch 702 was a recut along its north-western side, measuring 0.75m wide and of similar depth, the fill consisting of 0.12m of dark brown peaty silt flecked with charcoal (702.2) in the base and 0.33m of dark grey silt flecked with charcoal (702.1) above. The course of this to the north was not observed. A small fragment of an indeterminate brooch came from context 702.1 and a copper alloy bracelet fragment and iron ladle are recorded from 702.

Ditch 307 yielded a group of third- to early fourth-century pottery (Assemblage 7, p 99) but whether this was from the primary fill or one of the recuts is not known. This date range would, however, be in conformity with the earlier material from the lower fill of 302, cut by this ditch.

Possibly associated with 307 was ditch 303, set at right angles to it and extending northwards for some 11.5m. This ditch was 1.2m wide and 0.28m deep, with steeply sloping sides and a flat sump (Fig 6). A primary fill of dark brown clay (303.4) overlain by an organic layer (303.3) was capped by a thin layer of ash (303.2) and a dark grey brown clay silt (303.1). The ditch yielded no datable finds. If 307 formed the roadside boundary of enclosures facing the road then this ditch could have formed a division between two plots, the other sides of which have not been identified.

Immediately north of ditches 302 and 303 three parallel linear features (P8, P9, P10) aligned at right-angles to the road were traced for a distance of at least 12m. P8 was of rounded profile, 1.8m wide and at least 0.45m deep; P9 was 2m wide and 1m deep with a steeper-sided profile, and P10 was 1.5m wide and 0.8m deep with a more V-cut profile. All three features were recorded as filled with the same dark peaty fill and no dated finds were recovered from them. No details are available for P16 save that it was traced for approximately 18m and was approximately 1m wide. The relationship of this feature to the rest of the complex is uncertain but it may have formed the rear boundary to the earlier phases of enclosure. The more substantial features P8–P10 remain isolated and could represent recut and deeper continuations of 302 and 303 and part of a ditch line observed by Jim Bradshaw as continuing on this approximate alignment to the northern edge of the quarry. Ditch 302, however, was seen turning towards the west so may not be associated with this recut ditch alignment.

The latest activity in this area is represented by areas of metalling sealing ditches 301, 702 and 703, the surfaces apparently surrounding and respecting timber-lined tanks 333 and 701 respectively (*see* pp 32–3). A further area of metalling or 'road spill' is noted on plan between the road and the southern edge of 306, suggesting a widening of the road here or a surface allowing access to the enclosure. Further ditches are recorded as occurring in Area 7, but the exact position of the features has been lost other than that they are presumed to have lain near features 701–703 and were therefore part of the ditch system north of the road; the features are described below (p 42).

Mill channels (or watercourses) south of the road in Areas 1–4 *Christopher Sparey-Green and Paul Bennett*

Those linear features south of the road which are most easily interpreted as roadside features or boundaries have already been described. In the case of some of the larger linear features in these areas, however, the alignment, cross sections and presence of timber revetments suggest these were water channels associated with the mill structures. Here an attempt has been made to link features where their character and alignment suggest an association with specific mill structures which are described in detail below (pp 45–62). It should be noted that no absolute levels for the bases of the channels were recorded but comparison of sections drawn to common datum lines allows some tentative figures to be calculated for the falls in the base level of some channels and to give some idea of the relative levels of Channels A, C and D across Areas 1 and 6.

Although a number of timbers were retrieved from the structures, none survived for later study.

Channel A: (Features 118, 125, P13 in Area 1 and 310 in Area 3: Figs 4 and 10)

This watercourse was located against the far western edge of Area 1 close to the present line of the Little Stour and extended at least into Area 3 to the east. At the up-stream end the channel was represented by feature 118, sectioned in the trench extension of Area 1 (Fig 11, Section C). At this point the feature was 2.8m wide and 0.3m deep with a flat base and gently sloping sides, filled with grey silt and fine and coarse flint gravel (118.1). The presence of round-wood timbers set vertically on either side suggests it was revetted like the other channels. Two small round-wood posts lay on the northern side while a group of three 0.1m diameter round wooden posts (123.1, 123.2 and 123.3), were found on the south side, set as a group to provide stability since they penetrated the fill of an underlying pit (123). The nature of this feature is uncertain but it was at least 1.8m wide and 0.4m deep and filled with black silt (123.4). From the

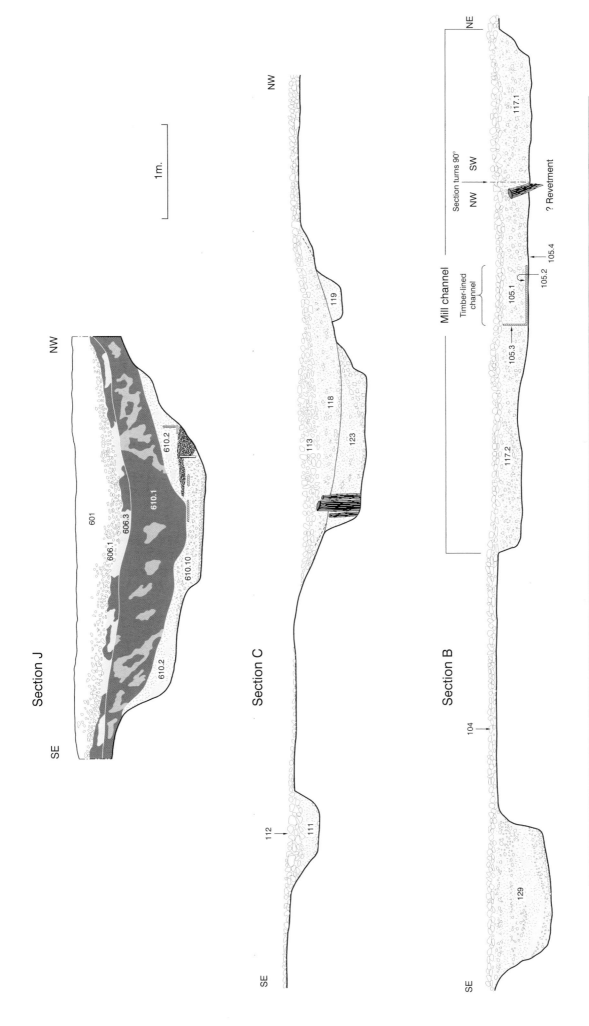

1m.

Section J

SE

NW

601

606.1

606.3

610.1

610.2

610.10

610.2

Section C

SE

NW

112

111

113

118

123

119

Section B

SE

NE

Mill channel

Timber-lined channel

Section turns 90°

NW SW

? Revetment

105.1

105.2

105.3

105.4

117.1

117.2

104

129

Fig 11. Sections J, C and B. Scale 1:40. (For key, *see* Fig 12, p 30.)

visible portion feature 123 was either the butt-end of a deeper channel or part of a pit extending beyond the trench. The western side of feature118 also overlay a similarly-aligned gully or drain (119), probably an earlier roadside drain or enclosure boundary.

The continuation of the channel may be represented by feature 125, observed in the quarry face 12m further east (Fig 10). The feature had a similar profile and fill, but was aligned more to the south-east and was somewhat narrower and shallower, being approximately 2m wide and 0.25m deep. Feature 125 was cut through an earlier linear feature (126) of similar profile and fill to ditch 119. Assuming that the continuous section showing 118 and 125 was correctly levelled then the base of this channel had dropped approximately 0.08m over a distance of 12m northwards, a fall of approximately 1 in 150.

Eastward, the projected line of 118 and 125 appears to coincide with feature P13, observed in the quarry face on the edge of Area 1, 3m distant, and by feature 310 in Area 3, a further 100m beyond. The former was a steep-sided trench 2.4m wide and 0.8m deep with a flat base and filled with peaty soil. Feature 310 was traced for 39m as a 2m wide cut but its depth and fill was not recorded. At the western end of the exposure, however, it was noted that gravel metalling occurred in the channel, suggesting its disuse or deliberate blocking. The upper fill yielded a small corpus of third- to early fourth-century pottery (Assemblage 8) but site records show that a group of significant finds, including a wooden figurine, were also recovered from this feature, in the section extending east from this blockage (*see* pp 215–17). An original site plan shows 310 as the findspot of the wooden figurine, a separate contemporary description of its discovery stating that it was found in a ditch close to a coin of Marcus Aurelius, a group of lead weights (p 219) and other unidentified pieces of wood. Fifteen metres distant, scraps of bronze, pieces of bangle and several fourth-century coins were recovered from the same feature.

Although the precise location of Mill 1 is unknown, based on such evidence as does survive it is felt unlikely that Channel A fed Mill 1. The watercourse may therefore have fed a mill predating Mill 1, located perhaps further to the east in the north-eastern part of Areas 8 and 9 or even in Areas 18 or 16. No trace of an early mill was found during the salvage brief and the function of the watercourse remains unknown.

Channel B: (Feature 314 in Area 3; P14 and P15 in Area 2)

The main component of this channel was an 11.5m length of ditch identified in Area 3 (314) (Figs 4 and 5). Few details are available other than this feature was 1m wide and that the easternmost observed section was sealed by a deposit of gravel. The recorded alignment and the size of the channel would be consistent with this being the feeder channel for Mill 1, which must be located within 10m of the eastern end of the recorded section.

The up-stream course of this is uncertain but may be represented by P14, 60m distant. P14 was traced for 24m parallel to the road and 16m from its southern edge. In section feature P14 was 0.8m wide, of a rounded profile 0.35m deep and was filled with peaty soil. The feature appeared to adjoin a similar feature, P15 which was only observed in section and was of uncertain alignment, but may have been an earlier cut of the channel or a boundary ditch on this side of the road. A continuation westward of this channel may be represented by P20 and Channel C.

Channel C: (Watercourse 105 and Feature P20 in Area 1: Figs 4 and 10)

This was the most fully recorded channel, discovered by Jim Bradshaw in Area 1 during the winter of 1973–4 when it was interpreted as a sunken-featured hut, and later recorded by Christopher Young in summer 1974. The wooden structures within this channel are now recognised as those of Mills 2 and 3, described below (pp 49–58). The channel consisted of a linear cutting in the natural brickearth set on a south-west to north-east alignment, and comprised features 105/106/120. Traces of a more irregular cut (128) on the south side may represent part of a preceding channel, the only recorded fill of which was a black silty gravel (128.1).[6] The later channel measured between 2.8 and 3.1m wide, the latter measurement to the north, suggesting that the feature was widening down-stream. Comparison of the two sections drawn towards the western end of the feature suggests that, if, as seems the case, they were drawn to a common datum level, the depth varied between 0.88m and 1.01m below datum over a distance of 8m, the former figure referring to the section on the boundary of the site (Fig 11, Section B). This would suggest a fall of approximately 1 in 60 in the channel at this point.

---

6.   Cut 128 is described as adjacent to Pit 107, but could not be identified on field drawings.

The basal fill of the channel comprised deposits of silt found under some of the structural timbers and probably resulting from the decay of the timbers. Underlying timber 15 was silt deposit (121); under timber 8 and its associated planking was silt (122); under timber 7 was silt (127) with some iron-panning; and under timber 42 was a very thin silt layer (105.4). Overlying timber 42 was a pure black silt (105.2). In the north-eastern part of the channel a more complex series of fills was recorded. Here, a primary deposit of light grey sandy angular gravel with flints (106.4: Assemblage 3, p 95) was overlain by a dark grey brown silt (106.3) with several large flints. An upper fill of very dark brown silt with flints (106.2) is recorded, this capped by a grey orange angular gravel (106.1). The numerous timbers set in the base of the channel and forming parts of Mills 2 and 3 are described below (3–42, 105.3, A, B, C, D and E, pp 47–55 and Fig 18).

The base of the channel, and possibly also its fill, were cut by Pits 107 and 115. These two features, originally interpreted as scour pits associated with the use of the mills, contained a small quantity of post-Roman finds suggesting that both were intrusive cuts; they are discussed below (p 70). The features also contained large numbers of coins that almost certainly derived originally from Channel C in the vicinity of Mill 3.

Comparison of the base levels of Channel A (118) in Area 1 with the corresponding base of Channel C (105) to the south suggests that the latter was approximately 0.2m deeper at a point 15m south of the point where 118 was sectioned. The course of this channel to the east is uncertain, but, during the initial recording of Area 1, an alignment of round-wood posts (P20) was traced eastward on a line that approximated to that of the northern edge of 105, although offset slightly to the north. This was traced eastward for a distance of at least 15m and was initially interpreted as a fence, but its location would suggest that the posts formed part of retaining timberwork for a continuation of the tail-race from Mills 2 and 3. Beyond this point a timber-revetted feature recorded in Area 4 may represent a continuation of the tail-race, 15–20m to the east. The location of this feature is far from certain, but, from the configuration of the adjacent channels it appears to have been located in the area between P22 and P23 on the south and P14 on the north. At a point approximately 13m north-east of the intersecting features (P22 and P23) a series of timbers was recorded over a distance of 7.5m on an approximately east–west alignment, the timbers comprising both vertical squared timbers and horizontal planks set along the southern edge of a cut. Traces of a parallel row of timbers 5m to the north were noted, the intervening space filled with an approximately 2m wide band of orange gravel running parallel to the south structure, the northern side occupied by grey ashy sand and bands of unspecified soil. A slot at the vertical interface of the gravel and soil could have held some decayed structure retaining the gravel. Overlying this complex of features and seemingly unrelated were small patches of burnt clay and charcoal. Interpretation of this partially recorded area, truncated by the drag-line, is problematic but the most salient features could have formed part of a wide timber-revetted channel later partially filled with gravel and narrowed to perhaps half its width. This possible channel would have lain on an alignment approximately parallel to P14 and P22 and mid way between them.

To the east no features were recorded for a distance of 40m, beyond which lay the cluster of features in Area 4 and Area 4 extension (below pp 39–42). It is noteworthy that in this area any down-stream continuation of this feature would coincide with the major river course identified on air photographs (*see* p 44).

Channel D: (Watercourse 610 Area 6 and Feature P22)

Channel D was a substantial linear feature cut into redeposited brickearth (613) and extending north-east to south-west for a distance of at least 5m as far as the southern limit of the excavation (Fig 5; Fig 10, Section D and Fig 12, Section J). The channel, 4.5m wide and 0.9m deep with a flat bottom and sloping sides, contained the timber structure of Mill 4, details of which are given below (pp 58–62). The fill consisted of three major deposits, 610.10, 610.2 and 610.1, but at the level of the timbers in the base a more complex stratigraphy was exposed.

Underlying the basal timbers was a primary deposit of black silt (610.9) 30mm thick containing a single sherd of late fourth-century pottery (Assemblage 14, p 109) as well as a fragment from a glass beaker (892) of late fourth- or early fifth-century date. Overlying the primary silt, in the area between the two main timbers, was a deposit of gravel (610.8) which yielded a group of sherds not closely datable (Assemblage 15, p 109). This deposit was in turn capped by another of gravel (610.7) which was banked up against the timber and which produced sherds of pottery and a number of metal small finds (Assemblage 16, p 109) dating to the second half of the fourth century AD. On the northern side of the channel the primary silt was capped by thin layers of black peaty silt (610.3) and gravel (610.7). Up-stream and south-west of the timber structure the basal deposit in the channel consisted of silt and gravel (610.10) while down-stream was a major deposit of gravel, banked against the timber but thinning to the north-east (610. 6 and 6a).

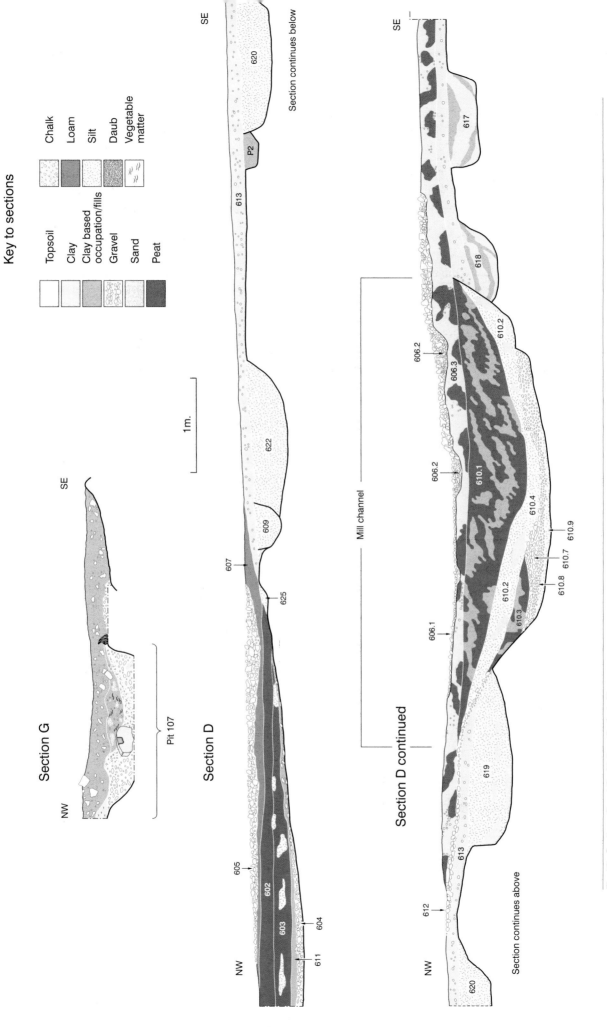

Fig 12. Sections G and D with key. Scale 1:40.

A central channel 1.1m wide and 0.14m deep was observed cutting the upper surface of gravel 610.7. The channel was filled with grey silt (610.4) which provided a small assemblage of late fourth-century pottery and a number of iron nails (Assemblage 25, p 118). The silt also capped gravel deposit 610.6 sealing the timbers.

These primary deposits were sealed by up to 0.25m of dark grey silt with lenses of brickearth (610.2) concentrated on either side of the channel. Finds from this deposit (Assemblage 26, p 118–19) included late Roman pottery, a copper alloy clasp for a box, a fragment from a wooden bowl (now lost) and three body sherds from an early Anglo-Saxon pottery vessel. Recorded as overlying this deposit, but respecting the central channel, was a 'daub' bank with wattle fencing (610.5). This structure provided an assemblage of late fourth- or early fifth-century pottery, as well as a shard from a glass vessel of similar date and a coin of the House of Theodosius (*c* AD 388–402) (Assemblage 24, p 118). The uppermost fill of the channel was a black peaty silt (610.1) up to 0.6m deep. A coin of Victorinus in the fill of pit 619, cut by the channel, provides a *terminus post quem* for the channel of AD 268, consistent with a date late in the third or fourth century.

At the time of its investigation this channel, like Channel C, had been truncated by the quarry but at an earlier stage of these operations a linear feature (P22) had been observed

on a similar alignment to 610 at a point 12m to the north-east. This was 2.5m wide and, from the single section, had been recut and contained at least one vertical timber; no other details are recorded. This probably represented the continuation of this channel to the north-east to a point 25m from the southern limits of the site where it was cut by another, later watercourse P23. Few details of the latter are available other than that this watercourse (as it was labelled on a site drawing) was 3.25m wide and was traced for at least 30m on a north–south alignmnet. The intersection of these two features is identifiable on a site drawing of Area 4, the later watercourse there turning eastwards to coincide with, and be subsumed within, the main watercourse.

No figure can be given for the fall in level of the base of this late channel but comparison between the base level of Channel D (Fig 12, Section D) and Channel C (Fig 11, Section B) suggest that the former, at its deepest point, was some 0.15m deeper than the base of Channel C. The later channel P23 provided no datable finds and has been interpreted as a post-Roman feature.

Wells, timber-lined tanks and other structures
Christopher Sparey-Green and Paul Bennett

In all, four timber-lined tanks or wells were recorded, the first identified north of the road and close to the quarry face

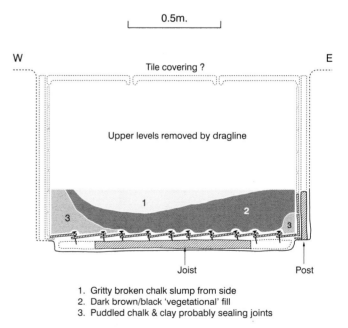

Fig 13. Plan of Pit 19. Scale 1:20.   Fig 14. Section through Pit 19. Scale 1:20.

Pl IX. General view of Pit 333 showing plank lining and loose plank lying diagonally across lower fill. Scale 2m.

at the north end of Area 1. The second was recorded at the south-west end of Area 1, while the remaining two occurred later at the north-eastern end of the enclosure complex in Area 3. In addition, a polygonal feature outlined by posts, (335, termed the 'shrine' in site records) may also have been a lined pit with a distinctive fill. A stake-lined structure (P24) in Area 2 may have been of a similar character.

An isolated wood-lined tank (P19 'Well 2') at the south-west end of Area 1 was identified in the area south of the road between Channels A and B. Few details of the feature are available, the structure being described as a 2m square well. It was located on or close to the projected line of a timber fence or post alignment P20.

The remaining two square timber-lined features (333 and 701) lay within the enclosure system north of the road. Of the first, few details were recorded other than the feature was a well approximately 2m square and lay against the north section of the quarry.

The second timber-lined structure (333) was set in a pit cut into the natural clay and measured some 1.38 by 1.35m and was approximately 0.8m deep (Figs 13 and 14; Pls IX and X). The feature had been badly truncated by the drag-line but the recorded timber lining survived to a height of 0.27m on all four sides and the base. The base planks were arranged with their overlapping edges nailed together to a series of five underlying horizontal joists set at right angles to them. The planks on the western side of the pit had given way during use and showed evidence of repair. The disturbed upper fill appeared to have been sealed by complete *tegulae* laid side by side, flush with the top of the natural clay. A gravel surface overlay this, co-terminus with the pit outline.

The remaining fill yielded a substantial group of pottery dating to the end of the fourth century and possibly the early fifth (Assemblage 22, pp 115–17).

The third tank (701) was located in Area 7 towards the north where a 1.2m square pit had been excavated to a depth

Pl X. Detail of Pit 333 showing plank lying diagonally across plank floor. Scale 20cm.

of 1.30m, cutting through the fill of ditches 702 and 703 (Figs 15 and 16, Pl XI). Set into this cut was a sub-square timber construction (P26) measuring approximately 0.7 x 0.8m internally and surviving to a maximum depth of 1.2m (Fig 16). The tank was formed of ten courses each of four planks joined together by simple cross lap joints, the planks on average 0.8m long, 0.12m wide and 0.02m thick. The uppermost timber course was surmounted by a lining of wattle (P27) about 0.1m deep. The construction pit backfill yielded no datable finds, but the tank infill provided a coin of Arcadius (*c* AD 388–95) together with a wide range of pottery dating into the second half of the fourth century (Assemblage 23, p 117) and a number of finds. These include at least two leather shoes, an iron stylus, part of a key, a knife with a bone handle and two shards from glass beakers of late third- or fourth-century date. A second fill (701.2) included four coins of mid fourth-century date. This feature also appears to have been surrounded by a contemporary metalled surface sealing the earlier ditch fill.

Two other features should be noted in the north-west section of Area 1. These were observed in the north-west quarry face and in early records made by Jim Bradshaw they were marked on plan as a metalled surface (P25) and a square feature (P18) identified as 'Well 1'. No written description of these features survives, but from the plan the metalled surface appeared to extend for 5m along the section, so is perhaps more likely to represent a metalled area or yard than a trackway. P18 was originally recorded as 3m square.

These timber-lined tanks and wells may have served the enclosure system or been a product of late industrial activity on that part of the site. They may have provided a clean water supply to the settlement or functioned as watering troughs for stock. It is also possible that they and the other substantial cut features in this area, such as P8–10, were used as retting pits in the preparation of flax (*see* pp 324–5), or perhaps for some other industrial process. From its shallowness and plank floor 333 was more likely of industrial use (*see* also p 138), while the depth and the form of lining in 701 suggests that was a well.

On the south side of the road two structures could represent the linings of pits. Firstly, context 335 in Area 3, consisted of a roughly rectangular structure measuring some 2m by 1.2m, set within a larger cut whose dimensions were not recorded but which was backfilled with clay (Fig 17, Pls XII and XIII). Gravel deposits visible in the photograph on the west and north may be the sides of this cut. The pit itself was defined by a rectangular setting of upright round-wood posts exposed to a depth of 0.2m The surviving posts were closely set along the angled northern end but were intermittent towards the southern end, the lower ends set in the unexcavated underlying soil. The base of the pit may have been partially formed by a layer of small stones or gravel. The fill of the pit was varied, including lenses of clay and fragments of sandstone, tile, flint and tree branches. A large number of animal bones including cattle lower jaws and shoulder blades were clustered at the north end of the pit, as if deliberately placed; it was this feature that gave rise to the appellation 'shrine'. A sizeable group of late Roman pottery (Assemblage 18, pp 109–10) from its fill also included one (possibly intrusive) early Anglo-Saxon pottery sherd. A small assemblage of metalwork and lead alloy waste was also recovered from the feature, including a number of items with hammerscale, suggestive of nearby metal-working. The objects include several fragments of copper alloy

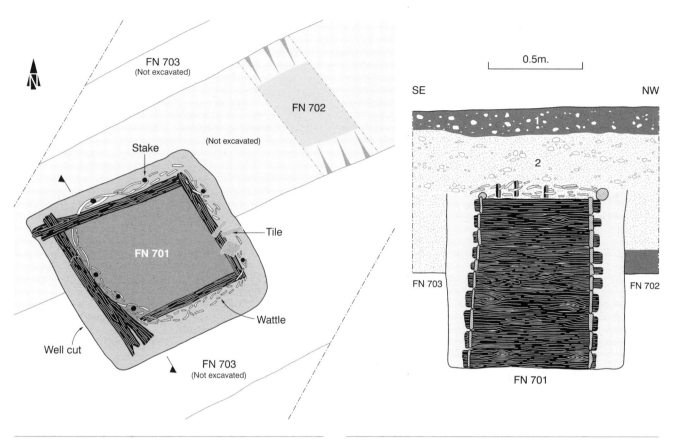

Fig 15. Plan of Well 701. Scale 1:20.

Fig 16. Section through Well 701. Scale 1:20.

and bone bracelets, an iron stylus, a knife, a fragment of a late Roman glass beaker, a bucket handle and an iron awl.

The second of these features, structure P24, lay a short distance north-east of Area 6 and was less clearly defined. This feature was formed of irregular alignments of stake-holes forming a three-sided trapezoidal structure with an open northern side although the most detailed site drawing suggests other arrangements are possible. No further details are available and no associated dated deposits were recorded. The feature may have been either the lining of a pit or part of a fish or eel-trap associated with the later river course passing through this area.

Miscellaneous features in Areas 1–16

The following description covers a miscellaneous range of features noted, firstly, in Areas 1 and 6 in the vicinity of Channels A, C and D and Mills 2–4, then in Area 3 and finally Areas 4 and 4 extension, in the area of the later river course, close to the site of Mill 1. The uppermost deposits in these

areas are treated separately in view of their stratigraphically late date and their possible association with the watercourse identified from air photography as passing through these areas.

Features in Area 7 have already been described where their position is certain; others, for which there are fewer records, are included in this section. For the remaining areas (Areas 8–16), few if any records survive, the existence of features in these areas indicated merely by the survival of labelled finds which indicated that, at least on site, context numbers had been assigned to the deposits from which these objects had been recovered.

Areas 1 and 6

The principal features in Areas 1 and 6 were the remains of three Roman watermills, Mills 2–4 associated with Channels C and D (Figs 18 and 19). These structures are described below (pp 49–62). Here, the remaining features in both areas are described, the majority of which represent fragmentary

Pl XI. Well 701 from the south-west showing part of the timber lining and surrounding wattles. The edge of Ditch 703 is in the foreground. Scale 2m.

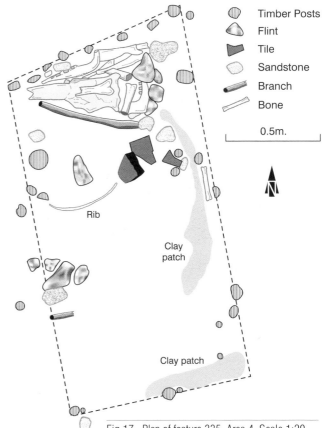

Fig 17. Plan of feature 335, Area 4. Scale 1:20.

elements of linear cuts from the preceding use of the area (Figs 4 and 10).

In Area 1, immediately south of Channel C, was a subrectangular pit (116) approximately 3.5m long and 1.5m wide, cut to a depth of 0.3m. No details of pit fill are recorded, although it included six coins spanning the period from AD 364–78, as well as a shard from a late Roman glass beaker and several fragments of querns. To the east of this feature was an irregular cut (129), traced for some 6.5m east from the southern section. The feature was 0.5m deep, filled with several layers of brickearth and silt (129.1). It included coins of Constantine I and Diocletian. A further cut (117), close to Channel C and containing fills of silt and gravel (117.1, 117.2 and 117.3), lay in the vicinity. It produced three coins covering the same time period as those from pit 116, as well as iron nails and a quantity of daub.

To the south, in the eastern part of Area 6, a number of minor ditches and cut features (P1–3, 609, 617–621, 623, 625 and 626) were found beneath a layer of brickearth (613) (Figs 10 and 19; Fig 12, Section D). A small group of post-

holes (614–616) was found to have cut the deposit and may have been associated with a structure constructed against the west side of a channel forming part of Mill 4. A deposit of destruction debris (612) capping the brickearth deposit may also have been associated with the structure.

One of the earliest features located in Area 6 was a north–south aligned flat-bottomed ditch (617) recorded in the south corner of the excavated area. The ditch, 0.8m wide and 0.3m deep, filled with silty brickearth (617.1) was traced for 3.5m and was truncated by Channel D (610). Extending parallel and adjacent to the ditch was a gully (618), 0.9m wide and 0.4m deep. The gully filled with a dirty yellow brickearth (618.1) was also cut by the mill channel.

A third early ditch or gully (621) was located approximately 4m north-west of Mill 4. This feature, aligned north-east to south-west, was 0.42m wide and 0.25m deep and could be traced for a total length of 2.4m from the southern section of Area 6. It was filled with a dark grey-brown silt (621.1). Ditch P2, possibly a recut on the north-western side of this, had a flat bottom and steep sides and was 0.5m wide and 0.16m

Pl XII. Detail of group of animal bones and flints within the timber structure 335. Scale 20cm.

Pl XIII. General view of structure 335 showing the framework of vertical timbers containing animal bones and flints. Scale 20cm.

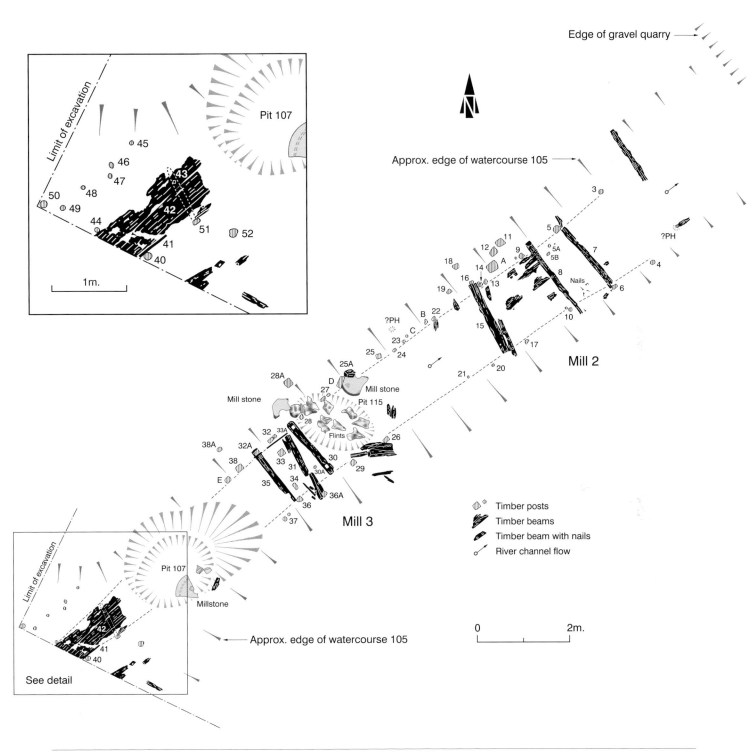

Fig 18. Detail plan of Channel C showing Mills 2 and 3 with pits 107 and 115. Scale 1:80.

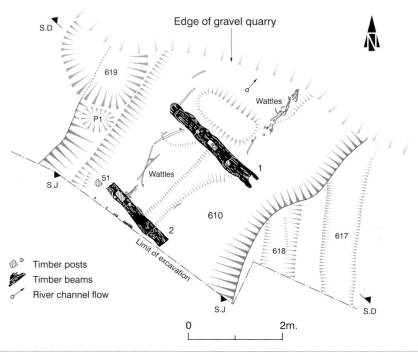

Fig 19. Detail plan of Mill 4. Scale 1:80. For Section J *see* Fig 11, for Section D *see* Fig 12.

deep. The ditch was traced for a length of approximately 3.65m from the quarry edge and terminated 0.5m from the southern edge of the excavation. Both these features were cut by 620, a ditch aligned east–west. This ditch, 1.37m wide and 0.4m deep with sloping sides and rounded base, was traced for 5.3m from the quarry edge to the point where it had been truncated by a later ditch (622). The feature was filled with a grey-brown silt (620.1) with bands of iron-panned brickearth incorporated in the fill.

Ditch 622, cut the western end of ditch 620. The late ditch, aligned north-east to south-west, 2.2m wide and 0.4m deep, was traced for 5m across the excavated area. The feature, cut with gently sloping sides and a flat base, was filled with grey silt (622.1).

Two subcircular features (623 and 625) were identified against the north-west side of ditch 622. Both features were approximately 0.9m in diameter and 0.2m deep and filled with mid grey silt flecked with brickearth (623.1 and 625.1). Cutting both features and ditch 622 was a narrow curving gully (609). The gully, 0.30–0.55m wide, was approximately 0.2m deep and filled with dark grey silt with brickearth flecks (609.1).

Approximately 7m north-west of 609 an irregular 'depression' (626), about 1.5m wide, was recorded together with a small cut feature (P3). Few details of either are available but the latter contained an iron key. To the south-east, Pit 619 was truncated by the quarry and by the edge of Channel D. This was an almost circular pit 2m wide and 0.6m deep with a rounded profile and filled with grey silt with lenses of brickearth. A coin of Victorinus (AD 268–70) is recorded as derived from this fill.

Capping the early features was an extensive deposit of discoloured brickearth and daub fragments (613) up to 0.15m thick (Fig 12, Section D), which included a coin of Constans (AD 337–40). Sealing the deposit was a layer of destruction material (612), comprising flint cobbles, large fragments of burnt daub, Roman brick, pottery and charcoal. Adjacent to these deposits were three post-holes (614–616) on average 0.25–0.5m in diameter and 0.08m deep. All three were filled with dark grey silt and chocked with angular flints, 615 also producing a fourth-century coin of the House of Constantine. A further possible post-hole P1, only recorded in plan as an oval feature 0.5 by 0.8m in diameter, and set on the edge of the cut for Channel D, lay to the south-east in line with 616, 614 and 623. The exact relationship of these deposits of building debris with the post-holes is not certain but they sealed the more substantial ditches and gully 609 and were concentrated in an area some 2.5m to the west of Channel

D and were cut by it. The association of layers of building debris with post-holes suggests the presence of a building here of fourth-century date, predating the mill channel. Features 623 and 625 could have formed part of the north-western end, the former lying at the western corner, the remainder forming part of the south-western side.

In view of the fragmentary nature of the features recorded, few conclusions can be drawn as to the nature of the occupation preceding the channels in this area. It should be noted, however, that features 617, 618 and 620 lie on alignments radically different to most of the features in this area and are approximately parallel with or at right angles to the line of the road to the north. It is therefore possible that they could represent elements of an early enclosure system, or perhaps beam-slots for timber buildings preceding dumped deposits 612 and 613. The curving ditch 609 must fall late in this sequence but was also sealed by the deposits of building debris at some date in the mid fourth century or later, before this was, in turn, cut by Channel D. Overall, the features may indicate the presence of two or more phases of building, predating the cutting of Channel D. Features 622 and 609 may perhaps have been successive phases of drainage gully located to the west of the putative buildings.

Area 3

Linear features and pits in Area 3 of the quarry have already been described where these were in close relationship to the road, enclosure systems and Channel A. Two groups of linear features were also planned in a narrow strip along the south-east edge of Area 3, south-west of Area 4, and adjacent to the south side of the major watercourse (Fig 4). The few details recorded are included here, the more easterly group of features comprising:

    Ditch 316: 0.65m wide and of unknown depth;
    Ditch 317: 0.8m wide and of unknown depth;
    Ditch 318: 1.7m wide and of unknown depth;
    Ditch 319: 1m wide and of unknown depth;
    Ditch 320: 0.55m wide and of unknown depth;
    Ditch 321: 0.35m wide found cutting ditch 322 and
       cut by ditch 323;
    Ditch 322: 0.3m wide, cut by ditch 321;
    Ditch 323: 1.55m wide found cutting ditch 321 and
       cut by ditch 324;
    Ditch 324: 1.35m wide found cutting ditches 325
       and 323;
    Ditch 325: 0.4m wide cut by ditch 324.

All ten ditches were relatively narrow and appear to follow two axes, the majority of features aligned approximately at

right angles to the road line, while two others (321 and 325) were set at approximately 45 degrees to its axis. The close clustering suggests that they either represent frequently-replaced timber foundation trenches or recut ditches.

To the south-east a further small group of three ditches was recorded. Feature 326 was a 1.5m wide ditch of unknown depth, set at an angle to 327, a ditch 0.3m in width. Feature 328 was a ditch 1.35m wide on an alignment approximately parallel to the road line. One site drawing makes mention of Anglo-Saxon pottery occurring in this feature but no details are available for this.

Little can be concluded from these scattered observations but it should be noted that 328 is approximately parallel to the road and as in Area 6 these features could be the surviving traces of an enclosure system preceding the system of channels, mills and the later river course, or substantial beam-slots for a timber building.

Area 4 and Area 4 extension

The main consideration in this area is the apparent coincidence of the complex of irregular pits and hollows with the course of the main watercourse (Figs 4 and 20). The latter will be further treated below but it would appear that the features in this area represent the remains of activity south of the road and the putative early mill Channels A and B, truncated by the later formation of the river course (*see* p 71) and sealed beneath alluvium and organic silt. Despite the proximity of this area to the position of Mills 1 and 2 no direct relationship can be drawn between any of these features and the mill.

The features identified in this area cut mixed natural deposits of gravel, brickearth and flint cobbles (413). The upper fills of these features were in turn sealed by extensive layers of gravel and peat which are probably to be associated with the later river course.

The earliest feature, stratigraphically, was an extensive and ill defined hollow (408), referred to as the 'midden' on account of the quantity of mixed occupation debris recovered from this feature (Fig 20). The hollow had been truncated on the north by the quarry while the southern edge was traced for at least 20m on an alignment approximately parallel to the road, the hollow measuring at least 5m wide but only 100mm in depth. The feature was only sectioned at one point where the waterlogged fill consisted of orange gravel mixed with peat, the deposit containing substantial quantities of finds including pottery (Assemblage 20, p 110–12) of fourth- to early fifth-century date. The finds included coins mainly of Constantinian or Valentinian date and a group

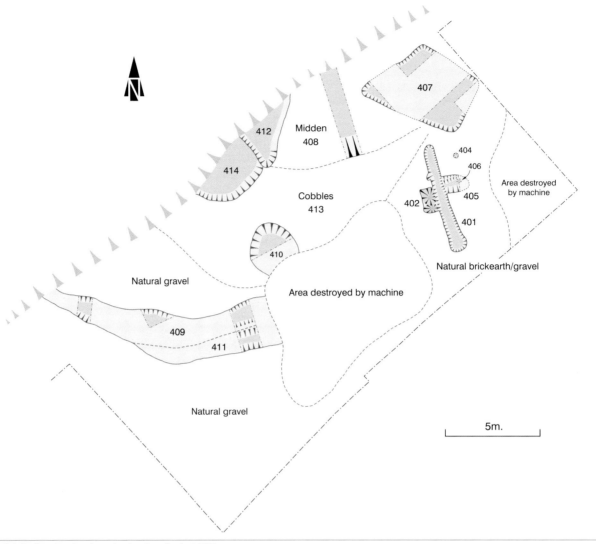

Fig 20. Detail plan showing Area 4 extension. Scale 1:200.

of objects of late Roman date including four lead alloy pendants (Pls XXI and XXII, 282–4, 287), several bracelets of copper alloy and bone, a strap-end, an iron finger ring, an iron stylus, two leather shoes and a small fragment of melted copper that represents debris from metal-working. The presence of copper alloy sheet and lead waste suggests that metal-working took place in the vicinity of this feature and this waste material may suggest that the lead pendants were made in this area of the site. An early Roman brooch (178, p 171) from this feature may have been retained as scrap for remelting .

Three features, 407, 412 and 414, are recorded cutting 408. Pit 407 was trapezoidal, approximately 5.4m long, 4m broad and at least 0.3m deep. The pit was filled with a sticky grey-brown silt (407.3) overlain by a peaty gravel (407.2) providing a group of pottery (Assemblage 19, p 110). Twelve coins attributed to 407 provide a date of AD 364–378 for the feature. No small finds are recorded from 407.3 but 407.2 included an assemblage of five iron styli, an iron penannular brooch, copper alloy and iron bracelet fragments, a knife, a bucket handle mount and a latchlifter. Further small finds are attributed merely to feature 407 and include several bracelet fragments, as well as structural ironwork.

A third pit (334/414, Fig 21), cutting the western edge of 408 and cut by the post-Roman pit (412), was 5m long and 2.3m wide. The pit had steeply sloping sides and was

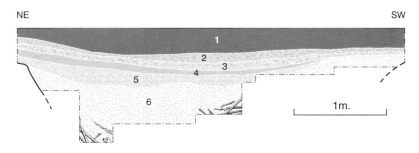

Fig 21. Section through pit 414 and palaeochannel. Scale 1:40. (For key, *see* Fig 12, p 30.)

at least 0.8m deep, the fill (334/414.6) consisting largely of dark brown silt and lenses of clay overlying large quantities of wood branches. The few sherds from this fill included pottery of the mid fourth century (Assemblage 10, p 100–1). The uppermost deposits (334/414.2–5) consisted of layers of sand, clayey occupation deposits and gravel, these deposits extending beyond the limits of the pit. The majority of the pottery from these contexts (Assemblage 11, p 101–3) dated to the fourth century. Other finds included objects with hammerscale adhering and a broken pair of blacksmith's tongs (Fig 119, 1236) indicative of nearby metal-working. These deposits (334/414.3 and 334/414.4) also contained much Roman brick rubble while 334/414.2 contained fragments of wood and other organic materials. Records of finds, including the blacksmith's tongs, from 'Section 2, layers 2–5' appear to be equivalent to 334/414.2–5 and therefore derive from these deposits. The deposits also yielded fragments of a glass 'Frontinus' bottle (846), window glass (1093), a copper alloy appliqué (38) and an iron lock (Fig 94, 667).

The uppermost deposits (334/414.2–5) extended beyond the pit to the north-east and were described as typical of the stratigraphy in the area. They may also be similar to the deposits of gravel and building rubble sealing Mill 1, approximately 25m to the north-east, but these more mixed layers may in part have been material reworked in the ancient river bed visible in the air photograph extending over this area. Overlying the area of the pit was a layer of brown peat, reeds and organic matter (334.1/414.1) which probably derives from the overlying, post-Roman river course. As elsewhere in this part of the site the full sequence was probably truncated, the topsoil and uppermost stratigraphy to a depth of perhaps 0.5m having been removed by drag-line.

Several features were identified in the area south of 334/414. To the east and approximately at right angles to its edge, feature (401) was a trench-like feature 5.8m long, 0.9m wide and 0.24m deep, with sloping sides and a rounded base

and a fill of gravelly peat. A flax heckle spike was retrieved from this feature. Two closely set square post-holes (402 and 403) were located mid way along the western side of the slot. The post-holes of sides 0.25m and cut 0.15m deep were filled with dark, organic silt. On the opposite side of the slot was an irregular post-pit some 0.9m wide and 0.2m deep, filled with peat. Set into the pit was a post-hole (406), 0.23m in diameter and 0.2m deep. The post 'ghost' was filled with peat and a little gravel (406.1). An isolated post-hole (404) was located a short way north-east of the slot. The roughly square post of side roughly 0.25m, and cut 0.15m deep, was filled with peat and a little gravel. The post-hole was packed with a number of large animal bones and a fragment of a leather shoe. These substantial features suggest the existence of a timber structure, the full extent and plan of which is unknown, but it is possibly associated with the mills or management of water supply.

In the area to the south-west and adjoining feature 408, three features, 409/411 could be identified. Feature 409/411 was a recut ditch of irregular outline on an approximately east–west alignment. Ditch 411, exposed for a length of some 6m, was 1.4m wide and 0.19m deep, cut with sloping sides and a rounded base. The ditch was filled with a grey silt (411.2) overlain by light grey silt and coarse gravel (411.1) and cut on the south by feature 409, approximately 1.75m wide and 0.38m deep. The recut, which removed most of the early ditch to the west, was filled with gravel (409.2) overlain by dark organic silt (409.1). There may have been a second recut of this feature (415), but no detailed information exists.

Adjacent to this ditch was a subcircular pit (410), approximately 2.5m in diameter and at least 0.5m deep. The pit was filled with dark grey silt (410.2) sealed by a deposit of coarse gravel mixed with peat (410.1).

It should be noted that irregular and ill-defined areas of gravel were noted in the area west of 409/411 but not overlying this feature; this may have been part of an extensive deposit represented by the adjacent layer 414.2 and reported as also extending east to overlie Mill 1. It is not clear whether these were part of metalled surfaces or, more likely, were water-lain deposits. The metalled surface and features in all but the north-east corner of the trench were capped by an extensive deposit of peat and water-lain gravel.

Areas 7–16

Area 7 lay towards the north-eastern end of the site, north of the Roman road (Fig 4). As already noted, part of an enclosure ditch and a later wood-lined pit (features 701–703), can be identified in this area but the exact position of the other features described in this area is lost although they are presumed to have lain nearby and were therefore part of the ditch system north of the road.

Gully 704 was aligned north–south and appears to have been dug into the gravel. It contained two deposits, the upper (704.1) light grey-brown silt, the lower (704.2) a light grey silt. At least five other ditches or gullies can be identified, details of which survive for only two. The section of 714 shows this to have been aligned north–south and apparently of two phases. The original cut was a steep-sided V-shaped channel at least 0.5m wide and 0.6m deep, recut to a U-shaped profile, 0.95m wide and 0.25m deep. This contained three deposits, the first phase filled with 714.3, a yellow brickearth silt, the second phase containing 714.1, a dark grey silt and 714.2, a grey silt. Ditch 715 appears to have been a linear feature, 0.65m wide, filled with yellow brickearth and adjoining 709. Part of a late Roman pewter vessel is recorded from 709.3 while another was recovered from 712, apparently a machine disturbance. Ditches 706 and 707 were two intersecting features.

Of two depressions the most significant was 713, an oval depression cut into the brickearth and measuring 3m by 1.1m and 0.35m deep and aligned east–west. This contained three deposits: 713.1, a black silt in the base; 713.2, dark grey silt on the upper part; 713.3, an orange silt filling the upper central part. The only finds were described as 'flints', raising the interesting possibility that this was a prehistoric feature. Another small depression in the gravel (705) contained one deposit (705.1) of orange brown fine gravel.

Areas 8 and 9 are noted as comprising a strip south-east of and parallel to Areas 3 and 4, in which case Area 4 extension and 10 and 14 must have overlapped with, or

extended into, this strip. Finds data from Area 8 includes mention of a smithing hearth base surviving in the base of the topsoil 801 while context 802 contained metalwork including an iron frying pan (below, p 69). The north-eastern end of Area 9 adjoined Area 7 since features 902, 903 and 905 refer to burials in the vicinity of Area 7. The records for 902 are confused and may be conflated with those from 802. 902 appears to have been a shallow depression cut into the clay and to have contained pewter bowls and an iron pan overlain by tiles, stone and preserved twigs. The photographs also suggest these vessels overlay human bones from a burial, but were not necessarily part of the grave fill. The remaining features 903 and 905 were undoubtedly burials (below, p 69).

Areas 10 and 14 appear to designate the area of Mill 1. The detailed records for this wooden structure and the associated finds from the area allow a full description of this structure to be given (below p 45).

Site records also refer to ditches being found in Areas 15 and 16, an area thought to be located south of the road and close to the watercourse in the eastern corner of the quarry. The ditches are significant in that they contained a collection of Roman leather objects, mainly shoes and other cut leather oddments indicating that the leather goods may have been manufactured nearby (below, p 211).

The Roman watermills [7]

Robert Spain

Introduction

In previous accounts of the Ickham mills (Young 1975; 1981), the existence of only two mill sites was reported but, as will be seen below, following a re-examination of the evidence, the situation is far more complicated. On the basis of new analysis, from the early third century until the late fourth century AD, it now seems that at least three watermills, and possibly four, were established on the Little Stour at Ickham.

The earliest mill (Mill 1), published in 1984 (Spain 1984a; 1984b) was thought at the time to have operated between *c* AD 150 and 280. A reassessment of coins and other finds associated with this part of the site now suggests

---

7.   Details of the millstones and querns associated with the mills are provided in Part 4, under the sections dealing with household implements (querns, pp 251–5) and crafts and industries (millstones, pp 277–89). A number of possible mill fittings are also described in Part 4.

that it was used between *c* AD 225–70 (*see* p 82). The site of Mill 1 in relation to other features was poorly understood in 1984. A re-examination of the site records has enabled a more accurate positioning of the mill structure to be proposed (Fig 4). The original Mill 2 is now recognised as having two distinct building phases, each with its own mill (Mills 2 and 3). Mill 2 (Fig 25) occupied the down-stream element of the original complex and Mill 3 the up-stream element (Fig 24).

Methodology

In the process of analysing the mill structures the writers have sought to determine the degree of certainty of the discoveries in particular areas of the site. Part of the examination of the evidence concerned the attempt to reconstruct and determine the building and machinery support structure of the mills. Critical to this analysis has been the evidence of earthfast posts and ground-plates on the edge of or outside the mill-race, especially those posts whose scantling is greater than that required solely for revetment work. In Mill 1 a complete earthfast 'foot-print' was revealed, facilitating a thorough reconstruction of the building and machinery support structure, including development and maintenance phases (Spain 1984a).[8] In Mills 2 and 3 the evidence was far less complete and for Mill 4 mostly lost. In order to qualify the integrity of the analysis and reconstruction that follows, it is necessary to establish whether evidence discovered on the margins of the mill-race, especially the north-west bank, could be considered to have been the entire earthfast foundations that existed within the Roman horizons.

As a prelude to this analysis all extant photographs of the excavation were examined to ensure that the recovered plan (Fig 18) was as comprehensive and accurate as surviving records would allow. For this exercise valuable evidence was provided by the near-vertical photographic shots taken from above watercourse 105. The views must have been taken somewhat later than those taken from the ground because one or two posts and a plank clearly evident in other photographs, were missing in the above-ground shots. Following this examination of the photographs there were two changes made to the plan of the structures, the first involving several features that were either not clearly

shown as posts or, shown as posts but not indexed.[9] The second change was that several of the posts at the north-east end of the watercourse were clearly larger in section than indicated on the original plan. Comparative measurements and photographic scales helped to re-assess the sizes, and a number of posts[10] have been increased in size. The reason for these differences is not difficult to ascertain. The waterlogged excavation conditions and the rapid decay of the projecting posts and timberwork over two seasons of digging made accurate recording difficult.

The water supply

The mill sites appear to have been carefully chosen so as to take advantage both of water from the Little Stour up-stream and access to a Roman road linking with Canterbury and Richborough. The exact course of the contemporary river channel is uncertain but the water supply needed to be relatively close to the millworks, whilst the stream's degree of seasonality needed to be carefully gauged because even the most powerful water-flow could run at greatly reduced levels during the summer months. Indeed, even water-powered mill sites established in more recent times often suffered from the seasonality of their watercourses. Millwrights could, of course, partially compensate for seasonal changes in water levels by being able to calculate the rates of flow available to them. However, earlier millwrights would have been almost wholly reliant on local observation of a watercourse or water supply over a long period of time. A further important consideration was the fall from the source to the proposed mill site, and to this end the mill-races had to be carefully laid out to maximize water-flow.

Within a 200-year period the Little Stour appears to have provided a consistent supply of water power for at least three and possibly four Romano-British watermills at Ickham. There can be little doubt that river water was directed to Mill 1 and, later, to Mills 2, 3 and 4 by means of artificially cut inlets or head-race channels, the course of which is only imperfectly understood. The up-stream supply is likely to have been drawn off at some point above the point where the road line crossed to the left or western bank of the river.

On the present site, the courses of four channels have been partially traced as described above. In the earlier

---

8.　The writer is deeply grateful to the late Jim Bradshaw, whose intimate knowledge of the site and patience in answering numerous and often exacting enquiries facilitated a thorough and exciting reconstruction.

9.　For ease of identification these have been indexed numeric-alpha, the number being from the nearest post. These are 5A, 5B, 25A, 28A, 38A, 30A, 32A and 36A. At the south-west end of the watercourse one bed plank (43) and several posts and stakes (44–52) were numbered.

10.　Posts 3, 4, 5, 6, 10, 17, 20 and 21.

occupation period two presumably successive watercourses were created along the south side of the road, one of these Channel B probably supplying Mill 1 (314: Channel B). The destination of Channel A (118/310) was not identified but the tail-races of both channels presumably emptied down-stream into the river after working the mills. In a later period major watercourses were built for Mills 2 and 3 (105: Channel C) and for Mill 4 (610: Channel D) and, although not identified, their tail-races must have flowed through Area 4.

The topography of the present valley floor suggests a negligible fall from the river to the millworks and this was, of course, the principal reason why undershot water-wheels were employed. A slight head of water might also have necessitated the artificial raising of the water level to facilitate its diversion into the head-races. At a similar site on Hadrian's Wall at Haltwhistle Burn Head, a small weir built with blocks of granite was constructed across an adjacent stream. The weir raised the water level sufficiently in the stream to accommodate its diversion to a head-race channel for an undershot watermill (F Simpson 1976, 33). In view of the evidence at Ickham, at which the hydraulic head relied on the diversion of water from an adjacent river, it is quite possible that a similar arrangement was originally in place. Unfortunately, no investigation of the head-race channels up-stream of the quarry was undertaken, but any dam might lie hidden within the woodland immediately up-stream of the site.

The shaded area on Fig 4 shows the outline of a sinuous and braided watercourse as revealed by aerial photographs (Pl I). This watercourse coincided with Roman features in Areas 1 and 6 and Area 4 down-stream and also, significantly, with extensive deposits of gravel and peat seen sealing these occupation features. This is particularly apparent in Section D in Area 6 (Fig 12) and the section of pit 334/414 in Area 4 where these deposits (layers 1–3) were described as extending over much of this area (Fig 21).

The nature and course of this feature suggests it was a natural development in the period after the abandonment of the mills, the passage of water eroding some areas and depositing riverine material over a wide area. While peat and gravel deposits accumulated immediately to the south-east near Channel D, the upper levels of Channel C and Mills 2 and 3 would have been eroded by water-flow at the bend of the observed watercourse, the course of which here turned through almost 90 degrees to the east. At this point on the outside bank both mills would have been subjected to the greater velocity of the flow, where its erosive forces were greatest; much of the structural evidence at this point may have been swept away. Although no trace of a constructed

channel coincided with this feature to the east the flow may have exploited the down-stream section of Channel C, erasing this feature here also. Further east, in Areas 15 and 16, the bifurcation of the channel could be due to its erosion of the earlier Channel A as well.

Channels and mills

As already noted, the four channels originated up-stream beyond the south-west limits of the Ickham site. The following section is concerned solely with the linear watercourses south of the road that appear to have served as mill-races for the four identified mills.

Channels A and B lay closest to the road, the former the larger of the two and traceable from the north-west corner of the quarry to a point beyond the conjectured position of Mill 1. The width of Channel A at 2m was much greater than Channel B, the head-race entering Mill 1, and it is therefore proposed that another water-power site may have existed close by and down-stream of Mill 1, and that its tail-race discharged down-stream in the area of the northern bifurcation of the later watercourse.

Only a 14m long section of the second watercourse Channel B (314) was located in Area 3. Although the watercourse may have been a continuation of features 111, 124 and P14, the size and profiles of the disjointed sections of channel do not match (*see* above, p 28) and a relationship between the elements is far from certain. Two alternative connections with Channel B may be proposed. The first links features P14 and 314 to a predecessor to watercourse 105 (Channel C) to form a continuous 1m wide watercourse and head-race for Mill 1. The second alternative connects Channel B to the larger and probably earlier Channel A. Channel A was recorded to have been blocked with purposely laid deposits of gravel and flints some 7m west of the excavated western terminus of Channel B. Channel B was aligned east–west on a converging line to intersect watercourse 310 just above the point where it is reported to have been blocked. Channel B and Mill 1 may therefore have been fed by an earlier watercourse (118/P13/310) which had been deliberately blocked just below the point of intersection of the channels. Given that Mill 1 was modified on perhaps more than one occasion, it is not impossible that during its working life the mill may have been provided with more than one watercourse connection to its head-race (Channel B). There are merits to all three alternative water sources, but without relative levels it is impossible to shed further light on the question of their commonality or separate existences. The source of supply to Mill 1 up-stream of Channel B must therefore remain conjectural.

The mill-races serving Mills 2 and 3 (Channel C) and Mill 4 (Channel D) were well defined, having fairly large revetted sections. These two parallel channels lay either side of the eroded hollow from the later watercourse but coincided with it down-stream and their tail-races may have been eroded away or masked by it.

Mill 1 (Figs 4, 22, Pls XIV–XVI) *Christopher Sparey-Green*[11]

Mill 1 appears to be the earliest on the site and was located in Area 10/14, down-stream of Channels A or B. The position of the structure cannot be exactly reconstructed, but it lay close to and immediately south of, the quarry face in June 1974, in the vicinity of features 310–312 and 314. The relationship to Channels A and B is not certain but it is likely that the latter fed this mill, feature 314 appearing to head towards the position of Mill 1. It is noteworthy that there are references to finds from context 14.01 as the channel leading into the mill but there are no details of its exact location.

The ground plan of a wooden building at least 6m by 3.5m was recognised from a pattern of vertical earthfast timbers and horizontal planks set on edge. Set with its long axis north-west to south-east, the structure was aligned at right angles to the general line of the watercourses and the Roman road. The north-western end of the building may have been lost in the quarry. Four major elements in the structure were recognised. Firstly, four groups of particularly stout timbers were interpreted as supporting the hursting for the millstones, this structure adjoining the wheel-race. Two posts on the other side of the race may have carried the hursting over the wheel and wheel-race to form a continuous platform some 3m by 1.5m. The group of posts nearest the race on the up-stream side appears to have rotated as if their position has been distorted or shifted under the pressure of water. The duplication of supports suggested that the ground was unstable and there was a need to reinforce the structure. The second element, contained by this framework, was the support for the wheel and driver gear. This consisted of two pairs of verticals which would have supported transverse beams carrying either end of the main shaft. The third element was the containing building which was of post and plank construction, retaining a slightly higher external ground level. Differences in the form of the timbers suggested that the building may have been extended during its life. Finally, there was the wheel-race 0.6m wide which led

into a tail-race 1.5m wide, both defined by uprights but not lined in any obvious way. The actual line of the head-race on the west side immediately up-stream could not be identified but posts either side of the channel on this side of the wheel pit may have supported some means of controlling or raising the water supply.

Since no dug channel on this side was identified the head-race may have have been raised above the surviving ground level and had left no trace. A substantial plank and post wall or barrier 1.5m on this up-stream side of the mill was, however, unexplained and this may have served as part of some dam to raise the water level before entering the head-race. Alternatively this may simply be part of a later structure unconnected with the function of the mill but the construction was generally similar to that of the mill. As with the other mills on the site, there was an associated small collection of millstones (*see* pp 277–85) and their presence suggests the use of the mill for flour production rather than any other purpose. Coin evidence suggests the mill was in operation between *c* AD 225–70. The building appears to have undergone a number of modifications during its working life, perhaps suggesting that it may have been poorly placed and ill-sited from the outset, with revisions to its design during its period of use implemented to improve or rectify its unfortunate situation.

Deposits of flint, gravel and rare tile fragments sealing the building did not obviously derive from the structure. These have been interpreted as a deliberate metalled surface lain over the remains of the structure but it is more likely that they represented a water-lain deposit. Metal-working debris from the area suggests industrial activity took place nearby but was not obviously connected with the working of the mill. This aspect can now only be studied from the portable finds (below pp 255 and 279).

Was Mill 1 a tide mill?

During the early Roman period, archaeology has shown that the tidal range in London was 2m for spring tides (Milne 1985, 79–86, graph 50).[12] Although many multi-disciplinary studies have been published concerning this complex subject of changes in sea level (eustatic change) and land subsidence and uplift (tectonic and isostatic change) the tidal range that existed in the Wantsum channel during the early Roman period is not clear. Moreover, the complex subject

---

11. The following account of this remarkably well-preserved structure is based on the detailed study and reconstruction by Robert Spain (1984a and b).
12. The range at mid first century AD has been proposed as *c* +1.5m OD (MHWS) to -0.5m OD (MLWS).

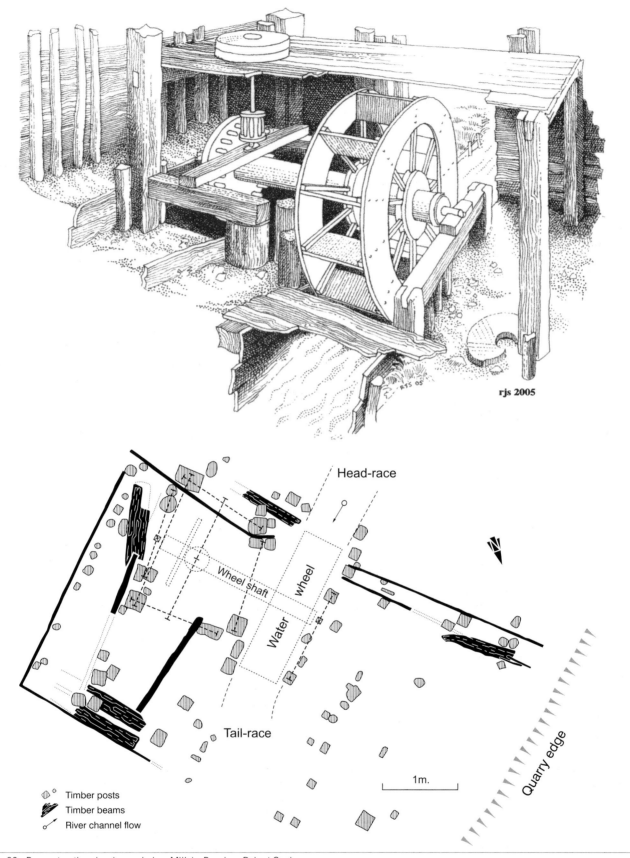

Head-race

Wheel shaft

wheel

Water

Tail-race

Quarry edge

1m.

Timber posts
Timber beams
River channel flow

rjs 2005

Fig 22. Reconstruction drawing and plan, Mill 1. Drawing: Robert Spain.

46

of estuarine tidal behaviour is most difficult to approach, especially in an historical context (Spain 2004, 17–21). If for the purposes of this analysis we assume that the relationship between the tidal ranges of London and Thanet in the Roman period was as it is today, then the tidal range for the early Roman period in the Wantsum channel would be approximately 1.6m for the spring tides, some 60 per cent greater than the *neap* tide range.[13]

As the most seaward of the water-wheel sites, Mill 1 should be considered as a possible tide-mill. With a tidal range of 1.6m the top of the mill-dam would need to be at least 1.8m above the tail-race. Such a dam would need to be immediately up-stream of the mill, roughly transverse across the valley or axis of the water flow. Otherwise its area and shape would be determined mainly by the natural contours and gradients of the main river valley above the mill.

One very obvious fact needs to be borne in mind when interpreting Mill 1 as a possible tide-mill. In Fig 22, the diameter and level of the water-wheel is such that the wheel-shaft, bearings and pit-gear would be under water at high tides – an impractical arrangement. A larger diameter wheel would mitigate or overcome this problem, but the structural analysis of the mill does not readily support the notion of a larger wheel. But of far greater significance, is that the entire lower structure of the mill would be regularly flooded, during normal spring tides to a depth of 1.3m above the tail-race, and deeper for perigean tides. Having regard to the design of the mill it is inconceivable that the structure was intended as an elevated building capable of operating and withstanding repeated tidal flooding. Most of the posts do not have sufficient scantling to form a structure to endure the forces of the sea, and the *in situ* weather-boarding would not have been placed under water. Finally, if the mill and its environs were repeatedly below the tides, sea-borne and landside erosion deposits would have been created, overlaying the whole area and none were found.

Given that an ample supply of continuous river flow existed that could be harnessed for power generation and for all the other reasons stated above, it is inconceivable that Mill 1 was a tide mill.

Channel C (Mills 2 and 3) (Fig 18)

The westernmost part of watercourse 105 (Channel C) contained the remains of two mills (2 and 3), one perhaps replacing the other. The channel was aligned north-east to

Pl XIV. Area 1 as first exposed in topsoil stripping Autumn 1973, looking north-east. The tapes outline the timbers first identified as a hut but later recognised as Channel C and structures of Mills 2 and 3.

south-west and at its south-west end (Fig 10; Fig 11, Section B) was approximately 0.5m deep and at least 4m wide. Moving towards the north-east the channel narrowed to a width of approximately 3m in a short distance, and thereafter the edges of the channel remained roughly parallel. Central within channel 105 was a collection of timbers whose remains spread over a distance of 16m. Most of the surviving timberwork was covered with shallow deposits of water-borne silt and gravel in places up to 0.2m thick. Erosion of the site following abandonment caused fragmentation, decay and scattering of the timberwork and artefacts.

The direction of flow in Channel C is beyond doubt, confirmed by the geography and the palimpsest of waterways in the entire area, both ancient and modern (see Figs 3 and 4). Water entered the timber structure from the south-west via the remains of a timber-lined channel (a mill-race). The width of the mill-race expanded from 0.6m at Section B, to at least 0.8m within a distance of 1.5m down-stream.

13. The writer is grateful to Martin Earlam of the Thames Barrier for the provision of advice regarding the tide ranges for London Bridge and Margate.

Pl XV. The remains of Mill 1, as exposed in July 1974, looking north and showing the main group of upright timbers supporting the wheel shaft and stones. The wheel would have lain to the left, the tail-race beyond to the north-east. Scale 6ft.

Unfortunately no further structural evidence was found for a distance of 3.4m between the remains of the timber-lined mill-race and the first post down-stream (E).

In the central area the remains of three transverse ground-plates[14] were found (30, 31 and 35). Two of these (30, 35) had a mortise at each end to support vertical posts. The mortises clearly indicated that the mill-race in this section was 1m wide between the posts. The remains of vertical boards were found on the north-west side of the mill-race between beams 30 and 35 and it was considered likely that the bed of the race was also boarded in this area. Within the mill-race and close to the structure several millstone fragments were found, indicating that a mill-house was nearby.

Moving down-stream, another collection of structural remains existed marked by transverse ground-plates, horizontal planks and substantial posts on the north-west bank of the mill-race (Mill 2). These ground-plates (7, 8 and 15) together with another, possibly displaced (1), were distinctly different from the three ground-plates up-stream, being generally longer and without mortises for posts. They also appeared to have been somewhat more decayed and according to the excavator's notes, of 'crude workmanship'. In this area the mill-race gave every indication of being wider, at approximately 1.4m according to the parallel sets of posts. Down-stream of posts 9 and 10, the mill-race expanded to a maximum width of 1.7m.

One other general observation has relevance to the analysis. If an axis is drawn between the centre of ground-plate 35 and the centre of the up-stream mill-race boards mid way between posts 40 and 44, and compared with the mill-race axis down-stream from ground-plate 35, it will be seen that the mill-race takes a distinct change of course. The axes coincide between ground-plates 30 and 35 and are displaced 7 degrees from each other (see Fig 18).

Posts 46 to 50 may have marked the north-west wall of the head-race, and it is thought likely that planks 42 and 43 had

---

14. The term sole-plate is also appropriate for a beam supporting a machine or structure but the writer favours the term ground-plate.

Pl XVI. The same area of Mill 1 as Pl XV, seen from the east with the race crossing the centre of the photograph diagonally and the quarry-edge in the top right corner. Scale 6ft.

swung out of position since abandonment. If this was the case then it would indicate a parallel channel more in line, though not perfectly so, with the axis of the mill-race down-stream. Plank 42 showed a rebate on its outer edge south-east but plank 43 did not, and overall an incomplete boarded section of mill-race may be indicated. A narrow ground-plate was identified underneath boards 42 and 43 adjacent to post 51. The ground-plate was not set at right-angles to boards 42 and 43 and this supports the notion that the fabric had shifted position since abandonment. However, the position of post 44, and details from Section B (Fig 11) indicated that the bed of the race was perhaps substantially complete and that the timber-lined channel was only 0.6m wide. On balance therefore, it does appear that the plank-lined race in this region was expanding as it extended down-stream as shown by the broken lines on Fig 18. Stakes 45–50 may have formed part of an earlier watercourse revetment (for Mill 2) or an outer revetment for the north-west edge of Channel C for Mill 3 (*see* below, p 57).

Differences in the ground-plates between the up-stream and down-stream groups have already been noted (see above) together with a change in the angle and width of the mill-race. In addition there appears to be a greater incidence of rectangular-sectioned posts in the up-stream group compared with the down-stream group. This might be explained by a difference in age or exposure prior to recording, but the most likely explanation is that two different mill structures (Mill 2 and Mill 3) existed on Channel C.

Mill 2 (Figs 23 and 25, Pl XVII)

The presence of large posts (A, 11, 12 and 18) on the north-west bank of the millstream indicated a substantial structure in this position, possibly a watermill. Unfortunately there is little evidence to assist in reconstructing the structure. In this area, the bed of the race was lined with planks, nailed down onto transverse ground-plates (15, 8 and 7), probably down-stream as far as posts 3 and 4. Remains of planks lining the bed of the mill-race (some still attached to a sole-plate) were recorded between sole-plates 8 and 15. The excavator recorded the ground-plate to have been of crude workmanship in comparison with those up-stream and longer; 7 and 5 were 1.6m long and 8 was 1.8m long.

Pl XVII. The timber structure of Mill 2 looking west, showing timbers revetting and lining channel. Visible section of scale 0.5m.

The posts on the south-east bank of the channel (4, 6, 10, 17, 20 and 21) were positioned opposite similar posts on the north-west bank (3, 5, 9, 13, 19A and 22). This pairing of posts suggested a relationship with the ground-plates. As the ground-plates were wider than the watercourse, with no obvious evidence of joints, the ends of the plates were probably buried under the boarded side walls of the channel, held by the posts. Provided that the ground-plates and the floor planks were maintained, the whole of the mill-race floor would have been structurally sound. The walls of this section of the mill-race were undoubtedly lined with planks secured to the earthfast posts.

Of the earthfast posts in this down-stream group numbers 11, 12 and A were the largest. Their minor axes were parallel and their proximity to each other indicated a load-bearing function. In Mill 1, four clusters of posts were identified as load-bearing for machinery or milling functions. In each cluster the minor axes were parallel, all in close proximity

to each other and they invariably had large sections. These primary features all existed in the cluster 11, 12 and A, and their position suggested that the gears and millstones were probably on the north-west bank of the millstream. Support for the bearings at each end of the wheel-shaft would have been provided either by a beam normal to the shaft axis or carried directly on the top of a large earthfast post.[15] On the south-east bank evidence of the larger posts necessary for supporting the bearing had disappeared. On the north-west bank, evidence for a reconstruction of the building and machinery is very limited and therefore conjectural.

In the suggested reconstructed plan for Mill 2 (Fig 23) the driver gear has been placed on the wheel-shaft on the 'water-side' of the driven gear and millstone spindle. This arrangement, which would have provided clockwise rotation of the upper moving millstone, has the advantage of the cogs and the staves of the lantern gear being clearly visible and readily accessible for maintenance.[16] This would have

---

15. This was the arrangement that could clearly be identified in Mill 1 and at the southern Roman watermill found near Fullerton villa.
16. The gearing within the up-stream mill has been shown with the driver gear on the 'landside' of the millstone spindle, simply to illustrate the other option.

Fig 23. Reconstruction view of Mill 2. Drawing: Robert Spain.

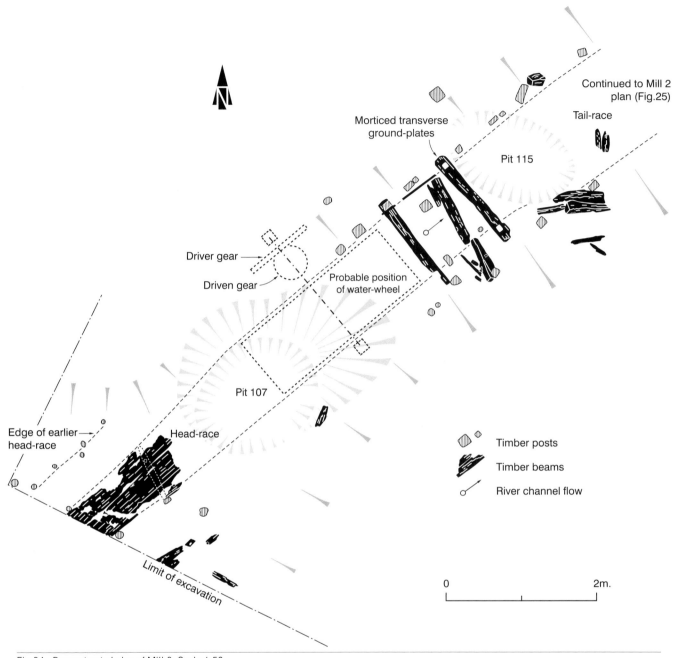

Fig 24. Reconstructed plan of Mill 3. Scale 1:50.

placed the position of the north-west bearing at least 1m away from the revetting wall of the mill-race, and there was no evidence for posts that would have supported it. It may therefore be concluded that at least two of the three posts (11, 12 and A) supported structures higher than the shaft. On the south-east bank, there was a similar lack of evidence for structural supports for the south-east bearing. Posts 10, 17, and 20, identified as supports for the plank walls, were of insufficient strength to carry the wheel-shaft. Wherever the millstone spindle was positioned, it had to be carried by a footstep-bearing supported on the bridge-tree. Posts 11 and 18 could have carried this, but this remains conjecture,

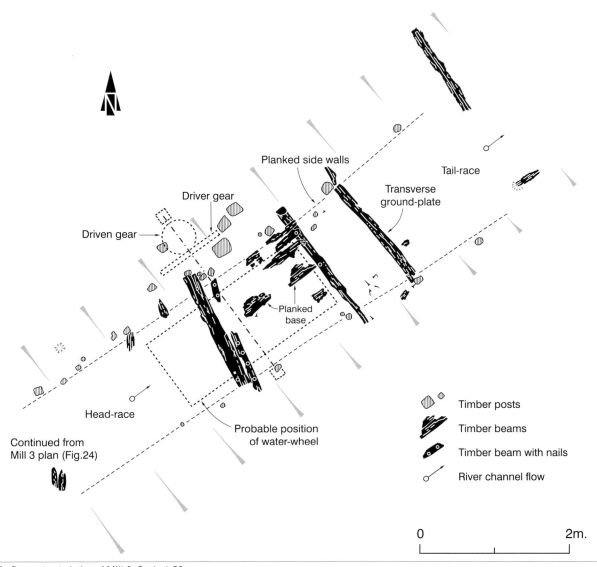

Fig 25. Reconstructed plan of Mill 2. Scale 1:50.

and in absence of other evidence preventing identification of possible building and machinery foundations, should be treated as uncertain.

The position of the wheelshaft shown on Fig 23 appears to be the only one that allows the axis to pass between the posts (ignoring the smaller revetment posts) and in so doing

retain the proximity of posts 18 and 19 etc. An alternative position, to the north-east of post 11, puts posts 18 and 19 further away, but in view of the posts that are clearly missing, this is another, though slightly less favoured, arrangement. Assuming that cluster (11, 12 and A) formed a principal support feature for the mill, it would need to have been supplemented by other earthfast posts singly or in clusters, to the north-west of posts 11, 12 and 18. With the risk of being increasingly unconvincing, it is considered imprudent to attempt any further reconstruction.

As to the size of the water-wheel, one can safely assume that its width probably filled most of the 1.4m wide boarded mill-race, simply to maximise the potential force of the flowing water. A width close to 1.25m is suggested. The diameter of the wheel is more uncertain, for as with the up-stream wheel (see below) there is no indication as to what this dimension could have been. A similar diameter to that proposed for the up-stream wheel, say *c* 2.4m, is tentatively suggested.

Mill 3 (Fig 24)

At the south-west end of the site, at the limit of the excavation (Fig 18) the remains of a wood-lined mill-race were found within Channel C. Two of the planks (42 and 43) lining the base of the race survived *in situ* as did a single vertical side-board (41). Planks 42 and 43 were 0.34m and 0.33m wide respectively and plank 42 exhibited a shallow rebate on its outer south-east edge intended to register and secure the lower edge of vertical board 41. The outer north-west edge of plank 43 may also have had a similar rebate but subsequent erosion prevented identification. The race was 0.6m wide and is 0.25m deep (Fig 11, Section B). The south-east wall of the race was supported by stakes 40 and 51 and a plank (41) which was 0.25m high and 0.024m thick was found *in situ*. This wood-lined race probably continued beyond the limit of the excavation beneath baulk A. The north-west wooden wall of the race was not preserved, although a single supporting stake (44) remained *in situ*.

In this area three ground-plates remained, two clearly *in situ* (35 and 30) and one (31), which had probably been displaced, from a position up-stream and became lodged in the position found. The *in situ* plates both had through-mortises at their ends for posts which indicated that the mill-race was 1m wide in this area, but plate 31, which was larger than plates 30 and 35, did not have such clear evidence of mortises at both ends. The mortises were subrectangular with rounded corners, suggesting that a spoon-bit was probably used to make them. The remains of a vertical board *in situ* between the north-west ends of beams 30 and 35 proved that the mill-race was lined with planks and it can be safely assumed that it was boarded on the base as indicated by the evidence up- and down-stream. The side posts that were tenoned into the ground-plates, were probably sufficiently stable and firm-jointed when first assembled, to take the

thrust of the backfilled earth thrown against the side boards. As time passed, the integrity of the joints may have failed, and top braces, parallel to and above the ground-plates, may have been installed (though obviously not where the water-wheel stood).

Numerous earthfast posts were recorded against the north-west edge of the mill-race following the same line as posts mortised into the ground-plates. Whilst the posts may have provided additional support for the planked sides of the mill-race, this is thought unlikely as they would have duplicated the function of the posts mortised into the ground-plates. Assuming a spacing of the ground-plates at 1m intervals (a distance that is matched by the average spacing that occurred down-stream) then posts E, 38, 32, 28 and 27 etc, although on the line of the mill-race would not have been needed as supports for the wall. This suggested that the additional posts may have formed part of a building abutting or spanning the mill-race. This proposal was strengthened by the presence of posts 26, 29, 36A, 36 and 37, which being up to 0.25m away from the south-east edge of the mill-race, were presumably also part of a building.

Ground-plates 30 and 35 were significant survivals, being the only timbers with mortised joints, which as noted above, provided a valuable dimension for the width of the mill-race (1m). One fragment of a vertical side-board was found *in situ* (33A) nailed to an upright post (32A) driven into a mortise of a ground-plate (35). Posts 33 and 34, located within the mill-race, present more of an interpretational problem. The presence of the posts clearly indicated that a water-wheel did not operate at this point. The posts, located mid-stream, either related to water control or a covering building. Although the minor axes of the posts were set parallel to each other and to the axis of the mill-race, they did not lie on the same transverse axis across the mill-race. This misalignment across the stream suggested that they were not intended for water control (a sluice gate), but rather for a building that would not have required accurate alignment. This would perhaps fit with the rather haphazard foundation posts evident in Mill 1, and to a lesser extent, those of Mill 2, a short distance away. A sluice in this position would have obstructed and reduced the water flow and would have needed a by-pass where excess water could be diverted. Such a by-pass would have needed to have been close to the sluice to be effective, and from the evidence recovered this arrangement clearly did not exist. The presence of the posts also suggests that a water-wheel did not exist immediately down-stream as the posts would have created turbulence and restricted water flow. Although it is possible that the posts may have been located for a 'debris grille' to prevent floating branches etc, from harming a wheel, the posts are unnecessarily large for this purpose and misaligned. A debris grille, perhaps consisting of small vertical stakes intertwined above water with hazel, would probably have existed at each of these watermills immediately up-stream of the mill wheel.[17]

The combined evidence suggests that a water-wheel may have stood up-stream of Beam 35, in the region of the pit 107, perhaps slightly nearer post E (Fig 24).[18] This suggestion is supported by the presence of a boarded race up- and down-stream of this position. To ensure reasonable laminar flow conditions approaching a mill wheel it would have been necessary to board the sides for perhaps 3 or 4m up-stream. Beyond this a wattle revetment would have sufficed to line the watercourse. The presence of a water-wheel in this position is also suggested by the width of the mill-race which expands in a distance of 2.8m from post 40 from 0.78m to 1m. This theoretical position for the leading edge of the water-wheel is coincident with the centre of pit 107. If the position of the water-wheel is accepted then boards 41, 42 and 43 may be interpreted as the remains of a head-race.[19]

It is unusual for a mill-race to expand as it approaches a water-wheel's position, because any head of water created and held by the boarded race, would be proportionally lessened as the width expanded. Depending on the gradient, a reduction in velocity is likely to occur as the stream became shallower, and so a reduced head and lower velocity would lessen the power potential at the wheel. A more likely arrangement is for the race to have parallel sides. One other minor and perhaps questionable observation can be made. Ground-plate 31 is assumed to have been dislodged from its original position up-stream. Its length and the absence of mortises might indicate that it originally lay close to, or perhaps under, the mill wheel.

With only three posts (38A, 28A and 36A) found away from the edge of the mill-race, and a lack of symmetry in the remaining posts it was impossible to reconstruct building or machinery frames. However the strength of posts on both sides of the mill-race suggests that the mill building bridged the water, and allowing for the narrowness of the stream it can be confidently suggested that it extended on one or both banks. As with the down-stream structure, there was slightly more evidence on the north-west bank, both in terms of the number of posts and their size, and so it is proposed that this is where the mill building was probably sited. The suggested position of the water-wheel immediately up-stream of ground-plate 35 would have required substantial earthfast posts to support the wheel-shaft bearings and the bridge-tree. But in this zone, both within and outside the delineated edges of watercourse 105, nature or the cutting of a later pit (107) has swept all evidence away. The width of the water-wheel is suggested as 0.9m, allowing for a nominal clearance between the boarded sides of the emplacement. Its diameter can only be guessed, but was probably a little over 2 metres. The position of the axis of the wheel-shaft and the bearings can only be postulated, although the gearing is favoured as being on the north-west bank simply because most of the large posts that were found are on that side of the watercourse.

Mills 2 and 3: discussion

Analysis of the millstone fragments recorded as being found in this area shows that two different driving arrangements had existed. Of the three millstones found where the dressing of the furrows allows a determination of the direction of rotation,[20] two rotated clockwise and one anti-clockwise. The writer has suggested that this might indicate that two watermills were operating simultaneously (Spain 1984a, 171), but we should also note that a mill might have changed its drive arrangement during its life. Figs 24 and 25 show two different drive arrangements purely for illustrative purposes, because we cannot tell what layout actually existed. In the up-stream mill the driver gear is mounted on the wheel-shaft on the landside of the driven gear. This results in the vertical

17. Good examples of debris grilles were found at both of the Roman watermills near Fullerton villa, where they were installed immediately up-stream of each of the water-wheels (Cunliffe and Spain 2008) and the settings for an iron grille survived at Janiculum (Wilson 2000; 2001a).

18. This area was originally interpreted as a scour pit (107) on the up-stream side of Mill 3. It contained a wide range of Roman material but its stratigraphic relationship to the channel fill and structures is not certain and it may be stratigraphically later (Fig 12, Section G). Pit 115 has been interpreted in the same way, but the evidence is ambiguous, the base fill including much stone rubble, either the fill of an intrusive feature or packing in the base of the scour hole.

19. Where a mill wheel is served by a head-race that does not have a recognisable change in section to create a hydraulic head and/or gradient approaching the wheel to accelerate flow, the use of the word penstock is questionable. In Britain there are many different terms for the various parts of watermills that vary from region to region and throughout time. For example the wooden or metal chute delivering the water to a wheel can be called either a trough, chute, lade, flume, penstock etc. For terms of more recent origin see Syson (1965, 163–6). For early medieval and old English mill terminology see Rahtz and Bullough (1977) and Holt (1988, 117–44).

20. Find numbers 1210, 1217, both clockwise and 1219, anti-clockwise.

millstone spindle rotating in an anti-clockwise direction when viewed from above. In the down-stream mill the driver gear engages the driven on the waterside that results in a clockwise millstone rotation. To change the rotation the miller would need to move the position of the gears relative to each other. To accomplish this, the driver gear had to be moved along the wheel-shaft, or the driven gear, vertical spindle and the millstones had to move. In either event the driver gear would need to be dismounted so that the cogs would face the other way. The latter alternative is the more major change because it involved shifting the bridge-tree (the beam supporting the vertical spindle) and the grain hopper and feeding mechanism etc. The least structural change occurs with moving the driver gear along the wheel-shaft, providing it was long enough, otherwise it became a major change of the wheel-shaft and the supporting structures of the bearing.

The various machinery components within a watermill suffer varying rates of wear, decay and replacement cycles. The combination of machinery and building fabric maintenance, natural decay, waterside erosion and the interaction of man's activity on an unstable estuarine landscape, eventually gave the miller opportunity to make change. A miller might make slight changes seeking operational improvement, but he was unlikely to undertake radical change affecting the building structure or machinery whilst incidental repair and replacement would ensure continuity of milling work. Therefore a reasonable and practical conclusion is that although the dressing of the millstones proves that two different drive arrangements existed, it is unlikely that they would have taken place sequentially in the same mill. If this is accepted, a corollary is that either a radical change to the design of the mills occurred or two different mills existed, not necessarily coevally.

In the above analysis of the two watermills, several differences have been identified. The down-stream mill-race was wider at 1.40m, and supported on longer ground-plates with planked side-walls attached to earthfast revetment posts. Up-stream, a narrower 1m wide mill-race was supported by ground-plates with supporting vertical posts mortised into the ends of the plates. The axis of the mill-race up-stream was aligned differently and expanded in width approaching the mill. Finally the down-stream structure had a greater incidence of less regular sectioned posts, was generally more decayed and was considered to be of cruder workmanship. We may conclude therefore, that the down-stream mill was very probably older than the upper mill.

All of the coins from watercourse 610 (Channel D) and the adjacent area fall into the period AD 260–402 and the

ceramic evidence in conjunction with that of the small finds, indicates a demise of the structures at *c* AD 370–400. It is disappointing that the great number of artefacts found in association with the mill structures were not recorded with greater accuracy to allow a separate analysis to explore the dating of the up-stream and down-stream watermills. No clear difference can be drawn from the analysis of the artefacts concerning the dating of the building and occupation of the mills, however, the analysis of the small finds identifies significant differences between the north-east and south-west areas. At the north-east end the assemblage was almost entirely of iron objects, mostly structural in nature, which it has been suggested could relate to the dismantling of the mill. Ian Riddler writes:

'Small finds are recorded from Mill 2 but also from the west of the mill and the east floor. The objects from the north-eastern part of the watercourse are made of iron, with just one exception, a copper alloy ferrule thought to be a possible plume holder for a helmet. An iron ferrule from a spearhead came from this end of the watercourse, alongside two knives, a padlock key and two fibre processing teeth stemming from a flax ripple. Structural ironwork is represented by nails, staples, several bindings and three split loops. Rods, bars and strips of iron were also present. It is noted below (p 299) that evidence for iron-working, in the form of rods, bars and strips, was particularly evident in Area 10, in the vicinity of Mill 1. Correspondingly, although the sample is smaller, iron-working may also have been carried out near to Mills 2 and 3.

Five complete horseshoes also came from the north-eastern end of the watercourse. Typologically, they can be compared with medieval and early post-medieval examples and although the possibility exists that they are of Roman date, the presence of other post-Roman material from this general area suggests that they represent later activity and may have been introduced during the cutting of pits 107 and 115.

The small finds to the south-west of the watercourse are of a slightly different character. Some of the objects reflect those seen to the north-east. Small quantities of nails are present, as well as single examples of bindings, bars and strips, staples and joiner's dogs. The range of materials extends however from iron to copper alloy, lead and glass. The copper alloy objects include several bracelet fragments, a U-shaped binding and two ear-rings, one of an unusual type. An iron steelyard was found, as well as a lock plate, and an iron smith's punch, which once again indicates the possibility of iron-working in the vicinity of Mills 2 and 3. Two copper alloy needles and one of iron represent three of the seven needles found in the area of Mills 2 and 3, itself 50 per cent of the entire sample from the site. Five small fragments of glass stem from one or more vessels of indeterminate type. Lead waste occurs in this area but not to the north-east. An iron flesh hook is of a post-Roman form. The small finds from the south-west of the watercourse are more varied in material and type from those to the north-east, although both assemblages indicate iron-working in the vicinity.'

These watermills were built on channels fed by the Little Stour not far from the river mouth in an estuarine landscape. In addition to the constant erosion of natural and revetted banks, the deposition of silt would have caused a continual problem to the maintenance of the mill-race, which would have been most troublesome where the water velocity slowed, due to widening of the bed, increased resistance or, a lower gradient. Whilst the timber lining of the mill-race made the task of silt and weed removal somewhat easier, down-stream the tail-race would have required regular and thorough work to maintain the gradient and clearance of the channel. Without such work the tail-race would have become increasingly ineffective in taking away the water from the wheel, such that in times of spate (ie river flood) the wheel suffered from working in backwater, a condition that reduced the efficiency of the mill and reflected badly on the miller. It is not unreasonable to conclude that with the inevitable passage of time the Little Stour and these tributaries experienced increasing deposition and consequent reduced bed gradients, until the impact upon the down-stream mill, in terms of tail-race maintenance and a reduced milling efficiency, became too burdensome. When this circumstance was reached, the miller had one solution to preserve his operational status – move up-stream. Such a move would be more attractive if it coincided with a need to undertake major structural repairs to the mill, whether due to wear, decay or settlement. Such conditions could easily have occurred within the time-span that we are dealing with, of 110–140 years, in this timber-framed earthfast structure. It may also have been influenced by the desire to improve the design of his machine.

Before we draw this conclusion of moving site, let us albeit briefly, consider the implications of two undershot water-wheels working simultaneously in close proximity on the same mill-race.

When an undershot vertical water-wheel is working, the velocity of its radial paddles is slower than the approaching water. Theory tells us that the maximum efficiency occurs when the floats are moving at 50 per cent of the water velocity, but the actual speed depends on the balance of power (the force on the floats compared with the resistance of all rotating masses, bearings, gears and millstones) that could vary considerably, being influenced mainly by millstone life cycles, dressing and grain, bearing lubricity and gear ratios etc. No matter, the average velocity of the water leaving the wheel would be noticeably less than that entering.

We do not know the gradient of this mill-race, but if its bed had a sufficient gradient, the water, after leaving the up-stream wheel, may have picked-up velocity before entering the down-stream water-wheel without obvious diminution. If the mill-race were level between the wheels, the up-stream wheel would effectively slow the down-stream wheel, though not necessarily to render grinding ineffective. An example of undershot water-wheels in series affecting each other is provided by those on the Janiculum hill at Rome (Wilson 2000; 2001a).[21]

In conclusion, we cannot be sure if the operation of the upper mill adversely affected the down-stream mill with one exception; if they co-existed, both water-wheels had to work at the same time because no by-pass existed between the two. Both mills would have shared a common by-pass somewhere up-stream of the upper mill.

Having regard to all of the evidence relating to the differences in design and condition, and mindful of the suggested dismantling of the lower mill (as suggested by the ironwork assemblage), it is proposed that the down-stream mill was built first and sometime later the up-stream mill was constructed. Whether or not the down-stream mill was dismantled at the time of building the upper mill, or it continued in use for some while working beside the other, is unknown.

Having arrived at this sequence of building, a final and logical view of the mill-race arrangements is that stakes 45–50, which align perfectly with the north-west edge of the mill-race through both mills, formed part of the original revetment prior to the building of the up-stream mill. This is surely the only explanation for their proximity to each other, their position and alignment. This explanation also

---

21. An extraordinary arrangement where four identical undershot mill wheels were operating as close together as possible. A hydraulic analysis of this series would be most interesting, for the resistance to the water flow caused by the wheels meant that they would work more slowly as you proceeded down-stream, a fact recognised by Wilson. This drawback might have been overcome by inclining the gradient of the mill-race bed, but there is no evidence of that, so that each mill's potential power and therefore output rate was less than its neighbour up-stream.

supports the idea that when the up-stream mill was built, an attempt was made to accelerate the head-race by constricting its width and directing it into a smaller and probably faster, water-wheel. We ought therefore to view the up-stream mill as having not only an improved mill-race construction but also an advanced hydro-mechanical arrangement.

Mill 4 (Figs 10 and 19, Pl XVIII)

Two large beams[22] were found in the base of Channel D located 25m to the south-east of Mills 2 and 3 against the western section of the excavated area. It has been suggested that the two beams (1 and 2) might be the remains of a sluice gate (Christopher Young, pers comm), with Beam 1 being the top section, which has been displaced from above Beam 2 and found inverted in the position excavated. The inspiration for this idea probably came from the duplicated side slots in the shoulders of the recesses on each beam, suggesting the position of a vertical sliding wooden gate or hatch, with the handle passing through the central mortise in Beam 1. The suggestion of a sluice gate being in this locality is sound and defensible having regard to the conjunction of a revetted watercourse, heavy transverse beams and nearby watermills and a millstream. But the suggestion requires further examination to determine the degree of probability.

A re-analysis of the beams within watercourse 610 suggests that Beam 1 was found in its original position. However, an annotated site plan of these beams shows that the mortise in the centre of Beam 1 was small and irregular on the surface of the timber but expanded to a rectangular cavity below. This suggests that the beam's original position must have been inverted. The suggestion is confirmed by a note on the site plan of a rough-cut cavity (0.27 by 0.15m in face area and 0.02–0.05m deep) on the underside of Beam 1. It appears likely therefore that the beam had an earlier function prior to being placed in the position found. The shape of the rectangular cavity suggested that it had acted as a mortise for a tenon when inverted, but the cavity was not made through the beam. Later, perhaps when placed in the position found, a smaller irregular-shaped mortise had been cut down into the larger cavity from the opposite face, which was now on top of the beam. The purpose of the large rectangular mortise, with its central position, is unknown, but we can say that it was unlikely to have been used as a sliding handle for a sluice gate, simply because the cavity was blind.

Pl XVIII. General view of Site 6 looking north-west, with the main timber of Mill 4 in Channel D in the foreground. Scales 2m.

If a sluice gate existed here, suffered decay and eventually collapsed, it is logical to expect the remains to be found down-stream of its original position. However, if this occurred it is most fortuitous that Beam 1 came to rest with its original downside facing upwards, parallel to Beam 2 and central in the transverse profile of the watercourse. It is also the case that Beam 1 had square cut shoulders to recesses in the centre top of the beam which appeared to align exactly with the recessed shoulders in Beam 2. It is difficult to envisage the collapse of such a substantial framed sluice gate without Beam 2 moving out of position, particularly with the position of a vertical side-frame indicated by a substantial (0.25 x 0.1m) mortise in its north-west end. It is worth noting that there was no evidence that the wattle revetment, found

---

22. We will refer to these as beams rather than ground-plates until we have resolved their probable function.

between the beams on the north-west bank, suffered damage or movement from such a collapse.

If a vertical sliding gate existed between the two beams it would have required the vertical grooves to continue in side-frames to facilitate movement. Such side-frames would need to be of a reasonable section to include the vertical grooves and there is no evidence to show how these were attached to beams 1 and 2.

Finally, and perhaps the most significant fact against the suggestion of a sluice gate, is the difference in width between the mortises or runners for the sliding gate. In Beam 2 (the 'bottom' of the gate) the shoulders were 0.76m apart and in Beam 1, (the 'top') 0.9m. Even if the sluice had a depth of over 1m, the divergence of the sides would have created a trapezoidal-shaped gate that would have required exceptionally deep side guides to retain a register on both sides, as the gate was lifted and opened. With a tapered frame, although the face pressure on the gate reduced as it was lifted to allow greater through-flow, the 'bearing area' on the side grooves would have also been reduced, creating increasing instability and loss of effective strength. As the gate ascended, water would have surged up the cavities created in the grooves. Beyond a certain height, the gate would have lost its registration with the side grooves. Given the shallowness of the grooves, this would have occurred quickly.[23] It would have then been virtually impossible to re-enter the guides if water was striking the face of the gate, especially if the handle was loose in its mortise in Beam 1.

In conclusion, the circumstantial evidence suggests that Beam 1 had not fallen but was found *in situ*, and a theoretical reconstruction and functional analysis of these beams as a sluice gate, highlights grave operational defects. It is therefore most unlikely that these two beams originally formed part of a single sluice gate.

It has also been suggested that the two beams in watercourse 610 may have represented the supports for the base of a casing for a vertical water-wheel. If an undershot water-wheel existed in this area it is difficult to suggest its position. With only two ground-beams found *in situ* there are three options: up-stream of Beam 2, down-stream of Beam 1, or between them. Analysis concerning the position of the wheel (if one was in this vicinity) relies wholly on interpretation of the two beams, Section J (Fig 11), the adjacent revetment work and nearby landscape features.

The primary supports for a vertical water-wheel are positioned beneath the bearings at each end of the wheel-shaft. Each bearing could be supported by one of two methods. A longitudinal beam supported in turn by posts, either earthfast or supported off a ground-plate, could carry it. Alternatively, the bearing could be supported by one or more (a cluster) earthfast posts. In addition to the bearings other foundation posts or ground-plates would be required for the building frame and the bridge-tree carrying the millstone spindle. The building frame may or may not have been integrated with the foundation supports for the machinery and millstones.

Apart from post 53, and a number of small stakes associated with wattle revetments, no other posts or post-holes were found. In view of the layers of deposition revealed by Sections D and J (Figs 12 and 11) and the survival of beams 1 and 2 in association with revetments, it seems unlikely, though not certain, that an earthfast building stood close to the beams. Analysis of Mills 2 and 3 above identified the advantages of using mortised transverse ground-plates for lining mill-races with planking. At the Fullerton villa, one of the Roman watermills used a 3.7m long transverse ground-plate that extended well beyond the mill-race wall into the mill. The advantage of using a transverse ground-plate is that it could serve simultaneously as a support for the building and machinery above and provide a base for boarding-out the race. Beam 2 has a mortise for supporting a substantial vertical post, but there was no matching feature on Beam 1 which could indicate longitudinal symmetry. The shoulder at the north-west end of Beam 1 may have supported a vertical post, matching what might be the remains of a mortise at the other end of the beam.

A water-wheel operating between the beams is also improbable, for the diameter of the wheel would be questionably small. Allowing for a small clearance between the beams the wheel would be limited to a diameter of approximately 1.8m although a few low-velocity Roman undershot wheels approach this diameter,[24] most of them have high hydraulic heads and are therefore high-velocity prime-movers,[25] quite different from the relatively low-velocity undershot wheels encountered at Ickham.

---

23. If the sluice gate was 0.5m deep and operated in a frame 1m high, a lift of 0.5m produces a gap each side (between the bottom corners and the rebate seat) of $(90-76)/2 \times 2 = 3.5$cm. At this position the gate would be close to falling out of the rebates.

24. Low-velocity undershot wheels include Ickham Mill 1 (2m diameter); Les Martres de Veyre (1.8m diameter) Romeuf 1978; Janiculum Hill (2.3m diameter) Wilson 2000; 2001a; Elfgen, Kreis Neuss (1.8m diameter) Arora and Franzen 1990. The writer considers that the interpretation of the San Giovanni evidence as an early first-century 1.4m diameter undershot watermill by Small and Buck (1994, 47–9, 305–9) is unconvincing.

25. Such as Venafro (1.85m diameter) Jacono 1938; Hagendorn (2.15m, 2.2m, 2.3m diameter) Gähwiler and Speck 1991.

Even if the wheel, with its shaft axis transverse to the water flow, projected beyond the beams, it is very difficult to propose a framing for the machinery and mill building, which is practical and coherent. Whilst two vertical mortises were evident, they did not relate to each other or others longitudinally, and the central mortise in Beam 1, although apparently re-used for a minor post, would have interfered with a centrally placed water-wheel.

If a water-wheel was located down-stream of the beams then the timbers may be interpreted as supporting elements for transporting and directing water. The size and strength of the timbers is excessive for supporting a boarded head-race, and suggest an additional function for supporting an oversailing building or structure. However the absence of mortises on a longitudinal axis common to both beams, combined with an apparent difference in length, belies this suggestion. Furthermore, the revetment remains down-stream of Beam 2 strongly suggests an expansion of the watercourse between the beams and further down-stream.

The two beams are massive, the largest on the Ickham site, being noticeably more robust in section than all of those on the site of Mills 2 and 3. The distance between the mortises in the ends of Beam 1 was 2m, twice the width as those in the ground-plates of Mills 2 and 3. Although roughly parallel to each other and central on the apparent axis of the watercourse, the up-stream Beam 2 was shorter than Beam 1. When Sections J and D are superimposed on the plan (Fig 19) it can be seen that the position of Beam 1 lay in the middle of the profile of the stream bed, especially as influenced by the shoulder formed by the south-east limit of the gravel bed. The stream bed profile provided by Section J corresponded reasonably closely to that in Section D, suggesting that Beam 2 may have lost its south-east end at some time. The symmetry of the surface features in Beam 2 in comparison with Beam 1 supports this notion. Whilst Beam 1 had vestiges of mortises at both ends, Beam 2 appeared to have square ends. Erosion was certainly evident on the south-east end of Beam 1 and Beam 2 may also have been reduced, perhaps deliberately.

But the most interesting feature of the beams is that they displayed several features that were not found at either of the other Ickham mills. Both beams displayed a recessed surface in the middle third of their top face, with opposing rebates

in the vertical face of the shoulders. There was a vertical mortise in the middle of Beam 1 in which was found the remains of a post. No other ground-plates or beams on the site had this central feature.

There was no evidence to support the existence of planking parallel to the water flow between the beams unlike the ground-plates in watercourse 105. The remains of two horizontal planks, however, were revealed in Section J, showing that boarding existed at one time up-stream of Beam 2.

The head-race of an undershot water-wheel is built to contain and direct water into the wheel and its bed is often graded to increase the velocity. Roman engineers were well aware of the advantages of an accelerated head-race[26] and the provision of keeping the width of the delivery penstock close to that of the undershot-wheel to bring all of the water to bear upon the radial paddles or floats and reduce the amount of water escaping past the wheel. In Channel C where the positions of two separate water-wheels (Mills 2 and 3) have been identified, there was clear evidence of longitudinal boards lining the mill-race to create smoother water flow and a more durable structure, in terms of erosion and scouring. Unfortunately in Channel D the only evidence of horizontal boards lining the watercourse occurs up-stream of Beam 2, where two end fragments were revealed in Section J. The level of the boards in relation to Beam 2 was not recorded. If base-boards had been attached to Beam 2, it is reasonable to suppose that some of their remains would have been found. It is also the case that no nail holes were recorded in Beam 2 (and only one at the end of Beam 1).

Two vertical planks, recorded in Section J and on plan (Fig 19), show the north-west bank revetment up-stream of Beam 2. These vertical boards, apparently found *in situ*, were displaced from each other by approximately 0.2m and were at different levels clearly suggesting that they were not part of a deep boarded channel with a single vertical side.

Further evidence of containment and channelling was provided by the remains of wattle revetments, which by their very nature were unsuitable for enduring water boundaries. Wattle fencing will readily yield to earth pressure, erosion and decay on the water face and would tend to slow the water, which in turn, encourages the deposition of silt. It is an unsuitable structure to be in close proximity to a vertical

---

26. A watercourse having an inclined bed where the generated power due to impulse, rather than gravity, is increased. For a general discussion on Roman accelerated head-races and their definition see Spain (1992, 212–43). The best example from *Britannia* is the Haltwhistle Burn Head watermill that produced a velocity of application of approximately 4.6m/sec, which is very fast for an undershot. Other examples of accelerated head-races, both overshot and undershot from elsewhere in the Empire include the Baths of Caracalla, Lösnich, Athenian Agora, Hagendorn and Venafro.

water-wheel where containment and water velocity and laminar flow condition is required. The presence of wattles was either supplementary to a boarded mill-race (which is very unlikely) or perhaps appeared later after the nearby prime-mover was abandoned. The wattling appeared to form part of a single and contemporary design providing an expanding width of channel between the beams. The wattle revetment down-stream of Beam 2 expanded further in width and overall this arrangement was difficult to relate to the presence of an adjacent water-wheel requiring a controlled watercourse.

Turning to the surface features of beams 1 and 2, it is tempting to recognise the shallow recesses in the middle thirds of the beams as emplacements to support a wooden trough or head-race that delivered water to an undershot wheel immediately down-stream of Beam 1. This might make sense were it not for the vertical grooves and 'mortises' on each shoulder of the recesses, and the mortise in the middle of Beam 1. As noted above, the recesses had different lengths so that if these held the base boards of a water-trough, the width of the race would have widened moving down-stream. The wider recess in Beam 1 could have been used with wedges, but this seems improbable.

There is at least one good example of a trough supported and held by ground-plates in a Roman watermill. At Avenches En Chaplix a first-century AD timber structure has been identified as an undershot Roman watermill (Castella 1994). The remains included several ground-plates, two of which that were 2.5m apart and parallel with each other, had recesses cut into their top surfaces. The up-stream ground-plate was 2.27m long and had a recess 1.33m wide, with one shoulder 0.17m high and the other 0.2m high. The down-stream ground-plate was 2.49m long with a recess 1.34m wide. No drawings or dimensions showing the depth of the recess in this plate are provided in the report but a photograph suggests that its depth was at least that of the up-stream beam recess (Castella 1994, fig 12). Immediately underneath this race was the remains of an earlier boarded race that laid on a slightly different axis. The later, higher trough rested directly on the base boards of the earlier one, which suggests that the builders must have caulked and sealed the joints of the trough, perhaps with moss as was used in many early Irish watermills (Rynne 1988).

An important feature of the remains at Avenches was a 7m long plank found nailed *in situ* in the recesses of several of the ground-plates. On the two ground-plates mentioned above, the plank lay 0.07m away from the north-east shoulder of both plates. This structure has been interpreted as the base of a mill-race, where the vertical side-planks would have been positioned in these gaps, nailed and wedged against the shoulders. Thus En Chaplix has provided us with important evidence of an early Roman construction mode for a mill-race, where the side-boards are supported by deep shoulders cut into the ground-beams.[27] With such a strong arrangement and sufficiently deep side-boards, top braces across the watercourse could have been minimal, and perhaps unnecessary.

In comparison with the En Chaplix evidence, the shoulders on beams 1 and 2 are very shallow, only 0.04 to 0.05m deep so that they would not have provided stability for vertical boards. This could have been overcome by using diagonal braces from the ends of the ground-beams, but no evidence for any type of fixings, including nail holes, was identified.

It is extremely difficult therefore, to envisage how a trough was effectively supported on these beams. The central mortise is also an obstacle to this suggestion, but could be explained as being a feature pre-dating a central trough or head-race because of its larger rectangular cavity on the underside.

Although we have examined the possibility of both beams being part of one sluice gate, another alternative is that each may have acted as a sluice gate, having boards sliding in the rebates. In Beam 2 a sluice gate would be helpful to control the flow down-stream but duplication of this function in Beam 1 makes no sense at all. A second water control gate 2m down-stream of another would be operationally useless and anyway, the suggestion is negated by the vertical mortise in the middle of Beam 1, if it was coeval with the shoulder rebates. This suggests that the boarding between the vertical grooves in Beam 1 was fixed rather than sliding; moreover if we accept this, the central portion of Beam 2 is equally unlikely to have been a water control gate, because, between Beam 2 and Beam 1 the watercourse would need to have bifurcated, separating and passing each side of the central portion of Beam 1. Such an arrangement is extremely unlikely because of the control implications.

If a plank wall existed in Beam 1 as part of an undercroft of a mill or other building, it would surely not have been

---

27. The evidence also shows that the side-boards were installed first into the shoulders rather than the bottom boards, which would give the slight advantage of full height shoulders for greater rigidity of the side-boards, and of the trough corner seams being closed by pressure from the horizontal planks and their caulking.

partly submerged receiving the weight of the stream against its south-west face, unless it formed part of a mill-dam holding back water. If the lower part of the plank wall was submerged it would have caused turbulence and settlement and silt would have built up against its face. Moreover, such an obstruction to water flow was counter to the objective of creating velocity, containing and directing the flow. But the suggestion of a mill-dam here can be quickly discounted because of the position of Beam 2. Beam 2 would have no function in the middle of a mill pond, especially with its surface features.

The above analysis shows that the possibility of a water-wheel existing either between or adjacent to Beams 1 and 2 is most unlikely. Having also rejected that Beams 1 and 2 were neither part of the same sluice gate nor the remains of two contemporary sluice gates, there is one alternative explanation that can be proposed. This is that the two timbers were not contemporary structures, but one replacing the other. If this did occur, we have to accept that we only have part of the sluice structures, and the suggestion of them having sequential operational functions might help to explain the differences between the beams. Further analysis is deemed too speculative.

Discussion and parallels *Robert Spain and Andrew Wilson*

The contribution that the Ickham evidence has provided to the corpus of Roman watermills from Britain is outstanding. The sites of at least three vertical-wheeled undershot watermills have been identified, including one (Mill 1) that has facilitated a comprehensive reconstruction of the building and machinery-supporting structure. In particular, the Ickham evidence sheds some light on the mill-races and hydraulic infrastructure associated with watermills, an important topic that has received little attention apart from a fundamental article by Wikander (1985b). Together with a growing body of evidence for other wooden watermills, it also points to continuities between the Roman millwrighting tradition in northern Europe and that of the early medieval period.

It is possible that two of the watermills (Mills 2 and 3) may have existed simultaneously, but equally the mills may have successively replaced each other, no more than one being operative at any one time. The timbers were too decayed for dendrochronological dating, and so the dating evidence for the mills relies mainly on assemblages of coins and pottery, whose find circumstances suggest they are more useful for giving a date range during which the structures were in use, rather than a clear *terminus post quem* for construction. For Mill 1, the coins suggest a period of use between AD 220 and AD 270; most of the pottery also falls within this range. For Mill 2, the coins (with one early third-century outlier) fall in the period 260–402, but the coinage of 260–273 is sparse compared to the norm for that period, suggesting that coin deposition began towards the end of that period. This might refine the likely period of use to *c* 270–400, and Mill 2 may, on chronological grounds, have directly replaced Mill 1. Ceramic evidence dates the abandonment of Mill 2 to *c* 370–400. For Mill 3, pottery and one coin of the House of Theodosius (AD 388–402) suggest a date of 390–400 for the assemblages from the water channel of this mill. It is thus possible that Mill 3 replaced Mill 2, and its use was relatively short-lived. This interpretation is perhaps reinforced by the consideration that Mill 3 lies immediately up-stream of Mill 2, creating flow conditions that would have hampered the operation of both mills had they operated concurrently. Deposits in Channel D provided no datable finds for the possible mill structure (Mill 4), but coins and pottery from Area 6 suggest activity into the early years of the fifth century.

The economic context of the Ickham watermills (AW)

Although a proportion of the 4,610 Ickham coins may have been the product of hoards, the discovery of some 450 coins in pits 107 and 115 in the mill-race of Mill 2, and further coins in the areas of Mills 1 and 3, suggests that a significant number may have been associated with customer transactions at the mills over a period of years. An assemblage of over 730 bronze coins was discovered in the remains of one of the watermills in the Athenian Agora. Many of the coins were small-denomination late fourth- and early fifth-century issues, which Parsons suggested came from customers visiting the mill (Parsons 1936, 88). An inscription of the 480s from the Janiculum Hill in Rome sets out prices for milling grain (3 *nummi* per *modius*), and stipulates penalties for millers who gave short measure to customers (*CIL* VI.1711), again demonstrating the practice of watermillers grinding grain for customers for cash transactions. Perhaps a significant proportion of the Ickham coinage may therefore also derive from such cash transactions for local customers. The mills' position alongside an arterial road, possibly as part of a somewhat larger settlement, would have facilitated such a role; despite the presence 1km away of the Ickham villa, it does not seem that the Ickham mills were necessarily tied to grinding the produce of a particular estate.

Watermilling in the Roman world (AW)

Besides the mills at Ickham, Roman watermills are known from six other sites in Britain: three on Hadrian's Wall

(Haltwhistle Burn Head, Chesters, and Willowford), two from villas (Fullerton and Spring Valley) and one from the small settlement at Nettleton.[28] Two spindles from watermills have been found in hoards of ironwork at Silchester and Great Chesterford; they may suggest the presence of watermills in the vicinity. But by far the largest body of evidence comes from stray finds of large, power-driven millstones. At least fifty-seven different sites in Britain (counting seven separate locations in London, but excluding the Blackfriars wreck) have yielded large millstones of Roman or probably Roman date, which were probably driven by water power (Fig 26). A further five sites have stones that were probably overdriven and animal-powered.[29]

Although the watermills on Hadrian's Wall are perhaps the best known mill sites from Roman Britain, the overall distribution of watermill sites and stray finds of powered millstones and spindles refutes any idea that watermilling was a technology connected specifically or particularly with the army. The overwhelming majority of finds come from the civilian zone in southern and eastern Britain, and many are demonstrably associated with villas – including a millstone from Wingham villa, under 2km from the Ickham site. Furthermore, both at Fullerton and Ickham there are clear indications of a quality of work in the design, building and maintenance that reflects the civilian artisan rather than the military mechanic. The making and maintenance of machinery in watermills, especially in vertical-wheeled mills (water-wheels, shafts, bearings, gears, millstones, sluice gates, etc) would have been well established as a specialised civilian craft, which in later centuries became known as millwrighting.

This is consistent with the wider picture that has emerged over the last two decades from archaeological evidence across the empire as a whole.[30] The watermill is now thought to have been invented in the mid third century BC, with overshot, undershot and horizontal versions appearing in quick succession (Lewis 1997). By the first century AD it had spread widely through the Roman world – a small undershot mill was built at En Chaplix near Avenches (*Aventicum*) in Switzerland whose timbers were felled in AD 57/58 (Castella 1994). During the early second century the first massive multiple-wheeled establishment appeared, at Barbegal in southern Gaul, and archaeological and epigraphic evidence

makes it clear that watermills were common in both the eastern and western parts of the empire throughout the second to fourth centuries. The increased number of written references to watermills from the fifth century onwards is a function of the appearance of new kinds of document (charters, law codes and hagiography in particular), and is not matched by a similar increase in archaeological evidence. Indeed, in the western empire, the number of watermills known archaeologically from the fifth to tenth centuries is somewhat less than that from the Roman period.

Wooden mills and mill-races: the development of a northern European millwrighting tradition (AW)

Nearly all of the watermill structures recognised to date in the Mediterranean provinces of the empire are built of stone or brick-faced concrete; by contrast, the use of timber was more common in the north-west provinces. The structural comparanda for Ickham thus come from Britain, Germany, Gaul and northern Italy. The closest parallel comes from Fullerton in Hampshire, where at least two successive mills were installed on a purpose-built leat running parallel to the River Anton. The earlier of the two excavated mills may have been built in the third century; at some point after AD 240 it was replaced by another mill immediately up-stream, which remained in use until the late fourth century. The mills seem to have lain within the estate of a farmhouse which in the late third or early fourth century was rebuilt as a villa with mosaics and a bath-house constructed on the bank of the mill channel *c* 105m up-stream from the second mill (Cunliffe and Spain 2008). The excavations at Fullerton revealed evidence for the replacement of a mill which had perhaps become structurally unsound, or whose wheel-race had degraded to the point where the wheel could not be properly constrained, by a new mill on a site immediately up-stream. This solution was presumably chosen so that the new mill and its wheel-race could be built on an area of undisturbed and unencumbered ground; it may find a parallel at Ickham in the possible replacement of Mill 2 by Mill 3 directly up-stream. Both the Ickham and Fullerton villa watermills are wholly wooden structures, having either earthfast or ground-plated foundations. It appears that at both sites the earliest watermill had wholly earthfast foundations. Ground-plates,

---

28. References conveniently collected in Wikander 1985a, nos 8–10 and 12–13.
29. Distinguishable because the rynd socket goes right through the thickness of the upper stone and the rynd could not therefore have served to support it.
30. For overviews of much of the recent evidence, see Wikander 1985b; 2000a; Brun and Borréani 1998; Wilson 2001b, 234–6; 2002, 9–15.

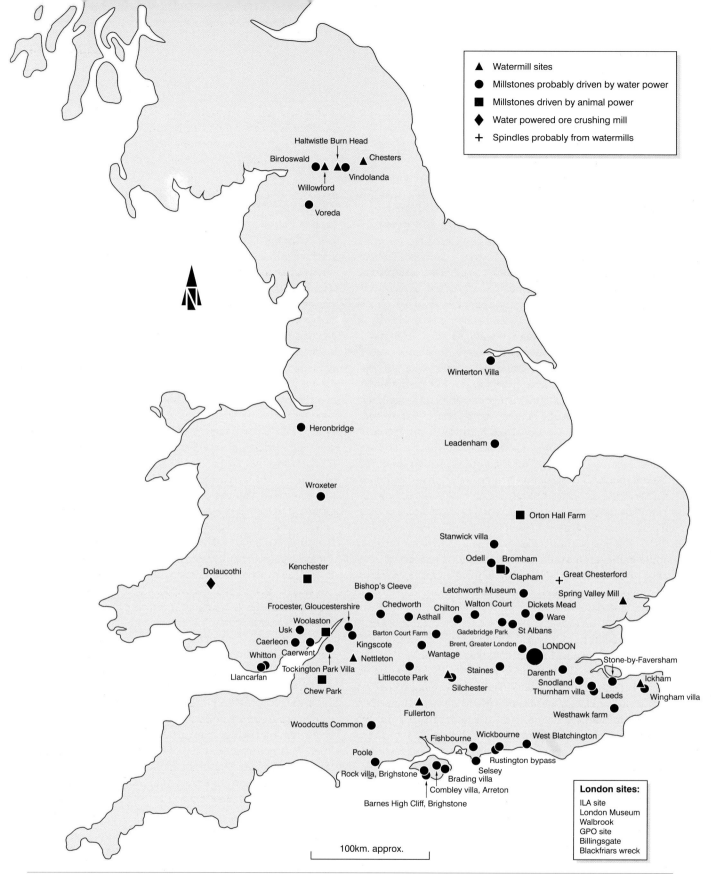

Legend:

▲ Watermill sites
● Millstones probably driven by water power
■ Millstones driven by animal power
◆ Water powered ore crushing mill
+ Spindles probably from watermills

Haltwistle Burn Head
Birdoswald
Chesters
Vindolanda
Willowford
Voreda

Winterton Villa

Heronbridge

Leadenham

Wroxeter

Orton Hall Farm

Stanwick villa
Odell
Bromham
Dolaucothi
Kenchester
Clapham
Great Chesterford
Bishop's Cleeve
Letchworth Museum
Spring Valley Mill
Frocester, Gloucestershire
Chedworth
Chilton
Walton Court
Dickets Mead
Woolaston
Asthall
Ware
Usk
Barton Court Farm
Gadebridge Park
St Albans
Caerleon
Kingscote
Brent, Greater London
LONDON
Whitton
Caerwent
Wantage
Stone-by-Faversham
Llancarfan
Nettleton
Staines
Darenth
Ickham
Tockington Park Villa
Littlecote Park
Silchester
Snodland
Leeds
Wingham villa
Chew Park
Thurnham villa
Fullerton
Westhawk farm
Woodcutts Common
Wickbourne
West Blatchington
Fishbourne
Poole
Rustington bypass
Rock villa, Brighstone
Selsey
Brading villa
Combley villa, Arreton
Barnes High Cliff, Brighstone

London sites:
ILA site
London Museum
Walbrook
GPO site
Billingsgate
Blackfriars wreck

100km. approx.

Fig 26. Distribution of Roman watermill sites and stray finds of powered millstones of Roman date in Britain.
Data collated by A Wilson from: *Britannia* 2001, 349, 367; Black 1987; Cardiff Museum Annual Report 1899; CBA 10 1972; Corder 1943; Crouch 1976; Cunliffe 1971 vol 2; Curwen 1937; Dix 1980; Dowker 1882; Frere 1972; Garrett and Harris 1938; Gilkes 1993; Holbrook and Thomas 1996; Jarrett and Wrathmell 1981; Jones 1980; King 1986; Lee 1862; Marsden 1967; McWhirr 1981; Neal 1974; 1989; Payne 1897; Pitt Rivers 1887; Rahtz and Greenfield 1977; Roe 1997; 2001; Rudling and Gilkes 2000; Spain 1984 a and b; 1996; St John Hope and Fox 1898; Stead 1976; Tilson 1973; Tomalin 1987; Wheeler 1931; Wikander 1985; Williams 1933; Wilmott and Rahtz 1985; Wilmott 1997; plus personal observation at *Vindolanda* and unpublished information kindly provided by Ruth Shaffrey and Örjan Wikander.

either for the mill-race or the mill itself, were probably a later development at both these sites.

The timber construction of the Ickham mill-races differs from those of some other Romano-British sites. The mill at Chesters Bridge on Hadrian's Wall, for example, was equipped with stone-lined head-race and tail-race channels, and is believed to have supplied an undershot water-wheel, 3–3.6m in diameter and between 0.61m and 0.91m in width (Spain 1984b, 105). This channel was shown to have varied in width from 1.85–1.93m, over a surveyed length of 39.6m (F Simpson 1976, 46; Spain 1984b, 104). A third-century date has been suggested for this mill (Moritz 1958, 136), which would make it broadly contemporary with the Haltwhistle Burn Head mill (*c* AD 250–70) and Ickham Mill 1. However, at the Chesters site the watercourse passes under a tower, which is believed to have housed the mill machinery, but in order to have operated within the tower the water-wheel and machinery would not have been parallel to the side walls. A further stone-lined mill-race associated with an early third-century mill site at Nettleton in Wiltshire has also been investigated (Wedlake 1982, 95–8), with a curved stone wheel trough for a low breast-shot wheel. At Haltwhistle Burn Head, on Hadrian's Wall, the head-race channel near the mill building was cut into bedrock to maintain the fall in the channel bed, as was the area accommodating the wooden wheel trough. This is the only mill channel from Roman Britain whose full extent is known and it demonstrates that little preparatory work was needed, and that the channel could be made short if necessary. It is also noteworthy that most of the available fall (*c* 1.4m) was concentrated in the six or so metres immediately above the wheel-race (F Simpson 1976, 26–40).

Outside the province of *Britannia* several Roman watermill sites have yielded evidence of timber mill buildings and wood-lined mill-races, with an earlier use of ground-plates than attested in mills from Britain. At En Chaplix (*Aventicum*) a Gallo-Roman site revealed a boarded race supported by ground-plates with mortised ends, overlain by a later boarded race 1.34m wide supported by rebated ground-plates. The timbers of the earlier race were felled in AD 57/58, those of the later race between AD 63 and 66, and the mill was used until *c* AD 80 (Castella 1994). These races, boarded on the sides and the bottom, suggest that an undershot water-wheel operated here, probably without shrouds. At München-Perlach in Bavaria the remains of a timber-lined mill leat and a rectangular wooden mill building (8.5 by 4.7m) have been discovered, together with fragments of millstones (Volpert 1997). The mill is apparently to be dated to the late second or third century; finds from the

burnt destruction layer date from AD 180–260. The wheel is assumed to have been undershot.

At Hagendorn in Switzerland, the remains of parts of three water-wheels, all with sole boards, were found in 1944 together with a solid oak curved wheel trough, an upper millstone and several fragments (Gähwiler 1984; Gähwiler and Speck 1991). The timbers of one of the wheels and of the trough were felled in AD 176 and the mill or mills were considered to have operated during the last quarter of the second century AD and the early third century. Their design showed that the wheels were breastshot, water probably being delivered to the wheel via a steep chute. Two of the wheels clearly had shrouded rims, whilst the third was unshrouded suggesting that it had operated within the curved trough. It is unclear whether the three wheels operated concurrently, or if they succeeded each other on the same site. The site also produced limited evidence that both the head-race and tail-race were boarded on the sides and bottom.

Two other sites have produced evidence for timber-lined channels probably associated with mills, but the mill buildings themselves have not been identified. At Dasing in Bavaria, Roman basalt millstones were discovered associated with a timber-revetted channel whose wood was felled AD 103/112; the Roman mill structure itself was not discovered, but a late seventh-century mill (built AD 696/7) was found nearby (Czysz 1994). At the second site, Oderzo in northern Italy, a timber-lined head-race probably serving a low-breast undershot water-wheel was discovered, dated to the later second century AD, although neither wheel nor mill structure or millstones were found (Trovò 1996). A timber barrier was constructed in the bed of a stream to divide the main channel from a probable mill-race on the western side. Sections of this channel, which may have been some 120m long in total, were excavated; at the down-stream end it narrowed sharply towards a boarded section investigated for a length of 4.8m. Here the boarded sides were held by vertical grooves in earthfast posts and the channel tapered further from 1.5 to 1.1m wide. The boarded bed of the channel was apparently inclined against the direction of flow by the addition of another layer of longitudinal boards tilted up at the (assumed) wheel end by an inserted cross beam lying across the top of the lower set of boards. The position of the wheel is assumed to have lain outside the area of excavation, shortly down-stream to the south-west. No ground-plates are shown on the illustrated reconstruction of the boarded race, but it is difficult to see how the base boards could have been held without cross-bracing on the underside. The design of the head-race, narrowing towards the boarded section which itself tapered in both width and depth, must have provided a very effective accelerated flow into the wheel. No evidence of the wheel design was found but the accelerated flow and consequent pressure indicates that it probably did not have sole-boards.

There is now therefore a considerable corpus of evidence from Britain, Germany, Switzerland and northern Italy showing a developed tradition of engineering head-races and tail-races, with timber linings and revetments, between the first and fourth centuries AD. Such timber-lined channels were to become regular features of early medieval and medieval watermills. In some cases, as at Ickham, we are now able to recognise the emplacements for vertical undershot mill-wheels by the indications of timber-lined sections of channels the rest of whose course is revetted with posts and wattles. For vertical undershot water-wheels, in addition to channelling the water so as to increase its velocity prior to impact with the wheel, it was also necessary to take steps to prevent incoming water from escaping around the sides of the wheel. Thus the head- and tail-race channels were tapered inwards and outwards, respectively, from the wheel area itself, and the lower part of the water-wheel was provided with either a trough or a wooden casing. These practices are widely attested in the archaeological, ethnological and documentary evidence for vertical undershot water-wheels from the early middle ages onwards (Rynne 1989, 30–1). Both Mills 2 and 3 at Ickham exhibit this basic configuration, and follow earlier examples of boarded wheel-races at En Chaplix (Avenches) and Oderzo, and the trough at Hagendorn. There can now be no doubt that this practice as recorded in early medieval contexts has its origins at least as far back as the Roman period.

The relatively well-preserved composite lower wheel-race casings investigated at Mills 2 and 3 provide valuable corroborative evidence for that excavated at Haltwhistle Burn Head. The remains of the wheel-race casing at the latter site consisted of three planks supported by a transverse timber, which had a half lap joint fixed with a wooden dowel (F Simpson 1976, 39). This trough, as was the case at Mill 2 at Ickham, is likely to have had side boards in order completely to enclose the lower section of the water-wheel.

The use of hurdlework to revet the sides of mill-races at Ickham is, on present evidence, the earliest known instance of this practice, although it is also known from early medieval contexts in Ireland (Rynne 1989) and Norway (Nielsen 1986). In many ways timber was a more flexible building material than stone for these purposes, being easily replaced in a mill-race without the need for skilled personnel, and would have been readily available at Ickham.

As seen above, there is now considerable archaeological evidence for wooden mill buildings in Roman Europe.

However, several other Romano-British sites, such as Great Chesters and Haltwhistle Burn Head, had masonry mill buildings. At Haltwhistle Burn Head the mill building had been built with well-squared stones, up to five courses of which were examined *in situ* (F Simpson 1976, 33). While the availability of either stone or timber locally was probably the main factor affecting the choice of building materials, the manner in which they were assembled on the later Ickham mills appears to ignore the generally high standards of Roman carpentry. The earliest mill, Mill 1, in building phases 1–4 as defined by Spain (1984a, 168–70), was more or less a well-executed timber building. But in its final phase the carpentry work was markedly inferior to that of the earlier periods. This latter phenomenon may be explained as extemporised repairs to what would have been, at this stage of its development, a run-down building. Extensive renovation of the building may already have been considered to be not worthwhile. But as this level of carpentry can be said to characterise the construction of Mills 2 and 3 throughout their working lives, an alternative explanation must be sought.

For the most part the standard of carpentry from Romano-British contexts is generally quite accomplished, particularly where the finish of large timbers is concerned (Weeks 1982). With exception of some of the flooring planks from Mill 2, however, the standard of carpentry in the later Ickham mills is extremely poor. Indeed, the generally low standard of timber finish on, for example, important structural members in Mill 3 such as beams 1 and 2 when compared to other timber structures within their immediate environs is extraordinary. The timbers received a rudimentary dressing with virtually no attempt to square them off, and this in structures which are supposed to be housing machinery, and which would, in normal circumstances, be expected to cope with abnormal stresses. In one mill we might explain this as an aberration but in two mills on the same site it appears to represent an established mill-building practice. But how localised is this practice and does it just apply to water-powered mills?

The expert use of wood in Roman water management is well-documented. The Roman pump house investigated at St Malo in France, for example, with its well-finished structural timbers and pump blocks represents the more accomplished end of Roman wood-working technology (Langouet and Meury 1976). In other timber structures, especially water-powered mills, we might well expect the same standards to apply. But even the earliest Ickham mill is by no means accomplished, and is a simple shed-like structure designed to provide cover for the mill machinery and the water-wheel.

The poor quality of carpentry in evidence in the two later Ickham mills, dating to the fourth century, could be taken as evidence that the quality of carpentry in general had fallen, were it not for the fact that better standards were being observed in other wooden structures, such as the wells, on the same site. Clearly there were two standards being observed here – one for the mills and one for other structures. There is compelling evidence from early medieval watermills from Ireland and Scandinavia that similar carpentry practices appear to have continued into the post-Roman period. In a vertical undershot watermill at Little Island in Cork harbour, Ireland, dated by dendrochronology to AD 630, there were six sleeper beams similar to those used in the tail-race of Mill 2 at Ickham (Rynne 1988, II, 288; Rynne 1992a). Furthermore, the quality of the timber finish was, like Mills 2 and 3, extremely poor. Similar timbers were also recovered from Omgard in Jutland, from a vertical undershot mill dated to *c* AD 840–41, again roughly-dressed (Nielsen 1986, 181). Both of these sites, as has been seen, also produced evidence for mill channels lined with wickerwork. In Ireland, however, the carpentry of early medieval watermills becomes more sophisticated by the eighth century AD. Nonetheless, the parallels with the later Ickham mills are striking. The horizontal- and vertical-wheeled mills at Little Island are currently the earliest-known post-Roman watermills to have been investigated in northern Europe. That these should apparently mirror late Roman practices as recorded at Ickham on the east coast of England may possibly fill an important gap in our knowledge of the technical development of watermills in the post-Roman period.

From the Ickham evidence two important possibilities arise. First, that a separate and distinct type of carpentry had developed for millwrighting by the end of the third century; and secondly, that this millwrighting tradition was continued throughout Europe in the immediate post-Roman period. On present evidence, the watermill was introduced into Ireland by the end of the sixth century, probably from sub-Roman Europe. There is nothing to suggest that early Irish mills were in any way different from those of continental Europe, and in point of fact traditional watermills in Iberia and the Balkans have very close affinities with those of early medieval Ireland (Rynne 1992b). Thus the Irish evidence reflects a greater European tradition in mill construction which, on the basis of the Ickham evidence, almost certainly has its origins in the late Roman period.

The discovery of ceramics and other finds dating from the fifth century to the middle Saxon period in Areas 3, 5 and 10 suggests some level of post-Roman occupation of the site. Although there is no evidence for an Anglo-Saxon watermill within the area of the excavations, we cannot rule out the possibility of other watermills lying up-stream from the excavated area. It is thus not impossible that Ickham, as the only known Roman watermill site with activity stretching into the early Anglo-Saxon period, might have been a site where late Roman watermill technology survived or was transmitted in the post-Roman period. But there is as yet no structural evidence to support this suggestion.

Bearing blocks (RS)

The bearing block fragments from Ickham Mills 2 and 3 are the first examples to be recovered from Roman Britain. They are described in detail below (pp 285–9), having already been published briefly by Robert Spain (1984b, 127 and fig 12). Their similarity to the other recorded examples from the early third-century watermills at the Baths of Caracalla in Rome (Schiøler and Wikander 1983, figs 8 and 9), third-century watermills on the Janiculum (Bell 1994, 79, 81; Wilson 2001a), an undated Roman watermill at Saepinum in Italy, and the early fifth-century mill in the Athenian Agora (Parsons 1936, fig 10) demonstrates that where these particular mill components were concerned there was relatively little variation throughout the empire – although the site at Hagendorn produced a wooden bearing block (Gähwiler and Speck 1991, 53). In the case of the Baths of Caracalla mills it was possible to estimate the diameter of the water-wheel's axle at *c* 0.3m, and for the mill in the Athenian Agora at some 0.2m; in both these cases overshot water-wheels were involved. Given a journal diameter of between 0.03m and 0.033m for the Ickham bearing blocks, an axle diameter of around 0.20–0.25m seems likely. However, whereas the bearing blocks from the three Italian sites and the Athenian Agora were set into masonry or brickwork, those from Ickham are more likely to have been positioned on wooden stands. This is the earliest known occurrence of a practice which is well-documented by the medieval period. In all of the Ickham mills the bearing blocks are likely to have been set into rebates cut into free-standing wooden frames, erected directly across the wheel-race trough from the mill building. Indeed, a number of the timbers examined *in situ* in the earliest Ickham site, Mill 1, were interpreted as being vertical supports for a bearing block, although the reconstruction drawing does not show the bearing block rebated into the timber support (Spain 1984a, fig 6).

The Ickham bearing blocks are also interesting in that they show modification through time, with new sockets being formed on an opposing face when the original one wore down. This clearly demonstrates long-term use of the watermills, and one must presume that the bearing blocks at the Baths of Caracalla and the Athenian Agora would have been replaced or redressed periodically. A not dissimilar instance of the redressing of a bearing stone was recorded at the third-century mill site at Haltwhistle Burn Head. A fragment of a basalt footstep bearing, which supported the spindle connected to the upper millstone, was found to have two holes on one surface of the stone, each displaying traces of where the spindle had rotated in it (F Simpson 1976, 389). The same practice evidently continued into the early medieval period, where similar stones have been recorded at the eighth-century undershot vertical-wheeled mill at Morett, County Laois in Ireland (Lucas 1953), while in a ninth-century Anglo-Saxon watermill at Tamworth in Staffordshire, a steel bearing block for a horizontal-wheeled mill was similarly re-used (Trent 1975). The re-use of discarded millstones as bearing blocks at Ickham, however, has as yet no known parallel in the Roman world.

Roman burials

Six inhumation burials were recorded from the site, but few details are available and their exact location is often unknown. Of the burials the first two were lost before any

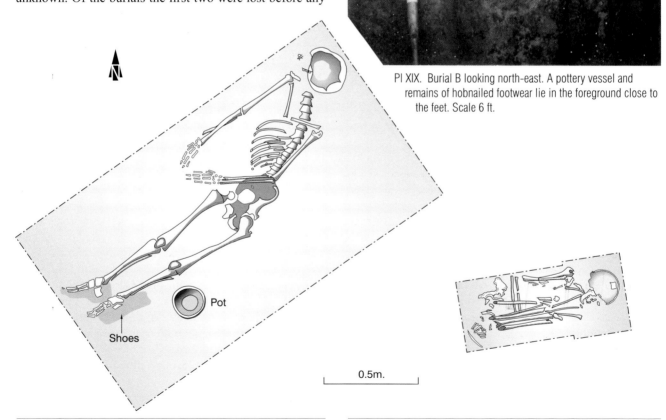

Pl XIX. Burial B looking north-east. A pottery vessel and remains of hobnailed footwear lie in the foreground close to the feet. Scale 6 ft.

Pot

Shoes

0.5m.

Fig 27. Plan of inhumation burial B. Scale 1:20.   Fig 28. Plan of inhumation burial A. Scale 1:20.

Pl XX. Group of folded pewter vessels buried beneath stones, feature (802) or (902). Scale 2m.

examination of the skeletons was undertaken. The remainder were reported, as summarised here. The skeletal remains were not retained. The first in the series was probably recorded in 1973–4 during observation of the northern quarry, reportedly associated with a curving ditch, presumed part of a ring-ditch. The second may have come from 'Surface or Area 7' within the main quarry. The remaining four were probably recorded later in 1974 in Area 9–14, located somewhere in the north-eastern corner of the site, north of the road.

Burial A (Fig 28): adult inhumation, fairly well preserved, crouched or tightly trussed, head east. Grave cut not recorded but at least 0.9 by 0.35m.

Burial B (Fig 27, Pl XIX): adult inhumation, well preserved, aligned north-east to south-west. The body lay on its right side, head to north-east, the hands together and placed in front of body. The south-east and north-east sides of the grave cut are visible in photographs, suggesting

a subrectangular cut 0.9m wide and 1.8m long and approximately 0.2m deep. There is a pottery vessel beside the lower legs (Fig 55) and hobnail shoes *in situ*. Film of the excavation, now transfered to videotape, shows both the pot and leather footwear.

Burial 902 Area 9: adult burial, either only partially excavated or in a decayed state; skeleton not examined. No details of the grave cut are visible on Pl XX. The photograph suggests that the visible bones of the skeleton were overlain by a group of folded pewter vessels (767–9, p 300), laid in an iron pan (723, p 242) and surrounded by stone and tile rubble. There is some confusion, however, as to whether these objects were from this context or from 802.

Burial 903, Area 9: no details of context. Adult female, poorly preserved. Examined by Justine Bayley and Carole Keepax (*see* p 319).

Burial 905, Area 9: no details of context. Adult male, 30–40, well preserved, stature 1.68m. Examined by Justine Bayley and Carole Keepax (*see* p 319).

Burial C: recorded December 1974 at a location unknown (but probably from one of the areas 8–14). Adult male, extended, head west, hands crossed on pelvis, legs straight, the body apparently laid on a bed of reeds. The skull was damaged but from examination by John Eley the skeleton was probably that of a male aged 45/50. A coin of Faustina the Younger (AD 161–75) was found in the grave.

Found close by, but not directly associated with the adult skeleton, were fragments of a neonate infant.

Post-Roman period

Christopher Sparey-Green

Evidence for the post-Roman period on the site is modest and for the earlier part is limited to a few objects of Anglo-Saxon date, some of which appear to derive from the features excavated or recorded during the watching brief on the main quarry and thought from their other, more numerous, contents to be of late Roman date. There appear to be no certainly Anglo-Saxon features and the only medieval and post-medieval deposits appear to be layers of peat, silt and gravel overlying the Roman stratigraphy. There is also one feature which can be identified with the line of a post-medieval field boundary.

Late Roman and early Anglo-Saxon periods

The majority of the late Roman features have already been described but the latest activity on the site is perhaps represented by scatters of metalwork and coinage recovered from the mill channels, a few isolated pits and one watercourse.

In Area 4 Pit 412 was stratigraphically of post-Roman date since it cut features 408 and 414. Only a small part of this irregular-shaped feature fell within the excavated area but it was at least 3.6m long, 2.2m wide and in excess of 0.24m deep. The lowest pit fill was of grey silt (412.2) overlain by a mixture of peat and coarse gravel (412.1).

The relationship to the extensive water-lain deposits in this central part of the site is uncertain.

In Area 1 Channel C was cut by two oval pits 107 and 115, both of which have been interpreted as scour pits associated with the working of the mills. The southernmost (107) lay immediately to the north of timber 42, and was approximately 1.6m long, 1.3m wide and about 0.17m deep. The depression, filled with a fine silt (108) yielded several large fragments of millstone. The depression was capped by a black peaty silt overlain by fine sandy gravel, the section suggesting stone rubble extended into the upper fill. The number (107.2) was allocated to finds from this area of the channel. All of the small finds from this feature are of late Roman date and they include a knife, a lift key, a fragment of a copper alloy bracelet and a fragment of a glass beaker. Thirteen coins were recovered from feature 107, the latest of which is an issue of Gratian (AD 378–83).

Adjacent to timber 30 was a second subcircular depression (115), approximately 1.75m long, 1m wide and 0.15m deep. A primary fill of orange gravel (115.1) was capped by a silt layer containing frequent large flints (115.2); a third deposit (115.3) was not described. The small finds assemblage is one of the largest to come from a single feature, with some of it recorded from individual deposits whilst the remainder was provenanced merely to 115. Almost fifty small finds are recorded from the primary fill 115.1 and they include a small fragment from a brooch, several copper alloy bracelets, a section of copper alloy chain and an ear-ring, two iron knives, a key, a fragment of a late Roman glass bottle, several copper alloy rings and a quantity of iron strips. Two items of late Roman belt equipment came from 115.2, alongside several iron strips and nails, a knife possibly of post-Roman date and a fragment from a late Roman colourless glass dish. Three items from 115.3 include a late Roman heart-shaped strap-end, a copper alloy strip and a lead offcut. Finds from 115 include several Roman knives and one of Anglo-Saxon type, a late Roman copper alloy strap-end, a set of copper alloy tweezers, a small drawknife possibly used in bone- and antler-working, two styli, two iron pins with broken stems, an iron snaffle bit link, lead and copper alloy sheet, iron strips, several iron bars and a small quantity of bindings. The pit produced some 435 coins, the latest dating to *c* AD 402.

Analysis of the many and various finds from these two pits (Assemblage 13, pp 103–5) suggests, however, the presence of several items of post-Roman metalwork, inlcuding one item certainly of Anglo-Saxon date and several others which may also be post-Roman, more than can be simply explained as contamination during excavation. This may indicate the features were cut to dispose of stone and metal debris removed from the surface of the meadow at a late date. Such an interpretation does not contradict the interpretation of the channel and Mills 2 and 3 but does mean that several items of metal and quernstone fragments must be treated as unstratified Roman finds, while others must be taken to be of Anglo-Saxon or early medieval date.

Watercourse P23, to the south-east of Channel D, must belong to a late phase of activity since it was recorded as cutting P22 at its north-eastern end. P23 was traced for at least 15m on a north–south alignment, but few details are recorded other than it was 3.2m wide and 'gravel-based'. This channel may have been associated with a post-Roman phase of water management and a mill beyond the site limits, in the area south-west of the quarry.

Medieval and post-medieval periods
Christopher Sparey-Green

The uppermost stratigraphy on the site was largely removed during the clearance of topsoil by drag-line and thus much of the evidence for later land-use has been lost. As already noted in relation to Channels A–D, extensive deposits in Areas 1, 4 and 6 sealed all the Roman features and are presumed to result from the action of a river course extending over this area. In its later stages the area served as water meadows, but there were however few signs of a managed system of drainage.

The most clearly defined post-Roman deposits were identified in Areas 1 and 6. In Area 1 deposits overlying Channel C (105), filled a broad and ill-defined hollow up to 20m wide and 0.7m deep, aligned approximately south-west to north-east while in Area 6 similar deposits could be traced a further 20m to the south-east (Figs 11 and 12, Sections B and D). The position of this hollow corresponds to the outline of the watercourse at this end of the site. The deepest point was located in Area 6, to the south-east, close to the steeper southern side while to the north the base rose almost imperceptibly to the level of the natural, 4m from the line of ditch 111. The primary fill was an extensive 0.1m thick deposit of silty, coarse gravel (104/112/113/114/604) which appears to have extended a considerable distance to the north, extending to seal ditch 111 and Channel A (118). Overlying the gravel spreads in the deeper part of this hollow a series of silt and peat deposits up to 0.4m thick are recorded (102, 103, 602, 603, 608, 611 and 624). On the south side of the hollow these deposits were, in turn, sealed by 607, a deposit of loam interpreted as post-medieval topsoil. These were capped by yet another intermittent deposit of gravel (605), possibly equivalent to 606.1 to the south and containing nineteenth-century finds. This possibly deliberately laid surface was sealed by a peaty topsoil (601/101) up to 0.30m deep.

This widespread deposit provided a substantial assemblage of pottery and a group of metal finds (Assemblage 27, p 119) many of which contained hammerscale within their corrosion products, suggesting that they were derived from metal-working activity in the vicinity. Most of the small finds came from context 104 and they are dominated by dress accessories, including bracelets, a stud and a buckle, all of late Roman date. There was also a spirally twisted link from a horse bit and fragments from several glass vessels, including a beaker, as well as a green glass biconical bead.

To the south-east, the main fill of Channel D, 610.1 also comprised a peaty deposit sealed by a 0.2m thick deposit of silty brickearth (606.3/607) (Fig 12, Section D; Fig 11, Section J). Several grooves identified in the surface of the deposit (606.2) were interpreted as nineteenth-century wheel ruts. Overlying the brickearth deposit was a 0.16m thick deposit of compact coarse gravel (110/606.1). A Constantinian coin came from 606.3; a nail, an iron cleat and an indeterminate glass body shard are recorded from 606.

The fills of this wide and ill-defined feature are broadly similar to the admittedly truncated stratigraphy recorded above pit 414 in Area 4 to the east (Fig 21, section, layer 1, and above, p 39).

On plan the extensive deposits of peat and gravel extending over these areas coincide with the watercourse identified on air photographs as crossing the site through Areas 1 and 6, 4 and further north-east (Pl I; Fig 4). The extensive layers of gravel and peat recorded in these two areas would be consistent with deposits laid down in a shallow river channel of post-Roman date. The origin of this may lie in the tail-race and mill ponds for the various phases of mill in the up-stream area, but since the putative water-lain deposits overlay at least Channel C, this river course could only have co-existed with the latest Mill 4 and Channel D and may be much later.

A detailed study of the post-Roman land-use will not be attempted here but certain features of the later topography should be highlighted. In Domesday four mills are recorded in Ickham and two in Wickhambreaux although the location of mills and the line of the mill streams is unknown. The course of the Little Stour in the later Anglo-Saxon and medieval periods is probably represented by the line of the Blackhole Dyke to the north of the site and north-east of Wickhambreaux (Fig 3). Up-stream, this river course is probably represented by a sinuous channel and oxbows in the valley south of the village, the channel continuing south-west towards Littlebourne and marking the line of the parish boundary between Ickham and Wickhambreaux. The Andrews, Dury and Herbert map of 1769 shows the approximate line of the river but also identifies the line of the Roman road as passing through Littlebourne and then Wickhambreaux before crossing the river and the present site on its way to Richborough. Although the line towards Canterbury is incorrect, the latter section would approximate to the recorded road and its postulated course to the Shore fort and harbour. By the time of the Tithe Apportionment map of 1838 the present course of the Stour had been straightened, the new canalisation now following the western side of the valley to serve the mill within the village of Wickhambreaux before crossing the old course of the river to the eastern side of the valley where it powered the mill at Seaton and then passed down the western side of the site to join the Wingham river.

Through all this period the greater part of the present site must have remained as meadow or pasture although the extent of the peat deposits and the record of the irregular river channels visible before quarrying commenced suggests there was no formal system of water meadows. One feature on site can be directly identified with early field enclosure.

Cutting through the 'occupation' deposits in the north-west corner of Area 1 was a broad ditch (109) extending roughly north–south, although its course was not traced over any distance. The ditch was approximately 5.2m wide and 0.5m deep. The feature contained a primary fill of dark grey silt (109.4) overlain by a grey-brown silty brickearth (109.3). Sealing these deposits was a grey silty brickearth and gravel (109.2) and a yellow-grey mix of brickearth and gravel (109.1). The feature was sealed by topsoil (101/601) and lies on the line of a field boundary between fields 30 and 32 of the Tithe plan, part of an extensive enclosure system laid out either side of the Little Stour. The river had, by this date, been harnessed to serve the nineteenth-century mills, these buildings surviving as part of the present landscape.

PART 3: THE COINAGE AND CERAMICS

Ian Riddler and Malcolm Lyne

Introduction

Ian Riddler

This chapter is concerned with the coinage and the ceramics. Virtually all of the coinage is Roman, although there is also a small quantity of Iron Age coins. Similarly, almost all of the ceramics are Roman, although in this case there are also a few early Anglo-Saxon sherds. These are described in this chapter and form part of the discussion of early Anglo-Saxon activity at Ickham in Part 5.

Of the 4,610 Roman coins, many were recovered through metal-detecting (*see* pp 76–8). Of this assemblage, 47.3 per cent is stratified, at least to area, whilst the remainder are surface finds. Outside of Richborough, this is a staggering quantity which, as noted below, exceeds that recovered to date from the city of Canterbury, where very many excavations have been undertaken from the nineteenth century until the present day. It is necessary to seek an explanation of the quantities of coins found at this site.

With such a sample, it is possible to provide a number of histograms, which can be set against 'standard' coin distributions for the various periods (Figs 29–45). In some cases, Ickham follows the norm; in others, it does not. The possible significance of the divergent distributions is set out below. A section is also provided on individual contexts which provided good groups of coins and are of particular interest, namely the four mills and a timber-lined tank or well in Area 7. Where these contexts provide good ceramic evidence, they have been designated as Ceramic Assemblages, and these are discussed below by Malcolm Lyne. In Part 5 further assemblages provided by the small finds are discussed, prior to describing activity on the site through and beyond the Roman period.

The coins

Iron Age coins

Colin Haselgrove

Standard references are as follows: 'VA' = van Arsdell 1989; 'BM' = Hobbs 1996. Dating after Haselgrove 1993.

1   Sf 278. Uninscribed half-unit ? Not certainly an Iron Age coin. Obv: crescent with pellets? Rev: possibly the curved leg of a horse, with ring ornament below. Weight 0.47g. Surface find. Identification of this coin is uncertain. Surface EDXRF analysis suggests that the object is made from a mixture of copper (50.65 per cent) and lead (47.39 per cent), which would be highly unusual for a regular Iron Age issue. If a coin, it could however originally have been plated. Tiny amounts of tin (0.94 per cent), silver (0.66 per cent), antimony (0.17 per cent) and arsenic (0.14 per cent) were also detected. A possible parallel is the silver half unit of the East Anglian early Pattern/Horse type, VA 683, BM 3784. Alternatively, the object might represent a poor attempt to copy a Kentish flat linear potin.

2   Sf 921. Uninscribed South-Eastern bronze unit, British LY7, VA 154–3, BM 2484. Obv: animal (bear ?) facing right with clawed feet, exergual line below; Rev: horse (?) facing right. Ring pellets in field around the animal. Weight 1.68g. Surface find.
Date: mid to late first century BC. The type is Kentish. Surface EDXRF analysis indicates that the coin is a tin bronze (91.08 per cent Cu, 5.74 per cent Sn, 2.29 per cent Pb; with 0.37 per cent Ag, 0.22 per cent Sb). This contrasts with two other early uninscribed Kentish types which have been analysed, which are both very low tin bronzes (Northover 1992, 294; Clogg and Haselgrove 1995, 49).

3   Sf 484. Cast British potin coin. Early British Massalia imitation or 'Thurrock type', VA 1402f, BM 662. Obv: Apollo head left. Rev: butting bull, right above pseudo-legend MA. Weight: 3.02g. Area 4.

Surface EDXRF analysis indicates a very high tin composition (50.76 per cent Sn, 47.29 per cent Cu; with 0.67 per cent Pb, 0.49 per cent As, 0.26 per cent Ni, 0.17 per cent Sb). Three early British potins analysed previously by Northover (1992, 296) had much higher copper (78–82 per cent) and lower tin (17.5–18.5 per cent). These are more likely to be representative of the normal composition. A fourth example in poorer condition produced results more similar to the Ickham coin.

Date: early to mid second century BC? The large number of early British Massalia imitations found in east Kent indicates that contrary to van Arsdell (1989), the series originated in the county (Haselgrove 1995; 2005). It was probably the first major British coin issue.

The presence of two or three Iron Age coins at a site with numerous Roman coin finds from the Flavian period onwards does not in itself provide conclusive evidence of Iron Age activity on the site, as the coins could all be post-Conquest losses. Two of the coins are unstratified and the other example can only be localised to Area 4.

Roman coins

Richard Brickstock and John Casey [31]

In total 4,610 Roman coins were recovered from Ickham by excavation and metal detecting, representing one of the larger coherent assemblages from Roman Britain: although smaller than that produced by nearby Richborough by more than an order of magnitude, it compares very favourably, for example, with that from Canterbury (total *c* 3,200 coins). A

summary of the various methods of recovery and recording is a necessary preliminary to the discussion of the coins themselves, since it will be necessary to discuss the levels of confidence attributable to component assemblages.

The majority of the initial cataloguing was undertaken by Ian Anderson at the Canterbury Archaeological Trust, though brief archive reports had already been produced by Kenneth Elks on both the Mill 1 coins (Area 14) and a small metal-detected hoard of Valentinianic date. The present updated and expanded catalogue, produced by Richard Brickstock, presents all the 1974 finds in numismatic order and is held with the excavation archive (on Microsoft Access) and at Durham University (on dBase III+ and Access).

Modern statistical methods of analysis of coin finds are dependent on the recognition of, firstly, a standard shape of coin histogram for a typical Romano-British site, and, secondly, variations from that pattern at a given site. These anomalies indicate variations in the numismatic site history which, when studied in detail, can often illuminate the archaeological sequence of that particular site. The accompanying histograms (Figs 29–42) are therefore constructed according to a now standard formula, which allows sites producing widely divergent quantities of coinage to be compared directly one with another: coins per period/ length of period x 1000 (a notional multiplier)/site total. It should be noted, however, that care must still be taken in the interpretation of very small assemblages, where a graph may be skewed by a very few coins.

Period divisions (Table 1) are of unequal length, following readily-identifiable date-brackets in order to maximise the percentage of partially-legible coinage that may be included in statistical calculations: in some instances this means the reigns of individual rulers, in others the issue life of important elements of the currency (Casey 1994a).

Published statistics for Richborough and Canterbury follow the slightly different date divisions preferred by Reece

Period	Date range AD	Period	Date range AD	Period	Date range AD	Period	Date range AD
1	43–54	8	161–80	15	244–49	22	317–30
2	54–68	9	180–92	16	249–53	23	330–48
3	68–81	10	193–217	17	253–60	24	348–64
4	81–96	11	218–22	18	260–73	25	364–78
5	96–117	12	222–35	19	273–86	26	378–88
6	117–38	13	235–38	20	286–96	27	388–402
7	138–61	14	238–44	21	296–317		

Table 1. Period divisions for Roman coinage used in the report. For an explanation of the various date divisions used by Casey, Reece and others, see Brickstock 2004.

31. Written in 1997.

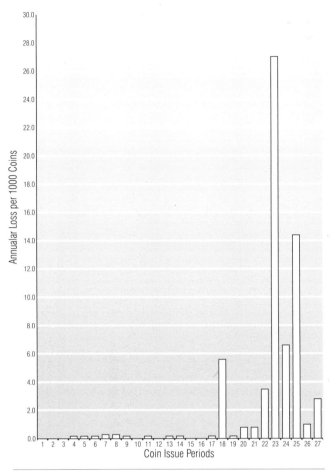

Fig 29. All coins.

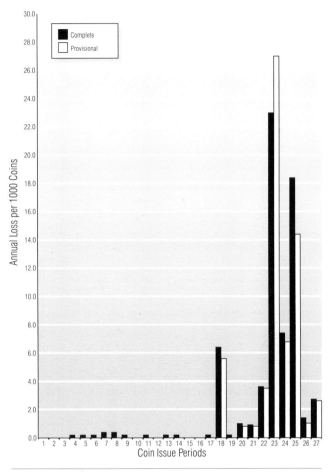

Fig 30. Comparison between provisional and complete coin totals (2,891 and 4,373 legible coins, respectively).

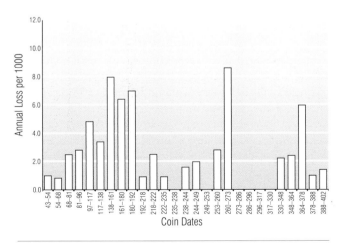

Fig 31. Areas 10 and 14 by coin dates. N=98.

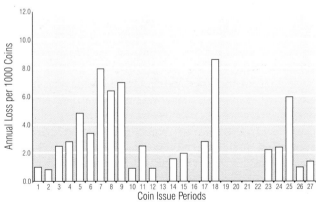

Fig 32. Areas 10 and 14.

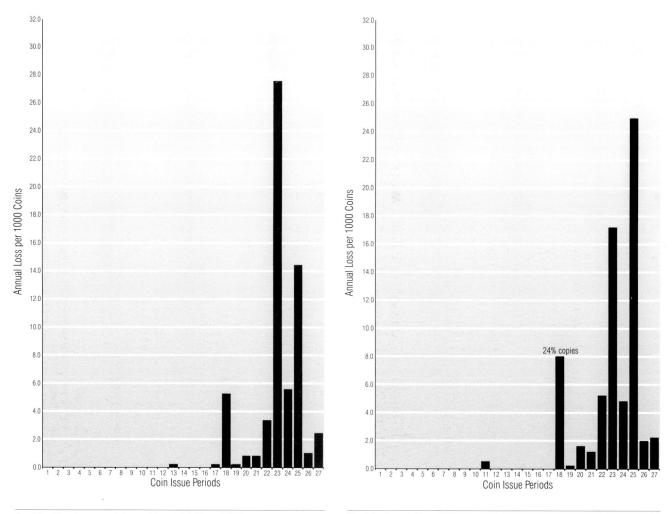

Fig 33. All coins except Areas 10 and 14: N = 4,275.

Fig 34. Area 1: N = 502.

(1991; Figs 43 and 44), but the two schemes are identical for the fourth century, allowing direct comparison between Ickham and those sites without the need for statistical conversion (Fig 45).

Included in the report are the site finds from no less than nine areas (Areas 1–7, 10 and 14) simultaneously investigated in 1974 whilst gravel extraction was taking place on the site. Coins from Areas 1, 6, 7, 10 and 14 were recovered through excavation. Virtually all the remaining coins (including those from Areas 2–5) were discovered through careful metal-detector searches of the site, as one of the first attempts in the region to use such instruments as an integral part of a controlled archaeological excavation. Nearly all of this material therefore has no stratigraphic context whatever and is of little use in elucidating the archaeological minutiae of

the site, but is nonetheless of considerable value in allowing an extended overview of the site. It is possible to offer an assessment of the effectiveness of the use of metal detection as part of a rescue excavation, through a comparison between excavated and metal-detected finds from the site as a whole and also from a specific area.

As a general principle, it might be expected that the detected areas would provide a better picture of the overall occupation sequence of the site, as represented by coins, whilst the stratified assemblages would be more likely to yield dating evidence specific to individual features. One might also anticipate, however, that the restricted 'reach' of the metal-detector (perhaps only 15–20cm below surface level) would lead to an over-representation of material from the uppermost surviving layers that would be readily apparent

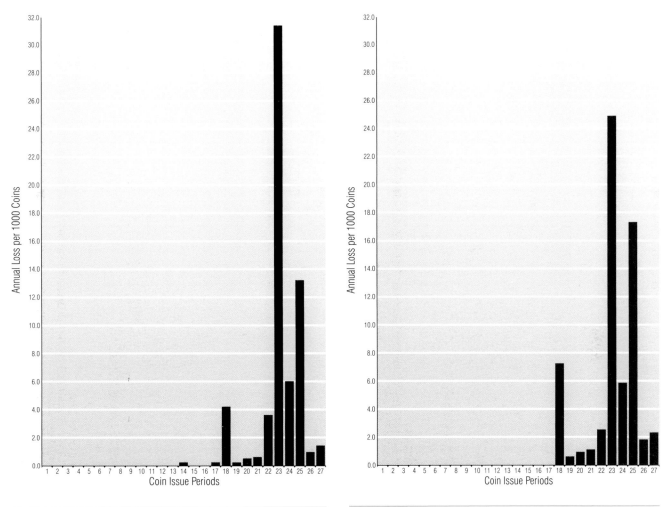

Fig 35. Area 4: N = 1,782.

Fig 36. 'Hut': N = 351.

in comparative histograms of metal-detected and excavated material. One might additionally predict that metal detectors would produce an increased proportion of the very small coinage so easily overlooked during excavation (and during rapid rescue excavation in particular), ie the smaller third- and fourth-century copies (of Periods 18, 23 and 24) and coinage of the House of Theodosius (Period 27). Where the depth of stratigraphy is such that the second/third centuries represent the extreme limit of the range of the metal detector, one might also expect to observe an over-representation of the larger small change (the brass *sestertii*, etc) relative to the smaller *denarii* (Brickstock 2007).

In reality, comparison between the excavated finds of Areas 1, 6 and 7 (Fig 41) and the metal-detected finds from Areas 2–5 (Fig 42) reveals a close correspondence between the two histograms, but differences in detail. This suggests that the metal-detection technique is of considerable use, both on its own (under controlled conditions) and in conjunction with excavation, but that allowance must be made in interpretation for the technical limitations displayed.

In this instance it appears that the lower stratigraphic levels have indeed been beyond the reach of the metal detectors. There is an almost total absence of coinage prior to AD 260 (Period 18) though, as predicted, the few coins that do appear are the larger and heavier bronze. This, however, is not of significance in the comparison between techniques of recovery on this particular site since, with the exception of a single *as* of Julia Maesa from Area 1, the located coins are confined to a timber-lined well (Area 7) and to Mill 1 (Areas 10 and 14) which will be discussed below. What appears to

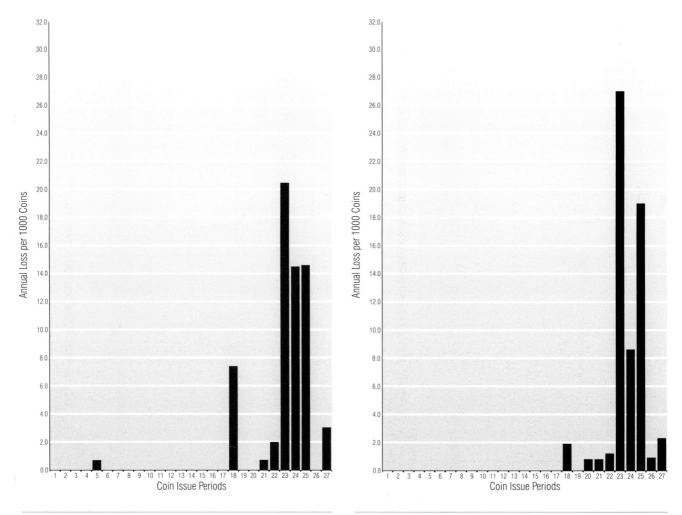

Fig 37. Contexts 407 and 408: N = 73.　　　　　　　　　Fig 38. Area 2: N = 118.

be of greater significance is the under-representation of the later third century (AD 260–96) in the metal-detected finds relative to the excavated finds. A similar contrast may be observed between the excavated finds of Area 1 (Fig 34) and the metal-detected finds of Area 4 (Fig 35), which (it has been noted above) extends over the location of Area 1. It should be also noted, however, that this divergence is by no means so apparent in that the proportion of the metal-detected finds that can be assigned with confidence to Area 1: several hundred coins were given the designation 'Hut' or 'Hut channels', a location subsequently recognised to be part of Channel C (Fig 36).

For the fourth century, the expected over-representations of certain categories of coins do not materialise: levels of Theodosian coin (Period 27) recovered by excavation are, if

any, higher than those produced by the metal detectors; and there is no noticeable difference in the proportions of smaller copies recovered. Very marked differences may be observed, however, between various histograms for the period AD 330–78 (Periods 23–25) which, given the similarities between the graphs for all other periods, may be indicative of the presence of scattered hoards amongst the site finds.

Given the low intrinsic value of the fourth-century bronze coinage, considerable, and increasing, quantities would have been required for everyday transactions. Large numbers of coins of the AD 330s and 340s may be identified within the Area 4 finds, indicated by similarity of type and condition as well as by consecutive small find numbers, which should perhaps be regarded as 'purse hoards' of everyday coinage, accidentally lost and subsequently dispersed over a wider

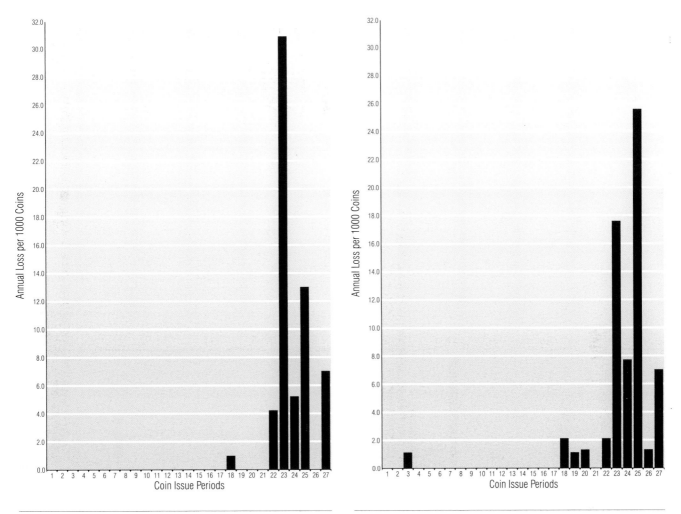

Fig 39. Area 3: N = 70.

Fig 40. Area 5: N = 73.

area. The presence of a scattered hoard may also be the explanation for the discrepancy in distribution between a preliminary histogram of some 2,700 coins and that produced subsequent to the addition of some 1,500 further coins representing the higher small find numbers (Fig 30).

Whilst the size of the Period 23 peak is readily explainable in terms of the presence of scattered hoards, it should, however, be noted that the Area 4 distribution is mirrored by other metal-detected areas, namely Areas 2 and 3 (Figs 38 and 39), although here the relatively low numbers of coins present, particularly in Area 3, make statistical calculations rather unreliable. Area 5 (Fig 40), another very small and therefore unreliable list, is the only metal-detected area to display a distribution similar to that of the excavated finds of Area 1 (Fig 34). An additional possibility is the

presence of a scattered hoard of Valentinianic date (Period 25) within Pit 115 of Area 1, which would otherwise display a distribution very similar to that of the detected finds from the same area (Fig 36).

Yet another hoard may be visible in the finds from Context 408 and Pit 407 (Fig 37): these two groups in Area 4 are the only specific coin contexts which can be isolated, other than the 'Hut' assemblage in Area 1. The distribution mirrors that of Area 4 as a whole (Fig 35) with the exception of Period 24 (AD 348–64), which appears over-represented because of the inclusion of what is probably a small hoard of Magnentian coins.

Whether or not hoards are contained within these deposits, a votive element is not precluded, but appears unlikely, since such activity is normally betrayed by the

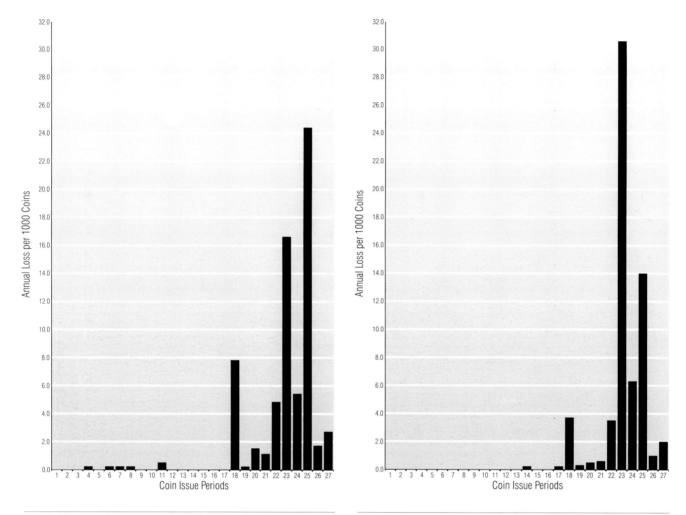

Fig 41. Excavated finds (Areas 1, 6 and 7). N = 553.

Fig 42. Metal-detected finds (Areas 2–5). N = 2043.

presence of obsolete or undesirable coin (*see* Area 7, below) rather than the coherent assemblages presented here. Rather, we appear to have evidence for substantial numbers of day-to-day transactions occurring over a considerable area of the site throughout the late third and fourth centuries.

Taking an overall view of the site from the cumulative numismatic material (Fig 29) produces a graph familiar from domestic, as opposed to military, environments in Roman Britain. It is immediately obvious that coinage of the period prior to *c* AD 260 (Period 18) is virtually absent from the site, an absence that is even more apparent when the coinage of Mill 1 is removed from the equation (Fig 33). Levels of activity in the years AD 235–60 (Periods 13–17) cannot be judged by the absence of coinage this period, since such a hiatus is normal in all histograms of British sites. This is a

function of the rapid debasement of the silver currency, which prompted the equally rapid disappearance from circulation (through withdrawal or hoarding) of earlier, intrinsically more valuable, issues.

The peak for AD 260–73 (Period 18) corresponds to the collapse of the silver currency, which reached a nadir of 2.5 per cent silver during the reigns of Claudius Gothicus (AD 268–70) and the Tetrici (AD 270–73). A large proportion of the coins of this period are copies of issues of the Tetrici ('Radiate copies'), probably produced to compensate for the dearth of Aurelian's reformed coinage in Britain in the following years (Period 19, up to AD 286). At Ickham the Period 18 peak does not reach the level achieved by sites with mature records of occupation in the last quarter of the third century, suggesting that coin deposits start only towards

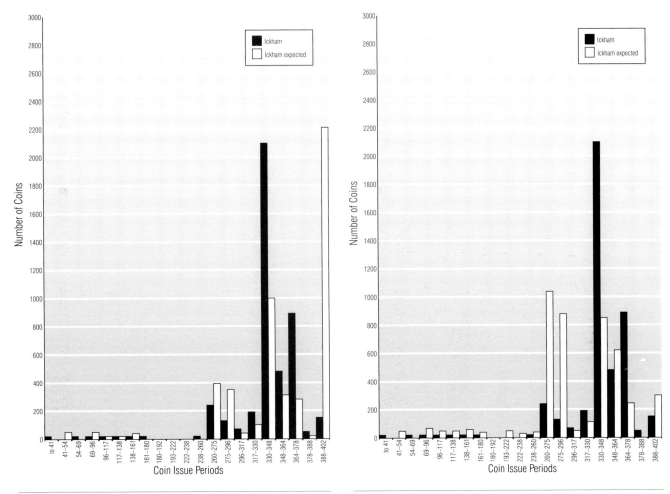

Fig 43. Actual number of coins and expected number in comparison to Richborough (total 50,767 coins).

Fig 44. Actual number of coins and expected number in comparison to Canterbury (total 3,215 coins).

the end of that period. This conclusion is reinforced by a relatively low proportion of Radiate copies and the absence of the smallest and crudest copies from the assemblage.

Thereafter the Ickham histogram conforms closely to a strongly-marked pattern of regional and national supply (Casey 1994a). The coinage of the usurpers Carausius and Allectus (AD 286–96; Period 20) is relatively common, for two reasons: firstly, there was a need for large quantities of coinage to secure the loyalty of the army, and secondly, this same coinage was almost certainly demonetised after the defeat of Allectus and the small change was dumped, often in virtually unworn condition. The coins of the following period (AD 296–317, Period 21) are uniformly rare, since they were of both relatively high intrinsic value and large module: they were both desirable and not easily lost.

Successive debasements and imperial indifference to the base-metal currency are responsible for the shape of the standard coin histogram in the following periods: a minor peak for the years AD 317–30 (Period 22) is followed by a major peak for AD 330–48 (Period 23), the latter further characterised by the presence of numerous copies (26 per cent of the total at Ickham) produced in response to a hiatus in the supply of small change between *c* AD 341 and 346. Regular coinage of the following years (AD 348–64; Period 24) is relatively scarce: this is explained by a combination of a coin reform in AD 348 and the subsequent suppression of the coinage of the usurper Magnentius (AD 350–53) following his defeat in August 353. The histogram peak for this period is provided largely by the copies that were once again locally-manufactured to fill the shortfall felt in the years *c* AD 354–64.

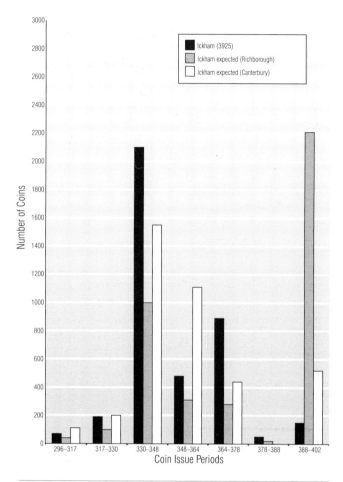

Fig 45. Fourth-century coins. Actual number of coins and expected numbers in comparison to Richborough (total 40,356) and Canterbury (total 1,541).

In the Valentinianic period (AD 364–78; Period 25) the addition of silver to the low denomination currency ceased entirely and in consequence the bronze coinage, since it was of very low intrinsic value, circulated in very large quantities, providing another major peak in both the 'standard' and Ickham histograms. The penultimate coin period (AD 378–88; Period 26) corresponds to both a further coin reform (by the emperor Gratian) and the usurpation of Magnus Maximus: coinage of this period is uniformly rare, perhaps because (unlike in Period 24) there was abundant small change already in circulation (the Valentinianic bronze) and in consequence no call for the wholesale copying of the AD 350s. The Period 26 peak at Ickham is normal or, if anything, slightly above the regional and national norms, particularly in the excavated areas of the site (Fig 41), and the

total is proportionally higher than that for either Richborough or Canterbury (Figs 43–45).

The last Roman small change which reached Britain in bulk is that of the House of Theodosius (AD 388–402; Period 27). The peak for this period is rather variable, not least because of the sometimes very low recovery rate of these very small coins by inexperienced excavators: it should be noted, however, that the proportion of Theodosian coin recovered through excavation at Ickham more than matches the metal-detected total (compare Figs 41 and 42). Nonetheless, the proportion is significantly lower than might be expected when compared to nearby Canterbury (Figs 44 and 47), in direct contrast to the situation pertaining in the preceding periods. An even more marked contrast may be drawn between Ickham (and all other British sites) and the wholly exceptional situation observable at Richborough, which has yielded the staggering total of 22,000 Theodosian coins, possibly indicative of coinage intended for, but for some reason never released into, general circulation.

Coinage supplied to Britain in the later fourth century was largely the product of the Gallic mints: by AD 388 the majority came from Arles, with smaller quantities from Lyons and Trier. With the closure of these mints in AD 395, supplies to Britain were sent from Rome itself and, to a lesser degree, from Aquileia. It is the post-395 issues in particular, ie the SALVS REIPVBLICAE types of Arcadius and Honorius, that are rare at Ickham: not all the coinage of this period may be readily dated to either before or after AD 395 (corrosion and wear often obscure the necessary details), but of ninety-one coins that are so identifiable only two belong to AD 395–402. There is a further coin of AD 394–402 and two more of AD 394–95. This meagre total strongly suggests that the site was not sharing fully in the regional inflow of late coinage, especially of issues later than AD 395.

Mill 1 (Figs 31–32)

The most striking deviation from the overall site pattern is that thrown up by Areas 10 and 14 (Mill 1) where a pre fourth-century dating of the structure is confirmed by the pattern of coinage (Spain 1984a). The exact location of this area is no longer known but the coins, once thought lost, have been isolated from the site records (Fig 31). In his preliminary study of the coins Kenneth Elks proposed a date of inception of *c* AD 150 and probable disuse by *c* AD 280. However, a start date in the middle of the second century is less probable than one in the early to mid third century given the extremely worn condition of the coins and the persistence in circulation of worn *aes* from the reigns of Trajan to Antoninus Pius until the demise of the base metal coinage with the collapse of the silver denomination in the late AD 260s. Even making allowance for the possible effects of water-rolling the recovered coins have been subjected to a marked degree of wear. The low volume of Period 18 issues (AD 260–73), and the generally early emphasis of this component of the assemblage points to a terminal date of *c* AD 270 for main activity on the site. The virtual absence of copies of the coinage of this period, a feature associated with the AD 270s and early 280s, confirms this view. The coins of AD 330–402 (Periods 23–27) do not appear to represent continued use of the site so much as casual losses from the general context of coin use in the late fourth century elsewhere in the vicinity.

Mills 2 and 3 (Figs 34 and 36)

The excavated finds from the mills at the south of the site probably do not represent the totality of coins from this area since, as was noted above, finds from this locality were included in a comprehensive detector sweep of the site, the finds from which were included with the material from Area 4. The bulk of the excavated coins associated with Channel C containing Mills 2 and 3 come from two contexts, 107 and 115. Originally identified as 'scour pits' associated with the working life of the mills, the presence of post-Roman finds in the material assemblage recovered from the features has led to a reinterpretation of the features as two pits cutting Channel C. Despite the change in interpretation, the coin finds have been linked with the use of Channel C and Mills 2 and 3. Other coins originally given the designation 'Hut' (Fig 36) can be directly associated with Mills 2 and 3 and Channel C. Context 107 produced fifteen and Context 115 some 435 coins, though the working total from the latter context is reduced to 363 coins when illegible material is deducted. It seems reasonable to regard the coins from both pits to have been dislocated from deposits associated with the south-west end of Channel C immediately up and down stream of the working gear of Mill 3.

Overall, the coins recovered from Channel C and the pits may be regarded as being derived from a common pool of coinage extending through the lifetime of the use of Mills 2 and 3.

Apart from an early third-century outlier, all of the coins associated with Mills 2 and 3 fall into Periods 18–27 (AD 260–402). As noted above, the pattern of coinage represented by the Area 1 histogram (Fig 34) is the product of two factors, the actual use of the site and the flow of coin issues injected by the state, the latter factor being dominant in any regularly occupied site. As was observed for the site as a whole (Mill 1 excluded), the coinage of AD 260–73 (Period 18) does not reach the peak normally achieved, again suggesting that coin deposits start towards the end of the period.

Unfortunately, a further area of uncertainty is created by the nature of the pottery deposits associated with the contexts discussed above, which are seen as the result of deliberate dumping and site clearance. At least one coin, said to have been found 'below the Mill floor', appears to give a *terminus post quem* for the construction of Mills 2 and 3 of later than AD 320–22, but the circumstances of the recovery of this item are not fully recorded.

In the fourth century the supply pattern dominates discussion except that, as was also observed above, one may note a high relative frequency, found only in this area of the Ickham site (and perhaps also Area 5), of Period 25 in relation to Period 23. This is probably due to the presence of a dispersed hoard, but is possibly suggestive of either a small decline in activity in Period 23 or an increase in Period 25. If this is the case, the latter suggestion might have the edge, since Period 26 is also, though the numbers are pitifully small, slightly more dominant than the norm.

Mill 4

There are too few coins from contexts associated with Mill 4 to merit graphical treatment (twenty-eight coins), but the assemblage conforms in broad outline with the conclusions drawn from the more abundant pottery, suggestive of activity in the second half of the fourth and early years of the fifth century. It is worth noting that the finds from this area (Context 604) form a rather eclectic group of coins derived from mints as widely dispersed as Constantinople, Rome, Nicomedia and Carthage. The general assemblage embraces the same time span as that from Mills 2 and 3, but a later bias is apparent even within such a tiny assemblage. It should be noted in particular that amongst the four Theodosian coins is one of the clearly later issues previously singled out for comment above, whilst the other three were recovered from Context 610.5 and can therefore be directly associated with Mill 4.

Timber-lined well 701: Area 7

Only twenty-three coins were recovered from this context, of which nineteen span the years AD 330–95, indicative of mid to late fourth-century activity and perhaps beyond: a coin of Arcadius (AD 388–95) suggests that it cannot have been backfilled until at least that date. The inclusion of four first- and second-century coins may represent the casting into the waters of curiosities long out of monetary circulation, a possibly-votive phenomenon not demonstrable in the assemblages of either of the later mills.

The pottery

Malcolm Lyne [32]

Introduction

The ceramic archive from Ickham consists of nearly 205kg of mainly Roman material, although much comes from poorly recorded contexts and is of limited value in understanding the nature of the site. There are, however, some well-stratified groups, including large assemblages from both the third-century Mill 1 and the post-AD 270 Mills 2 and 3. Areas 4 and 5 produced a number of mid to late fourth-century pottery assemblages associated with industrial activities.

The pottery from Ickham is important for a variety of reasons, including the very late date of some of the largest groups from Area 4 and Mills 2 and 3, the presence of a sub-Roman ceramic sequence on Area 6 and the evidence that some assemblages provide for specialised activities. The proximity of the site to the Continent means that the pottery also includes significant numbers of unusual fourth-century imports, which are reported in detail.

Methodology

Two different pottery retrieval systems were used during the excavations at Ickham. The larger assemblages from those excavations conducted by Jim Bradshaw have clearly been 'weeded' and consist almost entirely of rims and decorated pieces, whereas all of the sherds in Bradshaw's smaller assemblages and those from Christopher Young's excavations in Areas 1, 6 and 4 extension appear to have been kept. As a result, quantification of the various pottery assemblages by weight and numbers of sherds per fabric is only practical for Bradshaw's smaller groups and those from Young's excavation.

Quantification of pottery by these means has been shown to be of limited value, however (Fulford and Huddleston

1991) and (with the exception of the pottery assemblage from context 128, a precursor to Channel C) has only been used in this report to indicate the overall size of Young's pottery assemblages and Bradshaw's smaller groups. Fortunately both Bradshaw's and Young's pottery retrieval methods mean that their larger pottery groups can be quantified by the Estimated Vessel Equivalents (EVEs) method based on rim sherds per fabric (Orton 1975) and that system is used here. The samian and late Argonne wares, reported on separately by Joanna Bird, have also been quantified by EVEs.

Identification of fabrics and their inclusions was carried out with the aid of a x8 hand lens with built-in scale and the fabrics so defined are numbered and listed under the three prefixes of 'C' for coarse, 'F' for fine and 'M' for mortaria. Where Ickham fabrics can be correlated with those identified by the Canterbury Archaeological Trust at Canterbury, that system's reference is put in brackets after the Ickham coding. The Canterbury Archaeological Trust's fabric reference collection formed the basis for fabric attributions, and has been updated as a result of the Ickham analysis.

EVEs quantified assemblages have been tabulated with the fabrics listed vertically and the vessel forms horizontally under the four headings of jars, open forms, beakers and others. This system of tabulation not only indicates the relative importance of different suppliers of pottery at any one time but the varying emphases of these suppliers on different vessel types. Assemblages with unusual vessel form ratios could be regarded as indicative of specialised activities: several such assemblages were detected using this system of tabulation and they are described below.

Fabrics

The hand-made and tournette-finished coarsewares

C1A (B/ER 16)
Belgic grog-tempered ware. Soapy black hand-made ware with few visible inclusions. There are only a few sherds from Ickham, reflecting the dearth of first-century occupation material in general. A complete jar was, however, present in a pit sealed beneath the road (Fig 48, 39).

C1B
Belgic grog-tempered/native coarse 'transitional' ware (Pollard 1987, 298). Soft, soapy reddish-brown fabric with

---

32. Information from Didier Bayard, Kay Hartley and Françoise Vallet is noted in the text where appropriate.

few visible inclusions. Wares in this fabric developed from Belgic grog-tempered wares around AD 70 and were in turn replaced by Native Coarse Ware during the third quarter of the second century. There is a rather limited range of forms, comprising storage jars and cooking pots with everted and recurved rims (sometimes with fine body combing) as well as necked bowls with S profiles. There are considerable quantities of fabric C1B from Areas 10 and 14 (east of Mill 1). Some of the sherds from Area 10 have more visible inclusions than is usually the case and seem to belong to the transition of this fabric into true Native Coarse Ware.

Fig 46

1   Jar in soapy reddish-brown fabric with grey patches and sparse up to 4mm rounded red ferrous inclusions. External rim diameter 140mm. *Area 10, 1001.*

2   Slack-profiled grey-brown cavetto-rim jar. External rim diameter 170mm. *Area 10, 1005.*

3   Everted-rim jar in soft grey fabric fired grey-brown with up to 5mm rounded shale inclusions. *Area 10, 1001.*

Other forms are illustrated under the pottery assemblages of which they form part (Fig 48, 40, 41, 42; 54 and 55).

C1C (R1, 2 and 3)

'Native Coarse Ware' (Macpherson-Grant 1980a; Pollard 1995, 704). This is a somewhat variable hand-made and tournette-finished group of fabrics which tend to be pale grey with profuse coarse up to 2mm angular grey grog, sparse angular white grog and rounded black ferrous inclusions, fired flecky reddish grey with brown margins. Some vessels also have sub 1mm quartz filler. The predominant form is a necked jar with everted rim, sometimes fired almost to the point of vitrification and frequently with knife trimming on the body. Necked bowls and storage jars were also produced and Ickham is exceptional in having a few developed-beaded-and-flanged bowls of unusual design.

Native Coarse Wares are predominant in the late second- to late third-century Mill 1 assemblages and a kiln waster (Fig 46, 9) indicates that some at least of these wares were manufactured at Ickham and perhaps elsewhere in the neighbourhood of the site.

Fig 46

4   Everted rim jar fired black with knife-trimmed lower portion. External rim diameter 140mm. Paralleled at Marlowe Car Park, Canterbury in a third-century context (Pollard 1995, figs 308–75). *Surface.*

5   Everted rim necked-bowl with girth cordon and burnished decoration. External rim diameter 240mm. See St Margaret's Street Baths, Canterbury (Wilson 1995, F106 dated *c* AD 160–250). *Surface.*

6   Everted rim necked bowl/jar in patchy buff-black fabric with bosses on the girth. External rim diameter 160mm. *Area 10, 1047.*

7   Everted rim jar in grey fabric variant with moderate up to 1mm brown grit and flecks of shell, fired darker grey. External rim diameter 200mm. *Area 10, 1005.*

8   Hook-rimmed storage jar in grey fabric with up to 3mm brown and grey grog and patchy surface reddening. External rim diameter 320mm. See Simon Langton Yard, Canterbury (*ibid*, F169 dated *c* AD 130–60). *Area 10, 1005.*

9   Necked bowl waster in hand-made very fine sanded fabric variant fired black with split in rim surrounded by reddened patch. External rim diameter 220mm. A similar vessel type is recorded from Richborough (Bushe-Fox 1932, type 223) and Simon Langton Yard, Canterbury (Wilson 1995, F191, dated *c* AD 140–70). *Humus layer at north-east end of site.*

10   Developed beaded-and-flanged bowl in grey fabric fired polished black with buff margins. External rim diameter 140mm. *Area 10, 1001.*

11   Another variant in soapy grey-black fabric with polished surfaces. *Area 10, 1001.*

12   Devolved version of the previous type in dirty grey fabric fired grey black and with sharply in-turned rim reminiscent of that on a fourth-century Mayen ware dish form (cf Fig 52, 141 and p 112). External rim diameter 220mm. *Area 10, 1002.2.*

13   Lid in pale blue-grey fabric fired rough brown. External rim diameter 140mm.

14   Mortarium in reddish-brown fabric with profuse up to 0.30mm quartz and up to 1mm soft rounded red ferrous inclusions, and crushed flint trituration grits. External rim diameter 220mm. Local third century (KH). *Area 10, 1005.*

Other types are listed under their various assemblages (Fig 49, 70, 71 and 72).

C1D (LR 1)

Richborough grog-tempered ware (Lyne 1994a, industry 7B). Hand-made fabric with profuse up to 2mm crushed grey and black grog and occasional off-white siltstone inclusions, fired grey-black with irregular facet-burnished surfaces. Vessels in this fabric first appeared in east Kent during the mid fourth century and were the predominant local ware until the cessation of Romano-British pottery supply during the early fifth century. There is evidence for manufacture at Richborough, in the form of a number of grossly bloated wasters from above the ruins of the Chalk House (Lyne 1994a, 435). Production could also have taken place at Canterbury, where some very late fourth- to early

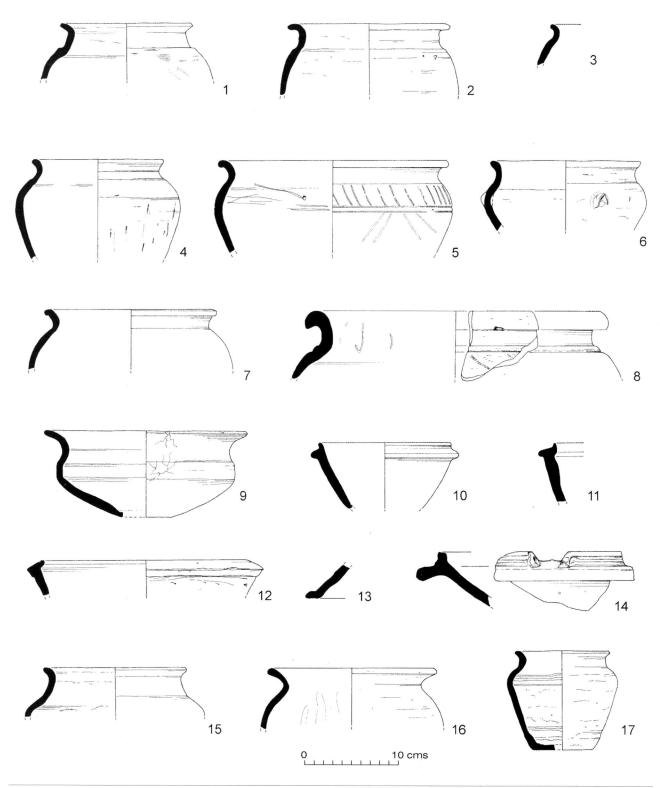

Fig 46. Coarsewares and finewares, Nos 1–17. Scale 1:4.

fifth-century assemblages have these wares, making up nearly three-quarters of all the pottery that is present (Pollard 1995, 712).

Figs 46–47

15   Slack-profiled cooking pot with slight shoulder carination fired black. External rim diameter 140mm. *Base of Channel C, Area 1.*

16   Cooking pot fired black. External rim diameter 180mm. *Mills 2 and 3, Area 1.*

17   Small everted rim cooking pot fired black. External rim diameter 110mm. *Area 5.*

18   Necked bowl in similar fabric. External rim diameter 200mm. *Rubbish pit/ditch end.*

19   Incipient beaded-and-flanged bowl. External rim diameter 180mm. This is the standard beaded-and-flanged bowl type made in this fabric. *Pit 107, Area 1.*

20   Deep convex-sided dish/bowl. External rim diameter 200mm. Another standard type.

Other types are illustrated under their respective assemblages (Fig 50, 87, 89, 90; Fig 52, 137; Fig 54, 170 and 178).

C2

Lympne grog-tempered ware (Lyne 1994a, industry 7A). Hand-made fabric with profuse up to 2mm crushed white and grey siltstone grog, fired grey-black with irregular facet-burnished surfaces. Wares in this fabric first appeared in east Kent during the late third century. Their arrival at Dover can be fairly closely dated: they are absent from the Period VI Painted House but tiny amounts are present in the AD 250–70 dated final occupation of the Period VII clay-walled building (Willson 1989, fig 34.219) and more in the Phase VIII destruction deposits immediately preceding the construction of the late Roman Shore fort during the 280s or 290s. A similar date for the appearance of vessels in this fabric is suggested at Canterbury (Pollard 1995, 702).

Fabric C2 vessels became more significant at both Canterbury and Richborough during the early to mid fourth century and continued to be supplied until after 400. They are particularly common at the Lympne Shore fort (Young 1980) and in the fourth-century rubbish pit at Wye (Pollard 1988, 151), suggesting a source either on the edge of the Weald or at the Lympne fort itself.

Fig 47

21   Necked bowl fired black. External rim diameter 160mm.

22   Developed beaded-and-flanged bowl fired black. External rim diameter 200mm. A standard form in this fabric. *Area 4 extension +.*

23   Another example of different form in similar fabric. *Area 4 extension +.*

24   Straight-sided dish in grey fabric fired black. External rim diameter 140mm. *Area 4 extension +.*

25   Deep dish/bowl in grey-black fabric fired patchy white/grey-brown/black externally. External rim diameter 180mm. *Area 3.*

C3

East Sussex Ware (Green 1980a; Lyne 1994a, Industry 5C). One of the most common fourth-century East Sussex Ware fabrics is fired black with profuse white siltstone grog filler in the manner of fabric C2 (Lyne 1994a, fabric 5-5) and can be virtually indistinguishable from that ware. East Sussex Ware developed beaded-and-flanged bowls were, however, made in a different way and frequently have a constriction just below the flange. One such bowl came from Context 610 and a couple of cooking pot bases with incised crosses on their undersides may also have an East Sussex origin.

Fig 47

26   Developed beaded-and-flanged bowl fired dirty grey-black (Lyne 1994a, type 5C-19 dated *c* AD 300–400). External rim diameter 160mm. *Area 6, 610, Channel D.*

C4A

Hampshire grog-tempered ware (Lyne 1994a, industry 6A, fabric 1A). Hand-made fabric with profuse up to 2mm crushed white and grey grog and sparse orange grog, fired grey-black with irregular facet-burnished surfaces. Recent research suggests that the bulk of wares in this fabric were manufactured in the northern half of the Isle of Wight during the fourth century and possibly as an adjunct to salt and tile production on the estuary of the Medina. There are just a few sherds from Ickham, including the following:

Fig 47

27   Stubby-flanged beaded-and-flanged bowl (Lyne 1994a, type 6A-17 dated *c* AD 300–70). *Area 4 extension, 'Section 2 Layers 2–5'.*

C4B

Hampshire grog-tempered ware variant (Lyne 1994a, industry 6A, fabric 1C). Hand-made fabric with profuse up to 1mm crushed orange ?tile and subangular up to 2mm buff grog, fired grey-black with irregular facet-burnished surfaces. There is only one sherd present in the Ickham material:

Fig 47

28   Beaded-and-flanged bowl with weakly developed flange and high bead (Lyne 1994a, type 6A-18 dated *c* AD 270–400). External rim diameter 160mm. *Area 1, Section 1.*

C5 (R13)

BB1 (Farrar 1973). Hand-made black fabric with profuse 0.30mm to 1mm white quartz filler and occasional coarse shale, flint and chert inclusions. BB1 has the widest distribution of any pottery in Roman Britain and is present in third-century assemblages from most sites. It is probable that one of the reasons for this widespread distribution is due to the wares being marketed with salt. Their rarity in Kent and Essex can be explained by the presence of local salt and BB2 pottery industries along the shores of the Thames estuary. As on most Kent sites, only nominal amounts of BB1 are present at Ickham and consist entirely of third-century forms (Fig 49, 73).

C6

Tournette-finished and slightly micaceous pale-grey fabric with profuse up to 0.10mm quartz, fired polished black with brown internal margin. There is a solitary convex-sided bowl from the fifth-century Context 610/2 in the upper fill of the re-cut water channel in Area 6 (Fig 54, 176).

Wheel-turned coarsewares

C7 (R69)

North Kent shell-tempered ware (Davies *et al* 1994, 101). Coarse grey-black fabric fired brown, with profuse up to 4mm fossil shell, sparse quartz sand and grog. There is a storage jar rim sherd from the lowest occupation levels within Channel C associated with Mill 2 (Fig 48, 43). Storage-jars of this type are dated *c* AD 60–160 and were made at Higham marshes on the Kent side of the Thames estuary. Some of the storage-jars from London and Staines have pitch adhering to the rim and shoulder, indicating that they were marketed with sealed lids as containers for some kind of commodity (Green 1980b; Lyne forthcoming a).

C8A (R14)

Thameside BB2 (Monaghan 1987). Medium grey to black fabric with profuse up to 0.10mm quartz, fired highly-polished grey-black with brown margins. Small quantities of dishes and bowls in this late second- to early third-century fabric are present at Ickham.

C8B (R14 var)

Thameside greywares (Monaghan 1987). Pale to medium grey fabric with profuse up to 0.10mm quartz, fired polished or rough medium grey. These wares lack the deliberate blackening of the BB2 variant and are less highly polished. Small quantities of late second- to early fourth-century forms occur at Ickham.

C9 (R9)

Canterbury ware variant. Biscuity reddish-brown fabric with moderate up to 0.20mm quartz and occasional similar sized white inclusions, fired smooth pinkish-grey. Lid-seated jar and bowl rims are present in the Mill 1 assemblages and are probably Antonine in date.

C10 (LR4)

Wheel-turned black fabric with sparse up to 1mm angular white and grey crushed flint grit. This may be a variant of the flint-and-sand-tempered ware encountered in mid fourth-century levels at Canterbury (Pollard 1995, 699) but differs in its lack of quartz sand and small size of the flint inclusions. This fabric is very rare at Ickham.

C11 (LR2.1)

'Scorched' sandyware (Pollard 1987). Wheel-turned greyware with profuse up to 0.20mm subangular quartz sand and occasional up to 1mm soft red ferrous inclusion, with rough, superficially reddened surfaces. The form range is almost entirely restricted to necked cooking pots with hooked or rolled-over rims. The distribution indicates that cooking pots in this fabric were made by the Thameside industry from the late second to the mid fourth century. The fabric is uncommon at Ickham.

C12 (LR5.1)

Alice Holt Type ware (Pollard 1995, 696).

C12A

Wheel-turned, high-fired blue-grey fabric with profuse up to 0.10mm subangular quartz and occasional up to 1mm angular red ironstone, fired rough grey-black with thick brown margins.

C12B

Wheel-turned reddish-brown to grey fabric with profuse 0.10 to 0.20mm quartz, fired smooth black or grey.

C12C

Similar fabric but with rough grey surfaces.

Some of the vessels in the above three fabric variants are thought to have originated at the local Preston kiln (Dowker 1878) and are moderately common in fourth-century assemblages from Ickham. The fabric variants (other than C12A) are not particularly distinctive, however, and may well include late Thameside wares and some from other production centres (Fig 50, 94). The putative Preston forms tend to closely imitate Alice Holt prototypes, even down to the use of a watery white or black-firing slip on some vessels. The fabrics are however somewhat sandier and harder than those originating from Alice Holt itself. The following is a brief introductory corpus of vessel forms thought to have originated at Preston.

Fig 47

29   Type 1. Necked bowl form with everted rim and girth cordon in fabric C12B with watery white slip over the upper part of the vessel. External rim diameter 170mm. This is the only surviving pot from Dowker's excavation of the Preston-by-Wingham kiln (Maidstone Museum 5PW3).

30   Type 2. Hook-rimmed jar form in semi-vitrified coarse blue-grey fabric C12A variant with pimply surfaces. External rim diameter 140mm. *Section 1–2.*

31   Type 3. Everted rim jar form in blue-grey fabric C12A fired black. External rim diameter 120mm. *Area 3, Ditch 307.*

32   Type 4. Developed beaded-and-flanged bowl form in buff fabric C12B fired polished black with groove on flange. External rim diameter 180mm spalled kiln second. *Area 7, Well 701.2.*

33   Type 5. Beaded-and-flanged dish form in bluish-grey fabric C12B with internal watery pale blue-grey slip and external diagonal burnished line decoration. External rim diameter 160mm. *'Floor'.*

34   Type 6. Convex-sided dish form with beaded rim in brown fabric C12B fired rough grey-black. External rim diameter 140mm. *Roman pit area.*

35   Type 7. Dish/bowl in reddish-brown fabric C12C fired pimply black and possibly imitating Argonne ware Chenet (1941) bowl form 320. External rim diameter 200mm. *Area 4, Section 2.*

36   Type 8. Flagon form in hard-reddish-brown fabric C12B fired polished black. External rim diameter 40mm. *Section 1–2.*

Other less certain Preston products are illustrated under their respective assemblages (Fig 50, 81, 82, 93, 94; Fig 52, 139 and Fig 53, 161).

In view of the proximity of the Preston-by-Wingham kiln to Ickham and the relatively small percentages of the fabric present in all quantified assemblages it seems clear that any pottery industry at Preston must have been small and probably short-lived. The highest recorded percentage is from the midden layer 414.4, Area 4 (18.4 per cent), the pottery from which dates between *c* AD 270 and 370. This suggests that the Preston kiln was in use at some time during that period.

C13 (LR5)

Alice Holt grey-wares (Lyne and Jefferies 1979). Medium grey fabric with profuse up to 0.10mm quartz and decorated with bands of iron-free clay slip which fire black or white depending on firing temperature. These wares were manufactured at Alice Holt, Farnham and Overwey on the Hampshire/Surrey border and marketed across Kent in small quantities throughout the fourth century.

C14 (LR6)

Overwey/Portchester D wares (Fulford 1975a, Lyne and Jefferies 1979). Distinctive cream-to-buff-surfaced fabric with profuse coarse to very coarse ironstained-quartz and red ironstone sand filler. Wares in this fabric first appeared during the second quarter of the fourth century and were made at Alice Holt, Overwey and elsewhere in south-east Britain until well into the fifth century. The range of forms is very limited, comprising a hook-rimmed jar with horizontal body rilling, beaded-and-flanged bowl, convex-sided dish and strainer. These wares became increasingly significant throughout south-east Britain during the late fourth century and small amounts were supplied to Ickham during that period (Fig 51, 97).

C15

Hadham Greyware (Harden and Green 1978). Extra-fine medium to leaden grey dense fabric with profuse sub-0.10mm quartz filler and polished surfaces. These wares were produced in eastern Hertfordshire and were supplied to London in appreciable quantities during the late third and fourth centuries. Much smaller amounts are found in Kent after AD 270. Ickham has produced just a few fragments from this source (Fig 51, 98).

C16 (LR3)

Harrold shell-tempered wares (Brown 1994). These wares were made at Harrold in Bedfordshire and at other sites on the Jurassic clays of northern Buckinghamshire throughout the Roman occupation. This industry was always an important supplier to the south-east Midlands and expanded its distribution zone south of the Thames during the mid fourth century. The late wares are never common in coastal areas of Hampshire, Surrey and Kent but most post 370 assemblages have sherds from at least one vessel. Ten stratified sherds are known from Ickham, of which eight come from horizontally-rilled hook-rimmed jars (Fig 51, 99) and two from a large storage jar with upright bead (Fig 48, 53). The hook-rimmed jars are likely to have arrived on site after AD 350 but the storage jar should be late third to early fourth century in date and is an unusual find from south of the Thames.

C17

Rettendon ware (Tildesley 1971; Going 1987a, fabric 48). Hard reddish-brown fabric with profuse angular up to

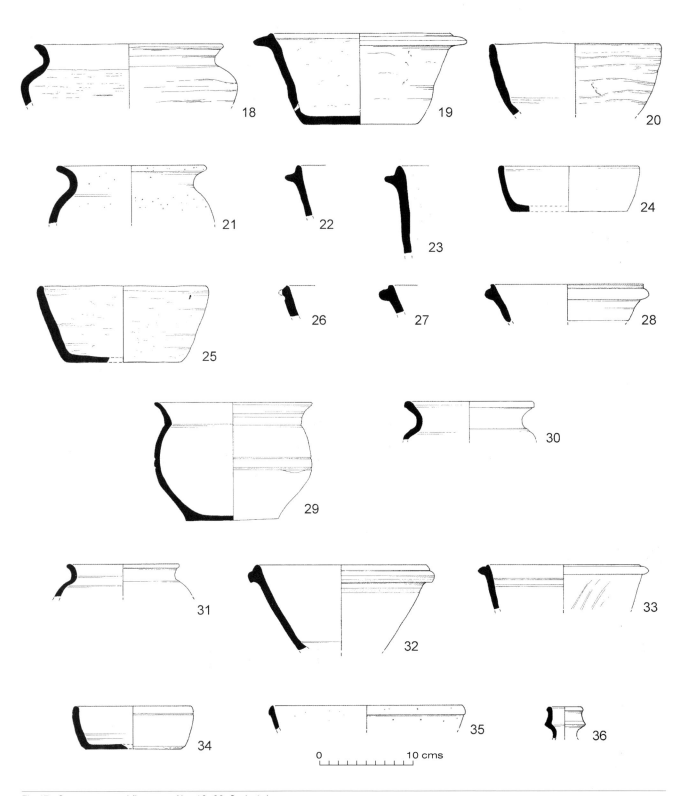

Fig 47. Coarsewares and finewares, Nos 18–36. Scale 1:4.

1mm white flint grit, up to 0.50mm subangular quartz and occasional flecks of shell. The industry which produced these wares was situated in the Chelmsford area of Essex and operated *c* AD 280–360+. Several kilns have been excavated (apart from those at Rettendon) at Moulsham Street, Chelmsford and at Inworth (Going 1987a, 73). One hook-rimmed jar and a large bead-rimmed storage jar (Fig 51, 100) are known from Ickham.

C18 (LR19)

Mayen ware (Fulford and Bird 1975; Redknap 1995). Hard vitrified fabric from the Eifel region of Germany with very coarse lava and quartz sand filler. Vessels tend to be fired in colours ranging from yellow through to black and have rough or pimply waxy-looking surfaces. There are twelve lid-seated jars of Fulford and Bird type 3 (Fig 52, 140) from the site as well as a bowl of type 5 (Fig 52, 141). Most of the limited importation of mainly type 3 cooking pots into south-east Britain took place after *c* AD 350/370.

C19 (LR2.2)

Coarse pimply blue-grey fabric with profuse up to 1mm subangular quartz and occasional up to 1mm angular red ironstone. There is a vitrified beaded-and-flanged bowl from Mill 2 at Ickham (Fig 52, 101). The source of this very distinctive fabric is unknown but is unlikely to be local.

C20

Verulamium region white wares. The pottery from Mill 1 includes fragments of a second-century screw-necked flagon from this source (Frere 1972, type 800, AD 140–90).

C21

Miscellaneous grey sandywares. As with most sites, Ickham has produced quantities of nondescript quartz-sanded greywares. The fabrics are not sufficiently distinctive for close identification of sources, but most of this material is either from the Thameside kilns or putative local east Kent equivalents and is probably of third-century and early fourth-century date.

C22

Miscellaneous oxidised sandywares.

Finewares

F1

?Canterbury white ware. Very fine pinkish-cream fabric with up to 0.30mm quartz and occasional red and black ferrous inclusions. There is a single double-handled lagena

from the 'humus layer in the ditch end at the north-east end of the site':

Fig 48

37   External rim diameter 150mm. There is a similar lagena from the Cranmer House, Canterbury cemetery (Pollard 1987, fig 111 Cremation 18A, dated to the second century).

F2A

South Gaulish samian.

F2B

Central Gaulish Les Martres-de-Veyre samian.

F2C

Central Gaulish Lezoux samian.

F2D

East Gaulish Trier samian.

F2E

East Gaulish Rheinzabern samian.

F2F

Argonne ware.

The samian and Argonne wares are described in a separate report by Joanna Bird (pp 121–31).

F3A (R16)

Upchurch ware. Wheel-turned sand-free medium-grey fabric with or without soft brown/grey up to 2mm grog inclusions. Biconicals, beakers and open forms from this source on the Medway marshes are fairly common in second- to early third-century assemblages from Ickham (Fig 48, 45, 46 and Fig 49, 69).

F3B (R84)

Sand-free blue-grey micaceous fabric. This fabric is rare at Ickham but there is a biconical pot from Preston in Maidstone Museum with tournette-finished and polished upper half and hand-made, knife-trimmed lower portion. Knife trimming is also a characteristic of Native Coarse Ware jars from east Kent and it would seem possible that vessels in this fabric were produced on a small scale by the Native Coarse Ware potters as a local version of Upchurch ware.

F4 (R18)

Hoo or North Kent white-slipped ware (Davies *et al* 1994, 40). Sand-free orange fabric with external white slip. Vessels in this late first- to second-century group of fabrics are rare at Ickham and consist entirely of flagon fragments.

F5 (R25)

Cologne white ware with brown colour-coat over rough-cast decoration (Davies *et al* 1994, 130). Bag beakers with corniced rims were imported into Britain from this source in appreciable quantities during the late second century. There is one example from Area 10.

F6 (R36)

Moselkeramik (Symonds 1992). Quantities of very fine beakers in this metallic colour-coated fabric were imported into Britain along with barrels of Moselle wine during the period AD 212–76 (Greene 1986, 167). One beaker sherd was present in Area 4 extension, Section 2 Layers 2–5 and another in Ditch 302, Area 3.

F7A (LR10)

Oxfordshire red-to-brown colour-coated ware (Young 1977, 123). Buff-orange sand-free fabric with sparse minute red and black ferrous inclusions and a reddish-orange to dark brown colour-coat. Ickham has a wide range of forms from the late third century onwards, including Young's types C3, 8, 23, 38, 46, 47, 50, 51, 68, 70, 71, 75, 77, 78, 79, 81, 83, 84, 93, 97 and 100.

F7B

An Oxfordshire red-to-brown colour-coated ware variant with profuse mica. Soft brown slightly sandy fabric with a tendency to laminate and with patchy maroon to chocolate-brown colour-coat. Forms include C47, 50, 51, 75, 78, 79, 81, 82, 84 and 97 (Young 1977). Micaceous Oxfordshire colour-coated wares are particularly characteristic of the Dorchester-upon-Thames kilns (Christopher Young, pers comm).

F8 (LR7)

Oxfordshire Parchment ware (Young 1977, 80). Hard, very fine sanded white ware with occasional tiny black and red ferrous inclusions and smooth surfaces with red-painted decoration. There are a few type P24 bowls from Ickham in late fourth-century contexts (Fig 53, 148).

F9

Soft orange-brown to buff fabric with matt chocolate-brown colour-coat and sparse up to 0.20mm red ferrous inclusions. The range of forms includes scale-decorated beakers, convex-sided dishes, beaded-and-flanged bowls, flagons, Dr 38 bowl copies and jars with rolled-over rims. Vessels in this late third- to fourth-century fabric have been seen in late

assemblages from a number of Kent sites and at Shadwell in East London, and may have been produced somewhere in Kent (Fig 49, 68, 76; Fig 50, 88; Fig 51, 109, 110; Fig 53, 154; Fig 57, 182 and 183).

F10

Soft grey fabric with sparse up to 1mm white grog and occasional shell flecks, fired polished micaceous brown-black. There are sherds from a poorly-finished Dr 38 copy and a wall-sided mortarium (Fig 52, 124) of probable local origin.

F11

Orange sand-free fabric fired buff-brown with profuse up to 1mm soft grey and brown ferrous inclusions. Some vessels are simply polished whereas others have patchy maroon to chocolate colour-coat. The forms are generally similar to Oxfordshire red-to-brown colour-coated ware ones but are less competently finished. There are just a few pieces from Ickham.

F12 (LR11)

Nene Valley white wares with brown-to-red colour-coat (Howe *et al* 1980). Both third- and fourth-century types are present at Ickham and include convex-sided dishes, beaded-and-flanged bowls and beakers. They are most significant in the AD 270–370 dated Assemblage 11 (Fig 50, 85, 86; Fig 53, 152, 153, 156 and Fig 54, 179).

F13 (LR13)

Hadham Oxidised wares. Polished orange fabric with profuse sub 0.10mm quartz filler. Vessels in this fabric are quite rare at Ickham (Fig 53, 155).

F14 (LR16)

German Marbled Ware. Very fine pinkish-brown fabric with patchy matt-brown colour-coat. A few unstratified fragments are known from Ickham, including Fig 48, 38, a flanged rim from a fourth-century double-handled flagon of Pirling type 72 (Bird and Williams 1983). External rim diameter 50mm.

F15 (LR12)

New Forest purple colour-coated stoneware (Fulford 1975b, fabric 1A). There are a few body sherds of an indented beaker from the ditches in Area 16.

F16

Very fine sanded orange fabric with matt black colour-coat and sparse up to 3mm angular white limestone inclusions, sometimes erupting through the surface. There are a couple of beaker fragments of fourth-century type from Ickham. Source unknown.

F17

Pevensey ware (Fulford 1973). Hard and lumpy orange-red fabric with coarse inclusions of haematite, limonite and other minerals. The vessels copy Oxfordshire red colour-coat forms and have deep-red colour-coat with applied stamped or white-painted decoration. There is just one small bowl rim fragment in this late fourth-century fabric from the so-called 'shrine' (335) in Area 3 (Fig 52, 125).

F18

Very fine pinkish-cream fabric with tiny red ferrous inclusions and patchy reddish-brown-to-chocolate-brown colour-coat. The few fragments from Ickham include a girth sherd from a rather squat beaker with white-painted scrolling. This may be a German Marbled Ware variant.

F19 (R95)

Terra nigra tardive (Bouquillon *et al* 1994). Hard very fine pale grey fabric fired polished blue-black. Vessels in this fabric were made at Arras during the fourth century. There is a bowl fragment in the pottery assemblage from Context 333 at Ickham (Fig 54, 167).

F20

Miscellaneous finewares.

Mortaria fabrics

Some of the mortaria from the site are in fabrics F7A and 7B but the majority are in the following specifically mortaria fabrics. Identifications by Kay Hartley made here and elsewhere in the report are indicated in brackets (KH).

M1

Underfired patchy cream/blue-grey fabric with no clearly visible inclusions and crazed surfaces.

M2

Soft pink-orange fabric fired buff-brown with crazed surfaces and mixed up to 1.50mm angular grey and white flint and black and red ironstone trituration grits.

M3

Very fine brown fabric with moderate up to 0.20mm quartz inclusions. A ?Kent product dated *c* AD 120–80 (KH).

M4

Sandfree pink fabric with external white slip. There is a single unstratified wall-sided mortarium sherd. A Kent product of Antonine date (KH).

M5

Lower Nene Valley white ware. Very fine pink fabric with minute red inclusions and black ironstone trituration grits.

M6

Rough medium-grey fabric with moderate up to 0.20mm quartz inclusions and up to 3mm pink and white quartz trituration grits.

M7

Oxfordshire white ware (Young 1977, 56). Very fine white fabric with minute black and red ferrous inclusions and occasionally pink-cored. This fabric is represented at Ickham by a significant number of mortaria with multi-coloured quartz trituration grits, of which the bulk are of Young's type M22 dated *c* AD 240–400+.

M8

Oxfordshire white-slipped ware (*ibid*, 117). Soft orange-brown sandfree fabric with sparse 0.10mm flecks of lime and occasional up to 3mm red ironstone inclusions. There is either a very thin and patchy white-slip or no slip at all: one mortarium from Area 4 extension has red dot decoration on the white-slipped flange (Fig 53, 162) and there are two from Area 7 with grey-to-grey-brown surfaces. There are fragments from thirteen mortaria in the Ickham material, all of which appear to come from post AD 370 contexts.

M9

Miscellaneous mortaria fabrics.

The assemblages

The nature of the archaeological investigations at Ickham was such that overall site phasing and a full understanding of the features uncovered has not proved to be possible. With this in mind, twenty-seven key ceramic assemblages have been isolated here and are presented in a chronological sequence. The first part of the samian report also follows this sequence. In each case, the small finds evidence which relates to these assemblages has also been presented here, in advance of the full description of those objects in the following chapter. Where appropriate, the relevant coins are also

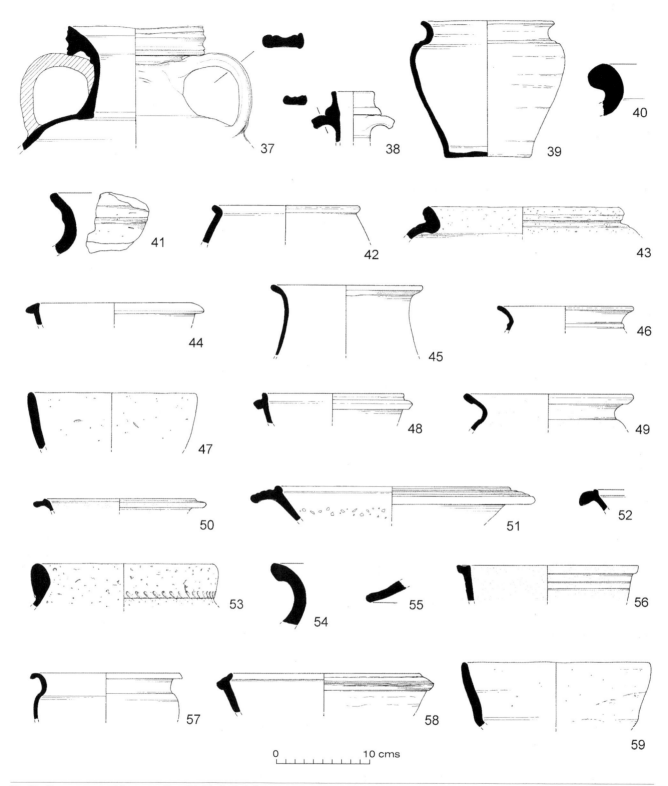

Fig 48. Coarsewares and finewares, Nos 37–59. Scale 1:4.

mentioned, thereby providing a dating framework for at least some elements of the site.

Ceramic Assemblages 1–3: late Iron Age to AD 80

The site produced very little pottery which could be dated to this period. There were, however, three features with pottery of this date in Area 1 and Pit 414 in Area 4 also had an Iron Age sherd (Assemblage 10). No small finds came from any of the ceramic assemblages of this period. There are small finds of early Roman date, however, and these are collated in Part 5 (Table 69, p 304).

Assemblage 1: pit sealed by the Roman road in Area 1

This feature contained the greater part of a cordoned and necked jar in soapy, hand-made, black fabric C1A (Fig 48, 39). A similar form is present at Richborough (Bushe-Fox 1949, type 388 dated *c* AD 70–85). External rim diameter 140mm.

Assemblage 2: ditch 111, Area 1

This feature produced five small sherds of pottery (20g), comprising four jar body sherds in calcined-flint-gritted Iron Age fabric and a rim sherd from a much later oxidised Hadham jar or necked bowl of late third- to fourth-century date. One type 1b nail was present.

Assemblage 3: the grey gravel in the bottom of Channel C down-stream of Mill 2 (106.4)

This context produced just two sherds of pottery, comprising a body sherd from a hand-made Iron Age jar with crushed flint filler and another from a North Gaulish white ware flagon. This material could be derived from an occupation layer through which the mill channel was dug.

Ceramic Assemblages 4–11: *c* AD 80–370

These assemblages are dispersed widely across the site, from the areas under and around each of the mills, the roadside ditches and contexts in Area 4.

Mills 2 and 3

There are several assemblages of Flavian to early fourth-century date associated with Mills 2 and 3 indicating activity on the site throughout this long period.

Assemblage 4: context 128: early watercourse preceding Channel C

The pottery from this context originated in gravel deposits beneath the transverse timbers and planking of the final mill-race. This context was dug first by Jim Bradshaw and then by Christopher Young. Jim Bradshaw's excavation yielded twenty-two fresh-looking sherds (644g) of *c* AD 70–250 date range including a single samian sherd (*see* p 122), a rim fragment from a Native Coarse Ware cooking pot and the following:

Fig 48

40   Storage-jar rim in soft reddish-brown fabric C1B with no obvious inclusions. External rim diameter 300mm+.

41   Recurved storage-jar rim in similar fabric, from vessel with corrugated neck and probable late first-century date.

42   Bead-rimmed jar in similar fabric, but fired patchy buff-black. External rim diameter 160mm. Late first century.

43   Bead-rimmed jar in reddish-brown fabric C7. External rim diameter 200mm. Type 3D.1 (Monaghan 1987) dated *c* AD 40/50–150.

44   Flanged dish in black-cored brown fabric C8A fired polished black. External rim diameter 200mm. Type 5A1-1 dated *c* AD 170/90–250 (*ibid*).

45   Biconical rim in grey fabric F3A. External rim diameter 160mm. Type 2G2–1 dated *c* AD 43/50–70/100 (*ibid*).

46   Rim from jar with cordoned neck in similar fabric. External rim diameter 140mm. Type 4A-1 dated *c* AD 70–120 (*ibid*).

The large sherds and their fresh appearance suggest that they were directly deposited soon after breakage and this in turn suggests that a precursor of Mill 3 was already functioning by the end of the first century. There is a possibility, however, that the later mill-race was constructed within a natural water channel which had rubbish thrown into it from a nearby occupation site during this period.

Young's excavation of the rest of the context produced four coins ranging in date between 260 and 322 as well as 133 sherds (1,838g) of first- to early fourth-century pottery. The assemblage is too small for quantification by EVEs but the following general observations can be made, based on numbers of sherds. The most common fabric is Native Coarse Ware (23 per cent), with small quantities of fabric C1B (8 per cent) indicating the presence of late first- and early second-century sherds as well. The second most significant fabric group consists of miscellaneous, unattributed sandy greywares (18 per cent). Hand-made grog-tempered ware fabric C2 of post 270 date accounts for 9 per cent of the assemblage. The following pieces are of particular interest:

Fig 48

47   Deep convex-sided dish in black fabric C4A with moderate up to 2mm white and orange grog. External rim diameter 160mm. A small everted jar rim in similar fabric was also present.

48   Developed beaded-and-flanged bowl in brown fabric C12B fired polished black. External rim diameter 140mm.

49   Everted jar rim with thickened bead, in coarse pale-grey fabric with profuse up to 0.50mm subangular quartz filler, fired rough dark grey. External rim diameter 180mm.

50   Incipient beaded-and-flanged bowl rim in coarse orange fabric with profuse up to 0.30mm quartz, fired rough grey-brown. External rim diameter 170mm.

51   Lower Nene Valley reeded-rim mortarium in fabric M6. External rim diameter 240mm.

52   Rim fragment from small mortarium in very fine sanded brown fabric with up to 0.20mm quartz filler and sparse coarse red ferrous inclusions, fired buff-pink. (Local Kent product of mid second-century date. KH.)

A small number of sherds in Richborough grog-tempered ware (2 per cent) and a rilled body sherd from an Overwey/Portchester D fabric cooking pot indicate that small amounts of material were still being added to this assemblage after AD 350. There was a single sherd of samian.

The presence of fragments from two Hampshire grog-tempered ware vessels in fabric C4A (Fig 48, 47) is particularly interesting, in that it demonstrates links of some nature between Ickham and Isle of Wight/Hampshire coastal areas during the period *c* AD 270–350+.

Another small late third- to early fourth-century pottery assemblage of twenty-one sherds (168g) came from the orange gravel layer with large flints (Context 106/3) in the bottom of the mill-race down-stream of the mill. This seems to be a continuation of the previous context and the assemblage includes an everted cooking pot rim in Native Coarse Ware, another in fabric C2, a black-slipped Alice Holt straight-sided dish of type 6A-4 (Lyne and Jefferies 1979) and an Oxfordshire fabric F7A flagon neck fragment of type C8, dated *c* AD 270–400+ (Young 1977). It also included a coin of Constantine (323–4).

Small finds were recovered from contexts 128 and 106.3. The former context contained a fragment of iron strip, five indeterminate iron fragments, six type 1b nails and thirteen nail shanks. There are also three fragments of vessel glass, two of which are also indeterminate. The third (893), however, stems from a beaker of Isings form 106, which is dated to the fourth or early fifth century. The earlier date should perhaps be preferred here, to accord better with the ceramic evidence.

Assemblage 5: features cut into the natural gravel east and west of Channel D (contexts 617, 618, 619, 620, 621, 622, 623, 624, 625 and 626)

These features produced very little pottery, but what there is suggests a late third- to mid fourth-century date. Contexts 623 and 624 produced fragments from the following vessel:
Fig 48

53   Bead-rim storage jar in black fabric C16 fired brown. External rim diameter 200mm. Vessels of this type are dated to the early fourth century at the Harrold kilns (Brown 1994, fig 34-253).

A single coin of Victorinus (AD 268–70) came from context 619. Context 626 contained the handle of a small iron casket key (703) for a lever lock and 2 type 1b nails. A biconical-headed iron pin (**29**), a type 1b nail and four nail shanks was found in the deposit 624.

Mill 1 (Areas 10 and 14)

Assemblage 6: context 1005 (?water channel)

The original archive for this mill could not be located but a footnote to Spain's paper on it (Spain 1984a) refers to it as being at Area 14. There were two pottery assemblages from this area; 1400 and 1401, the labels for the latter context also indicating that it was the fill of a water channel, presumably the mill-race. Labels in soil samples from Ickham do, however, indicate that Area 10 also related to the mill. There were five contexts of uncertain nature recorded for this part of the site.

The coins from the mill were used to date it to between AD 150 and 280 but, as noted above, they have been re-evaluated, and now provide a date of AD 220–70. Most of the pottery from Areas 10 and 14 falls within this range, but some could be Flavian or early second century in date. There were large assemblages of pottery from Area 10, one of which came from Context 1005. The slightly water-rolled nature of this assemblage suggests that the context may have been the fill of the water channel running under the mill.

More than 60 per cent of the assemblage consists of hand-made pottery, with a predominance of local wares in fabrics C1B and 1C. There are rim sherds from seventeen everted rim jars in fabric C1B, and eleven everted rim jars, one necked bowl, two beaded-and-flanged bowls, one straight-sided dish, a storage jar, two lids and a mortarium (Fig 46, 14) in fabric C1C. A necked bowl in fabric C1C from Context 1400 is closely paralleled at Canterbury Lane, where it was dated *c* AD 160–90 (Wilson 1983, fig 110.474).

Fabric	Jars EVE	Open forms EVE	Beakers EVE	Others EVE	Total EVE	%	% of coarsewares
Coarsewares							
C1B	1.90	0.05	0.12		2.07	24.80	32.10
C1C	2.44	0.19		store jars 0.07			
				lids 0.20			
				mortarium 0.15	3.05	36.50	47.40
C5		0.05			0.05	0.60	0.90
C11	0.44				0.44	5.30	6.80
C20				flagon 0.14	0.14	1.70	2.20
C21	0.11	0.23			0.34	4.10	5.30
C22	0.10	0.08	0.17		0.35	4.20	5.30
Total	4.99	0.60	0.29	0.56	6.44	77.20	
Finewares							
F2C		0.59			0.59	7.00	
F2D		0.08			0.08	1.00	
F3A	0.40	0.18	0.21		0.79	9.50	
F9		0.38			0.38	4.60	
M9				0.07	0.07	0.80	
Total of all	5.39 (64.60%)	1.45 (17.40%)	0.88 (10.50%)	0.63 (7.50%)	8.35		

Table 2. Ceramics from Context 1005.

Most of the wheel-turned greywares from 1005, 1400 and 1401 are unattributed but include a second-century lid-seated bowl from the Canterbury kilns, a developed-beaded-and-flanged bowl in BB1 and two late second- or third-century jar rims in the 'scorched' sandy grey fabric C11. The fabric F3A Upchurch ware vessels include Monaghan's types 7A-2 (AD 43–140) and 3F7.1 (AD 150–70).

Figs 48–49

54 Storage jar in soapy reddish-brown fabric C1B with recurved rim. *Context 1400.*

55 Lid in similar fabric. External rim diameter 200mm. *Context 1400.*

56 Lid-seated bowl in sandy reddish-brown fabric C9. External rim diameter 160mm. *Context 1400.*

57 Jar in very fine sanded reddish-orange fabric C12B fired polished grey-black. External rim diameter 160mm. *Context 1400.*

58 Bowl with inturned rim in very fine sanded grey fabric fired polished darker grey-brown. External rim diameter 200mm. *Context 1400.*

59 Dish in very fine sanded grey fabric C8B fired smooth grey-black with a little surface mica. Dated *c* AD 120 to early fourth century at Canterbury (Pollard 1987, 286). External rim diameter 200mm.

60 Mortarium of Gillam Form 255 in underfired fabric M1. External rim diameter 280mm. (Antonine. KH.) *Context 1401.*

61 Mortarium in dirty-grey-brown fabric M6. External rim diameter 200mm. (Local Kent product dated *c* AD 150–300. KH.)

62 Mortarium in soft pinkish-red fabric M2 fired buff-brown and heavily worn with internal knife-scoring. External rim diameter 240mm. (Northern Gaul. Early second century. KH.)

63 Mortarium in patchy brown/grey-black fabric M6. External rim diameter uncertain. (Dated *c* AD 150–300. KH.) *Context 1001.*

64 Mortarium in soft mauvish-grey fabric C1C fired patchy smooth brown/orange with angular white and grey flint trituration grits. External rim diameter 230mm. (Local copy of Oxfordshire mortarium dated *c* AD 240+. KH.)

There are three Dressel 20 and one carrot amphora sherd from Mill 1. The latter sherd is one of the earliest dated fragments from the site. There were also some fifteen Central and East Gaulish samian sherds (*see* p 122).

An early Roman copper alloy pin of Cool type 24 (**217**) came from context 1005. Beyond this, the context is notable for its assemblage of ironwork (*see* p 299), which is accompanied by a small amount of lead alloy waste. The ironwork includes craft tools, domestic items, agricultural tools, objects used in transport and structural materials, along with debris from iron-working. A fragment of undiagnostic iron-working slag, possible smithing hearth bottoms (1330–2) a formless fragment of iron and a fragment of burnt clay

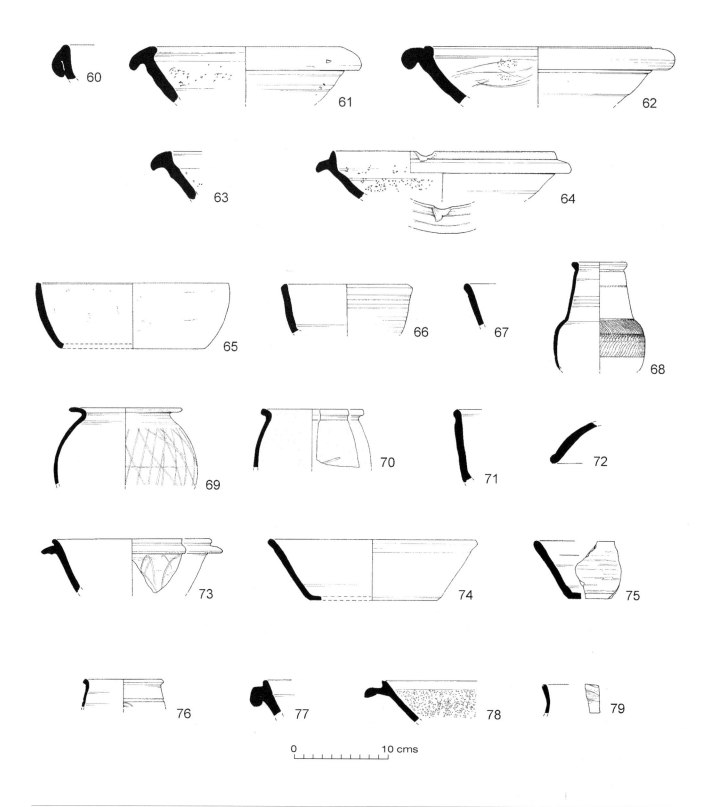

Fig 49. Coarsewares and finewares, Nos 60–79. Scale 1:4.

which may have been a hearth lining also came from this context (*see* p 298). The hammer (1235) may be no more than a thick bar with a central punched hole, as no distinct hitting faces are present.

The comments made concerning the dating of this assemblage associated with Mill 1, are confirmed by the small finds assemblage, but only on the basis of the dating of one object, the copper alloy pin. The remainder of the assemblage cannot be dated with any precision.

Ditches 307, 310 and Ditch 302

These three features were originally seen as ditches on either side of the road with 302 draining into the northern ditch 307. Ditch 310 is now seen as a continuation eastward of Channel A. Ditch 307 borders the northern side of the road and with 302 forms part of the enclosure system north of the road.

Assemblage 7: ditch 307 on the northern side of the road

This ditch produced fifty-three sherds of pottery (1,426g) of mainly third- to early fourth-century date. These include much of a necked bowl in fabric C2, an Oxfordshire red colour-coated type C71 bowl (*c* AD 300–400) and a type C47 dish (*c* AD 270–400). A rouletted body-sherd from a pentice beaker in the same fabric, a small everted rim jar in fabric C12B (Fig 47, 31) and the following are also present:

Fig 49

65　Deep, convex-sided dish in hard light grey fabric C1C with profuse, angular up to 2mm grey grog, fired flecky darker grey. External rim diameter 200mm. The form is similar to that of the deep dish characteristic of fourth-century Richborough grog-tempered ware (fabric C1D) and suggests that this vessel belongs to the end of the Native Coarse Ware tradition.

66　Straight-sided dish/bowl in wheel-turned, very fine sanded polished-black fabric. External rim diameter 130mm.

67　Straight-sided dish with rim edge beading, in grey-brown fabric 8B with smoothed surfaces. Type 5F4-2 dated *c* AD 140–210 at Canterbury (Monaghan 1987). External rim diameter 200mm.

The north-eastern continuation of this ditch in Area 7 (context 703) lacked pottery, but had been recut (context 702). This recut produced three sherds of late third- to early fourth-century character.

Assemblage 8: feature 310 (Channel A)

This feature produced just fifteen sherds of pottery (190g) of broadly third to early fourth-century date. This material

is noted on the plan as being confined to the top fill of the feature: the bulk of the ditch fill was totally lacking in pottery. This confining of rubbish to the top fill of the ditch may have also, on the evidence from Area 7, applied to Ditch 307.

Fig 49

68　Pentice beaker in sand-free buff fabric F9 with rouletted exterior over chocolate-brown colour-coat. External rim diameter: 60mm. A similar vessel came from Pit 293 at Richborough and was dated *c* AD 325–50 (Bushe-Fox 1949, 567).

The ditch also produced a developed beaded-and-flanged bowl in fabric C2, a type C97 Oxfordshire mortarium dated *c* AD 240–400+ and a stamped type C84 bowl dated *c* AD 350–400+. The presence of the latter vessel indicates that some rubbish was still being dumped in the top of the ditch after 350.

Assemblage 9: ditch 302 (field system north of road)

The much greater volume of pottery from Ditch 307 compared with that from Ditch 310 may be due to the proximity of a second- to early fourth-century focus of occupation in Areas 5 and 7 on the north-west side of the road. Although Ditches 307 and 310 may have been kept clear of rubbish for most of their lives, Ditch 302 was not and its pottery assemblage indirectly helps to date the digging of the roadside ditches and perhaps the construction of the road.

Ditch 302 produced 117 sherds (2,601g), some of which came from the primary silting. The overall assemblage had rim fragments from twenty-seven vessels and was quantified by EVES.

Despite this being a very small assemblage and therefore somewhat unreliable from the point of view of EVEs quantification, it clearly has abnormal characteristics. The most obvious of these is a deficiency of cooking pots and other jars and the domination of the assemblage by bowls, dishes and beakers. All other rural third- to early fourth-century pottery assemblages from east Kent quantified by the author consist very largely of cooking pots, whereas similarly dated urban and Shore fort pottery groups tend to be similar to this assemblage in having a preponderance of bowls and dishes. The significance of this is discussed in greater detail below.

The bottom fill of the ditch (Context 302.3) contained the greater part of the following vessel:

Fig 49

69　Small flat-rimmed jar in dark-grey fabric F3A with white margins and burnished acute-latticing. External rim diameter 120mm. A similar vessel came from Simon Langton Yard in

Fabric	Jars	Open forms	Beakers	Others	Total	%	% of coarsewares
	EVE	EVE	EVE	EVE	EVE		
Coarsewares							
C1C	0.08	0.19	0.10	Lid 0.09	0.46	15.40	34.80
C5		0.31			0.31	10.40	23.50
C8A		0.23			0.23	7.70	17.40
C8B		0.08			0.08	2.70	6.10
C12B		0.07			0.07	2.30	5.30
C21	0.12	0.05			0.17	5.70	12.90
Total	0.20	0.93	0.10	0.09	1.32	44.20	
Finewares							
F2C		0.11			0.11	3.70	
F3A	0.35		0.44		0.79	26.60	
F6		P			P		
F7		0.08		Mortarium 0.09	0.17	5.70	
F12				Lid 0.06	0.06	2.00	
F20		0.04	0.49		0.53	17.80	
Total of all	0.55 (18.50%)	1.16 (38.90%)	1.03 (34.60%)	0.24 (8.00%)	2.98		

Table 3. Ceramics from Ditch 302.

Canterbury, where it was dated *c* AD 140–70 (Wilson 1995, 689).

The pottery from the upper fills includes:

70　Small bead-rolled-rim jar in sandy grey fabric C1C fired rough pink with a little surface greying. External rim diameter 110mm. Paralleled at Marlowe III in Canterbury, residual in its context but dated to the late third century (Pollard 1995, fig 311–414).

71　Hand-made bead-rimmed bowl in pale grey fabric C1C with very fine sand and sparse up to 2mm black grog, fired lumpy dark grey with external residues.

72　Lid in pale grey fabric C1C with profuse sub 0.10mm quartz sand and sparse up to 0.50mm grey grog. External rim diameter 200mm.

73　Developed beaded-and-flanged bowl in BB1 with burnished external arcading. External rim diameter 160mm. Mid to late third century.

74　Dish with beaded rim in dirty grey fabric C8A fired black with reddish-brown margins. External rim diameter 220mm. There is another in fabric C8B. Type 5F4.2 dated *c* AD 140–210 at Canterbury (Monaghan 1987, 152).

75　Dish in charcoal grey fabric C8B with internal and external surface polish. Present at Canterbury from *c* AD 150–80 to 300+ (Wilson 1983, 273, fig 118, 647). External rim diameter 220mm.

76　Beaker rim in sand-free grey fabric F9 fired buff with chocolate brown colour-coat internally and externally. External rim diameter 60mm.

There were also a few residual samian sherds (p 126), fragments from a third-century Moselkeramik beaker, a biconical in Upchurch ware, an 'Alice Holt Type' beaded and flanged bowl with internal black slip, an Oxfordshire red colour-coat type C97 mortarium and a type C79 bowl dated *c* AD 340–400. The pottery suggests that Ditch 302 was dug during the early to mid second century and continued in use until the mid fourth century. This, in turn, indicates that the construction of the Roman road and its side ditches must pre-date 150 but be later than *c* AD 70, as indicated by Assemblage 1 sealed beneath the metalling.

Assemblage 9 includes a spherical-headed type 4 pin (230) of copper alloy, the length of the stem suggesting a late Roman date. A length of iron chain (1198), however, is similar to a bucket chain found in a pre-Flavian fortress pit at Usk. The wide triangular blade (**1242**) broken from a chisel for working hot metal, a wood-working adze or possibly a type of scraper is not readily datable. A small piece of offcut from a sheet of lead alloy, nine type 1b nails and five nail shanks also came from this context.

Pit 334/414, Area 4 (Fig 21)

Assemblage 10: pit 334/414, Layer 6

This large oval funnel shaped pit or well was not bottomed but produced thirty-five sherds (769g) of pottery. The assemblage is too small for any meaningful form of quantification but includes a prehistoric sherd with crushed calcined flint filler, an early second-century poppyhead beaker rim, a BB1 straight-sided dish of third-century type, an Alice Holt beaded-and-flanged bowl of type 5B-6 with internal black slip (Lyne and Jefferies 1979, *c* AD 270–420) and the following fragments:

Fig 49

77   Heavily burnt and eroded mortarium of type M22-14 in fabric M8 (Young 1977, dated *c* AD 240–400+). External rim diameter 270mm.

78   Burnt mortarium in soft orange-brown fabric M9 with patchy surface blackening. As with the similar example from Mill 2 this seems not to have been white-slipped. External rim diameter 200mm.

79   Rim from hand-made ?Frisian vessel in rough black fabric with sparse to moderate up to 0.20mm quartz filler. The rim has finger impressions.

A rim from a rouletted type C75 bowl in micaceous fabric F7B, dated *c* AD 325–400+ was also present. The considerable date range of these sherds suggests that the well was in use from the first to early fourth century. No objects or coins were recovered from this context.

Assemblage 11: layers 2 to 5 over pit 414

The pottery from the successive layers in the sinkage over Pit 414 was bagged as one assemblage (Section 2 Layers 2–5), but the archive indicates that the bulk of the pottery came from Layer 4.

The dirty pale sand (Layer 5) in Pit 414 also extended north-east from it. Few artefacts were recovered from this layer, which may have been a water-borne deposit. Capping Layer 5 was a black rubbish midden with much pottery, metalwork and bricks (Layer 4). There are eighty-nine sherds (2,192g) of pottery surviving from this layer but it is clearly selective as the overwhelming bulk of the pieces are rims and decorated sherds. Nevertheless this group of rim sherds is large enough for quantification by EVEs:

The predominance of fabric C2 wares, the presence of late third- to early fourth-century Nene Valley colour-coated beaker fragments and a third-century Thameside pie-dish suggests that this assemblage dates to the period *c* AD 300–70, but the presence of the post 325 fabric F9 bowl fragment in Pit 414 beneath indicates a mid fourth-century deposition of rubbish including earlier material. The pottery

Fabric	Jars	Open forms	Beakers	Others	Total	%	% of coarsewares
	EVE	EVE	EVE	EVE	EVE		
Coarsewares							
C1D	0.09	0.03			0.12	2.50	3.80
C2	1.14	0.29			1.43	30.20	44.60
C4A	0.10	0.07			0.17	3.60	5.30
C10		0.08			0.08	1.70	2.50
C12B	0.10	0.39	0.12		0.61	12.90	19.10
C12C	0.11		0.15		0.26	5.50	8.10
C13				Store jar 0.09	0.09	1.90	2.80
C16	0.14				0.14	3.00	4.40
C21	0.12	0.18			0.30	6.30	9.40
Total	1.80	1.04	0.27	0.09	3.20	67.60	
Finewares							
F2E		0.04			0.04	0.80	
F2F		0.08			0.08	1.70	
F6			P		P		
F7A		0.20	0.25	Mortaria 0.14	0.59	12.50	
F7B		0.06			0.06	1.30	
F9		0.05			0.05	1.10	
F12		0.20	0.32		0.52	11.00	
M7				Mortaria 0.19	0.19	4.00	
Total of all	1.80 (38.10%)	1.67 (35.30%)	0.84 (17.80%)	0.42 (8.80%)	4.73		

Table 4. Ceramics from Area 4, Layers 2–5, Pit 414.

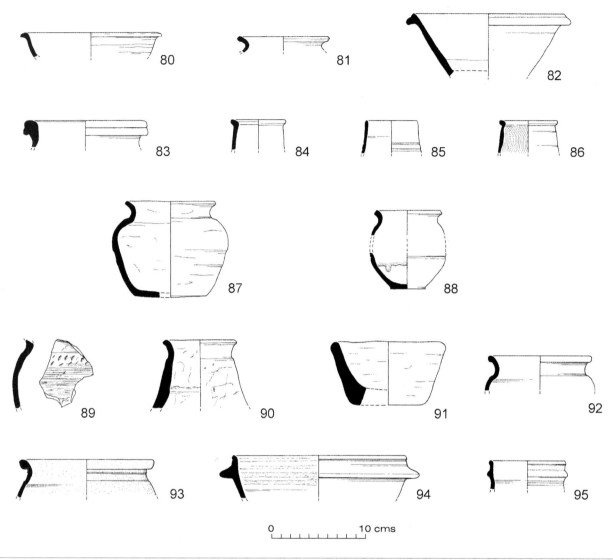

Fig 50. Coarsewares and finewares, Nos 80–95. Scale 1:4.

includes a cooking pot and a beaded-and-flanged bowl in fabric C1D, nine cooking pots, a straight-sided dish and a deep convex-sided dish-bowl in fabric C2 and:

Fig 50

80   Flanged dish in reddish-brown fabric C12B fired polished black. External rim diameter 140mm.

81   Rim from small everted-rim beaker in similar fabric. External rim diameter 80mm.

82   Developed beaded-and-flanged bowl in fabric C12B with partial internal black slip extending over the flange. External rim diameter 160mm. Further fragments from this vessel came from Context 408 and were unstratified in Area 7.

83   Rim from type 1A-16 storage jar in grey fabric C13 (Lyne and Jefferies 1979, *c* AD 300–400+). External rim diameter 130mm.

84   Rim from type C23 beaker in fabric F7A with brown-black external colour-coat (Young 1977, dated *c* AD 270–400+). External rim diameter 60mm.

Other Oxfordshire red colour-coated forms include a couple of type C68 bowls (*c* AD 300–400), a type C75 bowl (*c* AD 325–400+), a C100 mortarium (*c* AD 300–400+) and a C97 mortarium (*c* AD 240–400+).

85   Rim from funnel-necked beaker in fabric F12 with white-painted black colour-coat. External rim diameter 40mm.

86   Another beaker in similar fabric but with beaded rim. External rim diameter 50mm.

A dog-dish in similar fabric, an imitation Dr 38 bowl in fabric F9, a residual samian sherd and a few late Argonne vessels (p 126) and a fragment from a Moselkeramik beaker are also present.

Fragments of several glass Frontinus bottles, of second- to fourth-century date, were recovered from these layers. In addition, there is a small assemblage of iron objects, comprising a knife of later Roman type (631), a jaw broken from a pair of blacksmith's tongs (**1236**) showing signs of burning, a circular lock plate (**667**) comparable to an example dated to AD 280–315 at *Verulamium*, a ring-headed pin (**1139**), two nailed bindings and a length of bar iron, along with a small quantity of solidified molten lead alloy (75g). The tongs, lock plate and knife have hammerscale present within their corrosion products.

Ceramic Assemblages 12–23: AD 370–400+

Mills 2, 3 and 4 produced pottery dating evidence for their construction and occupation during this period. The dating evidence from the coinage has been summarised above. Apart from an early third-century outlier, all of the coins associated with Mills 2 and 3 fall into the period AD 260–402. As was observed for the site as a whole (Mill 1 excluded), the coinage of AD 260–73 (Coin Period 18) does not reach the peak normally achieved, suggesting that coin deposits start towards the end of the period. The ceramic evidence, viewed alongside that of the small finds, refines the dating for the demise of Mills 2 and 3 to *c* 370–400. The end date may, however, extend into the fifth century and Channel D and putative Mill 4 may have been constructed early in the fifth century.

Unfortunately, the contexts associated with the final, late fourth-century phase of activity at Mills 2 and 3 were largely removed by Bradshaw before Young started his excavation. The three main pottery producing contexts from the earlier dig are 'below hut floor', 'hut floor' and 'hut'. These contexts were so called because when the upright timbers lining the mill channel were found they were thought to be from the walls of a sunken hut. The transverse timbers in the bottom of the channel were thought to be the hut flooring and the mill-wheel scour pit fill (now interpreted as a post-Roman pit) was described as 'below hut floor'. In the following descriptions finds attributed to 'below hut floor', etc are now described as coming from amongst the timberwork in Channel C. The pits located immediately up- and down-stream of Mill 3 (107 and 115) are considered to contain largely residual material from Channel C fills. A hearth was also reported associated with the 'hut', but records of this feature have not been identified in the site archive.

Mills 2 and 3

Assemblage 12: 'hearth'

The assemblage derived from the hearth amounts to twenty-five sherds (740g). It includes the burnt rim from a 'Castor box', a type C78 Oxfordshire red colour-coat bowl (*c* 340–400+) and most of the following two vessels:
Fig 50

87   Hand-made cooking pot in black fabric C1D. External rim diameter 100mm.

88   'Small jar in light-brown fabric F9 with patchy brown colour-coat. External rim diameter 70mm.

Few finds were recovered from this context. They are limited to an iron lock plate or lock case fragment (**252**), two type 3 nails and a very small quantity of lead alloy sheet (offcut sheet 50g, broken sheet 50g). A small fragment of glass (**717**) from 'under the floor near the hearth' is Roman, but cannot be closely dated.

Assemblage 13: Channel C, contexts 107 and 115 (pits cutting Channel C)

Channel C contained large amounts of occupation and destruction debris derived from Mills 2 and 3 and pits 107 and 115. The pits also contained post-medieval metalwork (p 107) and appear to have been cut through the fabric of the mill-race up- and down-stream of Mill 3. Originally interpreted as 'scour' pits associated with the life of the mill, the features are now considered to be of post-Roman origin. Despite this, much of the material derived from their fills has been taken to be residual and originally from the fills of Channel C. The large amount of coinage mixed in with the occupation debris ranges in date from the mid third century to AD 402 but the rubbish must all have been deposited at some time after 350 because of the coin and pottery evidence from the pre-mill Context 128. There is 8,792g of pottery from the earlier excavation, although the high proportion of rim fragments indicates that many of the body sherds were discarded. Young's excavations produced a further 160 sherds (2,351g), including large numbers of body fragments.

This assemblage includes rim fragments from more than ten cooking pots (Fig 46, 15), four beaded-and-flanged bowls (Fig 46, 19) and two convex-sided dish/bowls (Fig 47, 20) in fabric C1D, as well as:

Fabric	Jars	Open forms	Beakers	Others	Total	%	% of coarsewares
	EVE	EVE	EVE	EVE	EVE		
Coarsewares							
C1C	0.15				0.15	0.90	1.50
C1D	3.52	0.82	0.19	Crucible 0.15	4.68	29.60	48.20
C2	0.79	0.57			1.36	8.60	14.00
C4A	0.05				0.05	0.30	0.50
C11	0.12				0.12	0.80	1.20
C12B	0.44	0.08		Flagons 0.11	0.63	4.00	6.50
C12C	0.39	0.05	0.14		0.58	3.70	6.00
C13	0.30	0.32			0.62	3.90	6.40
C14	0.44				0.44	2.80	4.50
C15		0.08			0.08	0.50	0.80
C16	0.08				0.08	0.50	0.80
C17				Store jar 0.07	0.07	0.40	0.70
C19		0.10			0.10	0.60	1.00
C21	0.38	0.08	0.30		0.76	4.80	7.90
Total	6.66	2.10	0.63	0.33	9.72	61.40	
Finewares							
F2C		0.40			0.40	2.50	
F2D		0.06			0.06	0.40	
F7A		1.29	0.31	Mortaria 0.18	1.78	11.10	
F7B		1.08	0.17	Mortaria 0.18			
				Flagons 0.59	2.02	12.70	
F9	0.13	0.09	0.08	Box 0.09	0.39	2.50	
F12			0.30		0.30	1.90	
F19		0.09			0.09	0.60	
M7				Mortaria 0.68	0.68	4.30	
M8				Mortaria 0.39	0.39	2.40	
Total of all	6.79 (42.90%)	5.11 (32.30%)	1.49 (9.40%)	2.44 (15.40%)	15.83		

Table 5. Ceramics from Contexts 107 and 115.

Fig 50

89　Cooking pot body sherd in similar fabric with stabbed decoration on the shoulder. Decoration on vessels in fabric C1D is unusual. *Channel C.*

90　Jug or flagon rim in similar fabric, fired patchy brown-black and polished externally and over rim. External rim diameter 80mm. A very unusual form.

There are also rim fragments from six fabric C2 cooking pots (Fig 47, 21, Fig 55, 186), one beaded-and-flanged bowl, two deep convex-sided dish/bowls (Fig 47, 25) and:

91　Crucible or crude bowl in dirty pale grey fabric C2 with profuse 2mm white grog. External rim diameter 120mm. *Channel C.*

92　Small hook-rimmed jar in orange-brown fabric C12B fired glossy black externally and matt-black internally. External rim diameter 110mm. *Channel C.*

93　Similar vessel but in coarse orange-brown fabric C12C fired rough grey-black. External rim diameter 140mm. *Channel C.*

94　Developed beaded-and-flanged bowl of unusual type in brown fabric C12B fired polished black with narrow matt horizontal bands around internal surface. A similar type but with rouletted flange was made at the Wattisfield kilns in Suffolk. Paralleled at Burgh Castle in Norfolk (Johnson 1983, 42–179). External rim diameter 140mm. *Channel C.*

95　Jug neck in orange fabric C12B fired polished black externally. External rim diameter 80mm. *Channel C.*

Fig 51

96　Developed beaded-and-flanged bowl in grey fabric C13 with bands of internal black slip over burnished acute latticing. External rim diameter 240mm. *Context 107 and Channel C.*

A white-slipped Class 3B cooking pot rim was also present (Lyne and Jefferies 1979. *c* AD 270–400+).

97   Rim from cooking pot in buff fabric C14 with external and rim top blackening. External rim diameter 170mm. *Channel C, west end.* One of two. *c* AD 330–400+.

98   Rim from developed beaded-and-flanged bowl in polished grey fabric C15 with darker surfaces. External rim diameter 160mm.

99   Hooked rim from cooking pot in brown-black fabric C16. External rim diameter 120mm.

100   Large bead-rimmed storage jar in soapy brown fabric C17 with sparse to moderate up to 0.50mm quartz and occasional up to 4mm crushed flint filler. External rim diameter 300mm. *Channel C.*

101   Beaded-and-flanged bowl rim in vitrified coarse blue-grey fabric C19. External rim diameter 180mm. *Channel C, west end.*

102   Beaded-and-flanged bowl rim in off-white fabric C21 with moderate sub-0.10mm quartz sand filler, fired soapy blue-grey. External rim diameter 160mm.

103   Small everted-rim jar in wheel-turned grey fabric with moderate up to 0.30mm brown ferrous and sparse up to 1mm rounded black inclusions, with black external slip extending over the rim. External rim diameter 100mm.

Sherds in Oxfordshire fabric F7A include the base from type C38 beaker (*c* AD 340–400+), three type C71 bowls (*c* AD 300–400+), a type C75 bowl (*c* AD 325–400+), a type C78 bowl (AD 340–400+), two type C79 bowls (*c* AD 340–400+), two type C100 mortaria (AD 300–400+) and rim fragments from several type C23 beakers.

104   Type C75 bowl in fabric F7B with rouletted decoration (*ibid* dated AD 325–400+). External rim diameter 180mm. *Channel C.*

105   Type C81 variant with rouletted decoration, in similar fabric (*ibid* dated *c* AD 300–400+). External rim diameter 180mm. *Channel C.*

106   Dr 38 copy in micaceous grey fabric F7B fired pink with patchy reddish-brown colour coat. External rim diameter 180mm. *Pit 107.*

107   Flagon in friable pinkish-brown fabric F7B with traces of maroon/brown colour-coat. External rim diameter 80mm. There is no exact equivalent in the Oxfordshire corpus. *Pit 107.*

108   Rim from bead-rim wall-sided bowl in micaceous pink fabric F7B with patchy maroon colour-coat and rouletted band. External rim diameter 120mm No exact Oxfordshire equivalent. *Channel C.*

109   Cordoned bowl in soft buff-orange fabric F9 with traces of external black and internal brown colour-coat. External rim diameter 180mm. *Channel C.*

110   Convex-sided dish in reddish-brown fabric F9 with internal brown and external patchy black colour-coat. External rim diameter 120mm. *Pit 115.1.*

111   Type M22 mortarium in pinkish fabric M7. External rim diameter 340mm. *Channel C, west end.*

112   Another type M22 mortarium with pinkish staining in similar fabric. External rim diameter 200mm. *Channel C.*

113   Another such mortarium. External rim diameter 200mm *Channel C.*

114   Type M23.10 mortarium in white fabric M8, dated *c* AD 350–400+. External rim diameter 260mm. *Channel C.*

115   Type M22.19 mortarium in pink fabric M9 fired cream/pink with multi-coloured quartz trituration grits. External rim diameter 220mm. *Channel C.*

116   Mortarium in soft orange-brown fabric M9 with no white slip surviving. External rim diameter 230mm.

There is a small amount of residual samian and a late Argonne bowl (*see* p 126). The bulk of the pottery dates to after AD 350 and is probably later than AD 370. Large quantities of small finds came from most of the contexts of this assemblage, and they can be used to test the dating evidence, and to establish something of the character of deposition in this area of the site. Elements of the assemblage are considered here, beginning with small finds assigned to Channel C.

Channel C produced a small assemblage of metalwork, little of which can be securely dated, unfortunately. A metal window grille must have come from a prestigious property and is likely to have been collected as destruction debris. It is better suited to a villa or a masonry structure than to a mill. A fragment of iron strip found burnt, also suggested destruction debris.

Channel C

The small finds from Channel C were assigned either to 'the Mill', 'the Mill area', the 'floor' or to its east or west ends. One hundred and sixty-seven items are recorded. They include artillery bolt heads (**4** and **5**), sheet copper alloy with repoussé dots (133–5), a ring with lozenge section (**168**) and a copper alloy stud (**86**). A possible copper alloy strap fastener (**42**) of first-century date is likely to be intrusive.

Eleven copper alloy bracelets, two brooches and five finger rings are also assigned to Channel C, alongside a pin with a facetted, cuboid head (234), which is a familiar late Roman form. The bracelets include examples of most of the types, although they are centred on strip forms (types 9, 11.1, 12 and 13). One of the brooches (**192**) is a penannular which is not, however, of a distinctive type; the other (197) is a fragment from a Nauheim and *Drahtfibel* type. The finger rings are simple forms which are not diagnostic.

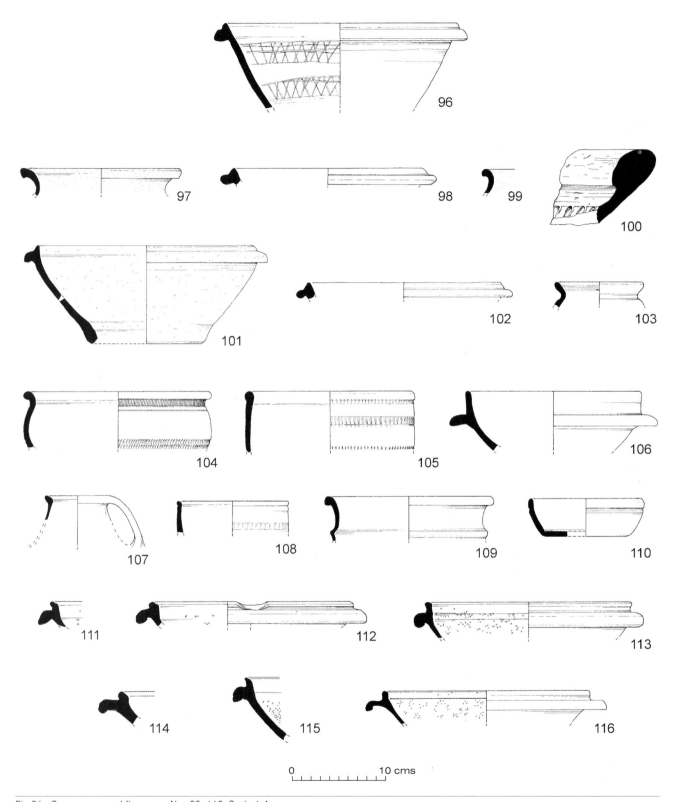

Fig 51. Coarsewares and finewares, Nos 96–116. Scale 1:4.

A helmet appliqué (**32**) is possibly of early fifth-century date. Alongside it lay two of the lead alloy pendants (286, 289), which are also thought to be of late fourth- or fifth-century date. It has also been noted that some of the glass beads are distinctive, late types, and they are represented here by several examples (267, **271, 272**). These, too, could well belong to the fifth century.

In general, the material from Channel C is chiefly domestic and structural in nature, although there is only a small quantity of nails. There is a good collection of knives, which includes examples of types 1.3, 1.4, 2.4, 3.3, 3.4, 3.6 and 4. There are equal numbers of knives with solid handles, and with centrally-placed tangs, and there appear to be no characteristic late forms. On the other hand, three heavy punches (**1254–6**) and an awl (1289), probably used in leather-working, also came from Channel C.

Copper alloy working is indicated by a manufacturing offcut, two sheet offcuts, and a partly made stem (1335). Three pieces of copper alloy folded sheet indicate scrap for remelting. Lead alloy working is represented by a candlestick foot or handle (**806**), a vessel foot-ring and eleven sheet offcuts. There is slight evidence for iron-working. Fifteen per cent of the objects had hammerscale within their corrosion products and it was noted in the nails also.

Two flesh hooks (**721 and 722**) can be paralleled by Anglo-Saxon examples and an iron key for a rotary lock is of a type commonly used in the medieval and post medieval period, suggesting that this context was not completely sealed. A decorative Roman copper alloy slide key handle (**691**) and a fragment of buckle frame of post-medieval date (sf no 918) were found on the surface nearby. A door latch (sf no 634) of medieval or post-medieval date and ring handle (**927**) of a similar date from the same general area also indicate the presence of some form of later occupation here.

The floor of Mills 2 and 3, Channel C

Small finds are assigned variously to the 'floor' of Mill 2 and to its west and east ends, and intriguing contrasts can be drawn between these assemblages. Fifteen fragments of vessel glass from the floor consist mainly of indeterminate pieces but include parts of a bottle (836), a bowl of first- or second-century date (**815**), a vessel of first- to third-century date (868) and two vessels, one a beaker, of late third- or fourth-century date (873 and **817**). None of the glass seems to be unduly late in date, and it may have been gathered for remelting.

Amongst the objects of copper alloy are a bracelet (**329**) of type 9, comparable with examples of the late fourth century at Lankhills, a suspension ring for an early Roman crescentic pendant (**63**), a pin (**219**) of type 4, a spoon (**758**) and a heart-shaped strap-end (**144**). All but one of these objects are late Roman, although none can be dated with precision. They are accompanied by one of the lead alloy pendants (**285**), an iron D-shaped buckle (**16**) and two fragmentary iron knives, one of which (**650**) is possibly from a razor of first-century date. Throughout the assemblage, therefore, there is an admixture of early and late Roman elements.

Thirty-five objects came from the west end of Channel C, just up-stream of Mill 3. Amongst them are five fragments of glass (906), all of which are indeterminate. Four strip bracelets (**336, 337, 343 and 374**) include examples of types 10.3 and 11.2, which are common late Roman forms. There is also an early Roman brooch (**184**) of Durotrigan type and a pin (**233**) of type 5 with a facetted, cuboid head. A flesh hook (**722**) is similar to another example (**721**) provenanced merely to Mill 2 and thought to be of late or post-Roman date.

The larger assemblage from the east end of Channel C, close to Mill 2 is of a quite different character to that at the west end. The material from the west end generally reflects that seen on the mill floor, with the admixture of early and late Roman forms and the range of dress fittings, domestic items and a little structural ironwork. At the east end, however, the assemblage consists almost entirely of iron objects, a significant number of which are structural in nature. Amongst them are bindings, handles, hinges, spikes, split-spiked loops, staples and wallhooks. Many of the same object types were also retrieved from Area 10 and were presumably associated there with Mill 1. It seems likely that these forms of structural ironwork stem directly from mill structures.

Other items of iron from the east end include four knives (**616, 646, 650, 652**), one of which (**616**) belongs to type 2.2, whilst the other three do not possess any distinguishing features. Five horseshoes (1051–55), three hooked blades used for agricultural purposes, an artillery bolt (**11**) and a padlock key (**698**) were also recovered. An ear-ring (**206**) is a fourth-century type and a possible helmet plume holder (**30**) is comparable with an example from late occupation at York dating to the late third or fourth century.

Contexts 107 and 115

Pit 107 is of interest because a considerable number of querns and millstones were deposited in it (Tables 48 and 58). The distribution of stone objects across the site is described below and it is centred on the mill areas, with thirty-three quern or millstone fragments from context 107. A small collection of metal objects also came from this context. Amongst them are a copper alloy crenellated strip bracelet (**375**), an iron knife (**634**) of type 3.2, an iron L-shaped lift key (**679**) and a formless fragment of iron. Fifty-two type 1b nails, four of

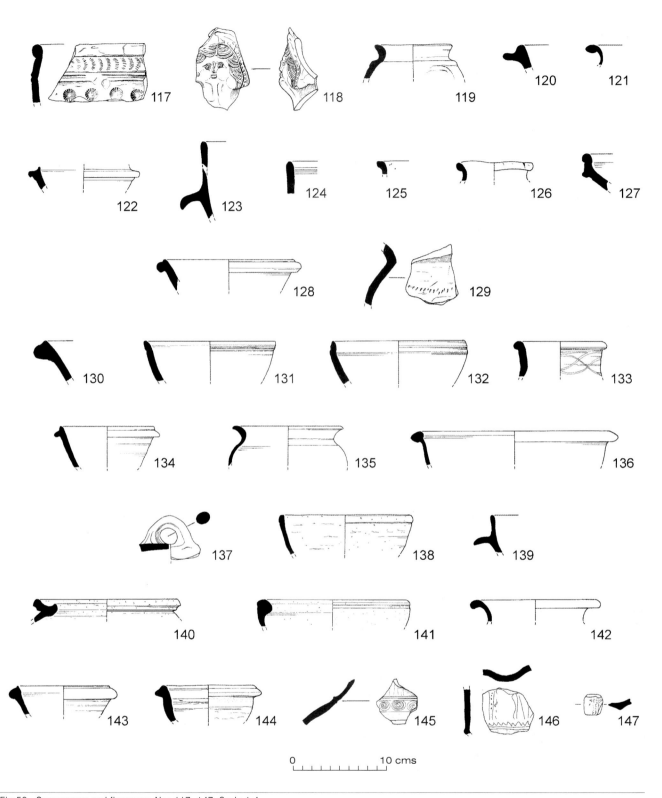

Fig 52.　Coarsewares and finewares, Nos 117–147. Scale 1:4.

type 1a and thirty-four nail shanks were found, including a quantity encrusted together with fifteen coins recorded as coming from the 'floor'. A fragment of glass (**877**) comes from a beaker of late Roman type.

A large assemblage of metalwork was recovered from context 115 consisting principally of domestic and structural items. In addition, a small quantity of late Roman belt fittings with forms broadly datable to 350–400 or later came from this context, including a buckle loop (**121**), buckle plate (**117**) and strap-ends of heart-shape (**150**), 'nail cleaner' form (**158**) and dart-shape (**155**). The ironwork from this deposit was distinctive in that much of it occurred in large concreted masses incoporating a variety of items of both copper alloy, including coinage (435 coins were recovered from this context), iron and lead alloy and flecks of hammerscale, apparently encrusted and corroded together, having been deposited in one episode. Hammerscale could be seen in the corrosion products of 6 per cent of the iron objects from this context and was frequently associated with the large amount of nails and nail shanks.

Mill 4

The water channel for this mill produced a sequence of fills containing small pottery assemblages.

Assemblage 14: black silt layer 610.9 in the bottom of Channel D underlying northern timber 1

This layer produced a single body sherd from a late fourth-century hand-made cooking pot in fabric C1D.

Assemblage 15: fine, washed gravel layer 610.8 above 610.9 and to the south of timber 1

Apart from a coin of the House of Theodosius dated *c* AD 388–402, this layer produced seven sherds of pottery (84g). These include three fabric C1D cooking pot fragments and a flagon handle stub in fabric F9.

Assemblage 16: gravel layer 610.7 abutting the south face of transverse timber 1 above 610.8 and gravel layer 610.6 abutting the north face of the same timber

Layer 610.7 produced twenty-seven sherds (352g) of pottery, including two C1D cooking pot fragments with internal residues, two cooking pot rim sherds in similar fabric and the rim from a type C94 Oxfordshire dish (*c* AD 300–400+).

Layer 610.6 yielded twelve sherds (142g) of pottery including:

Fig 52
117 Very large deep bowl of type C84 in abraded micaceous soft brown fabric F7B with patchy red colour-coat and rosette stamping. External rim diameter 300mm+. Dated *c* AD 350–400+.

The coin and the pottery indicate a date of *c* 390-400+ for Assemblages 13 to 16. It is possible that Mill 4 replaced Mills 2 and 3 towards the end of the Roman occupation and that the rubbish dumped in Channel C came from Mill 4 or elsewhere on the site.

Little can be said of the objects from contexts 610.6–9. There are three fragments of glass, one of which (**892**) comes from a beaker of late fourth- or early fifth-century type, whilst the other two are of indeterminate form. An iron knife (**603**) with a spirally-twisted handle, an iron box binding with a decorative pointed terminal (**933**) and a fragment of iron strip were also recovered. Twenty type 1b nails were found in context 610.7 and eleven type 1b nails and a nail shank were found in the fine washed gravel layer (610.8) to the south of Timber 1.

Assemblage 17: late roadside ditch south of road (context 309)

This feature yielded eighteen sherds (912g) of pottery of fourth-century character. The assemblage is too small for meaningful quantification but includes Oxfordshire red colour-coat types C84 (350–400+) and C115 (350–400+) as well as a type C46 dish in micaceous fabric F7B (340–400+). There were also two Oxfordshire white ware mortaria of type M22, two cooking pots in fabric C1D and one in fabric C4A. This suggests that Ditch 309 was in use during the late fourth century.

There is one piece of pottery of particular note:
Fig 52
118 Face flagon fragment in grey-cored brown fabric F7B with traces of maroon colour-coat (Young 1977, type C11 dated *c* 350–400+). Another flagon using the same face mould is known from Richborough (Franziska Dovener, pers comm).

There were no small finds from this context.

The late features in Area 4

Assemblage 18: timber-lined pit (context 335)

This feature contained seventy-one sherds (1,136g) of pottery including a sherd of samian (p 127), two late Argonne bowls (p 127), a single sherd in early Anglo-Saxon sandy brown-black fabric, a cooking pot in fabric C1D, four cooking pots and a deep convex-sided dish/bowl in fabric C2, an

Oxfordshire type C100 mortarium, a type C81 bowl, the neck of a Hadham greyware flagon, an Alice Holt white-slipped cooking pot rim and:

Fig 52

119　Cavetto-rim beaker in dirty-grey fabric C2 with profuse up to 2mm crushed white and grey grog, fired black externally. External rim diameter 80mm.

120　Developed beaded-and-flanged bowl in hand-made grey-black fabric C4A. External rim diameter 240mm.

121　Rolled over cooking pot rim in fabric C11. External rim diameter 140mm.

122　Crude developed beaded-and-flanged bowl in very fine sanded grey-brown fabric.

123　Copy Dr 38 bowl in soft, micaceous brown fabric F7B fired smooth grey-black with traces of maroon colour-coat. External rim diameter 180mm.

124　Wall sided mortarium rim in pale grey fabric F10 fired dirty micaceous brown with feeble maroon slip on the exterior and narrow slipped bands internally. External rim diameter 200mm.

125　Bowl rim in orange fabric F18 of Fulford's type 5, dated *c* AD 350–400+ (Fulford 1973, fig 1.10). External rim diameter 160mm.

126　Jar rim in smooth Oxfordshire fine white ware and of Young's type W33, dated broadly to *c* AD 50–400+ (Young 1977, fig 31, W33.2). The rim is warped and the vessel may be a 'second'. These jars normally had a very restricted middle Thames valley distribution (*ibid,* fig 29) and the finding of a 'second' so far from source is unusual.

A small assemblage of metalwork and lead alloy waste was recovered from this feature. The assemblage includes a pin (**241**) with the customary facetted, cuboid head, an artillery bolt head (**8**), a stylus (**590**) of type 2b, a ring-headed pin (**922**), a knife (**615**), two twisted strand bracelets, one with two strands (**305**) and the other with four (**322**). An open socket (**1014**) is probably broken from a hooked blade or pruning hook used to gather fodder. Hammerscale is present on the bolt head, knife, nails and shanks.

Despite previous interpretations of this feature as a 'shrine' (p 33), there is nothing obviously 'ritual' about the pottery or finds assemblage; indeed the presence of an early Anglo-Saxon sherd suggests the possibility that the material is entirely residual. It is equally possible, given that the feature was capped by deposits associated with a post-Roman watercourse, that the sherd was intrusive.

Assemblage 19: pit 407 (context 407.2)

The lowest sticky grey-brown silt fill of this unbottomed pit or well (407.3) produced no pottery at all but the dirty peaty gravel above (407.2) had 119 sherds (2,698g) of pottery. This assemblage is too small for reliable quantification but includes a cooking pot, beaded-and-flanged bowl and two deep convex-sided dish/bowls in fabric C1D and a cooking pot and beaded-and-flanged bowl in fabric C2:

Fig 52

127　Platter with wall-sided rim of type C41 in soft grey fabric F10 fired brown with maroon to brown colour-coat (Young (1977) dates the Oxfordshire red colour-coat version *c* AD 300–400+). External rim diameter 280mm.

128　Beaded-and-flanged bowl in similar fabric. The flange is less developed than that on the rare Oxfordshire type C93, which is dated *c* AD 350–400+ (Young 1977).

129　Shoulder of cooking pot in grey-black fabric C2 with stabbed decoration.

This assemblage also includes an Oxfordshire red colour-coat bowl of type C79 (*c* 340–400+), rim sherds from two late Argonne ware bowls (p 127) and a burnt 'Castor box' rim in fabric F9. A late fourth-century date is indicated for the pottery.

A small assemblage of domestic metalwork was found in Pit 407 (context 407.2) including a fragmentary iron penannular brooch (**195**) and three styli (**587, 588** and **592**), of type 2b and 2c. A knife with a spirally twisted handle (**605**) and a bucket mount (**921**) also came from this deposit, alongside a strip bracelet (**349**) with chip-carved decoration of type 13. Twelve coins are recorded from context 407, dated *c* AD 364–78.

Assemblage 20: fill of 408 and uppermost fill of pit 407

These fills produced 329 sherds (5,067g) of pottery and coins ranging in date between 328 and 402. The presence of a significant quantity of sherds in fabric C1D indicates that some of the pottery is post-370 in date, although the higher percentage of hand-made wares in fabric C2 and the low percentage of grog-tempered wares in general suggests that the bulk of the pottery belongs to the second and third quarters of the fourth century. This conclusion is supported by the fact that most of the fifty-six coins from this layer are late Constantinian and Valentinianic in date. The coinage from the lower fills of Pit 407 does however confirm that some at least of the 408 rubbish was dumped after AD 370.

This assemblage has something in common with the earlier one from Ditch 302 in that hand-made grog-tempered wares are poorly represented and bowls and dishes predominate. The large number of beakers present in the ditch assemblage, however, is not repeated here. Nevertheless the unusual breakdown of this assemblage may be indicative of specialised activities on this part of the site.

There are three cooking pots in fabric C1D, three cooking pots, a beaded-and-flanged bowl and two deep convex-sided dish/bowls in fabric C2. The following other pieces are of particular interest:

Fig 52

130   Developed beaded-and-flanged bowl in grey fabric C13 with internal slate-coloured slip. External rim diameter 240mm. One of five examples.

131   Straight-sided dish in grey fabric C13 with internal black slip. External rim diameter 130mm.

132   Convex-sided dish in medium grey fabric C13 fired black. External rim diameter 140mm.

133   Jar rim in charcoal-grey fabric with profuse up to 0.20mm quartz filler fired polished grey-brown with burnished decoration around the neck. External rim diameter 100mm. Similar decoration was used on the necks of jars made at the Moulsham Street kiln in Chelmsford (Going 1987a, fig 35-8) and at Mucking in Essex (Jones and Rodwell 1973, 26–8). Necked-bowl/jars of this type were made from the late second until the middle of the fourth century and the Ickham pot is probably a late Essex product of this type.

134   Developed beaded-and-flanged bowl in very fine greyware with profuse up to 0.20mm quartz filler. External rim diameter 100mm.

135   Rim from vase in very fine sanded pale grey fabric fired polished blue-black. External rim diameter 110mm. North Gaulish.

136   Bowl or dish rim in similar fabric. External rim diameter 200mm. This rim is paralleled in a mid fourth-century example from the Prefecture site in Arras (Tuffreau-Libre and Jacques 1994b, fig 4-1).

This assemblage also includes residual samian, late Argonne ware, Oxfordshire red colour-coated forms C51 (240–400+), C75 (2) (325–400+), C83 (350–400+), C97 (3) (240–400+) and C100 with rouletting (300–400+), two Oxfordshire white ware mortaria of type M22 (240–400+) and fragments from a scale-decorated beaker in fabric F9.

The forty small finds from context 408 are notable for the presence of four of the lead alloy pendants (**282–4** and **287**). Two are from the same mould. Other objects include two bracelets, one a wire bracelet of type 6 (**325**), the other (**377**) a strip bracelet of type 11 with a milled lower area. A

Fabric	Jars EVE	Open forms EVE	Beakers EVE	Others EVE	Total EVE	%	% of coarsewares
Coarsewares							
C1D	0.32	0.14	0.05		0.51	10.00	17.70
C2	0.24	0.34			0.58	11.40	20.10
C4A		0.06			0.06	1.20	2.10
C5	0.03				0.03	0.60	1.00
C12B		0.38			0.38	7.40	13.20
C13		0.21			0.21	4.10	7.30
C15	0.07				0.07	1.40	2.40
C21	0.70	0.34			1.04	20.40	36.20
Total	1.36	1.47	0.05		2.88	56.50	
Finewares							
F2C		0.05			0.05	1.00	
F2F		0.21			0.21	4.10	
F7A		0.26		Mortaria 0.39	0.65	12.70	
F9			0.15		0.15	2.90	
F12		0.25			0.25	4.90	
F19	0.32	0.05			0.37	7.20	
F20		0.05	0.30		0.35	6.80	
M7				Mortaria 0.20	0.20	3.90	
Total of all	1.68 (32.90%)	2.34 (45.80%)	0.50 (9.80%)	0.59 (11.50%)	5.11		

Table 6. Ceramics from Contexts 407.1 and 408.

strap-end of nail cleaner type is a late Roman type but, as noted above, there is little good dating evidence for this form. The slender padlock key (**699**), which may be post-Roman, was accompanied by a lever lock key (**707**). A small amount of copper-working is evident from a melt of solidified copper alloy and copper alloy wire (*see* p 299). Two fragments of querns also came from this deposit.

Context 407.1 contained a socketed candlestick of copper alloy (**716**), an iron joiner's dog and a nail shank.

Assemblage 21: surface material from Area 4 extension

This assemblage is strictly speaking unstratified material from an extensive deposit which equates to the fill of 408 and the upper fill of Pit 414. The assemblage is by far the largest from Ickham (33,809g) and was quantified by EVEs.

The make-up of this assemblage finds its closest parallel in the pottery from Mills 2 and 3. There is the same domination of the coarseware element by hand-made grog-tempered pottery and, as with the former assemblage, the bulk of such pottery is in fabric C1D. This strong showing by Richborough grog-tempered ware is in itself indicative of a post-370 date for most of the assemblage, as is the wide range of fabrics. There are a number of bowls and dishes in sandy grey fabrics, many of which are poorly made and very small. Small and poorly-finished straight and convex-sided dishes have been noted elsewhere in very late fourth- and early fifth-century pottery assemblages from Chichester (Lyne 1994a, 183), Eden Street, Kingston (*ibid,* 219) and elsewhere and may indicate declining technological competence at the end of the Roman period. The high percentage of bowls and dishes coupled with unusually large numbers of mortaria are strongly suggestive of some kind of specialised activity taking place on this part of the Ickham site. There are sherds from fifty-two cooking pots and necked bowls, fifteen beaded-and-flanged bowls and twenty deep convex-sided dish/bowls in fabric C1D, as well as approximately twenty-five cooking pots and necked bowls, ten beaded-and-flanged bowls similar to Fig 47, 22, three similar to Fig 47, 23, seven straight-sided and three deep convex-sided dish/bowls in fabric C2. The following other sherds are of particular interest:

Fig 52

137 Handle from lid in fabric C1D, of unusual design with central perforation. No parallels have been found.

138 Hand-made dish with beaded rim, in coarse brown-grey fabric C10 fired pimply black.

139 Dr 38 bowl copy in brown fabric C12B fired polished black. External rim diameter 180mm.

Three Alice Holt Class 3C rims, a Class 6A straight-sided dish, a convex-sided dish with internal black slip, a type 6C-1 beaded-and-flanged dish, four type 5B-8 bowls and a Class 3B cooking pot rim with black slip were also present.

140 Rim from Mayen ware cooking pot of type 3 in fabric C18 (Fulford and Bird 1975). External rim diameter 140mm. One of two examples.

141 Rim from bowl of type 5 in similar fabric (*ibid*). External rim diameter 180mm.

142 Rim from jar in high-fired slightly pimply blue-grey fabric with profuse up to 0.20mm quartz filler fired rough black with burnished horizontal lines on the neck. External rim diameter 140mm. A product from north-east Gaul dated at Arras to *c* AD 380–90 (Tuffreau-Libre and Jacques 1994b, fig 6-4).

143 Small hand-made beaded-and-flanged bowl in micaceous grey fabric with profuse up to 0.20mm quartz filler and very sparse up to 1mm rounded grey-brown grog, fired grey with brown margins and traces of external black slip. External rim diameter 100mm.

There is also a dish of Alice Holt Type 6A-13 in similar fabric.

Figs 52–53

144 Small hand-made beaded-and-flanged bowl in coarse grey-black fabric with profuse up to 0.50mm angular and subangular colourless quartz filler and occasional milky quartz inclusions, fired semi-vitrified bubbly blue-black. External rim diameter 100mm.

145 Body sherd from flagon in very fine blue-grey fabric fired leaden-grey internally and burnished blue-grey externally with burnished spiral decoration on the shoulder. Part of a similar vessel was found on Fishbourne beach, Isle of Wight at the emporium site (Lyne forthcoming b). Probably a continental import.

146 Part of the top of a ?face flagon in micaceous grey fabric with sparse to moderate up to 1mm black ferrous inclusions, fired smooth black externally with burnished linear decoration.

147 Fragment from *c* AD 350–400+ dated face flagon of type C11 in fabric F7A (Young 1977).

There were a large number of sherds from other Oxfordshire red colour-coat vessels including types C37, C46 (340–400+), C50 (325–400+), C51 (2) (240–400+), C55 (240–400+), C68 (5)(300–400+), C75 (2) (325–400+), C78 (2) (340–400+), C83 (350–400+), C97 (2) (240–400+) and C100 (4) (300–400+).

Fig 53

148 Bowl of type P24 in fabric F8, dated *c* 240–400+ but more common during late fourth century (Young 1977). External rim diameter 260mm. One of two examples; the other appears to have never had painted decoration.

149 Body sherd from bowl in micaceous fabric F7B with cordons and bands of rouletted decoration. The form is most closely

paralleled by Young's handled bowl type C85 but that is usually stamped rather than rouletted.

Sherds in this fabric also include Young's type C73 with rosette stamps (3) (350–400+) and type C74.

150 Dr 38 bowl copy in soft grey fabric F11 fired brown with orange margins and chocolate to maroon colour-coat. External rim diameter 180mm.

151 Bowl of Young's type C82 in similar fabric to Fig 54, 171 with red colour-coat and external white-painted scroll decoration, dated *c* 325–400+. External rim diameter 180mm.

152 Small convex-sided dish in white fabric F12 with reddish-brown colour-coat. External rim diameter 130mm. One of two.

153 Small beaded-and-flanged bowl in similar fabric with dull grey-brown colour-coat and rim edge blackening. External rim diameter 130mm.

The beaded rim of a beaker and a 'Castor box' rim in this fabric are also present.

154 Small convex-sided dish in grey fabric F9 fired buff-brown with chocolate colour-coat. External rim diameter 100mm. One of three examples.

A rim sherd from a tiny 100mm diameter beaded-and-flanged bowl in this fabric is also present.

155 Large bowl or dish rim in orange-brown fabric F13 with rim-edge greying and stabbed decoration. External rim diameter 320mm.

Fabric	Jars EVE	Open forms EVE	Beakers EVE	Others	EVE	Total EVE	%	% of coarsewares
Coarsewares								
C1C	0.18	0.08				0.26	0.70	1.10
C1D	7.39	3.19				10.58	29.40	45.30
C2	3.16	2.42				5.58	15.60	23.90
C4A	0.80					0.80	2.20	3.40
C5	0.10	0.01				0.11	0.30	0.50
C10		0.05				0.05	0.10	0.20
C12B	0.03	0.12				0.15	0.40	0.70
C12C	0.34	0.07	0.10			0.51	1.40	2.20
C13	0.79	0.69		Store jars	0.17	1.65	4.60	7.10
C14		0.04				0.04	0.10	0.20
C16	0.37					0.37	1.00	1.60
C18	0.38	0.09				0.47	1.30	2.00
C20	1.59	0.85	0.32			2.76	7.60	11.80
Total	15.13	7.61	0.42		0.17	23.33	64.70	
Finewares								
F2C		0.05				0.05	0.10	
F2E		0.37				0.37	1.00	
F2F		1.00				1.00	2.80	
F3A			0.36			0.36	1.00	
F7A		2.27	0.48	Mortaria	0.68	3.43	9.60	
F7B		0.72	0.19	Mortaria	0.08	0.99	2.70	
F8		0.23				0.23	0.60	
F9		1.70				1.70	4.70	
F12		0.67	0.15	Boxes	0.27	1.09	3.00	
F13		0.30				0.30	0.80	
F20		0.18				0.18	0.50	
M7				Mortaria	2.38	2.38	6.60	
M8					0.67	0.67	1.90	
Total of all	15.13 (41.90%)	15.10 (41.90%)	1.60 (4.40%)	4.25 (11.80%)		36.08		

Table 7. Ceramics from Area 4 extension.

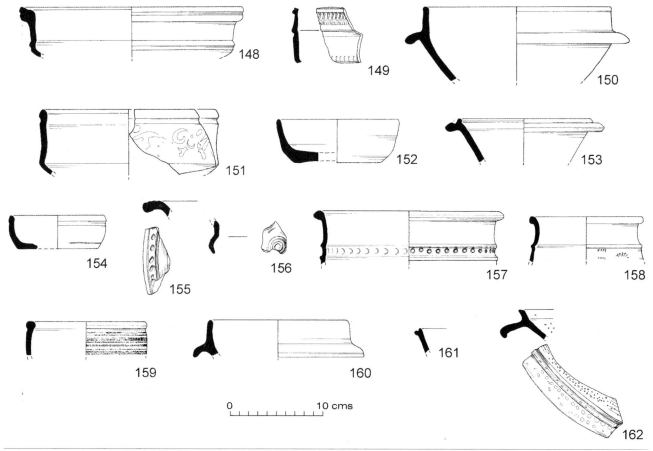

Fig 53. Coarsewares and finewares, Nos 148–162. Scale 1:4.

A fabric F13 Dr 38 bowl copy and form similar to Young's type C81 are also present.

156　Hollow boss with moulded raised spiral decoration from closed form in very fine buff fabric with occasional up to 1mm brown ferrous inclusions and external red colour-coat. Possibly from an example of the very late Lower Nene Valley three-handled jar type 74 (Howe *et al* 1980, fig 7) dated *c* AD 350–400+.

157　Deep ?handled bowl similar to Young's type C85 but in sand-free grey fabric with small white and brown inclusions, fired cream-buff with reddish-brown colour-coat and decorated with very small rosette stamps. External rim diameter 200mm.

158　Similar but smaller vessel in similar fabric. External rim diameter 120mm.

159　Bead-rimmed bowl in sand-free grey fabric with brown margins and moderate up to 1mm soft subangular grey inclusions. The horizontal black-fired bands on the exterior surface appear to have very fine diagonal line roller stamping. The lack of any real stamp impressions does however suggest

that the effect may have been achieved by the wet slip coming in contact with the threads in coarse cloth wrapped around the un-fired bowl (I am indebted to Joanna Bird for this suggestion) External rim diameter 130mm.

160　Dr 38 copy in very fine reddish-brown fabric with polished self slip. External rim diameter 160mm.

161　Beaded-and-flanged dish in very fine reddish-brown fabric C12B fired polished black. External rim diameter 140mm.

162　Mortarium of Young's type WC6 in soft orange fabric M9 with feeble white slip and red dot decoration on the flange, dated 350–400+. External rim diameter 320mm. There are three other smaller mortaria of similar form and in similar fabric but without the flange decoration.

Sixteen Oxfordshire white ware mortaria of type M22 are also present (Young 1977) as are significant quantities of samian and Argonne ware (pp 127–8).

A large assemblage of objects was recovered from the Area 4 extension. A discrepancy was discovered between the location of recovery of a number of items which, though recorded as coming from Area 4 extension on the original packaging, were listed as coming from Area 4 (not the extension) in the existing small finds notebooks. A minimum of twenty-six items were identified but not all of the small finds notebooks survive and this number may be an under representation. As both the original labelling on the packaging and small finds notebooks would have been produced at the same time it is now impossible to deduce which is correct. The metal finds from the Area 4 extension and Area 4 are quantified separately. However, there appears to be little significant difference in the range of items from each, so that the finds from Area 4 and Area 4 extension could be considered as one large assemblage. The same point has been made for the ceramics above and the same broad dating can be applied to each, as the small finds confirm.

The objects assigned to the Area 4 extension include eight bracelets of types 1, 3, 10 and 12 and three of the bone or antler bracelets. An Alesia/Hod Hill brooch (**185**) occurred alongside two semicircular buckle plates (**111** and **113**) and one rectangular plate (**108**), which are later in date than AD 350. The datable finger rings (**425**, **436** and **426**) are all of fourth-century types. Two copper alloy pins, of types 4 (**229**) and 5 (**240**) are accompanied by two spoons, one of which (**759**) is a rare iron tinned example. The glass includes one

bead (**279**) of a late fourth-century or later type, as well as several fragments of early Roman bottle glass.

Timber-lined features in Areas 3 and 7

Assemblage 22: fill of the timber-lined pit 333, Area 3

This feature, located at the north-east end of Area 3, close to the east end of the quarry, produced a quantifiable 219 sherds (5,385g) of pottery. The lateness of the assemblage is indicated by the same high percentage of fabric C1D as occurs in the Channel C and Area 4 extension unstratified material. There is one important difference, however, in that the other late assemblages are poorly stratified and could have accumulated over an appreciable length of time. In contrast, the pottery from the timber-lined pit has the advantage of being from a small well-defined structure with less chance of contamination by material from earlier or later contexts. Nevertheless, there is a little residual pottery, but the bulk probably belongs to the last years of the fourth and earliest years of the fifth century and has a considerably more limited date range than both the Channel C and Area 4 extension assemblages.

The high percentages of fabrics C1D and C2 are remarkably similar to those in the previous assemblage, but

Fabric	Jars	Open forms	Beakers	Others		Total	%	% of coarsewares
	EVE	EVE	EVE		EVE	EVE		
Coarsewares								
C1C		0.10				0.10	1.30	2.00
C1D	1.52	0.59		Lid	0.14	2.25	29.70	44.50
C2	0.91	0.43				1.34	17.70	26.50
C14	0.25					0.25	3.30	4.90
C21	0.11	0.09	0.14	Lid	0.05			
				Flagon	0.73	1.12	14.80	22.10
Total	2.79	1.21	0.14		0.92	5.06	66.80	
Finewares								
F2B		0.17				0.17	2.20	
F2C		0.05				0.05	0.70	
F3A	0.09			Biconical	0.49	0.58	7.70	
F7A		0.33				0.33	4.40	
F7B		0.24		Mortaria	0.30	0.54	7.00	
F12				Lid	0.07	0.07	0.90	
F19		0.09				0.09	1.20	
M7				Mortaria	0.52	0.52	6.90	
M8				Mortaria	0.17	0.17	2.20	
Total of all	2.88 (38.00%)	2.09 (27.60%)	0.14 (1.80%)		2.47 (32.60%)	7.58		

Table 8. Ceramics from Context 333.

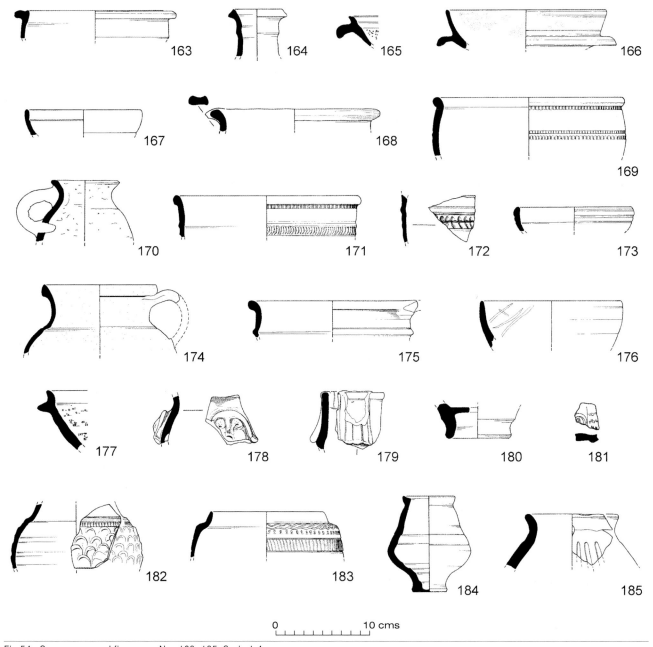

Fig 54. Coarsewares and finewares, Nos 163–185. Scale 1:4.

unlike the Channel C and Area 4 extension material there is a much more limited range of other coarse fabrics. There are no Alice Holt or Preston kiln wares; just rims from two Overwey/Portchester D horizontally-rilled cooking pots and a number of miscellaneous greyware vessels. This limited range of fabrics may reflect the lack of residual early fourth-century pottery but may also indicate that most of the late

greyware producers supplying east Kent had gone out of production by the time that the assemblage was dumped. This is supported by the evidence from Richborough and Canterbury, although the absence of Alice Holt greywares from this assemblage may be fortuitous. The presence of two cooking pots in fabric C14 is not surprising as production of such wares seems to have gone on after most other wheel-using pottery industries within the south-east of Britain had ceased to function.

The miscellaneous greywares include suspected continental imports:

Fig 54

163 Lid-seated jar rim in sandy off-white fabric with profuse up to 0.30mm quartz filler, fired grey internally and rough black externally. External rim diameter 130mm.

164 Flagon rim in buff-brown fabric with profuse 0.20mm quartz filler. External rim diameter 50mm.

The only fabric F7A Oxfordshire red colour-coat vessels are a C51 bowl and a stamped C84 example (*c* 350–400+). There is a considerably greater number of vessels in micaceous fabric F7B, including examples of Young's type C51 (2) and C97 (4). Rim fragments from three Oxfordshire white ware mortaria of Young's type M22 include a piece from a mortarium also present in the assemblage from Area 4 extension. The two mortaria in fabric F7B include the following piece:

165 Poorly made mortarium in a grey-brown fabric transitional between F7B and M9 and with a tendency to laminate. There are traces of external white slip. External rim diameter uncertain.

166 Dr 38 bowl in micaceous grey-brown fabric with marbled chocolate-brown colour-coat. External rim diameter 170mm. This is not an 'á l'éponge' ware product but may be a local attempt at copying a bowl from that source.

167 ?Dr 38 copy in fabric F19 with internal groove. External rim diameter 120mm.

A little residual samian is also present (p 128).

Assemblage 23: timber-lined well 701, Area 7

This feature produced a coin of Arcadius (388–95) indicating that it was backfilled at the end of the fourth century or later. There are 196 sherds (4,720g) of pottery, just enough for quantification purposes. This assemblage is similar to the previous one in that being inside a timber-lined structure it is not very susceptible to contamination from layers above and below. As with the pottery from the timber-lined pit the range of fabrics is quite limited but less so than in that assemblage. The sherds in the additional fabrics C5, 8, 11 and F3A are however clearly residual in the context and may have come from the fill of Ditch 702/703 through which the well was cut.

As with the assemblage from the timber-lined pit the most common fabric by far is Richborough grog-tempered ware fabric C1D with the Overwey/Portchester D fabric C14 coming second. The fabric C1D vessels include fragments from eleven cooking pots and two necked bowls, as well as a beaded-and-

flanged bowl and a convex-sided dish. The few fragments of fabric C2 are very largely from convex-sided dishes.

The fabric F7A Oxfordshire red colour-coated vessels include types C22 (240–400+), C51 (240–400+), C75 (3) (325–400+) and C115 (350–400+), all of which are consistent with a late-fourth-century date for the assemblage. The micaceous fabric F7B vessels include an example of Young's type C71 without colour-coat (300–400+), C75 (325–400+) and the following:

Fig 54

168 Handled bowl of Young's type C85 dated *c* AD 350–400+. External rim diameter 80mm.

169 Bowl of type C61 with rouletted body cordon, dated *c* AD350–400+. External rim diameter 200mm.

There are also fragments from an Argonne ware bowl of Chenet type 320.

The timber-lined well contained two fragments of glass beakers of fourth- or early fifth-century date (**899** and **878**), an early Roman bone knife handle (**651**), a fragmentary iron stylus (**593**), a nailed binding, a fragment of bar iron, a small quantity of spilt molten lead alloy (120g), three type 1b nails and one nail shank.

Ceramic Assemblages 24–27: early fifth century and later

Mill 4

The recutting of the Mill 4 water channel must surely be early fifth century in date. The associated contexts produced a number of small but very significant pottery assemblages.

Assemblage 24: daub bank with wattle fencing (610.5) defining Channel D

This feature produced seventy-eight sherds (1,346g) of pottery including fragments from five cooking pots in fabric C1D, two in fabric C2 and the following:

Fig 54

170 Rod-handled jug in grey fabric C1D fired black. External rim diameter 70mm. There is another slightly different rod-handled jug from Pit 30 at Richborough; the fill of which was dated *c* AD 360–70 (Bushe-Fox 1932).

171 Rim from handled bowl of type C85 in micaceous brown fabric F7B with maroon colour-coat, of type C85 dated *c* AD 350–400+ (Young 1977). External rim diameter 220mm.

172 Body sherd from another similar bowl, but in sand-free pale blue-grey fabric fired pink with all over reddish-brown colour-coat. There is a row of crescentic stamps applied over a double girth cordon.

173   Convex-sided dish in sand-free reddish-brown fabric with grey-black colour-coat. External rim diameter 100mm.

This context produced two fragments of glass stem from an early Roman jug or flagon (**860**) and a goblet or beaker (**869**) of fourth- or early fifth-century date. The context also contained four type 1b nails and four nail shanks, as well as a fragment of a millstone of lower greensand (**1220**).

Assemblage 25: fill of recut Channel D (context 610.4)

This fill accumulated after the mill went out of use. It contained sixteen sherds (378g) of coarse pottery including:

Fig 54

174   Three large joining sherds from a handled jug with collared rim, in high-fired pimply-grey fabric with profuse up to 0.50mm subangular quartz. External rim diameter 120mm. North Gaulish in origin and paralleled in *c* AD 350–420 dated deposits at Tournai (Brulet 1994, fig 5).

Fragments from two cooking pots in fabric C1D are also present. This context contained nineteen type 1b nails and seven nail shanks.

Assemblage 26: late fill of Channel D (context 610.2)

This context produced fifty-nine sherds (990g) of pottery, which includes three body sherds from a hand-made cooking pot in ?early Anglo-Saxon black soot-soaked fabric with profuse 0.10mm quartz sand filler, a cooking pot in black fabric C1D and:

Fig 54

175   Handled bowl of type C85 in sandfree grey fabric fired buff-brown with patchy dark-brown internal and external colour-coat (Young 1977). External rim diameter 180mm.

176   Hand-made or tournetted deep dish in pale-grey fabric C6 fired polished black with internal burnished linear decoration. External rim diameter 120mm. No parallels can be cited for this unusual ?sub-Roman vessel.

An interesting characteristic of this fifth-century sequence is the emphasis on handled bowls and jugs, from a variety of sources. The small amounts of pottery make conclusions difficult to draw, but it may be that such forms enjoyed a short-lived popularity during the early years of the fifth century.

This context contained an early Roman copper alloy box hasp (**47**), six type 1b nails and three nail shanks.

Assemblage 27: deposits sealing Channels C and D in Areas 1 and 6 (lower gravels contexts 104, 105.1, 113 and 604)

These contexts produced 5,650g (472 sherds) of pottery. The gravels could either be laid cobbling or the results of post-Roman flooding in the Stour valley and sealed both Channels

Fabric	Jars	Open forms	Beakers	Others	Total	%	% of coarsewares
	EVE	EVE	EVE	EVE	EVE		
Coarsewares							
C1C	0.27				0.27	5.40	8.60
C1D	1.44	0.20			1.64	33.00	52.40
C2	0.11	0.23			0.34	6.80	10.90
C5		0.10			0.10	2.00	3.20
C8		0.05			0.05	1.00	1.60
C11	0.16				0.16	3.20	5.10
C12B	0.21				0.21	4.20	6.70
C14	0.24	0.12			0.36	7.20	11.50
Total	2.43	0.70			3.13	62.80	
Finewares							
F3A			0.15		0.15	3.00	
F7A		0.76	0.23		0.99	20.00	
F7B		0.36			0.36	7.20	
M8				Mortaria 0.26	0.26	5.20	
M9				Mortaria 0.09	0.09	1.80	
Total of all	2.43 (48.80%)	1.82 (36.50%)	0.38 (7.60%)	0.35 (7.10%)	4.98	37.20	

Table 9. Ceramics from Well 701.

C and D. Their sealing of the latter feature would make the gravels of fifth-century date at the earliest. The pottery is all late Roman, however, of third- to fourth-century character in a wide variety of fabrics, but no unusual characteristics other than the presence of a face pot fragment (Fig 54, 181). It is likely, therefore, that most of the gravels are the result of post-Roman flooding and much, if not all, of the associated pottery derived from earlier contexts. Areas of larger flints within the gravel may however be the remnants of post-Roman areas of cobbling which have survived flood erosion, but unfortunately any pottery which may have been associated with these areas cannot be separated from the general assemblage. These residual sherds include a few samian fragments (p 128).

The small group of metal items from the lower gravels mostly derives from context 104, which contained two late third- or fourth-century copper alloy strip bracelets with punched and incised decoration (**346** and **352**), a lead-backed copper alloy stud (**85**), a spirally-twisted link from a horse bit (**1063**) and elements of structural ironwork. An oval buckle loop (**124**) is comparable with an example from Grave 81 at Lankhills, dated AD 350–70 (Clarke 1979, 270–2 and fig 34.70).

Ten per cent of the nails from the lower gravels (1 type 1a, 80 1b nails and 69 nail shanks) contained hammerscale within their corrosion products.

Miscellaneous sherds

A number of unstratified sherds and fragments from small insignificant assemblages are considered to be sufficiently interesting to be published in their own right.

Fig 54

177   Mortarium in dark blue-grey fabric fired reddish-brown with profuse angular flint trituration grits and occasional red ironstone. West Kent sand-and-calcite-tempered ware type 8B.14 (Lyne 1994a). Other examples are known from Context 501 at St Richards Road, Deal (late third to early fourth century), Rose Yard, Canterbury Trench 1 (6) and St Paul's Cray (unpublished, Bexley Museum). External rim diameter 240mm. *Surface.*

178   Fragment from jar in grey fabric C1D fired black with applied face plaque. It is unfortunate that the lower part of the face on this unique find is missing, so that we cannot tell whether the figure was male or female. The long hair with curled ends is certainly not in the late Roman or mainstream Celtic tradition but (allowing for the crudity of the rendering) comes quite close to that of the Franks as depicted in the royal bust on the gold ring of Childeric.

However, Françoise Vallet (pers comm) feels that the sherd, although possibly Merovingian, is not sufficiently close as a representation of this type. The face is probably that of a pagan deity. *Surface*

179   Fragment from face flagon depicting schematised hair at back of head, in white fabric F12 with black colour-coat. *Surface.*

180   Pedestal base or centre of lid in patchy brown-black fabric C1D with central perforation made before firing. *Surface.*

181   Fragment from vessel in micaceous fabric F7B with maroon colour-coat and depicting part of face. The eye was incised when the pot was in the leather-hard state and there is square-toothed roller-stamping across the raised ?nose. *104, Area 1.*

182   Fragments from large scale-decorated beaker in soft buff fabric F9 with matt chocolate colour-coat. *707.2, Area 7.*

183   Lid-seated bowl of similar design to 'Castor box' but in soft orange-buff fabric F9 with all-over chocolate colour-coat and elaborate stabbed, scribed and rouletted decoration. External rim diameter 120mm. *Well P19, Area 1.*

184   Small beaker in hard grey pimply fabric with profuse up to 0.20mm quartz filler. External rim diameter 50mm. *1003, Area 10.*

185   Hand-made jar in soft grey-brown fabric with sparse up to 1mm subangular flint, honey quartz and irregular up to 2mm haematite and chert inclusions, fired black with fluted body decoration. A quantity of similar style Jutish pottery came from east of the Marlowe Theatre in Canterbury and was dated to the mid fifth century (Stow 1995, 825). *Section 5 Area 4 in watercourse.*

The pot from Burial B

Fig 55

186   Necked-bowl in black hand-made fabric C2 fired patchy grey-black. External rim diameter 140mm. Two virtually identical necked-bowls in similar fabric are recorded from Richborough. One comes from the lowest silting in the outer ditch of the Shore fort and is not closely dated, but the other is from the AD 370–400 dated Pit 305 (Lyne 1994a, 421).

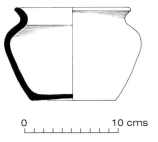

0   10 cms

Fig 55. Coarseware, No 186. Scale 1:4.

The Oxfordshire wares

Oxfordshire industry products form a significant part of the total Ickham assemblage and account for the vast majority of the late Roman finewares and mortaria from the site. The total EVE for the site in fabrics F7A/B (Oxfordshire red-to-brown colour-coated ware), F8 (Oxfordshire Parchment ware), M7 (Oxfordshire white ware) and M8 (Oxfordshire white-slipped ware) was quantified by vessel type.

Table 10 suggests that nearly three-quarters of the Oxfordshire Industry products being supplied to Ickham were in Oxfordshire red-to-brown colour-coated ware, predominantly bowls but with significant numbers of mortaria, flagons and beakers. Oxfordshire white ware and white-slipped ware mortaria make up more than a quarter of the assemblage. Mortaria in general account for an abnormally high 38 per cent of the material but Oxfordshire Parchment ware bowls scarcely register.

Bowl forms include Young's types C51 (240–400), C52 (350–400+), C55 (240–400+), C68 (300–400+), C70 (325–400+), C71 (300–400+), C73 (?270–400+), C75 (325–400+), C78 (340–400+), C79 (340–400+), C81 (300–400+), C82 (325–400+), C83 (300–400+), C84 (350–400+), C85 (350–400+), C112 (325–400+), C115 (350–400+) and P24 (240–400). The most common of these forms are C51, C75 and C84/85 which account for 21.6, 26.2 and 12.8 per cent of the bowls respectively.

Dishes are far less common but include types C46 (340–400+), C47 (270–400+), C50 (325–400+) and C94 (300–400+). Beaker types are difficult to determine because of rim forms being shared by more than one type: types C22 (240–400+), C23 (270–400+) and C38 (340–400+) are, however, present and it is likely that most vessels are of type C23. Flagons include types C3 (270–400+) and C8 (240–400+).

Mortaria are of types C97 (240–400+), C100 (300–400+), M17 (240–300), M18 (240–300), M22 (240/300–400+), M23 (350–400+), WC6 (350–400+) and WC7 (240–400+).

Of these, Oxfordshire white ware form M22 accounts for 46 per cent of all such vessels.

Areas 2 and 4 both produced large numbers of Oxfordshire products. As the two areas appear to be associated with different kinds of activity (milling in Area 2 and industrial activity in Area 4), the two Oxfordshire elements in their assemblages were quantified separately in order to compare them.

Tables 11 and 12 show that mortaria are far more significant in the Area 4 assemblage than they are in that from Area 2, confirming that activities in the two areas placed emphasis on different types of vessel. What these different types of activity may have been is discussed below (pp 138–40).

The amphorae

David Williams and Malcolm Lyne

All but one of the amphorae sherds belongs to the long-lived Dressel 20 form, the familiar globular-shaped olive-oil container from the Guadalquivir Valley region of Baetica (Peacock and Williams 1986, Class 25). The majority of the material consists of plain body sherds, including one with a rivet hole, indicating the re-use of a cracked vessel for ?storage purposes. Five handles are present, all in slightly different fabrics which suggest separate vessels in each case. One of the handles is stamped and, if correctly read, suggests a possible source from an estate close by to the Roman town of Arva on the north bank of the River Guadalquivir, nearby to the modern Alcolea del Rio. This handle is also complete and its shape points to a second-century date.

Of the thirty-one Dressel 20 sherds, seventeen are unstratified, three are from Mill 1, one from Channel C and four from Area 4 extension. Most of the Ickham contexts are later than the end of Dressel 20 importation during the mid third century and this may go some way towards explaining why there are so few pieces from the site.

Fabric	Bowls	Dishes	Beakers	Mortaria	Flagons	Others	Total	%
	EVE	EVE	EVE	EVE	EVE	EVE	EVE	
F7A/B	13.88	1.18	2.56	3.19	2.32	0.15	23.28	70.50
F8	0.30						0.30	0.90
M7				6.60			6.60	20.00
M8				2.83			2.83	8.60
	14.18 (43.00%)	1.18 (3.60%)	2.56 (7.80%)	12.62 (38.20%)	2.32 (7.00%)	0.15 (0.40%)	33.01	

Table 10. Oxfordshire industry products by vessel types.

Fabric	Bowls	Dishes	Beakers	Mortaria	Flagons	Others	Total	%
	EVE	EVE	EVES	EVE	EVE	EVE		
F7A/B	4.08	0.50	0.63	0.25	0.53		5.99	75.40
F8	0.07						0.07	0.90
M7				1.57			1.57	19.80
M8				0.31			0.31	3.90
	4.15 (52.30%)	0.50 (6.30%)	0.63 (7.90%)	2.13 (26.80%)	0.53 (6.70%)		7.94	

Table 11. Area 2 all contexts.

Fabric	Bowls	Dishes	Beakers	Mortaria	Flagons	Others	Total	%
	EVE	EVE	EVES	EVE	EVE	EVE		
F7A/B	6.06	0.35	0.58	1.67	1.00	0.05	9.71	65.20
F8	0.23						0.23	1.50
M7				3.93			3.93	26.40
M8				1.03			1.03	6.90
	6.29 (42.20%)	0.35 (2.30%)	0.58 (3.90%)	6.63 (44.50%)	1.00 (6.70%)	0.05 (0.40%)	14.90	

Table 12. Area 4 all contexts.

Two of the Dressel 20 handles show signs of sawing and conversion into pestles and another is still attached to part of the neck of the vessel but sawn through near its base. This suggests that the whole of the top of that vessel had been cut off to create an open vat, which would, perhaps, have been set in the ground. It may be that most of the few Dressel 20s on site were old vessels brought in for recycling during the fourth century.

The remaining amphora sherd belongs to the diminutive carrot amphora form, believed to have been used to carry fruit, in particular dates (*ibid*, Class 12). This intriguing type is commonly, but by no means exclusively, found on early military sites in Germany, Britain and Pannonia (Reusch 1970). However, it is also attested to in some numbers at Fishbourne in contexts dated *c* AD 75, and in second-century levels at *Verulamium* and again at Fishbourne (Wilson 1984; Cunliffe 1971). A *titulus pictus* on an example from Carlisle has led to the suggestion of a possible Egyptian origin (Tomlin 1992), although no finds of the carrot form have so far been discovered there. Moreover, thin sectioning shows that the fabric of carrot amphorae is quite different from the typical locally-made Egyptian amphorae, which were invariably made from the Nile silt (Williams and Tomber 2007). Carrot amphorae are also said to have been made in Beirut (Hayes 1997; Reynolds 2000), though it is not entirely clear if the vessels referred to are indeed of this form or

something similar. In addition, a comparison with known Palestine amphorae suggests that a source in this region appears possible and if, as appears likely, dates were carried in these vessels rather than doum palms, then perhaps in the Jericho region, which was famous for its date plantations (Carreras and Williams 2002).

Samian and Argonne wares

Joanna Bird with a report on the stamps by Brenda Dickinson

The samian ware from Ickham consists of a possible maximum of 174 identified vessels. Of these, only nine pieces (5 per cent of the total) come from South Gaul; they include two decorated fragments, a Dr 29 dating *c* AD 55–70 and a Dr 37 of *c* AD 90–110, and a single plain-ware stamp, of Flavius Germanus, dated *c* AD 85–120. The plain wares comprise four examples of Dr 27 and one of Dr 18, with a rim fragment of Dr 29. Set against the normal pattern for samian from British sites (Marsh 1981, fig 11.8), this low proportion of South Gaulish wares suggests little if any occupation on the site before the late first century.

Second-century Central Gaulish wares (137 pieces) make up 79 per cent of the total; they include only two sherds certainly from the early second-century potteries at Les

Martres-de-Veyre, a Dr 37 attributed to Secundinus I and a Dr 18/31. The remaining 135 pieces originate at Lezoux, and are of predominantly Antonine date. The nine decorated bowls include an unattributed piece dated *c* AD 125–50 and one by Sacer-Attianus or the Cinnamus group, *c* AD 135–70. There is also a Cinnamus bowl of *c* AD 150–70; the remaining six are of mid to late Antonine date, including a Dr 30 stamped by Advocisus, single bowls in the styles of Doeccus and Casurius and a small late bowl dated *c* AD 180–220. The plain-ware stamps follow a similar pattern, with two (of Albinus iv and Severus v) dating before *c* AD 155 and five (of Caletus, Caupirra, Crina, Habilis and an 'illiterate' potter) of mid to later Antonine date. The proportion of Dr 18/31 to Dr 31, approximately 1:5, reflects this predominantly mid to late Antonine range, with a high proportion of the later Dr 31R among the Dr 31s; however, the latest second-century forms are represented by only six to eight examples of the mortarium Dr 45 and two sherds of the late dish types.

East Gaulish wares make up 16 per cent of the samian; they include a single decorated sherd from the Antonine potteries in the Argonne and two other sherds from second-century workshops, but of the remainder around one quarter are assigned to Trier on the basis of fabric, and the rest are likely to come from Rheinzabern. The single plain-ware stamp, of Otonius on a Dr 32, has not been previously recorded, but is probably of late second- or early third-century date. Later East Gaulish wares are difficult to date at all precisely; many of the plain pieces can only be assigned broadly to the late second century or the first half of the third, while Trier and Rheinzabern decorated wares are, unusually, absent altogether.

The later Argonne wares (a possible maximum of thirty-four vessels) consist almost entirely of Chenet form 320 bowls; of these, fifteen have surviving roller stamped decoration, and there are a further fifteen rim sherds (Figs 56–61). The roller-stamp designs include simple repeated squares, alternately facing diagonal lines and more complex patterns incorporating ovolos, crosses and cross-and-pellet motifs. These bowls cannot be closely dated; they are clearly of the fourth century, and the present evidence would suggest that they were not imported to Britain before *c* AD 320/330 (Fulford 1977, 39–42). The Ickham material also included a few sherds of plain forms, including Chenet 303 and 304; these were probably produced from the later third century onwards.

Catalogue of Samian and Argonne wares

Abbreviations: x indicates number of vessels present; SG, CG, EG: South, Central and East Gaul; Oswald: figure-types from Oswald 1936–7

The ceramic assemblages

Assemblage 4
    Samian:
        Dish foot, CG, Hadrianic–Antonine.

Assemblage 4: context 128
    Samian:
        Dr 18/31 or 31, CG, Antonine.

Assemblage 6: context 1005
    Samian:
        Dr 37, CG; the bear (Oswald 1589) was shared by several later Antonine potters. *c* AD 150–90.
        Dr 37, CG; a triton in a corded medallion, as Stanfield and Simpson 1958, pl 138, no 1, a bowl in the style of Casurius with an added stamp of Apolauster. *c* AD 165–200.
        Dr 37, CG; the motif in the medallion is not identifiable. Mid to late Antonine.
        Dr 18/31, CG, Hadrianic to mid Antonine.
        3 or 4 x Dr 31, CG, mid to late Antonine.
        Dr 31, EG (Trier), late C2 to mid C3.
        2 x Dr 33, CG, Antonine; one burnt.
        Dr 33, EG, later C2 to mid C3.
        Dr 38, EG, late C2 to mid C3.
        Dr 45, CG, late C2.
        Dish (Walters 79, Ludowici Tg type), CG, mid to late Antonine.
        2 x CG sherds, C2.

Assemblage 9: ditch 302
    Samian:
        2 x Dr 31, CG, mid to late Antonine.
        EG sherd, later C2 to mid C3.

Area	Context	Date
1	Channel C	Ceramic Assemblage 13, AD 370-400+
4	Feature 335 ('shrine')	Ceramic Assemblage 18, AD 370-400+
4	407.20	Ceramic Assemblage 19, AD 370-400+
4	408.00	Ceramic Assemblage 20, AD 370-400+
4	extension	Ceramic Assemblage 21, AD 370-400+
7	701.00	Ceramic Assemblage 23, AD 370-400+
4	409.00	
5	'drainage gully'	
5	'floor'	
7	712.00	
16	1602.00	

Table 13. The distribution of late Argonne ware.

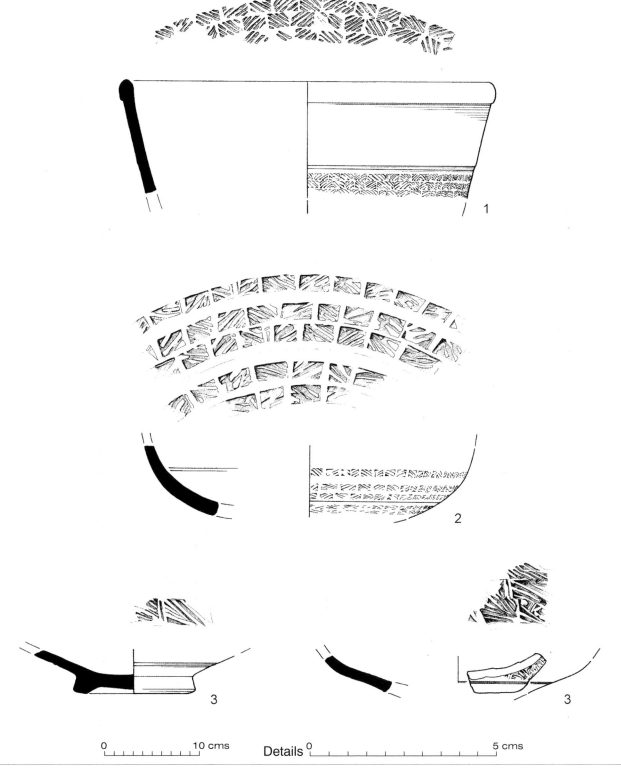

Fig 56. Argonne ware, Nos 1–3. Scale 1:4, detail scale 1:1.

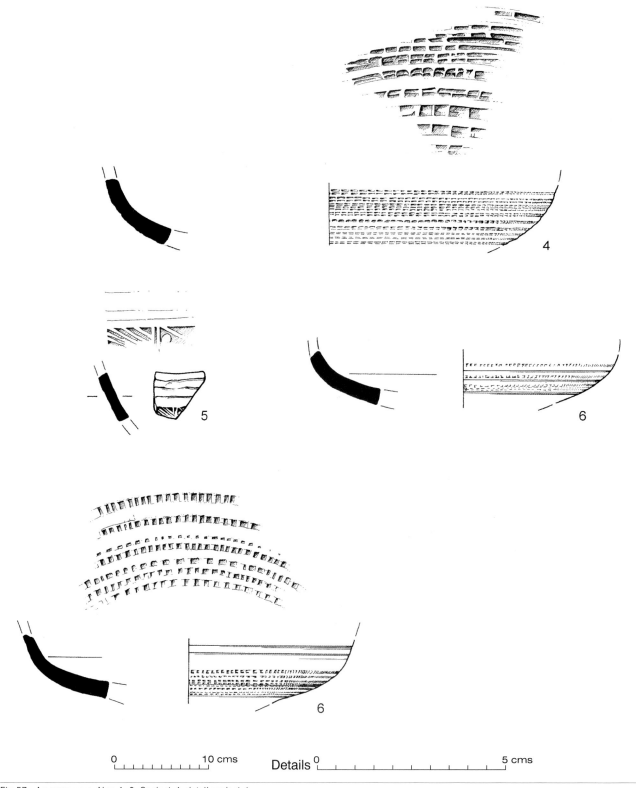

Fig 57. Argonne ware, Nos 4–6. Scale 1:4, detail scale 1:1.

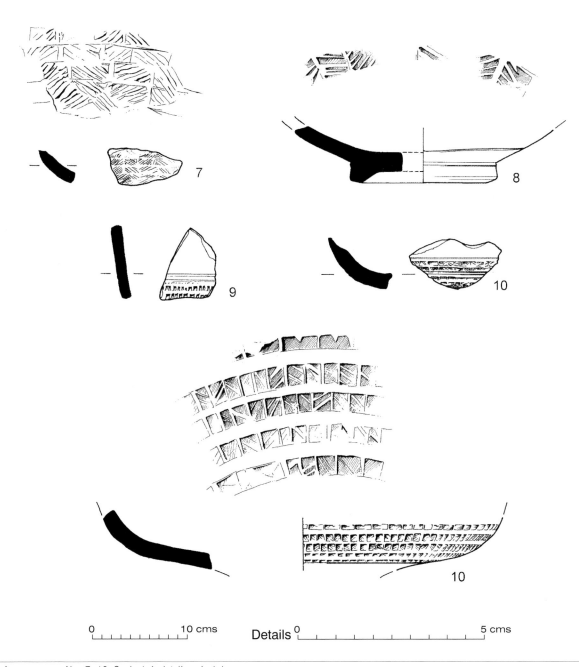

Fig 58. Argonne ware, Nos 7–10. Scale 1:4, detail scale 1:1.

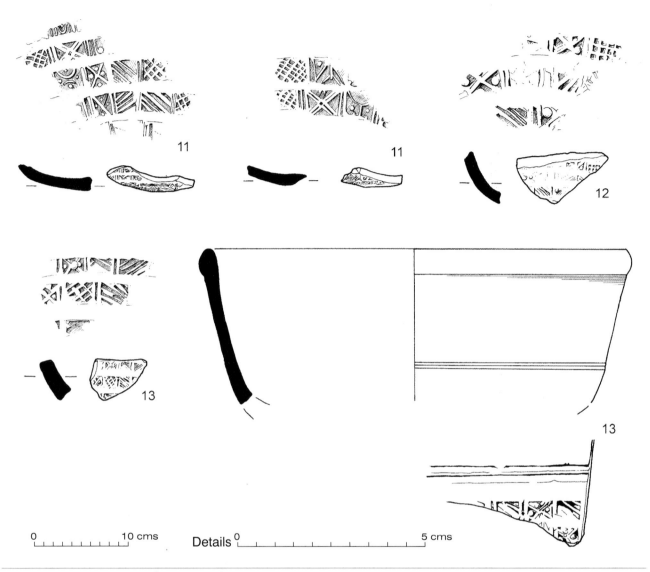

Fig 59. Argonne ware, Nos 11–13. Scale 1:4, detail scale 1:1.

Assemblage 11: layers 2–5 over pit 414
  Samian:
  Dr 37, EG (probably Rheinzabern), later C2 to mid C3.
  Argonne:
  Rims, 2 x Chenet 320, C4.
  Foot, small bowl, later C3 to C4.
  Dish sherd (as Chenet 304, etc), later C3 to C4.

Assemblage 13: pit 107
  Samian:
  Dr 18/31, CG, Hadrianic–early Antonine.

Assemblage 13: base of Channel C
  Samian:
  Dr 18, SG, Flavian.
  Dr 33, CG, Hadrianic–Antonine.
  Dr 31, CG, Antonine.
  Argonne:
  Chenet 320 with roller stamp of fine alternately-facing
  diagonals (cf Chenet 1941, pl 29, no 15). C4. Fig 58, 7.

Assemblage 18: timber-lined pit, context 335
  Samian:
  Dr 36, CG, Hadrianic–early Antonine.

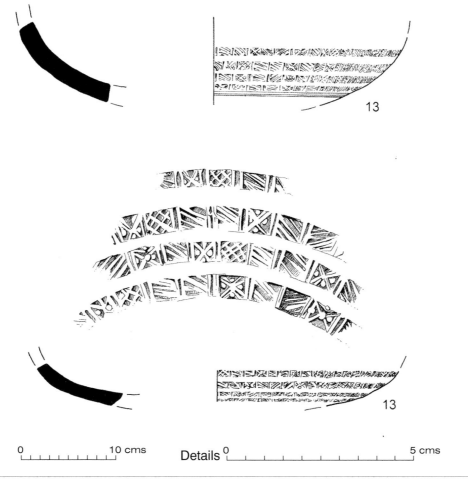

Fig 60. Argonne ware, No 13. Scale 1:4, detail scale 1:1.

Argonne:
Chenet 320 with roller-stamp of two rows of squares (cf Chenet 1941, pl 32, no 158). C4; partially burnt. (More of this bowl comes from Assemblage 21.) Fig 57, 6.
Chenet 320 rim, C4.

Assemblage 19: pit 407 (context 407.2)
Argonne:
Rims, 2 x Chenet 320, C4.

Assemblage 20: context 408
Samian:
Dr 18/31, CG, Hadrianic–Antonine.
Dish foot, CG, C2.
EG sherd (probably Trier), later C2 to mid C3.
Argonne:
Rims, 2 x Chenet 320, C4.

Assemblage 21
Samian:
Stamped Dr 32, *see* stamp report no 8.
Dr 30 stamped in the mould by Advocisus of Lezoux (*see* stamp report no 1). The figure, Oswald H, is shown on Stanfield and Simpson 1958, pl 113, no 17. *c* AD 160–90.
Dr 37 in the style of Doeccus of Lezoux. The ovolo, beads and terminal, rosette, figure, medallion and volute are shown on Stanfield and Simpson 1958, pl 149, no 32, the leaf on pl 151, no 61, and the circle on pl 151, no 55. *c* AD 165–200; worn inside. (More of this bowl comes from Area 5, surface.)
Rim, probably Dr 30 or 37, CG, Hadrianic–Antonine; burnt.
Dr 27, SG, Flavian.
Dr 18/31, CG, Hadrianic–early Antonine.
3 x Dr 31, CG, mid to late Antonine.
Dr 31/Ludowici Sa, EG, later C2 to mid C3.
Dr 33, CG, Antonine.
CG sherd, C2.

Argonne:

Chenet 320 with roller-stamp of alternately-facing diagonals, some separated by double verticals (cf Chenet 1941, pl 29, no 18). C4, burnt. Fig 56, 2.

Chenet 320; the surviving roller-stamped pattern comprises one-way diagonals, with part of a lattice at one point. C4. (More of this bowl comes from 701.) Fig 56, 3.

Chenet 320. More of this bowl comes from Assemblage 18, where it is described. Fig 57, 6.

Chenet 320; the roller-stamp is probably composed of three rows of squares (cf Chenet 1941, pl 37, no 304). C4. Fig 58, 9.

Chenet 320 with poorly impressed and worn roller-stamp decoration, apparently of alternately facing diagonals in single panels one way and double the other (cf Chenet 1941, pl 29, no 19). C4; partially burnt. Fig 58, 10.

Chenet 320. The roller-stamp of arches with pellets, cross-and-pellet motifs, double crosses, lattices and diagonals is probably the same as Chenet 1941, pl 35, no 250. C4; partially burnt. (More of this bowl comes from Area 4, 1–2.) Fig 59, 11.

Chenet 320. The roller-stamp of lattices, diagonals, squares, pellets and cross-and-pellet motifs is probably an inverted impression of Chenet 1941, pl 38, no 352, though the crosses on the Ickham sherd are composed of double rather than single lines. C4. Fig 59, 12.

Chenet 320. The roller-stamp of lattices, alternately-facing diagonals and single and double cross-and-pellet motifs has no precise parallel in Chenet 1941. C4; partially burnt. (More of this bowl comes from Area 4, 1–2 and surface.) Figs 59–60, 13.

Eleven rim sherds, Chenet 320, probably all different vessels, C4.

Chenet 303 (Dr 32), probably later C3 to C4.

Chenet 304 without grooving on the exterior, probably later C3 to C4.

Bowl, foot and two sherds, probably later C3 to C4.

Assemblage 22: fill of the timber-lined pit 335, Area 3
Samian:

Dr 37 in the fabric of Les Martres-de-Veyre. Apart from the trilobe pendant, the motifs are all found on bowls of Secundinus I: the cup is Rogers 1974, type U67, the beaded circle type C292, and the festoon type F74. *c* AD 110–30; slightly burnt.

Dr 18/31, CG, Hadrianic–Antonine.

Dr 46, CG; curved interior profile, angular exterior with a groove at the base of the wall. Hadrianic–early Antonine.

Assemblage 27: context 104
Samian:

EG sherd, later C2 to mid C3.

Assemblage 27: context 604
Samian:

Dr 31, CG, Antonine.

Other contexts [33]

Surface
Samian:

Dr 27, EG (from one of the earlier factories such as Blickweiler), mid C2.

Dr 33, CG, Hadrianic–Antonine.

CG sherd, C2.

Stamped Dr 33: *see* stamp report, no 5.

Stamped Dr 18/31: *see* stamp report, no 6.

2 x stamped Dr 31: *see* stamp report, nos 7 and 9.

Stamped Dr 31R: *see* stamp report, no 10.

Dr 37, SG. The Pan and satyr (Hermet 1934, pl 18, no 42, and pl 19, no 94) frequently occur on late South Gaulish bowls with this type of panel design (eg Hermet 1934, pl 86, nos 8, 8A). *c* AD 90–110.

Dr 37, CG. Cinnamus' ovolo 3 with a small bear (Oswald 1627); both motifs were shared by Sacer-Attianus and the Cinnamus group. *c* AD 135–70; worn and heavily burnt.

3 x Dr 33, CG, Hadrianic–Antonine.

At least 4 x Dr 31, CG, Antonine.

2 x Dr 31 / Ludowici Sa, EG, Antonine to mid C3.

Dr 31R, CG, mid to late Antonine.

Dr 45, EG (Trier), late C2 to mid C3.

Argonne:

Chenet 320 with roller-stamp of fine alternately-facing diagonals (cf Chenet 1941, pl 29, nos 5, 8). C4. Fig 57, 1.

Chenet 320: more of this bowl comes from Assemblage 21, where it is described. Fig 59–60, 13.

Plain sherd, late C3–C4.

'3'
Samian:

Dr 31, CG, Antonine.

Channel A, 118.1
Samian:

Dr 31, CG, Antonine.

Area 1, Channel C
Samian:

Dr 31/Ludowici Sa, EG (Trier), later C2 to mid C3.

Channel C, west end
Samian:

Dr 18/31, CG, Hadrianic–early Antonine.

Dr 33, CG, Antonine.

Base of Channel C
Argonne:

Chenet 320 with roller-stamp of small squares; insufficient survives to show whether the squares are arranged in two rows or three. C4.

Area 4 extension, 'section 1, layer 3'
Samian:

CG sherd, C2.

Area 4 extension, 'section 2'
Samian:

---

33. Material examined for Christopher Young, *c* 1975, with some revisions 1997.

Dr 31, cut and ground to make a spindlewhorl. Burnt, but probably EG and later C2 to early C3 [small find 537].

Area 4 extension, 'stone floor'
Argonne:
Chenet 320 base, C4.

Area 4, '1–2'
Argonne:
Chenet 320 with a narrow roller-stamp of two rows of squares. Chenet 1941 has several stamps with two and three rows of squares (eg pl 37, no 305) but none closely similar. C4. Fig 57, 4.
Chenet 320; the surviving fragment of roller-stamp decoration has diagonals and what is probably a cross-and-pellets motif. C4; burnt. Fig 57, 5.
Chenet 320: more of this bowl comes from Assemblage 21, where it is described. Fig 59, 11.
Chenet 320: more of this bowl comes from Assemblage 21, where it is described. Fig 59–60, 13.
Rims, 3 x Chenet 320, probably all different bowls; C4.
Body sherd, probably later C3–C4.

Area 4, 409
Samian:
Dr 31, CG, Antonine.
Argonne:
Rim, Chenet 320, C4.

Area 4, 410
Samian:
Dr 27g, SG, Flavian.

Area 5
Samian:
Dr 31, EG (Trier), later C2 to mid C3.

Area 5, u/s 'hollow area'
Samian:
Dr 18/31, CG, Hadrianic–Antonine.

Area 5, 'drainage gully 1'
Samian:
Dr 31, CG, Antonine.
Argonne:
Sherd, probably later C3–C4.

Area 5, 'drainage gully 3'
Samian:
Dr 45, CG, late C2.
CG sherd, C2.

Area 5, 'ditch 7'
Samian:
Dr 18/31, CG, early C2.
Dr 31, EG, late C2 to mid C3.

Area 5, 'floor'
Samian:
2 x Dr 18/31, CG, Hadrianic–Antonine.
Dr 31, CG, Antonine.
Argonne:
Rim, Chenet 320 or 321, C4.

Area 5, 'surface'
Samian:

Dr 37 in the style of Doeccus; more of this bowl comes from Assemblage 21, where it is described.
3 or 4 x Dr 31, CG, mid to late Antonine.
Dr 33, CG, Antonine.

Area 6, 624
Samian:
Dish base, CG, probably Antonine.

Area 7
Samian:
Dr 33, CG, Antonine.

Area 7, 'layer 1'
Samian:
2 x Dr 31R (one consisting of three joining sherds), CG, mid to late Antonine; the joined pieces have a possible graffito under the base.
Dr 31, CG, Antonine.

Area 7, 'layer 2'
Samian:
Dr 37, CG, a small bowl with the foot-ring clumsily applied. The borders are of coarse square or rhomboid beads, dividing the surviving decoration into small and narrow panels. The motifs include a bird (cf Oswald 2240), a beaded ring and probably a small figure. Similar coarsely modelled small 37s were produced at Lezoux in the later C2 and early C3. *c* AD 180–220. The surfaces and foot are very abraded.
Dr 18/31, CG, Hadrianic–Antonine.
Dr 31R, CG, mid to late Antonine.
Dr 46, CG, Hadrianic–early Antonine.

Area 7, Ditch 7 north
Samian:
Dr 33, EG (probably Trier), late C2 to mid C3.

Area 7, 704
Samian:
Stamped Dr 31R (two joining sherds): *see* stamp report, no 4.
Dr 33 (two sherds), CG, Antonine.
CG sherd, probably Dr 31 or 31R and Antonine.
Dr 45, CG, later C2.

Area 7, 705
Samian:
3 x Dr 31R, CG, mid to late Antonine.
Dr 31 or 31R, CG, Antonine.
2 x Dr 33, CG, Antonine.
CG sherd, C2; burnt.

Area 7, 706
Samian:
Dr 31R, CG, mid to late Antonine.

Area 7, 706.3
Samian:
Dr 33, CG, Antonine.
Dr 31 or 31R, CG, mid to late Antonine.

Area 7, 712
Samian:
Dr 31R, CG, mid to late Antonine.
2 x Dr 31 or 31R, CG, Antonine.

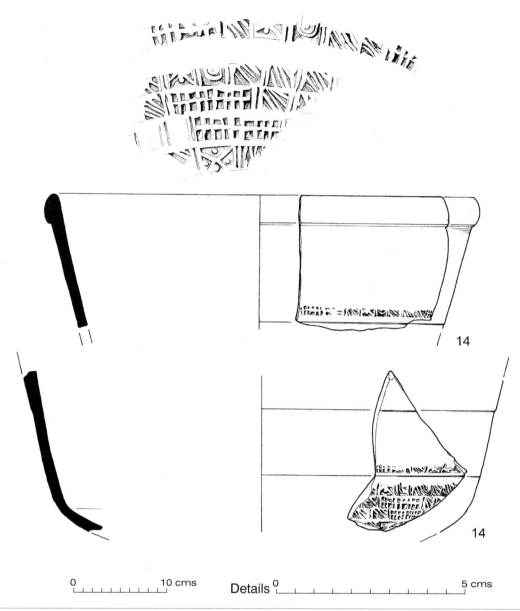

Fig 61. Argonne ware, No 14. Scale 1:4, detail scale 1:1.

Dr 37, a product of the Argonne samian industry. The ovolo is probably Chenet and Gaudron 1955, fig 54 bis, type T3; similar grapes are shown on fig 55, I, by Gesatus of Lavoye, while the corded motif is shown on fig 56, K, from Les Allieux. Antonine.
Dr 18/31, CG, Hadrianic–Antonine.
Argonne:
Chenet 320; the surviving roller-stamp decoration has alternately facing diagonals. C4. Fig 58, 8.
Rim, Chenet 320, C4.

Well 2, P19
  Samian:
  Dr 33, CG, Hadrianic–Antonine.
Well 2, interior
  Samian:
  Dr 31, CG, Antonine.
'C2 ditch north-west side lake'
  Samian:
  Dr 18/31, CG, Hadrianic.

Area 9, 905
Samian:
Foot-ring, Dr 18/31 or 31, CG, Hadrianic–Antonine.

Area 10, 1000
Samian:
Dr 29, SG, early to mid Flavian.
Mortarium, CG, late C2; heavily worn.
Dr 45, EG, late C2 to mid C3.
CG sherd, dish or bowl form, Antonine probably.

Area 10, 1001
Samian:
Stamped Dr 33 base: *see* stamp report, no 3.
Dr 29, SG. The decoration includes a row of lance-shaped leaves. *c* AD 55–70.
Dr 37, CG, with Cinnamus' ovolo 2 (cf Stanfield and Simpson 1958, pl 159, no. 27), here rather compressed to fit the space. *c* AD 150–70.
Dr 37, CG (two joining sherds). The decoration round the base includes a standing figure, perhaps a huntsman or gladiator, and a small ring. *c* AD 125–50. Heavily worn foot-ring.
2 x Dr 27, SG, Flavian.
Dr 27, CG, early to mid C2.
4 x Dr 33, CG, Antonine.
Dr 33, EG, Antonine–early C3.
Dr 38, CG, Antonine.
Curle 11 or Dr 38, CG, Hadrianic–Antonine.
Dish (Dr 32, Dr 36 type), EG, late C2 to first half C3; burnt.
Dish (Walters 79, Ludowici Tg type), EG, late C2 to first half C3.
Cup (Dr 27 or Dr 40), CG, Antonine probably; abraded interior, graffito inside foot-ring.
5 x Dr 31R, CG, mid to late Antonine.
2 x Dr 31, CG, Antonine.
Four foot and body sherds, Dr 31 or 31R, CG, Antonine.
3 x Dr 31 / Ludowici Sa, Sb (one consisting of two sherds), EG, late C2 to first half C3.
2 x Dr 45, CG, late C2; one burnt.
Mortarium, CG, late C2; heavily worn.
Dr 45, EG, late C2 to mid C3.
2 x mortaria, EG, late C2 to mid C3.
Four CG sherds, C2; two burnt.

Area 10, 1002.2
Samian:
2 x Dr 31R, CG, mid to late Antonine.
Ludowici Tg, EG, late C2–early C3.
Dr 43, EG, late C2 to first half C3; worn interior, hole for lead wire repair.

Area 10, 1002.3
Samian:
Dr 31R, CG, mid to late Antonine.
Dr 45, CG, late C2; abraded, slightly burnt.

Area 10, 1004
Samian:

2 x Dr 31R (one consisting of two joining sherds), CG, mid to late Antonine; one has three lines cut in the foot-ring.
Dr 18/31R or 31R, CG, Antonine.
Dr 31, CG, Antonine.
Dr 18/31 or 31, EG (Blickweiler or Argonne), mid to later C2.
Mortarium (two joining sherds), EG, late C2 to first half C3.

Area 14/Surface
Samian:
Dr 38, CG, mid to late Antonine.
Dr 45, EG, late C2 to mid C3.

Area 14, 1401
Samian:
Curle 11, CG, Hadrianic–early Antonine; burnt.
Dr 31, CG, Antonine.
Dish/bowl, EG, second half C2 to first half C3.

Area 14, 1400
Samian:
Stamped Dr 31 (two joining sherds): *see* stamp report, no 2.
2 x Dr 31R (one consisting of two joining sherds), CG, mid to late Antonine; the joining sherds are burnt.
2 x Dr 31, CG, Antonine; one burnt.
Dish, CG, mid to late Antonine.
3 CG sherds, C2.

Area 16, 1602
Argonne:
Chenet 320 (two sherds). The roller-stamp of squares, diagonals, ovolo and cross-and-pellet motifs is the same as Chenet 1941, pl 32, no 138. C4. Fig 61, 14.

Samian potters' stamps *Brenda Dickinson* [34]

Superscript a and b indicate: [a] stamp attested at the pottery in question; [b] not attested at the pottery in question, but the potter is known to have worked there.

Each entry gives: context number, potter (i, ii, etc, where homonyms are involved), die number, vessel form, reading of the stamp, published example (if any), pottery of origin, discussion, date.

1　'1974 4' Advocisus 8a 30 **ADVOC[ISI]** (Stanfield and Simpson 1958, pl 169) Lezoux.[a] Decorated bowls with this mould-stamp occur on Hadrian's Wall and at sites in northern Britain recommissioned *c* AD 160. It has also been recorded in the Wroxeter Gutter group. *c* AD 160–200.

2　Area 14, '1400'. Albinus iv 6a 31 **·A[LBINI·]M** (Ludowici 1927, 207, c) Lezoux.[a] One of the earlier stamps of a potter whose career continued into the mid Antonine period. It occurs on the Hadrianic and early Antonine forms 18/31, 27

---

34. This report was compiled in 1975 with some additions in 1997. The dating of the stamps has been revised to follow that given in the Index of makers' stamps (Hartley and Dickinson 2008–).

and 81 and is recorded in the Rhineland, where the supply of samian from Central Gaul seems virtually to have ceased by the middle of the second century. *c* AD 135–55.

3　　Area 10, '1001' Caletus 2a 33 **CAL·ETIM** (Dickinson 1986, 187, 3.24) Lezoux.[a] The final letter of this stamp appears to be a sloping **N**, but is almost certainly an incomplete **M**, to judge by other Caletus stamps in *manu*. Although the potter is known to have worked at the Terre-Franche kilns at Vichy, the uniformly British distribution of the stamp suggests that Die 2a was used only at Lezoux. Caletus was one of the latest Central Gaulish potters to export to Britain, down to at least the end of the second century. This particular stamp is known from Wallsend and there are several examples in a group of typologically late Antonine samian recovered off Pudding Pan Rock, Kent. *c* AD 180–200.

4　　Area 7, 704. Caupirra 2a 31R **CAV·PI[RI·AM]** retrograde Lezoux.[b] The earliest dating for Caupirra is a stamp from another die in Period IIC at *Verulamium* (*c* AD 140–50). However, 2a occurs in the burnt material from the Period IID fire there (after *c* AD 150: Hartley 1972, S132). It is also known from Benwell, where it will belong to the Antonine occupation. Caupirra's use of form 31R shows that he was still at work in the later second century. *c* AD 150–80.

5　　'1974 +'. Crina(?) la 33 **CRINA**. A Central Gaulish stamp, perhaps illiterate, though a stamp from the same die (from Vichy) seems to show the second letter as an **R** with a very small loop. Alternatively, this may be an illiterate stamp reading **CNNA** or **CAINA**. Antonine.

6　　'1974 +'. Flavius Germanus 9c 18/31 **[OF]FL·GER** (Bemmann 1984, 334) La Graufesenque.[b] Several of this potter's stamps have been found at Domitianic foundations; this particular one is known from Saalburg. Flavius Germanus's output includes a few examples of form 29, which should be earlier than AD 85, but also many dishes which are typologically 18/31, rather than 18. *c* AD 85–120.

7　　'1974 +'. Habilis 1a 31 **HABILI[SM]** Lezoux.[a] This stamp is noted from Chesters. It was used on both forms 27 and 80, which at Lezoux belong to the Hadrianic to early Antonine and mid to late Antonine periods, respectively. The balance in favour of form 27 suggests a date *c* AD 150–80.

8　　'1974 4'. Otonius la 32 **OTONIVSF**, East Gaulish. No other stamps of this potter have been recorded by the present writer. The form of this dish suggests late second- or early third-century date.

9　　'1974 +'. Severus v 6b' 31 **[SEVERV·]S<F>** (Curle 1911, 241, 95) Lezoux.[b] A stamp from a broken die, which originally ended in F. Examples of both versions occur in Antonine Scotland, while stamps from other dies come from the Birdoswald Alley find and from a pottery shop

at Castleford destroyed by fire in the 140s (Hartley and Dickinson 2000, 36–55). The potter's forms include 18/31, 18/31R and 27. *c* AD 130–50.

10　　'1974 +'. **IXIIILLMA** on form 31R (Durand-Lefebvre 1963, 262, 837) Lezoux.[a] One of the commoner Central Gaulish illiterate stamps, noted at Chesters and on the mid to late Antonine forms 79 or Ludowici Tg, 79R and 80. *c* AD 160–90.

The changing pattern of pottery supply

Malcolm Lyne

c AD 150–300

This is the first period to produce sufficient pottery for determining the pattern of supply to the site, although the length of time covered includes considerable changes in sources supplying east Kent during the third century. The map showing the origins of the pottery from Mill 1 (Figs 62 and 63) indicate, however, that the overwhelming bulk of pottery in use at Ickham came from the same very local sources throughout the period in question. These 'Native Coarse Wares' and the preceding Transitional wares make up nearly two-thirds of all the pottery from the mill (Table 2, p 97).

The Upchurch and Thameside kilns were the source of another 15 per cent of the pottery, including bowls and dishes in BB2 and Thameside fabrics C8A and C8B as well as beakers and other fineware forms in Upchurch fabric F3A. Tiny amounts of Romano-British pottery came from further afield and include a BB1 developed beaded-and-flanged bowl from Dorset, a lid-seated jar from the Canterbury kilns and a *Verulamium* region white ware flagon. One or two post-AD 240 Oxfordshire red colour-coated vessels were also present at Mill 1, indicating that such wares were already present in east Kent before the mill ceased to function during the last years of the third century. The local nature of Romano-British pottery supply to Mill 1 during most of its life was even more pronounced than is indicated in Fig 62, as BB1 and Oxfordshire wares only started to appear there towards the end of its use.

Continental imports include significant quantities of Central and East Gaulish samian, one or two Lezoux and Moselkeramik colour-coated beakers and a roughcast cornice-rimmed beaker from Cologne. Specialised wares include mortaria from various unspecified sources in Kent and Northern Gaul as well as Dressel 20 amphorae. One of the latter vessels shows signs of re-use in that a handle was sawn through at its base. This may have been part of an operation

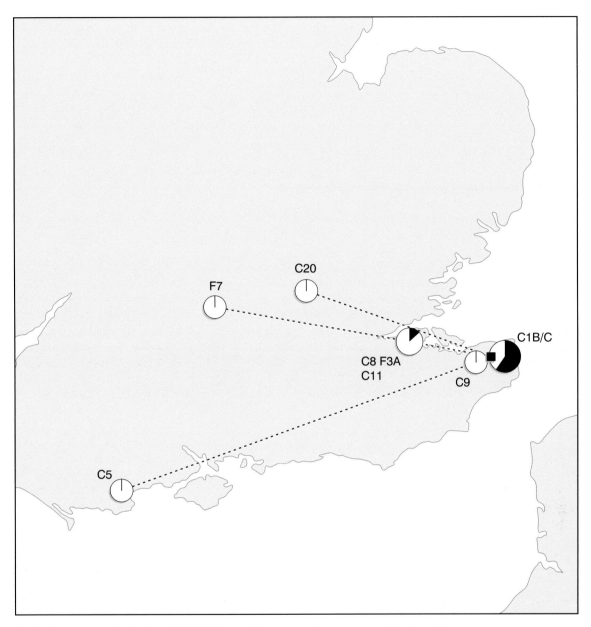

Fig 62. Pottery supply to Mill 1, *c* AD 150–300, from British sources. Percentages of pottery from different sources are shown in the form of pie-charts and should be used in conjunction with Table 2. Other, very rare, fabrics only present in other assemblages of similar date range are also included, however. Fabric codings are shown against their pie-charts where applicable.

to remove the entire top of the amphora and turn it into some kind of storage vat set in the ground. There are other examples of this kind of re-use at Staines and elsewhere and it may be that old amphorae were being brought to the site for re-use rather than olive-oil being imported from Spain.

The pottery assemblage from Ditch 302 differs from that associated with Mill 1 in having considerably higher percentages of Thameside and Upchurch products but no additional fabrics.

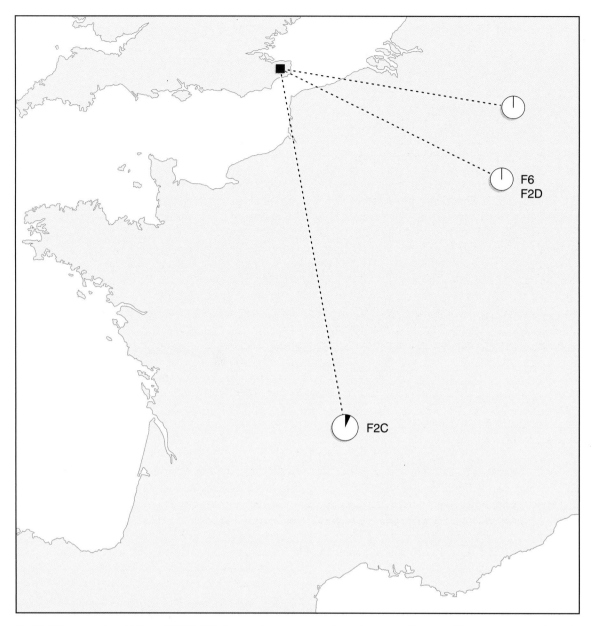

Fig 63. Pottery supply to Mill 1, *c* AD 150–300, from continental sources. Percentages of pottery from different sources are shown in the form of pie-charts and should be used in conjunction with Table 2. Other, very rare, fabrics only present in other assemblages of similar date range are also included, however. Fabric codings are shown against their pie-charts where applicable.

c AD 300–70

Assemblage 11 from layer 414.4 is the only relatively uncontaminated assemblage of any size which can be considered to be of this date. Hand-made grog-tempered wares make up over a third of all the pottery and come from at least three sources. The most common fabric is the kaolinite-rich siltstone-tempered fabric C2, which accounts for nearly a third of the pottery and indicates supply from an unspecified production centre on the edge of the Weald of Kent somewhere to the west of the Shore fort at Lympne and perhaps associated with salt production on the edge of Romney Marsh.

Very small amounts of Richborough grog-tempered ware are also present and must be some of the earliest products of that industry. A few pieces in the Hampshire grog-tempered ware fabric C4A indicate connections, trading or otherwise, with the Isle of Wight and Hampshire coastal areas. Tiny amounts of the crushed flint-tempered fabric C10 may be from the same unknown east Kent source as the flint-and-sand tempered wares encountered in mid fourth-century contexts at Canterbury.

The second most significant fabric present in 414.4 is Alice Holt type ware believed to originate at the nearby Preston kiln (18 per cent). The high percentage of these wares compared with their share of post-370 assemblages suggests that the *floruit* of this little industry was during the early to mid fourth century. True Alice Holt greywares from the Hampshire/Surrey borders account for a mere 2 per cent of all of the pottery.

The appearance of small quantities of Harrold shell-tempered and horizontally-rilled jars from Bedfordshire in southern coastal regions is a feature of pottery distribution during the second half of the fourth century and their presence here indicates that they had begun to circulate before 370.

The finewares include small amounts of imported roller-stamped bowls and plain dishes from the Argonne, somewhat larger amounts of Oxfordshire red colour-coated bowls, beakers and mortaria (13 per cent) and white ware mortaria (4 per cent). Colour-coated Lower Nene Valley white ware fabric F12 bowls, dishes and beakers were imported in similar quantities to their Oxfordshire equivalents (11 per cent) and like them were probably supplied out of London.

Rare imports, not present in the midden assemblage but known from elsewhere on the site, include a solitary New Forest purple colour-coated beaker and a few fourth-century Rhenish colour-coated examples.

c AD 370–400+

There are several large pottery assemblages of post-370 date from Ickham, but most of them suffer from being poorly sealed and having residual early to mid fourth-century elements. Nevertheless, the two largest of these assemblages (Assemblage nos 13 and 21) from Channel C and Area 4 extension (Tables 5 and 7), had their fabric percentages averaged out in order to produce Figs 64 and 65 which show the pattern of pottery supply to Ickham during this period.

The most striking feature of the map is the sheer variety of pottery sources compared with those supplying Ickham during earlier periods. The most significant supplier was the local Richborough grog-tempered pottery industry, which was the source of nearly a third of all the wares in use on the site and up to half of all of the coarse pottery. Amounts of Lympne grog-tempered ware fluctuate but an average of 12 per cent of all of the pottery came from this source. This material may, however, include vessels in a macroscopically indistinguishable East Sussex Ware fabric variant, as at least one beaded-and-flanged bowl from that source is known at Ickham. Small numbers of fabrics C1D and two vessels are present in contemporary assemblages from the Shore fort at Pevensey, indicating that the movement of hand-made grog-tempered wares was two-way between east Kent and East Sussex during the late fourth century.

Small amounts of Hampshire grog-tempered wares continued to arrive at Ickham. One beaded-and-flanged bowl type with exaggerated bead and in fabric C4B (Fig 47, 28) is paralleled at the Brading villa and also occurred at the Hastings Covehurst Wood site (Moore 1975). This and the fabric C4A fragments would seem to indicate coastal seaborne trade eastward from the Isle of Wight and Hampshire littoral.

The most significant fineware and mortaria supplier was the Oxfordshire industry: fabrics F7A, 7B, 8, M7 and 8 account for 30 per cent of the Mill 1 and 21 per cent of the Area 4 extension assemblages. The percentages of fabric C12 group wares from the local Preston kiln are down to 7 per cent of the pottery from Mill 1 and 2 per cent of that from Area 4: the pottery may all be residual in nature. Alice Holt wares are still present and form between 4 and 5 per cent of all the post-370 pottery.

The rest of the pottery brought to Ickham during the last quarter of the fourth century consists of very small numbers of pots from a great variety of sources. The coarseware element includes a beaded-and-flanged bowl of a type paralleled at Burgh Castle in Norfolk, Harrold shell-tempered wares, Hadham grey and oxidised wares from near Bishops Stortford in Hertfordshire and Rettendon ware from the Chelmsford area. Further coarsewares were imported from the Continent: Mayen ware from the Eifel in Germany, late *bandes-lustrées* wares from the Amiens area of north-eastern Gaul and a late *terra nigra* bowl from the Arras region.

Lower Nene Valley colour-coated wares make up between 2 and 3 per cent of the pottery, a figure well down on that for the mid fourth century. Brown colour-coat vessels in fabric F9 of possible Kentish origin account for between 3 and 5 per cent of the pottery, whereas they scarcely register in most assemblages of pre AD 350 date. One Pevensey ware bowl fragment from East Sussex is present at Ickham and there are a very small number of poorly made colour-coated vessels

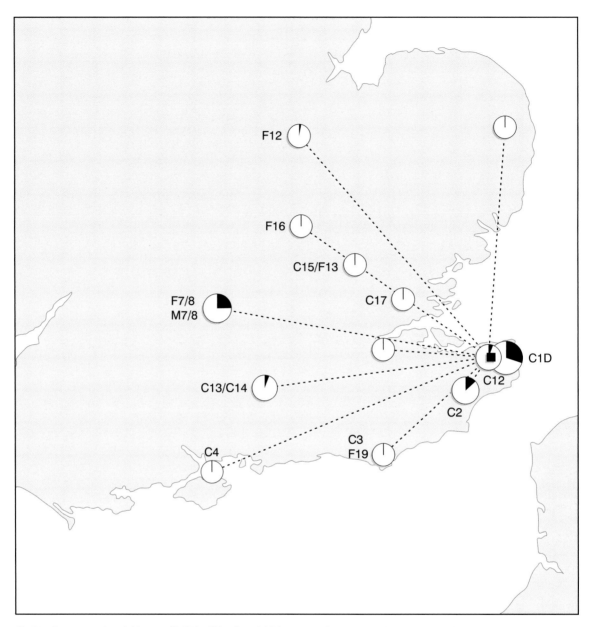

Fig 64. Pottery supply to Ickham, *c* AD 370–400+ from British sources. Percentages of pottery from different sources are shown in the form of pie-charts and should be used in conjunction with Tables 5 and 7. Other, very rare, fabrics only present in other assemblages of similar date range are also included, however. Fabric codings are shown against their pie-charts where applicable.

and mortaria in fabrics F10, 11 and M9, which are probably of local manufacture. There are appreciable quantities of Argonne ware from north-eastern Gaul and unstratified fragments from a German Marbled Ware flagon.

This great range of fabrics, some from far afield, suggests that Ickham may have been a port and engaged in British coastal trade and that with the Continent. There are however at least three other possibilities.

The first of these is that Ickham obtained much of its wide variety of imported wares through the known port at Richborough, not far to the east, at the entrance to the Wantsum channel.

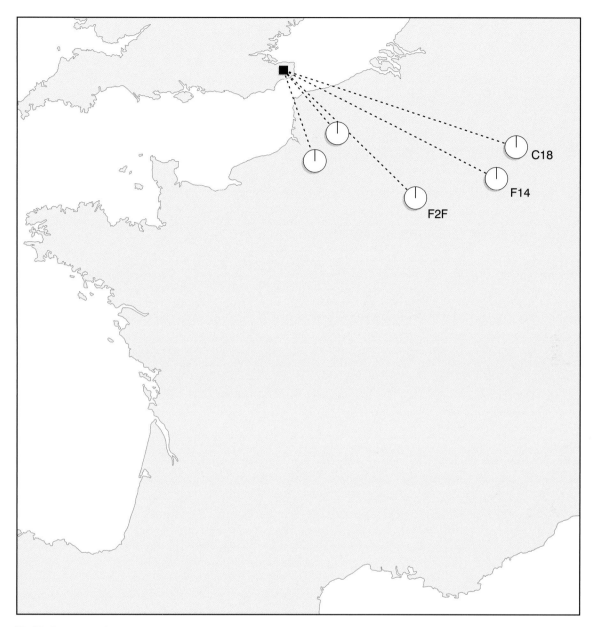

Fig 65. Pottery supply to Ickham, *c* AD 370–400+ from continental sources. Percentages of pottery from different sources are shown in the form of pie-charts and should be used in conjunction with Tables 5 and 7. Other, very rare, fabrics only present in other assemblages of similar date range are also included, however. Fabric codings are shown against their pie-charts where applicable.

The second possibility is that Ickham was a military supply depot. The wide variety of pottery may have got to the site via supply ships from the various Shore forts. The BB1 and Hampshire grog-tempered ware vessels could easily have come on ships out of Portchester, the Alice Holt, Overwey, Pevensey and East Sussex Ware similarly out of Pevensey and fabric C2 pots out of Lympne. The Suffolk style beaded-and-flanged bowl could have been brought to Ickham on a ship from the Burgh Castle fort and many of the continental imports from Gallic Shore forts across the Channel.

The third possibility relates to the fact that a number of very late fourth-century pottery assemblages from sites in southern Britain have pottery from a greater range of sources than previously. It is thought that this may reflect a situation where the various potteries had to distribute fewer wares more widely and thinly across each other's previous marketing zones because of declining demand. This decline may have been due to increased use of metal and glass vessels or other economic factors (Fulford 1975a; Lyne 1994a, 500).

Assemblage 22 from the timber-lined pit (333) with its more limited range of fabrics, may well have been deposited after AD 400 when most pottery industries had finally succumbed to economic pressures and only a few suppliers remained in the field.

The ceramic evidence for specialised activities

Malcolm Lyne

Before we can discuss any such evidence it is necessary to determine what constituted normal east Kent pottery assemblages, during both the third and late fourth centuries. It was decided to use quantification of a number of pottery assemblages from sites in east Kent carried out for the author's doctoral thesis (Lyne 1994a) and to work out average percentages of vessel types within the area. Too few early to mid fourth-century assemblages from east Kent sites have been quantified to carry out such an exercise for that period.

Four third-century rural sites (St Richards Road, Deal, Context 535; Worth, temple *temenos* ditch; Drapers Mill, Margate; Harville villa, Wye, midden) and four urban and military site assemblage quantifications (Northgate, Rochester Context 18; Richborough, Area XI, Layer 2; Dover, Shore fort rampart; Marlowe Car Park, Canterbury, Context R12A) were used (Table 14).

The assemblages from rural and urban/military sites show very different form breakdowns. Rural sites have a strong preponderance of cooking pots and other jar types, whereas the urban and military site assemblages are dominated by open forms and larger percentages of beakers. Mortaria and storage-jars are rare in all site assemblages.

The make-up of the pottery assemblage from Context 1005 (Assemblage 6) at Mill 1 has much in common with those from the rural sites in east Kent. Beakers and mortaria are slightly more common but there is no real evidence for specialised activities, despite the pot group having been recovered from the mill-race beneath Mill 1.

The assemblage from Ditch 302 is of very different character and has much in common with the pottery groups from urban and military sites. The bulk of the assemblage

is made up of open forms and beakers and compares most closely with the pottery from the construction of the rampart of the Shore fort at Dover. Is this indicative of a military presence at Ickham? We have to be somewhat cautious about arriving at any such conclusion because of the small size of the assemblage and the fact that the very high percentage of beakers differs from both urban and military form patterns.

There are fewer quantified post-370 pottery assemblages from east Kent to compare with contemporary Ickham groups. The two quantified rural assemblages are the Wye rubbish pit (Pollard 1987, 151) and Context 302 at St Richard's Road, Deal and the two urban ones Canterbury Rose Yard, Trench 1A.6 and Rochester Northgate C206. Thomas May's unpublished minimum numbers of vessels quantification of the very large pottery assemblage from the middle ditch fill outside the north postern at Richborough (Bushe-Fox 1949, 72) was also used (Table 15).

What these vessel form quantifications seem to imply is that the dichotomy between rural and urban pottery assemblages in east Kent, noted during the third century, had largely disappeared by AD 370. The assemblage from Richborough does, however, suggest that military sites in the area may have continued to show a dominance of open vessel forms.

The five Ickham assemblages, for the most part, have similar ratios of open forms to cooking pots to those from urban and rural sites elsewhere in east Kent, although the two from Area 4 have percentages of open forms approaching that in the pot group from Richborough. Where all of the Ickham assemblages differ from the other east Kent ones is in the unusually high percentages of mortaria which are present. This in itself suggests that specialised activities involving the grinding up or pulping of materials were taking place on the site; a suspicion reinforced by the presence of three Dressel 20 amphora handles converted into pestles. It is unlikely that the profusion of mortaria is due to the manual grinding up of grain to make flour being carried out at times when the mills were shut down for repairs: most of the mortaria are very small and unsuited for such a task. Furthermore, the highest percentages of mortaria are from Area 4 and its vicinity, where milling is not known to have taken place. It may be that other foodstuffs were prepared in this area or plants and minerals crushed to extract dyes for cloth. Support for the latter hypothesis lies in the fact that the highest percentage of mortaria comes from the timber-lined pit (333, p33), a structure admirably suited for use as a dye vat.

The predominance of handled bowls and jugs in the small early fifth-century assemblages from Channel D is

	Jars	Open forms	Beakers	Storage jars	Mortaria	Others	Total EVE	Estimated no of vessels
	%	%	%	%	%	%		
Rural Sites								
Deal	70.30	19.90	4.20			5.60	4.97	66
Worth	65.60	23.70	1.30			9.40	5.43	69
Draper's Mill	72.40	17.40	4.60			5.60	5.62	61
Wye	74.40	17.90	5.90		1.40	0.40	9.75	130
Average percentage	70.70	19.70	4.00		0.30	5.30		
Urban and Military Sites								
Rochester	46.90	41.00	7.30			4.80	6.69	110
Richborough	20.80	57.20	1.30		2.60	18.10		77*
Dover	16.00	46.70	14.00			23.30	4.30	41
Canterbury	23.90	45.60	16.80	2.40	1.50	9.80	15.69	90+
Average percentage	26.90	47.60	9.90	0.60	1.00	14.00		
Ickham Assemblages								
Context 1005	64.60	17.40	10.50	0.80	2.60	4.10	8.35	80+
Context 302	18.50	38.90	34.60		3.00	5.00	2.98	27

Table 14. Ceramic forms from third-century sites. * The Richborough percentages are based on Thomas May's unpublished minimum numbers of vessels quantification.

	Jars	Open forms	Beakers	Storage jars	Mortaria	Others	Total EVE	Estimated no of vessels
	%	%	%	%	%	%		
Rural Sites								
Wye	65.70	21.70	2.90		2.70	7.00	29.25	258
Deal	58.60	28.00	2.40	3.50	3.90	3.60	2.54	33
Average percentage	62.20	24.90	2.60	1.70	3.30	5.30		
Urban and Military Sites								
Canterbury	66.40	22.30		5.30	6.00		6.42	50
Rochester	49.80	39.80	8.00			2.40	7.42	115
Richborough	36.90	50.40	3.40		3.40	5.90		117*
Average percentage	51.00	37.50	3.80	1.80	3.10	2.80		
Ickham Assemblages								
Channel C	42.40	33.00	9.30	0.40	8.90	6.00	15.98	100+
408, Area 4	32.90	45.80	9.80		11.50		5.11	41
Area 4, extension	41.90	41.90	4.40	0.50	10.60	0.70	36.08	200+
Wood-lined pit 333	38.00	27.60	1.80		19.50	13.10	7.58	54
Well 701	48.80	36.50	7.60		7.10		4.98	42
Average percentage	40.70	37.00	6.60	0.20	11.50	4.00		

Table 15. Ceramic forms from post AD 370 assemblages. * The Richborough percentages are based on Thomas May's unpublished minimum numbers of vessels quantification.

particularly interesting, in that such vessels may have been used for ladling out measures of grain and flour. (I am indebted to Tony Wilmot for this suggestion.)

The scarcity of handled bowls and jugs in pre-400 mill assemblages may be due to the collection of grain at the Ickham mills in the form of an *annona* levied on local producers for the garrisons of the east Kent Shore fort system. Such an *annona* would have required the use of official *modii* to measure out the grain. Small scale civil milling after the end of the Roman occupation would not have required the use of a *modius*; grain and flour may have been measured out on a more *ad hoc* basis with whatever suitable vessel came to hand. It must be emphasised, however, that this is a highly-speculative explanation for the presence of these handled vessels.

PART 4: THE SMALL FINDS
Ian Riddler and Quita Mould

Introduction

Ian Riddler

In this report the small finds are described by functional category. This is followed by a discussion in Part 5 of their spatial distribution across the site. The chronology of a number of the objects has already been indicated above in Part 3, within the texts on the Ceramic Assemblages, which form the backbone to the dating framework for the site as a whole. The majority of the objects are of late Roman date and many can be placed within the period of AD 350–410, or beyond. The nature, distribution and possible significance of the fifth-century and later material is also highlighted in Part 5.

The quantity of material recovered, which amounts to over 3,000 objects, dictates that a detailed catalogue description of every single object from the site is not feasible, or even necessarily desirable. 1,337 numbers have been used to describe the 3,000 objects, with single numbers signifying multiple quantities of smaller, fragmentary items like fragments of glass, hobnails or iron nails. Every type of object or individual variant is mentioned and their quantities are given, so that the total assemblage is presented. Over 600 objects have been illustrated, providing a representative sample of the assemblage as a whole. Illustrated objects are indicated in bold type in any discussion.

A number of tables have been provided, which summarise some of the essential characteristics of each object. Individual discussions are followed, where appropriate, by these tables which show the publication number, material, context and relevant dimensions. Dimensions accompanied by a 'plus' symbol indicate that the object is broken and the incomplete measurement represents a minimum figure, to be used for guidance only.

The functional categories begin with a discussion of the military material. This is arranged in a broadly chronological narrative with weaponry and accoutrements followed by belt and harness fittings. These include belt equipment of late Roman date, although it is acknowledged, despite lingering reservations, that this material is more properly described as 'official' rather than 'military'. For the sake of consistency, it has been placed within this category, rather than with the dress accessories, hopefully without prejudicing its interpretation.

The sequence continues with the dress accessories, which include brooches, ear-rings, pins, beads, pendants, bracelets and finger rings. There are abundant examples of some of these items and the pendants, in particular, are rare and significant objects. It is true to say that the soil conditions at Ickham were favourable to the survival of organic remains and it is a little curious, therefore, that there are few items of organic materials. This point is made in relation to the bone pins, but it is relevant also for the leather shoes, and in terms of the lack of items of wood, with the exception of a single figurine. The shoes are described in the section on personalia, alongside combs and other toilet implements. The wooden figurine has been placed in the small section dealing with objects which may have had religious significance. Some of these objects are also considered elsewhere, as with the axe-headed pin, for example, which recurs in the section on dress accessories.

Small sections on weights and measures and objects relating to written communication are followed by a longer essay on household items. There is a noticeable lack of objects which provided services for buildings, like lighting equipment and locks. Keys, however, are reasonably abundant. The general absence of this material ties in well with the lack of structures on the site itself. Why then are there so many keys? Few of the keys are associated with the mills and they are concentrated in Area 4. There is no obvious reason why they should occur there in such numbers, but it is worth noting that the knives are also to be found there, rather than elsewhere on site, alongside the domestic implements, like frying pans, spoons, ladles and strainers. The situation is quite different for the querns, which were largely discarded in the same areas as the millstones, close to the mills themselves.

The millstones are considered under the heading of 'Crafts and Industries' (pp 276–89) for the evidence they provide for the grinding of grain. The querns could equally well have been placed in this section. There are few items associated with agricultural practices, strengthening the idea that the site served as an industrial centre, and not as a part of a rural estate. The grain would have been gathered locally, but not in the immediate environs of the site. The small quantity of fishing equipment reflects the presence of the river and its mill channels, as well as the proximity to the Wantsum channel. Few of the fishing implements are certainly Roman, however, and some do appear to belong to the Anglo-Saxon and later periods. The lack of samples of fish remains, to set alongside these implements, is another factor to be regretted. Other crafts which are represented include metal-working (copper alloy, lead alloy and iron), wood-working, leather-working, textile manufacture and bone-working.

The presence of a road inevitably means that there are items of transport within the assemblage, including spurs, hipposandals and horseshoes. The latter may possibly be added to the growing body of evidence for the existence of horseshoes in the late Roman period.

Structural equipment is reasonably well-represented and a significant amount is associated with the mills, suggesting that it was used in their construction and repair. Here again, however, there is also material in Area 4, and this does tentatively suggest that buildings may have lain close to this area of the site, possibly in proximity with the road, or perhaps further to the south, on ground which was not as low-lying and close to the river channels. The ceramic building material, however, comes largely from Areas 6 and 7 and the presence of a timber-lined well in the latter area may also suggest the presence of further buildings in that vicinity.

The small finds hint at a wide variety of activities, most of which were taking place during the late Roman period.

The majority of the assemblage belongs to the late third or fourth century and it forms a major corpus for southern England. Seen alongside the assemblages from Canterbury, and notably those from the Marlowe excavations (Blockley *et al* 1995), it provides an opening standpoint for considerations of regional practices which can, in time, be placed alongside the evidence from the ceramics, where concepts of location and the movement of objects are better developed.

Military equipment

Quita Mould

Weaponry

A small quantity of spearheads and artillery bolt heads were recovered from the excavations. The difficulties of classification and dating of 'projectile heads' are well known (Marchant 1990, 1–5; Bishop and Coulston 1993, 69). The difficulties of attempting to classify and date those from Ickham, with their inherent lack of stratification and independent dating, renders it unwise to stray far beyond the fact that they all appear to be of Roman date. The small, flat-bladed heads may be small spearheads, arrowheads or a type of artillery bolt head, according to choice. They, and the square-headed bolt heads, could all be of third-century date, although first-century examples are well known.

Spearheads

A near-complete spearhead (**1**) and a broken socket sufficiently large to come from a second example (**2**) were found on the surface of Area 14. The leaf-shaped, double-edged blade with mid rib of lozenge-shaped section (**1**) is comparable to a group of spearheads from Kingsholm, Gloucestershire (Manning 1985, 160–1 and pl 76, V30–V35) for which a first-century date is suggested. A triangular blade of flat section with a closed flanged socket (**3**) is of Manning's Group IIB, a crudely-made spearhead of a type which is commonly found on early military sites in Britain and Germany (*ibid*, 165 for extensive comparanda) but a group is also known in a third-century context at Baldock (*ibid*, 162). The spearheads are both low shouldered blades with a relatively long length of entry, a characteristic best suited to cavalry weapons.

Two small, flat-bladed projectiles from Channel C (**4** and **5**) have leaf-shaped blades and narrow, round-sectioned sockets. Manning has classified similar examples as flat-

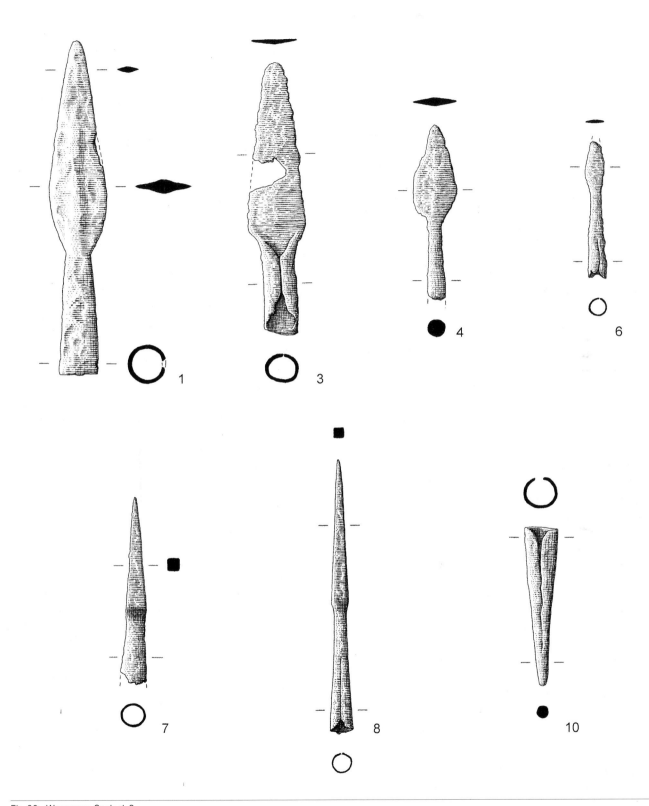

Fig 66. Weaponry. Scale 1:2.

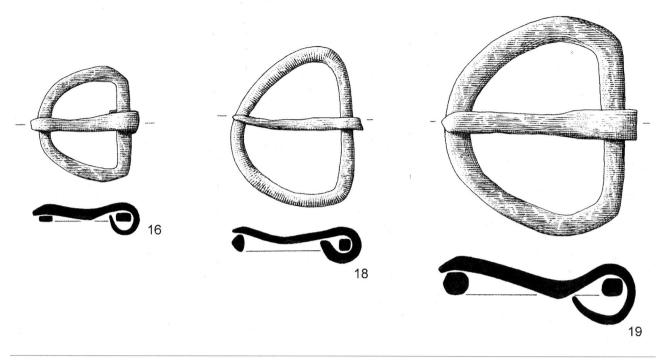

Fig 67. D-shaped buckles. Scale 1:1.

bladed artillery bolt heads of his type IIA (Manning 1985, 175) which can be paralleled by examples from the mid first century at Hod Hill. Daniels (in Allason-Jones and Bishop 1988, 103) has suggested that this type may be javelin heads. The third example (**6**) has the blade separated from the socket by a distinct neck. It would appear to come from a different, narrower, type of weapon such as an arrowhead or catapult bolt, indeed it has a similar socket diameter to the artillery bolt heads below.

Three examples of the more usual form of artillery bolt head with square-sectioned head and round-sectioned socket were also found, mostly occurring in Area 4 (**7, 8** and 9). Third-century parallels are common, occurring widely across the empire (Bishop and Coulston 1993, 139–41 and fig 99.1–7). Artillery bolt heads are usually considered to suggest the presence of the legionaries rather than auxiliaries during the first and second centuries AD. However, by the third century the use of artillery by auxilliaries has been suggested, based on two inscriptions mentioning *ballistaria* found at High Rochester (*ibid,*140).

Conical ferrules

Two conical ferrules from the tip of spear shafts were found, one in Area 4 and the other from the base of Channel

C (**10** and 11). A conical ferrule of lead alloy (12) has unidentifiable carbonised organic remains present within the round-sectioned socket (Watson 2000). Two smaller, crudely-formed examples (13 and 14) were also recovered. A lead ferrule would act as a counterweight to a heavy head at the opposite end of the haft, though whether they were used on military weapons is uncertain.

Armour

Seven small groups of ring mail (15), *Lorica hamata,* came from Area 4. They comprise single riveted rings alternating with pairs of unriveted rings of rectangular or flat section. No evidence for scarf-welded joints are visible, either by eye or in radiograph, on the plain rings, suggesting that they were punched in the manner described by Sim (1997). Ring mail was worn to the end of the Roman period and several examples and representations of late Roman ring mail are known (Coulston 1990, 147ff).

It has been suggested (Bishop and Coulston 1993, 60) that small pieces of mail in the archaeological record may represent damaged fragments which had been replaced and that their recovery may indicate the presence of a specialised workshop. In later times medieval metalworkers used small pieces of mail to highly polish the surface of metal items.

On that basis, the ring mail fragments here would indicate the activity of a metalworker.

D-shaped buckles

There are four iron D-shaped buckles, as well as four buckle tongues. The buckles appear to have integral rather than separate pin bars. Similar buckles are not uncommon finds on military sites and are thought to have been used on military equipment. The two smaller buckles (**16** and **17**) are of similar size to those on *lorica segmentata* from Hod Hill (Manning 1985, 146–7 and pl 71 T4, T5). The larger ones (**18** and **19**) can be paralleled by an example from Hod Hill (*ibid*, 147 and pl 71, T6) thought because of its size to have probably been used on a leather strap rather than attached to the plate. There is nothing to distinguish these buckles, however, from two iron buckles recovered from Lankhills, the smaller coming from a grave dating to AD 350–80 (Clarke 1979, 278, fig 35, no 25, 466). They are large enough to have served on horse harness. In discussing the two Lankhills iron buckles, Clarke cites continental examples, and Keller's proposition that they are not a Roman type and that those found within the Empire are likely to be of Germanic origin.

Two rectangular-framed examples were also found (**20** and **21**). Rectangular buckles are known in the Roman period (Manning 1985, 146). However, there is nothing to distinguish these from a large belt or harness buckle of post-Roman origin.

Helmets

A small number of items were recovered which could possibly come from a late Roman helmet. A curving fragment of sheet iron bowl (**26**) came from the Area 4 extension and it is associated with two strips, 19mm in width, each with a median ridge (**27**). One strip has a curved profile and the suggestion of a horizontal cross piece traversing one end. It is possible that these ridged strips could be strengthening ribs from a helmet. The remains of the bowl (**26**) are less convincing; it could possibly be a small fragment of helmet, but equally it could be the remains of a large ladle. The fragment had been burnt and radio-opaque specks are present within the corrosion products.

A fragment of copper sheet riveted with dome-headed rivets (**28**) from Area 4 is not dissimilar to the fragments suggested to come from the perimeter of the neck guard of a post AD 270 helmet from Richborough (Lyne 1994b, fig 1.1) recovered from the inner stone fort ditch fill.

An unusual iron biconical-headed pin (**29**) was found in a late third to mid fourth-century occupation layer (context 624, Assemblage 5). It may well be a simple, if unusual, hair pin or nail, however, it could possibly be a decorative crest rivet from a helmet of Berkasovo type 2 (Bishop and Coulston 1993, fig 123.4), although no sign of plating, necessary to prevent the iron from rusting, was discernible. Two other spherical-headed iron nails (nails of type 9, *see* p 265) were recovered from Ickham. In each case their shanks appear rather too long to have been used on upholstery, the function usually ascribed to them. A biconical-headed pin of copper alloy with a short stem (**243**), which could also have served as a crest rivet, is unstratified (*see* pins, p 181).

A tubular ferrule of copper alloy (**30**), decorated with a series of transverse mouldings, with a thickened rim at one end and a rectangular slotted terminal at the other, was found in the base of Channel C. It is comparable with a ridged tube from the fortress at York (Cool *et al* 1995, 1536 and fig 716.6312) which is thought to be a plume holder from a helmet or horse armour. Several other examples are recorded from military sites dating to the second century (*ibid*, 1536–7 for comparanda), the York example occurred associated with late occupation dating *c* AD 280–360 to 400.

Copper alloy decorative sheet appliqués

A minimum of six copper alloy sheet appliqués for a helmet were recovered. A complete double-lobed appliqué (**31**), a fragment apparently from a second example (**32**), and a small piece from a fitting of unknown shape (33) have a double line of repoussé dots around the perimeter, the better preserved examples having large ring-and-dot type motifs within. In addition, three small appliqués were found which have a single line of repoussé dots around the edge; a complete disc (**34**), a broken piece probably from a 'heart-shaped' fitting (**35**), and a triangular fragment (**36**) with nicked edges possibly cut-up for scrap.

They are comparable with the bronze plating from a late Roman helmet from Richborough found in the inner ditch and recently identified by Malcolm Lyne (1994b, 99–101 and fig 2). He suggests that the copper alloy sheet fittings were originally riveted to a helmet (helmet 2) of padded leather; whether a serviceable protective military helmet or ceremonial headgear worn by a priest is open to debate. The occurrence of sheet fittings decorated with both single and double lines of repoussé dots around the perimeter may suggest that the appliqué sheet fittings from Ickham derive from a minimum of two helmets. The complete sheet fitting (**31**) and a second fragment (**32**) have arms curving round a

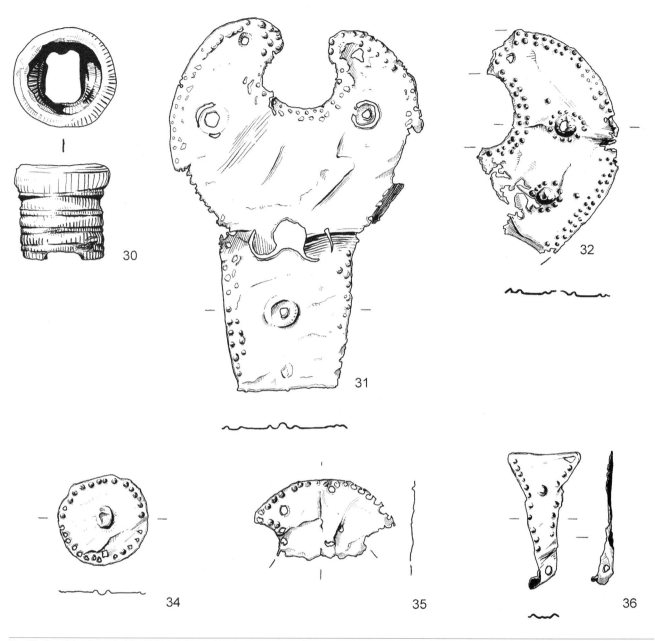

Fig 68. Possible plume-holder (30) and decorative sheet appliqués. Scale 1:1.

circular cut-out which Lyne suggests went around the crest holder on the top of the helmet (*ibid,* fig 2.1 reconstruction). Comparison with the Richborough helmet fittings suggests an early fifth-century date (*ibid*, 105). The appliqués were found scattered across the excavations, all show signs of wear and some are folded or bent suggesting that they had been removed from the helmet before being finally discarded.

Thirteen other pieces of copper alloy sheet with similar repoussé dots around the edge were found. Two objects with a border of repoussé dots and larger dots within may also be helmet appliqués (37 and 38). Repoussé dot decoration was commonly used in later Roman Britain particularly on belt-fittings, indeed Ickham produced a series of small buckle plates with this decoration (*see* below, p 154). These

No	Object	Total length mm	Blade length mm	Blade width mm	Socket/ring diameter mm	Context
1	iron spearhead	176	115	31	21	Area 14
2	iron spearhead?					Area 14
3	iron spearhead	141	90	30	18	Area 4
4	iron projectile	90	50	23	9	Channel C
5	iron projectile					Channel C
6	iron bolt head	73+		23+	11	Area 4, extension
7	iron bolt head	147	82	9	11	Area 4, extension, Pit 335
8	iron bolt head	100+	62	10	12	Area 4
9	iron bolt head	95	58	7	14	Area 14
10	iron ferrule	83			18	Area 4, extension
11	iron ferrule	51			10	Base of Channel C, east end
12	lead ferrule	75			22	Area 1, Pit 115
13	lead ferrule	30			24	Area 4
14	lead ferrule	30			23	Area 2
15	iron ring nail				8	Area 4

No	Object	Height	Width	Context
16	iron buckle	30	24	Base of Channel C
17	iron buckle	34	30	Area 3
18	iron buckle	58	45	Area 4
19	iron buckle	44	33	Area 4 'floor'
20	iron buckle	50	45	Area 16
21	iron buckle	32	30	Area 16
22	iron buckle tongue			Area 5
23	iron buckle tongue			Area 10, 1003
24	iron buckle tongue			Area 10, 1001, 1
25	iron buckle tongue			Area 7, 712

No	Object	Height mm	Width mm	Diameter mm	Context
26	iron helmet?	74+	19	103+	Area 4, extension
27	iron helmet?	69+	19		Area 4, extension
28	copper alloy helmet?	58+	12		Area 4
29	copper alloy crest rivet	60		12	Area 6, 624
30	copper alloy ferrule	26		26	Base of Channel C, east end
31	copper alloy appliqué	90	28–64		Area 4
32	copper alloy appliqué	58+			Area 3
33	copper alloy appliqué	32+			Area 2
34	copper alloy appliqué			25	Area 4
35	copper alloy appliqué	30+			Area 4
36	copper alloy appliqué	32			Area 4, extension
37	copper alloy appliqué	75	32		Area 4
38	copper alloy appliqué	46+	25		Area 4 extension, 'layers 2–5'
39	copper alloy mount				Area 3
40	copper alloy mount				Area 4

Table 16. Military equipment.

fragments of broken sheet may also come from these belt-fittings but equally well could have been used to decorate boxes and caskets.

In addition to the series of rectangular buckle plates decorated with repoussé dots and bosses, there is a collection of comparable sheet metal belt mounts (thirteen fragments) bearing the same decoration which must be of similar date. Two examples (39 and 40) are undoubtedly items of scrap. One of them (40) is associated with a collection of nineteen fragments of broken sheet, riveted sheet and offcut sheet fragments.

Military fittings

A relatively large collection of military belt and harness fittings was recovered from Ickham. Given the lack of secure dating evidence from the site some emphasis on the dating of comparative material is given here in order to show the presence of the military at Ickham during the first, second and third centuries, as well as the late Roman period. The military fittings are grouped by date, where possible, and are followed by other objects with a likely military association.

First-century military material

Harness fittings

A cast fitting (41), comprising a foliate design of four petals with knops around a central hole with a large loop above, was found in Area 14. It is comparable with a harness loop from Woodcock Hall, Saham Toney, Norfolk (Brown 1986, fig 30.222) found with other mid first-century military metalwork on the site of a hitherto unsuspected fort, and broken bearing rein attachments for harness from Wroxeter and *Margidunum*, also of mid first-century date (Webster 1958, fig 6.166, fig 7.175, fig 8.252).

Other possible first-century copper alloy harness fittings include a strap fastener (42) from Channel C and a junction loop hook (43) from Area 4. Each is now broken and cannot be unequivocally identified as harness fittings, however, sufficient variation between known examples exists to allow for their tentative identification as such here.

The possible hook from a harness junction loop (43) is poorly cast with a plano-convex section, having a pierced terminal with a transverse moulding at one end and the beginnings of a hook at the other. The range of designs of known junction loops is extensive. Bishop has ten types, with between three and seventeen sub-types within each,

recorded from the northern provinces (Bishop 1988, figs 5–10), so that the occurrence of a another possible variation should not, perhaps, be so surprising.

The strap fastener (42) of plano-convex section with a pierced ring terminal with decorative 'leaf-like' mouldings below, is comparable in both shape and size, if slightly longer, to a female strap fastener type 6e from Rheingonheim (Bishop 1988, 168, fig 54.6e and table 9).

Two gently domed bosses of flat-sectioned sheet are both centrally pierced. The complete example (44) resembles a small cymbal and it is possible that it could be one, as cymbals were used along with bells during religious rites. The more likely explanation, however, is that they are decorative bosses, probably decorative *phalerae* from horse harness. They are comparable with decorative *phalerae* found on cavalry equipment of first-century date, though they differ in profile (cf types 7a and 11a in Bishop 1988, 137 and fig 40). Similarly, the large size of an undecorated, circular mount of flat sheet (45) suggests that it is a *phalera* of type 16b (*ibid*, fig 40.12b). The lack of any diagnostic decorative features, however, makes it impossible to rule out a later date, similar to the openwork examples below.

The tip apparently from a large leaf-shaped pendant (46) was found in Area 5. It may come from a cavalry harness pendant of first-century date (Bishop 1988, type 4a or 4b, fig 45 and table 6, from Colchester and Hofheim respectively), but as only the terminal remains this can only be speculative.

A small copper alloy box hasp (47) with transverse mouldings and a decorative terminal can be paralleled by an example from a first-century context in subsoil under ovens at Chelmsford (Wickenden 1988, 236 and fig 3.9). It was found in context 610/2, associated with early fifth-century pottery (Assemblage 26), and would appear to be residual. The distinct leaf- or scallop-shaped terminal found on the hasp can be seen on a variety of pendants used on first-century military cavalry harness (Bishop 1988, fig 46.8a and 8e; fig 47.8g, 8k, 8n, 8o and 9c; fig 48.9n).

Second- and third-century military material

Belt-fittings

The lanceolate strap-end (49) is of a type commonly found in military contexts. Oldenstein suggests the main period of their use was in the second century continuing into the third with occasional later survivals (Oldenstein 1976, 144). At Caerleon they occurred in contexts ranging from mid second century to the fourth century (Webster 1992, 125 and fig 127, 99–103, for discussion of methods of attachment).

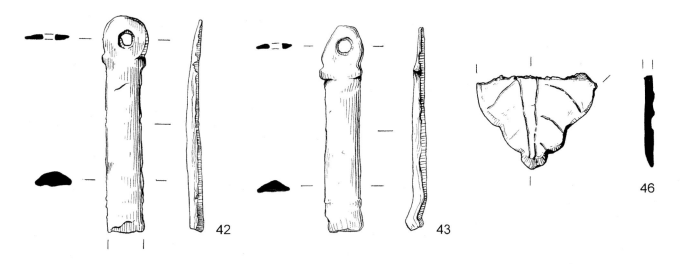

Fig 69. First-century harness fittings. Scale 1:1.

No	Object	Length mm	Width mm	Diameter mm	Context
41	copper alloy harness fitting	51	46		Area 14
42	copper alloy strap fastener	53+	10		Area 4
43	copper alloy junction loop	56+	12		Channel C
44	copper alloy domed boss			41	Area 7, 712
48	copper alloy domed boss			36+	Area 10, 1001
45	copper alloy domed boss			46	Area 5
46	copper alloy pendant?	26+	33		Area 5
47	copper alloy box hasp	50+	12		Area 6, 610.2

Table 17. First-century military material.

A broken belt mount (50) from Area 14 and a small fragment from a second example (51) from Area 4 are third-century belt-fittings and can be paralleled in the assemblage recovered from the upper sediments of the *frigidarium* drain (drainage group 4) at Caerleon (Brewer 1986a, 175 and fig 57) dating *c* AD 160–230. A cast decorative openwork mount (52) is reminiscent of a mount from the same deposits (*ibid,* fig 57.43). A cast belt-fitting (**53**) with a scroll-sided frame and small, triangular integral plate is also in the openwork tradition. The shape is reminiscent of certain categories of medieval and early post-medieval buckles but it lacks a bar or hole to attach a buckle pin. It is possible that the fitting is a casual loss of post-Roman date.

A broken openwork buckle (54) from Area 4 appears to be of a general type used by the auxiliary troops stationed along the Upper German-Rhaetian *limes* and Britain's northern frontier in the late second and early third century. The discovery of these buckles also in legionary contexts at Caerleon, Chester and Neuss (Webster 1992, 120–1 for discussion) supports the view that by the third century the distinction between the equipment of the legionary and the auxiliary had disappeared.

A double-headed copper alloy stud (74) that may have been used as a belt fastener is unstratified (*see* below, p 151–2)..

Harness fittings

The remains of a circular scrolled openwork mount (55) is in the same decorative tradition as the openwork buckle (54 above) and likely to be of the same date. The circular frame (56) broken from another openwork mount from Area 4 is

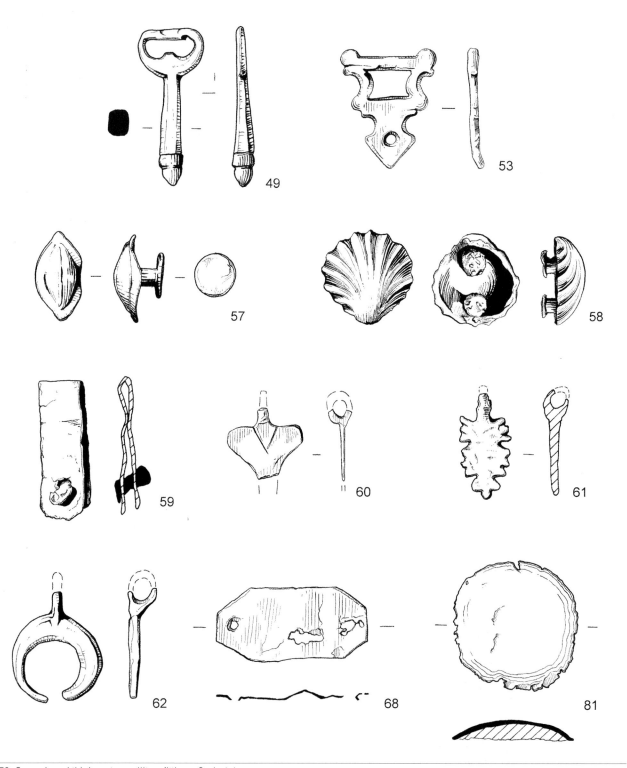

Fig 70. Second- and third-century military fittings. Scale 1:1.

also likely to be of third-century date. They are probably *phalarae*, comparable with other third-century harness and bridle equipment (Bishop and Coulston 1993, fig 112.1–4 and 6).

The elliptical vulvate stud (**57**) is comparable with the hexagonal harness mounts commonly found on military sites in the third century although they do come into use in the later second century (eg Allason-Jones and Miket 1984, 237 and 3.870, 3.871; Cool 1990b, 81, 86 and fig 70.27). The Ickham stud differs from the others in having a raised rib along the centre rather than the more usual incised line or depression.

A cast mount in the form of a cockle shell (**58**) was found in Area 2. It can be paralleled at Richborough by another example of late third- or early fourth-century date. The possibility that this mount was lost by a medieval pilgrim who had visited the shrine of St James de Compostela at Santiago in Spain, and was now perhaps travelling to St Thomas's shrine at Canterbury, cannot be entirely ruled out. On the other hand, the case for it being of Roman date is strengthened by the presence of a first-century parallel in silver from a temple site at Ménestreau, Nièvre (Garmier and Bouthier 1996, 17 and 56, no 38).

A simple folded sheet strap-end (**59**) with the open ends riveted together is similar to another from *Dobeta* in Dacia (Dawson 1989, 343 and fig 2.6) used to suspend a lanceolate strap-end pendant like the example (**49**) above. Three were used in conjunction with a decorative openwork strap distributor from *Buciumi*, also in Roman Dacia (Romania) (*ibid*, 351 and fig 6.1).

A broken heart-shaped pendant (**60**) was found in Area 5. A complete example was found at South Shields (Allason-Jones and Miket 1984, 3.660, where several other late second- and third-century military parallels are cited). Recently the context of an example from Caerleon has prompted Webster to suggest they may be military apron fittings rather than horse harness fittings (Webster 1992, 127.107) and the contexts of three Caerleon examples suggest an Antonine date (*ibid*, 126). They appear to be a long-used type, however, as another example came from a context dated AD 340/370 at Richborough (Malcolm Lyne, pers comm).

A small vine leaf pendant (**61**), worn through at the suspension loop, can be paralleled at Richborough (Malcolm Lyne, pers comm) where it is thought to be a horse harness trapping of pre-Diocletian date. A small crescentic pendant (**62**) with a broken suspension loop was found in Area 4. The crescent is a common pendant shape used on larger pendants associated with first-century horse harness and subsequently in smaller dimensions on late second- and third-century

harness. This small example is of third-century or later date and it is comparable to a silver pendant which was part of an armlet of jet, amber and glass beads and a pendant coin of Valens, 367–75, found in grave 402 at the Butt Road cemetery at Colchester (Crummy 1983, 51, no 1806). A suspension ring (**63**) with a scrolled terminal broken from another pendant came from the base of Channel C.

Plain sheet mounts

Ten undecorated copper alloy sheet mounts each have holes through which they were riveted to leather. Three mounts are of oval shape, one with a central rivet hole (64), the other two with a rivet hole at each end (65 and 66). One mount is lozenge-shaped (67) while two are of rectangular shape with clipped corners (**68** and 69). One mount (**68**) has a rivet hole at each end and possibly one near the middle close to the top edge. The left hand rivet appears to have been used twice, the middle rivet hole possibly three times, indicating extensive repair.

An undecorated oval-shaped mount with a pair of studs for attachment has been found at Balkerne Lane, Colchester from a *c* AD 250–400+ dump (Crummy 1983, fig 157.4238). Crummy cites other examples from Zugmantel and Saalburg and the fact that Oldenstein suggests they were made close to these forts from the middle of the second century (*ibid,* 136). An undecorated sheet mount was found with a variety of other harness fittings at *Buciumi*, Romania (Dawson 1989, fig 5.18). The mounts may not have been plain orginally; a small lozenge-shaped mount of brass decorated with sheet silver was found in a second-century context at Gorehambury (Wardle 1990, 129 and fig 125.185). These simple riveted mounts from Ickham may be in the same tradition.

Studs and bosses

A range of studs and bosses were recovered, which include examples of copper alloy and iron. They are commonly found on military sites and were probably used to decorate items of military uniform and harness.

A small copper alloy stud (74) with a domed head at one end and a flatter, circular head at the other, is comparable with other double-headed studs of second- or third-century date. It is thought that these were possibly used as belt fasteners (see the example from Aldborough (Bishop 1996, 74, no 454 and fig 39) where parallels from *Vindolanda* and Germany are cited).

Five decorative studs are made of iron, along with a copper alloy dome-headed stud adorned with a series of radiating grooves. Four have serrated (76) or milled (77 and 78) edges. Three (75, 76 and 77) have areas of tin/lead alloy present on the head, the remains of either a decorative plating or possibly a solder used to attach a metal foil covering, perhaps of copper alloy. A domed stud with a large flange with a serrated edge (76) has a clenched shank indicating it had been attached to leather or wood of 4mm thickness.

Eleven dome-headed copper alloy studs with lead backing occur in two general types; a smaller round-headed stud with a diameter ranging between 13–23mm (eg 80) and a larger shallow-headed type, the complete example with a diameter of 35mm (**81**). Lead-backed studs are often found in small numbers on military sites. The decorated example (82) is comparable with rosette stud baldric fittings, as with a third-century example from Saalburg (Bishop and Coulston 1993, fig 91.3) and another from Old Penrith (Mould 1991, 191 and fig 95.678).

A small number of flat, circular-headed copper alloy studs were also found (91, 92 and 96), along with two circular boss or stud heads with concentric mouldings (94 and 95).

Late Roman belt- and strap-fittings and other equipment

Introduction *Ian Riddler*

The late Roman belt-fittings should not be categorised simply as military equipment, and are better regarded as late Roman official issue. The collection from Ickham is extensive, and most of the assemblage has been published previously. In the following section, Barry Ager discusses forty-five examples of belt-fittings and Quita Mould describes a further selection of equipment of late Roman date.

Typology and dating *Barry Ager*

The various belt-fittings described here are almost all of types which are generally regarded as late Roman official issue, though whether for military or civilian use is a matter that will be considered below. They have largely been described and discussed already by Young (1981) and Brown (1981) and, as regards typology, it remains only to take into account here the items not previously dealt with and more recent discoveries and publications.

The two buckles with fixed triangular belt-plates cast in one piece with the loop, one solid and one with a central triangular opening (**97** and **98**; Brown's no 2), are of a form

that is easy to confuse with very similar, though usually composite, Anglo-Saxon and Frankish examples, but lacking their distinctive dome-headed rivets. The Roman buckles belong to Sommer's sort 3 type 'e' and occur in Britain, Gaul, the Rhineland and Danubian provinces and North Africa, eg the buckle from Furfooz, Belgium (Sommer 1984, 39, taf 16.8). They probably represent a simplified, one-piece form of Simpson's group II late Roman composite buckles with triangular plates (C Simpson 1976, 195–6). In addition to the British examples noted by Brown, Böhme (1986, 485–7) mentions buckles with both solid and openwork plates from Caerwent, Croydon and Dorchester. The three from Caerwent, including a fine example of a hinged prototype, are published by Knight (1996, 46–7, figs 2.4–5 and 4.6–7) and there are new finds from the late Roman cemetery at Bletsoe, Bedfordshire, and from Oxborough, Norfolk (Dawson 1994, fig 5.30; Gurney 2001, fig 4.e). A further example from a ditch with other fourth-century finds comes from a late Roman site at Enfield, Greater London (Gentry *et al* 1977, fig 30, 18 and pl 9; the attribution to the middle Saxon period by Going (1987b) is in error). The form is dated to *c* AD 310–60 in the Rhineland/Gaul region and more broadly to *c* 290–400 in the Danube region by Sommer (1984, 59 and 79), but in Britain a mid to late fourth-century date seems more appropriate, as buckle belts did not come into fashion here until *c* 340/50 and triangular-plated buckles, of Simpson's group II, seem to have been current in Britain in the third quarter of the fourth century (Clarke 1979, 266, 273). It is uncertain whether some remained in use or survived as old objects into the sub-Roman period (Knight 1996, 41).

One buckle (**99**) is so far unparalleled, and its use of enamel exceptional, though the form is broadly comparable with a late Roman buckle from Barton-on-Humber, Lincolnshire, which has clear dolphin heads on the loop, their tails curled up on either side of a bar for hinging the tongue, and a second bar for attachment either to a belt-plate, or perhaps directly to the belt itself in this case (Leahy 1984, fig 2.1). The loop of the Ickham buckle is quite similar in its zoomorphism to those of Hawkes and Dunning's late Roman buckle type IIA (Hawkes and Dunning 1961, 21–34, figs 17–18), though the dolphin heads on either side of the tongue-rest typical of the latter seem to have been reduced to just two round enamelled settings for the eyes, while the tails have sprouted animal heads as on Professor Evison's variant a[2] (Evison 1981, 129–30; further sub-groupings have been proposed by White 1988, 46–8). The feature of a second bar for attachment to a belt-plate occurs on continental buckles, eg from Furfooz, grave 1, from which Hawkes and Dunning's early Anglo-Saxon form IIC also developed

No	Object	Length mm	Width mm	Diameter mm	Context
49	copper alloy strap-end	42			Area 14
50	copper alloy belt mount	32	24		Area 14
51	copper alloy belt mount	14+	14		Area 4,'floor'
52	copper alloy mount		25	36	Area 14
53	copper alloy belt fitting	25	25	25	Area 14
54	copper alloy buckle	26		27+	Area 4, 'floor'
55	copper alloy mount			35	Area 10, 1001
56	copper alloy mount			53	Area 4, 'floor'
57	copper alloy stud	26	16		Area 7,712
58	copper alloy mount	25	25		Area 2
59	copper alloy strap-end	36	12		Area 4, extension
60	copper alloy pendant	19+	21		Area 5
61	copper alloy pendant	28	14		Area 4
62	copper alloy pendant	28+	28		Area 4
63	copper alloy pendant				Base of Channel C
64	copper alloy sheet mount	28	17		Area 4
65	copper alloy sheet mount	40	17		Area 4
66	copper alloy sheet mount	36	23+		Area 1
67	copper alloy sheet mount	44	22		Ara 4
68	copper alloy sheet mount	41	19		Area 2
69	copper alloy sheet mount	36+	14		Area 4
70	copper alloy sheet mount				Area 4
71	copper alloy sheet mount				Area 4
72	copper alloy sheet mount				Area 4, extension
73	copper alloy sheet mount				Area 7, 712
74	copper alloy stud	17	17		unstratified
75	iron stud		30		Channel C, west end
76	iron stud		38		Area 4
77	iron stud		43		Area 4
78	iron stud		38		Area 4, extension
79	iron stud				unstratified
80	copper alloy/lead stud	16	16		Area 5
81	copper alloy/lead stud		35		Area 4
82	copper alloy/lead stud		15		Area 5
83	copper alloy stud		21		unstratified
84	copper alloy stud				Area 10, 1001
85	copper alloy stud				Area 1, 104
86	copper alloy stud				Channel C
87	copper alloy stud				Base of Channel C
88	copper alloy stud				Area 2
89	copper alloy stud				Area 14
90	copper alloy stud		32		unstratified
91	copper alloy stud		23		Area 1, 115.1
92	copper alloy stud		31		Area 10, 1001
93	copper alloy stud		22		unstratified
94	copper alloy stud		37		unstratified
95	copper alloy stud		33		Channel C
96	copper alloy stud		28		Area 1, 129

Table 18. Second- and third-century military material.

according to Evison (1965, 63), and not directly from IIA. The simple bossed repoussé decoration of the plate occurs in various patterns on other buckle-plates from Ickham (**100**, **101**, **102**, **103**, **104** and **108**), as well as on other insular and continental examples, eg from Colchester, Lankhills cemetery, Winchester, the Aisne, France, and Oudenburg, grave 172, Netherlands (Crummy 1981, fig 15, 1–2; Clarke 1979, figs. 72, 126 and 100, 603; Sommer 1984, taf 2.8; Böhme 1974, taf 97.7). The Ickham buckle is typologically later than type IIA, which is datable to the mid to later fourth century (*see* **116** below), and so may belong to the later fourth, or even the turn of the fifth century.

There are two buckles of Simpson's group II, single-strap belts, with rectangular plates doubled over to form back-plates (**100** and **101**). They are very poorly made of thin sheet metal, with loops roughly cut from a strip and curved round. As with the buckle (**99**) the plates are simply decorated with repoussé dots, with the addition of rows of crescents on **101**. The D-shaped loops are typical of insular examples. The two similar, but longer, buckles from Colchester noted above were found paired with 'nail cleaner' type strap-ends with attachment-plates, but none of this type were found at Ickham, though one plate (**109**) is of similar size and proportion. The buckle from Oudenburg noted above appears to have been worn on a secondary belt to the main one with a larger buckle. By analogy with the buckles from Lankhills officers' graves 106 and 234, of *c* 350–90 (Clarke 1979, 272–3, fig 34.126 and 279), the Ickham ones can reasonably be dated to the second half of the fourth century.

The remaining nine rectangular buckle-plates (**102–10**; Brown's no 4 only; 105 and 107 *not illus)* could belong to either of Simpson's groups I or II, as the absence of loops makes their precise attribution uncertain, but the second group is usual in insular contexts; **109** is possibly a strap-end missing its hinged pendant (*see* 156 below). The plates are just as flimsy as those above (**100** and **101**) except for one example (**110**) which is cast and thicker, with neatly punched ring-and-dots around the rivets (and as its folded tabs are intact and rivets still in place it could not have gone with Brown's unbroken loop no 6, but may have had an open-ended loop). Two examples (105 and **106**) have holes punched through the centre which are not, however, for rivets, but for gripping the strap with their burred edges, as on the two Colchester buckles. This is indicative of a shared workshop tradition with the latter, though not necessarily of their being made in the same factory. However, the feature does not seem to occur on continental buckles, nor, for that matter, on other insular ones, so may be indicative of regional variation at least. The decoration of some (**102**, **103**, **104** and

108) is in repoussé bosses, as with others described above (**99** and **100**), and dating is as for the buckles with rectangular plates (**100** and **101**).

The five semicircular belt-plates from single-strap belts (111, **112**, 113, 114 and 115; Brown's no 3) are also of Simpson's groups I or II, but again the absence of loops makes it uncertain which, and some continental examples even have zoomorphic loops like those of Hawkes and Dunning's type IA (cf Sommer 1984, taf 1.4–8). The plate of a possible stray example has been recorded from Betchworth, Surrey (Higgins 1997, fig 1). At Lankhills examples of groups I and II were found in five graves dated between *c* AD 350 and 410 (Clarke 1979, 270–2 and fig 34), which is broadly consistent with continental dating (especially after the re-dating of the associated Roman crossbow brooches by Pröttel (1988); see now the revised brooch typology by Swift (2000), 13–88). At Canterbury two such buckles have been found at Marlowe IIB and Stour Street, the former from a context of *c* 350–75 and the latter from a third- to fourth-century demolition layer (Ager 1987, fig 1.e–f). The Ickham buckles can, therefore, be dated to the second half of the fourth/earliest fifth century and the Canterbury parallels are significant for the function and purpose of the site (*see* p 158 below). The Lankhills examples were associated with strap-ends of both heart- and amphora-shaped types (*see* below) and also with crossbow brooches in three cases (graves 23, 81 and 106), though how far the latter are indicative of the official or military status of the wearers is debatable (Clarke 1979, 262–3).

The openwork buckle-plate fragment (**116**; Brown's no 5) is from a dolphin-looped buckle of Hawkes and Dunning's type IIA, though from which variant is uncertain as the loop and tongue are missing. The insular examples of this type are distinguishable by paired dolphin heads on the loop, usually with curled tails interlocking with volutes on the base of a single tongue. The loop is hinged to the plate by a pin passing through lugs on both pieces (Hawkes and Dunning 1961, 21–34 and figs 17–18; Evison 1981, 129, British variant a[1]). Evison's variant a[2], with zoomorphic tails, does, however, occur on the Continent as well as in Britain, eg from Muthmannsdorf, Austria (Sommer 1984, taf 14.3). Such buckles probably came from single-strap belts (Clarke 1979, 273–6; Sommer 1984, 35). They were developed from a very similar west Roman type, from two-strap belts, also with an openwork plate, but usually with double tongues and dolphins with bobbed tails, found from Gaul to Pannonia (Evison's variant b). These continental precursors were mounted with amphora-shaped strap-ends and sets of propeller-shaped belt-stiffeners, as shown by grave associations; it seems probable that the insular form was, too. Hawkes (1974) has more recently suggested that the over thirty examples of type IIA found distributed evenly over the civil zone in Britain (many from walled towns, rural settlements and villas, and at least five from Anglo-Saxon graves) were modelled on 'dolphin' buckles from northern Gaul and introduced here in the 340s. The form had begun early on the Continent: in the western Danubian provinces it is dated *c* 290–400, and in Gaul and the Rhineland *c* 310–60 (Sommer 1984, 59, 79, sort 2 form B, taf 13.5–6 and 14.1–4). By the later fourth century the insular version had probably been superseded in Britain by Hawkes and Dunning's types III and IV (Clarke 1979, 275–6) and was being discarded as rubbish then and into the early fifth century. A new discovery from Dorchester, Dorset (more precisely of Evison's variant b, found mainly on the Continent), is discussed by Sparey-Green (1984; see also the updates in Böhme 1986, 476–84; Knight 1996, fig 2.2–3 for the two IIA buckles from Caerwent, one of variant a¹, the other approaching a²; and Marzinzik 2003, 17–18; fragmentary buckles have been noted from Stonea, Cambridgeshire and Stonham Aspal, Suffolk: Jackson and Potter 1996, 357, fig 115.126; Martin 2001, 77–9). It is important, however, to retain Evison's distinction between the variants to avoid over-generalisation about distribution patterns.

The openwork fragment (**117**) is possibly from a strap-end or buckle, but does not seem to be from any of the usual types.

The four buckle-loops (**118–21**; Brown's nos 7–8; 119 *not illus*) with pairs of stylised animal heads on either side of the tongue-rest, identifiable as dolphins by their crests in one case (**121**), belong to Hawkes and Dunning's type IA (Hawkes and Dunning 1961, fig 13), ie Evison's variant 'c', and would have been attached to their plates by the hinge-bar, which distinguishes them from the lugged loops of type IIA. They come from a narrow type of single-strap belt, and British examples often have long rectangular plates, whereas those from Roman Gaul have semicircular ones (Sommer 1984, taf 1.4–8, sort 1, form A). Hawkes (1974) suggests that in Britain they were being made in the last three decades of the fourth century and being worn out by the early fifth. They are more usually found here in walled towns, rural settlements and villas than in forts, eg the example from the walled town of Caerwent (Knight 1996, fig 2.1).

The small D-shaped loop (**122**; Brown's no 9) appears to be a crudely simplified version of Hawkes and Dunning's continental type IIIA, on which a pair of animal heads grips the ends of the hinge-bar (Hawkes and Dunning 1961, 10–21, figs 1.1 and 20a–f); it may be a local imitation. The type corresponds to Sommer's sort 1 form C, type f, on which

the plates are usually rectangular or square, and the animal heads appear to be of Germanic inspiration (Sommer 1984, 25–30, 70–1, taf 6–8, abb D; Swift 2000, 192–5, 202–5). It occurs in combination with a variety of other belt-fittings (disc and lancet-shaped strap-ends, tubular belt-ends and propeller or strip/triangular ended strip belt-stiffeners) mainly in northern Gaul, but also in Britain, Italy, North Africa, Spain, Germania Magna and the western Danubian region. It is datable *c* 364/70–407 in the Rhineland/Gaul area, with variants 4c and 5 continuing to *c* 450 (Sommer 1984, 62, 79, *passim*), while in Britain it came into fashion *c* 368–9 and continued in use into the first quarter of the fifth century, but is not known from Anglo-Saxon contexts, other than possibly one from Andrew's Hill, Easington (Hawkes and Dunning 1961, 20; White 1988, 47, group 3; Marzinzik 2003, 18). This dating is supported by the discovery of a further example at Lankhills, grave 376, which is independently dated 390–410 (Clarke 1979, 268, 276–7, fig 35.498). Other recent finds have been made, for example, at Crickley Hill, Gloucestershire, in the destruction layer at Bradwell villa, Buckinghamshire, and in the rubble overlying a third- to fourth-century building at Hibaldstow, Lincolnshire (Heighway 1987, illustrated on p 13; Böhme 1986, 473, abb 4). There is a rather atypical example from the Roman villa at Woodchester, Gloucestershire (Clarke 1982, fig 8).

The rectangular buckle-loop (**123**) is comparable in form with a composite loop from late Roman Silchester (Boon 1959, pl 3, A7) but, as similar, though cruder, buckles were used on military armour of the first and second centuries, the precise dating is unclear. The four remaining bronze loops (**124–7**) are of uncertain type, though the pinched-in front of one (127) suggests it may be from a buckle of Simpson's group I. This is a mainly continental form, though British examples are known, eg from Lankhills, grave 81, dated 350–70 (C Simpson 1976, 210–11; Clarke 1979, 270–2, fig 34.70). The stray tongue (25) is similarly unattributable.

The propeller-shaped belt-stiffener (**128**; Brown's no 10) belongs to Sommer's shorter group of such mounts (between 22–37mm long), which occur from one to eleven mounts per belt (not always matching), in association with heart or amphora-shaped strap-ends and buckles of Simpson's group I or Evison's variant 'b' (Sommer 1984, 5, taf 33.2–5 and 35.7–12). They are from narrow belts and are found largely in the Danubian region, but also in Gaul, as at Champdolent, and other European provinces (the longer form has a more general distribution and occurs on two-strap belts). British examples are few, though the number is increasing, eg from Colchester, Richborough, Stonea and Suffolk, and some may be imports, as one from Maryport (Cumbria), which is similar to the Ickham piece (except for double rivets at the ends), and could perhaps have belonged to a soldier from the Danube provinces, though this is not entirely certain (D Brown 1976, 78–9, fig 21; Böhme 1986, 485, abb 13; Jackson and Potter 1996, 357, fig 115.125). Another, with single rivets and grooves across the ends, has recently been found near Sutton Scotney, Hampshire, and there are at least four unpublished, with either single or double rivets, from various other locations in southern England (Iles 1997; Nick Griffiths, pers comm). The shorter propeller stiffeners were worn on civilian belts in the Danubian region in the second or third century and were in military use by the early fourth century (they are shown on the Arch of Constantine, erected in AD 315; Bishop and Coulston 1993, 173), but mainly in the second and third quarters of it and a little later. They were then superseded by longer forms on wider belts; two examples from Anglo-Saxon graves at Minster Lovell, Oxfordshire, and Harwell, Berkshire appear to have been kept as amulets (P Brown 1976; Clarke 1979, 267, 285 and 451–2; MacGregor and Bollick 1993, 212, nos 36.8 and 9).

Flat stiffeners of rectangular strip, which ultimately developed from the propeller-shaped form in the late fourth century (and were worn vertically across the belt, not on some sort of 'apron' as was once thought), are represented by three different examples (**129–31**; Brown's nos 11–13). The first is a finely nielloed mount, dated to the last quarter of the fourth century/*c* 400 by Brown on account of its nielloed decoration, which was used in northern France and Belgium at this time; its faceted ends and bevelled edges are comparable with a shorter stiffener from Treignes, Belgium, grave 137, still worn in combination with the propeller-shaped variety (Sommer 1984, taf 42.8). As with the propeller-shaped stiffener (**128**), it may therefore be an import. The narrow stiffener with bevelled edges (**130**) is broadly comparable with those of the Dorchester and continental belts, as noted by Brown, but is probably only half of a long strip broken across the centre and the undamaged end is differently shaped (cf similarly bevelled and faceted ones from Rhenen, Holland, grave 829, Trier (Maximinstrasse) and Bonn, Germany, associated with both hinged and late fixed-plate buckles of the end of the fourth century to second third of the fifth: Sommer 1984, tafn 53.5–6, 70.9, and 75.7–8; MacGregor and Bollick 1993, 212–3, no 36.11). However, there is no reason to disagree with his dating to *c* 390–410. It would have come from a two-strap belt with elaborate fittings, including buckle, strap-end, and probably additional stiffeners and tubular belt-ends. The third piece (**131**) is a strip stiffener from a wide belt, and so not earlier than the last quarter of the fourth century, as noted by Brown, while its crude manufacture suggests it is late in the series, say *c* 400 (cf Clarke 1979, 285).

The lozenge-shaped mount (132) is difficult to parallel, but is perhaps a belt-mount to match a buckle with a triangular plate and disc terminal (cf C Simpson 1976, fig 2, 4; and **97** and **98** above).

There are eight strap-ends from Ickham of Simpson's double-leafed, 'heart-shaped' type (**143–50**; Brown's nos 14–15, omitting three; 148 *not illus*; C Simpson 1976, 201–2); all are different, which is remarkable for such a standard form. They were all fastened to the strap by a single rivet (more usually there were two). On the Continent they occur mainly in the frontier regions of the western empire, from Gaul to Pannonia, with a variety of buckle types and propeller mounts, eg of Simpson's groups I and II and Evison's variant 'b' from Burgheim, Germany, grave 27, Zengővárkony, grave 4, Ságvár, grave 56 and Morichida, grave 111, Hungary, and Salzburg-Klessheim, Austria (Sommer 1984, 49, taf 24.2 and 4; 29.8; 31.2; and 33.6). They are rare in Britain, though two possibly insular examples were found at Lankhills, graves 81 and 426, dated *c* 350–70 and 350–90, both with Simpson group II buckles with semicircular plates (Clarke 1979, 282–3, fig 36, 75 and 534, noting an unusual piece from Frocester, Gloucester; cf buckles 111, **112,** 113 above). A plain example from Colchester was found in a late Roman deposit dated post-388 by coins, though was possibly residual (Crummy 1981, 14, fig 15.5). The ring-and-dot decoration of three of the Ickham strap-ends (**144, 149** and **150**) employs a typical motif, and both the triangular arrangement (**144**) and placing in 'line abreast' (**150**) can be paralleled on British and continental examples (C Simpson 1976, 202, fig 5). But the borders of smaller ring-and-dots (**149** and **150**) are perhaps a more local feature.

There are four examples of 'amphora-shaped' strap-ends, again of various forms of both hinged and riveted types (**151–4**; Brown's no 16, noting only two from this site). The type with pelta cut-outs at the 'neck' (**151–3**) is very widespread from Britain to Bulgaria, North Africa and northern Italy (C Simpson 1976, 198–200; Sommer 1984, 50–1, taf 19.5–11). On the Continent they are associated with Simpson group I buckles with rectangular plates and Evison variant 'b' buckles with propeller-shaped mounts (Sommer 1984, taf 28.2; 32.14; and 35.14), but opinions as to their dating, other than to the fourth century, seem to vary rather widely. In Britain two amphora strap-ends were found at Lankhills, graves 23 and 366, dating to 350–80 and 370–410, the first associated with a Simpson group II buckle with semicircular plate (Clarke 1979, 281, fig 36.26 and 489). One (**154**) appears to be a crude version of a slightly later form on which the two peltas at the 'neck' have been reduced to round holes, as on a ring-and-dot decorated strap-end from Lankhills, grave 106, dated *c* 350–70/90. This form is found from Gaul to Italy and the Danubian provinces. In Gaul and the Rhineland it is datable *c* 364/70–407, and in the Danube region *c* 380 to early fifth century (Sommer 1984, 79, group 2). The recent find of a damaged amphora-shaped strap-end at Culpho, Suffolk, is noted by Martin (2000, 502).

The exact original form of the fragmentary dart-shaped strap-end (**155**) is uncertain, but again it may represent a derivative of the amphora type, lacking a terminal lobe or knob, as with an example from Dalheim, Luxembourg (Sommer 1984, taf 21.6). Similar strap-ends occur mostly in south-eastern England and Gaul between the Seine and Rhine; a single plain leaf from one has been recorded as a stray find from near Saltwood Anglo-Saxon cemetery, Kent (Ian Riddler, pers comm). On the Continent they are datable to the early to mid fourth century, but British examples appear to be later, from the second half of the fourth century (Clarke 1979, 281–2; Ager 1987, 30).

Two of the three 'nail-cleaner' pendants (156 and 157) would have been hinged to a narrow, slotted, rectangular strap-end similar to two of the later fourth century from a child's grave at Butt Road, Colchester (Crummy 1981, fig 15.3–4). A plain example of such a strap-end from Ickham, missing its pendant, may be represented by a fitting (**109**) above. The single simple rhomboidal example (158) appears, from the leaf on the back, to have been riveted directly to the strap through its missing top. One (157) was found in occupation debris with pottery of the late fourth century (context 408) and the oval form with nicked, forked terminal of both (156 and 157) can be paralleled at Maiden Castle, Dorset (Wheeler 1943, fig 96.14). A 'nail-cleaner' strap-end with a rhomboidal outline like 158 was a surface find at Richborough (Cunliffe 1968, pl 43.177).

The putative rectangular strap-end (39) may be an example of Sommer's doubled-over square or rectangular form D, types a–b, belonging to his second belt group, dated *c* 364/70–407 (Sommer 1984, 79, taf 23).

The strap-fitting (159) is possibly a simple form of disc-attachment as on the well-known early fifth-century military belt from Dyke Hills, Dorchester, (Oxfordshire). Others are datable to the later fourth century (Hawkes and Dunning 1961, 4–6, fig 1.5–8). They would have served to suspend items of equipment, eg sheath-knives, as on the belt from Rhenen, Netherlands, grave 842, or to attach other straps (Ypey 1969, abb 13). As a rule, however, they

are secured by a single central rivet to a narrow tab at the back. An alternative explanation is that the fitting is one of two or three attached to the ring of a strap-distributor, such as a possibly Roman-influenced, fourth- to fifth-century, gilt silver example with three triple-rivetted discs from Kerch, in the Crimea (British Museum, reg no PE 1910, 4–16, 51); a Roman example with single rivets from Samson, Belgium is illustrated by Sommer (1984, taf 65.9).

The fragments of sheet bronze (160–3) include pieces clearly cut from, or broken off, unidentified objects, some of which may have been belt-fittings, but others are possibly from vessels or decorative mounts. Some have been folded up (as also 133–41), as if to be melted down for recasting. The riveted packet can be compared with two similarly crudely riveted, subrectangular scraps from Mucking, Essex, though these may be early Anglo-Saxon rather than late Roman (Hamerow 1993, figs 114.2 and 116.3).

The significance of the late Roman belt-fittings

The late Roman belt-fittings from Ickham, all of bronze, consist mostly of forms that could be described as of military type, though not necessarily of military use. Their military attribution is owed largely to their occurrence on military, cemetery and other sites in northern Gaul and the Rhine-Danube frontier areas (C Simpson 1976; Sommer 1984), or at Lankhills, Winchester, for example, in Britain (Clarke 1979; Bishop and Coulston 1993), and to comparison with chip-carved bronze versions from these areas (Böhme 1974, 188–94; Böhme 1985; Swift 2000, 201–2; unrepresented at Ickham) which seem likely to have formed an obligatory part of military uniform (as the fittings of *cingula militiae*, or belts denoting military rank). Many of the troops stationed here were of Germanic origin, whether as *foederati* or some grade of auxiliaries, though there have been varying estimates as to the percentage involved: only 15 per cent of officer ranks in the western Empire according to Welsby (1982), though the proportion could have been higher amongst the soldiery (see now also Halsall 2000) and, for simple practical reasons, the same equipment would no doubt have been supplied to units whatever their ethnic origin.

But even on the Continent rare representations in stone and ivory sculpture show that contrary to popular belief, belts with metal or jewelled mounts could be worn by Roman women in the second to fourth centuries. A gravestone from Intercisa shows propeller-shaped metal stiffeners on a woman's belt and another woman wearing a belt in the panel below (Bullinger 1969, taf 67 and 69), while on the late fourth-century Monza diptych a Roman woman, possibly

Stilicho's wife, wears a belt, apparently decorated with jewelled mounts, over her dress (Dixon 1976, illustrated on p 16), a fashion that is likely to have been imitated at court, if not in general society. It is debatable whether or not it shows Germanic influence. Also, in the Rhineland itself, belt equipment of 'military' type occurs in late fourth-/early fifth-century graves which, from their context, might be either purely civilian or have belonged to civil officials, as at Mayen, graves 5–6, 12, 16, and 21, and in three graves in civilian cemeteries at Speyer (Haberey 1942, abb 5–6, 11, 15, 18; Bernhard 1978, abb 8).

In Britain, Hawkes and Dunning's Type I, particularly, with very narrow belt-plates (cf 118–121), is better represented in walled towns, rural settlements and villas than in forts and may have been part of everyday civilian dress; it is probably significant that they are sometimes found in Anglo-Saxon female graves (Hawkes and Dunning 1961 and 1962–3; Hawkes 1974, 387, 393; Leahy 1984, 23, 31). Also, two buckles with thin rectangular plates of repoussé-bossed sheet, similar in construction to a number of the Ickham fittings, and forming sets with 'nail-cleaner' strap-end pendants like 156–7, have been found in a child's grave of the mid to later fourth century at Butt Road, Colchester (Crummy 1981, 12–14, fig 15, 1–4), so it is doubtful that the Ickham ones come from official belts. Various late Roman belt-fittings have been found at several sites in Canterbury in recent years, but, although soldiers could be temporarily billeted in cities in winter, it is unclear whether the finds by themselves indicate the presence of troops, or had been acquired by civilians (Ager 1987). A small group of such fittings has also been found at the roadside settlement of Each End, Ash, Kent (Garrard 1998, 157) and a hybrid version of the amphora and heart-shaped strap-ends (cf **143–54**, 148 *not illus*) was found in a late Roman midden deposit, perhaps associated with a temple or shrine, at Wayside Farm, Devizes, Wiltshire (Valentin and Robinson 2002, fig 13.3).

Research by specialists in such metalwork over the past couple of decades has shown that there is a range of possible interpretations to consider. It is now accepted that the late Roman civil service was organised on quasi-military lines, as a *militia non armata* (Hassall 1976; Tomlin 1976) and, after the reign of Valentinian (364–75), civilian as well as military officials wore belts (*cingula*) as part of a uniform, or at least as the insignia of one if in civilian dress, whereas previously only soldiers who had been appointed to civil posts had done so (Dawson 1990). The distinction by role is not always clear-cut either. In the fourth century some civilian officials held temporary military commands and could on occasion be permanently promoted to them

(Tomlin 1976, 195, 200–5). Furthermore, the extent to which civilians wore belts (*see* above), or even military-type clothing in the fourth century is uncertain. For example, in Rome itself, in 382 (Tomlin 1976, 191; James 1988, 313 note 275; Amory 1997, 341), laws had to be enacted to try and ban the wearing of battledress and belt equipment and the carrying of arms by civilian senators (though members of the imperial service were still allowed to buy it), and if this was happening at the centre of the Empire, to what extent was it mirrored in peripheral provinces? Was military garb worn for protection, fashion or economic reasons, or is it a sign that society itself was of necessity becoming more militarised, as it appears from Zosimus to have been in Gaul (parallels of a sort could perhaps be drawn with the youthful wearing of greatcoats and other military or official surplus in the more recent 1960s and 70s particularly)? A recent view of late Roman *Verulamium* is that, during the fourth century, it became more of a militarised taxation and administrative centre than a town (Faulkner 1996), and at Catterick some buildings seem to have been converted to military use late in the fourth century (James 1984, 167). Also, in Spain, it is now thought that finds of military-type belt and horse-equipment, etc, in the northern *meseta* and extending into the southern, are indicative of mixed military/civilian communities, while those from villa sites may have belonged to the owners, as possibly civil or military officials, or their staff (Aurrecoechea 1995–6; 1996).

The discovery of belt-fittings of military type on civilian sites need not therefore necessarily indicate a late Roman military presence, unless of course they are associated with weaponry or some other sign of military activity, such as inscriptional evidence. They might have been worn by veterans, the staff of a governor or procurator, or civil functionaries such as members of the judiciary, administrative officials, tax-collectors, officials in charge of goods requisition, communications, etc, and could be left by soldiers to their heirs in wills (see eg Sparey-Green 1984; Dawson 1990, 10–13). However, this is not to deny that where they occur in towns they may be indicative of city garrisons or of troops temporarily billeted there in transit or during the winter and not therefore documented in the late fourth-/early fifth-century official lists of the *Notitia Dignitatum* (Goodburn and Bartholomew 1976). But even city garrisons could have been formed by a citizen militia, as in late fourth-century Adrianople where one was under the command of the chief magistrate (Burns 1994, 36). Indeed, the Britons showed they were quite capable of taking up arms and themselves expelling one band of barbarians before ejecting the Roman magistrates in turn, so the imperial rescript telling them to look to their own defence need not have been as harsh as it seems (Zosimus, vi, 5 and 10: Buchanan and Davis 1967)! The mobility of units of *comitatenses* might provide an explanation for the widespread distribution of these finds. But discoveries on villa sites are harder to explain, though Black (1994) has argued that retired soldiers who had not had to hand in their uniform could have kept it as a souvenir of their service and there is the further possibility that villa-owners, some of whom are likely to have been middle and upper-ranking civil servants, maintained privately armed militias for their own and local defence - their rank might have enabled them to obtain official equipment. On the other hand, the lack of fortification of British villas poses a problem for such a hypothesis (James 1984, 168). Late Roman belt-fittings of military type from Anglo-Saxon female graves suggest that their owners might have been the wives or heirs of warriors who had served in Romano-British auxiliary units.

Most of the Ickham belt-fittings are finished pieces, but there is the quantity of scrap bronze, too, to consider, which was presumably for melting down for re-use. Also, one buckle (**122**) is bent and has transverse cracks, which suggest a rejected casting, and one strip belt-stiffener (**131**) appears to be unfinished. Taken together with other evidence for metal-working on the site (*see* below pp 289–93), these two pieces and the scrap bronze suggest that some, perhaps all, of the fittings were made here, some maybe for wear by administrators and guardians of the manufactory and others to order. Their quality is not very high (except for the enamelled buckle **99** and nielloed belt-stiffener **129**) and they would mostly have been mass-produced. This raises the question of the status of the site. In France, for example, unfinished items or failed castings have been found on non-military sites and indicate the existence of private local workshops. Although it is known from late Roman documents that there were centralised, state-run workshops for the production of arms, armour, etc, and official clothing (the *fabricae* for the former and *gynaecea* for the latter), the situation in Britain is unclear as, apart from a *gynaeceum* at *Venta* (Winchester or Caistor-by-Norwich?; Hassall 1976, 107), its list of official factories may be missing from the *Notitia Dignitatum* (James 1988, 258–63) and even then it is not recorded where the belt-equipment specifically was made; if they existed, such establishments seem unlikely to have survived the final withdrawal of the army (already largely depleted by late in the fourth century) followed by abandonment by the Roman

administration *c* 410. Before that date, state production may, however, have been complemented here by private production, particularly as the province no longer had a large army. The staff of the *fabricae* held military rank, though they were free men, if legally tied to their work. Could Ickham have been an unrecorded, small-scale *fabrica*, as mooted by Young (1981, 36) although known examples are all located at urban sites (James 1988, 274–6)? There is, however, some evidence from an earlier period, as possibly at Apulum, Dacia, for the leasing of private workshops to manufacture orders for official supplies (Dawson 1990, 10–13), and it may be that Ickham operated on a similar basis, though possibly under some form of official control, as the Imperial seals found nearby might suggest (Williams 2007, ill 5.37). In that case it could have been a production centre (rather than supply depot) both for the Saxon Shore forts of Reculver and Richborough and for civil officialdom in towns such as Canterbury, where military-type fittings have also been found. The range of metalwork found at Ickham has much in common with Richborough, and perhaps indicates the presence of a small military detachment to protect the workshop, but it appears that there was some degree of civilian occupation of the fort, too, at that time, which mirrors the situation at Portchester and makes it difficult to draw certain conclusions (James 1984, 168).

Clearly the above questions cannot be answered from the belt-fittings alone, as, with the possible exception of the three strip belt-stiffeners from broad military-type belts, they could have belonged to either military or civil personnel, or, in the case of the sheet metal buckles particularly, perhaps just to ordinary civilians. Furthermore, in the light of the evidence for the actual manufacture of such fittings at Ickham, there is the added complication that some, if not many of them, represent stock goods rather than worn items.[35]

Catalogue of late Roman belt-fittings

All objects listed below are of copper alloy. Dimensions given are across the belt or strap (width), or along it (length).

97   Fixed-plate triangular buckle (SF 88; Area 2). Plain triangular plate with bevelled edges and terminal disc, cast in one piece with D-shaped loop, of which only a stub remains; lobed at either end of loop; three rivets. Length: 54.8+mm; width: 33.7mm.

98   Fixed-plate triangular buckle (SF 153; unstratified). Openwork triangular plate with triangular cut-out, bevelled

---

35. Some time has passed since the submission of my report. For a number of additions to most of the types of fitting discussed the reader is referred especially to Appels and Laycock 2007, and for further debate on the role of the military in society to Gardner 2008.

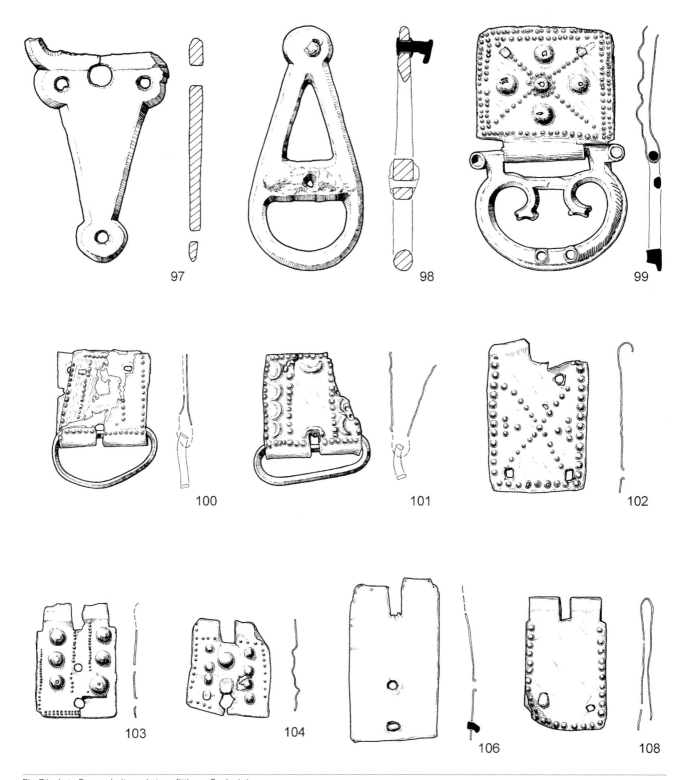

Fig 71. Late Roman belt- and strap-fittings. Scale 1:1.

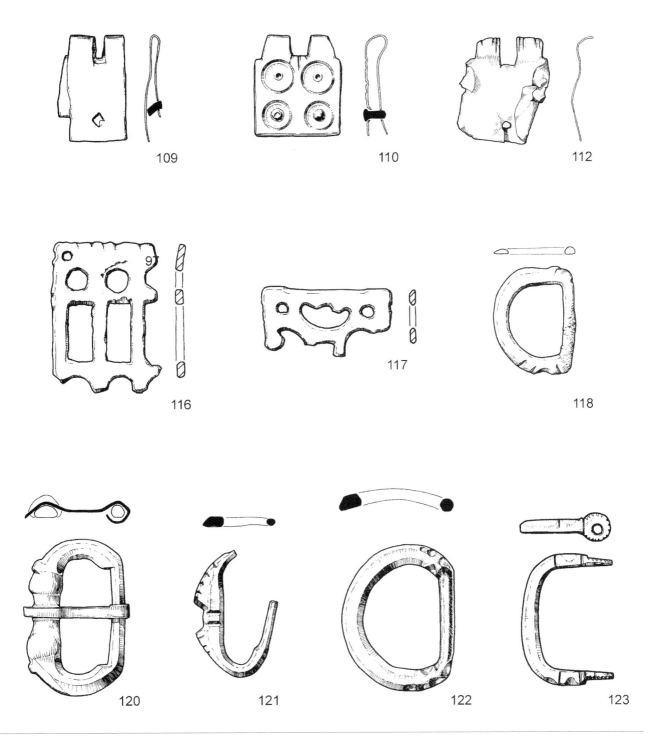

Fig 72. Late Roman belt- and strap-fittings. Scale 1:1.

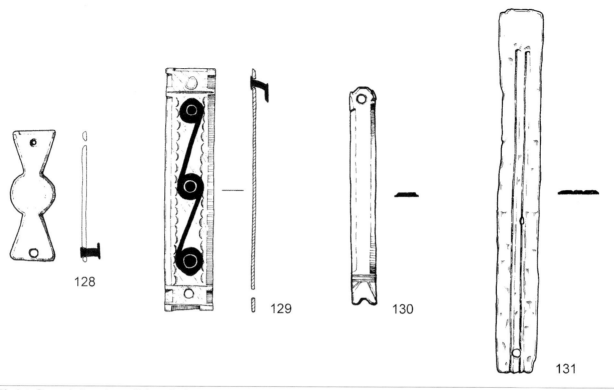

Fig 73. Late Roman belt- and strap-fittings. Scale 1:1.

sides and terminal disc, cast in one piece with D-shaped loop; three rivets, the one in the terminal being over twice as long as the two next to the loop (leather remains, 3.5mm and 1.5mm thick respectively). Length: 61.5mm; width: 28.9mm.

99 Buckle with zoomorphic loop and rectangular plate (SF 428; Area 4). The cast, D-shaped loop has a flanged edge and terminals in the form of small animal heads turned outwards and joined by a cross-bar, beneath which the loop is joined by two struts to a hinge-bar. The raised upper part is diagonally striated around the edge and the back is flat. There is a raised circular setting at each end of the hinge-bar and another pair forming a tongue-rest on top of the loop. One of the bar settings is empty, but the others are filled with a brownish-white material which may be enamel, as there are what appear to be a few burst bubbles on the surface in one case. The sheet-metal plate is folded double round the hinge-bar and fastened with two rivets. The front is decorated with five repoussé bosses within a saltire and borders of smaller ones. Length: 64mm; width: 40.5mm.

100 Buckle with rectangular plate (SF 1174; Area 4). D-loop of cut strip on edge, with ends overlapped. The plate is of

very thin sheet folded double round the loop and the front is decorated with lines of repoussé dots; fixed by two rivets, now missing. Length: 36.4mm; width: 28.2mm.

101 Buckle with rectangular plate (SF 1039; Area 4). Oval loop of cut strip on edge and inclined, with ends overlapped. The plate is of sheet folded double round the loop and the front is decorated with lines of repoussé dots and crescents; fixed by two rivets, now missing. Plate length: 27.6mm; width: 26mm; loop width: 31mm.

102 Rectangular buckle-plate (SF 1840; Context 610, Area 6). Of sheet metal, originally folded double round a loop, but the back is now missing; it is decorated with a saltire, borders and two triangles of repoussé dots; fixed by three rivets, now missing. Length: 40.3mm; width: 26.9mm.

103 Rectangular buckle-plate (SF 1040; Area 4). Type/condition as no 102; it is decorated with rows of repoussé bosses and dots; fixed by two rivets, now missing. Length: 30.4mm; width: 21.1mm.

104 Rectangular buckle-plate (SF 448; Area 4). Type/condition as no 102; it is decorated in repoussé with rows of large and small bosses and borders of dots; fixed by a single rivet, now missing. Length: 24.9mm; width: 22.6mm.

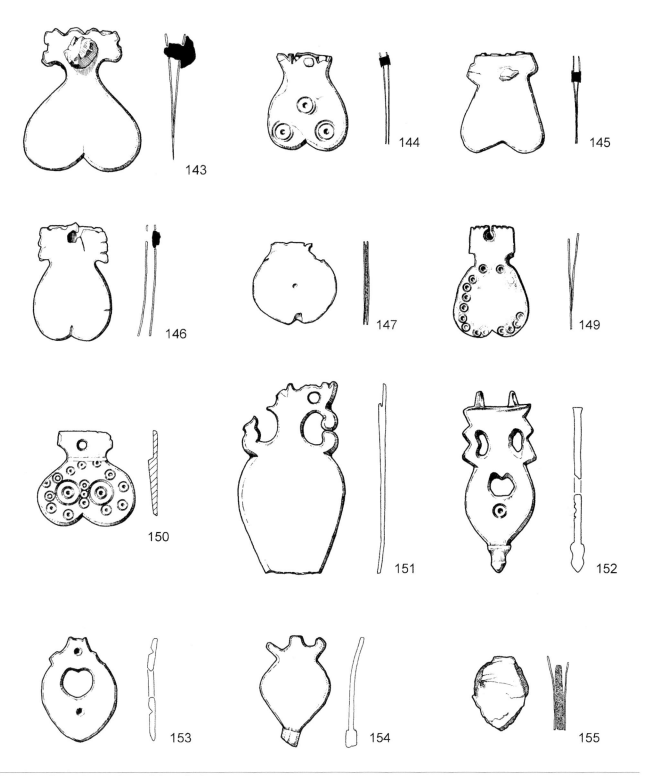

Fig 74. Late Roman belt- and strap-fittings. Scale 1:1.

105   Rectangular buckle-plate (SF 2343; Context 712; Area 7). Type/ condition as no 102, but plain, and front missing; fixed by two rivets, now missing. A third hole in the centre may have been made so that its rough edges would press into and help secure the strap. Length: 30.4mm; width: 22.6mm. *Not illus.*

106   Rectangular buckle-plate (SF 887; Context 105, Area 1; Channel C). Type/condition as no 105; fixed by a single rivet; the second hole may have been to clasp the strap, as on no 105. Length: 43.2mm; width: 23.9mm.

107   Rectangular buckle-plate (SF 2586; Area 14; Mill 1). Type/condition as no 105, and much corroded; fixed by two rivets, now missing. Length: 25.1 +mm; width: 20.9mm. *Not illus.*

108   Rectangular buckle-plate (SF 550; Area 4 extension). Of sheet metal folded double round a loop, now missing; the front is decorated with borders of repoussé dots; fixed by two rivets. Length: 34.9mm; width: 21.3mm.

109   Rectangular buckle-plate (SF 458; Area 4). Type/condition as no 108, but both leaves plain; fixed by a single rivet, now missing. Length: 23.3mm; width: 12.6mm.

110   Rectangular buckle-plate (SF 11; Context 110, Area 1; 'second metalling'). Of thicker, ?cast strip folded double round a loop, now missing. The front is decorated with four ring-and-dots and fixed by two rivets. Length: 27mm; width: 22.8mm; gap between leaves, +/- 35mm.

111   Semicircular buckle-plate (SF 400; Area 4 extension). Of roughly cut plain sheet, the opposite leaf, if once present, now missing; one hinge-lug remains; three rivet-holes, the central one adjoined by an extra fourth one. Length: 30mm; width: 30mm. *Not illus.*

112   Semicircular buckle-plate (SF 477; unstratified). Type/condition as no 111, but damaged and buckled. Both hinge-lugs remain and are decorated with parallel grooves. Length: 27.7mm.

113   Semicircular buckle-plate (SF 533; Area 4 extension). Type/condition as no 111, but both hinge-lugs now missing; three rivets and one rivet-hole in 'corners'. Length: 27.8mm; width: 31.1mm. *Not illus.*

116   Openwork rectangular buckle-plate fragment (SF 1930; unstratified). Cast, with bevelled and scalloped edge; two circular and two rectangular openings remain (originally there would have been a central row of four rectangles side by side, flanked by two rows of four circles each). Length: 35.8+mm; width: 26.4+mm (originally *c* 40mm).

117   Openwork rectangular buckle-plate fragment (SF 1860; Pit 115.2, Area 1). Cast, with bevelled edges; one crescentic opening and two rivet-holes remain. Width: 29.2mm.

118   D-shaped buckle-loop (SF 379; Area 5). Cast, with notched mouldings next to ends of hinge-bar and flat back. Length: 28.3mm; width: 21.8mm.

119   D-shaped buckle-loop (SF 393; Area 4 extension, 'Section 1.3'). Cast, with stylised animal-heads on either side of tongue-rest and flat back. Length: 19.9mm; width: 32.6mm. *Not illus.*

120   D-shaped buckle-loop (SF 200; Area 3). Type as no 119, with bevelled edges and tongue of strip bronze. Length: 25.4mm; width: 41.2mm.

121   D-shaped buckle-loop (SF 1868; Pit 115.2, Area 1). Cast, in the form of two confronted schematic dolphin heads with nicked crests, and flat back. Length: 21.9mm; width: 33.6mm.

122   D-shaped buckle-loop (SF 1076; Area 4). Cast, with very schematic animal heads biting the ends of the hinge-bar and flat back. The loop is bent and has transverse cracks, which suggest it might have been a rejected casting. Length: 30.4mm; width: 38.5mm.

123   Rectangular buckle-loop (SF 1098; unstratified). Cast, with bevelled top edge and flat back. At each end, next to a notched moulding, is a milled disc pierced to receive a hinge-bar, which is now missing. Length: 21.1mm; width: 30.3mm.

124   Oval buckle-loop (SF 1489; Context 104, Area 1). Narrow, of cut strip on edge and inclined, with butted ends and tongue of strip. Length: 10.7mm; width: 21.1mm . *Not illus.*

127   Concave buckle-loop (SF 157; unstratified). Cast, long and narrow, with bevelled, concave front edge. Length: 14.5mm; width: 32.2mm. *Not illus.*

25   Buckle-tongue (SF 1956; Context 712, Area 7). Of strip coiled at one end for hinge. Length: 35.2mm. *Not illus.*

128   Propeller-shaped belt-stiffener (SF 322; Area 4). Cast, plain, with bevelled edges; a rivet in one end and a rivet-hole in the other. Width (of belt): 34mm; thickness of leather: +/- 3mm.

129   Flat belt-stiffener (SF 483; Area 4 extension; 'Pit Section 4'). Of cast strip with faceted ends and bevelled edges; ring-and-dot scroll inlaid with niello between borders of punched crescents; a rivet in one end and a rivet-hole in the other. Width (of belt): 63.6mm.

130   Flat belt-stiffener (SF 337; Context 105, Area 1, Channel C). Of narrow cast strip with bevelled edges and double grooves across one end, which is broken across a rivet-hole; rivet-hole at other end, which appears to be shaped. Width (of belt): 54 +mm; (of strip): 6.4mm.

131   Flat belt-stiffener (SF 1058; Area 4). Crudely made of cast strip with two parallel, lengthwise grooves, a single rivet-hole in one end only, which suggests that the piece is unfinished. Width (of belt): 93.4mm; (of strip) 12.2mm.

132   Lozenge-shaped mount (SF 218; Area 3). Of plain sheet, with two circular terminals pierced for rivets; buckled and broken. Length: *c* 50mm; Width: 24.6mm. *Not illus.*

143 Heart-shaped strap-end (SF 97; Area 3). Of soldered 'double leaf' type, of plain sheet metal, opened at shaped top for strap and secured by an iron rivet. Length: 31.6mm; width: 30.7mm; thickness of leather: +/- 3mm.

144 Heart-shaped strap-end (SF 154; Context 105, Area 1; Channel C). Type similar to no 143, but front decorated with three ring-and-dots; bronze rivet. Length: 25.7mm; width: 21.1mm.

145 Heart-shaped strap-end (SF 370; Area 5). Type similar to no 143, with nicked top edge on front plate only; bronze rivet. Length: 26.1mm; width: 22.1mm; thickness of leather: 1.5mm.

146 Heart-shaped strap-end (SF 1077; Area 4). Type similar to no 143, with scalloped 'ears' at top; bronze rivet. Length: 30.7mm; width: 20.1mm.

147 Heart-shaped strap-end (SF 193; Area 2). Type similar to no 143; damaged and top missing. Length: 21.6+mm; width: 22.2mm.

149 Heart-shaped strap-end (SF 158; unstratified). Type similar to no 143, but with a rectangular strip soldered in place of the usual back-plate and raised behind the notched rectangular top part to accommodate the strap; the front has a border of ring-and-dots beneath the neck. Length: 29.3mm; width: 20.1mm.

150 Heart-shaped strap-end (SF 1919; Pit 115.3, Area 1). Form similar to no 143, but cast in one piece, with nicked split butt for strap and front broken off at top; front decorated with two large ring-and-dots and borders of smaller ones. Length: 25mm: width: 26.2mm.

151 Amphora-shaped strap-end (SF 424; Area 4). Cast, plain, flat and thick with a split butt, zoomorphic 'handles' and pelta-shaped cut-outs on either side of the 'neck'; terminal end broken off. Length 51+mm; width 27.9mm.

152 Amphora-shaped strap-end (SF 281; Area 4). Cast, with two pierced lugs at the top for hinging to strap-chape, dog-tooth 'handles' and pelta-shaped cutouts; a heart-shaped cut-out in centre above a single ring-and-dot and terminal knob. Length: 47.7mm; width: 19.6mm.

153 Amphora-shaped strap-end (SF 369; Area 5). Cast, thick, and broken at base of neck, with a ring-and-dot above and below central heart-shaped cut-out; pointed terminal. Length: 27+mm; width: 19.8mm.

154 Amphora-shaped strap-end (SF 138; 'Surface'). Cast, plain, and broken at base of neck and across terminal knob. Length: 29+mm; width: 18.8mm.

155 Strap-end fragment (SF 1882; Pit 115; Area 1). Pointed oval, of double leaf type, with leather remains in between; top broken off. Length: 20+mm; width 13.6mm; thickness of leather: 3.5mm.

Miscellaneous military fittings

Quita Mould

Buckle frames

An oval loop (164) from a buckle with the terminals set in the opposite plane to the frame, and a possible distorted second example (165), was found in Area 4. They are similar to another from Corbridge (site 49: Bishop and Dore 1989, fig 84, no 141). A similar buckle, described as a handle, was found along with late Antonine pottery in a robber trench of the tower granary at Gadebridge (Wardle 1990, fig 128.257).

Two angular buckle frames each have pierced ring terminals to hold a separate pin bar. The larger, rectangular frame (166) is plain. The square frame (167), decorated with a series of punched dots and grooves on the terminals, was used on a much narrower belt or strap. Angular buckle frames with separate pin bars are unusual but not unknown. Four angular buckles to take straps of varying widths were among the late Roman, mostly fourth-century, sacrificed war-booty from the Roman Iron Age bog-hoard from Nydam, Denmark (Engelhardt 1866, fig IX, no 55, 64–6. I am grateful to Barry Ager for making this known to me). The facet-and-grooved decoration on the Nydam buckles (*ibid*, nos 55, 64 and 66) suggests they have a provincial Roman origin (Barry Ager, pers comm).

Copper alloy rings

Five copper alloy rings with a lozenge-shaped section (168–72) vary in diameter between 17 and 23mm and in arm thickness between 3 and 4mm. Two similar examples found at Colchester (Crummy 1983, 139 and fig 162.4253–4) are thought to come from late Roman belt-fittings.

Other items

A most unusual and at present unparalleled object (**173**) was found in the bottom strata of the Area 4 extension. The cast brass openwork fitting comprises a 'basket-shaped' object of celtic 'trumpet' motifs with a round-sectioned finial. The finial was originally attached to another item, probably a stand, by a central iron shank. The *trompetenmuster* motif was commonly used on a variety of military fittings of second- and third-century date and there can be little doubt that the object is a military object of this date, though its precise use is unknown. It is not certain which way up the

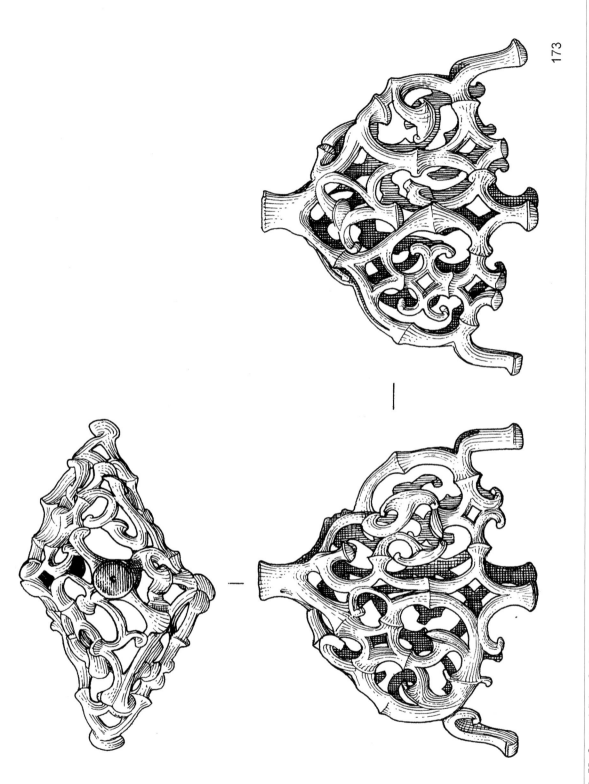

173

Fig 75. Openwork fitting. Scale 1:1.

Objects of personal adornment and dress

Quita Mould

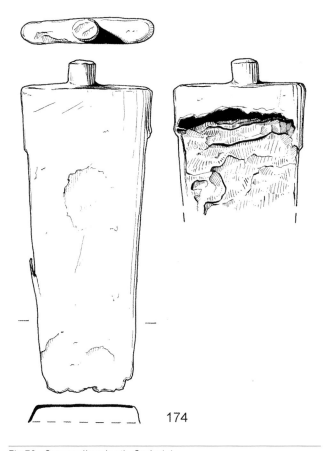

174

Fig 76. Copper alloy sheath. Scale 1:1.

The dress accessories from Ickham form one of the most important elements of the finds assemblage. In part, this is because there are good, representative examples of well-established late Roman objects, most of which have survived in good condition. Although the dating evidence from Ickham itself is relatively poor, it does tend to be consistent and late Roman objects turn up in contexts thought to be of that date. In addition, however, there is also a series of unusual items, of late fourth- and early fifth-century date, some of which are very difficult to parallel elsewhere. Amongst these, the lead alloy pendants deserve particular attention, as items for which some of the best parallels come from the Byzantine world.

The series of late Roman belt-fittings has been placed in the category of military items because they can then be seen in the context of the earlier material of that type from the site. Their position in that category should not be seen as affirmation that they were used exclusively by military personnel, and a discussion text on their function and usage is included in that section (*see* above pp 157–9).

The objects within this category include brooches, earrings, pins, beads, pendants, bracelets and finger rings. There are extensive collections of both pins and bracelets, most examples of which are conventional types, although there are also some rare items. The Celtic pin, in particular, is an unusual find for the south-east of England.

The issue of why such a large collection of jewellery came to be present at this site is deferred to the discussion section below (pp 340–1). Studies presented here relate to typological questions, as well as to the technology of some of the items.

Brooches [36]

Don Mackreth

The collection divides neatly into two parts. One is earlier than the second century, brooches **176–86** (176 *not illus*) and probably **194**, the other is later than the third, brooches **188–92** (192 *not illus*) and **195, 196** and 197. Brooches **184** and **196** may be a little equivocal, but the first is almost

object should be viewed. As illustrated it appears to be a stand, but turned the other way up it might be a decorative finial, possibly a sceptre head. If that way up, its basket-like shape suggests it may have originally contained an internal lining, possibly of glass. If the object had contained a vessel it may have been used as an oil lamp or incense burner, suggesting a possible ritual association.

A tapering copper alloy sheath (**174**) with an integral knob finial and an iron strap within appears to be a handle from a knife or other implement, possibly with a military association.

Fitting of uncertain use

A fragment of U-shaped binding of copper alloy sheet (**175**) is comparable with shield bindings. However, it could have bound the edge of box lid or a number of other items.

36. All the brooches described here are made from a copper alloy, unless otherwise stated.

No	Object	Length mm	Width mm	Context
97	fixed-plate triangular buckle	54.8	33.7	Area 2
98	fixed-plate triangular buckle	61.5	28.9	unstratified
99	buckle with zoomorphic loop and rectangular plate	64.0	40.5	unstratified
100	buckle with rectangular plate	36.4	28.2	Area 4
101	buckle with rectangular plate	27.6	26.0	Area 4
102	rectangular buckle-plate	40.3	26.9	Area 6, 610
103	rectangular buckle-plate	30.4	21.1	Area 4
104	rectangular buckle-plate	24.9	22.6	Area 4
105	rectangular buckle-plate	30.4	22.6	Area 7, 712
106	rectangular buckle-plate	43.2	23.9	Area 1, 105
107	rectangular buckle-plate	25.1	20.9	Area 14
108	rectangular buckle-plate	34.9	21.3	Area 4, extension
109	rectangular strap-end or buckle-plate	23.3	12.6	Area 4
110	rectangular buckle-plate	27.0	228.0	Area 1, 110
111	semicircular buckle-plate	30.0	30.0	Area 4, extension
112	semicircular buckle-plate	27.7		unstratified
113	semicircular buckle-plate	27.8	31.1	Area 4, extension
114	semicircular buckle-plate	30.0	22.0	Area 4
115	semicircular buckle-plate	34.0	21.0	Area 4
116	openwork rectangular buckle-plate	35.8	26.4+	unstratified
117	openwork rectangular buckle-plate		29.2	Area 1, Pit 115.2
118	D-shaped buckle loop	28.3	21.8	Area 5
119	D-shaped buckle loop	19.9	32.6	Area 4, extension
120	D-shaped buckle loop	25.4	41.2	Area 3
121	D-shaped buckle loop	21.9	33.6	Area 1, Pit 115.2
122	D-shaped buckle loop	30.4	38.5	Area 4
123	rectangular buckle-loop	21.1	30.3	unstratified
124	oval buckle-loop	10.7	21.1	Area 1, 104
125	oval buckle-loop	25.0	31.0	Area 1, Channel C
126	D-shaped buckle loop	24.0	30.5	unstratified
127	concave buckle-loop	14.5	32.2	unstratified
128	propeller-shaped belt-stiffener		34.0	Area 4
129	flat belt-stiffener		63.6	Area 4, extension
130	flat belt-stiffener		54+	Area 1, 105
131	flat belt-stiffener		93.4	Area 4
132	lozenge-shaped mount	50.0	24.6	Area 3
133	rectangular strip			Area 1, Channel C
134	rectangular strip			Area 1, Channel C
135	rectangular strip			Area 1, Channel C
136	rectangular strip	55.0	33.0	Area 2
137	rectangular strip			unstratified
138	rectangular strip			Area 4
139	rectangular strip			Area 4
140	rectangular strip			Area 4
141	rectangular strip			Area 4
142	rectangular strip			Area 16, 'ditches'
143	heart-shaped strap-end	31.6	30.7	Area 3
144	heart-shaped strap-end	25.7	21.1	Area 1, 105
145	heart-shaped strap-end	26.1	22.1	Area 5

No	Object	Length mm	Width mm	Context
146	heart-shaped strap-end	30.7	20.1	Area 4
147	heart-shaped strap-end	21.6+	22.2	Area 2
148	heart-shaped strap-end	31.0	22.0	Area 4
149	heart-shaped strap-end	29.3	20.1	unstratified
150	heart-shaped strap-end	25.0	26.2	Area 1, Pit 115.3
151	amphora-shaped strap-end	51+	27.9	Area 4
152	amphora-shaped strap-end	47.7	19.6	Area 4
153	amphora-shaped strap-end	27+	19.8	Area 5
154	amphora-shaped strap-end	29+	18.8	unstratified
155	strap-end fragment	20+	13.6	Area 1, Pit 115
156	strap-end pendant of 'nail-cleaner' type	27.0	13.0	unstratified
157	strap-end pendant of 'nail-cleaner' type	47.0	17.0	408
158	strap-end of 'nail-cleaner' type	29.0	12.0	Area 1, Pit 115
159	strap-fitting	22.5	13.0	unstratified
160	sheet metal scrap			Area 1, Channel C
161	sheet metal scrap	45.0	24.0	Area 4, extension
162	sheet metal scrap			Area 4, extension
163	sheet metal scraps			Area 4
164	oval buckle-loop	36.0	25.5	Area 4
165	oval buckle-loop?	38.0	27.0	Area 4
166	angular buckle	39.0	18.0	Area 4
167	angular buckle	17.0	18.0	Area 4
168	ring			Area 1, base of Channel C
169	ring			Area 4, extension
170	ring			Area 4, extension
171	ring			Area 4, extension
172	ring			Area 5
173	fitting	78.0	40.0	Area 4, extension
174	sheath with iron strap	86.0	35.0	Area 1, Channel C
175	sheet fitting			Area 1. Channel C, west end

Table 19. Late Roman belt- and strap-fittings, and other items.

certainly securely in the early group. Apart from that, there was gap of about 200 years in the occupation of the site. Displacement of items from one group to another could only occur by moving one or more Penannulars to the early period. Yet the available dating for those makes it seem unwise to do this for all three. Ignoring the Penannulars, the first group is normal for the ordinary British population in the Southeast, while the second should only have been worn by either soldiers or members of the civil service whose offices derived from military secondment under the Principate.

However, bringing in the Penannulars dating after the end of all manufacture of purely civilian brooches in Britain, these form a persistent percentage of brooches in use with third- and fourth-century official brooches. It is hard to tell whether they were worn mainly by native Britons as a clear mark that they had nothing to do with official ranks, or whether official ranks wore them for variety.

La Tène I

176 Now denuded of most of its foot and all the spring, the bow which seems to have a circular section remains with the catch-plate and the very start of the foot. *Not illus*.

The high hump to the profile of the bow places this brooch in Hull and Hawkes Type 1A (1987, 72–86), but without the foot the brooch cannot be placed in either of the defined subtypes. The lack of any observable decoration also prevents any further discussion. The overall date range is middle fifth

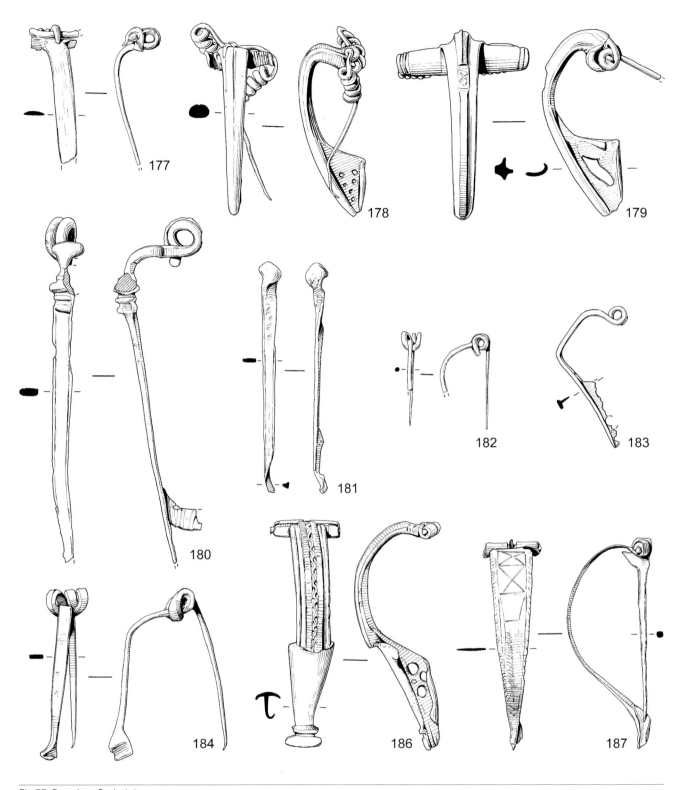

Fig 77. Brooches. Scale 1:1.

to early fourth decade of the first century BC (*ibid*). Several brooches of this type from Kent have been published recently (Parfitt 1999).

Colchesters

177 Half the spring and the lower bow with the catch-plate are missing. The hook is short, scarcely turning to run along the top of the bow. The plain wings are very short. The plain bow has a flat back, a rounded front and betrays little sign of tapering to a pointed foot.

The thin bow of Brooch **177** shows that this is a continental type, although the hook might be thought a little long as most continental brooches of this type have either a thin hook, as here, or a broad plate-like one, both tending to just touch the bow next to the chord. The British dating derives mainly from cemeteries, which contrasts with continental Colchesters which mainly come from occupation sites. The earliest are one from Phase 1 of the King Harry Lane cemetery (Stead and Rigby 1989, 342, fig141, g.270.3) and from Baldock where it was put in the first quarter of the first century AD (Stead and Rigby 1986, 112, fig 42.52). This dating may suit a pair from grave 17 at Swarling and another from grave group 19 (Bushe-Fox 1925, 40, pl12, 2; 42, pl12, 5). Thereafter there is another from the King Harry Lane, phase 2 (Stead and Rigby 1989, 330, fig 133, g.131, 5) and the Boxford cemetery (Owles and Smedley 1967) both of which should be counted as being earlier than the Roman conquest. The dating of the King Harry Lane cemetery is not securely established. The published dating cannot stand as there are no Hod Hills and only one Colchester Derivative. However, taking the earliest date allowed in the report, *c* 15 BC (Stead and Rigby 1989, 83) and moving the phases back in their entirety by fifteen years, the anomaly disappears. Therefore, the present specimen would belong to the earlier first century AD and be not perhaps significantly later than *c* AD 30.

178 Complete, the hook is very long, running over the head and just onto the front of the bow. The profile of the hook is shaped with an extra nick on either side of the tuck into the angle between the chord and the head of the bow, and there is a buried cross-moulding at the end. Each wing has a ridge at its end and a pair of vertical mouldings in the middle. The bow has a high kick in its profile at the top, a flattened hexagonal section and a groove running down the centre. The catch-plate has a flange along the top on both sides, and six circular holes punched through from the inner face. Both sides have scorper-graver decoration along the top and next to the bow.

The overall form and style of decoration show this Colchester as a member of the Kentish group. Decorative traits frequently include features found on Colchester Derivatives which shows that it is late in the Colchester's date range. Dating: Silchester, mid first century with early Flavian pottery (Cotton 1947, 144, fig 7,10); Colchester, AD 54–60 (Niblett 1985, 116, fig 74,11); Canterbury, Flavian to Trajanic, two examples (Bennett *et al* 1982, 169, fig 88,1; Blockley *et al* 1995, 959, fig 402,65); Canterbury, late first to mid/late fourth century (Frere *et al* 1987, 311, fig 118,1); Richborough, not later than AD 85 (Bushe-Fox 1949, 112, pl 27, 26). Any dating from the mid second century or later have been omitted. The picture presented is not particularly strong, save that there is no evidence for any in the earlier part of the *floruit* of the Colchester and those coming from Canterbury and Richborough derive from sites with a very considerable residual content: none should have survived in use much after AD 55/60.

Colchester Derivative

179 The spring is held in the Harlow manner: the axis bar in the coils of the spring passes through the lower of two holes in a plate behind the head of the bow, the chord being housed in the upper one. Each wing is curved to seat the spring and has a pair of grooves at the end. The bow has a flat back and a central face relieved on each side by a concave one. The plate behind the head runs over the top to form a skeuomorph of the Colchester's hook. Immediately below this is an incised X and the central face down the rest of the bow has a groove one each side. The catch-plate has a flange along the top on both sides and there is an ogee piercing with a rounded bottom and a concave top.

A chief variant of the main Harlow Type, the rocked-graver decoration down the central face is replaced by a pair of grooves and here the wings have a little ornament. The flange along the top of the catch-plate and the single opening in the catch-plate show that the dating should be early in the overall type, the X being reminiscent of that on the only Colchester Derivative from a context equivalent to those under the flood silts at Skeleton Green (Partridge 1981, 137, fig 69, 25) and which can, therefore, be said to be pre-conquest. It should be noted that the only Colchester Derivative from the King Harry Lane cemetery was also of this family, it came from a Phase 3 grave (Stead and Rigby 1989, 354, fig 154, g316.4). The dating for those conforming to the present example by having only one piercing in the catch-plate is: *Verulamium*, AD 49–60 (Frere 1972, 114, fig 29, 6); Baldock, AD 50–70 (Stead and Rigby 1986, 112, fig 44, 79); Harlow, temple, before AD 80 (France and Gobel 1985, 78, fig 40, 57); Chichester, late first century? and second century? (Down

1989, 185, fig 26.1, 7). The limited evidence points to a range running from the middle of the first century to AD 75/80 at most.

Late La Tène

180　The integral spring had four coils and an internal chord. The head of the bow, badly wasted by corrosion, had been a flattened trumpet wide enough for the spring to butt against. Beneath the sharp bend on the head of the bow are three mouldings. The top two ran all the way around, the upper being the larger. The third moulding is a small projection on the front face alone. The rest of the bow has a flat front face with a groove down each side and tapers to the foot which is now missing, along with most of the catch-plate. This had obviously been pierced and the top of the one partially surviving opening is curved.

Belonging to a group of brooches discussed by Stead (1976), the chief features, apart from its great size, are the incipient trumpet head, the mouldings on the bow and indications of a fretted catch-plate. Unfortunately, none of the examples collected by the writer has a date. The incipient trumpet head is later first century BC and runs on into the earlier first century AD. The small projecting moulding under the two more prominent ones points towards the Birdlip and so should have the same date range as the head. The fretting in the catch-plate had curved bars and these do not really run into the first century AD. Finally, such large brooches are not really of the first century AD either. The best assessment of date is that the brooch belongs to the second half of the first century BC.

181　A brooch of the same type as the previous one with all the head missing, the blob of corrosion possibly masks traces of mouldings. The bow has a flat back. The front has a ridge down each side and an arris down the middle. The catch-plate has been reduced to a stub.

Although the head is missing, there would have been a three or four coil spring probably with an internal chord. The very straight profile with the hint of a sharp bend at the top suggests that this brooch owes something to Continent brooches of the latter part of the first century BC and the first two decades of the first AD. The lack of any sign of fretting or of any piercing in the remains of the catch-plate possibly indicates the later part of this range and a brooch of this size should not date significantly after *c* AD 25/35.

182　Iron. The integral spring has three coils and an internal chord. The bow has the same diameter as the wire forming the spring and is well curved as far as it survives.

This is a *Drahtfibel* and iron ones are not well dated. One

from Skeleton Green belongs to the period 10 BC to AD 20 (Partridge 1981, 132, fig 66, 1), and another from Great Oakley, Northants, came from a context dated to the late first to near the end of the second century (Meadows 1992, 93, not illustrated). This example is likely to be earlier than later in the very roughly indicated range.

183　The remains of the integral spring show that it had had three or four coils probably with an internal chord. The bow has a thin rectangular section and had had a blunted foot. The position of the trace of a circular hole in the catch-plate suggests that there had been a series of these.

The form is distorted and the sign derived from the catch-plate, which was obviously long in proportion to its width, is that the profile of the bow had been more or less upright like that of Brooch **181**. The circular holes in the remnants of the catch-plate are not typical of a standard Nauheim Derivative and should not be expected much after *c* 25/30, nor far back into the first century BC on this kind of brooch.

184　The integral spring has three coils and an internal chord. The whole brooch had been forged, possibly from bar and not from rolled or folded sheet. The bow has a thin rectangular section and the catch-plate is very short and a little rudimentary.

If this brooch had had four coils, the conclusion would have been that it was probably first century AD, but possibly not after *c* AD 80. However, when it comes to three-coil copper alloy brooches the dating is overwhelmingly after AD 100, and there is a reasonably strong presence right through the fourth century.

Alésia-Hod Hill sequence

The axis bars of the hinged pins are housed in the rolled over heads of the bows.

185　All the original surface has gone. The upper bow has a panel of two curved faces, divided by a narrow vertical flute, separated from a bordering ridge on each side by another flute. Above and below is a pair of narrow cross-mouldings. On each side was a wing the surviving one of which has a knob at the end rising from a pair of ridges. The lower bow has a small panel at the top and a pair of cross-mouldings under that. The foot is bent and may have only have had a simple elongated knob. *Not illus.*

The Hod Hill arrived fully developed from the Continent at the time of the conquest; none has been shown convincingly to have arrived before then. The type was immensely popular and remained in common usage until *c* AD 70/75, after which time only one major strand carried on to exercise great influence on a school of second-century designs. This is not an example of that element and may be counted as being earlier than 65/70.

186   Carefully finished, the brooch is sturdy and large. The rolled-over head is tucked behind a beaded cross-ridge. The upper bow has a ridge down each side and a central raised section with a finely beaded edge and a sunken ridge distorted by a punch into a wavy line. The lower bow has a wide top and tapers to a two-part foot-knob whose elements are exaggerately elongated. The front of the lower bow seems to have been heavily worn: there is evidence for a punched-dot design which has been completely lost over most of the surface.

The dating shows a good run up to AD 75/80 and just a hint that it might run on a little. Looking at the brooch itself, the great care taken over its finish probably points to a date after 55/60 at least: the early run of brooches seldom show much care over the cast detail, even if given a silvery finish.

Durotrigan

187   The axis bar of the hinged pin itself is a pin whose head butts the roll-over at one end, the point being bent to secure the whole. The sheet bow has a waist at the head and was given shoulders. The incised decoration on the front is made up of diagonal marks running away from a line down each side. There are two panels at the top also with diagonal lines, a line beneath these curving in slightly with a small empty panel at the top and a herringbone beneath. The bottom of the bow is crudely shaped like that of an Aucissa and there may be the remains of a peg for a separately made foot-knob. The catch-plate is very narrow.

A member of the Durotrigan family owing a lot to the Alésia (Duval 1974), but this falls short of actually being one of those as it has a rolled-over head and there is no sign in the catch-plate of the transverse rod carrying knobs, a *sine qua non*. However, the elaborate decoration down the front of the characteristically thin, triangular-shaped bow is reminiscent. Although the Durotrigan family, almost to a fault, has the rolled-under head of the Alésia, the whole appearance, including the feathered ornament, more strongly recalls that family than any other. The overall decorative effect owes much to Colchester Derivatives found in the deep south-west of England (eg Exeter, Holbrook and Bidwell 1991, 232–3, fig 100, 5, 7; Nor'Nour, Dudley 1967, 38, fig 16, 83). The bias of the dating for the family is before the later first century AD, and there is no reason not to suppose that that does not apply here.

Crossbows

All have or had hinged pins.

188   Each wing has a circular section and a reel at the end. On the head is a knob on a pedestal. The bow has a hexagonal section much deeper than wide. The lower part of the bow and foot are missing.

The loss of the foot would have been serious had it not been for the form of the head and the bow section. Neither belongs to the fully developed Crossbow series. The collections from Saalburg and Zugmantel (Böhme 1972) show that the undeveloped knob on the head (*ibid*, taf 17,727) and the section of the bow (*ibid,* taf 19, 800) were to be found before 260, the terminal date of both forts (*ibid*, 9–10). While this only provides a slight indication, the likely date range runs from the middle to the end of the third century.

189   The lower bow and foot only survive, the section of the bow is hexagonal but the rear chamfers are small. The bottom of the bow has a stop to the front chamfers with a concave chamfer between that and the top of the foot. The foot has a rounded back, the front being flat with a cross-groove at the top and two pairs below separated from each other by a concave flute on each side. The slot in the foot for the pin is on the right.

The foot has a parallel in a brooch from Winchester (excavations M Biddle, unpublished) and both are reflected in a silver one from Hethersett, Norfolk (private collection), and one from Wroxeter (Rowley's House Museum, Shrewsbury, X.16). None is usefully dated and all might be related to Keller's (1971) *Typ* 1. Dating is unfortunately absent and the style of the heads of those which have them suggests a range from the later third century into the fourth.

190   Again the lower bow and foot only, the bow has a triangular section with the apex cut back to form a very narrow central face. The sloped sides are stopped near the top of the foot so that the flat face of that runs up the bow. The foot has a small projecting moulding across the bottom and, under the corrosion, can be seen three narrow chamfers on each side. There may even be two pairs on the lower part of the bow, but this is not certain. The slot for the pin is on the right.

A distinctive feature of the developing Crossbow series is the moulded decoration at the base of the bow. This is commonly in the earlier part of the series chamfered, but was succeeded by a projecting moulding either in the casting itself or applied commonly in the form of wire wound round the bow. Neither is present here where, in effect, the face of the foot runs up the lower part of the bow. Normally, when discussing the Crossbow before the advent of the fully developed forms (eg Brooch 192), the collection of brooches from Saalburg and

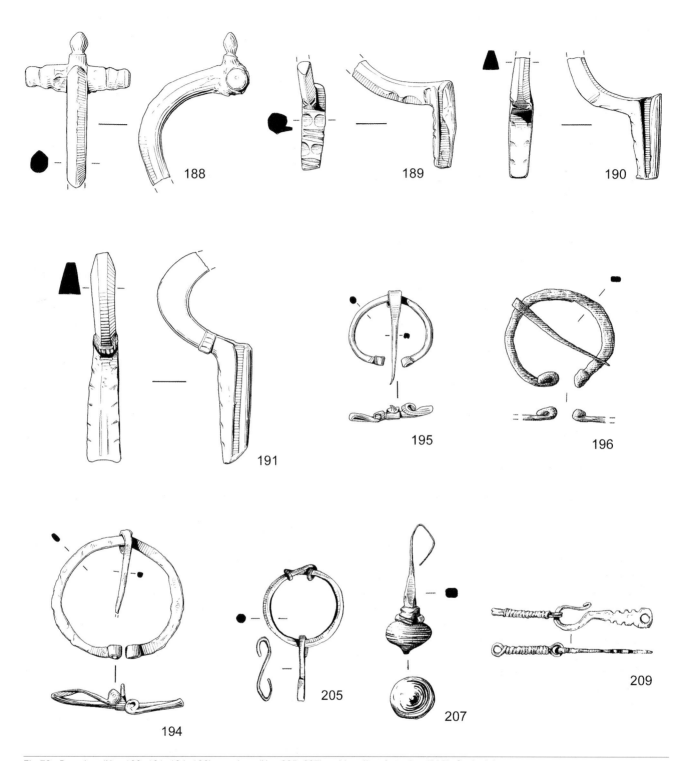

Fig 78. Brooches (Nos 188–191, 194–196), ear-rings (Nos 205–207) and jewellery fastening (209). Scale 1:1.

Zugmantel, where the earlier stages of the Crossbow make their appearance, is examined. The advantage of doing this is neither site really survived the troubles of 260 (Böhme 1972, 9–10) and so to a large measure what is not there is later. The treatment of the foot and lower bow as effectively one face is absent, but this was never a common feature and its absence may have been chance. The loss of the head is unfortunate as it would have been how that matched into the sequence as demonstrated at these two forts on the German *limes* which would have also have helped to place this brooch. As it is, the thin section of the bow should place the brooch into the Crossbow series before the arrival of the fully blown late series. A date between 260 and the end of the third century may be suggested.

191 The head is lost. The bow is deep and narrow and its section is as that of the last brooch. The bow near the bottom has a ridge on the sides and front face, the bridge from that to the foot has a rounded front. The foot tapers outwards towards the bottom, has a flat front face and five pairs of chamfers like those of Brooch **188**, and a pair of grooves down the middle. The slot for the pin is on the right.

Although the head is lost, the design of the foot is paralleled on others which may be loosely ascribed to Keller's (1971) *Typ* 4 to which he gives a range of 350–80. There is no British dating. The slot in the catch-plate for the pin may be on either the left or the right-hand side and it seems that only as the fourth century advances that the slot on the left appears.

192 Each wing ends in a large onion-shaped knob, and there is another on the head of the bow. Each wing has chamfers above and below with a narrow rounded front ending in a diagonally cross-cut moulding next to the knob. The bow has the same section as those of the previous two. The foot is also of the same form as that of the last, but with a more elaborate design: a concave chamfer on each side at the top, a straight one below that with diagonal ends the end of the foot has a mixture of nicks and small concave flutes. Dot-and-circle motifs occur in pairs, one in the middle of the long chamfers and two on the bottom section. The slot for the pin is on the left. *Not illus.*

This is the only Ickham Crossbow to be complete, apart from the pin. The slot for the pin is on the left and this is a more frequent feature in the group which has basically the same design of foot. British dating is again not available. The dating may not be much different from that suggested for Brooch **191**.

Plate

193 The pin was hinged. The main part is a rectangular plate set lozenge-wise. The centre is recessed for enamel, now missing, and on each side is a projection consisting of a semicircle rising from a straight line. Top and bottom is a moulded projection which is set slightly back from the main face and made up of a wide flute and ending in a bead under a cross-moulding. *Not illus.*

One of many designs produced possibly by more than one factory. The present example has no British dating and the indications on the Continent are only for a general second-century one. What is of note, however, is that it and its close relatives occur in Britain in the area south of a line drawn from the Wash to the mid-Severn and east of that river valley.

Penannulars

194 The brooch was forged from folded or rolled sheet. The ring has a circular section and each terminal was hammered flat and each terminal coiled. The pin is straight.

This is a common form, the terminals being coiled more or less so that at the least they lie flat on the ring, and at the most so that there are at least two complete coils. The dating is: West Stow, Suffolk early to mid first century (West 1990, 71, fig 166); Weekley, Northants, AD 25 to mid first century (Jackson and Dix 1987, M77, fig 23, 17); Maiden Castle, AD 25–70 (Wheeler 1943, 264, fig 86, 6); Colchester, AD 49–61 (Hawkes and Hull 1947, 326, fig 59, 2); Hod Hill, earlier than AD 50 (Brailsford 1962, 12, fig 11, E8); Poundbury, Dorchester, AD 70/80–100/110 (Sparey-Green 1987, 97, fig 67, 21); Gussage All Saints, before AD 75 (Wainwright 1979, 112, fig 86, 3044); Fishbourne, before AD 75 (Cunliffe 1971, 107, fig 40, 44); Chichester, Flavian to early second century (Down 1978, 287, fig10.28, 57); Castleford, AD 100–80? (Cool and Philo 1998); Scole, Norfolk, AD 110–60 (Rogerson 1977, 134, fig 55,12); Thetford, second century to mid third (Gregory 1991, 128, fig 115, 42); Rudston, (Stead 1980, 95, fig 62, 20); Peterborough, Stanground, late second to early third century (Dannell *et al* 1993, 66, fig 13, 1); Wakerley, third century (Jackson and Ambrose 1978, 220, fig 57, 7); Baldock, third century (Stead and Rigby 1986, 122, fig 49, 154); Ilchester, late third and early fourth century (Leach 1982, 247, fig 117, 27); Peterborough, Werrington, fourth century (Mackreth 1988, 92, fig 20, 4); Nettleton, Wiltshire, dated by coins to mid fourth century (Wedlake 1982, 133, fig 55, 78), Chichester, mid fourth century (Down 1981, 259, fig 10.2, 23); Canterbury, AD 375 to early fifth century (Blockley *et al* 1995, 981, fig 410, 121). The following are from Anglo-Saxon burials: Wakerley, (Jackson and Ambrose 1978, 228, fig 65.1); Mildenhall, Suffolk, two examples (White 1988, 11, fig 4, 2, 3); Barrington, Cambridgeshire (*ibid*, 11, fig 2,

5); Droxford, Hampshire (*ibid*, 10, fig 3, 1); Willoughby on the Wolds, Nottingham (Kinsley 1993, 22, fig 43, 14.2).

There is a reasonable spread of dates through the whole Roman period. Those from Anglo-Saxon burials were not necessarily scavenged from abandoned Roman sites; the Anglo-Saxons themselves used penannular brooches and had what may be called a reflux Iron Age culture. The point is brought out in the number of such brooches recovered from the Morning Thorpe cemetery in Norfolk (Green *et al* 1987, 165–6): too many were of iron for them to be items long lost on Roman sites. To return to the dating, those from third- to early/mid fourth-century contexts come from sites which had earlier occupation and should perhaps be regarded as residual. The coiling on the present specimen seems to be too great for it to be anything other than an early one.

195   The same as the last only the terminals are bent so that the straight end touches the ring. The pin was similarly made, has a simple wrap-round and is straight.

In this case, there is no real coil and a different set of criteria come into play. The dating is: Chichester, probably mid first century (Down 1978, 287, fig 10.28, 57); Canterbury AD 70/80 to 300/320 (Blockley *et al* 1995, 982, fig 410, 124); Portchester, AD 340–60 (Cunliffe 1975, 199, fig 109, 7); *Verulamium*, AD 365–80 (Frere 1984, 31, fig 9, 56). The following all come from Anglo-Saxon cemeteries: Barrington, Cambridgeshire (White 1988, 10, fig 2, 4); Kingsworthy, Hampshire (*ibid*, 15, fig 6, 9); Linton Heath, Cambridegeshire (*ibid*, 15, fig 6, 8); Mildenhall, Suffolk (*ibid*, 11, fig 3, 6); Morning Thorpe, Norfolk (Green *et al* 1987, fig 427, E); Sleaford, Lincolnshire (White 1988, 12, fig 4, 6); Willoughby on the Wolds, Nottingham, two examples (Kinsley 1993, 22, fig 13, NP7; fig 13, 66).

The result is that this variety should perhaps be seen as being late Roman, or even later, if one has to accept that there are different cultural allegiances at play here. Whatever may be the case when it comes to those from Anglo-Saxon cemeteries, the dating allows none to have been earlier than the early fourth century.

196   Iron. The section of the ring is a narrow rectangle and each terminal is of the same form as those of the last brooch. The pin is straight.

A distinction has been made in the section of the ring and for the material, although the terminals are as those of the last. The dating is: two from Phase 1 of the King Harry Lane cemetery (Stead and Rigby 1989, 310, fig 114, g146.3; 370, fig 168, g384.7); two more from Phase 3 graves (*ibid*, 318, fig 120, g178.4; 390, fig 180, g460.5) and one from the same site but unphased, which should still mean that it is earlier than *c* AD 60 (*ibid*, 358, fig 156, g327.2; *see* comment on dating under Brooch **177**); Weekley, Northamptonshire, AD 25 to mid first

century (Jackson and Dix 1987, M79, fig 24, 25); Lullingstone, fourth century (Meates 1987, 102, fig 47, 277); Barnsley, Gloucester, later than AD 350 (Webster 1981, 144, fig 37, 162). The following come from Anglo-Saxon cemeteries: Morning Thorpe, five examples (Green *et al* 1987, fig 378k; fig 394f; fig 399, 38c; fig 402a; fig 440, a); Sewerby, Yorkshire (Hirst 1985, 57, fig 38, 2, 3); Mildenhall, Suffolk (White 1988, 11, fig 4,1); Great Chesterford, two examples (*ibid*, 11, fig 3, 4, 5). One from an Anglo-Saxon grave at Mucking was specifically given an early fifth-century date (*ibid*, 13, fig 5, 10).

These brooches fall into two clear groups: those basically of the mid first century or earlier, and those which are fourth century or later. The number from Anglo-Saxon burials, being specifically of iron, cannot have been recovered from long abandoned Roman sites. The Introduction will have made it clear that this brooch could have come from occupation on this site at either of these periods.

197   The section of the ring is the same as the last, but with a line of nicks around the outer edge. *Not illus.*

The available dating is: Colchester, AD 49–61 (Hawkes and Hull 1947, 326, fig 59, 3); Canterbury, AD 70/80–100/110 (Blockley *et al* 1995, 981); Baldock, late third century (Stead and Rigby 1986, 122, fig 49, 153); one from Lydney and another from Baldock are fourth century (Wheeler and Wheeler 1932, 79, fig 14, 29; Stead and Rigby 1986, 122, fig 49, 155); Towcester, AD 350–75/400 (Brown *et al* 1983, 105, fig 35, 4); Chichester, late fourth century (Down 1978, 305, fig 10.39, 127); Canterbury, AD 375 to early fifth century (Blockley *et al* 1995, 981, fig 410, 123); *Verulamium*, fifth century (Frere 1984, 31, fig 9, 55). The following are from Anglo-Saxon cemeteries: Fairford (White 1988, 12, fig 4, 9); Ferring, Sussex, two examples (*ibid*, 13, fig 5, 2, 3); Fimber, Yorkshire (*ibid*, 12, fig 4, 10); Girton, a pair (*ibid,* 13, fig 5, 1); Kenninghall, Norfolk (*ibid*, 13, fig 5, 6); Long Wittenham, a pair (*ibid*, 13, fig 5, 9); Morning Thorpe (Green *et al* 1987, fig 454, 409k); Nassington, a pair and a single one (White 1988, 14, fig 6, 1; 13, fig 5, 9); Ruskington (*ibid*, 14, fig 6, 3).

The emphasis is again on the late Roman and Anglo-Saxon periods and the chances that the present specimen may be an early example is perhaps less likely than might be the case for Brooch **195**. One may note the pairs in the Anglo-Saxon cemeteries, but a note of caution is needed: the decoration is not uniformly like that of the present brooch.

Fragments

198   The pin and two coils and half the chord from a brooch belonging to the general Nauheim and *Drahtfibel* families.

As it is preserved, the chord might be external, but there is no proof that this is really the case. *Not illus.*

199 Iron. Part of the pin and two and a bit coils from a spring. There are too many coils for the brooch to be other than from the Colchester and its progeny. *Not illus.*

200 The pin from a hinged-pin brooch. *Not illus.*

201 Hinged pin. *Not illus.*

No	Material	Type	Context
176	copper alloy	La Tène I	Ickham B
177	copper alloy	Colchester	Area 1, 105
178	copper alloy	Kentish Colchester	Area 4, 408
179	copper alloy	Colchester Derivative	Area 7, 712
180	copper alloy	Late La Tène	west end of gravel pit
181	copper alloy	Late La Tène	Area 10, 1006
182	iron	Drahtfibel	Area 10, 1002
183	copper alloy	Late La Tène	Area 4, extension, section 1
184	copper alloy	Late La Tène	Area 10, 1001
185	copper alloy	Alésia-Hod Hill	unstratified
186	copper alloy	Alésia-Hod Hill	Area 4, extension
187	copper alloy	Durotrigian	Area 1,105
188	copper alloy	Crossbow	unstratified
189	copper alloy	Crossbow	Area 1, 120.2
190	copper alloy	Crossbow	Area 14, unstratified
191	copper alloy	Crossbow	unstratified
192	copper alloy	Crossbow	unstratified
193	copper alloy	Plate	unstratified
194	copper alloy	Penannular	Area 1, Channel C
195	copper alloy	Penannular	Area 4, extension, section 1, layer 3
196	iron	Penannular	Area 5, unstratified
197	copper alloy	Penannular	unstratified
198	copper alloy	Nauheim/Drahtfibel	Area 1, Channel C
199	iron	Colchester or Colchester Derivative	Area 4, unstratified
200	copper alloy	Pin only	Area 1, 121
201	copper alloy	Pin only	Area 10, 1004

Table 20. Roman brooches.

Ear-rings

A maximum of seven possible ear-rings were found at Ickham. An ear-ring of rectangular-sectioned wire with overlapping, slightly flattened and expanded terminals (202) came from 115/1. A larger example of round-sectioned wire (203) came from Area 3. They are both of Allason-Jones type 1 (1989, 2–3), a type found throughout the Roman period.

A hooked length of fine copper alloy wire (204), pointed at each end with series of incised transverse ridges decorating the outer face, appears to be a mis-shapen ear-ring of type 2a/b (Allason-Jones 1989, 3); being straight it appears to be partly formed into the circular shape of the ear-ring, less likely it could have been straightened after removal from the ear. It is comparable with an example from a fourth-century context from Portchester (*ibid,* fig 4, 406).

A complete annular wire ring with adjustable fastening articulating with an S-shaped link (**205**) is of type 3 (Allason-Jones 1989, 5–6). This ear-ring type has a very long history; the majority of Roman examples date to the third century.

A fragment of a spirally twisted ear-ring (206) of type 4 (*ibid,* 6–7), a fourth-century type, was found at the east end of Channel C.

A fine drop ear-ring with an 'onion-shaped' terminal (**207**) was found at the west end of Mill 2. This does not appear to be a usual Roman form and parallels are not obvious. In addition, a fine hook with a scrolled terminal (208) used to suspend a bead or other small pendant, may come from an ear-ring or another item of jewellery.

No	Material	Diameter mm	Length mm	Context
202	copper alloy	24		Area 1, Pit 115.1
203	copper alloy	34		Area 3
204	copper alloy		40	unstratified
205	copper alloy	21	link: 17	Area 3
206	copper alloy		32	Area 1, base of Channel C, east end
207	copper alloy		34	Area 1, Channel C, west end
208	copper alloy			unstratified

Table 21. Ear-rings.

Miscellaneous jewellery

A fastening (**209**) from Area 4 is of a type found on late Roman necklaces, such as the examples from the southern extra-mural area of Alcester, from early to mid fourth-century contexts (Lloyd Morgan 1994, 178–9, fig 84 nos 35 and 36 and comparanda). The denticulated sides are comparable to the fastening on a bead necklace from a grave dated between AD 350–80 at Lankhills (Clarke 1979, Grave 336, no 363).

Lengths of chain comprising fine S-shaped links of copper alloy wire were found, the individual links ranging in length from 16–32mm. The finer is likely to come from jewellery, the larger from suspension chain for scale pans or other items.

No	Material and type	Context
209	copper alloy, fastening	Area 4
210	copper alloy, chain	Area 14
211	copper alloy, chain	'Site 1 road surface at west'
212	copper alloy, links	Area 1, Channel C
213	copper alloy, links	Area 4, extension
214	copper alloy, links	Area 1, Pit 115.1

Table 22. Chain fragments.

Pins

Quita Mould, Ian Riddler, Adrian Tribe and Susan Youngs

Pins of metal, principally copper alloy, bone and antler were recovered from Ickham, most examples being of late Roman date, although several of the metal examples are early Roman. Analysis of the metal content of the pins was carried out by Adrian Tribe. The most spectacular example within the assemblage is undoubtedly the large dress pin, which is described here by Susan Youngs.

Metal hair pins

Eight different types could be recognised within the thirty-two metal hair pins, although the majority had either spherical or faceted cuboid heads, the two predominant types in late Roman Britain. A small number of pins dating to the earlier Roman period were also recovered. The pins were found predominantly in Area 4 and Channel C. The small number from Area 10 is confined to types 1 and 3. A further fourteen broken pin stems were also recovered.

No pins of jet or shale were found. Usually, where hair pins are recovered those made of bone outnumber those of metal; however, this was not the case at Ickham. Whilst this discrepancy may be the result of collection bias resulting from the use of metal detectors for retrieval, it could be the case that the metal pins were being deliberately deposited or collected for scrap for melting down and re-use of the metal. Each of the eight types of metal pin is described in turn here.

Type 1

A pin which has a very small head with bead-and-reel decoration (**215**) belongs to Cool's (1990a, 154) group 3 sub group A, dated to the first to second century. Our example, measuring slightly over 100mm, supports this early Roman date.

Type 2

A silver pin with a conical head with lattice decoration and small finial knop (**216**), found on the surface, is difficult to parallel in metal. The cross-hatched lattice decoration is a common decorative device occurring on several types of pin (Cool 1990a, groups 4, 5, 9, 11, 14, 22 and 23) all of which have examples from contexts of second-century date. Given this and the length of the pin (81mm) a second-century date (*ibid,* 173) is suggested for the Ickham example.

Type 3

Two simple pins (**217,** 218) of leaded bronze have no heads, just a pointed top to the shaft, and belong to Cool's group 24 (1990a, 170 and fig 12.7). This simple pin form could have been in use throughout the Roman period but is most likely to be a second-century type. The complete Ickham example measures over 100mm in length supporting the earlier Roman date suggested (*ibid,* 173). The type occurs in both metal and bone, and may have been used for other purposes than as a hair ornament.

Type 4

Fourteen pins have spherical heads, including one with a head made of green glass. They are of Cool's group 1 (1990a, 151), a type found across southern Britain and in use throughout the Roman period, but most popular in the later period. Eleven examples are complete and only one example measures over 80mm in length, suggesting they belong to the later Roman period, as does the pin with the spherical green glass head (**220**) from Channel C. Glass-headed pins are of fourth-century date, well-dated examples coming from the later half of the century (*ibid,* group 16, 165); this pin can be paralleled by another found in a grave dated AD 370–90 at Lankhills (Clarke 1979, 316 Grave 351, no 397). Examples of Cool's sub-group A (onion-shaped) and C (spherical-headed) were found but not sub-group B (with a groove at the neck) which appears to have a restricted distribution in the west country (Cool 1990a, 151). Differential corrosion

No	Material	Type	Length mm	Head diameter mm	Context
215	copper alloy	1	100		Area 10, 1001
216	silver	2	81		unstratified
217	copper alloy	3	78+	4	Area 10, 1004
218	copper alloy	3	109	3.5	Area 10, 1005
219	copper alloy	4	74	7	Area 1, Channel C
220	copper alloy/glass	4	53	5	Area 1, Channel C
221	copper alloy	4	82	10	Area 1, Channel C
222	copper alloy	4	64	7	Area 2
223	copper alloy	4	42	6	Area 4
224	copper alloy	4	44+	6	Area 4
225	copper alloy	4	66	6.5	Area 4
226	copper alloy	4	72	8	Area 4
227	copper alloy	4	64	7	Area 4
228	copper alloy	4	71	6+	Area 4
229	copper alloy	4	54	5.5	Area 4, extension
230	copper alloy	4	80		Area 3, 302
231	copper alloy	4	63	9	unstratified
232	copper alloy	4		11	unstratified
233	copper alloy	5	64	5.5 x 7	Area 1, Channel C, west
234	copper alloy	5	46	4 x 2	Area 1, Channel C
235	copper alloy	5	30+	6 x 6	Area 1, Channel C
236	copper alloy	5	70	5 x 5	Area 4
237	silver	5	65	4 x 4	Area 4
238	copper alloy	5	63	3 x 3	Area 4
239	silver	5	71	6 x 4	Area 4
240	copper alloy	5	73	5 x 4	Area 4, extension
241	copper alloy	5	65	5 x 5	Area 4, extension, shrine
242	copper alloy/glass	5	70	bead length: 11	Area 4
243	copper alloy	6	19	7 x 7	unstratified
244	copper alloy/tin	7	60		Area 5
245	copper alloy	8	65	9 x 4.5	Area 4
246	copper alloy	8	59	18 x 9	Area 1, Channel C
247	copper alloy		364	5	Area 4, base of Channel C

Table 23. Metal hair pins.

showed that many of the metal pins had heads and shanks of differing composition and this was confirmed by analysis. Those with 'onion'-shaped heads of Cool's sub-group A were found to be made of brass. Unusually, eight of the other pins were found to have separate heads of pewter attached to shanks of bronze, principally of leaded bronze, as noted below in Table 24 (p 186). This combination of a pewter head on a copper alloy shank has not been recorded from other Roman pin assemblages to date. It is tempting to see these pins as a product of local manufacture, in the light of the evidence for pewter-working on site.

One pin (**246**) from Channel C, thought to have a heavily-corroded, spherical head was found during investigative conservation to have a head in the form of a bird modelled in the round. This should perhaps be best considered along with the axe-headed pin and accordingly, it has been placed in Type 8. It accords with Cool's group 18B (Cool 1990a, 168), another late Roman form.

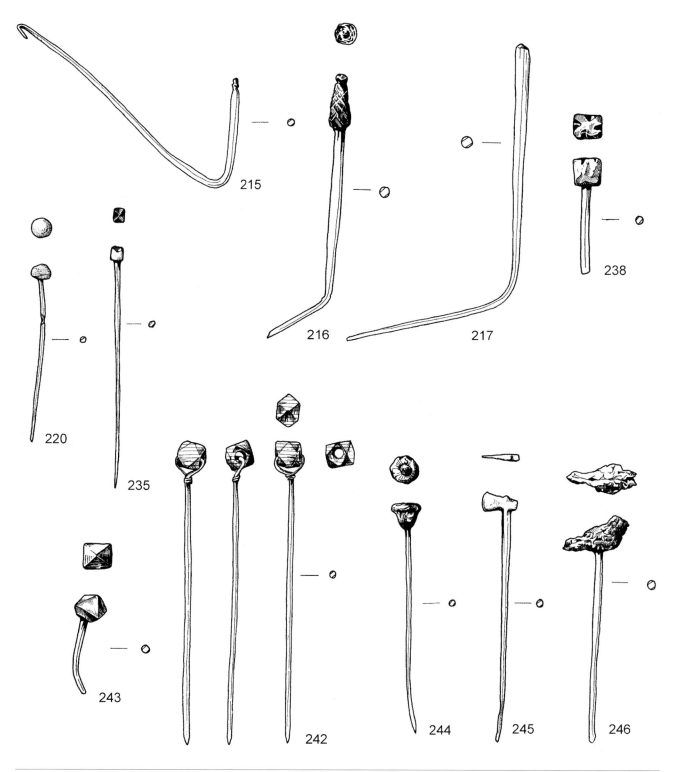

Fig 79. Metal hair pins. Scale 1:1.

Type 5

Seven pins with faceted, cuboid heads of varying size are a late Roman type (Cool 1990a, 164) found in late third- and fourth-century contexts in southern Britain. A further two pins (**235** and **238**) are in the same decorative tradition with nicks taken from the cuboid head, and are likely to be of similar date. These pins were found to have been made in a variety of metals: silver, brass and leaded bronze. Two pins from Channel C (233–4) had pewter heads attached to shanks of leaded bronze. Again, the use of such a hitherto unusual combination of metals may suggest local production for these items.

A pin with a blue faceted bead head (**242**) held by a loop of wire to the stem was found in Area 4. Along with the glass spherical-headed pin, it is a late fourth-century type (Cool 1990a, 165 group 16); it can be paralleled by a pin in a grave dated AD 350–70 at Lankhills (Clarke 1979, 316 Grave 336, no 332).

Type 6

A pin with a short, probably repointed stem and a biconical, eight faceted head (**243**) is unstratified. The stem is not long enough to be used in the hair and it may have been used as an upholstery pin or a decorative feature on a helmet crest. The pointed head is comparable with a hair pin with a pyramidal head from Grave 336 at Lankhills dated to AD 350–70 (Type C: Clarke 1979, 316 and fig 89.333). Richborough (Bushe-Fox 1949, pl LII, 200) and Woodeaton (Kirk 1949, 45, pl II, A7) have similar examples.

Type 7

A pin (**244**) from Area 5 has an inverted conical head, the flat top with an annular groove possibly originally holding enamel; however, no trace of this was detected. The stem was made of leaded bronze, the head of tin. The short length (60mm) suggests a late Roman date for the pin, although a pin of brass with a flat head with a similar annular groove was found in a first-century level at Gadebridge (Wardle 1990, 124, fig 123, no 105). The pin has similarities to those in Cool's group 21 (1990a, 170, cf fig 11:8) which have all been found in Colchester and may have been produced there. The composition of the Ickham pin (**244**), comparable with some examples with spherical and facetted heads, suggests it was made locally.

Type 8

An axe-headed pin of copper alloy, originally tinned (**245**), was found in Area 4 and belongs to Cool's group 18 sub group C. None of the metal examples from southern Britain have been recovered from dated contexts but those in both bone and metal from elsewhere in Europe are of fourth-century date (Cool 1990a, 168). They are often found on temple sites and may have a religious significance as the axe motif may be linked with the cult of a sky god (*ibid*).

A copper alloy dress pin *Susan Youngs*

A long, slender pin (**247**) cast in leaded bronze with a shank bent in two places, was recovered from Area 4. It is not well-stratified although, as noted above, the majority of finds from this part of the site are of late Roman date.

247   A long, slender pin cast and worked in leaded bronze, complete, but with the shank bent in several places, length approximately 36.4cm. The head (width 0.50cm) is rounded at the top and D-shaped in cross-section as is the upper shank. The cross section of the rest of the shank is roughly circular and it tapers to the tip. Cast decoration is found on the front of the upper section with a flat back, the extended shank having been worked from the lower rod after casting. The pin head has a raised frontal disc filled with three lobes springing from the centre, with deep recesses between them and a shallow dot on each lobe and one in the centre (**247**, detail). A second panel at a lower level has opposed lobed scrolls meeting in the centre against a recessed background with a broad curved rim. The depth of the background recesses and their unfinished surfaces, where these are not obscured by corrosion, indicate the original presence of an opaque inlay which will certainly have been red enamel. The shank below the head has a pattern of fine angled grooves; first a deep band of lines across the shank above two groups of diagonal lines, followed by another worn section of transverse lines.

Function

This pin is of non-Roman type in that it is patently not a hair pin, exceeding as it does the normal length of such pins by about 300 per cent (see Cool 1990a for Roman examples, as well as the Roman pins noted above). By default and decoration it must be a native product and it is one of forty or so related by their skewer-like form and size, although no other class of indigenous pins of this size is known from Britain or Ireland in the first four centuries AD. It must have

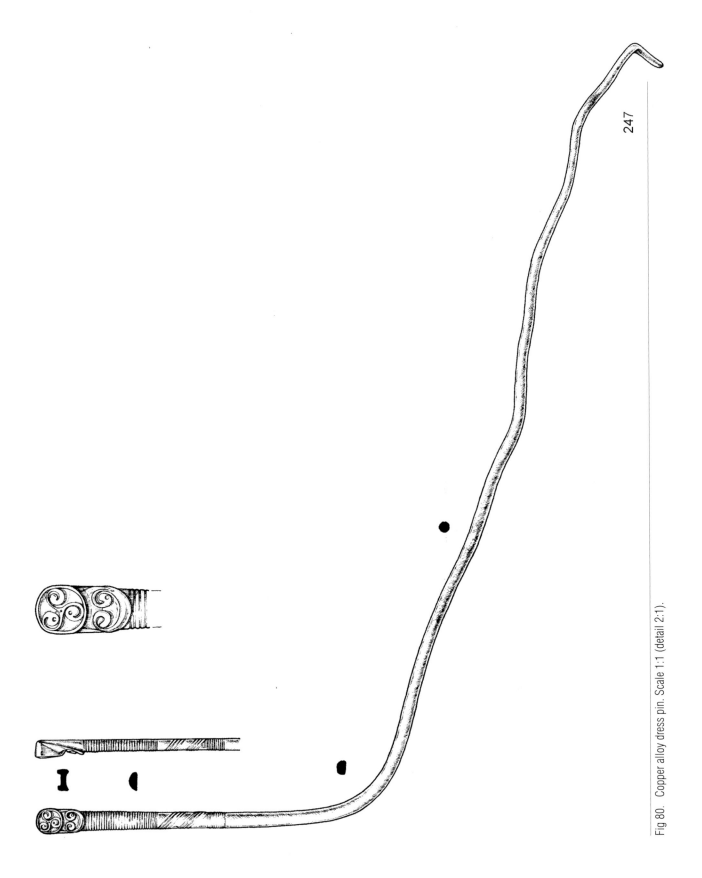

247

Fig 80.   Copper alloy dress pin. Scale 1:1 (detail 2:1).

functioned as a dress fastener and two later types of sturdy dress pin of large size are known from Britain and Ireland in the early medieval period, discussed below. As a dress item its manner of wearing without injury to wearer or bystander remains unclear, although pins of this exaggerated length were worn in the Bronze Age and they are also found on brooches in the ninth and tenth centuries worn in Hiberno-Norse areas. Two smaller Ickham-type pins excavated at Skaill, Deerness on Orkney both have a loop on the head and two other Scottish finds have similar perforated plates on the head for attachments or linking chains (Buteux 1997, 102–3, fig 8.10; Bourke and Close-Brooks 1989, 227). There are signs of wear on the ribbing below the head on the Ickham pin and wear has been observed in this position on other examples (Boon 1975, 401–2). An item of this size must have signified the status of the wearer or donor and been prominent on an outer garment.

Origin, terminology and date

This is the forty-second example of this distinctive large pin type coming both from sites in Britain which extend from south Wales to Orkney, and from Ireland (Fowler 1963, Type E, 121, Appendix 8, with several later finds). The distribution shows, firstly, an association with eleven Roman military sites and towns from Hadrian's Wall and the North-west to the lower Severn and south Wales. These are mainly single finds, but include two from Wroxeter, Shropshire, and three from Chesters, Northumberland. The remainder were recovered from ten native or non-diagnostic find places in Britain, with a remarkable concentration of eight pins from a native stronghold and manufacturing site at Traprain Law, East Lothian (Burley 1955, nos 102–9; Kilbride-Jones 1980, 5–8; this new total was confirmed by Fraser Hunter, National Museum of Scotland). There is a concentration of finds from northern Scotland in Pictish islands and territories, with three from Orkney sites (Bourke and Close-Brooks 1989, 227; Hunter 1997, 28–9; Buteux 1997, 139, fig 8, 10). Of three examples from Wales, two are beach finds from Margam, and one from Caerleon (Boon 1975). Six pins have been found in Ireland, but only one has a more precise provenance of Crumlin, County Dublin. These last are particularly important in confirming that we are not looking at a purely Romano-British hybrid like the dragonesque brooch which has no Irish distribution.

Precise contexts are often unknown or not clearly datable by independent means. An unstratified find associated with a Romano-British village at Rushall, Wiltshire, should probably be in the 'native site' category (British Museum P&EE 1868, 6–25, 1, unpublished). This pin, together with a recent metal-detected find from the Stour valley, west Dorset, also alters what had appeared to be a predominantly northern distribution from a trickle of finds down to modern Wales in the west. The Ickham pin is the only pin from south-east Britain and also had the most finely and elaborately decorated pin head.

Dated contexts range from a pin associated with an early second-century building in the Roman fort at Newstead, Roxboroughshire (Curle 1911, 337, pl 92, 11), to an Anglo-Saxon furnished burial of the sixth century in Oxfordshire (Leeds and Riley 1942, 70, fig 16, b–d). A late Pictish context for two Orkney pins has, fortunately, been discounted (Hunter 1997, 28; Buteux 1997, 102–3).

The Ickham pin type clearly raises questions which cannot be answered fully here; to echo Elizabeth Fowler (as Burley 1955, 169) 'These pins ... constitute a major problem'. The pins published by Fowler, as her Type E (1963, 121, appendix 8), Boon (1975) and Kilbride Jones (1980) have been recently re-assessed in the context of other early medieval Celtic metalwork by Raghnall Ó Floinn (2001) and there was a review by Dr Kate Pretty with the publication of two more excavated at Wroxeter, Shropshire (Barker *et al* 1997, 211–12).

These large pins, referred to variously as stick or skewer pins, fall into two groups by head type, either 'proto-zoomorphic', with heads rounded at the end and 'beaks' below, like the Ickham example (35 out of 42), or 'zoomorphic', having square-ended very stylised heads with ears and eyes indicated and a raised snout which swallows the rod (a group of seven). The latter are not as long and heavy (although there are some smaller versions of proto-zoomorphic form). Ó Floinn has made the important observation that the zoomorphic pins, relatively small and finely detailed are closely associated with sites on Hadrian's Wall and the intra-mural area, with one outlier in Ireland (Ó Floinn 2001, and unpublished Glasgow paper for an important revision of dating and origins). The same zoomorphic decoration is used on a major class of British and Irish penannular brooch up to the sixth or possibly early seventh centuries (Graham-Campbell 1991, Class 1; Fowler types E and F; Kilbride Jones 1980; Youngs 1995; 2007). Fowler believed the rounded head-type to be earlier than the fully zoomorphic squared head on the basis of the difficult stratigraphy at Traprain Law (*ibid,* 169) dating them to the third century, and this was the view of Boon and Kilbride-Jones (Burley 1955, 169; Kilbride-Jones 1980, 5–11). Boon (1975) was convinced by the evidence then available that the very large pins were made in Ireland. Spiral shafts and heads with loops suggest also the existence of local Scottish forms of the 'proto-zoomorphic' forms, something which a detailed re-evaluation of all the pins should clarify.

The term proto-zoomorphic reflects the evolutionary view that this type was ancestral to the zoomorphic form. It was used most recently by Kate Pretty (Barker *et al* 1997, 211–12) for the Wroxeter pins which are dated by context to the second half of the fourth or early fifth century. A sequential view of the proto- and full zoomorphic sub-types of pin creates considerable difficulties. Firstly, both the earliest and latest contexts produced round-headed 'proto-zoomorphic' pins. The apparent problem of the three Orkney pins excavated using modern techniques from what were described as late Pictish levels prompted Fraser Hunter (1997, 28) to write 'the main recognisable items are *all* of generally earlier chronological distribution than the phases in which they were found: indeed some even have Romano-British origins' (my italics). The 'late Pictish' date is resolved with the full publication of the Skaill excavations in which the stratigraphical evidence is seen as consistent with a fourth- to fifth-century date for the pins, but this date is arrived at from the published dates given to other pins of the type because the contextual evidence is very broad, apparently also not inconsistent with a second-century date (Porter 1997, 102–3, fig 8.10). The best that can be said about these two round-headed pins is that their context is not incompatible with the dated contexts of the Wroxeter and Ickham finds.

For the critical early context of an enamelled, round-ended pin from Newstead Fort near Melrose, we were dependent on Curle's published statement that the level on which the pin was found was the same as that of a building close by, reinforced by the fact that his excavation of the fort produced no material later than the second century, which supports this unique very early context. This puts the round-headed pin type back two centuries before the next reasonably datable context (Curle 1911, pl xcii, 11). The Newstead pin-head is enamelled which may have lead the excavator to assume it belonged to the same chronological horizon as most of the Roman enamelled brooches; we cannot tell whether the context dated the pin or *vice versa*, but the published text certainly reads like the former. However, recent excavation by Richard Jones, University of Bradford, together with contextual re-evaluation by Fraser Hunter, National Museum of Scotland, confirm the context was likely to pre-date a wall built *c* AD 140 (Richard Jones and Fraser Hunter, pers comm). The earliest example is then an enamelled pin of the round-headed 'proto-zoomorphic' type.

We are certainly dealing with a dress fastener with a long cultural history in the north of Britain. Remembering that the Fowler type G penannular brooch remained in circulation with some variation from the late fifth to the ninth century AD (Dickinson 1982), it is unlikely but not impossible that production of these big pins lasted from the second to the sixth century. In the light of other more recently excavated examples from Wroxeter, Ickham and Orkney a second-century date *ante quem* for an enamelled form is startling, for all of these pins are of 'proto-zoomorphic' type and come from fourth-century, possible early post-Roman contexts, a label which may have had a different significance between Kent in the east and the west Midlands. The decades about 400 would be acceptable in the present state of knowledge. They are much more like each other in length and weight than the plain Irish and Margam beach finds; these last have been dated to the third century, but not from independent evidence but because of their relationship to the dated Newstead find (Boon 1975). The presence of a 'proto-zoomorphic' enamelled pin in a sixth-century furnished grave at Purwell Farm, Cassington in Oxfordshire carries the contextually dated examples through to the early medieval period, with the proviso that here as elsewhere, context gives a *terminus ante quem* for manufacture and Romano-British jewellery is well represented in Anglo-Saxon furnished burials (Leeds and Riley 1942, 70; P Brown 1976, 21, fig 3.1 no 2; White 1988).

These large pins could also be classified by the use of enamel, with eight possible examples, but work on the early zoomorphic penannular brooches indicates the contemporary production of enamelled and non-enamelled versions (Youngs 1995), just as the unique silver pin from Halton Chesters Roman site is a de luxe version of the zoomorphic type (Smith 1960). The use of yellow enamel on a pin from Vellaquie, North Uist, is unparalleled and of considerable interest in the history of enamelling, whether the pin be third century or of later date (Bourke and Close-Brooks 1989, 227). The Ickham example is unlikely to have carried anything other then red enamel. Length is a possible indicator of sub-grouping in the round-headed pins, reflecting different time or place of manufacture, but it puts three of the plain, relatively heavy finds from Ireland and Margam in the same group as the elaborately decorated Ickham pin and would appear to be too crude an indicator. Head width may be a more reliable distinguishing factor or, more plausibly, a combination of attributes. Ó Floinn's persuasive argument that there is a geographical distinction between the zoomorphic and non- (or proto-)zoomorphic pins and that the find places indicate that the zoomorphic pins were developed in the intra-mural area of north Britain has been supported by the recent additions to the corpus of purely round-headed types from Ickham in Kent, Rushall in Wiltshire and Wroxeter in Shropshire, and by the evidence from the Orkney sites (Ó Floinn 2001, 3–4). Despite the variations in the treatement of the heads, ribbing and diagonal banding of the shank below and behind the head are found on several examples of both round and square-headed pins.

The other major difficulty with the proposition that the round-headed, or 'proto-zoomorphic' pins preceded the more finely decorated zoomorphic type is that this means a development from a huge and exaggerated pin whereby the basic moulding of the head is zoomorphised by added detail to become a smaller, finely decorated type. This is a development which appears to run contrary to the development of other native dress fasteners in Britain and Ireland from the fourth century into the early medieval period, both pins and brooches. For example, the related zoomorphic penannular brooch increased in weight and elaboration before and after its introduction from Britain to Ireland, with the addition of coloured glass inlays. This change in size in the brooch from the Roman to post-Roman world is a development paralleled on the other large dress pins of the fifth to seventh centuries, the great disc-headed pins and 'hand-pins'. The former are of interest because they are linked by their enamelled head decoration to the disc on the Ickham find. Disc-headed pins are a rare type with distinctive offset head of which six decorated examples are known, and they are the only pins to match these great dress pins in size, for example the unprovenanced silver 'Londesborough' pin is 32.4cm long and was originally slightly longer (Youngs 1989, nos 10–12, another two examples should be added to the ones listed there). Their decoration is continued in panels on the shaft below the head and is non zoomorphic and enamelled. The little disc on the Ickham pin is a miniature of the dotted lobed scrolls on enamel seen on the discs of three of these pins, while a stick pin from Cirencester (which lacks a context) has a long pointed panel of paired triangles on the shaft, a motif found later on the large disc-headed pins. The latter is itself closely similar to the Cassington find (both are discussed by P Brown 1976, 21, fig 3.1 no 2, who points out that Fowler's 1963 drawings are unreliable).

Despite the Newstead evidence, a fourth-century date of manufacture for the Ickham pin, which would allow overlapping production with the early medieval disc-headed pin and the revival of enamelling in the fifth and sixth centuries, is most acceptable. The association is not a great aid to dating given the lack of precise dating for the disc-headed pins, although we know that a small undecorated disc-headed pin was manufactured at Garranes, County Cork probably early in the sixth century (Ó Ríordáin 1941, fig 3, 252). Provenances where known are in Ireland, with one find from southern England, and they are not dated by archaeological evidence any more secure than the great pins of Ickham type. They have been generally accepted as an exclusively non-Roman early medieval pin type and dated broadly on stylistic grounds to the sixth century, but I would now date the origin of the decorated disc-headed pins as early as the fifth century on the evidence of the context and decoration of the Ickham dress pin and the Cirencester/Cassington finds. A direct relationship, equivalent to that between the late Roman proto-hand pin and the medieval hand pin, is not defensible because the disc is set forward on a short shank, but it is the suggested relationship of the ornament of the Ickham pin to the post-Roman revival of enamelling which is significant. The dotted lobe or 'dodo head' of the Ickham pin is a motif of great antiquity in Celtic art but it is one which remained in the repertoire until at least the late sixth century. While it is therefore no help in dating the pin more precisely than its context, the date proposed gives the Ickham pin a potential role in the transmission of this archaism into the medieval repertoire. In my opinion the use of two fields of reserved ornament against enamel places the pin from Kent in the second half of the fourth century or later.

Conclusion

The great pin found at Ickham was a sport, an offering, a piece of scrap, or a chance loss, it was not the sort of dress item for suburban Romanised provincials, but something native and rural, even strongly regional. In the present limited state of our knowledge, independent of context, it sits most comfortably within the period 350–450, while the enamelled decoration suggests to me a date of manufacture in the period 375–430, a date which cannot be empirically supported. We are, however, no closer as yet to understanding the origins or circulation of these large pins than in 1975 when George Boon commented on the possible development of the round-headed form in Ireland, except perhaps to say that later additions to the corpus indicate manufacture at centres in Britain over a long period (Boon 1975, 403). The Ickham pin has extended our knowledge of the range of form, context and the geographical spread of these huge pins.

Investigative analysis of the metal pins *Adrian Tribe*

Forty-six metal pins and pin or needle fragments were selected to undergo investigative conservation. In broad terms the form and length of most of the intact pins appeared to support the interpretation that they were of Roman date. When present, the heads were almost all of forms that have been found in Roman contexts before, and many could be assigned to one of the groups as defined by Cool (1990a), as noted above. An obvious exception is the Celtic-type pin (**247**).

The results of the detailed visual and x-radiographic examination and XRF analysis of forty-three of the pins and pin fragments are summarised in Table 24. Full details are given in the conservation record cards retained in the archive. While Caple's study of copper alloy pin production

(Caple 1986) gives a good account of Anglo-Saxon and later techniques of pin manufacture, to the author's knowledge no similar detailed study of pre fifth-century pins has ever been published.

As Table 24 shows, while some of the Ickham pins were cast or wrought in one piece, some were two-piece pins, with head and shank made separately of either the same or a different material. Of the latter, the most striking category to note are those that had bronze or leaded bronze shanks with cast-on heads made from tin-lead alloy. Pins with cast-on lead heads are known from Anglo-Saxon times, one of which

No	Construction	Composition
215	wrought: head details may have been cut into the top of the shank	brass
216	wrought? in one piece	silver, containing very small amounts of gold, lead and copper
217	wrought?	very lightly leaded bronze, with a trace of zinc present
218	cast, possibly with some subsequent working	heavily laded bronze/gunmetal (low zinc content)
219	cast-on head, shank made from folded/rolled strip	head: *c* 63% tin/37%lead. Shank: leaded bronze
220	softended glass wound round top of shank	head: green glass. Shank: leaded bronze
221	cast-on head; shank made from folded/rolled strip that had been slightly twisted	shank: bronze, with traces of tinning
222	cast-on head: shank made from folded/rolled strip	head: *c* 73% tin/27% lead. Shank: leaded bronze
223	cast-on head: cast? shank	head: *c* 73% tin/27% lead. Shank: leaded bronze
224	cast? in one piece	brass
225	cast-on head; cast? shank	head: tin/lead/copper alloy, with a trace of zinc present. Shank: leaded bronze
226	cast-on head; cast? shank	head: *c* 65% tin/35% lead. Shank: leaded bronze
227	cast-on head; wrought? shank	head: *c* 46% tin/54% lead. Shank: leaded bronze
228	cast-on head; wrought? shank	head: 61% tin/39% lead. Shank: bronze
229	cast? in one piece	brass
230	cast in one piece; head decoration could have been incised after casting	leaded bronze
231	cast-on head; shank made from folded/rolled strip	head: *c* 81% tin/ 19% lead. Shank: bronze
233	cast-on head; shank made from folded/rolled strip	head: *c* 58% tin/42%lead. Shank: leaded bronze
234	head soldered round the top of the shank; shank wrought?	head: brass. Shank: brass. Solder: not analysed
235	cast-on head; shank made from folded strip	head: *c* 72% tin/28% lead. Shank: very lightly leaded bronze
236	wrought in one piece, with the shank worked from a folded/rolled strip and very well finished	brass
237	wrought in one piece with the 'seam' visible on shank	silver, containing very small amounts of copper and very small amounts of gold and lead
238	head soldered round the top of the shank, after which the notches were cut; shank wrought	head: leaded bronze. Shank: leaded bronze. Solder: not analysed
239	cast in one piece	silver, containing a little copper, gold and lead
240	wrought? in one piece	brass
241	cast-on head: wrought? shank	head: lead-tin/copper alloy. Shank: leaded bronze
244	cast-on head: wrought? shank	head: *c* 98% tin/2% lead. Shank: lightly leaded bronze
243	wrought? in one piece	copper plus 1–2% each of tine and lead
245	wrought? in one piece	copper with traces of tinning
246	cast-on head; cast shank	head: *c* 79% tin/21% lead. Shank: heavily leaded bronze
247	cast in one with final detail applied subsequently?	leaded bronze: enamel in roundel

Table 24. Investigative analysis of selected metal pins.

was found at nearby Richborough (Lyne 1994b), but in these the shanks are invariably made of iron and are usually quite narrow, with the heads being spherical and decorated with dot-in-circle motifs, a design absent from the Ickham cast-on headed pins. Caple reports that copper alloy pins with spherical lead or lead-tin cast-on heads are known as a late medieval type (Caple 1986, 66), but at Ickham the presence of considerable Roman pewter-working evidence would lend support to these pins being Roman rather than much later intrusive items, as would the Roman head forms, and the greater thickness of the shanks than was usual with late medieval pins. Three iron pins with globular heads of lead alloy were found in deposits ranging in date from eighth or ninth century to 1195 to early fourteenth century at Fishergate, York (Rogers 1993, 1230 and 1367, nos 5054, 5056 and 5061).

Table 24 also shows that some of the pins had shanks made from folded and/or rolled strip, which would subsequently have been worked to disguise as far as possible any evidence of the 'seam'. This method of manufacture is certainly reported by Caple for later pins (Caple 1986, 117), but has not been noted before, to the author's knowledge, for Roman pins.

Bone pins *Ian Riddler*

Eleven of the fifteen bone or antler pins from Ickham are fragmentary and only three are complete. The heads survive on six of the pins, however, which enables them to be assigned to type. In several other cases the presence of a noticeable swelling along the pin shaft allows them to be placed within a broad late Roman category. Two fragments of pin shaft from Area 10 (257 and 261) belong, in all probability, to the same pin.

It is generally difficult to distinguish between the use of bone and antler in pin production. Many Roman pins are made of bone and this situation is borne out by the study of assemblages of pin waste (Greep 1995, 1135). Equally, however, it is clear that pins were also manufactured from antler, as well as bone. This is certainly the case with one of the Ickham pins and two further examples are probably made of antler. The remainder were made from either bone or antler and their precise material of manufacture cannot be readily distinguished.

Several of the pin shafts are relatively crude and they have not been smoothed and polished. This does not necessarily mean that they are unfinished, however. In four cases the shafts have been shortened, presumably by breakage, and the pin has been repointed. This situation is commonly seen with Roman bone and antler pins.

The typology for Roman bone pins devised by Greep has been utilised here, and reference has also been made to the Colchester sequence (Greep 1995, 1113–21; Crummy 1979; 1983, 19–25). The identifiable head forms can be quantified by type, as follows:

No	Material	Greep type	Length mm	Context
248	antler?	B1.5	67	Area 10, 'layer 2'
249	antler	B1.6	84 estimated	Area 10, 'layer 3'
250	bone or antler	B1.9		Area 10, 'layer 3'
251	antler?	B1.10		Area 10
252	bone or antler	B3.1	69	Area 5
253	bone or antler	B3.1	69	Area 4, 'floor'
254	bone or antler	B5		Area 4, 'floor'
255	bone or antler	B		Area 4, 'floor'
256	bone or antler	B		Area 1, Channel C
257	bone or antler	B		Area 10, 'layer 1'
258	bone or antler	B		Area 1, Channel C
259	bone or antler			Area 1, Channel C
260	bone or antler			Area 14, 'layer 1'
261	bone or antler			Area 10, 'layer 1'
262	bone or antler			Area 16, 'ditch 1'

Table 25. Bone pins.

No early Roman pin forms are present in the assemblage. Those for which a part or all of the head survives can be separated into three late Roman groups. Four of the pins are variants of Greep's type B1, which is broadly equivalent to Crummy's type 3 (Greep 1995, 1117; Crummy 1979, 161; 1983, 21–2). A few pins of this type are of second-century date but the majority belong to the third and fourth centuries. It is interesting to note that the head forms seen here are comparatively rare in Canterbury, where those of type B1.1 (which are entirely absent at Ickham) dominate most assemblages (Greep 1995, 1117). At Colchester, also, pins with globular heads were the most common group within those of type 3, and the same situation occurs elsewhere (Crummy 1983, 21; Béal 1983, 189–93; Bíró 1994, 31–2). All four of the Ickham examples of type B1 pins come from Area 10. In one case (248) the shaft has been repointed, producing a pin of truncated form.

Two pins belong to Greep's type B3 and Crummy's type 5 (Greep 1995, 1119; Crummy 1979, 162). This type belongs essentially to the fourth century (Crummy 1983, 24). Both examples have also been repointed and are relatively short.

Two pins with fragmentary heads form a third group, which cannot be readily assigned to any typological sequence. Both pins come from Area 4. One example (255) includes incised grooves just below the point at which it is broken. The pin shaft is lightly hipped and it cannot therefore belong to any early Roman form like Greep type A2 or Crummy type 2. It is likely to be a Greep type B1 pin, with the addition of grooves below the head. This corrugated variant of the B1 form can be seen elsewhere, as at Poundbury, for example (Bíró 1994, pl XXVIII.307 9 and pl XXIX.310 313; Greep 1993, fig 76.5; but cf Béal 1983, fig XXXVI.709).

The second example (254) is the only pin from Ickham which has been lathe-turned. Its hipped shaft leads to a well formed reel, above which lies a small moulded area, representing the vestige of the head. The hipping of the shaft and the presence of the reel suggest that it is a fourth-century form. The head may conceivably have been of composite form (Bíró 1994, pl XXII.355), but its original shape cannot now be identified. Similar pins, which have broken at the same point, are known from the Lyons area (Béal 1983, fig XXXVII).

Approximately half of the bone and antler pins came from Area 10, with the remainder stemming largely from Area 4. Unfortunately, however, only a few pins are stratified. It is interesting to note that pins of type B1, with its numerous variants, come entirely from Area 10, whilst the distinctive late Roman forms (B3.1 and B5) are confined to Areas 4 and 5.

Glass beads

H E M Cool [37]

The majority of the beads from Ickham belong to types that were commonest in the late Roman period, and there is a noticeable late fourth- to fifth-century element amongst them. One bead is definitely a first- to second-century type (**280**), and it is possible that some of the others which belong to types that have long life spans (**263–5**, 266–70) might represent earlier activity.

Frit melon beads such as **280** are very common on sites occupied during the first to second centuries, but become much less common in the later second century. This is clearly demonstrated by comparing the proportion of melon beads in the late first-century drain deposits at the fortress baths at Caerleon with those in the later second and earlier

third-century deposits at the site (Brewer 1986b, 148–51). Examples found in third-century or later contexts are very likely to be residual from earlier activity.

The two glass annular beads (**263** and **264**) could be contemporary with the melon bead. The yellow/green example **263** (Guido 1978; 66 Group 6iiia) belongs to a type that is known in the later Iron Age but which continued in use into the Roman period. Though some are known from third-century contexts (see for example Cool and Price 1993, 167 no 163, fig 88), the majority that are found closely stratified tend to come from first- to second-century ones. On balance, therefore, an early Roman date is most likely for **263**. In the light of the late fourth-century beads at Ickham, however, it may be significant that Guido (1978, 150) records an annular bead of similar size to **263** in the same colour glass from the signal station at Scarborough. Occupation at the Yorkshire signal stations can be dated with some security to the last third of the fourth century whatever the precise building date is preferred (Wilson 1989, 144). The bead from Scarborough thus suggests that large annular beads in this colour glass may still have been in use at this time. Blue/green annular beads such as **264** (Guido 1978, 66 Group 6iia) are a post conquest type that made use of broken fragments of vessel glass for their raw material. They have occasionally been found in fourth-century contexts, for example at Birdoswald (Wilmott 1997, 274, nos 14–5) and *Segontium* (Allen 1993, 226, no 47). The context in which **264** was found also contained late fourth-century pottery so it is possible that this is a late example, though again an early Roman date would be most likely.

Hexagonal-sectioned green glass beads such as **265** were in use throughout the Roman period with ones made of translucent green glass being recovered from contexts as early as AD 75–85 (Brewer 1986b, 148, nos 3–5), and as late as the third quarter of the fourth century (Clarke 1979, 298–300, nos 140, 424 and 436). This bead could thus be contemporary with the late fourth-century pottery found in the same ditch. Green cylindrical beads (**271–4**) are known from second- and early third-century contexts (Brewer 1986b, 149, no 35; Cool and Price 1998, 187 nos 114–5, 128, 176–8), but the bulk of dated examples come from late third- and fourth-century ones.

A good case can be made for all of the other beads being of later fourth- or early fifth-century date. Opaque green disc cylindrical beads such as **271–4** have been found repeatedly in contexts of that date (Cool 2000), and unlike many other types such as those discussed in connection above (**265**, 266–70) are conspicuous by their absence in second- to

---

37. This report was written in 1999. The references have been updated, but the text is otherwise unaltered.

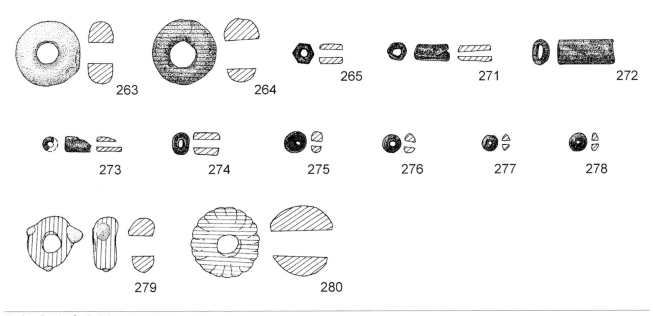

Fig 81. Beads. Scale 1:1.

early fourth-century contexts. The only example known to me that is possibly stratified in a second- to third-century context is from Catterick (Wilson 2002, 260, no 26). The annular opaque green bead (**275**) should probably be viewed as a poorly made example of this type, because though it has a more rounded outline than is normal, on a necklace it would have been virtually indistinguishable from several others (**271**, **272**, **273** and **274**).

Three short biconical green beads beads (**276**, **277** and **278**) are also present. The form made in translucent deep blue glass is a common mid to late Roman type, and a number have been recovered from second- to third-century contexts. Examples may be noted in the Caerleon fortress bath drain deposit of AD160–230 (Brewer 1986b, 149, nos 62–5), the Antonine fire debris at *Verulamium* (Frere 1972, 214 no 4) and in an early to mid third-century context at Birdoswald (Wilmott 1997, 275 nos 29–32). The same shape made in green glass as here is again conspicuously absent from early contexts. There are none, for example, in the large mid second-century bead assemblage at Castleford (Cool and Price 1998, 186–8), the late second- to early third-century one at the Caerleon fortress baths (Brewer 1986b), and the group of beads associated with the mid third-century burials at Brougham, Cumbria (Cool 2004, 385–90). Apart from a single example from a context of AD 49–125 at the Gilberd School, Colchester (Crummy 1992, 211, no 67) and one from a context of AD 270–330 at Towcester (Price and Cool 1983,

124, no 62), the rest of the stratified examples come from mid and late fourth-century contexts. Examples may be noted on the necklaces associated with inhumations of that date at the Lankhills School cemetery, Winchester (Clarke 1979, 300, no 443) and Butt Road, Colchester (Crummy 1983, 220 nos 683–7, 724–802). Single examples are known from Towcester in a context of AD 330–70+ (Price and Cool 1983, 124 nos 63), and from Caerleon (Allen 1992, 185 no 41), Silchester (Allen 1997, 118, no 11) and Catterick (site 433 unpublished) in ones belonging to the second half of the fourth century. At present, therefore, it appears likely that green short biconical beads are a late fourth-century variety and that the unusually early example found at Colchester is intrusive. These are, after all, very small beads easily displaced within the archaeological record.

The final glass bead (**279**) is an unusual polychrome bead. It could be classified as belonging to Guido's somewhat disparate group 3 (miscellaneous horned beads) even though only one of the yellow spots is really pronounced enough to be described as a horn (Guido 1978, 60). A black bead with green or yellow horns is recorded by Guido (*ibid,* 125) as coming from a hoard of about AD 400 found at Icklingham, Suffolk. This is presumably the 1902 Icklingham hoard that had coins running up to *c* AD 393–5, a silver spoon and some rings and beads (Pearce 1929). The 'black' glass both beads are made from would strongly suggest a late fourth-century or later date as 'black' beads are rare prior to this (Guido 1999, 17). Where examples come from narrowly dated

No	Shape	Colour	Length mm	Diameter mm	Context
263	annular	translucent yellow/green	6	17	Area 4, extension, 'section 1 layer 3'
264	annular	translucent blue/green	9	17	Area 5
265	hexagonal	translucent emerald green	6	5	Area 5
266	long cylindrical	translucent green/blue	9	4.5	Area 1, 101
267	long cylindrical	translucent green/blue	15	6.5 x 4.5	'IH'
268	long cylindrical	cloudy translucent mid green	7		Area 4
269	cylindrical oval	cloudy translucent mid green	6	5.5 x 4.5	Area 4, extension, 'section 2'
270	cylindrical	translucent emerald green	5.5	4.4	Area 6, 602
271	disc cylindrical	opaque mid green	4	4	Channel C
272	disc cylindrical	opaque mid green	3.5	5	Channel C
273	disc cylindrical	opaque mid green	3.5	5	Area 5
274	disc cylindrical	opaque mid green	3.5	5	Area 4
275	annular	opaque mid green	3.5	5.5	Area 5
276	short biconical	translucent green/blue	3	5	Area 6, 610.5
277	short biconical	opaque mid green	2	3.5	Area 1, 104
278	short biconical	opaque mid green	2	5	Area 5
279	annular	very dark, with opaque yellow spots spaced equidistantly	6	14 x 12	Area 4, extension
280	melon bead	turquoise frit	15	18	Area 12
281	setting	cloudy translucent greeb/blue	5	8.5 x 8	Area 1, Pit 115

Table 26. Glass beads.

contexts, they belong to the end of the century. In addition to the bead in the Icklingham hoard, a black cylindrical bead on a necklace deposited in a grave dated to AD 390–410 at the Lankhills School cemetery, Winchester (Clarke 1979, 298, no 315) and a black disc cylindrical bead with a group of other beads including the late opaque green disc cylindrical form in a late fourth-century (or later) context at Feltwell, Norfolk (Gurney 1986, 13, 38, no 51) can be noted.

The contexts of the nine beads for which a late fourth-century date has been suggested can be identified in six cases (**273**, **275**, **276**, **277**, **278** and **279**), and it is interesting to note that in all but one case (**278**), late fourth-century pottery has also been identified in these contexts.

The glass hemisphere (281) is not closely datable as such settings are occasionally found throughout the Roman period, though more often in blue/green glass than the green/blue shade seen here. It is likely that it forms a setting for a pendant of the type described below.

Pendants (Pls XXI–XXIV)

Martin Henig

The Ickham pendants are extremely rare objects, although their salient features can all be matched in Roman jewellery.

All of them (except **290**) are double-sided and have beaded edges like coins; four are set with what must have been intended as imitation emeralds. In a society where jewels and coins were often mounted and worn as pendants the creation of such objects in base metal should not occasion surprise.

The iconography belongs to a late Roman secular *milieu*; the only subject which I have not been able to match from the art of the period is the boxing match (pendants **282**, **283** and **286**). The hound and stag (**286**) is very reminiscent of a motif engraved in intaglio on one of the sides of a bronze cube perhaps used for making lead sealings found at the Imperial estate centre at Kingscote, Gloucestershire (Henig 1977, pl lvii g); the subject is also found in *venatio* scenes on contorniate medallions (Alföldi and Alföldi 1976, 35–6 no 122, taf 41, 1.12), dating from the second half of the fourth century. Friezes of running animals are familiar from other items of late Roman metalwork such as the hunt figured on two of the engraved and pierced gold bracelets from Hoxne, Suffolk (Johns 1996, 116, pl 11 on right). The device of a horseman (often the emperor) with a spear is widespread and can be seen on the Belgrade cameo (Weitzmann 1979, 83, no 71) and the gold medallion from Arras which shows Constantius I entering *Londinium* (Kent 1978, pl 152, no 585; Sutherland 1974, pl 516). Standing soldiers occur on the late Roman coinage (Sutherland 1974, pl 530), but also

Pl XXI. Lead alloy pendants nos 282, 283, 284 and 285 (top to bottom).

Pl XXII. Lead alloy pendants nos 286, 287, 288 and 289 (top to bottom).

on other objects such as an officer's badge said to be of late third-century date, where vexillations of the second and twentieth legions are shown in connection with animals including a hound and a stag (Casey 1994b, 94 and fig 5). The vine frieze is a very widespread motif in late Roman art as earlier, for example in relief on two bowls in the Mildenhall treasure (Painter 1977, 28–9, nos 9 and 10, pls 23 and 25) and on another Hoxne bracelet.

Despite the genre of the representations being apparent the specific sources are not. The immediate prototypes do not seem to have been numismatic as neither coins nor contorniates provide exact parallels even if the style of execution is not unlike local imitations of coins in both the third and fourth centuries. There are, in fact, very few truly analogous pendants from Roman Britain. A bronze roundel evidently depicting a vase upon a calyx within a beaded surround was found at Richborough, Kent (Bushe-Fox 1949, 125–6, no 91) and there are two gold pendants, one set with a cameo and the other with an intaglio from the Thetford treasure (Johns and Potter 1983, 103–5, nos 39 and 40). Amongst late Roman jewellery from outside Britain an early fifth-century pendant from a treasure found in Rome, one side set with little gems and the other ornamented in repoussé (Weitzmann 1979, 309, no 283) may be noted: with regard to the obverses of two pendants (**282** and **284**), a gold pendant in St Petersburg, said to be sixth century which depicts the crowning of an emperor, has two surrounding registers one showing a scroll and the other running animals (*ibid*, 72, 4, no 62).

Beyond what would normally be considered the Roman sphere is a fifth-century gold bracteate from Viken, Norway showing on one side a man and a woman either side of a tree and on the other a horseman with spear and shield. This has been explained (Magnus 1997, 1967 and fig 87) in terms of Norse myth but the images closely recall those of an Ickham pendant (**287**). It is tempting to look for a common prototype.

A lead alloy pendant with central glass jewel similar to nos 282–5 was found in a late or post-Roman context at Alington Avenue, Fordington, Dorchester, Dorset (Henig and Morris 2002). Here the ornament consists of a beaded border and a series of raised dots on both obverse and reverse, while the 'jewel' is of red, not green, glass.

In late fourth- and fifth-century Britain a style of animal art developed, which is manifested on quoit brooches and other objects which belong within a provincial development of Roman art (Hawkes 1961; Henig 1995a, 170–3). Within our area, an oval plate showing a hare (Hawkes 1961, 38, no 16, fig 4) and the running hounds on a fragmentary quoit

brooch, both from Howletts, Kent (*ibid*, 31–2, pl xv b; Evison 1965, 123–4, pl 10c), provide examples. A simplified vine scroll on a penannular brooch related to the quoit brooch style from Alfriston, Sussex (*ibid*, 39, no 17, pl xviie; Evison 1965, 126, pl 15a) also displays what is essentially a Romano-British development from the classical original. The incorporation of glass *cabochons* in a pair of drop-shaped pendants from Bifrons (*ibid*, 32–3 no 4, pl xv c; Evison 1965, 125, pl 12a), a buckle plate from High Down, Sussex (Hawkes 1961, 36, no 10, pl xvi d) and above all a disc brooch from Faversham, where the jewel is surrounded by a running scroll and another register of stylised animals (*ibid*, 33, no 5, fig 1; Evison 1965, 123, pl 10a) exhibit features linking them with the style of the Ickham pendants, even if they also reflect new influences from the Anglo-Saxon and southern Scandinavian world. *Romanitas* was not forgotten neither by the 'sub Roman' population nor by new settlers and in fact the developing art of Kent is best explained by cultural symbiosis.

There is a possible connection with the Quoit Brooch style, even if that style itself does not include discoidal pendants (Hawkes 1961, 30–40; Ager 1985; 1990). The Faversham disc brooch has a central, blue glass setting as also does a buckle plate from High Down, where the setting is red glass (Hawkes 1961, pl XVId and fig 1). The Higham disc brooch would have included a similar setting, strongly redolent of the Ickham pendant design (*ibid*, 35 and pl XVIa).

The Ickham pendants seem to belong early in the process of the creation of the later Kentish jewellery. The use of coins as pendants at the end of the sixth and in the seventh century, for example in the Canterbury St Martin's (or St Augustine's) cache (Webster and Backhouse 1991, 23, no 5 a–e) and in a group from Faversham (*ibid*, 53, no 34 a–f) marks its continuation, as does the use of superbly crafted and often jewelled gold pendants at this time (*ibid*, 26–7, no 10 from Canterbury; 50–1, no 32c from Kingston Down, Kent; 51–2, no 33b from Ipswich, Suffolk; 54–5, no 36 from Milton next Sittingbourne, Kent). In this regard the jewelled disc brooches such as the famous example from Sarre (*ibid*, 48–9, no 31a) should also be noted.

Four of the pendants were found together in context 408, an occupation deposit in Area 4 thought to date to the late third to early fourth century, on the evidence of its coins. The ceramics, however, point to a date after AD 370 (*see* Assemblage 20, p 110), and a late Roman date would appear to be confirmed by the pendants. A second group of three pendants was retrieved from Channel C, for which a late fourth- or early fifth-century date is well established. One further example came from the Area 4 extension, which

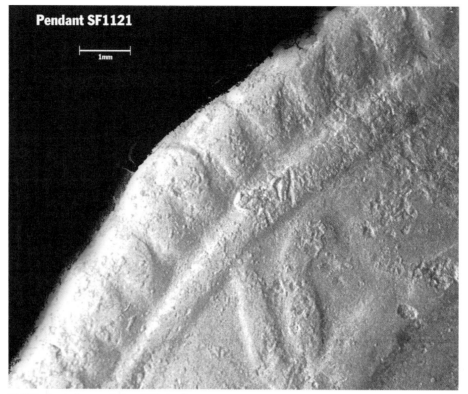

Pl XXIII. Lead alloy pendant no 282, detail.

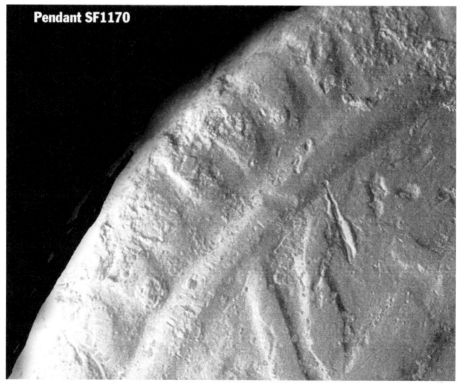

Pl XXIV. Lead alloy pendant no 283, detail.

is substantially late Roman in date, whilst the pendant or sealing (**290**) was retrieved from Area 10 and could, therefore, be slightly earlier in date.

All of the pendants were found by quantitative XRF analysis to be made of almost pure tin (95–99 per cent) or tin-lead alloy with a high proportion of tin (73–90 per cent) and sometimes a little copper also (up to around 5 per cent) (Fig 82). All had been cast in two-piece moulds and examination by Adrian Tribe at high magnification using a Scanning Electron Microscope confirmed that two examples (**282** and **283**) were cast in the same mould, strongly suggesting that they would have been manufactured on site (Pls XXIII and XXIV). It is notable also that very similar casting flaws are present on three pendants (**282**, **283** and **284**), where an air bubble had evidently been trapped behind the glass gem, preventing the metal from completely filling the mould at this point and disrupting the design on the reverse face.

The importance of the assemblage of pendants is hard to exaggerate. The dating will primarily have been done on the basis of coins and of ceramic evidence itself ultimately based on coins. The pendants are of a rare type, hardly attested in 'Roman' Britain and which I believe to be later. The Ickham finds may be evidence for Roman continuity and the metamorphosis of classical culture in late antiquity (see Henig 2002, chapter 7 and Henig 2004, 19–20, where the Ickham pendants are cited).

Catalogue of pendants

Pendants set with a jewel of green glass in a central raised setting:

282 *Obverse.* A frieze of four or five running animals (two confronted) encircles the setting. Line and hatched border around.
Reverse. Two confronted boxers; within the field are four small arcs, two on either side. The figures stand on a ground line below which a row of pellets imitates an inscription. Line and hatched border around.
Diameter 25mm; loop 5mm; diameter of setting 11mm; diameter jewel 7mm. Context 408.

283 Size and type (Obverse and Reverse) the same; clearly from the same moulds. This example is bent and some details are less clear. Context 408.

284 *Obverse.* Vine frieze encircles the central setting. Line and beaded border.
Reverse. A horse in profile to the right: upon its back sits a rider holding the reins in his right hand and a spear in his left hand. Line and beaded border.
Diameter 25mm; loop 7mm. Context 408.

285 *Obverse.* Two registers of beading around the central raised setting. The glass jewel is conical.
Reverse. Horseman. The type is the same as the reverse of 284 above but is not taken from the same die. Line and beaded border.
Diameter 27mm; loop 4mm. Base of Channel C.

Pendants without central setting and glass jewel:

286 *Obverse.* A hound chases a stag towards the left. One hound is set vertically in order to contain it in field, a second hound below. Line and hatched border.
Reverse. Two boxers. A central circle between them may be intended to represent a target, or else is a version of a central setting. No ground line. Line and hatched border.
The boxers are similar to those on 282 and 283 above but are larger. Diameter 28mm; loop 6mm. Channel C.

287 *Obverse.* Two standing figures one on each side of a column. They both wear tunics. The figure on the right holds a spear or sceptre with a pellet at each end. Above the column is an object composed of three pellets, evidently supported by the figures. Beaded border.
Reverse. Horseman, holding a spear, to right. The horse turns its head to face the rider. Ground line. Beaded border.
Diameter 26mm; loop not pierced. 3mm. Area 4, Context 408.

288 *Obverse.* A warrior holding a shield in his right hand and a spear in his left hand, set within a stellar field composed of four arcs. Line and hatched border.
Reverse. Horseman with spear in right hand; horse in profile to right: in front what appears to be a standard composed

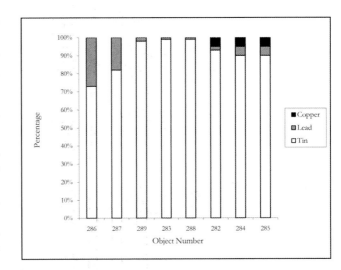

Fig 82. Composition of pendants by XRF analysis.

of three small crosses. Zigzag under ground line. Line and beaded border.

Diameter 29mm: loop 5mm. As well as a loop this pendant is pierced. Area 4 extension.

289   *Obverse.* Wheel like device composed of hub with radiating spokes. Beaded border.

Reverse. Woman (?nude), Side saddle on donkey (note long ears) to left. Beaded border.

Diameter 20mm: loop missing. Channel C.

290   Pendant, spoon or sealing. The edges have only been roughly cut. Only one side bears ornament and it is not at all certain that this is a pendant. It might be one side of a sealing made with a *bulloterion*. Equally, it might well be the bowl of a pewter spoon. Accordingly, it is described in detail below with the other spoons. The field bears a combination of raised, curving lines set within a circle and hatched border.

Diameter 24mm; no loop. Area 10.

No	Diameter mm	Area	Context
282	25	4	Area 4, 408
283	25	4	Area 4, 408
284	25	4	Area 4, 408
285	27	1	Area 1, base of Channel C
286	28	1	Area 1, Channel C
287	26	4	Area 4, 408
288	29	4	Area 4, extension
289	20	1	Area 1, Channel C
290	24	10	

Table 27. Lead alloy pendants.

Bracelets

Quita Mould and Ian Riddler

No less than 115 copper alloy bracelets were recovered from Ickham, as well as thirteen of bone or antler. Burial evidence shows that these light copper alloy bracelets were worn in groups so that a large quantity must have been produced during the fourth century. Good comparable assemblages are known from Canterbury, and particularly from the Marlowe excavations, where sixty-three examples came from Period 4 (late Roman) deposits (Blockley *et al* 1995, 1026–8 and figs 433–6). Eight per cent of the copper alloy bracelets are complete, the majority are broken fragments. Examples with chisel-cut ends suggest scrap collection for re-use of the metal.

The various forms of copper alloy bracelet are described here, beginning with wire bracelets (types 1–5) and continuing with cast copies of wire bracelets (type 7), snake's head bracelets (type 8), strip bracelets (types 9–10) and crenellated, grooved or chip-carved examples (types 11–13). The final type (14) consists of those with 'cut-out' decoration. Each type is described in turn here, and the section concludes with a discussion of those objects which began as bracelets but were subsequently transformed into simple forms of finger ring.

Copper alloy bracelets   *Quita Mould*

Wire bracelets

A total of thirty-two bracelets or fragments of bracelet were made from strands of copper alloy wire, either a single strand, plain (type 1) or twisted (type 2), or several strands twisted together (types 3–5). The cable twist bracelet (types 3–5) was the principal bracelet type throughout the Roman period (Cool 1983, 120 bracelet group 1) in use from at least the early second century to the fourth century.

Type 1

The single strand bracelet with adjustable fastening was a common form found throughout the Roman period, although often occurring in late Roman contexts (Cool 1983, 130 bracelet group III). Two complete examples occur (**291** and 292) along with lengths of wire from two other examples (293 and 294) In addition, a strand of wire with each end pointed (295) could represent a partly-made bracelet of this type.

Type 2

This type is formed of single strand, spirally twisted wire bracelets with a hook and eye fastening. Two examples were found (**296** and 297), of Cool's bracelet group IV (Cool 1983, 135–8) which was in use during the late third and fourth century.

Type 3

This variant encompasses the two-strand, spirally-twisted bracelet. Ten examples were found, none of which are complete, and two (301 and 302), appear to have cut ends suggesting the deliberate collection of scrap; the rest are broken. One example (298) has a hook from a hook and eye fastening, two others (**299** and 300) have a sheet collar wrapped around the terminal, from one of which the looped fastening eye protrudes (**299**).

Type 4

Type four consists of three-strand, spirally-twisted bracelets. Thirteen examples were found, all of which are broken. Three of the bracelets have hooked terminals, remnants of which survive (318, 314 and 310). Two (312 and 320) have a sheet collar wrapped around the base of the looped wire terminal. The bracelets vary in thickness from 2–5mm, individual strands ranging in diameter from 1–3mm.

Type 5

Four strand bracelets are defined here as Type 5. Three bracelet fragments (321) consist of four strands of fine wire spirally wound around a thicker central stem which was bent into a hooked fastening at the terminal.

In addition two fragments of bracelet were found whose exact number of individual strands could not be discerned. They have been assigned here to Type 6.

Type 7

Cast copies of spirally twisted bracelets form Type 7. Two bracelets from Channel C were cast with a series of oblique transverse mouldings in imitation of spirally-twisted cable bracelets like those above. One (**326**) has a hook and eye fastening and the other (327) appears to have had a riveted fastening.

Type 8

This type consists of distinctive snake's head bracelets. A complete bracelet (**328**) of oval sectioned wire has flattened leaf-shaped terminals, a simple snake's head terminal form. It is comparable with a bracelet from Caister-on-Sea (Cool 1993, fig 49, no 168). Snake's head bracelets are another long-lived form found throughout the Roman period, but at its most popular during the third to fourth centuries (*ibid*, 84).

Strip bracelets

A large number of lightweight bangles were recovered. These bracelets are commonly found in large numbers on late Roman sites, dating to the fourth century although possibly first occurring in the late third century (Cool 1993, 84). A small quantity of undecorated strip bracelets were found (type 9) but the majority (type 10) were decorated with various combinations of incised geometric patterns of transverse or oblique or cross hatched lines, dots or ring-and-dot motifs. Although similar in design and execution, few are exactly the same, nor can many be exactly paralleled by examples found elsewhere, indicating the wide range of styles in which they were produced during the later third and the fourth centuries. Multiple unit bracelets comprise a variety of these simple decorative motifs in alternating bands. These are more highly decorated versions of the single motif bracelets, often combining notched edges to produce a sinuous profile. Multiple unit bracelets are difficult to distinguish from those comprising a single motif when only a small fragment of the original bracelet is found. However, those which can be so identified are indicated as such in Table 28, p 200.

Crenellated bracelets (type 11) and similarly decorated types (types 12 and 13) occur widely and can be exactly paralleled on many late Roman sites. The wider strip bracelet (type 14) is more unusual and appears to have a much more limited distribution.

Type 9

Undecorated strip bracelets are defined here as Type 9. Seven fragments of undecorated strip bracelet were found, five with the remains of either a hook or eye fastening. One fragment (**329**) may be scrap from a partly made bracelet.

Type 10

Strip bracelets with punched and incised decoration form Type 10. Many fragments of strip bracelets decorated with incised geometric designs, punched motifs or combinations of the two were recovered. Only two complete bracelets were found; one decorated with a series of punched squares (**336**) had a hook and eye fastening, the other decorated with punched 'dumb bell' like motifs (337) had a riveted fastening. A bracelet with transverse grooved ornament (361) has a flat, round terminal in the form of a crude animal head.

One of the bracelets (353) is comparable with an example from grave 378 in the Butt Road cemetery at Colchester, dated *c* AD 320–450 (Crummy 1983, fig 47, 1730). One small fragment of bracelet (397) from Area 4 is decorated with very fine cross hatching similar to that found on snake bracelets. The hooked terminal from another (**398**) which is unstratified has distinctly serrated edges. A single strip bracelet (399) fragment is decorated by a series of horizontal grooves.

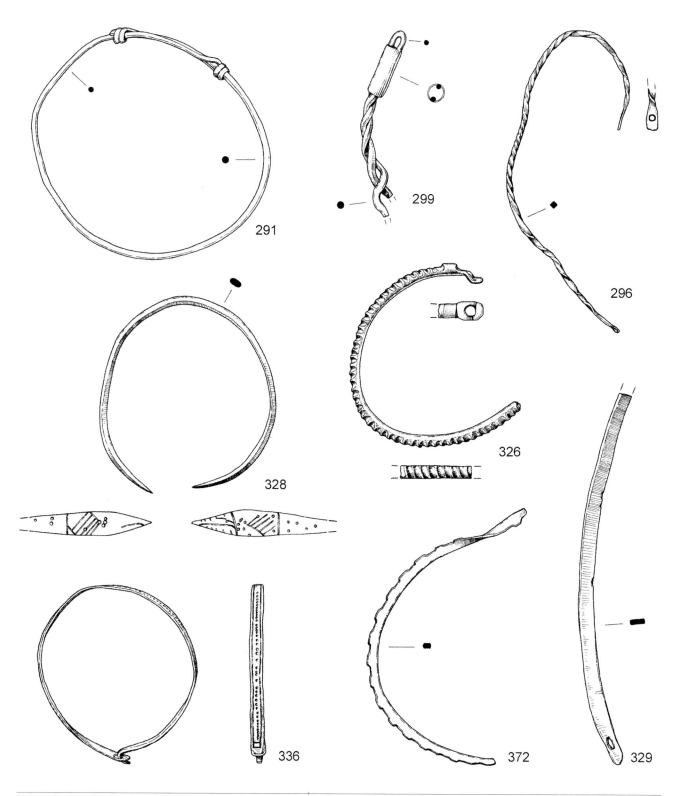

Fig 83. Copper alloy bracelets. Scale 1:1.

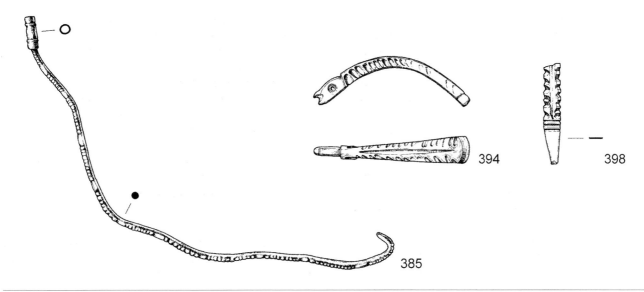

Fig 84. Copper alloy bracelets. Scale 1:1.

Type 11

Amongst these light bracelets are a distinct group with crenellated decoration flattened in the vertical rather than the horizontal plane. Examples with and without milled decoration on the lower areas were found. Three bracelets (371, **372** and 373) with no milled decoration present are comparable with two bracelets from graves dated AD 350–70 at Lankhills (type D1d; Clarke 1979, 305). In addition, two fragments of similar bracelets which are flattened in the vertical plane but uncrenellated were recovered from the excavations (380 possibly from the west bank of the lake by Jim Bradshaw). They are of similar dimensions to the crenellated bracelets and it is possible that they could be bracelet blanks awaiting decoration. Where terminals survive, the bracelets can be seen to have been riveted together. These crenellated bracelets occur widely throughout Roman Britain in fourth-century contexts.

Type 12

Comparable with the crenellated bracelets are those decorated with a series of simple parallel grooves. A complete bracelet of this type (381) has a riveted fastening.

Three bracelets were found with this decoration separated by plain areas in the manner of the crenellated bracelets; a similar bracelet was found in a grave dated AD 350–70 at Lankhills (type D2c in Clarke 1979, 306; Grave 142, no

163). One bracelet (384) was joined by the pointed terminal at one end fitting into a simple socket at the other, another (**385**) had a separate collar. Where the plain areas are small (**385** and 386) the appearance of a mock bead is created (cf bracelets from the Butt Road cemetery, Colchester: Crummy 1983, fig 44, no 188, fig 46, no 1721).

Type 13

Another distinct group of light bracelets has chip-carved decoration. At its most simple small notches are cut in each edge (387 and 388). Two bracelets (389 and 390) are flattened in same plane as the crenellated bracelets and decorated with a series of notches cut from alternate edges to produce a zigzag pattern. Another example (391) of flat strip has the same zigzag decoration produced in the same way. A further bracelet (392) is a more elaborately decorated variant. These light chip-carved bracelets are of fourth-century date (Cool *et al* 1995, 1540). It is interesting to compare these chip-carved bracelets with a flat strip bracelet with similar zigzag decoration produced by incised lines (393) which may be a simplified version of them.

An unusual bracelet (**394**) may be considered a variant of the chip-carved assemblage. The surviving fragment of plano-convex section with feathered chip-carved decoration tapers to an animal head terminal, set in the opposite plane, similarly executed with an open mouth and ring-and-dot eyes. It is reminiscent of a zoomorphic-headed buckle.

No	Type	Diameter mm	Context
291	1	65	Area 4, 'floor'
292	1	50	Area 4, extension
293	1		Area 1, Channel C
294	1		Area 4
295	1?		Area 4, extension
296	2	80	Area 4
297	2		Area 5. 'hollow floor'
298	3		Area 4
299	3		Area 4
300	3		Area 4
301	3		Area 4
302	3		Area 4
303	3		Area 4
304	3		Area 4, extension
305	3		Area 4, 335
306	3		Area 5. 'hollow floor'
307	3		Area 2
308	4	45	Area 1, Channel C
309	4		Area 1, Channel C
310	4		Area 1, Channel C
311	4		Area 1, Pit 115.2
312	4		Area 1, 122
313	4		Area 4
314	4		Area 4
315	4		Area 4
316	4		Area 4
317	4		Area 5. 'hollow floor'
318	4		'road surface area at west'
319	4		unstratified
320	4		Area 16, 'ditches'
321	5	41	Area 4
322	5		Area 4, 335
323	5		Area 1, Channel C
324	6		Area 1, Pit 115.1
325	6		Area 4, 408
326	7	49	Area 1, Channel C
327	7		Area 1, Channel C
328	8	47	Area 10, 1003
329	9	98+	Area 1, base of Channel C
330	9		Area 1, Channel C
331	9		Area 1, Channel C
332	9		Area 3
333	9		Area 14
334	9		'road surface at west'
335	9		unstratified
336	10	57	Area 1, base of Channel C
337	10	89	Area 1, Channel C, west
338	10.1		Area 1, Channel C
339	10.1		Area 4
340	10.1		unstratified
341	10.2		Area 1, Channel C
342	10.2		Area 4
343	10.3		Area 1, Channel C, west end
344	10.3		Area 1, Channel C
345	10.3		Area 1, Channel C
346	10.3		Area 1, 104
347	10.3		Area 1, Pit 115.1
348	10.3		Area 4
349	10.3		Area 4, 407
350	10.3		unstratified
351	10.4		Area 1, Channel C
352	10.4		Area 1, 104
353	10.4		Area 3
354	10.4		Area 4
355	10.4	49	Area 4
356	10.4	46	Area 4
357	10.4		Area 4
358	10.4		Area 4, extension
359	10.4		Area 4, extension
360	10.4		Area 5. 'hollow floor'
361	10.4		Area 16, 'ditches'
362	10.4		Area 7, 702
363	10.4		Area 7, 710
364	10.4		
365	10.4		
366	10.4		
367	10.5		Area 1, Channel C
368	10.5		Area 1, Channel C
369	10.5		Area 4, extension
370	10.5		
371	11.1		Area 1, Channel C
372	11.1		Area 4
373	11.1		unstratified
374	11.2		Area 1, Channel C, west end
375	11.2		Area 1, 107
376	11.2		Area 1, 102.2
377	11.2		Area 4, 408
378	11.2		Area 4
379	11.2		Area 5. 'hollow floor'
380	11.2		unstratified, possibly west end of quarry
381	12	69	Area 1, Channel C
382	12		Area 5. 'hollow floor'
383	12		road surface at west'
384	12		Area 1, Channel C
385	12	114	Area 4, extension
386	12		Area 1, Channel C
387	13		Area 1, 122
388	13	63	Area 4, 407.B
389	13		Area 1, Channel C
390	13		Area 10, 1001
391	13		Area 4
392	13		
393	13		Area 1, Channel C
394	13		Area 4
395	14	38+	Area 1, 120.2
396	14	28	Area 1, base of Channel C
397	10?		Area 4, unstratified
398	10?		unstratified
399	10?		Area 10, 1001
400			Area 4
401			Area 10, 1001
402			Area 2
403			Area 4, extension
404			Area 1, Channel C
405			Area 4, unstratified

Table 28. Copper alloy bracelets. Bracelets of types 10 and 11 have been subdivided by motif as follows: 10.1, strip bracelets with ring-and-dot motifs; 10.2, ring-and-dot with transverse grooves; 10.3, ring-and-dot, transverse grooves and notched edges; 10.4, geometric motifs (transverse or oblique grooves); 10.5, geometric and ring-and-dot motifs; 11.1, plain crenellations; 11.2, milled lower areas.

Type 14

Two examples of strip bracelets with 'cut-out' decoration have been assigned to Type 14 (395 and 396). Each is decorated with large cut-out circles separated by groups of smaller ones, all within a milled border. A fragment from a similar bracelet has been found occurring residually at Canterbury (Blockley *et al* 1995, 1025, fig 435, no 384); another was found at Lankhills in a grave dating between AD 360–70/380 (Clarke 1979 type D1j, fig 99, Grave 438, no 566), where examples from Bokerley Dyke, Silchester and Woodeaton are also cited.

Six small decorated strips bent into a circle may be broken from light strip bracelets or be finger rings of similar style, indeed they could well have started life as the former and been re-used as the later. Two (400 and 401) have remains of pierced terminals, indicating they derive from bracelets originally. The decorative motifs include punched dots (402 and 400) and incised 'feathered' (403) and transverse lines (404 and 405). One (401) can be paralleled by a finger ring found occurring residually at Colchester, as well as examples from Monkton and Canterbury (Crummy 1983, fig 50, no 1764).

Bone or antler bracelets *Ian Riddler*

Most of the thirteen examples of bone or antler bracelets are fragments which are broken at one end, generally across a rivet hole. In six cases, however, one or more of the terminals of the bracelets survive, which enables them to be ascribed to a particular type (Table 29).

As MacGregor has observed, it is difficult to define the precise material used in the manufacture of these bracelets (MacGregor 1985, 112–3). Deschler Erb has noted, however, that most of those from Augst are made from antler, and this may well be the case here (Deschler Erb 1998, 167). One fragment from Ickham (416) includes traces of cortile tissue on the inner face, which indicates that it is made from antler. No traces of soft tissue can be seen on the remaining pieces, which have been cut with some skill from the raw material. Various parts of red deer antler are curved and the bracelets may possibly have been cut from a section of brow tine, or from a length of the beam. Equally, however, it is possible (if less likely) that bone examples were fashioned from solid elements of the edges of animal ribs.

Most of the fragments are curved, although several are almost straight and others are slightly twisted. Clarke has noted that the Lankhills examples tended to decay and to straighten, following burial (Clarke 1979, 313). The Ickham

pieces have also been reduced in curvature and only one example (408), which has a diameter of 85mm, can be considered to have retained its original shape. Even this example is quite massive, in terms of its diameter, when compared with those of the copper alloy bracelets described above. It is inherently likely that the bracelets were softened, prior to being fastened, although the precise methods used in this process have not, as yet, been conclusively identified (Zurowski 1973; 1974; MacGregor 1985, 64).

The bracelets vary in width between 3 and 8mm, and are mostly between 1.5 and 3mm in thickness. Similar dimensions have been recorded for comparable examples from both Lankhills and York (Clarke 1979, 313; MacGregor 1985, 112; 1995, 424 and fig 160.15.1). All are rectangular in section, although the small example (411) is virtually square.

One bracelet (415) is decorated with two parallel linear grooves. Similar forms of simple decoration can be seen on bone or antler bracelets from Lankhills, Orton Hall Farm and Poundbury (Clarke 1979, fig 77.511; Mackreth 1996, 96; Greep 1993, fig 76.8). It is surprising that so few of these bracelets are decorated, particularly when this is the case with almost all contemporary examples of bracelets made of copper alloy (Johns 1996, 123–4).

Clarke distinguished three types of late Roman bone or antler bracelet on the basis, essentially, of the nature of their fastening (Clarke 1979, 313–4; MacGregor 1985, 112 3). All three types include two or more rivet holes at the terminals, although rivets are only an integral part of the fastening mechanism with bracelets of types B and C. Bracelets of type A are secured with ribbed metal sleeves and the terminals of the bracelets themselves are also corrugated. With type B the metal sleeves are plain and rivets of copper alloy or iron assist in securing the ends. Those of type C have distinctive, pared and tapered ends which are rivetted together and do not have metal sleeves.

In considering the smaller assemblage from Poundbury, Greep amalgamated types A and B and he defined two forms of bracelet, rather than three, on the basis of the presence or absence of a metal sleeve (Greep 1993, 105–8). In reviewing a sample from Tác, Bíró distinguished six types of bracelet on the basis of their decoration (Bíró 1987, 53–4 and figs 34–6; 1994, 27–8). Only one of the Ickham bracelets is decorated, however, and Clarke's threefold system has been adopted here, in preference to these other schemes.

One example (412) of a bracelet of type A can be identified, alongside two of type B and two of type C. One further example may belong to type C, although it is only slightly tapered. It is interesting to note that no metal sleeves remain

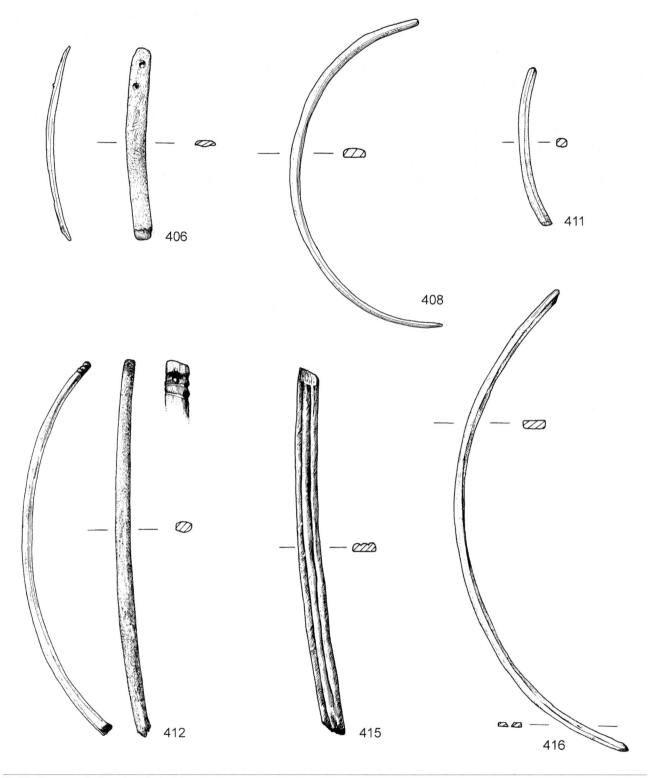

Fig 85. Bone or antler bracelets. Scale 1:1.

on these bracelets and there are virtually no rivets present at all. Indeed, the only metal fastening which survives is a trace of one copper alloy rivet on a bracelet of type C (**406**). There is little evidence to suggest that more than one of the Ickham bracelets was ever fastened together. No traces of metal can be seen at any of the surviving terminals (Adrian Tribe, pers comm). This situation contrasts vividly with the evidence from burials, where metal fastenings are much more common and where bracelets were clearly buried when complete and worn on the body (Clarke 1979, 313 4; Greep 1993, figs 76 7; McWhirr *et al* 1982, 129 and fig 80, 196A; Keller 1971, 107). In Hungary, at least, it was more common for them to have been worn on the left arm of the deceased (Bíró 1987, 53).

The contrast between the surviving elements of bracelets from cemeteries and settlements is repeated elsewhere in the late Roman period. At Canterbury only one of five bone or antler bracelets retains its metal fastening, and no metal fastening remains on any of the six bracelet fragments from Portchester, or on any of those from Bayeux (Greep 1995, nos 926, 997 and 1006 8; Webster 1975, 218 20; Delacampagne 1997, 149, nos 365, 453 and 921). It is not necessarily the case therefore, that the Ickham examples are fragments discarded during the latter stages of the production process, although this is possible.

Bone or antler bracelets belong essentially to the fourth century, and are not seen before that date (Clarke 1979, 314; Greep 1993, 308; Mackreth 1996, 96; Bíró 1994, 27; Deschler Erb 1998, 167). The majority may belong to the second half of the century (Keller 1971, 106 7). Stratified examples from Canterbury, with just one exception, are of late fourth-century date (Greep 1993, nos 926, 997 and

1006–8; Johns forthcoming). Clarke felt that those of type B could have been introduced slightly before those of type A, but there has been no subsequent confirmation of this suggestion and no chronological distinctions have been identified elsewhere (Clarke 1979, 314; Bíró 1987, 54; Greep 1993, 308).

The majority of the bracelets come from Area 4 (Table 29). Greep has noted that exceptional numbers of bracelets have come from Lydney, where it has been suggested that a ritual purpose lay behind their deposition (Greep 1993, 108; Wheeler and Wheeler 1932, 42). Unfortunately, however, too little is known of the precise location of the Ickham sample to be able to compare it, in spatial terms, with the Lydney assemblage.

Finger rings

Martin Henig

Most of the rings are what might be expected from any late third- or fourth-century Roman site. Some are diagnostic of the fourth or fifth centuries. Three simple rings are paralleled at Lankhills (**436** and **438**). Of special interest is a signet ring with a biblical subject, Moses striking the rock (**425**) which probably belonged to a Christian (though of course notionally it could have been worn by a Jew). Three rings have raised box bezels (**426** and **428**) which evidently held intaglios (? in silver), two of which remain. One displayed a single (male) portrait, now largely decayed; the other still has two facing portraits, they were almost certainly secular tokens given at betrothal or marriage. Two of the rings may belong in the fifth century, namely the ring with the biblical scene (**425**) as well as that with confronted heads (**426**).

A detailed catalogue of the finger rings is provided here. As noted above, several of the bracelets were also re-used as simple slip-knot rings; they are catalogued with the bracelets.

Catalogue of finger rings

No	Material	Type	Length mm	Context
406	bone or anter	C	50	Area 16, 'ditches'
407	bone or anter		37	Area 16, 'ditches'
408	bone or antler	C	122	Area 1, Channel C
409	bone or antler		158	Area 4
410	bone or antler		67	Area 4
411	bone or antler		43	Area 4, extension
412	bone or antler	A	110	Area 4, extension
413	bone or antler	B	41	Area 4, extension
414	bone or antler		52	Area 4, 335
415	bone or antler		96	Area 4, 335
416	antler	B	148	Area 7
417	antler?		128	Area 1, Channel C
418	bone or antler	C?	69	Area 7, 712

Table 29. Bone or antler bracelets.

419 Silver. Keeled ring (Henig type VIII see Henig 1978, 35, fig 1) with expanded leaf-shaped shoulders ornamented with three longitudinal grooves. Oval bezel contained a setting, now lost. Similar shoulders to those of a ring from Grovely Wood, Wiltshire (Johns 1996, 63, fig 3, 24). Diameter across shoulders 23mm; bezel 14mm by 10mm. Third century/ fourth century. Area 10, Context 1001.

420 Silver. Keeled ring (Henig type VIII) flattened above the shoulder but no defined bezel. Channel C.

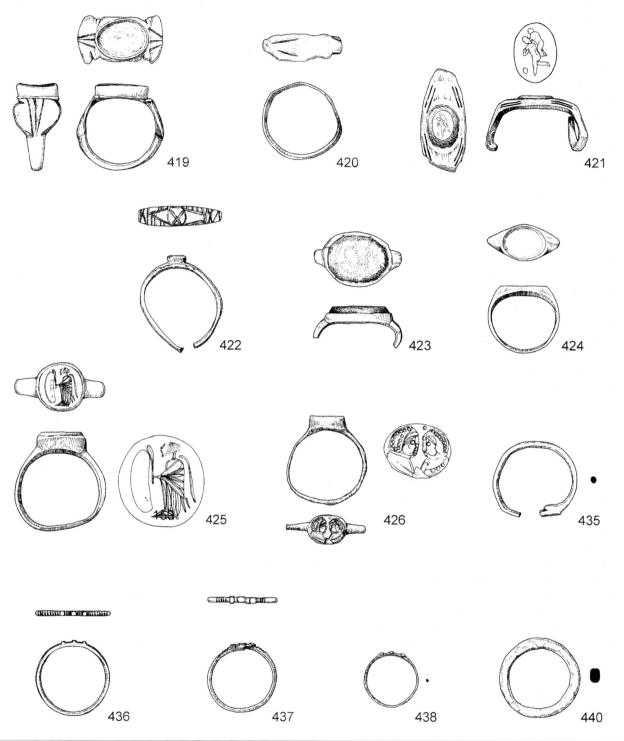

Fig 86. Finger rings. Scale 1:1.

421 Copper alloy. Ribbon hoop expanding towards bezel which is set with a glass intaglio imitating nicolo. The lower part of the hoop is lost and what remains has been flattened. The ring is of Henig Type XI. The intaglio depicts an adult male satyr carrying a young satyr on his back. For the type on a gem from Caerleon see Zienkiewicz 1986, 138, no 65. Length of ring fragment (bezel and shoulders) 20mm: intaglio measures 11mm by 8mm. Probably third century. Unstratified.

422 Copper alloy. Keeled ring (Henig type VIII) with expanded shoulders ornamented with grooved decoration and raised circular bezel with a simple cross incised upon it. Compare Henig 1994, 272, no 582 with crescent and star (from Egypt), and not engraved, Henkel 1913, 126, pl xx, no 1377 (Trier museum). For a rather broader ring but with similar bezel engraved with a cross see Allason-Jones and Miket 1984, 121 2, no 3, 161 (South Shields). Diameter 22mm. Third century/fourth century. Area 4.

423 Copper alloy. Ring with narrow, everted shoulders and raised bezel set with a glass setting imitating nicolo, but now badly shattered so no device can be discerned. Hoop below shoulders lost. Ring type as Henig 1995b, 1001, no 206. Diameter (shoulder to shoulder) 22mm; bezel 16mm by 11mm. Third century. Area 7, Context 712...

424 Copper alloy. Simple hoop expanding towards the oval bezel, now empty of its setting. Type XI. Compare Henig 1995b, 1004, no 224. Diameter 18mm. Second/third century. Area 14.

425 Copper alloy. Simple ribbon hoop with circular bezel. The device is Moses, wearing a long mantle like a philosopher, standing to the left and striking the rock. Compare, for ring type and subject, Chadour 1994, 134, no 461, there (mis)interpreted as Christ the fisherman. For the subject of Moses striking the rock note also the sheeting from a casket found at Intercisa in Hungary (Weitzmann 1979, 429, 30, no 3). Diameter of hoop 24mm; of bezel 12mm. Fourth to fifth century. Area 4 extension.

426 Copper alloy. Simple ribbon hoop with raised box bezel containing what appears to be a paste like substance. This preserves the form of an intaglio device of two confronted heads. For the ring type with box bezel see also below nos 427 and 428; also Henkel 1913, 98, pl xlii, no 1057 (from the Mosel at Coblenz). For the subject see Chadour 1994, 131 no 449 for a silver ring with confronted busts; also the well known gold ring from Brancaster (Henig 1978, no 790; Johns 1996, 53, fig 3, 12). Presumably a marriage ring. Diameter 21mm; bezel 8mm by 7mm. Fourth to fifth century. Area 4 extension.

427 Copper alloy. Thin hoop of circular section and pronounced raised oval box bezel. A label with the ring says, 'When found wet, the centre appeared to have an impressed surface. Possibly a human head, similar to a Constantinian AE4 Barbarous imitation. This later disintegrated'. A trace of the head seems to remain. Two silver bezels of about the same size from Silchester may be noted, Henig 1978, nos 786 and 787, especially the former which carries the legend *Iul, Bellator Vivas*, suggesting it is a love token. This is not unlikely here given the similarity of the ring to the 'marriage type', 426 above. Other human heads with fourth-century hair styles are featured on glass bezels from Richborough (Wilson 1968, 99 100, pl xlii, nos 162 and 163). Diameter 23mm; bezel 12.5 by 11mm. Fourth to fifth century. Area 10, Context 1006. *Not illus.*

428 Copper alloy. Similar ring with more flattened hoop; circular box bezel, now empty. Diameter 20mm; bezel 6 by 6mm. Fourth century. Channel C. *Not illus.*

429 Copper alloy. Ring with leaf-shaped expansion of bezel which is ornamented with four ridges each scored along its length with diagonal notches. Diameter 20mm. Area 4 extension. *Not illus.*

430 Copper alloy. Simple ring ornamented across the band with horizontal grooving. Bent. Diameter 17mm. Area 4 extension. *Not illus.*

431 Copper alloy. Simple ring; a little grooving on one side. Terminals originally hammered together, now sprung apart. Diameter 16mm. Channel C. *Not illus.*

432 Copper alloy. Simple ring with notches on each shoulder; flattened above where a bezel could have been affixed terminals now sprung apart. Diameter 18mm. Area 4 extension. *Not illus.*

433 Copper alloy. Simple ring with overlapping terminals, broad hoop. Diameter 21mm, width of hoop 5mm. Area 10, Context 1001. *Not illus.*

434 Copper alloy. Simple band with some notching across. Bent. Diameter 19mm. Area 14. *Not illus.*

435 Copper alloy. Simple band, snapped across at bezel. Diameter 22mm. Channel C.

436 Copper alloy. Ring with three small bosses at bezel, a notch between each boss and upon each shoulder. For the type M Wilson 1968, 100 and pl xcii, no 165 (Richborough) Clarke 1979, fig 75 no 146; fig 87, no 389; fig 90, no 337; fig 78, nos 567, 571, dated *c* AD 350–80. Diameter 19.5mm. Fourth century. Area 4 extension.

437 Copper alloy. Ring of same type as **436**. Three bosses mark bezel three notches on each shoulder. Diameter 19mm. Fourth century. Area 4.

438 Copper alloy. Diminutive and very thin ring, for a baby or young child, with three bosses marking bezel. Type as for **436**. Diameter 14mm. Fourth century. Area 2.

439 Iron. Possibly a key ring. Very broad and wide hoop with short raised ridge at one point, where a projection, perhaps the lever of a key has been broken off. Diameter 29mm. Area 4, Context 408. *Not illus.*

440 Copper alloy. Simple junction ring. Diameter 20mm. Area 10, Context 1001.

No	Material	Context
419	silver	Area 10, 1001
420	silver	Area 1, Channel C
421	copper alloy	unstratified
422	copper alloy	Area 4
423	copper alloy	Area 7, 712
424	copper alloy	Area 14
425	copper alloy	Area 4, extension
426	copper alloy	Area 4, extension
427	copper alloy	Area 10, 1006
428	copper alloy	Area 1, Channel C
429	copper alloy	Area 4, extension
430	copper alloy	Area 4, extension
431	copper alloy	Area 1, Channel C
432	copper alloy	Area 4, extension
433	copper alloy	Area 10, 1001
434	copper alloy	Area 14
435	copper alloy	Area 1, Channel C
436	copper alloy	Area 4, extension
437	copper alloy	Area 4
438	copper alloy	Area 2
439	iron	Area 4, 408
440	copper alloy	Area 10, 1001

Table 30. Finger rings.

Personalia

Quita Mould

This category is largely concerned with leather footwear, although it also includes toilet implements and combs. The footwear consists largely of multi-layered bottom unit components for nailed shoes although small fragments possibly deriving from one-piece shoes were found also. The footwear is principally of late Roman type, though there are a few exceptions that appear to be earlier in date.

The small collection of toilet implements is restricted to tweezers, spoon-probes, a spatula, a cosmetic grinder and a nail cleaner. There are no examples of *ligulae*, which would

be expected in this category, given that they are common implements. In addition, there are also two fragments of composite combs. One is of a conventional late Roman form, although it is relatively small and fine. The other fragment comes from a type of triangular comb that is otherwise seen in early Anglo-Saxon burial and settlement contexts.

Hobnails and cleats

Forty-eight hobnails from shoes were found scattered across the site. Three small cleats (455, 456 and 457) were also recovered and are of a type thought to have been hammered into the leather shoe soles to prevent wear. Similar cleats with traces of leather preserved were found associated with hobnails in six late Roman graves at Lankhills (Clarke 1979, 321 and fig 323), while seven were found at the feet of a skeleton at Rotherley (Pitt-Rivers 1887, 86, pl XXVIII, 16) and others at the feet of a skeleton at Bokerley Dyke (Pitt-Rivers 1892, 128). The author has no personal experience of an example found *in situ* on a shoe sole and the possibility exists that they come from a separate object placed at the feet of the burial.

No	Quantity	Context
441	1	Area 1, 103
442	2	Area 1, 104
443	1	Area 1, 105
444	9	Area 4, 408
445	1	Area 1, 115
446	2	Area 1, 115/2
447	2	Area 10, 1001
448	1	Area 10, unstratified
449	5	Area 4, 408
450	12	Area 4, extension
451	2	Area 4, 335
452	1	Area 1, Channel C, east end
453	4	Area 16, ditches
454	3	Area 5

Table 31. Hobnails.

No	Quantity	Length mm	Tang height mm	Context
455	1	36		Area 1, base of Channel C
456	1		13	Area 4, 407
457	1	30+	10	unstratified

Table 32. Cleats.

Leather shoes

The leather was first catalogued by John Thornton in 1975, shortly after excavation, and has been looked at subsequently, more than twenty years later, by the present author. The leather has air-dried and is extremely fragile and friable. Certain items observed by Thornton are now in a highly fragmentary condition and his original comments have been noted and used to inform the interpretation of the material given in this report.

Ninety-two items were examined from the excavations and principally comprise fragmentary remains of multi-layered bottom units from shoes of nailed construction, the most commonly recovered shoe type throughout the Roman period. Features on those from Ickham indicate a late Roman date, with certain exceptions discussed fully below. A small number of fragments possibly from shoes of one-piece construction were also identified, along with limited evidence for shoemaking. The majority of the leather appears to be the result of rubbish disposal save a pair of shoes worn by an adult body buried in the later fourth century. None of the leather finds have been illustrated.

The leather is recorded as coming from four locations. The majority, 72 per cent of the assemblage, came from the ditches (which particular ditches are not specified). A small quantity came from Channel C, Area 4 and Area 7. A pair of shoes, now represented by their nailed bottom units only, are known to have come from an unlocated burial, identified here as Burial B (Pl XIX, p 68).

Although much of the assemblage is fragmentary, ten complete or near-complete individual bottom units were recovered, and a further thirteen bottom units had approximately half of their original length remaining. This provides a conservative estimate of a minimum of twenty-three individual nailed shoes represented by the leather recovered, but this is likely to be an under representation of the true figure. To this should be added the possible fragments from shoes of one-piece construction (a minimum of one shoe).

Although shoes of nailed construction are the most commonly found Roman shoe type, one might expect a wider range of shoe constructions to be represented in what is principally a late Roman assemblage. Too much should not be read into the apparent lack of shoes of one-piece or stitched construction in the Ickham assemblage. The hurried salvage operation under which much of the excavations were conducted may have influenced the leather recovered and it is possible that only leather which contained iron hobnails came to the attention of the excavators and metal detectors.

The majority of the leather finds are highly fragmentary shoes of nailed construction. These survived principally as nailed multi-layered bottom units comprising an insole, middle often with additional middle lamina (packing strips), and a sole. The lasting margins of the shoe uppers were often preserved sandwiched between the insole, middle and sole. Occasionally, larger fragments of the uppers were recovered and small lengths of seam (a minimum of five examples) were recognised. The shape of the toe was preserved on six bottom units, the majority were pointed, a single example (520) from Area 4, was oval. Constructional thonging was noted on nineteen bottom units or fragments, and where discernible (in five cases) the thonging was found to be of type 1, that is running vertically down the centre of the bottom unit from toe to seat (520, 532 and 533). A further three bottom units were seen to have been made without constructional thonging. Twenty-five bottom units or bottom unit fragments were sufficiently complete for their individual attributes to be recorded and these are given in Table 33. Smaller fragments (459–85) are listed in Appendix I (p 347), along with the rest of the leather recovered.

Shoe sizes are calculated from measurements of complete insoles. Eight bottom units from shoes of nailed construction were sufficiently complete for this component to be measured. The figures presented here (in Table 33) are unadjusted with no allowance for any shrinkage that may have taken place following excavation. Shrinkage does seem to have occurred during storage (see discussion of the shoes from Burial B below) but the extent is uncertain as one cannot be certain that the same measurements were taken nor the condition of the item when measured. What is clear is that footwear for both adults and children is present; indeed children's shoes were also noted amongst the broken shoe parts that make up the bulk of the assemblage. The few shoes of Adult 3 (continental size 35) and above are likely to have been worn by men, the shoes in the larger child and smaller adult sizes to be worn by women and adolescents, while child size 7 (continental size 24) was for a child. A 'normal' population appears to be represented though little inference can be drawn from this as the numbers measured are so small.

Nailing patterns (Fig 87)

Nailing patterns could be discerned on twenty-two bottom units or bottom unit fragments. The majority (64 per cent, fourteen examples) were of Type A (Fig 87, A) with a closely spaced row of nails around the perimeter with a decorative pattern of nails infilling the tread and seat (Mould 1997a,

Nailing patterns found at Ickham

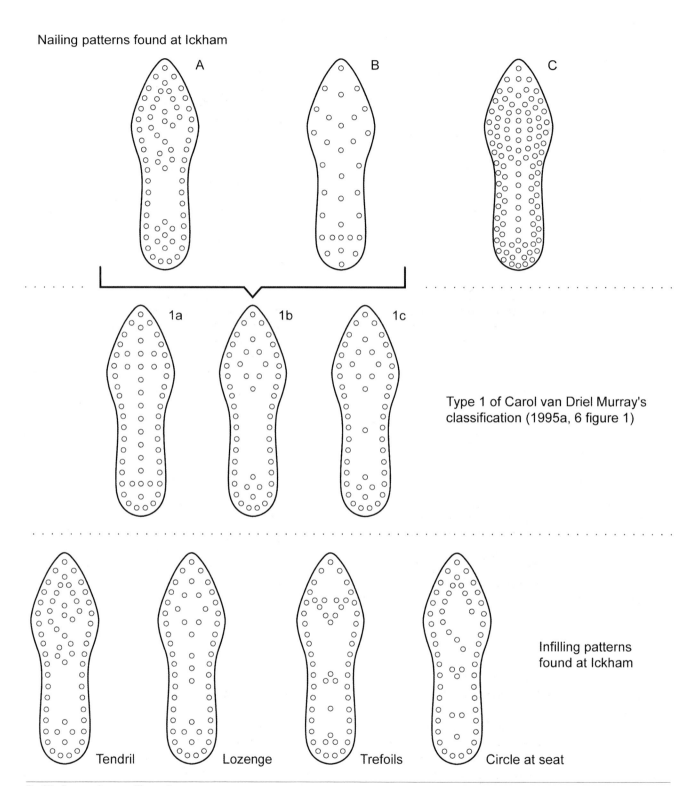

Type 1 of Carol van Driel Murray's classification (1995a, 6 figure 1)

Infilling patterns found at Ickham

Fig 87. Roman shoes: nailing patterns.

331 and fig 243). A further six examples (27 per cent) were of Type B (Fig 87, B) with a widely spaced row of nails around the perimeter and widely spaced infilling at the tread and seat. Three bottom unit fragments could be said to be heavily nailed, Type C (Fig 87, C), with many closely spaced rows of nails (523, 524 and possibly 525).

Type A and Type B nailing patterns, having a single line of peripheral nailing, both fall into Type 1 of Carol van Driel-Murray's nailing pattern classification (van Driel-Murray 1995a, 6 and fig 1), see Fig 87. At *Vindolanda* (*ibid*, 7), where a suitably large assemblage is available for study, the single row of nailing around the edge (Type 1) is by far the most popular pattern of nailing from the later second century onwards. Insufficient remained of the small fragments with heavy nailing of Type C at Ickham to categorise beyond van Driel-Murray's Type 2 or 3, which predominated in the earlier periods. Nine examples of van Driel-Murray's Type 1a (with a central line of nailing Fig 87, 1a) and three examples of van Driel-Murray's Type 1c (with a single nail at the waist Fig 87, 1c) could be recognised at Ickham. No examples of Type 1b without infill nailing at the waist were identified.

Infilling patterns at tread and seat (see Fig 87)

Within both the closely spaced (Type A) and widely spaced (Type B) peripheral nailing distinct patterns of infill nailing could be recognised. Seven bottom units had a tendril pattern of nails at the tread (525, 526, 527, 528, 529, 530 and 531), and two had a lozenge pattern (534 and 535). The tendril nailing pattern is common (see Mould 1997a, 331 for British comparanda) occurring widely, along with the S and lozenge pattern, from the AD 160s onwards (van Driel-Murray 1995a, 6). Two examples had a distinctive circular pattern at the seat with a single nail at the centre (536 and 527). They also had a distinct trefoil nailing motif at the waist. Individual groups of three nails (trefoils), a popular nailing pattern on fourth-century footwear (van Driel-Murray 1995b, 116), were a notable nailing pattern motif amongst the Ickham assemblage, occurring on two other bottom units (533 and 542). One example (533) shown in Fig 87 (trefoils) can be paralleled by that on a nailed shoe from Well 1 at Dalton Parlours (Mould 1990, 231 and fig 142, no 11) in use from the third quarter of the third century and abandoned shortly after AD 370 (Wrathmell and Nicholson 1990, 244).

Thornton noted that two distinct sizes of iron hobnail were used on one shoe sole (452) and that a particularly large square-headed nail occurred amongst the hobnails on another (537), the latter likely to be the result of repair.

Nailed shoe upper styles

Twelve heel stiffeners were noted. Used to support the heel area of the quarters of shoe uppers, they indicate that the nailed shoes had a closed upper. Thornton noted a heel stiffener measuring 50mm in height. Though relatively little of the shoe uppers survived, a small amount of evidence exists for shoe styles of second-century date (489, 537 and 463) and a little more for shoe styles belonging to the later Roman period. The few upper fragments sufficiently well preserved to allow identification appear to be of goatskin.

A highly fragmentary shoe with a small fragment of upper decorated with a series of small punched squares (517) is likely to date to the beginning of the second century. When initially examined following excavation it was seen to be part of the toe area of a shoe vamp with an internal lining. The vamp upper had a turned-in lasting margin with a scalloped edge and grain/flesh holes. The vamp upper was decorated above the height of the lining with a grid of small cut-out squares and a line of holes below. While it is dangerous to place too much significance on such a small piece of surviving evidence it would appear to come from a 'fishnet' openwork shoe upper. Nailed shoes with such elaborate openwork uppers are found in both military and civilian contexts from the last quarter of the first century to *c* 130 (van Driel-Murray 1987, 36). They were a quality shoe and likely to have belonged to someone of high status. At *Vindolanda* shoes of this style are thought to have been worn by the commander's household (van Driel-Murray 1993, 45 and fig 19).

517   Length of internal shoe lining with a skived top edge and a corresponding fragment of upper with a line of awl made grain/flesh stitch holes and another line of regular small holes above. Also a fragment of upper with a lattice design of regular small square holes *c* 1.5 x 1.5mm with 1.5mm between the squares and a small fragment of nailed bottom unit. Leather goatskin. *Not illus.*

There is a small amount of evidence of later second-/early third-century footwear, though it would be unwise to place too much reliance on it. A fragmentary shoe (537) includes the remains of an area of folded hem secured by a line of grain/flesh stitching with a stitch length of 3mm, in awl-made holes. An impressed line of decoration was noted when it was originally examined. This may come from a closed latchet fastening shoe characterised by having a hemmed top edge with crescentic lace holes within the fold (for example style 4 at Birdoswald: Mould 1997a, 336 and fig 244, no 4) in a

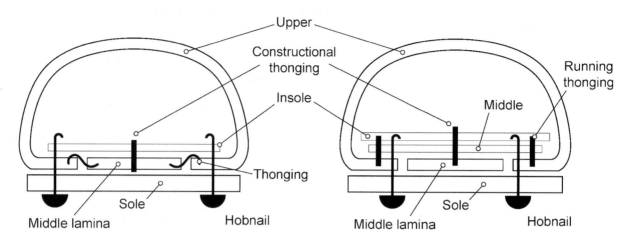

Fig 88. Roman shoes: constructional details.

style commonly found in contexts dating to the later half of the second and into the third century.

The remainder of the shoes of nailed construction, where discernible, had features which indicate a later Roman date. The method by which the lasting margins of the uppers were held in place between the bottom unit components prior to nailing (illustrated in Fig 88) and the style of the uppers themselves are diagnostic.

Examples were found with the edge of the upper lasting margin sewn to the edge of a middle lamina by fine thonging, *see* Fig 88 (left) (518, 519, 466 and 538). Others were secured to the middle by a line of fine thonging running around the perimeter parallel to the edge, *see* Fig 88 (right) (519, 520, 481 and 539), and one apparently by both (519). These are constructional features characteristic of shoes of third- and fourth-century date. Evidence for side seams were found on three shoes. One fragment (518) had a side seam sewn with fine thonging; this lapped seam had its edge whipped to the interior of the upper. Whipped stitching to secure a free seam edge on the interior of a shoe upper also occurred on the back seam of a one-piece shoe from the late third-/fourth-century assemblage from Well 1 at Dalton Parlours (Mould 1990, 233 and fig 142, no 12). Another fragmentary upper with a side seam (520) had tunnel stitching running down the vamp toward the toe. When originally catalogued this was described as decorative thonging. A vertical line of decorative stitching or thonging is a feature found on a small but increasing number of shoes from later Roman contexts in Britain. To date nine examples are known to the author, occurring chiefly in the south-east of the country in well deposits of fourth-century date. Decorative thonging on the

vamp can be paralleled on a shoe from fourth-century well backfill at Skeldergate, York (MacGregor 1978, 31, fig 28, no 353), the most northerly example recorded, and a shoe found at Piddington, Northants, in a well with coins and pottery dating AD 330–60 (Friendship-Taylor 1997). The dating of other examples await confirmation from other independent dating evidence.

518   Upper lasting margin fragment with small area of vertical seam. The lasting margin has a closely-spaced row of nail holes and thonging at the edge to attach to a middle lamina. The vertical seam is lapped with a well sewn line of running thonging. The edge of the seam was originally whip stitched to the interior of the upper to ensure it laid flat. Leather heavily worn. Surviving length: 105+mm, Height: 40+mm. Probably from the same shoe as 519. *Not illus.*

519   Fragment of delaminated bottom unit component, middle or insole and an area of upper lasting margin present with thonging along the edge and running thonging on the interior parallel to the edge. Length: 62+mm. *Not illus.*

520   Shoe of nailed construction for the right foot, comprising a complete insole of narrow shape with an oval toe and medium tread tapering to the seat, with no distinct waist. Delaminated tread area of middle and possibly sole with widely spaced nailing and constructional thonging of type 1. Part of the heel stiffener present with top edge and nailed lasting margin broken. The toe area of the vamp also present with nailed lasting margin with holes for thonging or bracing at the edge and suggestion of running thonging parallel to the edge. An orginal edge at the left side of the vamp suggests the position of a side seam. Vamp throat area torn away, a line

of tunnel stitching runs vertically down the vamp toward the toe. Leather dried out and much delaminated. Insole length: 160mm, tread width 53mm. *Not illus.*

The burial

Two nailed bottom units (530 and 531) are labelled as 'sandals from extended burial'. Though the location of this burial is unknown, a note made when initially catalogued suggests 'Surface or Area 7?' (*see* p 69). The burial was that of a 45/50 year old interred with a complete pot dating to the second half of the fourth century (*see* above p 119). Photographs of the burial (eg Pl XIX) show the shoes *in situ* at the feet of the skeleton, the shoes appear to have been worn by the body when buried and not placed alongside it in the grave. The tendril pattern of nailing dates the shoes to post AD 160. The surviving upper fragments indicate a closed upper with a side seam. As the bottom unit components were firmly secured it was not possible to see how the upper lasting margin was attached. Estimation of the equivalent modern shoe size was hampered by the fact that the shoes appear to have undergone some post-excavation shrinkage whilst in storage. One shoe (530) was the equivalent of Adult size 6 when originally examined but found to be Adult size 4 when examined twenty years later. Despite this discrepancy, the shoe size suggests the burial to be of an adult male (van Driel-Murray 2001, 360).

530   Complete nailed bottom unit, virtually straight for left foot, with insole, middle lamina and sole. Short pointed toe, medium tread and wide waist and seat. Closely spaced single line of nails around edge with infilling at tread and seat (tendril pattern). Type 1 constructional thonging. Heel stiffener present at seat, height originally recorded as 50mm. Insole leather worn ?goatskin. Length originally recorded as 265mm, surviving 240mm. *Not illus.*

531   Nailed bottom unit, for right foot, as above. Toe area missing. Areas of upper including heel stiffener preserved around the perimeter. When originally catalogued a small triangular fragment of upper present at the inside waist with a edge/flesh side seam stitch length 4mm and loose fragment of upper present. Length surviving: *c* 230+mm. *Not illus.*

Shoes of one-piece construction

Three fragments may come from shoes of one-piece construction. A fragment of grain/flesh seam (504) possibly from a seat seam, and the left side of the seat and waist area (505) from a one-piece shoe were found in the ditches. A broken fastening loop (503) of a type usually found on shoes of one-piece construction came from Channel C. In addition, a rectangular thonged patch was recovered from the ditches. Similar patches have been found covering the interior of seat seams of one-piece shoes and patching other un-nailed shoes elsewhere. It is comparable to a similar patch attached to what is described as a *solea* sole recovered from well II from Scole, Norfolk, backfilled between *c* AD 160 and the late third century (Adams 1977, fig 88, no 6A/B).

Evidence for shoemaking

A very limited amount of evidence for shoemaking in the form of waste leather was recovered from the site. A single intersectional cutting piece of goatskin (480) from the cutting out of shoe soles, and four delaminated trimmings (508) from pattern cutting were found in the ditches. Waste leather cannot be independently dated and this secondary waste may date from the Roman or medieval period, being associated with Roman footwear, however, it is assumed to be of Roman date. The large quantities of waste leather produced by shoemaking and the repair and refurbishment of other leather goods were not recovered here.

Several small fragments of scrap with no distinguishing features were found. They were, however, heavily compacted and therefore likely to come from shoe bottom unit components.

The leather by context

Channel C, Mills 2 and 3, Contexts 107 and 115: Ceramic Assemblage 13

Eight finds are recorded as recovered from these contexts. The peripheral nailing on the fragmentary shoe components of nailed construction suggests that a minimum of two shoes were represented. Surviving features on the remaining uppers suggest a late Roman date. A fastening loop possibly from a shoe of one-piece construction (503) was also recovered.

701: timber-lined well in Area 7: Ceramic Assemblage 23

Fragmentary remains of at least two shoes of nailed construction (483 and 499) were recovered from the timber-lined well in Area 7, backfilled at the end of the fourth century or later. Constructional features used to attach the upper lasting margin to the middle bottom unit component suggest a late Roman date.

712: unstratified

A bottom unit from a shoe of nailed construction (540) with no constructional thonging and the upper lasting margin attached to the middle lamina by thonging was found in this context. Its nailing pattern comprised a line of closely-spaced nails around the perimeter with a single vertical line down the centre (Fig 87, van Driel-Murray 1995a, type 1a, fig 1). Two other fragments from a bottom unit of nailed construction were also found (484 and 485).

406: post-hole

Fragmentary remains of the quarters area of a shoe upper supported by a heel stiffener from a shoe of nailed construction was found in context 406 (498).

408: Ceramic Assemblage 20, fill of 408 and uppermost fill of Pit 407

Fragments from two bottom units of nailed construction were found in context 408 (475 and 476).

Area 4

At least three bottom units from shoes of nailed construction were recovered from Area 4. These included a shoe for the right foot (520) with remains of a side-seamed upper with a line of tunnel stitching running vertically toward the toe likely to date to the fourth century.

Area 4 extension, Pit 414.3: possibly Ceramic Assemblage 11, Layers 2–5 over Pit 414

A fragment of bottom unit of nailed construction was recovered from this context (459).

The 'ditches'

Thirty-five bottom units or bottom unit fragments from shoes of nailed construction were found in 'ditches' without specified context numbers. While most appear to date to the later Roman period, two examples may be earlier. A nailed shoe with a possible 'fishnet' openwork upper (517) dating to the end of the first/beginning of the second century was found and a small hemmed fragment of upper possibly of later second-/early third-century date (537). One bottom unit (533) had a distinctive trefoil nailing pattern (*see* Fig 87) also seen on a shoe from a well abandoned shortly after AD

No	Length (mm)/size	Parts present	Nailing type	Foot	Context
1340		S M IN	B		Area 4
458		S M IN HS		R	Area 4
525		S M IN U	?C		Area 4
520	160 CD7	?S M IN CT U	B	R	Area 4
526		S M U	B		'ditches'
536		S ?M IN U HS	A		'ditches'
536		S M IN CT	A		'ditches'
1341		S ?M IN CT HS	B		Channel C
538		S M IN CT			'ditches'
534	195 CD11	S M IN CT U HS	A	R	'ditches'
1342		S M IN CT	A		'ditches'
1343		S M ML CT	A	L	'ditches'
528	205 CD12	S M IN CT U HS	A	R	'ditches'
524		S M IN	C		'ditches'
533	222 AD2	M IN CT	B	R	'ditches'
527, 1344	236 AD3	S ML IN HS	A		'ditches'
542		S M IN CT	B		'ditches'
529		S M IN	A	L	'ditches'
1345	200 CD12	IN CT	A	L	'ditches'
537		S IN U	A		'ditches'
539		ML IN CT U			701
540		S M IN	A		712
535		S	A	R	surface
530	240 AD4	S M ML IN CT HS	A	R	'Grave 4'
531	230 AD3	S M IN CT U	A	L	'Grave 4'

Table 33. Shoes of nailed construction. AD, equivalent modern shoe size, adult; CD, equivalent modern shoe size, child; S, sole; M, middle; ML, middle lamina; IN, insole; CT, constructional thonging; U, uppers; HS, heel stiffener.

370 at Dalton Parlours (Mould 1990, fig 142, no 11). Nine other small fragments of shoe upper and three fragments of narrow thonging used to secure uppers to bottom unit components occurred. Two fragments possibly from a shoe of one-piece construction (504 and 505) were also found. An intersectional cutting piece (541) and four trimmings (508), the only indication of leather-working on the site, were recovered from the ditches. In addition, a further eight small fragments had no distinguishing features preserved.

Toilet implements

The small collection of toilet implements includes tweezers, spoon-probes, a spatula, a cosmetic grinder and a nail cleaner. Five sets of copper alloy tweezers have narrow arms varying

No	Object	Length mm	Width mm	Context
543	copper alloy tweezers	51	4	Area 1, Pit 115
544	copper alloy tweezers	46	4	Area 1, Pit 115.1
545	copper alloy tweezers	39	4	Area 1, Pit 120.2
546	copper alloy tweezers	43	3	Area 4
547	copper alloy tweezers	62	5	Area 4, extension
548	copper alloy spoon-probe	100+		Area 10, 1002
549	copper alloy probe	92+		Area 10, 1001
550	copper alloy spatula			Area 10, 1001
551	copper alloy grinder	39		Area 4
156	copper alloy nail cleaner	27	13	unstratified
157	copper alloy nail cleaner	47	17	Area 4, 408
552	copper alloy stem			unstratified
553	iron stem			Area 4

Table 34. Toilet instruments.

in length from 39–62mm and width from 3–5mm. A spoon-probe *cyathiscomeles* (**548**) and a probe from a second instrument (549) were both recovered from Area 10. The spoon-probe was used as a surgeon's curette or sound, as well as for more everyday purposes like extracting cosmetics from bottles and applying them to the face. A flat blade from a spatula was found (**550**) in the same area, and such instruments often formed part of a double-ended implement. The spatula-probe *spathomele* was used to mix and apply ointments, or in conjunction with a scalpel as a surgical blunt dissector (Crummy 1983, 60–3). It is surprising that the simple cosmetic spoon with a small, flat scoop, *the ligula*, commonly found at other sites, does not occur at Ickham.

A small, undecorated cosmetic grinder (551) was found in Area 4. It is thought that such implements were used as a pestle in conjunction with a 'grooved pendant' to grind and apply eye cosmetics, although it would have served well as a nail cleaner. The decoration on the more elaborate cosmetic grinder sets recovered has been interpreted as having a connection with fertility and virility and the recovery of examples in proximity to temple sites and in burials may suggest a religious or ritual use (Trett 1983, 220). It should be mentioned here that a small piece of galena (554) was found on the surface, which when ground could be used to make a pigment or cosmetic.

Two nail cleaners (156 and 157) were found. One (157), with a disc-shaped body decorated with a series of chip carved nicks and punched dots, was found in occupation debris with pottery of late fourth-century date. The suspension loop, set at a right angle to the body, is worn through, indicating that it is likely

to be a casual loss. Such decorated nail cleaners were worn as strap-ends at this time and are included in the catalogue of late Roman belt-fittings above (Table 19, pp 168–9).

In addition, a stem with decorative transverse mouldings (552) and a fragment of spirally-twisted iron wire, covered with a white metal coating probably of tin (553), both appear to be the stems derived from other toilet implements.

Combs

Ian Riddler

Fragments of two antler combs were recovered from Ickham, one of which is a double-sided composite, whilst the other is a triangular comb. Each is described in turn here.

The fragmentary double-sided comb (**555**) is of a familiar late Roman type. It has a lightly indented back and a curved graduation to the teeth as they lengthen towards the connecting plate. The profiled back to the end segment, alongside the shallow, bevelled connecting plate and the presence of both fine and coarse teeth, all serve to identify the comb as late Roman.

The profiling of the back of the end segment is very subtle and understated. It can be compared in this respect with combs from Darenth, Woodhall and York, although the Woodhall comb is more elaborate in design (Philp 1973, 153 and fig 46.451; Ottaway 1993, fig 71; Manby 1966, 343 and fig 2.7). Unpublished combs from Canterbury and London are also similar for this particular characteristic and both also include perforations beyond the line of the connecting plate, as is the case here. It is likely that this single perforation is decorative and it is not a suspension hole.

In contrast to most combs of this type, the Ickham example is relatively narrow and has noticeably fine teeth. Late Roman combs are short and stout in proportions (MacGregor 1985, 92) and it is unusual for them to be less than 50mm in width (Fig 89). The only other late Roman comb from Britain which is of a similarly slender width came from a grave at Lynch Farm, Orton Waterville, and the teeth of that comb appear to be unusually truncated (Jones 1975, 113 and fig 14.36).

The teeth of the Ickham comb are also noticeably fine, with a spacing of one tooth per millimetre on one side. Late Roman double-sided composite combs generally include both fine and coarse teeth, and most sets lie within the range of four to eight per centimetre.

The majority of combs of this type can be dated to the fourth century, and to the last third of that century in particular (Keller 1971, 112; Galloway 1979, 247; Hills 1981, 97; Riddler 1988,

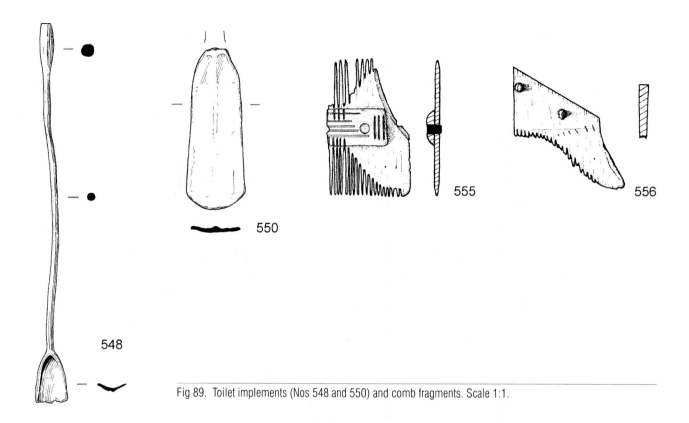

Fig 89. Toilet implements (Nos 548 and 550) and comb fragments. Scale 1:1.

374). It is difficult to judge the extent to which they continued in use into the fifth century. At least a dozen are now known from early Anglo-Saxon contexts, but none of these contexts can be set unequivocally in the early or middle part of the fifth century, and it is likely that these were collected, retained and used in the same manner as other Iron Age and Roman *spolia* (Riddler 1988, 374; White 1988). A case has been made for the fifth-century or later dating of a comb of this type from Queensford Mill, Dorchester, but it is not entirely convincing (Chambers 1987, 58 and figs 5 and 7).

Keller has noted that combs with straight backs to their end segments were produced in central Europe from as early as the fourth century, and this suggestion has been echoed subsequently (Keller 1971, 112–3; Cüppers 1984, 334). Although double-sided composite combs with straight backs were present in Europe at this early date, the English series retains curved, concave backs in the fifth century. Examples are known from Abingdon, Barton Court Farm, St Mary Cray and Spong Hill and some, at least, can be provenanced to an early workshop in the Abingdon area (de Hoog 1984, 5: F3 and fig 108.3 and 4; Hart 1984, fig 6.3; Hills and Penn

1981, fig 174.2192; Hills *et al* 1987, fig 110.2600/7 and 2560/4). Similar combs are seen also in Frisian contexts (Boeles 1951, pl XXVII.5; Roes 1963, pl XV.2–3). All of these combs come, however, from Germanic or early Anglo-Saxon contexts.

An end segment (**556**) can be identified as a part of a comb of Thomas *Typ* II Variante 1, and Böhme type C (Thomas 1960, 94–101; Böhme 1974, 122–6). The lack of any accompanying connecting plates means that it can only be assigned to a type, and not to a sub-group, and this is essentially on the basis of the subdued outward flaring of the end segment. For both Thomas and Böhme, this is taken to be a typologically early feature and more overtly extended end segments are thought to be later in date (Thomas 1960, 98; Böhme 1974, 123). Böhme has noted that with combs of type C the graduation of the teeth echoes that of the line of the end segment, and that is the case here (*ibid*, 123). With earlier Germanic triangular combs, like those illustrated by Pescheck, the graduation of the teeth does not generally coalesce with the line of the end segments (Pescheck 1978, 48–50 and taf 10.5, 100.16 and 136.15).

Combs of Böhme type C belong to the fifth century, and most have been assigned to the second half of that century (Böhme 1974, 123). The subdued flaring of this end segment may suggest that it is early in this series. Other combs of type C from English contexts include examples from cremation cemeteries at Lackford, Loveden Hill, Newark and Spong Hill (*ibid*, 123 note 553; Kinsley 1989, fig 90i; Hills and Penn 1981, fig 173.2161). Although triangular combs of Böhme types B, D and E have been found in late Roman contexts (Hills 1981, 98–9) those of type C have not, and almost all have come from early Anglo-Saxon cremation burials. This situation echoes that seen in north-western Europe, as at Trier, for example (Gilles 1981, 336 and taf 69).

Objects with possible religious significance

Quita Mould

The most obvious item of potential religious significance from Ickham is a wooden figurine, which is described in detail below. In addition, small copper alloy bells and a possible cymbal may have been used during religious ceremony. The unusual openwork fitting (Fig 75, **173**) of brass which is described above (pp 165–7) in the section on military items may have a ritual significance, as also in the case of the copper alloy finger ring (Fig 86, **425**, p 203) with an image of Moses striking the rock. A small copper alloy mount (561, Table 35) in the form of an antelope or gazelle head should also be noted here. An axe-headed pin of copper alloy (Fig 79, **245**) is described above (Type 8, p 181) and this too may have religious connotations.

The spatial distribution of these items is not unduly helpful. The bells and the axe-headed pin came from Area 4 and their location may relate to their gathering as scrap material. The same can be said for the fragment of a lead tank (**563**) from context 115. The copper alloy mount came from a ditch; another of the bells is unstratified. The figurine, however, came from context 310. It is therefore the only of these items to be found in the vicinity of the feature 335, which was originally identified as a shrine (*see* p 33).

Bells

Three hemispherical bells were recovered from Area 4. One (557) is decorated with a series of compass drawn double ring-and-dot motifs. The bells are comparable with a hemisperical bell threaded along with a glass bead onto a two strand bracelet from grave 1 at Butt Road, Colchester dating to *c* AD 320–450 (Crummy 1983, fig 41.1808) and a second example from grave 278 dating from the second century to *c* AD 320 (*ibid,* fig 54.1811) thought to have been deposited with other trinkets within a chain link purse. A fourth bell of differing form was found with gently concave curving sides similar in shape and size to a bell-headed stud.

Mount

A flat sectioned mount (561) in the form of an animal head was found in a ditch. It has a pair of inward pointing horns with oblique mouldings depicting spiral twisting in the manner of an antelope or gazelle.

Figurine

Peter Clark

The wooden figurine (**562**) was found lying on its left side in context 310 (the eastern end of Channel A) running parallel to the road; other finds from this context included a number of fourth-century coins, a *sestertius* of Marcus Aurelius, scraps of copper alloy, two pieces of broken bracelet, a group of eighteen rolled lead tubes, thought to be net sinkers, and several fragments of lead waste (these were within 2 metres of the figurine).

A sample of wood from the figurine was submitted for dating by the Oxford Radiocarbon Accelerator Unit in 1998. This returned a date of 1850 ± 50 BP (sample ref CK74; OxA no OxA-8047). This has been calibrated by Alex Bayliss to AD 30–320 (at 95 per cent confidence), using the maximum intercept method of Stuiver and Reimer (1986) and the calibration set of Stuiver *et al* (1998). The figurine is almost certainly Roman in date (98.4 per cent probable).

Preliminary discussion of the object (Coles 1993) has drawn attention to its similarity with objects of prehistoric date, but there seems no compelling reason to question the Roman date of the figurine. A number of other figurines found at various places in the British Isles, such as Roos Carr, Kingsteignton, Ballachulish, Dagenham, Ralaghan and Lagore do offer some similarities with the Ickham find (Coles 1990). However, radiocarbon dating has demonstrated that these figures are of prehistoric date, ranging from about 3000 BC to 350 BC, and have been fashioned from pine, oak, yew and ash. The Ickham example is the only one from Britain to be made of maple, and the only one of Roman date.

Within the boundaries of the Roman empire, wooden figurines are not unknown, such as those retrieved from

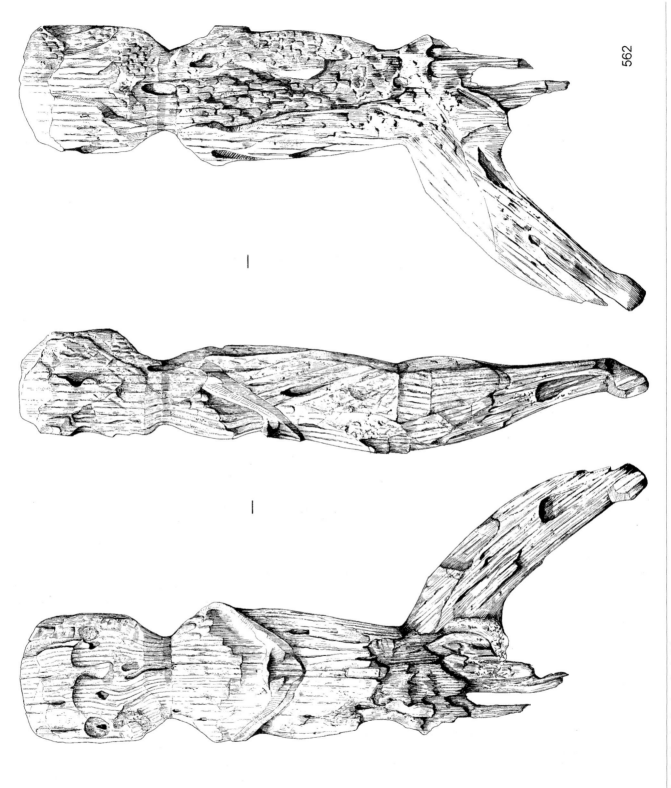

562

Fig 90. Wooden figurine. Scale 1:2.

Sources de la Seine (Deyts 1983; Martin 1965), Chamalières (Dumontet and Romeuf 1980; Vatin 1972) and Villimpenta, Italy (Deyts 1983, 162, plate xciv, c); however, the majority of these examples reflect classical expressions of form and few offer good parallels with the Ickham figure.

Some wooden figures from northern Europe dating to the Roman period offer better parallels with the Ickham find, however; an oak example from Skjeberg, Ostfold in Norway was radiocarbon dated to around AD 260 +/- 50 (Johansen 1980), whilst a German example from Alt Friesack, Brandenburg was radiocarbon dated to AD 480 +/- 100 (Hermann 1985, 539). Other examples, such as those from Oberdorla, Kr Muhlhausen have been dated from the late Iron Age through to the third century AD (Kruger 1978; Deyts 1983, 169). The use of a naturally branching stem to help create the legs of a figure can be seen in a few examples from the pre-Roman Iron Age. Among the twenty or so wooden figures found at Braak, Germany (Struve 1975; Deyts 1983, 168), the use of a natural split for the legs can be seen, though these figures, dated to around 500–400 BC offer few other similarities with the Ickham find. The figure found in 1880 at Broddenbjerg, Denmark (Glob 1971, 127, pls 74–5) possibly suggests the original form of the now damaged and partially missing lower half of the Ickham figure. The head is more massive and bearded, whilst the torso is undifferentiated with no carved arms, but the oak-fork from which it is made has a side-branch jutting out from the point of bifurcation which has been fashioned into the image of a penis. This is very reminiscent of the damaged Ickham figure, where the right leg (perhaps originally formed by a forked maple branch) has been lost, but the fragments of wood extending the axis of the torso below the junction of the left leg may represent the vestiges of a penis like the Broddenbjerg figure.

Perhaps the best parallels for the Ickham figurine may therefore be sought in the pre-Roman and Roman Iron Age of northern Europe. Elements of northern European material expression would not be unexpected in fourth-century Britain, but given our lack of knowledge regarding religious matters during this period there is no pressing reason to view the figurine as anything more than an indigenous, Romano-British creation. Figures of this type are universally perceived as symbolic or religious objects, and it is unlikely that the find can be explained as a child's toy or secular ornament. We would therefore see the Ickham figurine as a pagan religious or cult object. The piece may have been an object of veneration, originally housed in a small shrine, and was discarded along with the mass of other material when Channel A went into disuse or was deliberately blocked at its eastern end.

562 An anthropomorphic wooden figurine made of maple (*Acer* sp), approximately 330mm high, 50mm thick and 70mm broad. The main body of the figure appears to be formed from a round wood stem, the pith running through the vertical axis of the head and torso; judging from photographs and drawings made nearer the time of discovery, the figure has substantially degraded, with splits appearing along the rays of the original stem. A crude face is carved on the front of the head, formed by two scoops in the wood leaving proud a slightly flattened nose flanked by curving 'eyebrows'. Earlier drawings of the figure show two irregular eyes about 5mm in diameter flanking the nose, the left slightly higher than the right; these are no longer visible. An irregular oval depression about 9mm long and 3mm broad forms the mouth, immediately below the nose. A waisted neck broadens out to form the shoulders of the torso, which then tapers down to the junction with the surviving leg. Two crude arms are carved in relief, the hands clasped in front of the stomach. The bottom part of the figurine has been badly damaged, but the left leg survives, extending sideways from the torso at an angle of about 45 degrees, *c* 140mm long. This leg appears to be fashioned from a natural branching of the stem. Earlier drawings show what may be a crude depiction of a foot, but this has subsequently broken off. No trace of a right leg survives, though damaged fragments of wood extend the line of the torso below the junction with the left leg. No clear tool marks survive on the figurine, though earlier drawings show marked facets suggesting that the figure was carved from greenwood with a sharp blade. It is not possible to ascertain the type of tool(s) used in its manufacture. Sf 1699, Context 310.

Circular tank fragment

A piece cut from the rim of a thick sheet vessel of pure lead (563), was found in context 115 (Channel C, Assemblage 13). It is decorated along the rim with a simple feather or herringbone pattern, with a faint circle visible below. The decoration, the thickness of the sheet and slight discernible curvature allow it to be identified as a small piece of rim cut from a circular tank.

The circular motif was commonly used to decorate circular lead tanks; the motifs and their significance have been fully described and discussed by Watts (1988, 211–22, for the circular motif in particular see p 214). In her article Watts sets out an interesting case for the tanks having been used for ritual feet washing (*pedilavium*) as part of the Christian ceremony of baptism.

It is said that a 'circular piece of lead 5 feet in diameter' was recovered during the excavations at Ickham but

No	Object	Diameter mm	Width mm	Height mm	Context
557	copper alloy bell	30		17	Area 4, extension, 'section 1, layer 3'
558	copper alloy bell	32		crushed	Area 4
559	copper alloy bell	27		12	Area 4
560	copper alloy bell	19		13	unstratified
561	copper alloy mount		9	27	ditch
562	wooden figurine		50	330	Area 3, 310
563	lead alloy tank offcut				Area 1, Pit 115

Table 35. Objects with possible religious significance.

difficulties in arranging for its removal and storage resulted in the object not being retained. It is highly tempting to see this as the base of such a circular tank which was, presumably, in the course of being dismantled for recycling of the metal. The suggested diameter of 5 feet (*c* 1520mm), however, does present difficulties, making it significantly larger than the largest example known to date (965mm) and three times the size of the smallest (Guy 1981, 275; Watts 1988, 217).

Circular lead tanks of Roman date have been described and discussed by Guy (1981, 271–6) and Watts (1988, 210–22). Recent work has identified the fact that the circular tanks fall within two size ranges: the larger, all decorated, appear to be of Roman date, while the smaller, some undecorated, are likely to be of Anglo-Saxon date (Jane Cowgill, pers comm). The use of the tanks is the matter of current debate. The Roman tanks, being better made, were capable of storing liquid; the poorly sealed Anglo-Saxon examples do not appear to have been water-tight and amongst other uses that of a grain measure or storage for other dry goods has been suggested (Jane Cowgill, pers comm). It is possible that the size of the Ickham base has become exaggerated with time, even so, its size would reflect a large vessel. It may have been the base of a liquid storage vat for dyeing, fulling or brewing or simply water storage (Watts 1988, 214) but its occurrence at Ickham alongside a fragment decorated with a potentially early Christian motif is difficult to ignore.

The fragment of circular tank rim (563), the possible base and the late fourth- or fifth-century signet ring (425) engraved with a biblical subject may point to a Christian 'element' present at Ickham.

Roman circular lead tanks have been found principally in East Anglia and the east Midlands, Pulborough in Sussex being the most southerly (Watts 1988, 215). Two circular tanks of later date, however, are known from Kent; a seventh-century tank said to contain the bones of St Eanswythe is housed in the church dedicated to her in Folkestone, another, said to be of Saxon date, dredged from the River Medway is in Maidstone Museum (Jane Cowgill, pers comm). The Roman tanks appear to have fallen out of use in the middle of the fourth century, possibly associated with the 'pagan resurgence of the second half of the fourth century' (*ibid*, 218), although the evidence for resurgence has been questioned (Dark 1994, 32–4). The question remains, was the tank originally used at Ickham, whether for Christian baptism or for large scale storage, or was it, or part of it, brought there for recycling having originated elsewhere? The difficulties in transporting the base have already been mentioned but it would certainly be possible; though surely it is more likely to have been cut into more manageable pieces if being brought some distance.

Weights and measures

Quita Mould

There are few items which can be placed within this category, although this situation broadly reflects that to be seen elsewhere, as at Colchester, for example (Crummy 1983, 99–101). There is one example of a small iron steelyard, alongside a copper alloy balance, nine lead weights, a set of iron dividers and a fragment possibly from a folding foot rule.

Steelyard

A small example of the most common form of iron steelyard (564), comparable with others of fourth-century date from Icklingham, Suffolk (Manning 1985, 106–7) was found in Channel C. It can also be compared with a larger example of iron from east Kent at Monkton on Thanet (Macdonald *et al* 2008, 199–200).

In addition, a complete arm of a copper alloy equipoise balance (565), from which a pan was originally suspended at each end, was found in Area 12. Its small size indicates it was used to weigh comparatively light items such as powders, precious metals or coins.

Calculations establishing the approximate range of the steelyard are thus:

1st fulcrum

    distance to loading hook (a) = 17mm

    distance to end of beam (b) = 190mm

    Ratio of (a) to (b) is 1:11.2.

    By using a counterbalance of 1 Roman pound a load of up to 11 Roman pounds could be weighed.

2nd fulcrum

    distance to loading hook (a) = 40mm

    distance to end of beam (b) = 168mm

    Ratio of (a) to (b) is 1:4.2.

    By using a counterbalance of 1 Roman pound a load of up to approximately 4 Roman pounds could be weighed.

Lead weights

The nine lead alloy weights include a two and a half *unciae* weight (**568**), a weight now weighing a little over three *unciae* (566) and another a little over three and a quarter *unciae* (567). The biconical weight (566) of approximately

No	Height mm	Diameter mm	Weight (g)	Context
566	32	31	85.3	Area 3
567	31	30	91.3	Area 7, 710
568	22	28	68.4	unstratified
569	32	40	267.3	Area 5
570	24	40	182.8	Area 3
571	25	37	222.0	Area 4
572	20	20		Area 3, stone floor
573	8	46	139.0	Area 5
574	10	23	26.0	Area 7, 712

Table 36. Lead weights.

three *unciae* from Area 3 is unusual in having a seating for a suspension loop at both ends rather than one. Another weight (**569**) almost spherical in shape and also with a broken iron suspension loop, weighs between nine and a half and

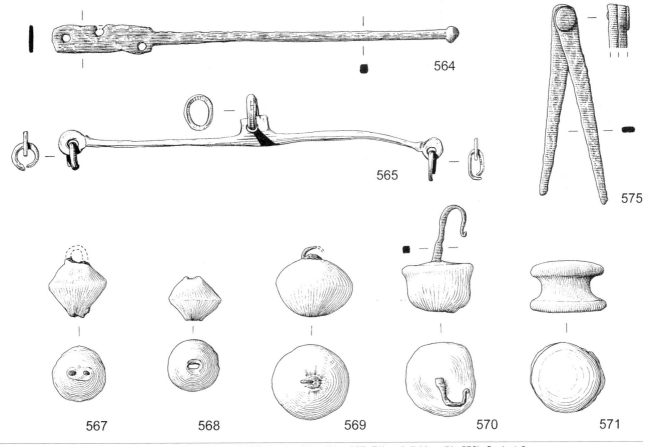

Fig 91. Weights and measures. Steelyards (Nos 564 and 565), lead weights (Nos 567–71) and dividers (No 575). Scale 1:2.

ten *unciae*. A truncated conical weight (**570**) with an iron suspension loop projecting from the flat upper face weighs a little over six and a half *unciae*. A 'cotton-reel' shaped weight (**571**) weighing approximately eight *unciae* was found in Area 4, with a fragment cut from another example coming from a stone floor in Area 3 (572). A centrally-pierced, circular weight (573) of rectangular section from Area 5 weighs approximately five *unciae*, whilst a waisted, one *uncia* weight came from context 712 (574). Analysis found this object to have been made of tin. Three of the weights, two coming from Area 5 (**569** and 573), the other from the stone floor in Area 3 (572) were made of pure lead. The majority had a low percentage of tin in their composition (13–25 per cent); one (**570**) with a tin content of 60 per cent was made of low grade pewter.

Measuring instruments

A pair of simple iron dividers (**575**) was found on the surface. Dividers were used in a number of crafts, including metal-working and carpentry, for measuring and marking out. A small copper alloy hinge (576), from Area 2, with an iron pivot and a fragment of one arm remaining, was found to have a complex structure when examined in detail. Two copper alloy strips held an organic strip of either wood or horn, with wooden scales on the exterior, and all of this was held together with a pair of copper alloy rivets. The precise identification is uncertain but it is comparable with the hinge mechanism found on the arm of a folding foot rule (cf two copper alloy examples from the pre-Flavian fortress at Usk: Webster 1995, fig 74.3 and 4).

Written communication

Ian Riddler

Objects of written communication from Ickham are limited to examples of iron styli. There are no seal-boxes but there are abundant examples of styli, a situation which is, in effect, the reverse of that to be seen at Colchester (Crummy 1983, 103–4). However, given that most seal-boxes belong to the second or third centuries, their absence from Ickham may not be entirely surprising. Nonetheless, there are examples (which may possibly be residual) from late Roman contexts at Canterbury (Blockley *et al* 1995, 1032 and fig 437.419–21).

Equally, the other instruments of writing, like inkwells and tablets, are also missing here. Even for a late Roman assemblage, there are few types of objects from Ickham that can be placed in this category and the tools of the scribe, as indicated by Merten (1987) and Bilkei (1980) are largely absent.

Styli

Styli were principally used to write upon recessed wooden tablets or *tabellae* and instruments of iron appear to be the most common in Roman Britain, reflecting perhaps the use of the word *ferrum* as a synonym for *stilus* by Ovid (*Metamorphoses* 9.522: Gostenčnik 1996, 109). It has been noted, however, that they were versatile tools which could also be used to incise notes on parchment or vellum, and that they were also suitable devices for manuscript lineation (Merten 1987, 311; Bischoff 1979, 36).

Twenty-one examples of styli have been identified from Ickham, all of which are made of iron. There are no examples made from other materials, although copper alloy and bone styli are known from other Romano-British sites. The latter are known, in particular, from Puckeridge-Braughing, and there is one possible example from Colchester, as well as a further example from Dover (Potter and Trow 1988, 85 and fig 87.1–2; Crummy 1983, 104 and fig 107; Philp 1989, fig 26.46). The situation at Magdalensberg, where styli of bone outnumber those of iron, has yet to be repeated elsewhere, although this is partly because the styli from that site are relatively early in date (Gostencnik 1996, 109; Deschler-Erb 1998, 144).

Most of the Ickham styli are complete or near-complete, although six are fragmentary. At the same time, comparatively few examples within the assemblage can be described as both complete and entirely undamaged. In a number of cases, either the points or the stems of the objects are bent over and a few of the points have also snapped at their ends. Few of the styli would have been discarded when still in a reasonable condition.

Iron styli are normally defined by the presence of a point at one end and a broad, spatulate area for erasure at the other (Wheeler 1946, 56; Manning 1976, 34; 1985, fig 24). Wheeler also illustrated one example of a stylus of iron from London which includes the point but does not have an eraser (Wheeler 1946, pl XXIV.5). There are several examples of similar objects from Ickham, which are described below. It is possible that these styli did not include erasers although, given the slender nature of their stems, it is more likely that the objects have fractured and the erasers are missing. Gostencnik has noted that some metal styli invoke the same form as those of bone, which customarily have rounded ends, rather than spatulate erasers (Gostencnik 1996, 110).

Ickham	Manning	Gostenčnik
1a	1a	
1b	1	
2a	2a	1
2b	2	
2c	3	2

Table 37. Concordance of stylus typologies.

Manning has set out a typology for iron styli which was based, in the first instance, on assemblages from sites along Hadrian's Wall (Manning 1976, 34; 1985, 85–7). Four types of styli have been identified, as well as several variants. The criteria used to distinguish between types vary between formal and decorative attributes, however, which slightly diminishes the overall value of the classification. It is inherently likely, for example, that any iron stylus with decoration on its stem will be assigned to type 4, irrespective of any variation in its shape. Conversely, however, if decoration on the stem is not recognised, the stylus could be placed within one of several groups.

An alternative typology has therefore been adopted specifically for the Ickham assemblage, which represents a slight modification of that presented by Professor Manning. It is based principally on the shape of the stem, although the form of the eraser and the length of the point are also considered. The decoration of the stem varies considerably, even within the Ickham sample, and it has not been considered in detail within the typology, although it is noted below. In general terms, this classification is closer to that proposed by Gostencnik for bone styli from Magdalensberg (Gostencnik 1996, 110–14). A concordance of types is included here (Table 37).

Within the Ickham assemblage, two principal forms of stylus can be identified. The first has a long point which extends to at least a half of the length of the entire object. The eraser is not distinguished from the stem and flows evenly from it. Two styli (**577** and **589**) can be placed in this group. One comes from Area 3 and the other from context 408, an occupation spread to the south of the road. This is likely to be an early type although the simplicity of its design may mean that it remained in use for a long time. A related stylus (**582**) includes the lengthy point, but the eraser is clearly distinguished from the stem and a raised moulding lies between the point and the stem. It comes from Area 4.

No	Object	Type	Length mm	Point	Stem	Context
577	iron, complete	1a	113			Area 3
578	iron, fragment	2c		34		Area 2
579	iron, complete	2c	100	28	57	Area 4, extension
580	iron, incomplete	2c	72	10	54	Area 4, extension
581	iron, fragment			26		Area 4, extension
582	iron, complete	1b	100		89	Area 4
583	iron, incomplete	2c	102	53	43	Area 4, extension
584	iron, complete	2c	10	31	59	Area 4
585	iron, incomplete?	2a	66	9	52	Area 2
586	iron, complete?	2c	120	27	93	Area 4
587	iron, complete	2b	127	62	52	Area 4, 407/B
588	iron, incomplete	2b	106		82	Area 4, 407B
589	iron, incomplete	1a	114	63	51	Area 4, 408
590	iron, complete	2b	111	30	66	Area 4, 335
591	iron					Area 4, extension
592	iron, fragment					Area 4, 407/B
593	iron, fragment					Area 7, 701
594	iron, fragment	2c		20		Area 1, 115
595	iron, fragment	2c		27		Area 7, 712
596	iron, incomplete	2c	103	9	86	Area 10, 1002
597	iron, complete	2c	95	31	51	Area 7, 712

Table 38. Styli.

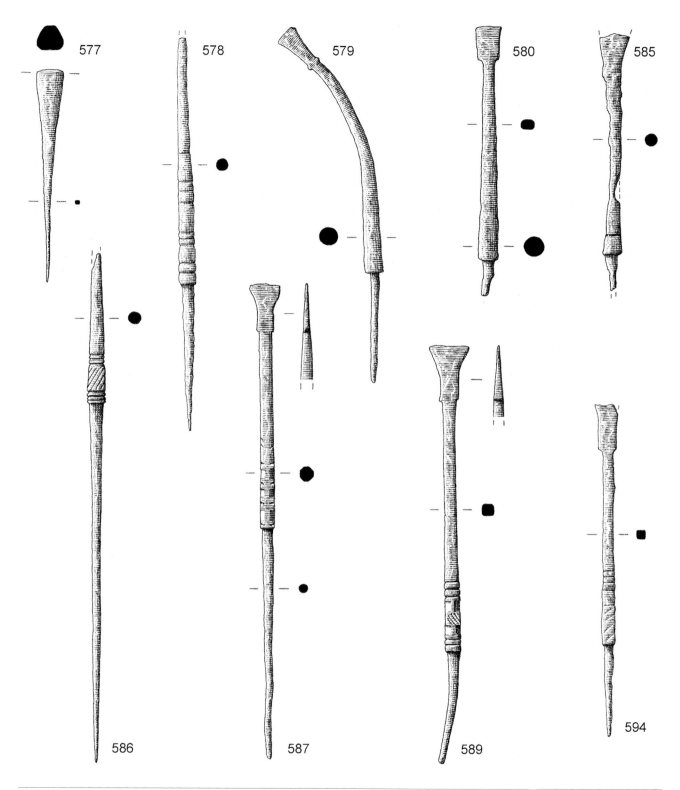

Fig 92. Styli. Scale 1:1 (No 577, scale 1:2).

The second form of stylus has a relatively short point, which is overtly distinguished from the stem, which is thicker at this point and may be emphasised by decorative mouldings. Three types of stylus can be identified within this group. The first (**585**) has a short point leading to a thickened stem with a slightly enlarged eraser, which is not separated from the stem. A band of inlay lies a little above the point. The second type (**587**, 588 and 590) is a little more conventional and common, and consists of a point which is separated from the stem by raised mouldings. A spatulate eraser, with curved sides, lies above the stem. With the third type (**579**, **580**, 583, 596 and 597) the stem narrows from the point to the eraser. The same is true also of a further series of examples, most of which should also be placed in type 2c (**578**, **586**, **594** and 595) where the eraser is now missing in each case, as a consequence of the narrow shape of the stem.

Decoration occurs in the form of raised mouldings and non-ferrous inlays. It can be seen on examples of practically all of the types identified here. Where it has been placed just above the point, it may have been intended to aid the grip of the writer.

Nineteenth-century discoveries of styli from Canterbury include examples of types 2b and 2c (Brent 1879, pl 2.2, 7 and 5). More recent excavations have provided a few more examples which, although fragmentary, look to belong to type 2b (Blockley *et al* 1995, 1071 and fig 463.686). The assemblage from Nettleton, which is largely late Roman, also includes comparable examples of types 1a, 1b, 2b and 2c, and examples of types 2b and c can be seen at Birdoswald (Wedlake 1982, 236 and fig 103; Summerfield 1997, 299 and fig 211). It is possible that a typological sequence exists within the variations of point, stem and eraser, but it is not possible to identify it clearly from the Ickham assemblage.

Household implements

Quita Mould

This category encompasses a wide range of object types and includes a considerable number of objects. Amongst them are knives, hones, locks and keys, candlesticks, cooking utensils (flesh hooks, frying pans, ladles and strainers), spoons, vessels of copper alloy, pewter and glass, and handles from implements. Also included here are box fittings and querns. Knives are well-represented, although not all of the examples described here are Roman; several post-Roman forms can be clearly identified. The same can be said for the locks and keys, which are equally numerous and varied in date. In contrast, items used for heating and lighting are not common.

The presence of frying pans can evoke a military image, in the light of the Roman assemblages from Thebes, but in Roman Britain they are not associated with specifically military contexts (Manning *et al* 1995, 198). One of the frying pans was found in association with three pewter plates. The context information from Ickham is poor, but it does not look as if sets of cooking utensils were discarded as complete groups.

Few of the twenty-four spoons from Ickham possess any unusual features and, as with so many other items, the majority can be assigned to the late Roman period. Details of XRF analyses of their metals by Adrian Tribe are provided in this section, alongside a consideration of the metals of the pewter vessels by Rebecca Sutton, which form one of the more important components of this assemblage.

The supply of early glass to Ickham appears to have been very limited and the absence of pillar-moulded bowls, in particular, is of some interest. The late Roman glass, in contrast, conforms readily to expectations and serves to emphasise, once again, the nature of the overall finds assemblage. There can be less certainty about the dating of the fragments of querns, although the Ickham assemblage is noticeably large and it can be compared with similar groups from both Canterbury and Monkton.

Knives

The assemblage of iron knives consists of forty-nine complete or near-complete examples and fifteen blade fragments. The majority are of known Roman forms, but examples of later, Anglo-Saxon types were also recovered. While many of the knives were general purpose, domestic implements, certain blades (eg 647) may well have been used for specific craft functions.

The knives have been loosely classified according to the shape of the blade and the type of handle. The position of the tang and the shape of the back have been considered as the blade edge may change considerably during its life as a result of resharpening. Where relevant, cross reference is made to the classification adopted by Manning when cataloguing the collection at the British Museum (Manning 1985, 108–23 and figs 28–9).

A variety of broken knife blade fragments were found which cannot be classified. They include a fragment of a narrow knife blade (649), along with a second possible

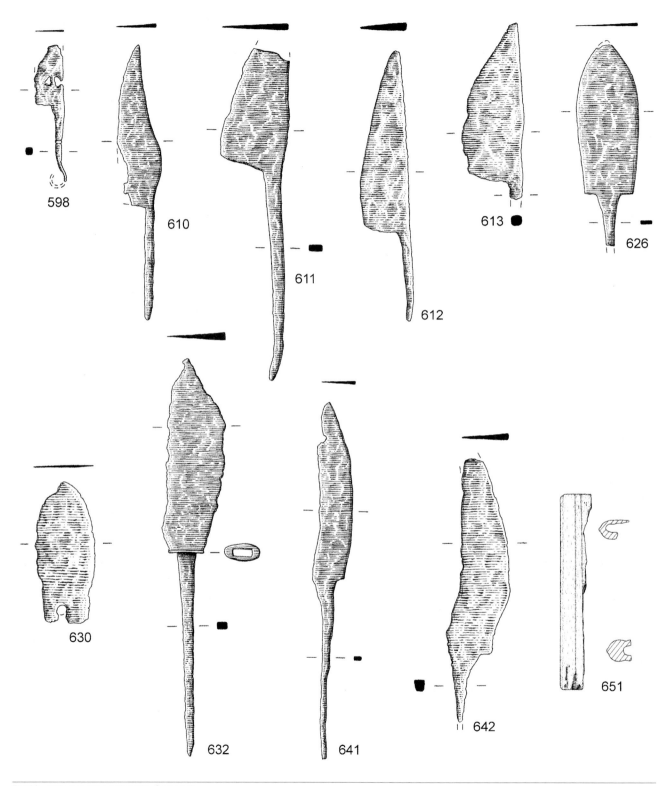

Fig 93. Knives and bone handle. Scale 1:2.

fragment (650), with a downward pointing tip similar to that occurring with Manning's type 7 (Manning 1985, 111–12 and fig 28) which he suggests may have been a razor of early Roman date. Also there are a few types which are normally found in early contexts but probably have a long lifespan, eg Manning type 9, but our example (609) is significantly smaller than the examples illustrated by Manning from London (*ibid*, 113 and pl 54).

Knives with solid handles

This is a relatively large group, which consists of solid handled knives. Two small objects (**598** and 599) are, in strict terms, more likely to be razors than knives, but they have been included in this category. Five subdivisions of this type have been made here.

Type 1.1. A small blade (**598**) has a solid handle with decorative mouldings, apparently accompanied originally with a ring terminal. It is comparable with a knife from London (Manning 1985, 117 Q59, pl 55).

Type 1.2. A small hooked blade (599) with a straight back and edge curving toward the tip and a spirally-twisted handle with a looped ring terminal falls into Manning's type 6 (*ibid*,111) a catch-all category for hooked blades. It is likely to have been used as a razor rather than a knife.

Type 1.3. Seven knives have spirally-twisted handles with scrolled ring terminals (eg 600, 602). The complete blades have a sinuous back and a convex edge rising to meet it at an upward pointed tip. The ring terminals on this and the following category of knives puts them into Manning's type 11B (*ibid*, 114 and fig 28)

Type 1.4. Two knives have plain handles with ring terminals (eg 607).

Type 1.5. A single straight-backed knife (609) has a sinuous solid handle with a triangular knobbed finial. The knobbed handle is similar to that of Manning's type 9 (*ibid*, 113 and fig 28), though the knife is smaller than the examples he cites from the Walbrook, which date to no later than the end of the second century.

Knives with tangs on a line with the back

The fifteen knives of this group all include tangs that continue directly from the back of the blade. They include knives with sinuous backs, straight backs and convex curving edges, and straight backs dropping to meet the edge at a pointed tip.

Type 2.1. A single knife (**610**) has a sinuous back and is of the same blade shape as the Manning's type 9, though tanged for an organic handle. Like its solid-handled counterpart

above (609) it is smaller than the comparable examples from London quoted by Manning (*ibid*, 113, type 9).

Type 2.2. Nine knives have straight backs and convex curving edges. These knives vary from large blades with long, pointed tips (**611** and **612**), comparable with Manning's type 11a (*ibid*, 114 and fig 28) to smaller, wider blades of Manning's type 12 (**613**).

Type 2.3. A group of knives have a straight back that drops to the edge at a pointed tip. Three correspond to Manning's type 17 (*ibid*, 116 and fig 29). A small knife with a facetted antler handle (620) has a distinctly thickened back, producing a horizontal ridge along one side of the blade, suggesting it was used for a specific craft function. A smaller knife (623) of the same general type with a more rounded tip may be of Manning's type 13 (*ibid*, 115 and fig 28).

Type 2.4. Two knives with a straight back and edge are broken before the tip, so that their exact type is unknown. One (625) has the minerally preserved remains of the wooden handle surviving. Wood on the knife tang was too degraded to identify but that present on fragments broken from it were found to be of ash (*Fraxinus* sp) (Watson 2000).

Knives with centrally-placed tangs

Three types of knife can be identified, for which the tang is centrally-placed in relation to the blade.

Type 3.1. This type consists of small, wide blades with convex curving backs and edges meeting at a central tip, with short wide tangs. Six examples of this style of blade (**626**, 627–9, **630**, 631) of Manning's type 21 (Manning 1985, 117 and fig 29) were recovered. The type is thought to be of later Roman date and it is not surprising to see examples at Ickham. X-ray of knife (**630**) showed VICTOR stamped along the back.

Type 3.2. This type includes knives with long tangs and convex or straight backs which meet the straight edges at a central tip. One knife (**632**) has an oval hilt plate of bronze present. Other copper alloy hilt plates (652 and 653), one (Brown 1981, fig 5, no 17) with decoratively scalloped sides, and an iron end plate (654) have been found separately. These knives are comparable in shape with those deposited in graves dating between AD 350–410 at Lankhills (Clarke 1979, 249), one of which has a hilt plate and an end plate remaining (*ibid*, no 93 from Grave 37, other knives found have an end plate only). The Lankhills knives were recovered from male graves, most being associated with belt-fittings, although others have been found in female graves in fourth-century continental cemeteries and fifth-century Anglo-Saxon cemeteries (*ibid*, 250). One knife (634) had remains

No	Material	Type	Length mm	Blade length mm	Width mm	Context
598	iron	1.1	73+	30	15	Area 4
599	iron	1.2	118	60	13	Area 8, 802
600	iron	1.3	138	75	27	Area 1, Channel C
601	iron	1.3	160	80	30	Area 1, Channel C
602	iron	1.3	138	69	19	Area 1, 122
603	iron	1.3	112	67	22	Area 6, 610.6
604	iron	1.3	84	50	20	Area 1, Pit 115.1
605	iron	1.3				Area 4, 407.B
606	iron	1.3				Area 4, 408.U
607	iron	1.4	159	110	29	Area 1, Channel C
608	iron	1.4	115+		32	unstratified
609	iron	1.5	109	68	22	Area 14, unstratified
610	iron	2.1	141	85	24	unstratified
611	iron	2.2	174+		35	Area 4, extension
612	iron	2.2	150	105	24	Area 1, Pit 115.1
613	iron	2.2	90+		33	Area 4
614	iron	2.2	65+		22	Area 4, extension
615	iron	2.2	113+		43	Area 4, 335
616	iron	2.2	80+		34	Area 1, Channel C, east end
617	iron	2.2	70+		20	Area 4, extension
618	iron	2.2	70+		21	Area 1, Pit 115
619	iron	2.2	130+		30	Area 1, Pit 115
620	iron	2.3	130	71	25	Area 10, 1001
621	iron	2.2	157+	121	30	Area 4, extension
622	iron	2.2	138+		25	Area 4
623	iron	2.3	89	56	23	Area 4, extension
624	iron	2.4	100+		39	Area 4, extension
625	iron	2.4	146+		28	Area 1, Channel C
626	iron	3.1	106	79	33	Area 4, extension
627	iron	3.1	72	66	30	Area 4, extension
628	iron	3.1	82+	80	27	Area 3
629	iron	3.1	60+		33	Area 7, 712
630	iron	3.1	74+		31	Area 4, extension
631	iron	3.1	83+		29	Area 4, extension
632	iron	3.2	210	100	29	Area 4
633	iron	3.2	165	98	26	Area 4
634	iron	3.2	180	93	38	Area 1, 107
635	iron	3.2	158	72	23	Area 4, extension
636	iron	3.2	160	74	32	Area 4
637	iron	3.2	92+		25	Area 3
638	iron	3.3	126	81	24	Area 1, Channel C
639	iron	3.4	120	85	24	Area 1, Channel C
640	iron	3.4	85+		25	Area 4
641	iron	3.4	190	93	18	Area 1, Pit 115
642	iron	3.5	138	102	26	Area 10, 1002.2
643	iron	3.5	87+	66+	16	Area 7, 712
644	iron	3.5	65+	33+	16	Area 4, extension
645	iron	3.6				Area 1, Channel C
646	iron	3.6				Area 1, Channel C, east end
647	iron	4	126+	80	27	Area 1, 115.2
648	iron	4	180	95	30	Area 1, Channel C
649	iron	7	50+		10	Area 7, 712
650	iron	1	46+		10	Area 1, base of Channel C
651	bone	7				Area 7, 701

Hilt and end plates		Group	Length/diameter mm	Width mm	
652	copper alloy hilt plate	3.2	23	11	Area 1, base of Channel C
653	copper alloy hilt plate	3.2	24	14	Area 4, extension, section 1, layer 3
654	iron end plate	3.2	19		Area 1, Pit 115.2

Table 39. Knives, hilt and end plates.

of the minerally-preserved wooden handle present on the tang, the wood was too degraded for species identification (Watson 2000).

Type 3.3. A single knife (638) with a straight back and edge meeting at a central tip has a pair of grooves in one face running parallel to the back. No trace of any inlay was found within the grooves. Grooves have been found on a number of Roman knives (Manning 1985, 116, types 17 and 18a) and are relatively common on blades from the later fifth or sixth century onwards (Ottaway 1992, 580).

Type 3.4. Three knives have a straight back dropping at an angle to the edge. Two (639 and 640) meet the edge at a central tip, similar to Manning's type 20 (Maning 1985, 117 and fig 29). One knife (**641**) has a narrow blade with the back dropping at an angle to the straight edge in a pointed tip. It has a very long tang. Small knives with an angled back are known from Roman contexts (*ibid*, type 14, fig 28, type 20, fig 29). The extreme length of the tang on the narrow blade (**641**) suggests a post-Roman date, it being a common feature of knives of ninth- to eleventh-century date in northern Europe (Ottaway 1992, 577 and comparanda).

Type 3.5. Two narrow knives (**642** and 643) have short tangs and blades with gently convex backs and concave edges produced by frequent sharpening. A broken knife (644) probably represents a third example. These knives are comparable with Manning's type 14 (Manning 1985, 115 and fig 28) but are also of a type commonly found on sites of Anglo-Saxon and Saxo-Norman date. The heavily whetted edge seen on these knives is a common feature of knives of ninth- to eleventh-century date and may be result of using the 'sandwich' technique of blade construction (Ottaway 1992, 574) with a steel core which resulted in a cutting edge that could be sharpened many times and still remain hard, however thin the blade became (*ibid*, 598–9).

Type 3.6. A small number of knives with centrally-placed tangs have broken blades preserving no distinguishing features.

Knives with a scale tang

One knife (647) has a convex back and a thick scale tang originally riveted to organic handle plates. The heavy handle and relatively wide, flexible blade suggests a special purpose knife. A similar knife (648) with a convex curving back and edge has a scale tang attached to a pair of decorated bone handle scales with a pair of solid non-ferrous rivets. The handle is decorated with ring-and-dot motifs and has an oval end cap of non-ferrous metal. Knives with this blade shape occur in post-Roman as well as Roman contexts and

while both scale-tanged blades and knives with end caps (though usually of iron) are known in the Roman period, the combination of scale tang and non-ferrous metal end cap on this knife makes a date after the middle of the fourteenth century a distinct possibility.

Tangs

A small number of iron tangs were found which may be broken from knives. However, they could equally be discarded smithing handling rods; smithing scrap with handling rods attached is discussed below (p 299).

Handle

An elegantly crafted example of a bone handle (**651**) belongs, in all probability, to a whittle-tanged knife or similar implement. It can be compared with a first-century example from *Verulamium* which has only two raised cordons, however, instead of four (Goodburn and Grew 1984, 69 and fig 29.259). Similar knife handles, which are generally of first-century date, are known also from *Vindonissa*.

Item of uncertain use

An iron strap (**655**) (117mm long, 20mm wide) for which no edge to the blade is present, with a tang aligned with the back, a straight choil, and the other end deliberately scrolled, could be for crushing rather than cutting. It is comparable to an example from Alchester (sf 910 context 339) found in a late fourth-century context which has a centrally-placed, round-sectioned tang and a simple folded end. The Ickham example, having a scrolled end, could have been hammered vertically into wood and used to suspend a hanging lamp. If hammered into wood horizontally the scrolled end may have held a taper. However, it may well be a blank, partly-worked by the smith, the tang being a handling rod.

Hones

Ian Riddler

Five hones were retrieved from the site, three of which are complete. Four of the five have been made from a fine-grained, micaceous, glauconitic sandstone, whilst the fifth example (658) has been produced from a softer, dark grey siltstone. All five are rectangular in form, with rounded edges and roughly-finished ends. They are all of similar

No	Material	Length mm	Width mm	Depth mm	Context
656	fine-grained sandstone	46	29	19	Area 4, extension
657	fine-grained sandstone				Area 1, 'hearth site, layer 2d'
658	grey siltstone	68	17	12	Aea 1, Pit 115
659	fine-grained sandstone	51	32	38	Area 1, 128
660	fine-grained sandstone				unstratified

Table 40. Hones.

dimensions, although one example (658) is a little larger than the remainder. In one case (660) prolonged use of the object has indented the central area, and marks from sharpening are visible.

The hones have been produced from stone types that are local to Kent, and similar examples have come from contemporary Roman sites in the area. A series of five fine-grained grey sandstone hones was recovered from the Marlowe excavations at Canterbury, and these are similar to the Ickham examples for both their form and their stone type (Blockley *et al* 1995, 1210, nos 1399–1403). Those from Roman contexts in Dover are also comparable for their fabric descriptions, and several of them are rectangular in form (Philp 1981, 169, nos 245–7 and 249). On this basis, it is inherently likely that the hones from Ickham are Roman, although they cannot be dated more closely.

Locks and keys

A reasonable collection of both locks and keys came from the site and, as with most other categories, it appears to consist largely of items of late Roman date, although in this case there are several keys which are either Anglo-Saxon or medieval. The Anglo-Saxon material is further reviewed below (p 308). A large range of keys was found, including simple iron latch-lifters, lift keys and slide keys along with keys to open padlocks and lever locks.

Lock plates

The best preserved fragment (**661**) of three copper alloy lock plates with decorative raised concentric borders around the keyholes is of rectangular shape with a border of repoussé dots around the perimeter. A similar example of lead alloy (**931**) was found in Area 3 and is discussed with other box fittings below. Fragments of iron lock plates also occurred, along with a circular keyhole escutcheon of copper alloy (**664**).

Locking mechanisms

A circular iron plate (**667**) comes from a lever padlock with a cylindrical case like that from *Verulamium*, dating to AD 280–315. Other examples are known from the villas at Lullingstone and Fishbourne, as well from Caerleon (Manning 1972, 182 and fig 67, no 71). Another broken lock plate or case fragment with a keyhole (668) was found in the 'hearth' associated with Channel C. Among the nine fragments of internal lock mechanism recovered is a barb-spring padlock bolt (695) and three sprung fasteners of varying size (**669, 670** and 671), including one articulating with a split spiked loop. Sprung fasteners were used to secure two of the wooden casket burials of Antonine date from Skeleton Green, Puckeridge, Hertfordshire (Partridge 1981, 317 and fig 112 BXXX, fig 115 BXLV).

Latch-lifters

The remains of six latch-lifters were recovered several of which are complete or near-complete (eg **672, 673, 675**). They occurred in Areas 3, 4 and 10 and all are simple, plain forms.

Lift keys

Two broken examples (679 and **680**) of T-shaped lift keys are of a standard Roman form. However, the small, complete key (**678**) is an Anglo-Saxon type.

The seven L-shaped lift keys are mostly of a common Roman form. More unusual is a decorated key with notched edges and a moulded collar (**681**). Similarly notched edges on the bow and upper handle occurred on an L-shaped lift key from Well 1 at Dalton Parlours (Scott 1990, 203 and fig 121, no 86) which was in use up to the abandonment of the villa in the late fourth century (Sumpter 1990, 244). A copper alloy L-shaped lift key with notching has also been found at Canterbury (Blockley *et al* 1995, 1041 and fig 443,

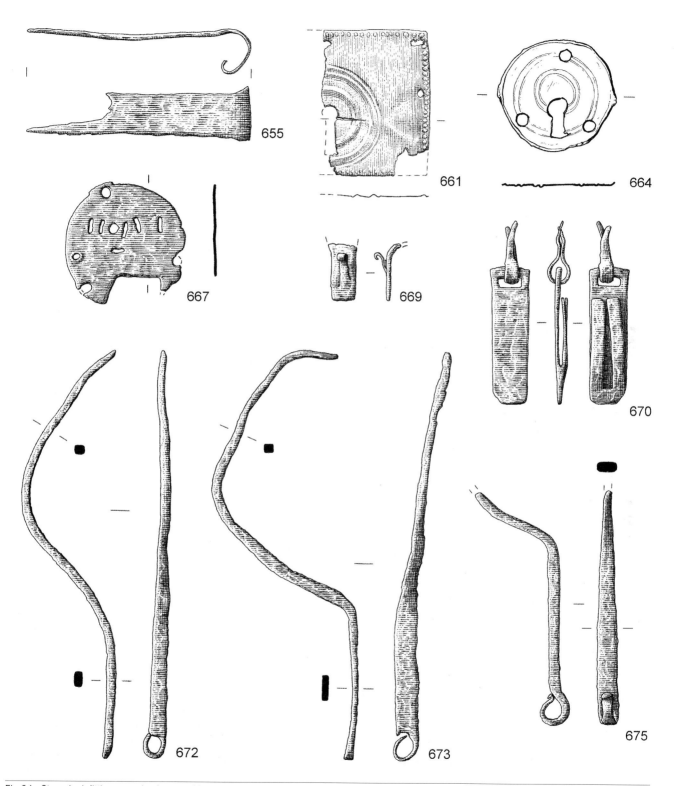

Fig 94. Strap, lock fittings, mechanisms and latch-lifters. Scale 1:2 (Nos 661 and 664, scale 1:1).

No	Object	Length mm	Width mm	Diameter mm	Context
661	copper alloy lock plate	77	56+		Area 4
662	copper alloy lock plate				Area 4
663	copper alloy lock plate				Area 4, extension
664	copper alloy lock plate			30	Area 4
665	iron lock plate				Area 1, Channel C, west end
666	iron lock plate				Area 4
667	iron lock mechanism			64	Area 4, extension, Pit 414.2–5
668	iron lock mechanism			41	Area 1, Channel C, hearth
669	iron lock mechanism	30+	14		Area 3
670	iron lock mechanism	105	25		Area 3
671	iron lock mechanism	71	20		Area 4
672	iron latch-lifter	214			Area 3, 'floor'
673	iron latch-lifter	215			Area 4
674	iron latch-lifter	220			Area 10, 1004
675	iron latch-lifter				Area 3
676	iron latch-lifter				Area 4
677	iron latch-lifter				Area 4, 407.B
678	iron lift key	84	16		Area 4, extension
679	iron lift key	71+	20		Area 1, Pit 115.2
680	iron lift key	47+	27+		Area 10, 1005
681	iron lift key	106	32		Area 4
682	iron lift key	113	30		Area 4
683	iron lift key	120	28		Area 4
684	iron lift key	63	8+		Area 4
685	iron lift key	104+	32		Area 16
686	iron lift key	122+	50		unstratified
687	iron lift key	90			Area 1, 107
688	iron slide key	88	30 x 16		Area 14
689	iron slide key	48+			Area 1, Pit 115.1
690	iron slide key	60			Area 7, Layer 5
691	copper alloy slide key	35	18		Area 1, Channel C
692	iron padlock key	140	19		Area 16
693	iron padlock key	146	27		unstratified
694	iron padlock key	78+	17		Area 4
695	iron padlock bolt				Area 1, Pit 115
696	iron padlock key	36+			Area 10, 1004
697	iron padlock key	70+			Area 10, 1005
698	iron padlock key		86+	13	Area 1, base of Channel C, east end
699	iron padlock key	122	6		Area 4, 408
700	iron key handle	89			Area 14
701	iron key handle	100+			Area 14
702	iron key handle	80			Area 4, 411
703	iron casket key handle	60+			Area 6, 626
704	iron padlock key handle	85+			Area 10, 1005
705	iron lever lock key	100		41	Area 1, Channel C
706	iron lever lock key	42		29	Area 4, 'floor area'
707	iron lever lock key	28	11 x 10		Area 4, 408
708	copper alloy lever lock key	33	20		Area 1, Channel C
709	copper alloy lever lock key	35		13	Area 1, base of Channel C
710	copper alloy lever lock key	37		17	Area 2
711	copper alloy lever lock key	33		18	Area 4
712	copper alloy lever lock key	44		14	Area 4, extension
713	copper alloy lever lock key	34		15	Area 4, extension
714	copper alloy lever lock key	61		18	Area 5
715	copper alloy lever lock key	32		13	unstratified

Table 41. Locks and keys.

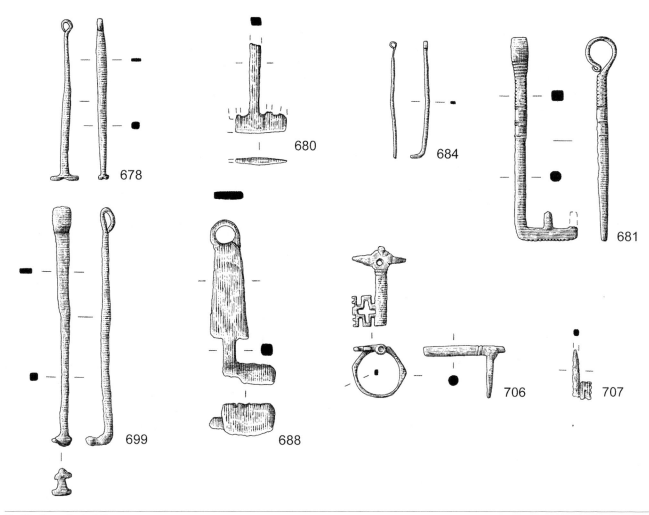

Fig 95. Keys. Scale 1:2.

no 467) for which Webster tentatively suggests a date in the late sixth or seventh centuries. Another particularly slender lift key (**684**) is likely to be of similar date.

Slide keys

Three slide keys include a complete example (**688**) of Manning's type 2 (Manning 1985, 93 and fig 25, no 7) and remains of a possible type 1 (*ibid* 92 and fig 25, nos 4–6). In addition, a cast copper alloy handle (691) is comparable to an example, complete with its iron slide key bit, which came from a fourth-century context at Canterbury (Blockley *et al* 1995, 1074 and fig 464, no 697).

Padlock keys

Seven padlock keys are of a common Roman type with angular cut outs in the bit at right angles to the strap handle (eg 693, 694). A key with a slender handle and an H-shaped bit (**699**) is comparable to examples of Anglo-Saxon date (Brown 1972, fig 40, nos 181 and 186).

There are also five broken key handles. One handle (700), probably broken from a lift key, has a five-petaled flower or five-pointed star-shaped maker's mark visible in radiograph. This could not be located during investigative cleaning. However, XRF analysis revealed the presence of lead and copper, suggesting that a maker's mark had been present in the area, and indicating that the object is of post-Roman date.

Lever lock keys

One of the three iron keys for lever locks (705), with an oval bow and stem projecting below the square notched bit, is of a type commonly found in the medieval and later periods. The other two iron keys are small and were used to work small lever locks on caskets, like the copper alloy keys discussed below. The iron finger ring key (**706**) is comparable with an example from London (Manning 1985, 95, O64). Key rings are more frequently found in copper alloy, see for example those from the South Shields Roman fort (Allason-Jones and Miket 1984, 144–5, 3.348–3.352 and comparanda). The other iron key (**707**) has a small tang to attach a separate bow of copper alloy or possibly an organic material.

A collection of eight small, copper alloy lever lock casket keys have piped stems and decorated bows. One (708) has a trefoil lobed bow of a type frequently found, albeit in a larger size, on military sites throughout the northern provinces (Allason-Jones and Miket 1984, 3.347). The others have round bows, all but one (710) with a decorative finial knop, with mouldings at the neck and small, notched bits. They are comparable with a larger example with a finial knop found in late occupation (*c* 280–360/400) of the southern buildings of the Fortress at York (Cool *et al* 1995, 1589 and fig 750, no 6354). A key of similar size was found occurring residually at Canterbury (Blockley *et al* 1995, 1032 and fig 438, no 430). Their presence suggests that the security of valuables in small caskets or chests was considered a priority by part of the population.

Possible Anglo-Saxon keys

The very narrow, slight T-shaped lift key (**678**) and broken L-shaped lift keys can be paralleled by similar keys from site F of the Anglo-Saxon settlement site at Shakenoak Farm, and they are presumed to be Anglo-Saxon in date (Brown 1972, fig 40, no 181, fig 44, no 209).

Domestic implements

Quita Mould

The sub-category of 'domestic implements' can cover a wide range of household devices, designed for lighting, heating, cooking and crafts practised within the domestic environment. In the following section items relating directly to lighting and cooking are discussed. This is followed by a contribution on spoons by David Sherlock, and by a consideration of vessels and containers of glass, lead alloy, copper alloy and iron. A

discussion of the evidence for caskets is also included here, and the section concludes with an analysis of the querns.

Lighting

Lighting equipment is not well-represented, although it includes a broken copper alloy candlestick (**716**) with the remains of a flat circular base or drip pan and central socket. The pewter socket (**806**, *see* Fig 101) cut possibly from a candlestick should be noted here. A candle pricket (**719**) and two iron candleholders (**717** and 718), comprising simple tanged sockets, were also recovered.

Cooking utensils

Two forked implements (**721** and 722), each with a tang which would have been hafted into a wooden handle, are likely to be flesh hooks. They are comparable with examples from site 2N at Thetford (Goodall 1984, 95 and fig 133, nos 193–5) and Fishergate, York (Rogers 1993, 1330 and fig 643, no 5043) where it is noted that the implement was in use from the late Anglo-Saxon period through to the thirteenth century. This has been observed also by Manning (1985, 105) and the implement type changes little over time. The Ickham examples, although not well-stratified, could therefore be of late Roman date. Manning has also indicated that flesh hooks can be found in association with ladles, but that was not the case here. Another double-pronged fork (**720**) is discussed below in relation to possible fishing equipment (*see* p 258, Fig 106).

Frying pans

The remains of four iron frying pans, either have a shallow oval or a circular pan and open flanged sockets to hold a pivoted handle (**723**, 724–6). One of these (**723**) was found together with three pewter plates. The best preserved example (**723**) has been repaired by a patch riveted to the left side of the base. A similar pan with a hinged handle was found in the post-fortress drainage gully by the *via principalis* at Usk (Manning *et al* 1995, 198–9 and fig 54, no 16) dating to the third century or later; most appear to date to the later Roman period. Manning suggests they were sufficiently valuable to indicate that a reasonable standard of living was enjoyed by their owners (Manning 1985, 192).

Ladles

The remains of a minimum of two ladles (**727** and **728**) can be identified, although there are fragments from a possible third example (*see* p 145, above) and the long, curving

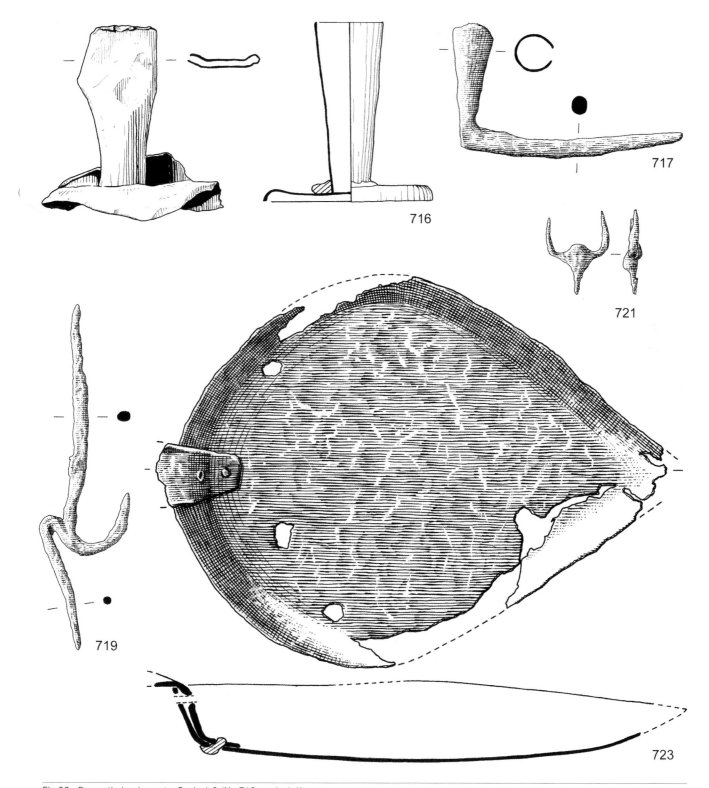

Fig 96. Domestic implements. Scale 1:2 (No 716, scale 1:1).

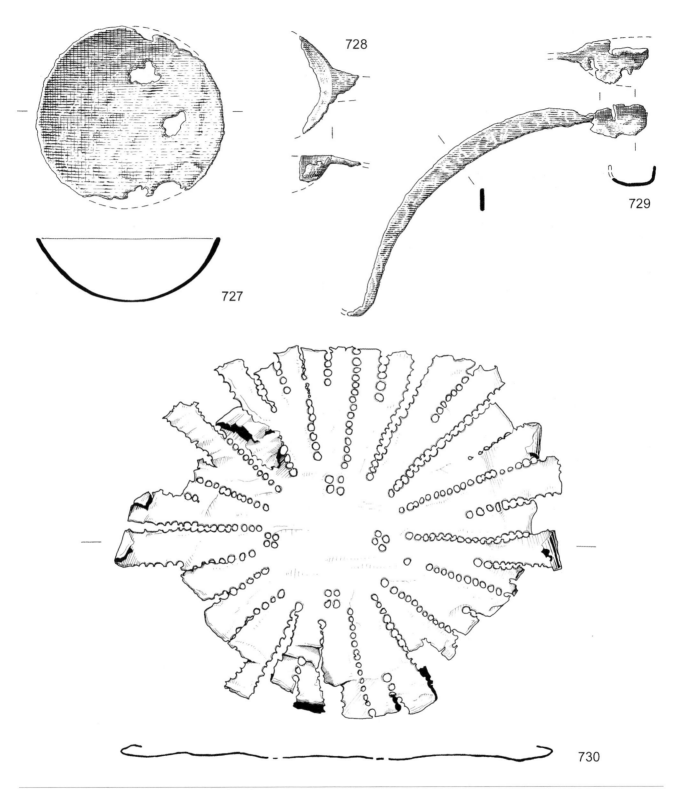

Fig 97. Domestic implements. Scale 1:2 (No 730, scale 1:1).

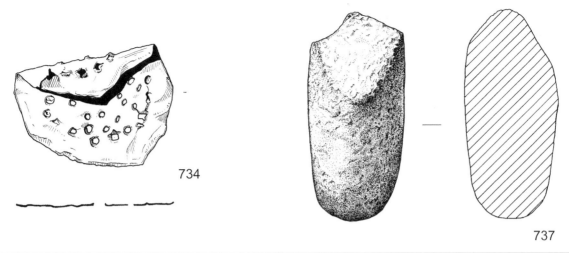

Fig 98. Domestic implements. Strainer (No 734) scale 1:1. Pestle (No 737) scale 1:2.

handle of another distorted ladle or bucket (**729**) was found at a separate location.

Strainers

The remains of the circular bowl of a copper alloy strainer (**730**) has a series of radiating lines of evenly punched circular holes, and small fragments (731 and 732) have probably been broken from it. Some of these fragments came from the same context, whilst others had been dispersed elsewhere. The highly fragmentary remains of a possible handled iron strainer or vessel (733), formerly with a riveted repair, were also found in Area 4. A small circular plate (**734**) perforated with a series of less well executed holes likely to be a strainer plate from the spout of a wine jug or flagon was recovered from Area 4. The plate was folded, suggesting that it was scrap.

Pestles and rubbing stone

Tania Wilson

Four possible grinding or pounding stones were recovered from the Ickham site. The stone selected for this use consists exclusively of elongated pebbles of flint, and the fortuitous size and shape of these pebbles may have been instrumental in their selection. The suggestion that these artefacts were used as grinders or pounders arises from limited areas of crushing located at one end of each of the pebbles and in addition two examples (**737** and **738**) have further modifications. Whilst the crushing is almost certainly evidence of use as a pounder there

is no direct evidence, in the form of scratches or striations, to demonstrate that the objects were used for grinding. However this may not be readily apparent due to the nature of the pebble cortex, which is hard and chatter marked.

Table 42 shows the dimensions of the stones. Whether the crushing on two of the examples (**737** and **738**) was made to facilitate handling of the object or serve some other purpose is uncertain. Interestingly three of the objects were recovered from the same context (107, Ceramic Assemblage 13), whilst the fourth is unstratified.

In addition to the grinding stones, one artefact (739) was possibly used as a rubbing stone. This piece was in fact originally used as a hammerstone and has extensive crushing over much of its surface. The stone, now unfortunately incomplete, would probably have been spherical and has a very smooth surface. The crushed areas are worn quite smooth and, where crushing is not present, multi-directional striations on the surface can be seen with slight magnification. Unfortunately, the object is unstratified.

Spoons

David Sherlock

Twenty-four Roman spoons were found at Ickham and are here published for the first time, not having been mentioned in Dr Young's interim report on the site (Young 1981). There are five complete spoons and fragments of sixteen bowls and three handles. They are listed here according to types rather than their contexts which, because of the nature of the

No	Object	Length mm	Width mm	Diameter mm	Context
716	copper alloy candlestick	46+			Area 4, 407.1
717	iron candle holder	68			Area 4
718	iron candle holder	70			Area 10, 1002.3
719	iron candle pricket	180			Area 4, extension
720	iron ?boat hook	124			unstratified
721	iron flesh hook	43	33		Area 1, Channel C, west end
722	iron flesh hook		58		Area 1, Channel C, west end
723	iron frying pan	260+ 213			Area 8, 802
724	iron frying pan				Area 4
725	iron frying pan				Area 4, extension
726	iron frying pan				Area 4, extension
727	iron ladle	32		99	Area 4
728	iron ladle			51+	Area 14
729	iron ladle	190			Area 7, 702
730	copper alloy strainer			104+	Area 10, 1001
731	copper alloy strainer				Area 10, 1001
732	copper alloy strainer				Area 1, Pit 115.2
733	iron ?strainer				Area 4
734	copper alloy strainer plate			41	Area 4
735	stone pestle	136	56		unstratified
736	stone pestle	130	55		Area 1, 107
737	stone pestle	112	51		Area 1, 107
738	stone pestle	94	72		Area 1, 107
739	stone rubbing stone		85	60	unstratified

Table 42. Domestic equipment.

excavations, have little bearing on their date. All the bowls are oval, with one exception.

Provenance

About half of the spoons are surface finds or come from contexts about which little is known. The context of one spoon (746) is of the earlier, possibly late third century in Area 10. There was earlier, second- to third-century, occupation at Ickham into which the spoon with a circular bowl (740) would fit, but this spoon was a surface find. Area 14, where a fragmentary spoon (760) was found, is thought to be a part of the site which is earlier than the rest, but the form of this bowl, although fragmentary, does not suggest an early date.

Styles and parallels

There has been no general classification of Roman spoons by type from the first to the fifth century since Strong (1966),

but his classification is still broadly accepted, both for silver spoons which were his subject and for those of other metals - namely that circular bowls are early, oval bowls are later and that the so-called fiddle- or purse-shaped bowls come between, overlapping the earlier and the later. There are of course exceptions: there are some early oval bowls and a few late circular ones. The former are characteristically small and the latter large. Large spoons mostly occur later in the Roman period. Spoons may be further classified into types according to details such as the design of the join between the handle and the bowl, or the decoration on the handle or on the back of the bowl.

The Ickham spoons exhibit no unusual types, except for three examples. One of these (741) is the only fiddle-shaped bowl although it is not a good example of one. The spoons have no graffiti and no decoration, with one exception (290). This spoon has a circular pewter bowl, and the rim, which is incomplete, includes raised decoration. The interior appears to be decorated with a poorly executed fruit basket or vase

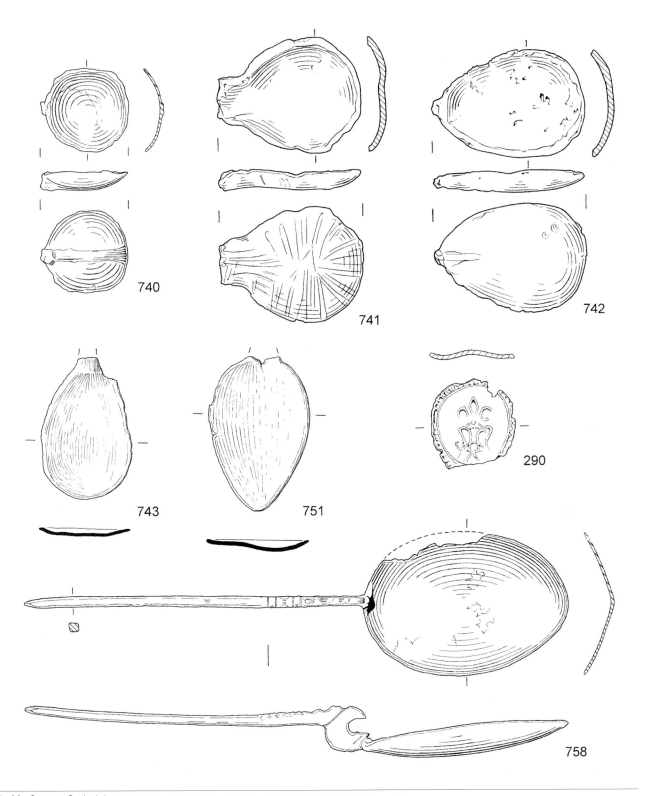

Fig 99. Spoons. Scale 1:1.

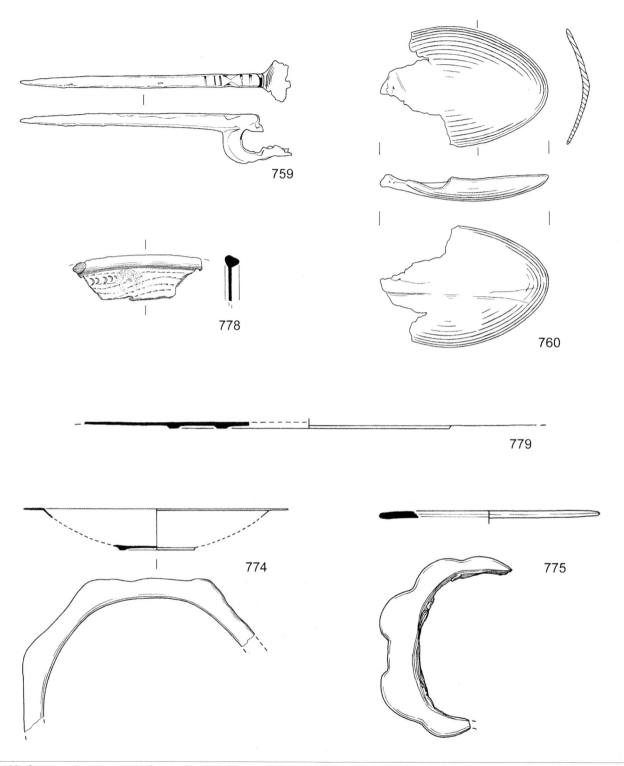

Fig 100. Spoons and pewter vessels. Spoons (Nos 759–60, scale 1:1), vessels (Nos 774–5, 778–9, scale 1:2).

No	Material	Bowl shape	Width mm	Length mm	Context
740	copper alloy	circular	22	22	unstratified
290	pewter	almost circular	23.5		Area 10, 1001
741	pewter	fiddle	31	48	Area 3
742	pewter	oval	29	42	Area 4
743	pewter	oval	24	37	Area 4, extension
744	pewter	oval	24	40	unstratified
745	copper alloy	oval	25	45	Area 4
746	copper alloy	oval	27	46	unstratified
747	copper alloy	oval	23		unstratified
748	copper alloy	oval	31	54	Area 4
749	copper alloy	oval	49		Area 3
750	copper alloy	oval			Area 1, Channel C
751	pewter	oval	27	41	Area 5
752	pewter	oval		60	Area 1, base of Channel C
753	silver	oval	25	142	unstratified
754	copper alloy	oval			
755	copper alloy	oval		86	
756	copper alloy	oval		63	Area 4
757	copper alloy	oval	31	166	Area 4, extension 'section 2'
758	copper alloy	oval	38	145	Area 1, base of Channel C
759	iron	oval		74	Area 4, extension
760	copper alloy	oval	32		Area 14, Mill 1
761	copper alloy	oval	31	165	Area 4, extension
762	copper alloy	oval		190	Area 4

Table 43. Spoons.

similar to examples on oval bowls from early Roman London (Jones and Sherlock 1996, fig 20.3, nos 7 and 9) although the design is difficult to make out because of damage and the alloy is a little different; nor can it be stated here with certainty that this is the bowl of a spoon, but the similarity is sufficient for it to be included here, rather than with the pendants with which it was boxed after excavation. It comes from 1001, Area 10. This area has produced other early finds. A date comparable with the second-century London spoons would not be out of place.

One spoon of heavily leaded bronze (**740**) has a raised rib on the back of the bowl, continuing the line of the missing handle and splayed at the end. Such ornamental ribs, a development from the 'rat-tail' used to join handle and bowl, are common to a small group of some dozen spoons from various sites in southern England (Sherlock 2000). A spoon of leaded bronze from Area 4 (745) is very similar to a bowl from the 1905 Lansdowne excavations, now in the Pump Room museum, Bath (RB 1451, unpublished).

The size and pointed tip of the bowl of a pewter spoon (**751**) from Area 5 suggest a stylistic date rather later than the other pewter spoons. It is interesting to note that the remaining pewter spoons were dispersed across the site, and only two of them (**742** and **743**) came from Area 4. The only example of a silver spoon (753) can also be assigned to the late Roman period. It is similar to one of two examples from a burial of *c* 300 from Lullingstone (Sherlock 1987, fig 23). The curved 'bite' taken out of the join with the handle on a leaded bronze spoon (754) is common and it can be compared with unpublished examples from Silchester. A damaged bowl of leaded bronze (756) includes notched decoration of the join for the handle, which is similar to a spoon from an unstratified context at Nettleton (Sherlock 1982, fig 83.4). Notched decoration can also be seen on two further spoons (**758** and **759**).

A fragment of a short, tinned iron handle with a join for the bowl (**759**) came from Area 4 extension. It is rare to find iron tinned in the Roman period but the design of the

No	Position of analysis	Composition
740	bowl, underside	heavily leaded bronze
740	break edge at rat's tail	heavily leaded bronze
741	bowl, underside	pewter (ie lead/tin alloy)
741	bowl, topside, rim	pewter (ie lead/tin alloy)
742	bowl, underside	pewter (ie lead/tin alloy)
742	bowl, topside, rim	pewter (ie lead/tin alloy)
743	bowl, underside	pewter (ie lead/tin alloy)
743	bowl, topside, rim	pewter (ie lead/tin alloy)
745	bowl, underside	leaded bronze
745	bowl, topside	leaded bronze
745	handle offset	leaded bronze
746	bowl, underside	leaded bronze
746	bowl, underside patina	leaded bronze
746	bowl, topside, rim	lightly leaded bronze
746	handle offset	leaded bronze
748	bowl, underside	leaded bronze
748	bowl, topside at junction with handle	bronze (a very small amount of lead was detected)
749	bowl, underside	very lightly leaded bronze
749	bowl, topside	very lightly leaded bronze
750	bowl, underside	leaded bronze
750	handle/bowl junction	leaded bronze
751	bowl, underside	pewter (with very high tin content)
751	bowl, topside, edge	pewter (with very high tin content)
752	handle, mid point	pewter (ie lead/tin alloy)
752	handle/bowl junction	pewter (with a higher proportion of lead)
753	handle	silver (plus a little copper, lead and gold)

No	Position of analysis	Composition
753	bowl	silver (plus a little copper, lead, gold and a very small amount of zinc)
756	handle, mid point	leaded bronze
756	handle at offset	leaded bronze
757	handle	leaded bronze
757	bowl	leaded bronze
758	handle	leaded bronze
758	bowl	leaded bronze
758	bowl edge	leaded bronze
759	handle	iron
759	inlay on handle	pewter (ie lead/tin alloy)
760	bowl, underside edge	leaded bronze (plus a little zinc)
760	bowl, underside rat's tail	leaded bronze (plus a little zinc)
760	bowl, topside, rim	leaded bronze (plus a little zinc)
760	bowl, topside at break	leaded bronze (plus a little zinc)
761	handle, tip	very lightly leaded bronze (plus a small nickel peak)
761	handle, golden area	underlying metal, leaded bronze. No gold detected. Golden area due to presence of sulphide corrosion products, probaby predominantly chalcopyrite, a copper-iron sulphide
761	bowl	leaded bronze (only a very tiny nickel peak was present this time)
761	handle, near bowl	leaded bronze (no truly discernable nickel peak)
762	handle	lightly leaded bronze
762	bowl	lightly leaded bronze

Table 44. Spoons: qualitative analysis results.

spoon itself is widely known in Britain, as with the spoons from Nettleton, for example (Sherlock 1982, figs 83.4 and 7, 84.8 and 9).

Coming from various parts of the site, the spoons cannot be considered as part of a scattered hoard destined for melting and re-use, although metal-working is known to have occurred here. They could have been made at Ickham but more likely at a nearby urban centre such as Canterbury, given the fact that their shapes are widely known from southern England. They are not associated with burials. They have no *prima facie* connection with the military or any other class of Roman society. As eating implements they must originate from everyday domestic contexts.

Roman spoons have been found at many other Roman sites in Kent, ranging from those in the late silver hoard from Canterbury, thirty-six from Richborough, to numerous small numbers from villas. The Ickham spoons are noteworthy for two main reasons. Firstly, there is the quantity of spoons,

perhaps partly due to the accident of systematic excavations. Comparable sites for such numbers (apart from the great silver hoards of East Anglia) are Camerton (Somerset [now Avon]) and Nettleton (Wiltshire) which have yielded about twelve and twenty-seven respectively. Camerton was a Romano-British settlement which had industrial development. At Nettleton there was a shrine of Apollo around which grew up a hostelry, shop and domestic buildings. The twisted handles and notched decorations on the Ickham spoons have particularly close parallels with the late Roman spoons from these sites as well as with those from many other sites in southern England.

The description of metals in the table is based on the results of XRF qualitative analysis, kindly carried out by Adrian Tribe. In summary, there are fifteen spoons made of leaded bronze (with variable amounts of lead), seven made of pewter (with some variation in the proportions of lead and tin), one iron spoon handle coated with tin, and one silver spoon. Many of the base metal spoons bear traces of

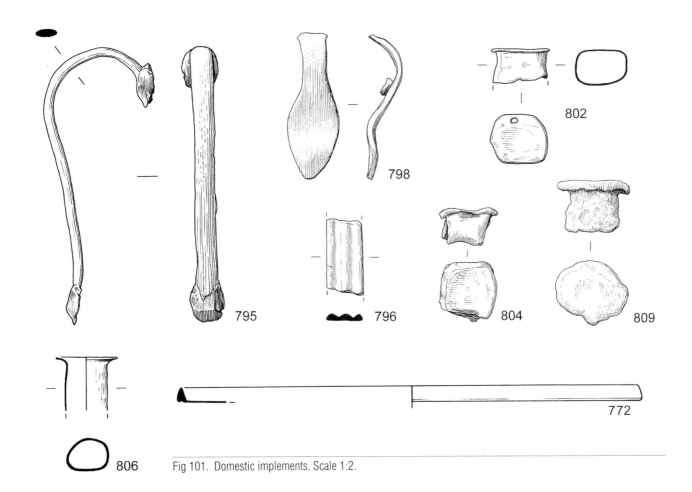

Fig 101. Domestic implements. Scale 1:2.

tin plating, generally a late Roman practice, presumably to make them look like silver.

Vessels

The range of vessels from Ickham encompasses examples of copper alloy, pewter and glass. The pewter vessels, in particular, form an important collection which is largely of late Roman date. Copper alloy vessels, in contrast, are poorly represented.

Copper alloy vessels

Three fragments of copper alloy rim possibly from cups or bowls were recovered, but too little remains to indicate their original diameters. A piece of thick sheet (766) with a pair of parallel incised lines on one surface and possible turning lines on the other may also come from a vessel.

Pewter vessels

Ickham produced a large assemblage of pewter tableware, though all in fragmentary condition, alongside other items of lead alloy and much scrap and spillages which are discussed in relation to metal-working elsewhere (p 300). The remains of eight vessels and twenty-three other rim fragments were found, occurring principally in Area 4. They are broken or deliberately cut and some are folded, indicating that they represent the collection of scrap awaiting melting down for recasting. Several of the vessels show distinct turning rings and others have three marks on the base from the impression of the lathe plate prongs, showing that they had been spun on a lathe. The highly fragmentary and often distorted nature of many of the pieces made it impossible to estimate the number of vessels represented and difficult to be sure of the original style or size of the vessels from which they derived. Attempts to classify the vessels according to type proved impossible as previous typologies rely on the shape of the entire vessel and do not easily relate to small, cut or broken pieces. What is certain is that a wide range of vessel types is represented including, plates, bowls, saucers, small drinking vessels (cups/beakers) and flagons. In addition the lids or bases of canisters were also recognised along with a possible socket from a candlestick (**806**).

The approximate estimated original diameter of nine of the rims suggests they come from plates measuring between 140 and 260mm in diameter. Two other rims are smaller at 120 and 95mm (**772**, 807). Other broken fragments retain either fragments of a supporting ring (788 and 792) or concentric rings (779 and 785) also characteristic of plates and dishes. The size of three fragments suggest small plates or saucers (787, 788 and 789), while rim fragments from small drinking vessels such as a plain cup or beaker (793 and 794) were also recognised.

A rim of triangular section was noted (786) from a flat serving platter. Another rim fragment (**778**) was decorated on its upper face, an unusual feature, and also appears to have a circular punch mark present below the rim.

Half of a small dish (**774**) with a faceted-edged or 'wavy' rim, slightly fluted in profile, and a small support rim was found in Area 3. It is distorted, the edge is torn and possibly cut in one area. A scalloped rim (**775**) was also found which appears to have been deliberately removed from the neck of a small bowl to which it had originally been soldered.

A complete flagon handle (**795**) and fragments cut from six others were found. Three (799) are cut above the terminal, two of which are leaf-shaped (**798** and 800). The handles are plain or reeded (**796** and 797). No other flagon components were recognised. It was also notable that though pedestal bowls are a common form, none were recognised at Ickham, though they may possibly be represented in highly fragmentary form amongst the scrap material recovered.

Four lids or bases from canisters of varying size were found (**802**, 803, **804**, 805). Two were unusual (**802** and 805) in being of D-shape, another had a small suspension hole present in the flange (**802**).

Two circular bases deliberately cut from the rest of the vessel were found (789 and 790). One (790) has a much larger central spindle mark than is normal, and appears never to have been polished, suggesting it may be a poor casting re-used for a secondary purpose possibly as a weight.

Three plates were found together (767–9) in Area 7 context 802, and are said to have been found stacked inside a shallow oval iron frying pan (**723**, Fig 96). The small finds notebook entry for 1970 lists a bowl, and not the remains of three vessels, so that the possibility exists of a transposition of

small finds numbers in the years between excavation and study. All three plates are folded and appear to be scrap awaiting remelting. Analysis showed them to be made of pewter of varying compositions. One plate (768) of high quality pewter (99 per cent tin content), had been folded and melted around the edges. Another (767) of slightly lower quality (85 per cent tin content) had been partially melted after being folded. The third (769), of poor quality pewter (45 per cent tin content), had been deliberately cut away from the rest of the plate. Two of the plates (767–8) with flanges *c* 30mm wide are of Peal's type 4 (Peal 1967), the other (769) cannot be categorised with certainty but may be of Peal's type 3d or type 1.

A plate fragment (772) has a solidified molten lump of metal present on the interior face, again suggesting it to be a scrap vessel awaiting remelting. Another piece of tableware (770) had been folded into four.

It is clear that the pewter material represents the collection of scrap, deliberately cut up for remelting and casting. Lead alloy can be easily melted and cast again and again, so why such a valuable commodity should be discarded, rather than gathered up and taken with them when the metalworkers moved on, is unclear. It would suggest a deliberate act of abandonment.

Pewter analysis

The following text is adapted from Ancient Monuments Laboratory Report 32/98, 'Analysis of Roman pewter tableware and debris from Ickham, Kent' written by Rebecca Sutton.

All the items recognised by eye as being of tableware (3.75kg) were analysed and their tin content plotted. The plot showed a peak occuring between 50–70 per cent tin content, a smaller number between 70–90 per cent tin, and a large peak at 90–100 per cent tin. These peaks are similar to those found in compositional studies of Roman pewter tableware previously undertaken by Tylecote (1962, 68–9, tables 25 and 26), Pollard (1983, 83), and later summarised by Beagrie (1989). Beagrie's groupings centred on 50, 75 and 90 per cent tin composition. He suggested three principal reasons for the wide range of varying compositions observed: the deliberate addition of other metals to the tin to improve its hardness, casting properties or cost; impurities deriving from the original tin ores or fluxes, and their incomplete removal during smelting; and the recycling of tin and its accidental contamination. The eutectic composition of the metal is one which would produce the best castings by allowing the pewter to solidify quickly, and it is certain that this composition would have been aimed at by the Roman

No	Object	Diameter mm	Height mm	Context	No	Object	Diameter mm	Height mm	Context
763	copper alloy rim			Area 1, Pit 115.1	786	pewter plate			Area 7, 712
764	copper alloy rim			Area 3	787	pewter plate/saucer			Area 4, 408
765	copper alloy rim			unstratified	788	pewter saucer			Area 10, 1001
766	copper alloy			Area 4	789	pewter plate base	86		Area 7, 709.3
767	pewter plate	225		Area 8, 802	790	pewter plate base	69		Area 1, Channel C
768	pewter plate	240		Area 8, 802	791	pewter plate base			Area 4
769	pewter plate	265+		Area 8, 802	792	pewter plate/bowl	140		unstratified
770	pewter plate	170		Area 1, Channel C	793	pewter cup/beaker			Area 4, extension
771	pewter plate	162		Area 1, Channel C	794	pewter cup/beaker			Area 10, 1001
772	pewter plate	120		Area 4	795	pewter flagon handle			Area 2
773	pewter plate			Area 4, extension	796	pewter flagon handle			Area 4, extension
774	pewter dish	130	40	Area 3	797	pewter flagon handle			Area 1, Pit 115.1
775	pewter bowl	100		Area 4, extension	798	pewter flagon handle			Area 1, Channel C
776	pewter plate	100		Area 4	799	pewter flagon handle			Area 4
777	pewter plate	225			800	pewter flagon handle			Area 10, 1005
778	pewter plate/dish	260		Area 4, extension	801	pewter flagon handle			Area 2
779	pewter plate			Area 3	802	pewter canister socket	30	18	Area 4
780	pewter plate			Area 4, extension	803	pewter canister socket	17	15	Area 10, 1001
781	pewter plate			Area 4, extension	804	pewter canister socket	30	19	Area 4
782	pewter plate			Area 2	805	pewter canister socket	40	54	Area 7, 712
783	pewter plate			Area 4	806	pewter candlestick/pipe fragment			Area 2
784	pewter plate			Area 4	807	pewter plate	95		Area 5
785	pewter plate			Area 4					

Table 45. Metal vessels.

pewterers. Hughes (1980) has suggested that this would be represented by a 60–80 per cent tin content range. Pliny's 'recipes' for pewter (*ibid*, 43–4) consist of two parts tin to one part lead (67 per cent tin/33 per cent lead), one part tin to one part lead (50 per cent/50 per cent) and one part tin to two parts lead (described as solder). These recipes may also explain the groups found in the tin content analyses of the Ickham tablewares.

The tableware plot also showed a small number of items with a low tin content which may represent pieces which were either misidentified as tableware or may come from the bases of vessels, as sometimes bases were made of a higher lead content than the rest of the vessel.

Vessel repairs

Eleven lead cramps to repair pottery were scattered across the site, one still holding a fragment of greyware (808). In addition, three crude lead plugs (**809**, 810–11) also appear to be pot repairs. Two copper alloy folded sheet clips for repairs to wooden bowls were also found (812 and 813) alongside a narrow copper alloy strip (814) which may have served a similar purpose.

Glass vessels *John Shepherd and Sasha Smith, incorporating notes by the late Dorothy Charlesworth*

A total of 311 items of glass were submitted for identification. Of this total, 265 are vessel fragments and twenty-seven are fragments of window glass. Nineteen glass objects, eighteen of which are beads, the other object being a pendant setting, have been described elsewhere. The window glass is described below (p 264) with other structural materials.

Of the 265 vessel fragments, eighty-seven come from identifiable vessel shapes, twenty-five of which come from the rims of late Roman conical beakers. The remaining 188 come from the bodies of vessels of indeterminate forms.

In general, all of the fragments of glass from this site are small and many show signs of abrasion due to redeposition. As a result it is very difficult to be precise about the forms of every single fragment. In fact, for the greater majority it is only possible to identify the general vessel type for the

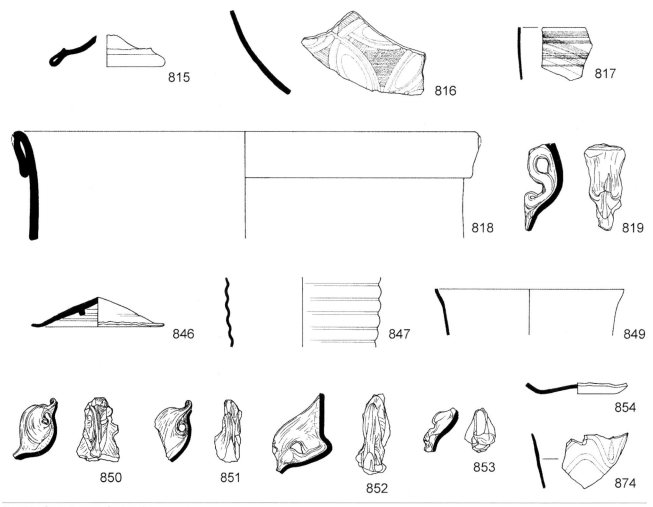

Fig 102. Glass vessels. Scale 1:2.

fragment. This accounts for the large number of wheel-cut fragments among the indeterminate groups.

The following discussion examines the main vessel types represented in this assemblage, giving parallels from elsewhere which contribute towards the accepted date for such forms. These lists are not intended to be exhaustive and, indeed, the geographical range of the locations may not be representative of the real distribution of the vessel type.

Discussion

Only three vessels made from colourless glass could be identified. One (**815**) is the base of a vessel, probably from a beaker or cup, which is of a common type of the late first and second century. The other two examples (**816** and **817**)

with wheel-cut and cross-hatched decoration are much later, coming from bowl or cup forms of the third or fourth century. Examples, some with cross-hatching similar to these Ickham vessels, can be seen at Trier (Goethert-Polaschek 1977, 29, no 71, taf 32; 54, no 182, taf 38; 31, no 2, 77–9) and further east at Dura-Europos (Clairmont 1963, 72, no 273, pl 27).

A fragment (**818**) comes from the rim of a large urn which would appear to be of the type commonly used for cremation use (eg Isings (1957) form 67a and see RCHM 1928, 159, fig 65.32 for an example from Bishopsgate, London). Its presence here, however, is not unusual since such jars were commonly used on domestic sites (Cool and Price 1995, 109–12 for a full discussion of the wide range of jars with rolled rims).

The oil-flask or aryballos, represented by just the single handle fragment (**819**), would have been used for containing oils and unguents required while bathing. It is one of the most common types of toilet vessels. A handle or chain between its two small, dolphin-like handles allowed it to be suspended from the wrist or from a thong around the waist. The type first appears during the Claudian period (at *Carnuntum*, see Isings 1957, form 61) and continues into the third century with some variations (eg colourless with deep wheel-cutting such as from the legionary bath-house at Caerleon (Allen 1986, 107–8, no 52). This particular site produced a very large number of these oil-flasks dating from the early Flavian period to the mid to late third century). The form is rare in the fourth century.

Thick-walled bottles, the square-sectioned form (Isings form 50) and its associated cylindrical form (Isings 1957, form 51), are perhaps the most common forms in assemblages of the late first and second centuries and are well-represented here at Ickham (Table 46). These vessels, very sturdy and functional in design, were produced in very large numbers throughout the Empire and were used, in the first instance, for the transport and storage of liquid foodstuffs, cosmetics and pharmaceutical preparations. The associated jar form, which only differs from the bottle in the finishing of the vessel above the mould-blown body, could be used for more solid products (unpublished examples from Pompeii in the Naples Museum contained pulses). The bottles came in a variety of sizes and the largest were used as cinerary urns, such as the bottle from Blomfield Street, Moorfields, London (RCHM 1928, 161, fig 66, 35i).

A particular feature of these bottles (and jars) is the relief base designs. These mould-made features are a very useful tool for mould-linking individual examples. Unfortunately, the scale of production of these bottles, and the fact that so much glass was removed from the archaeological record in antiquity for recycling, makes this difficult. Although a large number of bottles and their designs still exist for study only a very small percentage can be linked to common moulds. The variation in the patterns of the moulds, however, does suggest that particular designs existed only in certain areas of the Empire (Shepherd 1978, 46). This being the case, the comparison of similar designs is still a valid exercise and the more elaborate the design, the more likely it is that two bottles with that design were part of the same manufacturing and distribution mechanism. Unfortunately, the only base design which comes from Ickham is incomplete and consists of part of a circle (828), the most common single element of all the known designs.

Three fragments come from 'Frontinus' bottles (**846–7, 848**), so-called because of the name and its abbreviations included in the decoration on the bases of these bottles. The

one-handled example (Isings 1957, form 89) appears first during the second century and should not be confused with the two-handled form (Isings 1957, form 128) which is fourth century in date, although both forms obviously follow the same tradition and function.

There are some fundamental differences between the early and late one-handled bottles. The earlier bottles are in a naturally coloured, green blue metal, such as the Ickham fragments, whereas the later examples tend to be in the late Roman greenish colourless metal. Another difference would appear to be in the rim and handle forms (Cool and Price 1995, 204). The early bottles have a rim that has been folded outwards then inwards onto itself and then flattened, and they usually have reeded handles. The later vessels, however, have more funnel-shaped rims with the lip simply rolled over, and the handles are usually plain. Unfortunately it is not possible to equate any of the bottle rim fragments from this site with this form. The base fragment (**846**), shows part of a single circle which usually accompanied part of the abbreviated name, for example 'FRO'.

In 1978 Price was able to locate such bottles, irrespective of their date, on only eleven sites in this country, although they are very common indeed in other parts of the north-western provinces. However, in writing about a fourth-century bottle from Colchester, Cool and Price were able to list at least thirty sites with Frontinus bottles, emphasising that they were probably not as rare as the earlier study had suggested (Cool and Price 1995, 205 for references to published and unpublished examples). However, these are small fragments and their comparison with the distribution of complete and fragmentary examples in the rest of the north-west provinces still shows that the form is relatively scarce in Britain.

A fragment (**849**), from a hexagonal-sectioned bottle decorated with low relief diagonal vertical ribbing comes from a form which is not common in Britain. Seventeen fragments are known from Barnsley Park (Price 1982, 183–4, nos 46–7 and a–i inclusive, fig 60, 46–7) one from Colchester (Cool and Price 1995, 207, no 2264, fig 11.18) and one from Marlowe, Canterbury (Shepherd 1995, 1244, no 406, fig 547). The form, a variant of Isings (1957, 119) form 100 dates to the late third and early fourth centuries (see also Morin-Jean 1913, 66, form 18, fig 58, an example from the Boulonnais, Musée de Boulogne sur Mer, inventory no 2647, and Pirling 1974, fig 103,5 for a Krefeld-Gellep example).

The bottle form represented by nos **850–4**, with twin dolphin handles, is one of the more well-known late Roman bottle types. Isings cites an example from Remagen which is

No	Colour and form	Type	Typological dating	Context
815	colourless bowl		late first or second century	base of Channel C
816	colourless dish		third or fourth century	Pit 115.2
817	colourless vessel		fourth century	base of Channel C
818	naturally coloured urn	63–5	late first or second century	Area 4
819	naturally coloured oil flask	61	late first or second century	Area 4
820	naturally coloured bottle	50–1	late first or third century	103
821	naturally coloured bottle	50–1	late first or third century	Area 4, extension
822	naturally coloured bottle	50–1	late first or third century	Area 2
823	naturally coloured bottle	50–1	late first or third century	1001
824	naturally coloured bottle	50–1	late first or third century	Area 14
825	naturally coloured bottle	50–1	late first or third century	Area 4, extension
826	naturally coloured bottle	50–1	late first or third century	104
827	naturally coloured bottle	50–1	late first or third century	Area 4, extension
828	naturally coloured bottle	50–1	late first or third century	1004
829	naturally coloured bottle	50–1	late first or third century	Area 5, 'Ditch 2'
830	naturally coloured bottle	50–1	late first or third century	Area 4
831	naturally coloured bottle	50–1	late first or third century	Area 4
832	naturally coloured bottle	50–1	late first or third century	Area 4, extension
833	naturally coloured bottle	50–1	late first or third century	Area 4, extension
834	naturally coloured bottle	50–1	late first or third century	Area 4, extension
835	naturally coloured bottle	50–1	late first or third century	Area 7, 'Layer 4'
836	naturally coloured bottle	50–1	late first or third century	base of Channel C
837	naturally coloured bottle	50–1	late first or third century	Area 4
838	naturally coloured bottle	50–1	late first or third century	Area 4
839	naturally coloured bottle	50–1	late first or third century	Area 4
840	naturally coloured bottle	50–1	late first or third century	1002.2
841	naturally coloured bottle	50–1	late first or third century	1004
842	naturally coloured bottle	50–1	late first or third century	604
843	naturally coloured bottle	50–1	late first or third century	1001
844	naturally coloured bottle	50–1	late first or third century	1001
845	naturally coloured bottle	50–1	late first or third century	1001
846	naturally coloured frontinus bottle	89/128	second to fourth century	'Section 2' L2-5
847	naturally coloured frontinus bottle	89/128	second to fourth century	Area 4
848	naturally coloured frontinus bottle	89/128	second to fourth century	Area 4, extension
849	naturally coloured late Roman bottle	100	late first or fourth century	Area 4
850	naturally coloured late Roman bottle	100	late first or fourth century	105.1
851	naturally coloured late Roman bottle	100	late first or fourth century	Channel C
852	naturally coloured late Roman bottle	100	late first or fourth century	411
853	naturally coloured late Roman bottle	100	late first or fourth century	Pit 115.1
854	naturally coloured late Roman bottle	100	late first or fourth century	408
855	naturally coloured phial	82	late first to third century	Area 4, extension
856	naturally coloured phial	82	late first to third century	Area 4, extension
857	naturally coloured phial	92	late first to third century	Area 4, extension
858	naturally coloured phial	82	late first to third century	Area 4, extension
859	naturally coloured phial	82	late first to third century	base of Channel C
860	naturally coloured jug or flagon		late first or second century	610.4
861	naturally coloured jug or flagon		late third or fourth century	Area 4, extension
862	naturally coloured jug or flagon		late first or second century	Area 5
863	naturally coloured jug or flagon		late first or second century	Area 4
864	naturally coloured jug or flagon		late first or second century	'Along fence'
865	naturally coloured bowl	44	late first to third century	Area 4

No	Colour and form	Type	Typological dating	Context
866	naturally coloured bowl	44	late first to third century	Area 2
867	naturally coloured beaker or bowl	34/44	late first or second century	Area 4
868	naturally coloured cup or bowl	34/44	late first to third century	base of Channel C
869	naturally coloured goblet or beaker	106a	fourth or early fifth century	610.5
870	naturally coloured bowl	115	fourth or early fifth century	base of Channel C
871	naturally coloured bowl		fourth or early fifth century	Area 4, extension
872	naturally coloured beaker	106c?	late third or fourth century	602
873	naturally coloured beaker	106c?	late third or fourth century	base of Channel C
874	naturally coloured cone-shaped vessel		fourth or early fifth century	unstratified
875	naturally coloured beaker	106	late third or fourth century	'Ditch 6'
876	naturally coloured beaker	106	late third or fourth century	601
877	naturally coloured beaker	106	late third or fourth century	107
878	naturally coloured beaker	106	late third or fourth century	701
879	naturally coloured beaker	106	late third or fourth century	'Ditch 8'
880	naturally coloured beaker	106	late third or fourth century	Area 4, extension
881	naturally coloured beaker	106	late third or fourth century	Area 4, extension
882	naturally coloured beaker	106c	late third or fourth century	Area 4
883	naturally coloured beaker	106c	late third or fourth century	Area 4
884	naturally coloured beaker	106c	late third or fourth century	122
885	naturally coloured beaker	106c	late third or fourth century	Area 4
886	naturally coloured beaker	106c	late third or fourth century	Area 4
887	naturally coloured beaker	106c	late third or fourth century	Area 4, extension
888	naturally coloured beaker	106c	late third or fourth century	Area 4, extension
889	naturally coloured beaker	106c	late third or fourth century	121
890	naturally coloured beaker	106c	late third or fourth century	116
891	naturally coloured beaker	106c	late third or fourth century	335
892	naturally coloured beaker	96/106c	fourth or early fifth century	610.9
893	naturally coloured beaker	96/106c	fourth or early fifth century	128
894	naturally coloured beaker	96/106c	fourth or early fifth century	Area 7, Layer 4
895	naturally coloured beaker	96/106c	fourth or early fifth century	104
896	naturally coloured beaker	96/106c	fourth or early fifth century	408
897	naturally coloured beaker	96/106c	fourth or early fifth century	712
898	naturally coloured beaker	96/106c	fourth or early fifth century	Area 4
899	naturally coloured beaker	96/106c	fourth or early fifth century	701
900	brown indeterminate fragment			Area 4
901	green indeterminate fragment			Area 4
902	blue indeterminate fragment			1001
903	colourless fragment			'Ditch 8'
904	2 colourless fragment			1001
905	13 colourless fragments			Area 4; Area 4, extension; base of Channel C
906	13 naturally coloured fragments			base of Channel C; Channel C, west end
907	8 naturally coloured fragments			Area 4; Area 4, extension; Area 5
908	97 naturally coloured fragments			213; Area 4; base of Channel C; Channel C, west end; Area 4, extension; 335; 104; 127; 128; 710; 712; 1001
909	10 natural green fragments			Area 2; 'Ditch 8'; Channel C, west end; Area 4, extension; 408, 408.4
910	2 natural green fragments			Area 4, extension; 712
911	29 natural green fragments			Area 2; Area 4, extension; Area 4; Area 5; 104; Pit 115.1; 408; 408.4; 610.8; 610.9; 710

Table 46. Glass vessels. Type numbers are those ascribed by Isings (1957).

said to date from the end of the second or early third century (Isings 1957, 119, form 100) but, as Harden (1979, 220) has pointed out, this comes from an old excavation on which the dating may be unreliable. He believed that the form could not have begun much earlier than the middle of the third century with a main period of production and use during the late third and fourth centuries. A fragment of one of these bottles came from a third-century ditch fill at Chew Park, Somerset (Harden 1977, 289, no 5, fig 113), a bottle from Andernach dates to the second half of the third century (Isings 1957) as too does a bottle from Strasbourg-Koenigshoffen (Arveiller-Dulong and Arveiller 1985, 118–9). There are many more examples from the late third and fourth century, such as at Lankhills, Winchester (Harden 1979, 220, 20–1 and 411), York (Harden 1962, 141, no HG 182), Shakenoak Farm (Harden 1973, 104, nos 232–3, fig 52), Colchester (Cool and Price 1995, 207, no 2263), Lullingstone, Kent (Cool and Price 1987, 121–2, no 382), Barnsley Park, Gloucester (Price 1982, 182), Ospringe, Kent (Whiting *et al* 1931, pl 38, no 448), The Beeches, Cirencester (Shepherd 1986, 120, no 623), Frocester Court (Price 1979, 44, no 42), and *Verulamium* AD 350–400 (Charlesworth 1984, 169, no 276, fig 68,129).

A surface find (**874**) comes from a type of late Roman beaker, conical and decorated with trailed festoons, which is well-known on Romano-British sites, eg Canterbury (Shepherd 1995, 1249, nos 506–9, fig 549), Chichester (Charlesworth 1974, 134, no 22, fig 8.13), Barnsley Park (Price 1982, 177, nos 16–17, fig 59), Lankhills (Harden 1979, 213, no 385 and 214–15, no 633, fig 27), Shakenoak (Harden 1973, 100, nos 196–7, 102, no 206, fig 52), Frocester Court (Price 1979, 42, no 10–23, fig 17), and the Beeches, Cirencester (Shepherd 1986, 121, no 655 and 658, fig 87). Price (1979, 43) cites complete examples from *Verulamium*, Colchester Hospital, Hauxton Mill (Cambridge) and Chilgrove near Chichester, Sussex.

The conical beakers, either with or without abraded decoration and with either cracked-off or fire-rounded rims, are common in Britain during the late third and, particularly, the fourth century. For example, see Shakenoak (Harden 1973, 103), Portchester (Harden 1975, figs.197–8) Frocester Court (Price 1979, 41–2), Bath (Shepherd 1985, 162–3, nos 1–6) and Cirencester (Shepherd 1986, 120, nos 625–41).

Conclusion

The fragmentary nature of the glass and the state of the site records make it difficult to reconstruct the nature of the supply and use of glass to this site throughout the Roman

period. The absence of a number of distinctive and common types must be noted - for example monochrome glass other than the few indeterminate pieces and pillar-moulded bowls which would seem to exclude supply here during the first century. Bottles, dating from the late first through to the third century, are present in profusion but there are very few vessels here which could be described as contemporary with them. Of particular note are the late Roman vessels, the bottles with dolphin handles, the hexagonally ribbed vessels, and the numerous conical beakers which would point to an active supply of glassware during the late Roman period, in particular the late third and fourth centuries.

Buckets and handles

Bucket fittings

Wooden stave-built buckets are represented by iron handles and their mounts. Five iron bucket handles were recovered, three being spirally twisted (913–15). Bucket handle mounts of nailed iron strap with either pierced-ring or hooked-ring terminals to articulate with the bucket handles were also found (eg 918–21). A group of thirty-nine nailed binding fragments (912) came from Area 4, comprising three bucket handle mounts and fragments of binding of three distinct widths [*c* 36–40mm, 20–22mm and 15mm] probably representing the remains of a minimum of two wooden stave built buckets with iron bindings which rotted *in situ*.

Handles

A range of iron and copper alloy handles and iron handle mounts come from domestic implements. The iron handles include a spirally-twisted fragment (929) likely to come from a fire shovel or other hearth implement and a broken, rectangular-sectioned handle (930) of iron with a non-ferrous metal inlay or plating. Three iron handles for furniture were recovered from Area 4 extension and a cast copper alloy dome-headed finial (925) may have served as a heavy handle.

Large ring handles

A large waisted ring (927) articulating with a large U-shaped staple may be a tethering ring or a large handle. It is comparable with a post-medieval coffin handle from Norwich (Margeson 1993, 82 and fig 46, no 521) and could have been made and used at any time from the Roman period onward. A large ring handle or terret of lead alloy of round section (**928**) is comparable with another from Colchester recovered from a context dated *c* 60/75–*c* 100/150 (Crummy 1983, 168, no 4703, fig 208).

No	Object	Length mm	Width mm	Diameter mm	Context
912	iron fittings (39)		96+	12	Area 4
913	iron handle				Area 1, base of Channel C, east end
914	iron handle				Area 1, Channel C, west end
915	iron handle				Area 4
916	iron handle				Area 3
917	iron handle				Area 10, 1001
918	iron handle mount		118	28	Area 4
919	iron handle mount		57+	25	Area 4
920	iron handle mount		37+	29	Area 4
921	iron handle mount		111	24	Area 4
922	iron handle		111	20	Area 4
923	iron handle		70+	44	Area 4
924	iron handle		110		Area 4, extension
925	copper alloy handle			31	Area 14
926	iron handle		95		Area 10, 1006
927	iron handle		62	80	Area 1, Channel C
928	lead handle			88	unstratified

Table 47. Bucket fittings and handles.

Box fittings

The remains of a rectangular box fitting of lead alloy (**931**) came from Area 3 and a fragment from another, decorated with repoussé dots (932) came from the stone floor in the same area of the site. The sheet is decorated with concentric raised mouldings in the centre and a border of impressed dots around the edge. It had been nailed at the surviving corners.

An iron hasp from a box fitting (933) was found along with twelve fragments of nailed bindings with decorative rounded or pointed terminals. Fifteen angled strap bindings were used to strengthen box corners. A small hasp of copper alloy (47) possibly with a military association, is described above.

In addition, six fragments of similar flat-sectioned strap found scattered across the site are likely to come from box fittings. All fall between 47–63mm in width and, where they survive, have deliberately rounded corners. Three have series of rivet holes present, both round and square rivet holes are found on the same straps suggesting that they had been repaired.

Other fixtures and fittings

Two copper alloy bell-shaped studs (**934** and 935), with integrally cast rectangular shanks riveted at the straight terminals, are of Allason-Jones type 2 (Allason-Jones 1985, 95–108). One, complete example (935) had been burnt. Used in groups to attach lock plates to boxes and caskets, there is also evidence for them being used singly as decorative pommels for knives or daggers.

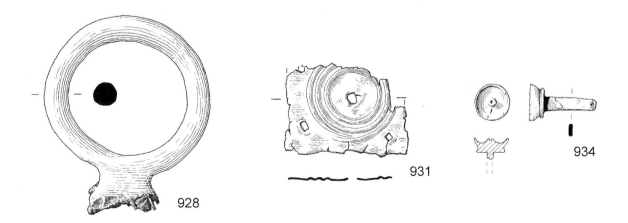

Fig 103. Bucket and box fittings. Fittings (Nos 928 and 931, scale 1:2), stud (No 934, scale 1:1).

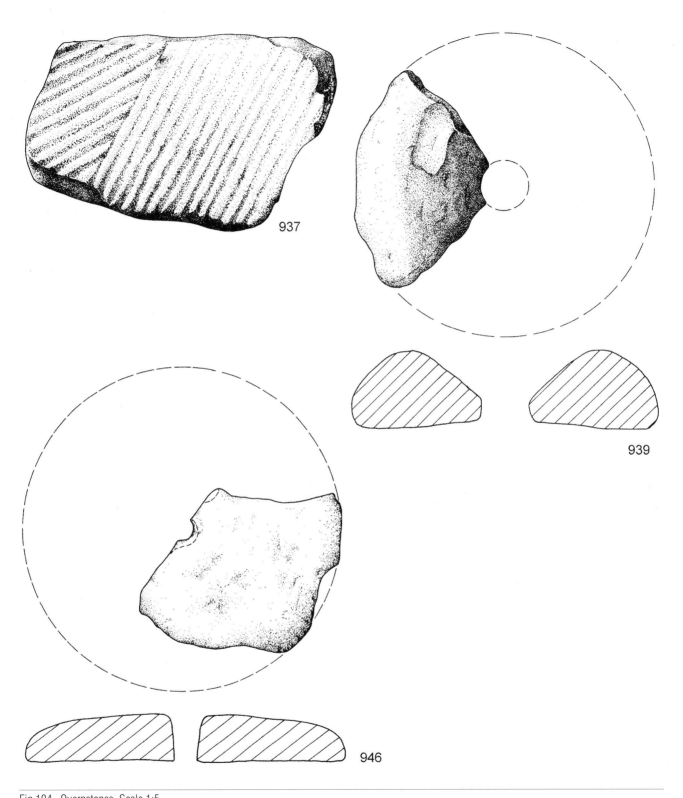

Fig 104. Quernstones. Scale 1:5.

Querns

Ian Riddler

The sequence of worked stones from Ickham includes both querns and millstones of Roman date. The millstones are described below (pp 277–89). The querns can be differentiated from the millstones by virtue of their smaller size and thickness, their lack of features diagnostic of millstones and, in some cases, because of their stone type. They can be separated into four basic groups by stone type and general form: 1, Greensand oscillatory hand querns; 2, basalt lava rotary querns; 3, coarse gritstone querns; 4, querns produced from other local sandstones.

These four divisions correspond with those to be seen elsewhere in southern England during the Roman period. Similar stone types were used for the millstones, which invoke both Greensand and Millstone Grit, with one example of a tertiary sandstone. Basalt lava was only used for querns, however, and not for millstones. In the following text the querns are considered in a broad chronological sequence which is based, in the first instance, on the stone type.

Greensand querns

The argillaceous Lower Greensand used for these querns probably comes from the Thanet beds. Indeed, these particular querns almost certainly come from the Folkestone quarries, which were used extensively during the Iron Age and Roman periods (Keller 1989). The harder greensands still found today on the beach at eastern Folkestone provided a durable stone which did not wear down as quickly as the softer, Upper Greensand found further to the north. Although it is still possible that further Greensand quarries remain to be discovered within the Weald, previous studies of Iron Age and Roman stone quarries indicate that they were widely dispersed (Peacock 1987) and this suggests that Folkestone formed one of the few areas for east Kent quern quarries.

The lack of a detailed chronology for deposits at Ickham is to be regretted, but some tentative indications of dating are provided by the worked stone objects themselves. Early forms of rotary quern are scarce. Elsewhere in east Kent these are of Iron Age and early Roman date (Blockley *et al* 1995, 1206 and fig 532.1368). They are represented here by four examples (936, **937**, 938 and **939**), two of which come from Area 10. Only one fragment (**939**) can be reconstructed and this represents an upper stone from a quern 330mm in diameter.

Eight further fragments of querns (940–7) have a shallower profile and a broader diameter, and they can be

identified as rotary querns of a distinctive Roman type. There are three upper stones and four lower stones, as well as one fragment which is of indeterminate form. Furrows are present on the grinding surfaces of five examples.

The best-surviving example of an upper stone of this type (**946**) shows a small part of the central eye and has a grinding surface that has been worn smooth. The shallow, broad profile recalls that of contemporary millstones but this example has a diameter of 430mm, and the others range between 380 and 560mm, well below the dimensions of millstones.

Evidence from Canterbury, Monkton and Harrietsham suggests that querns produced in Greensand were not in use to any extent after the second century (Bennett *et al* 1982, 185, no 119; Blockley *et al* 1995, 1206 nos 1368–81; Riddler 2008). Examples from Canterbury in particular were generally retrieved from contexts of Periods 1 and 2 at the Marlowe excavations, which extend only a few years into the second century. However, a few examples came from late Roman Period 4 deposits there, and these are paralleled by the examples from Ickham, two of which come from late Roman contexts (Table 48). In both cases they may be residual in those deposits.

As seen in Table 48 below, one of these stones (alongside one of the earlier forms of Greensand quern) came from context 107 and one was also found in the nearby context 116. Many of the objects retrieved from these contexts, and from 107 in particular, are of late fourth-century date. One came from Area 10, and another was retrieved from Area 6, indicating that their distribution mirrors that of millstones, in terms of their general proximity to the mills themselves.

Basalt lava rotary querns

A number of querns from Ickham were produced from basalt lava. This is probably of Rhenish origin, although it could, in theory at least, have come from the Auvergne (Röder 1953; Peacock 1980; Biddle 1990, 881). It is widespread in Kent, as elsewhere in Roman Britain, and it occurs throughout the Roman period. Every *contubernium* and century in a legion probably possessed some form of hand-mill and it has been argued that basalt lava was the preferred stone type for hand querns carried by military personnel (Childe 1943, 25; Frere and Wilkes 1989, 181; McIwain 1980, 132). It may be significant that basalt lava querns are predominant on a number of military sites, almost to the exclusion of other stone types (Manning *et al* 1995, 214). On that basis, can a military connection be proposed for Ickham?

The seventeen examples of basalt lava querns (948–64) can be compared with nineteen examples of querns of

QUERNS

No.	Area	Context	Stone type	Object	Quantity	Ceramic Assemblage	Dating	Diameter (mm) Skirt (rim)	Diameter (mm) Eye	Thickness (mm) Skirt (rim)	Thickness (mm) Eye	Max
936	1	105.1, Mills 2 and 3	G	EQ	1	27	400-450					
937	1	107, Mills 2 and 3	G	EQ	2	13	370-400+	-	-	-	-	-
938	10	1001, Mill 1	G	EQ	1			-	-	-	-	-
939	10	1001, Mill 1	G	EQ	1			330	45	-	-	-
940	1	107, Mills 2 and 3	G	RQ	1	13	370-400+	c 380	-	30	-	37.5
941	1	115, Mills 2 and 3	G	RQ	1			-	-	-	-	80
942	1	115.2, , Mills 2 and 3	G	RQ	1	13	370-400+	c 540	-	60	-	-
943	1	116, Mills 2 and 3	G	RQ	1			c 475	-	77.5	-	-
944	4		G	RQ	1			446	50t 56b	47	58	-
945	6	610.1, Mill 4	G	RQ	1			450	c 60	82	98	-
946	10	1001, Mill 1	G	RQ	1			c 430	-	-	63	-
947		u/s	G	RQ	1			560	-	54	-	60
948	1	107, Mills 2 and 3	BL		1	13	370-400+	-	-	-	-	50
949	1	107, Mills 2 and 3	BL		1	13	370-400+					
950	1	116, Mills 2 and 3	BL		1			300				
951	1	116, Mills 2 and 3	BL		1							
952	4		BL		4							
953	4	407	BL		1	19	370-400+	380				
954	4	414	BL		1	10	50-325					
955	7		BL		1							
956	7		BL		12							
957	7	'layer 5'	BL		3							
958	7	712	BL		3							
959	7	'layer 4'	BL		6							
960	10	1001, Mill 1	BL		1							
961	10	1001, Mill 1	BL		2							
962	10	1001, Mill 1	BL		1							
963	10	1001, Mill 1	BL		1							
964		u/s	BL		1							
965	1	107, Mills 2 and 3	MG		1	13	370-400+	-	-	-	-	22
966	1	107, Mills 2 and 3	MG		1	13	370-400+	c 600	-	min 67.5	-	-
967	1	107, Mills 2 and 3	MG		1	13	370-400+	min 465	85-96	c 20	45	-
968	1	107, Mills 2 and 3	MG		1	13	370-400+					
969	1	107, Mills 2 and 3	MG		1	13	370-400+	-	-	-	-	59
970	1	107, Mills 2 and 3	MG		1	13	370-400+	c 540	-	43	-	-
971	1	107, Mills 2 and 3	MG		1	13	370-400+	470	50	-	60	-
972	1	107, Mills 2 and 3	MG		1	13	370-400+	480	-	45	c 70	-
973	1	107, Mills 2 and 3	MG		1	13	370-400+	c 380	-	45	-	-
974	1	116, Mills 2 and 3	MG		1			c 380	-	30	-	-
975	1	116, Mills 2 and 3	MG		1			-	-	-	-	37
976	4	'extension'	MG		1			-	-	-	-	-
977	4	408	MG		1	20	370-400+	-	-	-	-	-
978	4	414	MG		1	10	80-370	-	-	37.5	-	-
979		u/s	MG		1							
980		u/s	MG		1							
981		u/s	MG		1			-	-	-	-	-
982		u/s	MG		1							
983		u/s	MG		1							

FRAGMENTS OF QUERNS OR MILLSTONES PRODUCED FROM MILLSTONE GRIT

No.	Area	Context	Stone type	Object	Quantity	Ceramic Assemblage	Dating	Diameter (mm) Skirt (rim)	Diameter (mm) Eye	Thickness (mm) Skirt (rim)	Thickness (mm) Eye	Max
984	4	408	MG		1	20	370-400+	-	-	-	-	-
985	5	'gully 3'	MG		1							
986	7	'layer 2'	MG		1							
987	10	1001, Mill 1	MG		1							

EQ: Early Quern, RQ: Rotary Quern, G: Greensand, MG: Millstone Grit, BL: Basalt Lava, X: Convex, V: Concave

Notes
The number of harps to view include whole and parts of harps.
Where either no evidence exists or the information cannot be ascertained the column is left blank.

Table 48. Querns.

| Grinding face | | | | | | | Rotation RH stone (C) |
| Harps | | | Furrows | | | | LH stone (AC) |
X or V	No. to view	Probable no.	Depth (mm)	Distance apart (mm)	Width (mm)	Incline of face	
X	1	-	1	16	3.4	?	-
flat	2	-	very	13	worn		-
X	2		2	14	3-5	-	-
X	-	-	-	-	-	3°	-
X	3	10 max	shallow	9.5-10	3.5	4.5°	?
V	-	-	-	-	-	?	-
V	1	-	-	-	-	-	-
V	2	-	2.3	8-10	4	-	-
V	1	-	1.2	8	2.4	?	-
V	1	-	worn	11	worn	-	-
V	-	-	-	-	-	-	-
X	-	-	-	-	-	11°	-
V	-	-	-	-	-	?	-
?	1	-	2.3	18	6-8	?	-

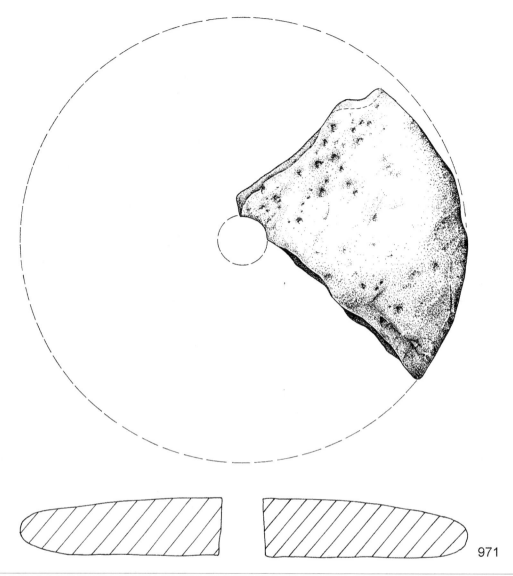

Fig 105. Quernstone. Scale 1:5.

Millstone Grit. Basalt lava querns were widely distributed in Kent from the late Iron Age onwards (Riddler and Vince 2005, 80). Doubts have been raised about their presence in late Roman deposits, based on London evidence (Symonds 1999, 331), but within east Kent they are common throughout the entire Roman period. Indeed, it is difficult to find a Roman site in east Kent, whether rural or urban, that does not provide examples of them. It is notable that rural sites of Roman date in south-east Kent, lying in the vicinity of the Greensand quarries at East Wear Bay, Folkestone, nonetheless provide copious examples of basalt lava querns, particularly in late Roman deposits (Riddler forthcoming b).

The Greensand quarries may have ceased to function after the second century, leaving basalt lava as the principal material for querns of the late Roman period in east Kent (Riddler and Vince 2005, 80). The Ickham sample has to be judged in part against this background, which has no military connotations whatsoever. Moreover, as has been noted above (p 45), the presence of millstones and querns relates to flour production and that itself explains why there is a reasonable sample at Ickham. Here they occur alongside querns of other stone types and although they may conceivably be a little more dominant in the later Roman period, the dating evidence cannot be used to substantiate this military association.

Most of the fragments of basalt lava querns are too small for metrical analysis. This situation is commonly seen during both the Roman and the Anglo-Saxon periods, and is often caused by the re-use of lava quern fragments as hard-core (Blockley *et al* 1995, 1206).

For those querns which do survive to any extent, it can be established that lower stones are concave below and convex above. The latter surface provided the working area and it is generally smoothed from extensive use. The upper stones are concave below and are flat above with a raised rim around the edge. There are no traces of any hopper sockets of the type that has been seen elsewhere, as at Colchester for example (Crummy 1983, 75 and fig 78.2057). The working surfaces are furrowed and in some cases the patterning can be established, albeit only for small fragments. The querns may have been of relatively small diameter, given that the only two measurements that could be taken provided 300 and 380mm. However, the rim of the quern did not survive to any extent in either case, and the measurements may not be completely reliable.

Basalt lava querns occur in Kent from the early Roman period onwards and because so many survive only as small fragments there are no obvious distinctions between those of early and later Roman date. Unlike the other quern forms, therefore, they do not provide any independent dating evidence. On the other hand, it has been suggested elsewhere that the lava querns are a feature of the earlier Roman period, and there are relatively few securely-dated examples from late Roman deposits (Peacock 1980, 50). More recently, however, fragments of basalt lava querns have come from stratified late Roman deposits in Canterbury (Blockley *et al* 1995, 1206 nos 1387–9).

The Ickham sample can be correlated against the dating evidence for some of the relevant contexts. There are five fragments from Area 10, which may have been associated with activity during the life of the third-century Mill 1. Twenty-five further fragments come from Area 7, for which, unusually, there is no association with a mill. Four fragments from contexts 107 and 116 lie near to Channel C and are of late Roman date, and there are six fragments from contexts in Area 4. No pieces of basalt lava quern came from Area 6.

Coarse gritstones

Nineteen examples of quern made from Millstone Grit can be identified which, alongside many other fragments, came from the dump of stone in context 107. In six cases their diameters can be measured, and these range from 380 to 600mm. These are mostly from upper stones, although there is also one example (**971**) of a lower stone. The smaller fragments of Millstone Grit cannot always be assigned securely to querns or millstones and five of these pieces have not been placed into either category. There remain a further fourteen pieces, however, which appear to stem from querns, on the basis either of their size or of the presence of central spindle holes which do not include any traces of rynds. Traces of furrows can be seen on several although other fragments have remarkably smooth faces and had clearly been discarded because of this characteristic. The relatively high proportion of querns of Millstone Grit within the assemblage, which is an unusual situation for east Kent, may well stem from the redressing of millstones to create querns. In two cases (982 and 967) the querns themselves were re-used as broad whetstones.

Querns produced from this stone type occur also in Roman contexts at Canterbury and here too the fragments were re-used as whetstones (Blockley *et al* 1995, 1206, nos 1382–6). The only stratified example came from a Period 2 context, of AD 70–110. At Ickham, however, the majority of querns of Millstone Grit came from late Roman contexts, and particularly from pit 107, cutting Channel C.

Agricultural implements

Quita Mould

The small collection of agricultural implements includes shears (which are not necessarily agricultural), harvesting tools, an interesting group of socketed hooked blades, a spud and a number of collar ferrules. In general terms, this is a small collection of implements, particularly when it is viewed against the more extensive east Kent assemblage from the rural settlement at Monkton (Macdonald *et al* 2008, 215–19). This suggests that the areas of the site which were investigated were adopted for industrial purposes, and that structures which were used for agriculture and the storage of food have yet to be found in this area.

Shears

Ten blades of shears were recovered. Those with complete blades measured below 80mm, and were probably for domestic and personal use (Manning 1985, 34–5, type 3). No large 'industrial'-sized shears were found, but these are rarely recovered in any case. Three shears (**991**, 989 and 995) have omega-shaped springs which are stronger than the U-shaped springs, suggesting differing use. Another example (**992**) has a thickened back, indicating that it was intended for heavy

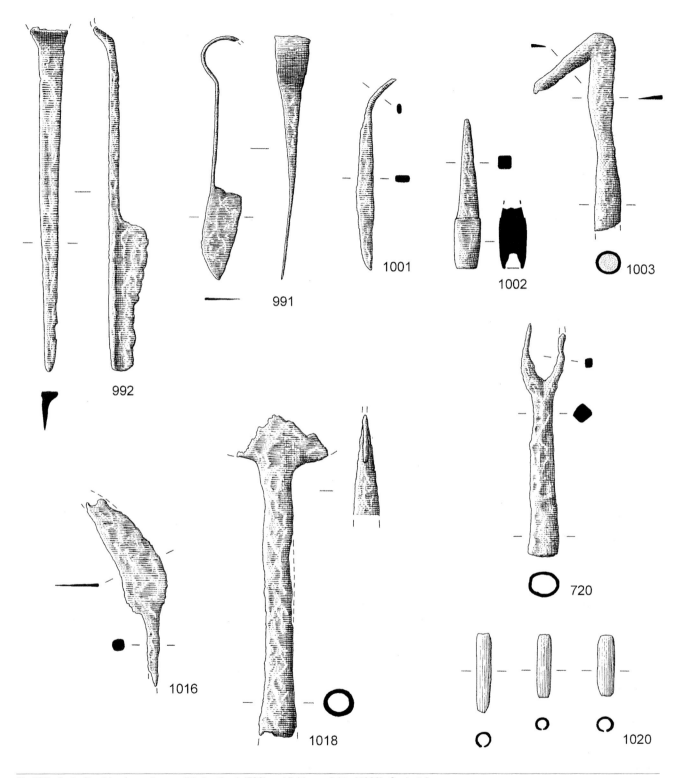

Fig 106. Agricultural implements, possible boathook (720) and fishing weights (1020). Scale 1:2.

No	Object	overall length mm	blade length mm	width mm	Context
988	iron shears	135	58	15+	Area 1, Channel C
989	iron shears	122+	47	18	Area 1, Channel C
990	iron shears	108+	42	14	Area 4
991	iron shears	130	48	19	Area 4
992	iron shears	181	75	15+	Area 4
993	iron shears	104+	48	16	Area 4
994	iron shears	128+	50	17	Area 4, extension
995	iron shears	110	58	17	Area 10, 1001
996	iron shears	111+	?	25+	Area 5, 'roadway ditch'
997	iron shears	123+	62	20	unstratified
998	iron scythe				Area 4
999	iron scythe				Area 10, 1005
1000	iron scythe				Area 10, 1005
1001	iron rake tine	105		8	Area 4
1002	iron hay fork?	79		14	Area 4
1003	iron hooked blade	110+		13	Area 1, base of Channel C, east end
1004	iron hooked blade			18	Area 10, 1004
1005	iron hooked blade	106+		16	Area 1, base of Channel C, east end
1006	iron hooked blade	85+		12	Area 1, base of Channel C, east end
1007	iron hooked blade	98+		14	Pit 115.1
1008	iron hooked blade	102+		14	
1009	iron hooked blade	95+		10	
1010	iron hooked blade	105		12	
1011	iron hooked blade	87+		18	Area 4, extension
1012	iron hooked blade	92+		15	Area 4, extension
1013	iron socket, flanged				Area 3
1014	iron socket, flanged				Area 4, 335
1015	iron socket				Area 7, 710
1016	iron hooked blade				Area 10, 1005
1017	iron socket, nailed				Area 1, Channel C
1018	iron spud	179+			unstratified

Table 49. Agricultural implements.

use. It is of medium size (Manning type 2) and is practical either for shearing sheep or for cutting cloth.

Harvesting tools

Three blade fragments are likely to be broken fragments from scythes. One is from a large blade with a curving back (998) and the others (999 and 1000) have a distinctly thickened back.

A rectangular-sectioned hay rake tine was also found (**1001**). The tang was originally secured to a wooden head, a surviving example of which from Borough Hill, Northants was found to be of oak (*Quercus* sp) (Manning 1985, pl 25 F63–4). A socketed point (1002) could be the protective tip for the prong of a wooden hay fork.

Hooked blades

An interesting collection of ten socketed, hooked blades was recovered. They are all of similar size, though varying slightly in the style of the cutting edge, and they fall into the small hook category classified by Manning (1985, 57). Two (**1003** and 1004) have the edge set at a right angle to the handle, which both Manning and Rees (1975) suggest to be mainly an Iron

Age type (*ibid*, type 1, 57 F44 and comparanda). The others have U-shaped blades of Manning type 2 (*ibid*, 57). They are probably a general purpose tool used as small reaping hooks and leaf hooks for gathering fodder for livestock. Mineral-preserved remains of the wooden hafts were found in the sockets of six of the hooks. The wood in one (**1003**) was probably hazel (*Corylus* sp), that in the sockets of the other examples (1004, 1007, 1008, 1010, 1012) was generally too degraded for identification (Watson 2000, 1–2).

In addition, there are also three small sockets, two of which (1013 and 1014) have open flanged sockets with an exterior tang which are likely to derive from other examples of hooked blades (cf Manning 1985 pl 24, F49 and F52).

A single hooked blade (**1016**) has a tang set midway between the back and edge. The curvature of the blade suggests a wider, more arched blade than the socketed examples; more an open curved knife than a hook. An open, nailed socket (1017) has broken away from a larger implement, and several small fragments (six) broken from the sockets of other objects, which cannot be identified to type, were also recovered.

Spud

The remains of a broken, apparently crescentic blade with a long, central, socketed handle (**1018**) were found on the surface. Although the crescentic blade shape can be paralleled on Roman leather knives (eg Gaitzsch 1980, Teil i, abb 13) the slender, socketed handle suggests a different use. It may be a slender spud for weeding or cleaning mud from the share and mould board of the plough. However, it does have a particularly narrow socket (20mm in diameter, although no narrower than a modern hoe), perhaps suggesting weeding between closely-set plants.

Fishing equipment

Quita Mould

Fishing equipment from Ickham is limited to a fragmentary netting needle, a possible boathook and a group of eighteen lead alloy cylinders, which may have served as net weights or spacers. The lack of any well-developed sampling programme for the recovery of environmental remains inevitably means that there is little evidence of the riverine component of the local diet in the Roman period, and the objects associated with fishing cannot, unfortunately, be correlated with any environmental material.

Netting needle

A broken iron netting needle (1019) from Area 10 has one of its characteristic forked terminals remaining. The needle was used to produce a knotted mesh, the thread being wound along the length of the stem and held between the forked ends. Rather more delicate needles of copper alloy were used to work knotted silk hairnets (Walton Rogers 1997, 1790 fig 836, no 6634). This robust iron example may have been used for a stronger mesh such as fishing net.

Boathook

A small double-pronged fork (**720**), recovered from the surface of Area 1, can be paralleled by examples from Anglo-Scandinavian Coppergate (Ottaway 1992, 599 and fig 247) and at Thetford (Goodall 1984, fig 133.196) which are interpreted as flesh hooks used in cooking to take meat from the cooking pot and roast meat at the fire. However, six comparable implements from Dorestad (van Es and Verwers 1980, 179–81 and fig 134.1–6) are said to be boathooks, an alternative interpretation which is particularly attractive for the Ickham example coming, as it does, from the close vicinity of a river and watermill.

Lead alloy weights

Eighteen small cylinders of rolled lead alloy sheet fishing weights (**1020,** 1021–37) were found in a ditch near the figurine (310, eastern part of Channel A). They range in length from 30–41mm and in diameter from 7–8mm, with an average weight of 10.8g. The fact that they were found in numbers together suggests that they were associated with a fishing net that subsequently rotted, leaving just a group of associated weights/sinkers remaining. Similar objects of medieval date have been regarded as weights used to hold down the underside of net openings (Devenish 1979, 129).

Another pierced lead alloy disc (1038) may have been used for a similar function (*see* miscellaneous objects, p 276 and Table 57).

Transport

Quita Mould

The range of items related to transport extends to spurs, hipposandals, horseshoes, bridle-bits, curb-bits and cart fittings. A significant number of items come from Area

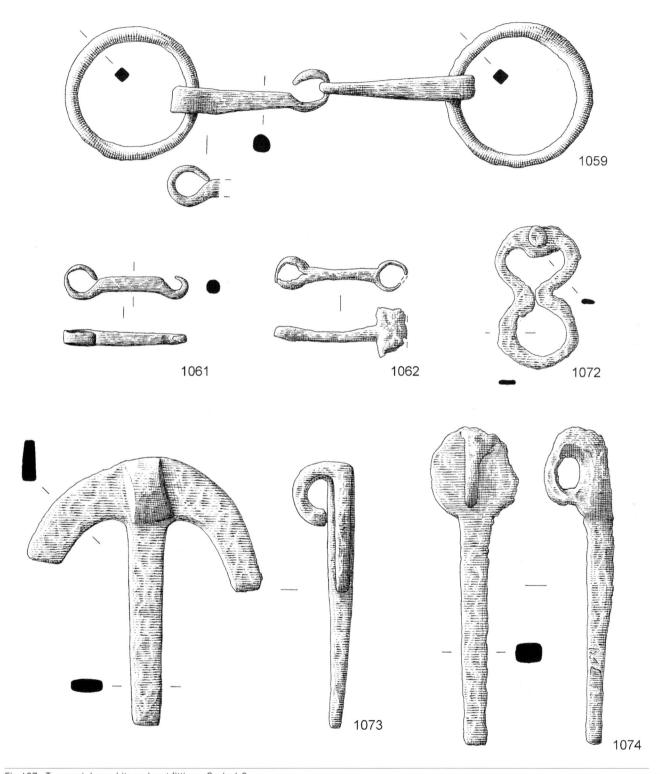

Fig 107. Transport: horse bits and cart fittings. Scale 1:2.

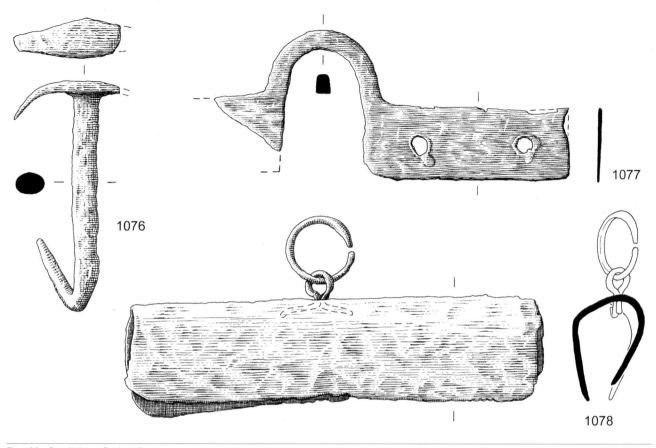

Fig 108. Cart fittings. Scale 1:2.

10, including five hipposandal fragments, three bit links, a trefoil cheek-piece, two linchpins and a T-clamp which may have served as a cart fitting. Not all of these need be of late Roman date. In contrast, a group of five horseshoes came from the east end of Channel C, and these may have been gathered for re-use. Although the horseshoes from Ickham are not securely stratified, there is a possibility that they are of Roman date, even though they can be paralleled by examples of the medieval period.

Spurs

Terminals broken from two copper alloy Romano-British rivet spurs (1039 and 1040) were found which date to the end of the third or the fourth century (Shortt 1959, 69). Each has a plano-convex sectioned arm and a flat, round terminal remaining. One example (1039), which has been published previously (Brown 1981, fig 5.18), with transverse mouldings at the neck, has the disc terminal capped by a

separate sheet with a serrated edge held in place by a central iron rivet.

Hipposandals

A maximum of ten fragments of hipposandals were recovered. No complete examples were found and half of the fragments came from Area 10, which lay close to the Roman road. Examples of types 1 and 2 are represented (Manning 1985, 64–6 and fig 16) with a possible heel loop (1047) of type 3 also. The front hook (1041) and two wings (1042, 1043) came from type 1 hipposandals, a front hook (1044) came from a type 2 along with two possible toe loops (1045, 1046). The sole-plate of another example has grooves to aid grip, as seen on examples from London (*ibid*, H1 and H6, pls 26 and 27). Hipposandals were in use from the late first/early second century to the end of the Roman period as temporary shoes for unshod animals travelling on metalled roads.

No	Object	Length mm	Width mm	Web width mm	Context
1039	copper alloy spur				Area 4
1040	copper alloy spur				Area 1, 121
1041	iron hipposandal				Area 10, 1001
1042	iron hipposandal				Area 10, 1006
1043	iron hipposandal				Area 7, 710
1044	iron hipposandal				Area 10, 1005
1045	iron hipposandal				Area 4
1046	iron hipposandal				Area 4, extension
1047	iron hipposandal				Area 10, 1002.3
1048	iron hipposandal				Area 10, 1002.3
1049	iron hipposandal				Area 14
1050	iron hipposandal				Area 1, Channel C
1051	iron horseshoe	110	105	25	Area 1, Channel C, east end
1052	iron horseshoe	120	113	33	Area 1, Channel C, east end
1053	iron horseshoe	106+	100	27	Area 1, Channel C, east end
1054	iron horseshoe	90+		33	Area 1, Channel C, east end
1055	iron horseshoe	48+		26	Area 1, Channel C, east end
1056	iron horseshoe	63+		20	Area 5
1057	iron horseshoe	100		34	Area 6, 601
1058	iron horseshoe	125	131	32	unstratified
1059	iron bit link	275			Area 4
1060	iron bit link	86+			Area 14
1061	iron bit link	66			Area 1, Channel C
1062	iron bit link	72			Area 10, 1001
1063	iron bit link	76+			Area 1, 104
1064	iron bit link	77			Area 1, 115
1065	iron bit link	71			Area 4, extension
1066	iron bit link	71			Area 4, extension
1067	iron bit link	55+			Area 4, extension
1068	iron bit link	68+			Area 4
1069	iron bit link	53+			Area 10, 1005
1070	iron bit link	56+			Area 10, 1005
1071	iron curb-bit	70			unstratified
1072	iron curb-bit	76			Area 10, 1001
1073	iron linchpin	145			Area 10, 1005
1074	iron linchpin	167			Area 10, 1001
1075	iron linchpin	58+			Area 7, 712
1076	iron T-clamp	120			Area 10, 1001
1077	iron binding	186			Area 4
1078	iron binding	222			unstratified

Table 50. Items relating to transport.

Horseshoes

In addition to the hipposandals, five complete horseshoes and five fragments were recovered from the site. While half may simply be the result of loss when passing across the area, a group of five (1051–5) recovered from the east end Channel C are less easily explained. Two horseshoes (1051 and 1053), one with rolled calkins and both with rectangular nail holes within narrow, rectangular countersunk holes, were found together with a horseshoe with small rectangular nail holes without countersinking (1052) with a thickened heel on one side. The broken branches of two other horseshoes, one (1054) with an oval nail hole within a rectangular countersunk hole, were found in the same context.

Two (1051 and 1053) fall in to Clark's type 3, dating to the thirteenth and fourteenth century (J Clark 1995, 86–7 and 96), another (1052) is of type 4, of fourteenth- to fifteenth-century date (*ibid*, 88–91, 96–7), whilst the broken branch with the wavy outline (1054) is of type 2A, known as early as the tenth century but common until the end of the twelfth century (*ibid*, 86 and 95–6).

Despite the discovery of comparable horseshoes from well stratified Roman contexts at Usk and more locally at Chartham near Canterbury (Manning *et al* 1995, 43–4 and fig 16, nos 23–6 and discussion; Chartham example unpublished) their Roman origin at Ickham is a possibility, rather than a certainty. Their occurrence together at the east end of Channel C may be the result of deliberate scrap collection for eventual re-use.

Bridle-bits

Two complete two-link snaffle-bits (**1059** and 1060) and ten individual links from other examples were recovered. Most of the links have simple ring terminals although some have collar rings to articulate with the cheek-pieces (1060 and **1062**). Two links are spirally-twisted (**1061** and 1063) though this is not visible in the illustration. Some of the assemblage of fifteen plain annular iron rings may be cheek-pieces; *see* the section on rings in the miscellaneous category below.

Curb-bits

Two trefoil-shaped cheek-pieces (1071 and **1072**) come from curb-bits of type 1 (Manning 1985, 68 and fig 17). The curb-bit was used when the horse was ridden (*ibid,* 67), rather than when used to carry loads or for traction, and are widely found in civilian contexts throughout Britain.

Cart fittings

The three linchpins include two (**1074** and 1075) of type 2b (Manning 1985, 73 and fig 20) with a spatulate head and turned-over loop, and one (**1073**) of type 1b with a cresentic head.

A T-clamp (**1076**) with an anchor-shaped head is of a type which may have been used as a cart fitting to attach the pole to the body of the wagon (Manning 1985, 132, pl 62 R70–2 and comparanda). Four other examples were found, all coming from Area 10. Each has downward curving arms, they are not as pronounced as the other example (**1076**) but they do suggest a function distinct from those with straight heads which are frequently found.

A heavy strap binding with an upstanding U-shaped collar (**1077**) and a semi-cylindrical binding (**1078**) are also likely to be cart fittings. The semi-cylindrical binding is similar to another example from Benwell, Newcastle-upon-Tyne (Manning 1976, no 101, fig 20). The Ickham binding has a split-spiked loop passing through the centre, while one edge is serrated in the manner of a semi-cylindrical curry-comb blade. However, no attachment points for a handle are present.

Structural fittings

Quita Mould

The structural materials gathered from the site include timbers from the mills, which have been separately described above, as well as a conventional range of iron fittings. Amongst these are collars, window grilles, bindings, hinges, split-spiked loops, staples, ring-headed pins, wallhooks, joiner's dogs, cleats and nails. In addition, there is a small collection of fittings of lead alloy, as well as an assemblage of ceramic building material. The latter material does not fit readily with this site, where the few buildings to have been discovered were made, in part at least, of wood. A scatter of material was reported (p 4) and it should be noted that the villa at Ickham lies nearby so it is possible that the material stems from that structure, or related buildings of the estate.

Collars

Nine examples of angular collars with straight, butted ends made of rectangular-sectioned strap (**1079**, 1080–7) have diameters ranging from *c* 35–50mm They occur principally in the area of Mill 1 and were possibly used to strengthen

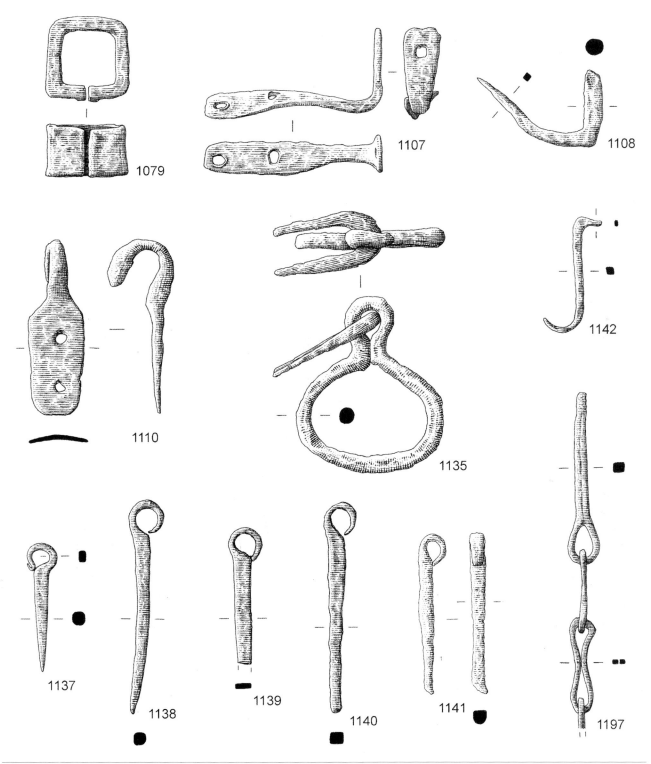

Fig 109. Structural fittings. Scale 1:2.

wooden components associated with the mill construction or mechanism in some way. At present their precise function is not clear.

Window grilles and glass

Quita Mould, John Shepherd and Sasha Smith

The cross from the intersection of a window grille (1088) was found in the base of Channel C. It stems from a type of window grille most commonly found in the northern provences (Manning 1985, 128). Occasionally these window grilles appear to have been used with glass window panes as with those from Wall, Staffordshire and Holstein, Switzerland, which were found associated with window glass (Manning and Painter 1967, 126). It is interesting to note, in this respect, that quantities of window glass were found in this area.

Sixteen fragments of window glass were identified, all of which were of the cast matt/glossy variety. This type of window glass is common throughout the Roman period and its presence here is not a surprise. Eleven fragments of free-blown, cylinder process window glass were also discovered. This technique was in use during the late Roman period, possibly first being used during the late second century.

A broken rectangular-sectioned plate (1089) originally nailed at the corners, with a central, circular hole, may be a pivot base from the threshold of a door (and see other hinges below)

Nailed bindings

A large quantity (154) of broken, nailed fragments derive from a variety of bindings used on boxes, buckets, carts and structural strapwork such as hinges. The heavier examples are likely to be broken hinge fittings and strapwork, whilst lighter pieces come from box fittings and bucket handle mounts, which have been discussed above. One group of forty-eight fragments of nailed binding (1182), including a small hooked-loop terminal from a hinge, were found together in Area 4 extension. Fourteen of the fragments had non-ferrous metal specks present within the corrosion products, indicative of their having been in close proximity to a smithing hearth and suggesting that they had been collected together by the smith for recycling.

Hinges

Drop hinges used on doors and shutters were represented by heavy nailed straps (**1107**) and thirteen L-shaped hinge staples (**1108**, Fig 109) with upstanding round-sectioned arms. The smaller L-shaped hinge staples were probably used on shutters and cupboard doors.

Loop hinges (1109) used on chest and large box lids, and vertically mounted shutters, comprise heavy straps with pierced ring terminals (five examples) which articulate with similar straps (**1110**) with hooked terminals (ten examples).

Split-spiked loops and staples

The split-spiked loops include eighteen examples of iron and one of copper alloy (1120). One split spiked loop was found associated with a cart fitting (**1078**), another with a sprung fastening (1115), and a third with a broken sprung fastener or simple hinge (1118).

Complete examples vary in arm length from 32–78mm Two noticably small iron examples (1116 and 1119) and the example in copper alloy (1120) have straight arms, more like modern cotter pins, and are likely to have been for furniture fixings rather than structural fittings. Two with clenched arms (1125 and 1127) suggesting they had been secured to timber *c* 1 inch in thickness, are likely to be from a simple box hinge.

One (**1135**) of the eight U-shaped staples (eg 1129) was used to secure a large ring handle, as noted above. Complete examples varied in arm height from 35–110mm.

Ring-headed pins

A total of fourteen ring-headed pins could be identified. Those with broken stems (**1139**, **1140** and **1141**) may be the handles from keys and other small domestic implements. Others are complete with well-formed points (**1138**) and scrolled heads (**1137**) and were driven into wood to provide points of attachment or used as other fastenings, like that with the figure-of-eight chain links (**1197** below).

Wallhooks, joiner's dogs and cleats

Two of the eleven examples of wallhooks are U-shaped (1144 and **1142**), whilst the remainder (eg 1143) are L-shaped. There are also sixteen examples of joiner's dogs and thirty-one examples of cleats (including many broken arms) for joining timbers. They either have a rectangular central shank or a flat central strap with an upstanding arm at either end. Three small, round-bodied shoe cleats are discussed with the hobnails above (*see* p 208). Many of the cleats are represented by fragments of broken upstanding arms only

	Surface	Area 1	Channel C	Area 2	Area 3	Area 4	Area 5	Area 6	Area 7	Area 10	Area 14	Area 16
1a		20	5			27		1	4	24	4	
1b	13	1506	340	4	30	333	27	115	114	1776	59	6
2		2	4			3	1		2	17	1	
3		9	3		1	2	1		1	13		
7		2	1		1	2	1		1			
8		1				5			1			
9						1				1		
Total	13	1539	354	4	34	373	31	116	123	1831	64	6
Shank only	5	552	102	5	19	215	29	45	78	1258	49	3

Table 51. Iron nails by type and location.

which may result in an over-representation of the actual original number.

Timber nails

A large quantity of iron timber nails were scattered in contexts throughout the site but they also occurred in two notable concentrations, in contexts 115 (Ceramic Assemblage 13, pp 107–9) and 1005 (Ceramic Assemblage 6, pp 97–9). In total, 4,488 nails were classifiable according to the typology established by Manning (1985, 134–7 and fig 32). As is usually the case, the vast majority of the nails (96 per cent) fall into type 1b, however types 1a, 2, 3 and upholstery nails type 7, 8 and 9 were also found in small numbers. Larger nails of type 2, with triangular heads, and heavy nails for structural timbers of type 1a occurred in small numbers. The large nails (type 1a) with pyramidal heads may come from boat timbers, as might be expected at a location so close to the river.

Two spherical-headed nails of type 9 (1184 and 1185) have previously been mentioned in the discussion of the biconical iron pin (29) and these could possibly be a variant. They vary in size, with lengths of 121 and 42mm and head diameters of 22 and 13mm and while the shorter object could have been used as a decorative upholstery nail, this could not be the case for the longer example. In addition, a spherical-headed nail of copper alloy (1186) from 1001, is likely to be an upholstery nail comparable to the iron nails of type 9.

Three small nails of lead alloy were found in Channel C, including a flat, round-headed nail (1187) and a dome-headed nail (1188); the other example is fragmentary (1189).

Six recognisable post-Roman nails, including modern cut nails and a wire nail, are not included in the quantifications below. 2,360 nails had the shanks only remaining, their heads having broken off, and these could not be classified.

Lead alloy structural fittings

The small collection of structural fittings of lead alloy includes a crude seating (1180) from 1001, a fragment of a masonry cramp (1181) and a semicircular fragment with a length of iron strap embedded into it. The masonry cramp (1181) was used to seat a large iron cramp into building stone deriving from a large structure, not located during the excavations and salvage work. Three small offcuts of lead pipe were found and a large quantity of lead sheet fragments (4.4kg), which no doubt derive from the leadwork associated with Roman buildings. The sheet offcuts and trimmings (4.8kg) with blade cut edges were produced when cutting the sheet to shape during the installation and repair of lead fittings.

Ceramic building material

Louise Harrison

The Roman brick and tile retrieved from the excavation was generally in a fragmentary and abraded state. The entire assemblage amounts to 206 pieces, weighing a total of 58.72kg.

Fabrics

The material was primarily recorded by fabric type, using a system based on the fabric type series developed at the Canterbury Archaeological Trust. The fabrics were studied under x10 and x20 magnification. All of the fabrics are red or orange in colour unless otherwise stated. The varying quantities of quartz present in fabrics 1, 2 and 3 do not necessarily indicate a different tile source, but may only reflect variations in the original clay source. The fabrics present are described briefly.

No	Material	Object	Quantity	Context
1079	iron	angular collar	1	Area 10, 1101
1080	iron	angular collar	2	Area 10, 10/01
1081	iron	angular collar	2	Area 10, 10/01
1082	iron	angular collar	1	Area 10, 10/02, layer 3
1083	iron	angular collar	1	Area 10, 10/05
1084	iron	angular collar	2	Area 10, 10, layer 4
1085	iron	angular collar	2	Area 10, 10, layer 4
1086	iron	angular collar	1	Area 7, 710
1087	iron	angular collar	1	Area 14, 1400
1088	iron	window grille	1	Area 1, base of Channel C
1089	iron	pivot base?	1	Area 10, 1004
1090	glass	window, cast	4	Area 1, base of Channel C
1091	glass	window, cast	1	Area 1, Channel C
1092	glass	window, cast	2	Area 1, Channel C
1093	glass	window, cast	2	Area 4, extension, 'section 2, layers 2–5'
1094	glass	window, cast	1	Area 4, 408
1095	glass	window, cast	2	Area 6, 608
1096	glass	window, cast	1	Area 6, 611
1097	glass	window, cast	1	Area 6, 613
1098	glass	window, cast	2	Area 10, 1001
1099	glass	window, free-blown	1	Area 4
1100	glass	window, free-blown	1	Area 1, Channel C
1101	glass	window, free-blown	1	unstratified
1102	glass	window, free-blown	2	Area 1, 104
1103	glass	window, free-blown	1	Area 1, 115/1
1104	glass	window, free-blown	1	Area 1, 118/1
1105	glass	window, free-blown	3	Area 1, 122
1106	glass	window, free-blown	1	Area 4, 408
1107	iron	drop hinge	1	Area 1, Channel C, west end
1108	iron	staple hinge	1	Area 4, extension
1109	iron	loop hinge	1	Area 10, 1002, layer 4
1110	iron	loop hinge	1	Area 4
1111	iron	split-spiked loop	1	Area 1, base of Channel C, east end
1112	iron	split-spiked loop	1	Area 1, base of Channel C, east end
1113	iron	split-spiked loop	1	Area 1, base of Channel C, east end
1114	iron	split-spiked loop	1	Area 1, Channel C
1115	iron	split-spiked loop	1	Area 4
1116	iron	split-spiked loop	1	Area 4
1117	iron	split-spiked loop	1	Area 4
1118	iron	split-spiked loop	1	Area 4
1119	iron	split-spiked loop	1	Area 4, extension
1120	copper alloy	split-spiked loop	1	Area 5
1121	iron	split-spiked loop	1	Area 6, 604
1122	iron	split-spiked loop	1	Area 1, 115
1123	iron	split-spiked loop	1	Area 1, 115
1124	iron	split-spiked loop	1	Area 10, 10/01
1125	iron	split-spiked loop	1	Area 10, 10/01
1126	iron	split-spiked loop	1	Area 10, 10/01
1127	iron	split-spiked loop	1	Area 10, 10/01
1128	iron	split-spiked loop	1	Area 10, 10/06
1129	iron	staple	1	Area 1, Channel C, west end
1130	iron	staple	1	Area 4
1131	iron	staple	1	Area 4
1132	iron	staple	1	Area 4

No	Material	Object	Quantity	Context
1133	iron	staple	1	Area 4, extension
1134	iron	staple	1	Area 1, Channel C, east end
1135	iron	staple	1	Area 1, Channel C, unstratified
1136	iron	staple	1	Area 1, 104
1137	iron	ring-headed pin	1	Area 4
1138	iron	ring-headed pin	1	Area 4, 407
1139	iron	ring-headed pin	1	Area 4
1140	iron	ring-headed pin	1	Area 1, 115
1141	iron	ring-headed pin	1	Area 4
1142	iron	wall hook	1	Area 1, 115
1143	iron	wall hook	1	Area 10, 1105
1144	iron	wall hook	1	Area 1,115
1145	iron	wall hook	1	Area 1, base of Channel C, east end
1146	iron	wall hook	1	Area 10, 10/01
1147	iron	wall hook	1	Area 10, 10/04
1148	iron	wall hook	1	Area 10, 10/05
1149	iron	wall hook	1	Area 4, extension
1150	iron	wall hook	1	Area 3
1151	iron	wall hook	2	Area 1, base of Channel C, east end
1152	iron	wall hook	1	Area 6, 601
1153	iron	joiner's dog	1	Area 4
1154	iron	joiner's dog	2	Area 4
1155	iron	joiner's dog	1	Area 4, extension
1156	iron	joiner's dog	1	Area 4, extension
1157	iron	joiner's dog	1	Area 3
1158	iron	joiner's dog	2	Area 3
1159	iron	joiner's dog	1	Area 1, Channel C
1160	iron	joiner's dog	1	Area 1, Channel C, west end
1161	iron	joiner's dog	1	Area 4, 407B
1162	iron	joiner's dog	1	Area 14, 1401
1163	iron	joiner's dog	3	Area 10, 10/05
1164	iron	cleat	1	Area 3
1165	iron	cleat	1	Area 4
1166	iron	cleat	2	Area 4
1167	iron	cleat	1	Area 1, base of Channel C
1168	iron	cleat	1	Area 4, extension
1169	iron	cleat	1	Area 4, 407A
1170	iron	cleat	1	Area 1, Channel C
1171	iron	cleat	1	Area 1, 101
1172	iron	cleat	1	Area 1, 101
1173	iron	cleat	2	Area 6, 606
1174	iron	cleat	1	Area 1, 1152
1175	iron	cleat	1	Area 1, 120.2
1176	iron	cleat	4	Area 1, 122
1177	iron	cleat	3	Area 10, 1001
1178	iron	cleat	3	Area 10, 1002, layer 2
1179	iron	cleat	1	Area 10, 1002, layer 3
1180	iron	cleat	1	Area 10, 1001, layer 4
1181	iron	cleat	2	Area 16, 16/ditches
1182	lead alloy	seating	1	Area 10, 1001
1183	lead alloy	masonry clamp	1	Area 7, 710

Table 52. Structural metalwork and glass.

	Brick	Flue	Imbrex	Tegula	Misc	Total
Fabric 1	2	16	7	40	11	76
Fabric 1?		4				4
Fabric 1 or 2	2		3	3		8
Fabric 2	1	6				7
Fabric 1 or 3		2	3	3	8	16
Fabric 3	1	1	5	7	2	16
Fabric 6 or 7		1				1
Fabric 8	1		1	9	2	13
Fabric 10	5	15	8	19	1	48
Fabric 11	1	1?			1	3
Fabric 17	1					1
Total	14	46	27	81	25	
Weight (kg)	15.73	8.57	17.9	27.45	5.18	

Table 53. Quantification of tiles by type and fabric.

Fabric 1: a fine sandy fabric with a scatter of small-sized (under 0.5mm) quartz grains. There are few other inclusions apart from very occasional larger-sized quartz grains and calcareous inclusions. This fabric is very similar to material excavated from tile kilns situated at Whitehall Gardens and St Stephen's in Canterbury, and was probably produced at one of these two kilns (Jenkins 1956; 1960).

Fabric 2: a very fine non-sandy fabric. Very occasional quartz grains or calcareous inclusions are sometimes present in the matrix. No other inclusions are visible. It is possible that this fabric is a non-sandy variant of fabric 1.

Fabric 3: a fine, sandy matrix with moderate quantities of medium-sized white and clear quartz grains, approximately 0.5mm across. Occasional calcareous inclusions are also present. This could be a sandy variant of fabric 1.

Fabric 6: contains a moderate quantity of large-sized quartz grains (up to 1mm in diameter), frequent flecks of iron oxide and occasional calcareous inclusions.

Fabric 7: fine and faintly sandy. It is characterised by frequent flecks of iron oxide and red clay pellets up to 0.5mm across.

Fabric 8: is characterised mainly by its colour, which can vary from a pale orange to a white/cream colour. It contains a moderate quantity of small-sized quartz grains (up to 0.5mm), moderate flecks of iron oxide and occasionally lenses or pellets of red clay. Additionally, the moulding sand present on the back of the tile usually consists of large rose coloured quartz grains (up to 1mm). This fabric is thought to have been produced at Eccles and dates in London from the early first century (*c* AD 50–60/1) to the second century (AD 175/80) (Betts 1992).

Fabric 10: a fine sandy fabric with characteristic abundant black specks, thought to be iron oxide. Occasional red clay pellets and quartz are also present. A similar fabric has been identified in London and is thought to come from Radlett in Hertfordshire. However, the examples found in or near Canterbury are less sandy and have fewer flecks of iron oxide, suggesting that the tile could have been produced at a kiln nearer Canterbury, probably somewhere in Kent.

Fabric 11: a fine and slightly sandy fabric with distinguishing silty swirls and lenses present in the matrix. A scatter of small-sized quartz grains (0.5mm) are also present. This fabric is dated in London to AD 100/120 and was probably produced there.

Fabric 17: a fine, sandy fabric with numerous black inclusions up to 0.25mm in diameter. These are thought to be iron oxides or unusually red quartz grains. The only other inclusion is that of occasional white, clear and 'rose' coloured quartz grains. A large quantity of this fabric type (including some wasters) was found at Doon's Farm in Reigate, Surrey. No kiln for this tile has been discovered at the present time. The kiln is thought to have produced brick and tile from AD 140/180 to the early third century (Ian Betts, pers comm).

Fabric 18: very few examples of this fabric have been found. They are all reduced, causing difficulty in the identification of inclusions, etc. The tiles are grey on the inside and red/ orange on the outside. The fabric has a fine matrix which is not particularly sandy. The most common inclusion appears to be ferruginous clay pellets; occasional calcareous inclusions are also present.

Table 53 shows the quantity of different tile types present in each fabric. Where a fabric is classed as two fabrics, for

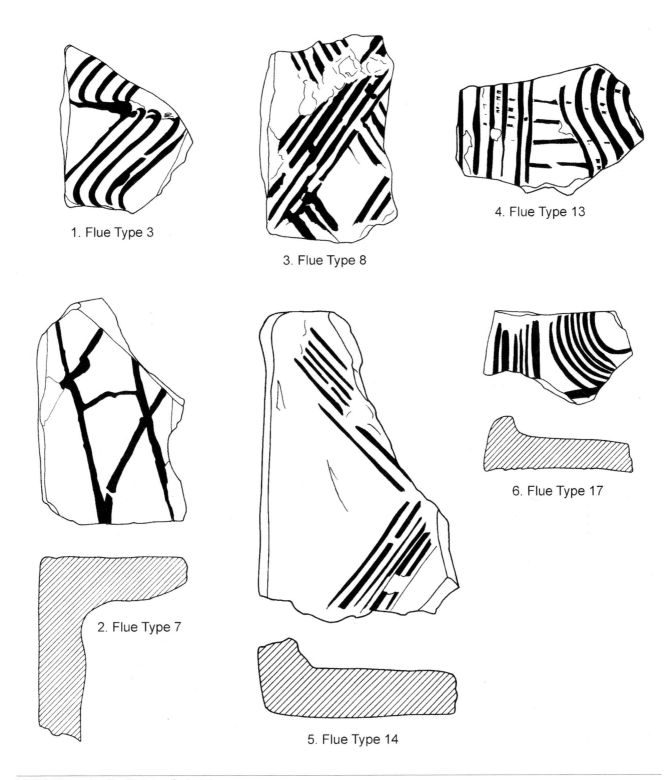

1. Flue Type 3

3. Flue Type 8

4. Flue Type 13

2. Flue Type 7

5. Flue Type 14

6. Flue Type 17

Fig 110. Roman tile: flue tile types. Scale 1:4.

example 1/2, it indicates that the fabric cannot be positively identified as one single fabric. It implies that the fabric is very similar to both, for example, 1 near 2. This tends to happen when there are sandy and non sandy variants of the same fabric. A good example of this is fabric 1 which has two variants, fabric 2 (non sandy) and fabric 3 (sandy). Table 53 indicates that fabrics 1 and 10 are the most common, representing 39 per cent and 25 per cent of the assemblage respectively, while the imported fabrics 11 and 17 appear rarely and amount to only 1.5 per cent and 0.5 per cent respectively.

Brick

No complete or virtually-complete bricks were present in the assemblage. The surviving fragments have thicknesses ranging from 29–56mm, suggesting that they were most likely to be *Bessalis*, *Pedalis* or *Lydion* type bricks.

Flue tile

The tile has been assigned to a particular type primarily by the combing present on the surface. Other features such as dimensions and the presence of cutaways have also been considered, where possible. In some cases, a combed fragment with no corner may be assigned a flue tile type when it could conceivably be a part of a voussoir.

Only flue tiles displaying clear or diagnostic keying and/ or dimensions have been included in this report. Additionally, only clear examples of keying have been illustrated. Other, more fragmentary examples have been described but not illustrated; details of the remaining material is held in archive.

Flue tile types (Fig 110)

Type 3 is characterised by its fabric, which is type 8; additionally the combing consists of wavy bands. Teeth: 5–6. Width of stroke: 35mm.

Type 4 is represented by one fragment, probably part of a face. The combing consists of a diagonal cross with a horizontal band through the centre. Teeth: 6. Width of stroke: 32mm. *Not illus.*

Type 5 is also represented by a single fragment. It is combed with a diagonal cross with a vertical band through the centre. Teeth: 5/7. Width of stroke: 27mm/40mm. *Not illus.*

Type 7 is characterised by the type of keying employed, which consists of scoring with the use of a sharp implement, forming a lattice pattern.

Type 8. Here the tile has a combed lattice pattern employed as keying. Only fragmentary examples were retrieved and no lengths or widths were present which would have helped determine the basic dimensions of a complete tile. However, a number of previously recorded tiles from other sites (St George's Church, Canterbury and the Mount Villa, Maidstone) bore the same keying and were complete enough to provide a width measurement. This was only 107mm, suggesting a small sized tile. Teeth: 5/6. Width of stroke: 23–30mm

Type 10. The keying consists of wavy vertical bands. Teeth: 5. Width of stroke: 24mm. *Not illus.*

Type 13 bears combing which is both straight and wavy. Teeth: 6? Width of stroke: 41mm.

Type 14. Combing here consists of a diagonal cross with no border. The combing is similar to voussoir type 5 but as no side survives it cannot be identified as a voussoir. Teeth: 6/7. Width of stroke: 35/41mm approx. Height of tile: 195mm (face).

Type 17 (new type). Combing on this type appears to consist of a diagonal stroke, probably forming a cross, with vertical borders on either side. There are also two semicircles, one above and one below the cross. Teeth: 6/7 Width of stroke: 28mm.

Type 18 (possible new type). Combing appears to consist of two slanting strokes. It is possible that this is an incomplete example of type 8. Teeth: 7. Width of stroke: 43mm. *Not illus.*

Type 19. A plain side with a round cutaway. It is positioned approximately 96mm from top/base and 65mm from corner. The face bears combing consisting of a diagonal stroke probably forming a cross. Teeth: 2+. Width of stroke: 7mm+. *Not illus.*

Voussoir types (Fig 111)

These were all fragmentary, which caused difficulty in identification of the type. Where possible, tiles have been allocated a tile type based on the combing visible. A number of fragments bore diagonal strokes, probably forming crosses. These were too incomplete to be given types and have been placed together as type V5.

Type V2. Combed on both face and side, although only one surface is complete enough to identify the combing type. This consists of a diagonal cross with vertical borders on either side. Teeth: 9?. Width of stroke: 60mm.

Type V5. A number of fragments bore diagonal strokes, probably forming crosses. These were too incomplete to be given types and so have been placed together as type V5. This voussoir type bears diagonal strokes or diagonal

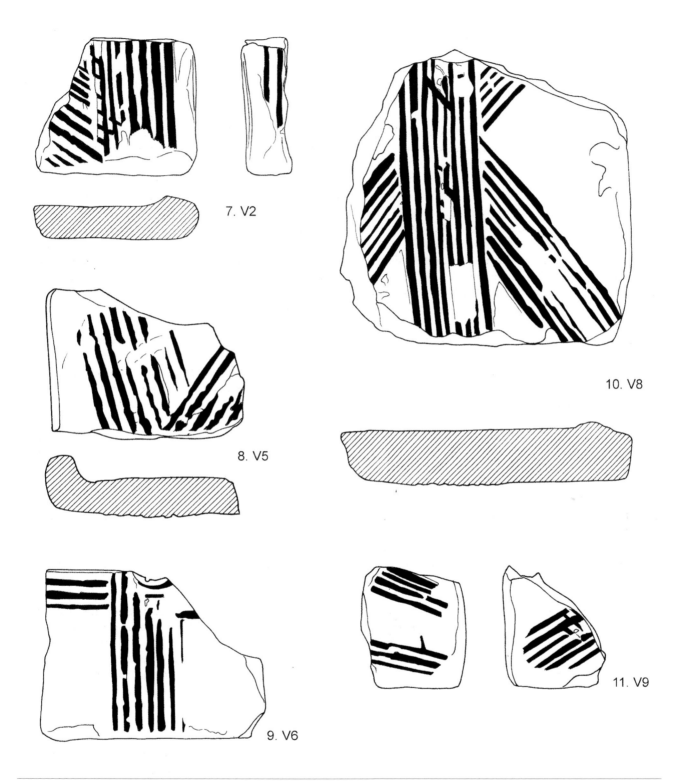

Fig 111. Roman tile: voussoir types. Scale 1:4.

crosses on either face or side or both. Teeth: 5–8. Width of stroke 23–50mm.

Type V6. A round cutaway is positioned 82/72mm from top/base. It is probably combed with a cross. Teeth: 5/7. Width of stroke: 40/51mm.

Type V7. Combed with a diagonal cross with a horizontal band through centre. Teeth: 3/4. Width of stroke: 16mm. *Not illus*.

Type V8. Combed with a diagonal cross with a vertical stroke going through the centre on one surface. The other surface has combing consisting of a diagonal stroke, probably forming a diagonal cross. Teeth: 8. Width of stroke: 43mm.

Type V9. Combed with a diagonal stroke, probably forming a cross on one surface, while the other has two diagonal strokes going in same direction. Teeth: 6. Width of stroke: 29mm.

Type V10. Combing consists of vertical strokes on both face and side. Teeth: 7+. Width of stroke: 38mm+. *Not illus*.

Type V11. Combed with a vertical stroke on one surface, while the other bears a diagonal stroke, probably forming a cross. Number of teeth: 6. Width of stroke: 42mm. *Not illus*.

Flue type	Fabrics	Voussoir type	Fabrics
F3	3, 8	V2	2
F4	10	V5	1, 11
F5	10	V6	10
F7	2	V7	1
F8	1	V8	1
F13	1, 2	V9	3
F14	1, 2, 3, 10, 11	V11	1, 3
F17	1		
F18	1		
F19	8		

Table 54. Fabrics present in flue/voussoir types.

The table indicates that fabrics 1 and 10 were the most common, appearing in a number of different flue and voussoir types. There is no obvious difference between the fabrics being used for flue tile and the fabrics being used for voussoirs. However, it should be noted that a large number of tiles could not be classed as voussoirs, due to their fragmentary state.

Roof tile

All of the *imbrex* tiles are fragmentary with no complete or virtually complete tiles surviving. With respect to the *tegulae*, although the flanges are functional, it is thought that certain styles were favoured by different tile makers working at different kilns. Although this assemblage from Ickham is relatively small, an attempt at comparing the fabric types with the flange/cutaway types was carried out. The flange and cutaway types listed and illustrated are based on the type series developed and used at the Museum of London.

Flange type	Cutaway	Fabrics
F1	E	1, 2, 3, 7, 8, 10
F2		1, 2, 10
F4	C	1
F6		1
F7		1, 10
F8		8, 10, 13
F12		1, 2, 3, 8, 10
F13		1, 3, 8
F31	C	1, 11, 18
F32		8
F38	E	1

Table 55. Roof tile flange and cutaway types.

A large number of different flange types were present in the assemblage (Fig 112). In addition, a number of these appear in a variety of different fabrics. This suggests that *tegulae* were being made both locally (perhaps at Canterbury rather than Ickham) and also imported from further afield.

The most common flange type (1) was found most often to be fabric type 1, the Canterbury fabric. Rare flange types, predominantly 8, 31 and 32, mostly appear in imported fabrics.

Despite the small assemblage, study of the *tegulae* suggests that flange types 1 and 2 (and to a certain extent 12) were made and used at a number of different kiln sites and at a number of different locations. The flange types which appear less frequently may have been made at a limited number of places. Future study of comparisons between flange and fabric types may enable a more definite conclusion to be drawn as to whether certain flange types were made at particular kiln sites or whether they were made on more of an *ad hoc* basis.

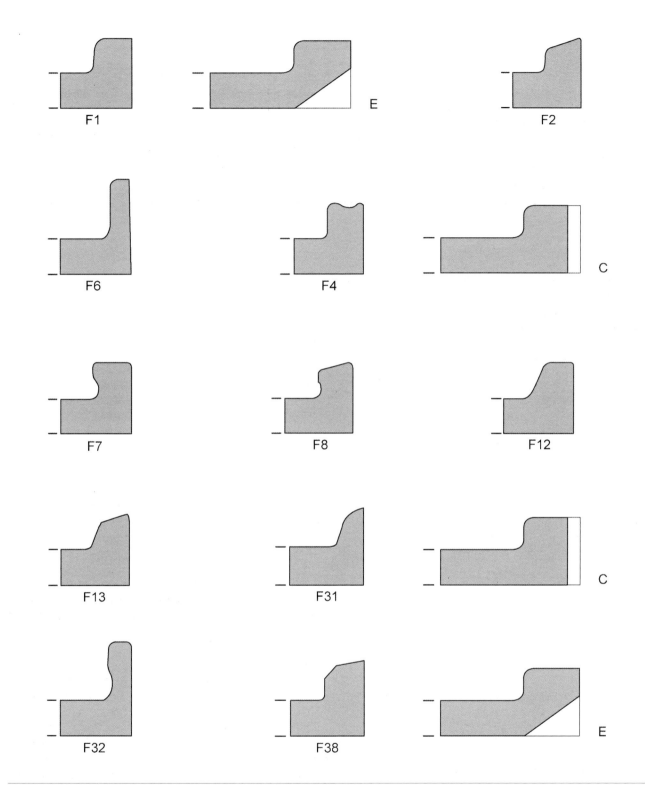

Fig 112. Roman tile: roof tile flange and cutaway types.

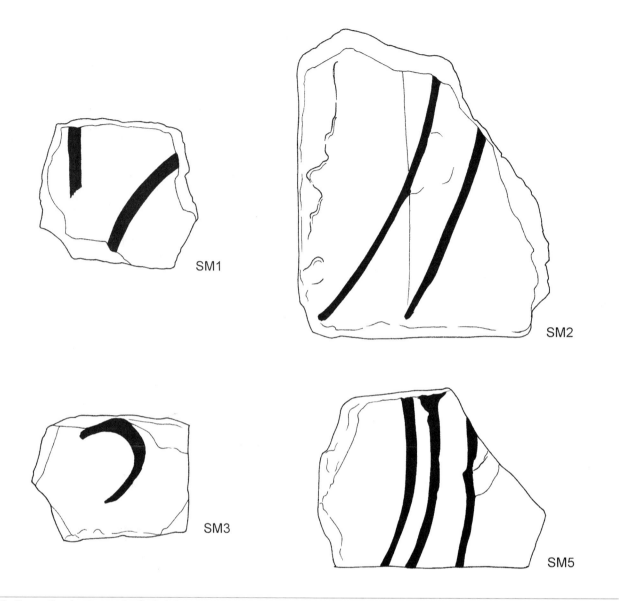

Fig 113. Roman tile: signature marks. Scale 1:4.

Signature marks and impressions

Signature marks types 1, 2 and 5 (Fig 113) are the most common, being present on both brick and *tegulae*, and in a number of different fabric types.

Very few tiles bore impressions such as animal paw prints and only one dog paw print (fabric 1 or 2) was recorded. Additionally, one *tegula* body fragment has a nail hole with a diameter of 11mm. It was applied before firing, which tends to be a feature of tiles dated from the mid second century onwards (Ian Betts, pers comm).

Discussion

The majority of the material is datable on the basis of its fabric to the early Roman period, from the early first century to the late second century. Fabric 1 represents 39 per cent of the assemblage while fabric 10 represents 25 per cent of the assemblage. Fabric 1 is similar to clay that was probably used in Canterbury in the early Roman period. Fabric 10, although abundant, cannot be dated at the present time. The only fabric that definitely dates to the later Roman period is fabric 17, which was produced in Surrey from the late second

Signature mark	Tile type	Fabrics
SM1	brick, misc	1, 1/3, 8, 10
SM2	brick, tegula, misc	1, 1/2, 1/3, 3, 8
SM3	misc	1
SM5	misc	1, 3
new type	brick	2
new type	misc	1

Table 56. Signature marks.

century to the early third century (Ian Betts, pers comm). This fabric was very poorly represented with only one brick fragment being recorded.

The large quantity of pottery from the site is generally dated to the later Roman period. The relatively small assemblage of (mainly fragmentary) early Roman brick and tile seems to be scattered throughout the area with no obvious concentrations other than that observed near the northern quarry (*see* pp 4 and 20). The material was probably derived from elsewhere, most likely from one of the other Roman structures which are known to be situated in the

area. Apart from the villa situated at Wingham (Dowker 1882; 1883; Jenkins 1984), remains of a substantial structure were discovered in 1863 to the east of Ickham church, near Britton Farm (Taylor 1932, 119). Additionally, another substantial Roman structure was examined at Wenderton by James Ogilvie (P Clark 1995). The large quantity of flue and voussoir tile present suggests that the structure probably had a hypocaust system and may have had a vaulted roof.

The material varies greatly both in terms of its form and fabric. A large quantity of the tile studied is very similar to material thought to have been produced at Canterbury (Fabric 1). Additionally a number of other fabrics, thought to have been imported into the Canterbury district were identified. These vary in provenance from Eccles in north-east Kent, Reigate in Essex and London. This suggests that tile was being imported for use in the Ickham area, mostly in the early Roman period.

A wide variety of different keying techniques were evident on the flue and voussoir tile. The *tegulae* appeared to have been made using a number of different flange types and cutaways in similar fabrics. This would seem to suggest that a number of tile makers were producing tiles from a single kiln.

No	Object	Diameter mm	Width mm	Weight g	Context
1190	copper alloy collar ferrule	12			Area 1, base of Channel C
1191	copper alloy collar ferrule		19	20.0	Area 1, Channel C
1192	copper alloy collar ferrule	15	7		Area 1, base of Channel C
1193	copper alloy collar ferrule	26	36		Area 4
1194	lead disc	24	8	12.2	Area 4
1038	lead disc	37	5	42.0	Area 4, 408
1195	lead disc	22	1.5	5.0	Area 1, Channel C
1196	iron chain		50 (link)		Area 3
1197	iron chain		38 (link)		Area 3, 302
1198	lead caulking	40	25	123.3	Area 1, 115
1199	lead caulking	33	19	100.0	Area 1, Channel C
1200	lead caulking	24	13	25.0	Area 1, Channel C
1201	lead caulking	18	10	12.8	Area 1, Channel C
1202	lead caulking	17	9	15.0	Area 3
1203	lead caulking	24	17	50.0	Area 3, 'stone floor'
1204	lead caulking	20	8	14.1	Area 4
1205	lead caulking	16	4	6.3	Area 4
1206	lead caulking	24	12	25.0	unstratified
1207	lead caulking	26	12	25.0	Area 4
1208	lead caulking	20	9	20.0	Area 1, base of Channel C, east end
1209	lead caulking	15	10	15.0	unstratified

Table 57. Miscellaneous metal objects.

Miscellaneous metalwork

Quita Mould

This small category encompasses a number of metal objects, mostly of lead alloy and iron, which cannot be placed in other sections with certainty. Each object type is described in turn.

Collar ferrules

Twelve iron collar ferrules range in diameter from 15–42mm and they may have been used on a variety of hafted implements. A small collar ferrule (1190) of copper alloy sheet is unusual in having a pair of widely-spaced teeth projecting from one side. Although reminiscent of a pen nib the teeth are too widely-spaced to have functioned in this fashion and its use is unknown. Mounted on a wooden handle it could have been used to inscribe paired parallel lines or evenly-spaced dots into a soft medium such as clay, plaster or wax. Another example is known form Richborough (Malcolm Lyne, pers comm).

Three other small collar ferrules of copper alloy sheet were also recovered. One is of oval section (1191) and appears to have fibres within suggesting it may be the binding from a small brush, possibly for cosmetic use. Another (1193) has three concentric layers of organic material from the haft remaining. Lying directly next to the metal collar was a layer *c* 3mm thick of a black glassy material, thought to be possibly bitumen. Beneath this was a 3mm thick layer of 'paper or felt-like' material, with fragments of the ash wood (*Fraxinus* sp) haft in the centre (Watson 2000, 3).

Lead discs

Three centrally-pierced lead alloy discs may have had a number of uses. One (1195) is made of low quality pewter and it appears to have been suspended; it may have been used as a net sinker. The others (1194 and 1196) are made of lead alloy with a low tin content.

Chains, links and rings

One of the four lengths of iron chain with figure-of-eight shaped links (**1197**) is attached to a ring-headed pin which may have been used as a simple fastening for a gate. Another (1198) has chain links with a central oval link between and is comparable with a bucket chain from a pre-Flavian fortress pit at Usk (Manning *et al* 1995, fig 55.19). Nine individual links were found, the complete examples of which are of oval shape.

Lead caulking

Nine pieces of lead caulking of conical shape with a central hole (1198–1206) and a further three unpierced examples (1207–9) can also be placed in this section. They are comparable with other examples from South Shields (Allason-Jones and Miket 1984, 333, nos 8.92–9). The largest (1198) weighs the equivalent of four and a half *unciae* and may be a crudely-made weight.

Other metalwork

In addition, a range of other miscellaneous metalwork was recovered from the site. This included eight iron washers, fragments of broken sheet of copper alloy (120 including thirty-three riveted fragments) and iron (ninety-six including two riveted fragments), five rods of lead alloy and a small quantity of formless fragments of copper alloy (seven) and iron (thirty-one). A small amount of metalwork (sixteen) certainly of medieval or post-medieval date could be recognised, along with items of cast iron (forty-five) of recent manufacture.

Crafts and industries

Quita Mould

A wide range of tools was found at Ickham, representing the working of wood, metals, leather and textiles, as well as the grinding of grain. Waste from the working of iron, copper and lead alloys was found and small quantities of other waste materials were also recovered. There is also evidence for flax processing. Inevitably, the form of some tools is such that they may have been used for a number of purposes and they cannot be allocated to any one category with certainty; hammers, chisels, punches and certain awls fall into this group. Several of the tools are broken, again making their original purpose ambiguous. An attempt has been made to assign individual tools to particular crafts but hammers, chisels and punches have been considered together and, with some broken tools, have been cross referenced to a number of crafts, as appropriate.

This section begins, however, with a consideration of the millstones. These form indirect evidence for the milling of grain, which clearly formed one of the major activities at the site during the late Roman period.

Millstones

Robert Spain and Ian Riddler

Introduction

The Ickham millstones and querns were first examined by Robert Spain, who produced a comprehensive archive report (Spain 1977). Seventy-eight stones were catalogued, some of which can be identified as millstones, whilst others are clearly querns. The quernstones have been separately considered above (pp 251–5). The report by Robert Spain forms the basis of the text presented here, with additional observations from Ian Riddler. Spain concentrated on the millstones, rather than the querns, and provided a detailed account of their characteristics. His archive text has been summarised and is augmented by an analysis of their distribution across the site and a description of their broader significance. Stone identifications were originally carried out by Robert Spain, and these have been ratified by Joan Blows.

Relatively large assemblages of millstones and querns were recovered from Mills 1–3, a small number from Mill 4 and a few examples from other contexts (Tables 48 and 58), though as might be expected they were all largely found in the vicinity of the mills. All of the millstones show signs of excessive wear and they were discarded in a fragmentary condition, presumably having broken during use. In a working situation the lower stone would usually last longer than the thinner upper stone, and one would expect that both millstones would be periodically redressed. In some cases it is also likely that a lower stone could be re-used as an upper stone (see below).

In attempting to distinguish between millstones and quernstones within assemblages, the principal distinctions include diameter and thickness, as well as the presence or absence of handle sockets and the diameter of the spindle hole in the case of lower stones. Stones with an estimated diameter of 650mm and a thickness of 50mm or more are considered to be millstones. Querns and millstones may overlap in terms of their diameters (Spain 1984a, 123–4) and querns can also be found in the vicinity of mills, as was the case here, but in general terms it is thought that the two forms of implement have been accurately differentiated. Size cannot always be relied upon to make the sole distinction as large-diameter millstones with pick-dressed furrows are also associated with Roman geared hand or animal mills (Jacobi 1912). Nonetheless, the existing corpus of water-powered millstones from the Roman world leaves little doubt that by the end of the third century, the basic characteristics of water-powered millstones were already well-defined.

Smaller fragments of stones may fall into either category, although in some cases the type of stone used provides an important clue. Most of the stones which can be identified with some certainty as millstones, for example, are made of Greensand. The same stone was also used for querns, both at Ickham and elsewhere in east Kent, but not as frequently in late Roman contexts, as noted below. Equally, basalt lava was used commonly for querns throughout the Roman period but is scarcely found at all with the millstones from Ickham, although it was used for millstones elsewhere..

Alongside the consideration of size, there is also that of structural features. Two of the millstones, for example, possess elements of central rynds. Others show the harps of the dressing of the grinding surface on both faces and this suggests that they were used initially as upper stones, and subsequently as lower stones. Two of the millstones (Nos 1217 and **1213**) show evidence of serving first as a top stone (runner) and then as a bottom stone (bedstone) and no 1217, found in two pieces, showed evidence of being originally driven and carried by a two-winged rynd (see below).

Millstones that have both surfaces dressed for grinding began life as top stones and then were used as bottom stones. The reason often put forward for this is that as the stone wore away it became too light to achieve proper grinding and a new and heavier stone then replaced it. The original top stone, while still whole, could be used as a bedstone where its weight was not important. To take up its new position however, its grinding face, hitherto concave, would require reshaping and dressing as a convex surface. If the original grinding face was re-used for grinding, this had two disadvantages. First, more stone would have to be removed from this surface than from the original top face to achieve the convexity required and, secondly, the rynd cavity would interfere with the grinding process.

Analysis of the millstones shows that thickness of the top stones was, on average, 590mm at the rim and 93mm at the eye, compared with 54mm at the rim and 85mm at the eye for the bottom stones. The thickest stone found happened to be a bottom stone which measured 165mm at the eye (**1210**, Fig 115) whilst the thinnest examples, as one might expect were all rim fragments, and mostly from bottom stones. This thickness analysis appears to support the theory of minimal weight top stones, which is also reflected in the two stones identified as having been first top stones and then bottom stones (1217 and **1213**). Probably the best examples of minimum weight grinding stones are from the Athenian Agora (Parsons 1936) where one or two of the top

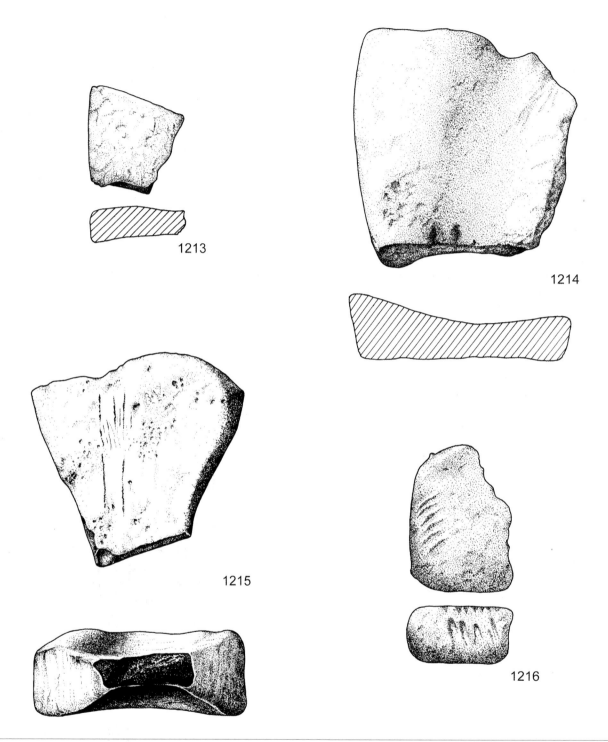

Fig 114. Millstones (1214–16 re-used as whetstones). Scale 1:4.

stones were extremely thin in relation to their diameter and the thickness of the rynd cavity.

Other Roman watermill sites that have yielded millstones that have served as top and bottom stones include Fullerton, Barbegal and Janiculum. At Ickham this form of re-use occurs with the millstones, but is not seen with the querns.

Five of the millstones come from Area 10 and can be associated with Mill 1. The millstones are fragmentary and only two of the collection can be identified for their original position within the mill. One is a lower stone and the concave surface of the other (**1222**) suggests that it was an upper stone, although no traces of the grinding surface can now be seen. The fragments include millstones of both Greensand and Millstone Grit in relatively equal numbers, with diameters of 750 and 1000mm for the two measurable examples.

The largest collection of millstones comes from Area 1. On the plan of Mill 3 (Fig 18) several stones can be seen to be dispersed about the mill, but these are mostly querns. Eight millstone fragments were recovered from context 107 (*see* p 107). A further twenty-eight pieces of quern were also found in this context. Single examples of millstones were assigned to 'Mill 2' and context 116 and two pieces came from Mill 4 (contexts 610 and 642). The five millstone fragments from Area 10 stem from Mill 1. The character of the late Roman assemblage is substantially similar to that seen with the earlier Mill 1. It includes millstones of Millstone Grit and Greensand, with examples of both upper and lower stones extending in diameter from 670 to 1030mm. In general terms, however, they survive to a greater extent than the fragments from Mill 1.

Of the fourteen stones identified as millstones, ten had evidence of furrows on their grinding faces which, having regard to the degree of degradation and their terminal condition on abandonment, suggests that it was the normal practice to dress the stones. On most of these stones the furrows could be seen arranged in 'harps',[38] a design feature which prevailed in millstone dressing until its demise in the early twentieth century. One example (**1210**) is dressed as a right-hand stone so as to rotate clockwise. At least three concentric striations are in evidence at its mid-working zone, where the grain was either shelled or crushed, depending on the millstone setting. This feature has not been previously

recorded on Roman millstones dressed with furrows, even though one would expect it to be present. The well-defined convex working surface is dressed with furrows. Its lower surface is flat-bottomed, which presumably facilitated its positioning on a hursting (a wooden framework supporting the millstone assembly) or on the floor of the mill's grinding room.

A second example (1217) includes furrows on both of its sides, suggesting that it began as an upper or runner stone, and was subsequently used as a lower stone. The wing emplacements of a rynd are visible on one face. It was dressed as a right-hand stone in its original configuration, as also was the smaller fragment (1211) and a piece from the centre of a further stone (1218), also of Greensand. The Greensand millstones from this context are dressed as right-hand stones, with the exception of a small fragment (**1219**) with prominent furrows, which comes from a different context and is probably a lower stone. This is dressed so that the upper stone rotates in an anticlockwise direction. This was previously noted in the published account of Mill 1 (Spain 1984a, 171) and it was observed that perhaps two or more water-wheels were in operation simultaneously. The right-hand dressed stones are all from context 107 in the area of Mills 2 and 3, which largely confirms the hypothesis outlined above that the mill building was on the left-hand side of the wheel-race. The 'aberrant' example (**1219**) comes from context 116. Its deposition may, therefore, represent a different episode from that of the clearance of millstone fragments into context 107. None of the millstones had radial furrows although Roman examples of this style of dressing do exist at the Museum of London (personal observation). Although the evidence was insufficient to determine the exact number of harps on the stones, the angles that the sectors represented on the rims suggested three stones with seven harps, one with eight and one with nine. The distance between the furrows varied from 11–15mm, their width from 2–6mm and their depth from 1–3mm.

From the fragments we are able to determine the lead[39] on thirteen separate harps. On nine of these the lead was positive varying from 20mm to 60mm from the axis of the stone. On four harps the lead was negative, in one instance by as much as 78mm. On five of the stones, where the lead can be determined for more than one harp, it is clear that

---

38. The modern term for the circular sectors within which the furrows are all parallel to each other. Strictly the shape is a 'circular ring sector' allowing that the eye of the stone creates an inner radius.

39. The leading furrow in a harp should be tangential to an imaginary circle around the eye of the stone. The radius of this circle is the lead or 'draft'. The main reason for this is to ensure that the scissor movement of crossing and converging furrows induces the grain and meal towards the rim or 'skirt' of the stones.

MILLSTONES

No.	Area	Context	Stone type	Position	Diameter (mm) Skirt (rim)	Diameter (mm) Eye	Thickness (mm) Skirt (rim)	Thickness (mm) Eye	Thickness (mm) Max	Harps X or V	Harps No. to view	Harps Probable no.	Furrows Depth (mm)	Furrows Distance apart (mm)	Furrows Width (mm)	Incline of face	Rotation RH stone (C) LH stone (AC)
1210	1	107, Mills 2 and 3	G	L	880	150	72-97	165	-	X	3	7	1-2	11-12	5-6	12.5°	A
1211	1	107, Mills 2 and 3	G	U	min 560	-	max 650	min 90	-	V	2	-	2	-	4	?	A
1212	1	107, Mills 2 and 3	G	U	1030	-	90	123	-	V	-	-	-	-	-	4.5°	-
1213	1	107, Mills 2 and 3	MG	U	710	-	35-40	-	-								
1214	1	107, Mills 2 and 3	MG	U	825	-	65	-	-								
1215	1	107, Mills 2 and 3	MG	L	670	-	57.5	-	-								
1216	1	107, Mills 2 and 3	MG	U	-	-	-	-	-								
1217	1	107, Mills 2 and 3	G	U	860	120	92-102	c 88	-	V / X	5 / 1	9 max / -	1-3 / -	11-12 / 13.5	2-4 / 2-4	8° / 6°	C / C
1218	1	Mills 2 and 3	G	U	c 560	120	-	-	182	V	2	7 max	2	17	3.5	0.5°	C
1219	1	116, Mills 2 and 3	G	L	c 730	-	30	-	c 40	flat ?	2	-	4.8	16	3.4	0	A/C
1220	6	610.5, Mill 4	G	U	c 730	-	c 40	-	c 50	flat	1		worn	16.8	fairly wide	0	C
1221	6	624	G	L	920	144	25-80	95	-	X	7	7	1.5-2	11-15	2-4	6°	C
1222	10	1001, Mill 1	MG	U ?	max c 750	-	67.5	-	-								
1223	10	1001, Mill 1	G		1000	-	-	-	-								
1224	10	1001, Mill 1	G	L	-	-	-	-	125								
1225	10	1001, Mill 1	MG														
1226	10	1001, Mill 1	MG		-	-	-	-	c 115								
1227		u/s	G	U	-	-	-	-	105	V	1	-	1 (worn)	13	5	-	-
1228		u/s	G	U	860	150	70	102	-	V	3	8 max	-	10.8	-	7.5°	C
1229		u/s	TS	U	620	-	68	-	-								
1229a		u/s	MG		600	-	40	-	-								

BEARING BLOCKS

No.	Area	Context	Stone type	Position	Diameter (mm) Skirt (rim)	Diameter (mm) Eye	Thickness (mm) Skirt (rim)	Thickness (mm) Eye	Thickness (mm) Max	Harps X or V	Harps No. to view	Harps Probable no.	Furrows Depth (mm)	Furrows Distance apart (mm)	Furrows Width (mm)	Incline of face	Rotation RH stone (C) LH stone (AC)
1230	1	107, Mills 2 and 3			c 560	-	140	-	-								
1231					780	-	-	-	140	X	1	-	unclear	15	unclear	-	C
1232					c 770	-	85	-	-								

G: Greensand, MG: Millstone Grit, TS: Tertiary Sandstone, U: Upper stone, L: Lower stone, X: Convex, V: Concave

Notes
The number of harps to view include whole and parts of harps.
Where either no evidence exists or the information cannot be ascertained the column is left blank.

Table 58. Millstones and bearing blocks.

the miller or stone-dresser did not mark out his stone face in preparation for dressing and furrow cutting. Not only does the area of each harp vary but also the lead is different on the same face. These irregularities (especially the negative lead evidence) tell us that their knowledge of millstone and quern dressing was rather basic.

At Ickham, the stone favoured for millstones was Greensand. This is probably due to its fine-grain and homogeneity (which would be easier to dress than Millstone Grit) and also its closer availability. The inclusions found in the coarse-grained grit-stones, especially pebbles, would make it very difficult to produce accurate furrows. The extant evidence would seem to support this suggestion; Fig 118 shows that two-thirds of the Greensand millstones and rotary querns that were not subsequently degraded, were dressed with furrows, whereas on the grit-stones, only one fifth have furrows. If subsequent degradation in the form of whetstone and bearing use is ignored on the basis that it is unlikely to have obliterated the furrows, the difference becomes greater.

The stones of Millstone Grit include one example (**1213**) which has been ground on both faces and three others (**1214–16**) which had been used as whetstones, once they had broken.

Just two millstones can be associated with Mill 4. Both are of Greensand and one is an upper stone whilst the other is a lower stone. The lower stone (**1221**) is the best surviving millstone from the site, with a good indication of the patterning of its furrows, which are set in seven segments and dressed as a right-hand stone (Fig 116). The smaller fragment of an upper stone (**1220**) is dressed to rotate in the same direction.

Four of the millstones are unstratified. One fragment of an upper stone (**1228**) has a similar diameter to a stone from context 107 (1217) and it may possibly have acted as the pair for this stone, once the latter had ceased to function as an upper stone. The upper surface near the eye is extensively worn, possibly because of a later loosening of the rynd. A further stone (**1229**) is unusual in that it has been formed from a tertiary sandstone; it is the only stone from the site of this stone type.

The profile of some of the stones is worthy of attention. A section shows that the inclination is rarely straight. On the bottom stones, the radial section from the centre (eye) to the rim is either convex-concave (as **1210** and **1221**) or concavo-convex (as quern 944). However the evidence of three top stones where we have reliable profiles (1271, 1221 and **1228**) all· have concavity adjacent to the eye on radial sections. This seems to match the bottom stone profiles but

we do not know if such shapes are the result of dressing or wear or perhaps a combination of both.

It is probable that the stones would be dressed to admit whole grains from the eye and that the surfaces would then come closer together as the meal passed towards the rim. This is the design of modern millstones and notwithstanding the crudity of dressing and absence of skill as depicted by the Ickham evidence, we should assume that the Ickham millers were aware of this essential fact of milling. Without such a lead-in at the eye the stones would choke with grain. Evidence that the Ickham millers were aware of this is suggested by the flattening off of the convex profiles on bottom stones adjacent to the eye. In addition, on stone (**1228**) the surface adjacent to the eye out to a distance of 90mm from the eye, is rough-pecked, which is surely an attempt to break and crack the grain immediately on entering between the stones and before passing into the furrows.

On six of the millstones it is possible to determine the inclination of their grinding faces, which vary from 3.5 degrees to 12.5 degrees with the average being 7 degrees. This range of inclination may be due in part to the amount of use and working age of the stones, but it also may reflect natural wear between the surfaces, of which little is known. In the twelve stones where the grinding slope is known, nine of them are Greensand which appears to rule out the possibility that slope relates to material. The only meaningful conclusion that can be drawn from this evidence is that variation in slope or experimentation appears to have occurred throughout the period, and no clear development can be identified. It is possible that different millers favoured different slopes.

Students of molinology have noted that as the centuries passed the slope of the grinding faces of millstones reduced, being generally steeper in the Roman period and becoming flatter by the medieval period. By the nineteenth century, the heyday of corn milling with discoidal stones, the grinding faces were virtually flat. The modern bedstone was cut and dressed flat but the runner stone was slightly concave to admit grain between the stones. It is interesting that the slope of the Ickham millstone faces vary so much. This characteristic is not confined to a particular mill and does not appear to change over time.

As has been noted above, the evidence of the timbers examined *in situ* around mills 2, 3 and 4 supports the suggestion that clockwise and counter-clockwise stones were in use: three mills were in operation in Areas 1 and 6, perhaps not simultaneously, but certainly as separate entities. In each case different gearing arrangements were involved to facilitate either clockwise or counter-clockwise rotation. The central perforation or eye in all of the surviving millstones is

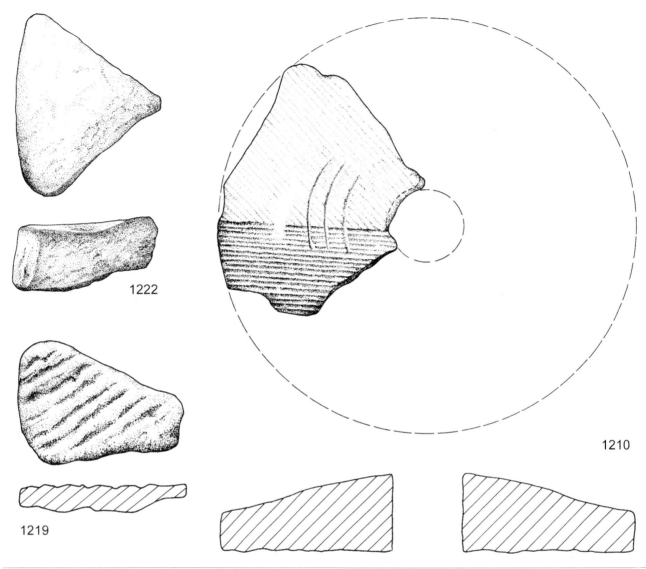

Fig 115. Millstones. Scale 1:4 (No 1210, scale 1:8).

cut vertically, which suggests that a collar bearing was not used to support the spindle.

Discussion

The Ickham assemblage of powered millstones is the largest thus far recovered from a Romano-British watermill. Roman water-powered millstones have been recovered from numerous Romano-British sites (Fig 26), although of these only Haltwhistle Burn Head and Fullerton exhibited features which could clearly be ascribed to a watermill (Wikander 1985b, 163–4). Many, indeed, were recovered out of context, where the millstones were being re-used as building material in other structures. At Woolaston, Gloucestershire, for example, two upper stones had been incorporated into the pavement of an outhouse in a Roman villa, around AD 320 (Garrett 1938, 122–4), while at Chew Park, Somerset, a complete upper stone and a fragment of another was recovered from a late third- or early fourth-century corn-drying kiln (Rahtz and Greenfield 1977).

The depositional histories of Romano-British millstones vary considerably. At Barton Court Farm, Oxfordshire, fragments of four millstones had been dumped into a fourth-century well; all except one had been built into the stone shaft of the well (Spain 1984b, 114; 1984c, 5: A13). Nonetheless, the existence of such stones, regardless of their context, clearly indicates the existence of water-powered mill sites. In one instance, millstones were found in a Roman smithy at Caerwent in Gwent, where it was assumed that their presence indicated that some sort of repair was being carried out (Spain 1984b, 123, note 67). This seems unlikely, however, as while the rynd may have been repaired at the forge it would have been much more practical to fit the rynd at the mill, rather than carry the heavy millstone to the forge.

All of the Romano-British upper stones appear to have been equipped with a single pair of rynd sockets, and although iron mill spindles have been recorded at Great Chesterford and Silchester (Neville 1856, 1–13; Manning 1964; Spain 1984b, 125–7) thus far no Romano-British mill rynds have come to light. Cruciform rynd sockets are also known from the eastern Mediterranean. Upper stones with four rynd sockets have been found at *Alba Iulia* and *Micia Deva*, in the former Roman province of Dacia (Romania), which date to the second or third centuries (Bucur 1978, 194–6). Similar stones were also recovered during the excavation of the fifth-century overshot watermill in the Athenian Agora (Parsons 1936, fig 17). However, stones of this type do seem to have the pick-dressed furrows of the Romano-British stones and a number of examples from central Europe. The generally high quality of the Romano-British variety suggests that this may well have become a specialised trade by the end of the third century, for not only is the dressing carefully executed, but great care has to be taken to impart a proper balance to the stones. The dressing of lands and furrows on early medieval millstones from Ireland and Anglo-Saxon England has not been recorded (Rynne 1989; Rahtz and Meeson 1992) and indeed seems not to have become common in Europe again until the post-medieval period.

Yet although the stone may have been manufactured by a specialist craftsman, its upkeep and redressing is likely to have been the responsibility of the miller. As the Ickham millstones clearly suggest, used millstones could be discarded into the mill channel or re-used as other parts of the mill plant such as bearing blocks (see below). In more recent mills, indeed, used millstones were often dumped near the mill, while there is at least one early medieval horizontal-wheeled mill, at Cloontycarthy, County Cork in Ireland (AD 833) where a disused runnerstone was dumped in the tail-race channel (Rynne 1988, 11, 313). The depositional histories of power-driven stones, on present evidence would suggest that used millstones were re-used within the immediate environs of the watermill, as has previously been suggested (Spain 1984b, 114). The Ickham millstones are a case in point, where demonstrably what was a presumably useful hydro-power site continued to be used over almost 200 years. Within this period many mill components would have needed repair or replacement and the millstones, when entirely worn out or broken during normal use, were finally dumped out of harm's way in the tail-race.

A millstone from Selsey in West Sussex has a recorded diameter of 1090mm (Curwen 1937, 144), which, on present evidence, appears to be the largest Romano-British water-powered millstone known. An example in the Musée St Germain has a diameter of 1.30m (Andrew Wilson, pers comm). The Barton Court farm examples range from 650 to 800mm and the single example from Usk is 625mm in diameter (Spain 1984c; Manning *et al* 1995, 236, no 79). A millstone from Birdoswald extends to 830mm in diameter (Wilmott 1997, 291 no 133). These measurements suggest that stones of 650mm or more in diameter should be treated as possible millstones, rather than querns.

The extent to which certain types of water-wheel have traditionally been site-specific can often provide important clues with regard to local hydrology. Generally speaking, the overshot and high breastshot water-wheels were used at upriver locations where the fall of water would normally compensate for any insufficiency of water flow. Breastshot and low breastshot wheels, on the other hand, are normally to be found at down-stream sites, as are undershot water-wheels. What would appear to have been the clear preference for Romano-British millwrights in using undershot water-wheels would suggest that a suitably chosen down-stream site as at Ickham could be utilised without the need of aqueducts or other expensive engineering works. The continuity of use of the Ickham site through successive mills corroborates this suggestion. Thus the size of millstone, if an appropriate source of hydro-power is available, need not be affected by type of water-wheel used, provided that the water-wheel is suited to the site.

The incidence of degradation, from rotary discoidal millstones and querns, to saddle querns, whetstones and bearings, found at Ickham is unusual. At Fullerton, where the later mill continued in use until *c* AD 380, only three millstones among a total of twelve found show evidence of subsequent degradation including rubbing and whetstone work. At Ickham, the incidence is much higher.

A study of Fig 118 suggests the following: two thirds of the millstones were made of Greensand, mainly Lower

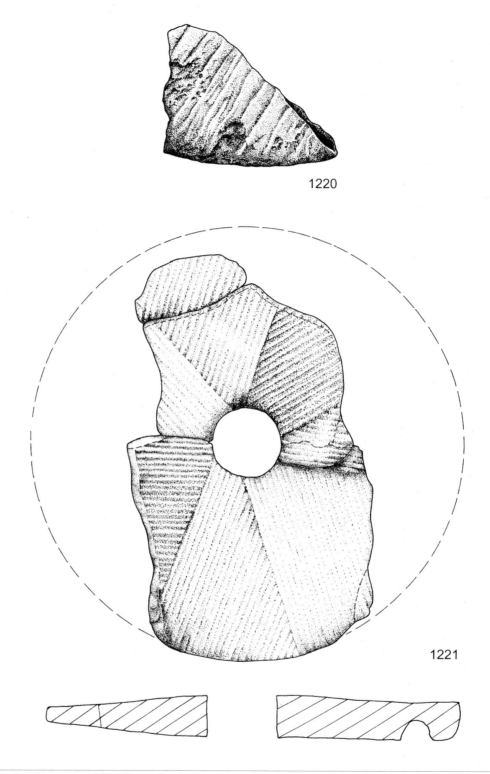

1220

1221

Fig 116. Millstones. No 1220, scale 1:4, No 1221, scale 1:8.

No	Small find no	material	slope (degrees from horizontal)	Top or bottom stone
millstones				
1210	1663	Lower Greensand	12.5	bottom
1212	1817	Lower Greensand		
1217	1799	Lower Greensand (two fragments of a millstone that served as a top then a bottom stone)	8 .0 6.0	top bottom
1218	900	Lower Greensand	0.5	top
1221	1652	Lower Greensand	6.0	bottom
1228	1653	Lower Greensand	7.5	top
	2594	Mayen basalt	c 10.0	top
	1937	Carstone	c 10.0	?top
quernstone				
944	1053	Lower Greensand	3.0	bottom
945	1589	Upper Greensand	4.5	bottom
972	1687	Millstone Grit	11.0	bottom
	945	Tertiary Sandstone	c 10.0	bottom

Table 59. Millstones and querns: slope of grinding surface.

Greensand; the majority of the rotary querns were made of Millstone Grit; four-fifths of all the saddle querns occur on Millstone Grit; five-sevenths of all the instances of whetstone work occurs on Millstone Grit; Greensand was the material favoured for bearings.

On the subject of degradation, the degree occurring with Greensand was minimal; with Millstone Grit it was considerable and was obviously the material favoured for nearly all non-rotary grinding and abrasion. It would appear that for all quern and whetstone work a coarse-grained hard stone with gritty or pebble inclusion was favoured. A degree of porosity may also have been desired.

All of the seventy-three millstone and quern pieces discovered were fragments; not a single stone was complete. With millstones, this is not too surprising because they would normally be worked until they became so thin that they broke. The great majority of all Roman millstones found are incomplete but there are exceptions (Parsons 1936). In spite of a detailed and meticulous examination of all the pieces, such was the fragmentation, degradation and erosion of the stones that it was not possible to put together a complete stone. It is possible however that two or more pieces could have come from the same original stone that we are now unable to identify. This is more likely to occur with the smaller fragments, generally the querns. We must also admit that the original use of some of the pieces cannot be confidently identified. This particularly applies to five saddle querns that may have started life as either a millstone or quern.

With a relatively large site like Ickham, where a wide variety of industrial and craft activities were taking place in the late Roman period, we can expect that good quality grinding stones would be used for other purposes when their primary function ceased. This was clearly the case for both millstone and querns. A common use for both millstones and querns is for them to be re-used as building fabric, such as walls, foundations (Cunliffe and Poole 2008), pavements (Wilson 2003) or hard core (Blockley *et al* 1995). But at Ickham, they were all apparently discarded without further purpose, many of them thrown into the boarded mill-race, presumably after the cessation of water-power generation.

The bearing blocks

Robert Spain

All three of the bearing blocks were cut to support journal bearings as distinct from supporting vertical spindles (footstep bearings) and have been made from re-used Greensand millstones. Two are unstratified, whilst the other came from context 107 (*see also* discussion pp 67–8).

1230 Upper Greensand. Spindle footstep bearing. A light grey whitish stone with a little iron staining. This loaf-shaped fragment, was probably originally part of a millstone rim. If so, the rim had a very rough profile and no remains of the grinding surface is evident, for both flanks appear to be

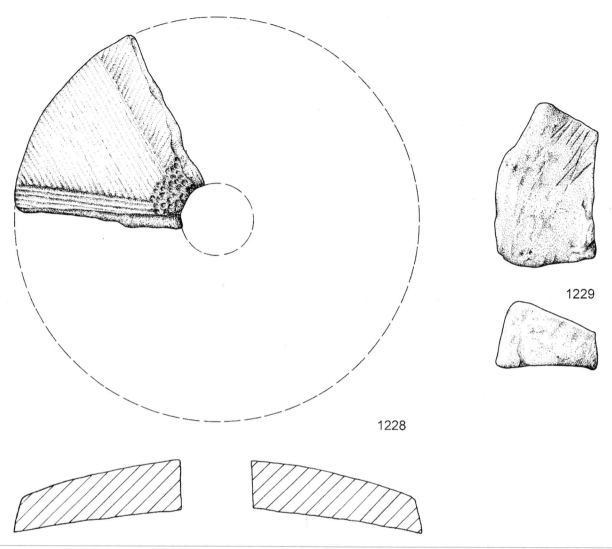

Fig 117. Millstones. No 1228, scale 1:8, No 1229, scale 1:4.

roughly dressed. On one flank there are three definite areas of wear, where the stone was apparently used for whetting, for they are not flat and do not lie in a single plane.

In the centre of the rim is a bearing emplacement where a spindle was supported. The semicircular cavity is 65mm long and its shape shows that the spindle was close to 30mm diameter. Surprisingly, the cavity does not have smooth radial areas of wear which are usually generated by rotating elements, or a flat circular area where the stone was subjected to thrust by the end of the spindle. However, that this stone was intended to serve as a bearing is in no doubt, for the cavity is semicircular in form (very obvious from an axial view), lies on the centre-line of the rim and its axis is parallel to the rough base of the stone; moreover, the face below the cavity is rough dressed at right angles to the spindle axis.

On the underside of the stone there is a dressed cavity, roughly rectangular in shape, some 40mm wide, 175mm deep and 55mm long. This surely served some purpose when the stone acted as a bearing, but it is not easy to ascertain its use. Two possibilities can be suggested; that it may have been cut to clear an iron strap or bolt head, or, and, this seems more likely, that the stone was kept in place by a keep-iron that fitted this cavity. As a bearing this stone would have been supported by a horizontal beam normal to the spindle axis in plan. In such a position lateral movement of the stone could easily be prevented by iron spikes or wood blocks against the flanks, but if the stone length was close to the width of the beam an alternative method had to be found for preventing movement in an axial direction. One method would be to introduce an iron bar under the stone, keyed to the beam; this cavity could have served just such a purpose. *Not illus.*

1231 Lower Greensand. Journal bearing. A hard light-grey stone. Originally a fragment from the rim of a lower millstone. The grinding face is dressed with parallel furrows which are well-worn and rather indistinct. On this surface there is an unusual ring-shaped natural fault in the stone. The rim of the stone is very roughly dressed and the underside so rough as to suggest that it has not been dressed since it left the quarry. At *c* 140mm thick, this is one of the thickest stones found on the site. That it should have fractured in use or when being re-dressed is surprising. One is tempted to suggest that the stone may have been abandoned because of the faults that occurred in its surface. This stone was one of a pair, the upper of which rotated in a clockwise direction. The two or three leading furrows have zero lead.

The bearing cavity is on the underside of the millstone so that the stone, when acting as a bearing, rested on the remains of the grinding face. This cavity, which is a maximum of 65mm long, is very irregular in its axial and longitudinal sections. Its sides are splayed and there is no evidence that the cavity was prepared to receive the journal spindle. The main area of rotary wear occurs at the back of the cavity, where some end thrust probably occurred and it is here that the approximate diameter of the journal can be ascertained, at 55mm. But the figure must be treated with caution because the wear in the cavity is consistent with the stone being tilted at some stage and, furthermore, the journal may have moved sideways slightly thus elongating the semicircular section. Such movement between journal and stone was probably attributable to the fact that the stone was resting on its convex grinding surface. This instability could have been partly overcome by wedges but their use must be questioned in view of the irregularity of the cavity. Indeed, one conclusion that is difficult to avoid is that this bearing was made and maintained by someone who was lacking in basic engineering knowledge and skills. *Not illus.*

1232 Lower Greensand. Journal bearing. A hard fine-grained grey stone. This is a large fragment, some 85mm thick, again cut from the rim of a top millstone. The top surface is well dressed and a small portion of the rim shows that its face was inclined to the vertical. The former grinding face is interesting; it is concave and has circular striations or scores and a large spall. Some of this scoring is deep and shows

that the stones were completely defaced before grinding was abandoned.

Part of the stone has split off, probably when the bearing weakened the stone. The bearing emplacement is 42mm long and the diameter of the journal was close to 33mm. The journal was probably bronze or iron and over time as it wore the stone away it settled deeper into the stone. On the assumption that the original position of the axis was not lower than the surface of the stone (a half round bearing), the journal settled down at least 15mm. The profile of the bearing emplacement shows that either (a) the stone tilted relative to the journal so that its end bit deeper into the stone or (b) the journal wore away in the centre reducing its diameter. *Not illus.*

In Roman vertical-wheeled watermills, the outer extremity of the horizontal axle was fitted with a metal gudgeon or journal, upon which the axle rotates. The journal formed a bearing with a horizontal socket cut into a flat stone, where one end of the socket was left open to receive it. One bearing block would have been positioned within the millhouse and the other on a support on the opposite side of the wheel-race or wheel pit. In this way the water-wheel's axle could freely rotate over its watercourse, supported at both ends in a bearing block. One would expect that the journals for each wheel-shaft would be forged in pairs, having similar diameters. Each pair of bearing stones would therefore be expected to display similar cavity diameters although the lengths could vary according to the physical arrangement at each end of the shaft. Bearing stones 1230 and 1232 might be pairs were it not for the fact that number 1230 does not appear to have been used.

Evidence of Roman bearings is rare, and so the three stone bearing blocks found at Ickham are a valuable contribution to our knowledge of the technology. A single example of a stone footstep bearing was found at the Haltwhistle Burn watermill site on Hadrian's Wall (F Simpson 1976; Spain 1984b, fig 12) and another specimen was apparently found at Dolaucothi, but neither the type nor age has been confirmed (Lewis and Jones 1971, 297). A possible footstep bearing stone was found at the Fullerton Roman watermill site, in Hampshire (Cunliffe and Poole 2008, stone no F995). The stone has a small hemispherical cavity in the centre of its face 40mm diameter and 10mm deep. Its regular shape and smoothness suggest that it could have been generated by rotary action, although the radius of the cavity is large compared with known examples. Additionally, a stone from Orton Hall was thought to be a footstep bearing (Spain 1996, 110–12). At the Athenian Agora mill, the wheel-shaft bearings, made

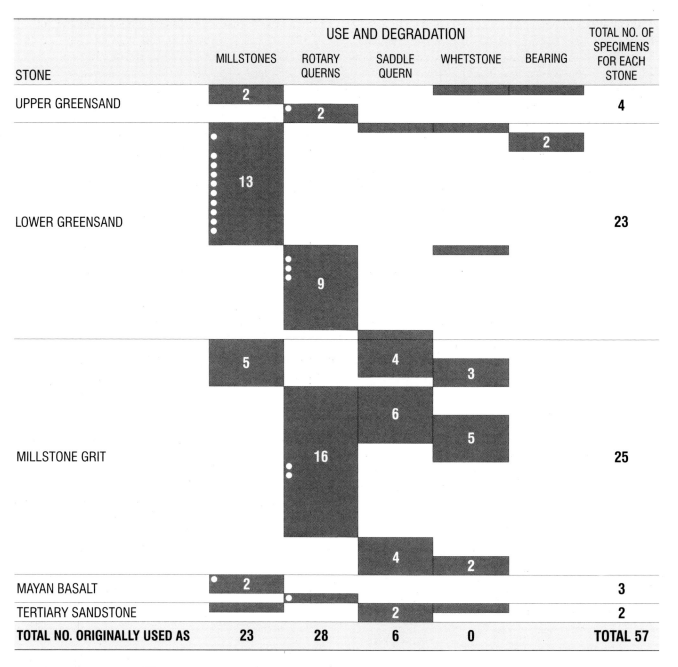

| STONE | USE AND DEGRADATION | | | | | TOTAL NO. OF SPECIMENS FOR EACH STONE |
	MILLSTONES	ROTARY QUERNS	SADDLE QUERN	WHETSTONE	BEARING	
UPPER GREENSAND	2	2				4
LOWER GREENSAND	13	9			2	23
MILLSTONE GRIT	5	16	4 / 6 / 4	3 / 5 / 2		25
MAYAN BASALT	2					3
TERTIARY SANDSTONE			2			2
TOTAL NO. ORIGINALLY USED AS	**23**	**28**	**6**	**0**		**TOTAL 57**

Evidence of furrows denoted by ▢

Notes: 1. Subsequent use (degradation) for the same stone is shown when a shaded unit occurs on the same level to the right-hand side of the original use.
2. The total number of units is given in each block except for single units.

Fig 118. Use and degradation of stones.

of wood or stone, were clearly set into and supported by stone blocks.

Hardwood Roman bearings for water lifting wheels have been found in the Rio Tinto mines in Spain and elsewhere (Benoît 1940, 53; Boon and Williams 1966; Palmer 1926/7). Our experience through the centuries tells us that the favoured materials for watermill bearings were hardwood, metal and certain stones.

Stone, including pebbles, appears to have been a popular material for footstep bearings and occurs in post-Roman periods (Graham 1986). Several stone footstep bearings have been found at the sites of horizontal-wheeled watermills in Ireland but they all belong to post-Roman periods (Lucas 1953, 15 and 24; MacAdam 1856; O'Reilly 1902–4). An iron footstep bearing was found at the Anglo-Saxon watermill at Tamworth (Wilson 1976, 89, 90, 276; Rahtz 1981; Trent 1975, 19–25), but no parallel Roman specimen has come to light. In more recent times evidence of widespread use of iron journals on hardwood bearings was found in extant watermills in Southern Europe (Hunter 1967, 446–66), and the practice of using hardwood for bearings, often *lignum vitae*, prevailed through the eighteenth and nineteenth centuries millwright work.

Metal-working

Hammers

The largest of the three iron hammers (**1233**, Pls XXVIII and XXIX), weighing over 10lbs, has a large, round face and a smaller, rectangular one, each being domed and burred. The round face shows a pronounced wear pattern suggesting repeated blows at the same angle. The small, round eye (31mm) contains remains of the minerally preserved haft

of box wood (*Buxus* sp). Box has been selected for the handles of hammers from the Iron Age through to recent times (Watson 2000, 3). This haft was made from a young stem or branch wood, more likely the former as a sapling combined the desirable properties of strength and elasticity. The relatively slender haft appears rather flimsy for the weight of the head and it may be that the hammer was steadied by one person by way of the handle, and hit by a second person. The distinct angle present on the larger face suggests that the hammer was possibly set on end and re-used as an anvil. Specks of non-ferrous metal are present within the corrosion products. A compelling argument has also been put forward that the object may have been a stonemason's hammer and used in the production of millstones (Robert Spain, pers comm).[40]

The rectangular hammer (**1235**) has two straight panes without an edge and is comparable with a modern mason's 'spalling' hammer. There do not appear to be any distinct hitting faces, however, so that it may be no more than a wide bar with a central hole made by a drift. A large cross-paned hammer (**1234**) has its gently domed face burred, which is suggestive of heavy use. Although more of a general purpose tool, it could certainly have been used for metal-working.

Blacksmith's tongs

Two broken jaws from metalsmith's tongs (**1236** and **1237**) were found, along with two tong handles with knobbed finials (**1239** and **1240**) The jaws (**1236** and **1237**) are of similar length with slightly extended gripping faces, one (**1237**) being relatively straight and finer jawed than the other (**1236**), which is bowed. Although broken, they come from small tongs used for handling small pieces of hot metal. Larger tongs are more commonly found, being a general blacksmithing tool

No	Object	Length mm	Width mm	Weight (lbs)	Context
1233	iron hammer	208	60	10	Area 4, unstratified
1234	iron hammer	180	25		surface
1235	iron hammer	160	43		Area 10, 1005

Table 60. Hammers.

No	Object	Length mm	Width mm	Context
1236	iron tongs	85+	20	Area 4, extension, 'section 2, layers 2–5'
1237	iron tongs	73+	19	Area 1, 122
1238	iron tongs	139+	19	Area 4
1239	iron tongs handle			Area 10, surface
1240	iron tongs handle			Area 10, 1001

Table 61. Tongs.

40. The hammer was x-rayed again in 2006 in the hope that more information might be forthcoming about its function and whether early thoughts that it might be part of a mechanical trip hammer were justified (see Appendix II).

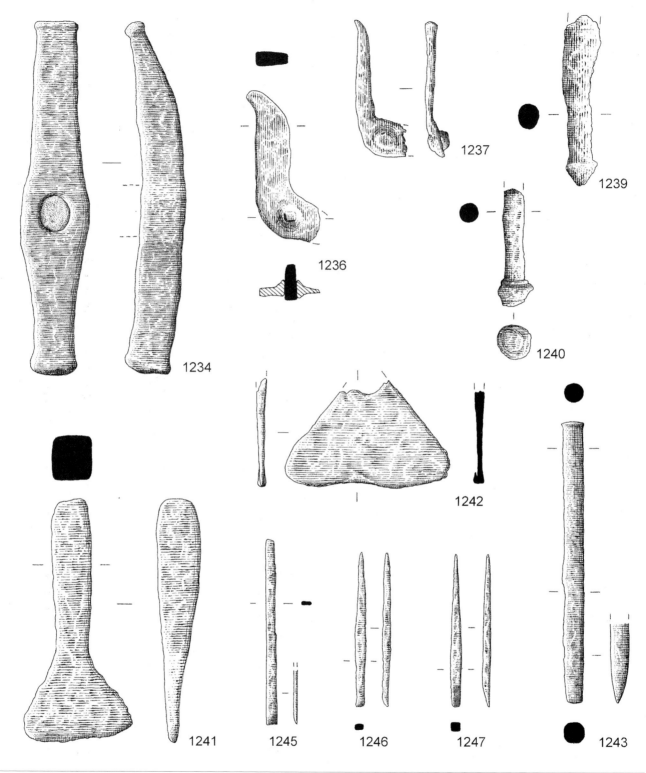

Fig 119. Metal-working tools. Scale 1:2.

(Manning 1985, 6–8 for full discussion and comparanda). The general blacksmith would have little use for the smaller types, suggesting a specific function for the Ickham examples. The pivoting jaw from a pair of small tongs possibly used for handling non-ferrous metal (1259) was also recovered and is described below (p 293).

What appears to be a broken jaw from a third example (1238) comes from a large set of tongs with straight jaws with a distinctly hooked gripping face, indicating a specialised use. A working blacksmith has suggested that jaws of this type would be needed to make disc-shaped items. The rectangular washer present appears to be a crude repair.

Chisels

Heavy chisels to cut hot metal, sets to cut cold metal and masons' chisels to cut soft stone are difficult to distinguish. Similarly, certain lighter chisels could have be used equally well to work wood or metal. It may now be unproductive to agonise over how particular tools were originally used; what can be said with certainty is that tools used by the blacksmith and carpenter are present.

A heavy chisel or set (**1241**) with a splayed blade for cutting hot metal was found in Area 10. A triangular splayed blade with a straight edge (**1242**) may be broken from a large chisel, comparable with that from Coldham Common, Cambridgeshire (Manning 1985, 9 A20 and comparanda)

Two round-sectioned stems with flat heads and narrow bevelled edges (**1243** and **1244**) are solid-handled chisels

No	Material	Length mm	Head diameter mm	Stem diameter mm	Context
1254	iron	125+	29	19	Area 1, Channel C
1255	iron	30+	33	20	Area 1, Channel C
1256	iron	44+	26	16	Area 1, Channel C, west end
1257	iron	20	47		Area 4, extension, 'layer 4'

Table 63. Punches.

which may have been used to cut hot metal, as a mortise chisel for wood or to cut stone.

Three slender, tanged implements (**1245–7**) of angular section with straight, bevelled edges represent fine chisel-like tools and may be a carpenter's bradawls (comparable with Manning 1985, pl 12 B77, B78) or a metalworker's tracer to decorate metalwork (comparable with Manning 1985,11 pl 6 A33).

In addition to the chisels above, seven broken blades were found with wedge-shaped sections and straight edges, five of which possess a bevel, and these may be broken chisel blades. They range in width from narrow blades of 10–17mm, and medium of 27–33mm to wide blades of 40mm, suggesting a variety of uses in working wood.

Punches

Three heavily battered heads of round-sectioned smiths' punches (**1254–6**) for working hot metal, each broken before the edge or point, were found in Channel C. A large example with an oval head and thick rectangular section (**1257**) was found in Area 4 extension.

Three thick stems of round section and two of angular section, each tapering to a blunt tip, may be lighter punches. None shows signs of battering at the head, however, and in the light of the amount of bar iron recovered from the site they are best considered under that heading. Accordingly, they are discussed below.

Non-ferrous metal-working

A possible doming punch (1258) was found in Area 2, comprising a sphere of copper alloy set onto an iron shank, which is now broken and encrusted. It is comparable with two similar objects from Poole's Cavern, Buxton, Derbyshire (Branigan and Bayley 1989, 42 and fig 4.109

No	Material	Blade width mm	Blade length mm	Head diameter mm	Context
1241	iron	55	125		1002, layer 2
1242	iron	88	56+		302
1243	iron	9	148	14	408
1244	iron	9	128	11	712
1245	iron	6	92+		Area 4, extension
1246	iron	5	82		Area 4, extension
1247	iron	4	81		1001
1248	iron	40			Area 14, surface
1249	iron	27			1002, layer 3
1250	iron	33			Area 2
1251	iron	10			1005
1252	iron	17			Area 2
1253	iron	16			Area 16/ditches

Table 62. Chisels and other implements with bevel-edged blades.

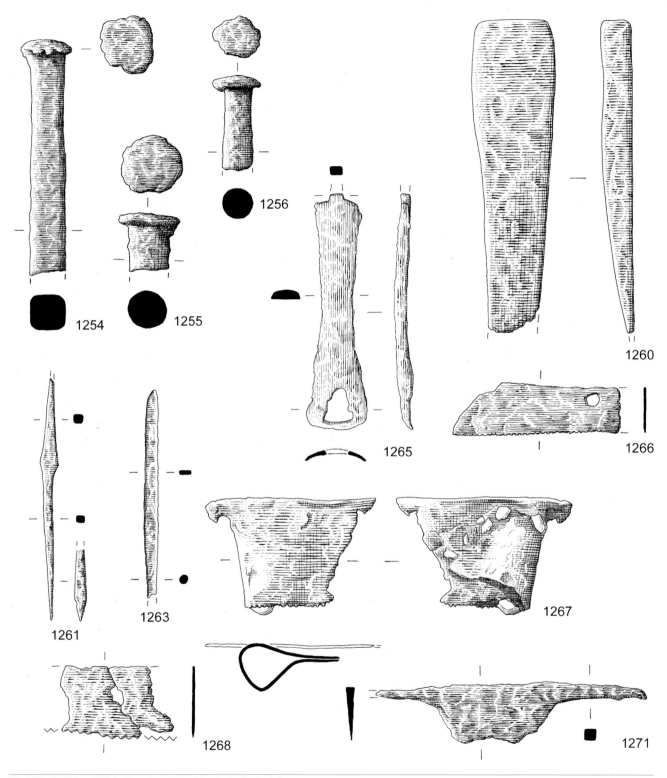

Fig 120. Smithing (1254–6) and wood-working tools. Scale 1:2.

and 110), indeed it is of exactly the same diameter as one of them (*ibid*, 42, no 109). Such punches would be used along with a corresponding doming block to make sheet metal hemispheres such as stud heads and bosses. A doming block was also found at Poole's Cavern (*ibid*, fig 4.108). The principal use of Poole's Cavern is believed to have taken place in the second century with the possibility of small-scale activity extending to the middle of the third century (*ibid*, 48). The method of use and an analysis of the composition of the copper alloy heads of these tools are provided in the discussion of the evidence for metal-working from Poole's Cavern (*ibid*, 47) which confirms the casting and cold working of sheet metal copper alloy.

A pivoting jaw broken from a small pair of metal-working tongs (1259) was also recovered. The back is curving, ending in a curved tip. No distinct back or edge is visible, suggesting it to be for gripping rather than a cutting blade, and prompting an identification as a small pair of tongs rather than metal shears or snips. The item had been burnt.

Wood-working

Various tools can be placed in this category, including wedges, drill bits, gouges, saws and particular forms of knife. Each object type is discussed in turn here.

Wedge

A rectangular-sectioned wedge (**1260**) with a slight shoulder may have been used to split wood.

Drill bits

A complete spoon drill bit (**1261**) was found (cf Manning 1985, fig 5, no 3), along with the head of another (1262) broken before the bit, and the stem broken from a twist bit (**1263**), a type which has rarely been identified. Another broken fragment (1264) may come from a pyramidal bit head.

Gouge

A gouge with a splayed blade (**1265**) has a strap handle and the beginning of a small tang remaining. Other fragments of U-shaped section (1272 and 1273) may be broken from gouges of various sizes. However, they have been considered with the open sockets, from which they are indistinguishable when broken.

No	Object	Length mm	Width mm	Thickness mm	Context
1260	iron wedge	168	41	16	Area 7, 710
1261	iron drill bit	129	7		Area 14
1262	iron drill bit	110+	13		Area 5
1263	iron drill bit	83+	9		Area 10, 1003
1264	iron drill bit	43+	10		Area 4, extension
1265	iron gouge	125+	32		Area 10, 'Layer 4'
1266	iron saw	88+	28		Area 14
1267	iron saw	94+	58		Area 10, 1005
1268	iron saw	58+	32		Area 10, 1002, 'layer 3'
1269	iron saw	53+	14		Area 1, Channel C
1270	iron saw	116+	19		Area 4, extension
1271	iron knife	145	30		Area 1, 115

Table 64. Wood-working tools.

Saws

No great differences in teeth size were represented (all are 30–40mm) with the five saw blades but they do vary in blade width. One example (**1268**) has distinctly asymmetrical teeth, indicating that it cut on the backstroke in the manner of a handsaw. Another (**1266**) with a nail hole, had symmetrical teeth suggesting it came from a bow saw which, being tensioned, cut on both the forward and the back stroke (Manning 1985, 21). A fragment of a wide blade has a distinctly thickened back (**1267**) possibly indicating a specific craft function.

Knife

A small knife blade (**1271**) has a straight back and a tang at each end. The double-handled blade appears either to be a very small draw knife used in wood-working or a scraper. It is significantly smaller than the similarly-shaped fleshing knives used in the preparation of hides to remove hair and other debris in the tanner's and currier's trades, Roman examples of which have been found in Pompeii (Gaitzsch 1980, taf 25, nos 128–30).

Leather-working

A number of tools recovered may have been used in leather-working though, with the exception of the fine awls, other uses for them cannot be excluded. Some of the thicker pointed tools found are comparable with others identified as

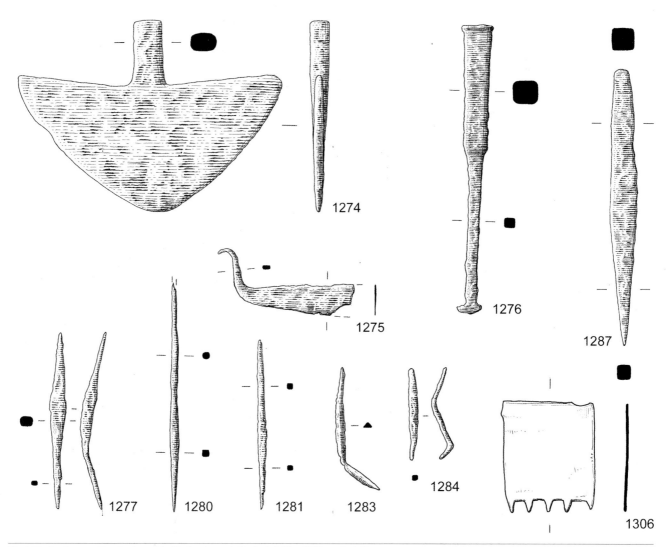

Fig 121. Leather-working tools and textile implement. Scale 1:2 (No 1306, scale 1:1).

leather-working awls in the past but may perhaps be more likely to have been used for piercing other materials. The half-moon knife and possible creaser are implements that are rarely found while awls are commonly recovered in small quantities from Roman excavations.

Half-moon knife

A leather cutting knife found in Area 4 (**1274**) is similar to an example from Pompeii (Gaitzsch 1980, taf 23, no123). Knives of this distinct shape are relatively uncommon finds (Manning 1985, 39 E3 for parallels). In the light of the pewter-working debris recovered from the site it may

be worth noting here that the half-moon stake used by the pewterer to work the edges of vessels takes the same form (Glass 1927, 42 and fig 24).

The identification of a small broken blade with an upstanding clenched tang remaining at one end (**1275**) is uncertain. It may possibly be a slicker or sleeker used by the currier on tanned hides during the beginning of the leather dressing process.

Creaser?

An unusual tool (**1276**) has a square-sectioned handle and a long stem ending in a small, flattened, crescentic blade. It has

No	Object	Length mm	Width mm	Context
1274	iron knife	101	140	Area 4, extension
1275	iron slicker?	73+	15	1001
1276	iron creaser?	153		Area 4, extension
1277	iron awl	93	7	Area 4, extension
1278	iron awl	56+	6	Area 4, extension
1279	iron awl	95	5	1005
1280	iron awl	121	4	408
1281	iron awl	90	4	Area 4, extension
1282	iron awl	88+	9	1006
1283	iron awl	70 (bent)	4	1001
1284	iron awl	70		335
1285	iron awl	65	7 (diameter)	Area 4, extension, layer 1–2
577	iron awl/punch	122	15	Area 2
1286	iron awl/punch	112	12	Channel C
1287	iron awl/punch	146	16	1400
1288	iron awl/punch	123	12	408
1289	iron awl/punch	105	13	Channel C
1290	iron awl/punch	81	11	706
1291	iron awl/punch	64+	10	Area 10, surface

Table 65. Leather-working tools.

proved difficult to parallel. It may have been used as a creaser to impress linear decoration or marking out lines on to leather or as a burnisher for pewter.

Awls

Seven fine awls of Manning's type 4a (Manning 1985, fig 9) have slender points, separated by a shoulder from the tangs for insertion into an organic handle. Three have square-sectioned points (**1277–9**), three have round points (**1280–2**) and one has a triangular section (**1283**). One awl (**1280**) has remains of the wooden handle preserved on the tang. In addition, a fine stem of square section, pointed at each end, appears to be a fine awl (**1284**), although it has no obvious shoulder. It is comparable with the possible partly-made needle (1303) from Channel C which is discussed with textile-working below.

A fine point tapering from a flat, circular head (SF197) might possibly be a variant of a Manning's type 3a awl (*ibid*). An awl with a small domed head (1286) can be paralleled by an example from Niederbieber (Gaitzsch 1980, taf 47, no 241). Each of these fine points could be awls or fine punches. A fine point with a small socket (1285) is also likely to be

an awl of Manning's type 5 (Manning 1985, fig 9), a type rarely recognised amongst the large quantities of nail shanks encountered.

Five thicker pointed tools of Manning's awl type 3b with a tapering handle to be held in the hand were also found (Manning 1985, pl 16, E8). The points appear rather thick for the piercing of leather; indeed, the largest example (**1287**) is sufficiently robust to suggest this tool is more likely to be used as a drift or punch for metalwork.

Textile manufacture

The various forms of textile implements of the Roman period have been summarised by Wild (1970), and more recent discoveries have been noted by Manning (1985) and Deschler-Erb (1998). These texts enable textile implements of the Roman period to be identified with some certainty, and to be distinguished from those of post-Roman date.

The implements from Ickham are all made of copper alloy or iron and include needles, a selvedge stretcher and fibre processing teeth. They are discussed in turn here.

Needles

Eight needles of copper alloy were found, five of which came from Mill 2. In addition, one example from Area 5 (1297) which is pointed at each end and has a flattened area with two faint parallel grooves visible on each face marking the position of the eye, which is not actually pierced, appears to be partly-made. The five complete examples are all similar, with the eye set within a groove, a characteristic of Crummy's type 3 which she suggests is a late Roman type, occurring at Colchester in third- and fourth-century contexts (Crummy 1983, 67). Complete examples from Ickham vary in length from 61–75mm. They are slender (maximum diameter 2mm) with either pointed or straight heads suitable for sewing fine fabrics. No examples of Crummy's type 2 needles with spatulate heads were recovered which, given that they are thought to have been used throughout the Roman period (*ibid*, 65), may indicate a particular use or sewing a specific type or weight of material not in use at Ickham.

Three fine, round-sectioned iron needles were found; each had been broken across the eye (eg 1301). One other broken iron stem (1304) came from a needle or a pin. A complete iron stem (1303) from Channel C is deliberately pointed at each end and appears to be a small partly-made needle, awaiting the forming of the eye. The iron needles are small, with diameters of 2mm, ranging in surviving length

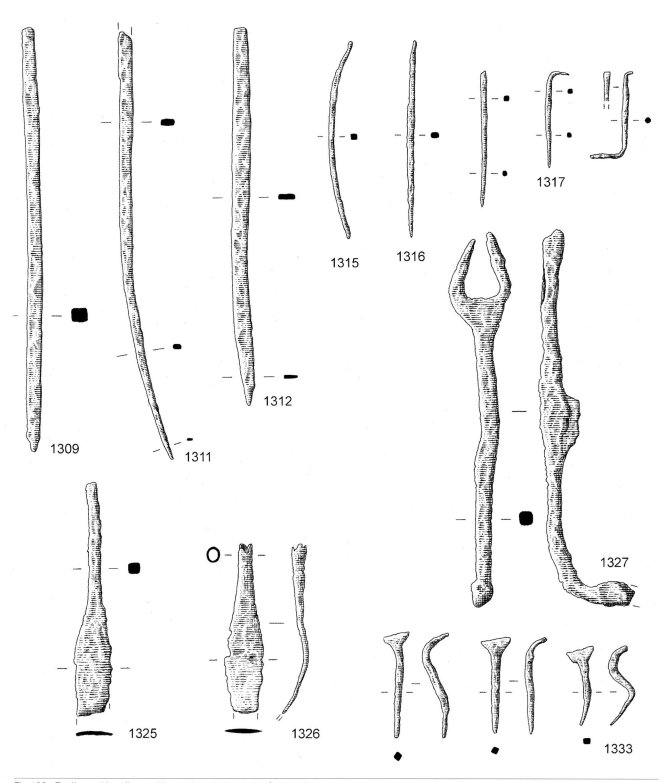

Fig 122. Textile-working, flax-working and modelling tools. Scale 1:2.

No	Object	Length mm	Eye length mm	Diameter/ width mm	Context
1292	copper alloy needle	56	4		Area 1, Channel C
1293	copper alloy needle	61	5		Area 1, Channel C
1294	copper alloy needle	75	5		Area 1, Channel C, west end
1295	copper alloy needle	67	5		Area 1, Channel C, west end
1296	copper alloy needle	70	5		Area 4
1297	copper alloy needle	70			Area 5
1298	copper alloy needle				Area 1, Channel C
1299	copper alloy needle				Area 1, 104
1300	iron needle				Area 1, Channel C
1301	iron needle				Area 4
1302	iron needle				Area 10, 1005
1303	iron needle	46	2		Area 1, Channel C, west end
1304	iron needle				Area 2
1305	iron needle				Area 1, 122
1306	copper alloy selvedge stretcher	29			unstratified

No	Object	Length mm	Eye length mm	Diameter/ width mm	Context
1307	iron flax heckle spike			7.5 x 7.5	Area 4
1308	iron flax heckle spike	222		7	Area 4
1309	iron flax heckle spike	197		7.4 x 5.5	Area 4
1310	iron flax heckle spike	226		8.2 x 4.7	Area 4
1311	iron flax heckle spike	200		10 x 6.8	'Ditch 7, north'
1312	iron flax heckle spike	180		3.5 x 2.6	Area 4, extension
1313	iron flax heckle spike			3.8 x 3.8	Area 1, base of Channel C, east
1314	iron flax heckle spike	55		3.7 x 3.2	Area 1, base of Channel C, east
1315	iron flax heckle spike			2.7 x 2.3	Area 2
1316	iron flax heckle spike	90		5 x 4.9	unstratified
1317	iron flax heckle spike	170		5 x 4.9	Area 4
1318	iron flax heckle spike	130		5.2 x 4.8	Area 4, 401
1319	iron flax heckle spike	70		3.4 x 2.8	Area 4, extension
1320	iron flax heckle spike			3.8 x 3.7	Area 4
1321	iron flax heckle spike	125		4.4 x 3.3	Area 4, extension
1322	iron flax heckle spike	106		4.2 x 3.9	Area 4
1323	iron flax heckle spike	105		2.9 x 2.8	Area 4

Table 66. Textile-working implements.

from 37–60mm, and are comparable for their sizes with the copper alloy examples.

Selvedge stretcher or temple

A copper alloy selvedge stretcher (**1306**), an implement known to weavers as a temple, consists of a rectangular plate with five small teeth along the top edge. When mounted onto either end of a wooden batten they are used to stretch the selvedge edge during textile weaving to help prevent the sides of the material becoming irregular. Several other examples have come from Roman contexts, including one which was found at Caister-on-Sea, Norfolk from refuse dumping on the ramparts (Cool 1993, 115 and fig 94.647 and comparanda) and six were found together in a pot at Chalton, Hampshire in a fourth-century context (Frere 1957, 219; Roes 1958, 244). More recently a group have been found at Stanwick, Northants, in lower plough soil (Angela Wardle, pers comm). Similar toothed plates, but not identical, have been found at Portchester, *Verulamium*, Chedworth, Winchester and Ivy Chimneys, Essex.

Spindlewhorl

A single, disc-shaped lead spindlewhorl (1324) came from Area 7. It weighs 24.8g and has a central hole 6mm in diameter. Several other centrally-pierced discs of lead are described above in the section on miscellaneous metalwork.

Flax processing

Penelope Walton Rogers, The Anglo-Saxon Laboratory

There are five sturdy iron spikes with square cross-sections and blunt tips which almost certainly come from flax ripples (1307–8, **1309**, 1310, **1311**). The spikes are 180–230mm long and each has a tapering lower end, which is common in spikes which have been set in a wooden block. Flax ripples have a single row of these spikes mounted vertically and are used to remove the seed pods from flax stalks (Heinrich 1992, 20). The head of a bundle of flax is pulled through the teeth so that the seed pods drop off and the seeds are then collected for linseed oil and the empty pods fed to cattle.

A further twelve spikes are more slender, with sharper tips (**1312**, 1313–14, **1315–17**, 1318–23). They occur in a range of sizes, 55–130mm long, are square or rounded square in cross-section and one (**1316**) has remains of a crossways wood-grain reaching up to 30mm from the base. These represent spikes from flax heckles. Heckles consist of groups of spikes mounted vertically in a wooden block. The flax is brought down on to the heckle, so that the teeth bite into the stems and the flax is then pulled towards the user, so that the stems split lengthways (Walton Rogers 1997, 1726–31). Two or three heckles with different grades of spike are used, one after the other, which explains the different sizes of spike recorded here.

Flax production was established in Britain by the Iron Age and linens (textiles woven from flax) have been recovered from a number of Roman period sites (Wild 1970, 13–15 and 91–4). No flax ripples or heckles seem to have been recorded so far, although this is probably due to a lack of accurate identification. Flax tools are often confused with those used for wool processing, although the Roman woolcomb, which is cut from a single plate of iron, is quite different from the objects described here. The flax plant, *Linum usitatissimum* L, is an annual, often grown in river valleys and coastal districts, and would be easy to cultivate in the vicinity of Roman Ickham.

Modelling tools

Two leaf-shaped, flat-bladed tools were found, one (**1325**) with a tang, the other (**1326**) with a narrow round-sectioned socket for a wooden handle. These large spatulas appear to be modelling tools for working soft, plastic material such as clay or plaster. Modelling tools of different forms are known, principally from London (Manning 1985, 31–2) but the Ickham examples are closer in shape to an item from the Waltham Abbey hoard, Essex (*ibid*, 28, B76) which, having sharp edges and a point, was thought to be a type of auger.

Miscellaneous craft tools

A pulley and hook found in Area 4 (**1327**) was used to lift heavy weights and could have been used during construction of the buildings or subsequently to raise heavy bags of flour in the mill. Continental examples with pierced lugs similar to the Ickham example are cited by Manning (1985, 138).

A slightly curved fragment of copper alloy originally from a cylindrical object with subtriangular section and a serrated edge (1328) was found in Channel C. The unusual serrated edge is reminiscent of the iron tubular drill bit from Niederbieder (Gaitzsch 1980, taf 50.233). If copper alloy was sufficiently hard and durable, then this fragment could be broken from a similar tool used to bore holes in soft materials such as bone. It was perhaps used in conjunction with an abrasive agent such as corundum.

Metal-working debris

In addition to the craft tools described above, quantities of debris from metal-working, of both copper alloy, iron and lead were recovered.

Iron-working evidence

It is not known whether iron-working slag was present at Ickham in any quantity. If it was, it was not collected or recorded. A small amount of 'industrial waste' was retained but what proportion this represents of that originally recovered cannot be ascertained. The samples include a subrectangular block of iron (1329) from Area 4 which may be an unusually-shaped bloom brought in as trade iron from the area of smelting for use by the smith. It is not the typical bun-shaped bloom, however, and it could be of post-medieval date. Three smithing hearth bottoms were also identified from Area 10 (1330–2).

No	Object	Length mm	Blade mm	Width/length mm	Context
1325	iron spatula	122+	57+	18	Area 3
1326	iron spatula	90+	58	20	Area 7, 710

Table 67. Modelling tools.

No	Diameter mm	Length mm	Width mm	Context
1334	17 x 15		2	Area 10, 1001
1335		46	5	Area 1, Channel C

Table 68. Unfinished objects of copper alloy.

Dr David Starley writes: 'The Ickham assemblage included a few hundred grammes of iron-working debris. Three fragments were considered to be possible smithing hearth bottoms - indicative of the hot working of iron. Most of the remaining debris was classified as 'undiagnostic iron-working slag' which, in the absence of positive evidence of ironsmelting, probably also derived from ironsmithing. The significance of such a small assemblage must be considered very limited, perhaps the product of very short term smithing, no more than one day's activity would be required to produce this quantity. Alternatively the small quantity could have spread to the area excavated from a larger focus in the vicinity.'

In addition, a large quantity of broken iron strap, strip, heavy shanks, rods and bar iron was recovered which represent the bar iron, blanks and scrap used in iron smithing.

One hundred and seventy-six fragments of flat-sectioned iron strap (more than 21mm in width) and 166 fragments of strip (less than 21mm in width) were found. Over half were recovered from Area 10 (strap 58 per cent, strip 52 per cent). While some of these fragments may be broken from nailed bindings, a proportion is undoubtedly associated with iron-working.

One hundred and thirty fragments of bar iron with rectangular or square section were found, as well as twenty-seven offcut shanks, likely to be from bar iron, along with a further twenty-seven lengths of iron with round section (rods and wire), many showing signs of working. A further eight pieces of smithing scrap with handling rods were recognised, again chiefly deriving from Area 10 (five out of eight). The handling rods were projecting tangs by which the hot metal was gripped by the smith's tongs.

Approximately half of all the smithing stock came from Area 10, suggesting that this part of the site may have been the location of the smithing hearth/s or a dump for iron-working debris. It was notable that radio-opaque specks were present in the corrosion products of only a few items of 'smithing stock' suggesting that the non-ferrous metal-working activities did not occur in close proximity to the smithing hearth.

A maximum of thirty-six short tangs with flattened ends (eg **1333**) were found, again principally from Area 10. The hammered ends lie at roughly right angles to the square-sectioned tangs, sometimes slightly rolled under at the straight end, giving the appearance of having been snapped off. They vary in length from 43–59mm and in head width from 13–20mm. All appear to be quickly and crudely made which prompted the author to suggest that they are scrap

from a manufacturing process, being handling rods, that is, the tang gripped by the backsmith's tongs when forging an object (Mould 1997b, 83 and fig 4.4 no 2). Alternatively they could be nails or clips with a specific function. They are comparable to the small fittings found at Saalburg (Jacobi 1897) used to hold iron tyres onto wooden cartwheel rims. An example has been found from Asthall (Mould 1997b, fig 4.4, no 2), a late Roman settlement also with much evidence for smithing, in third- or fourth-century pit fill (*ibid*, 83).

Evidence for the working of copper alloy

A small number of items provided evidence for the working of copper alloy. An oval flan or blank (1334) is unfinished and is possibly an item in the course of manufacture. It may be the bezel from a finger ring. A partly-made stem (1335) which changes from a rectangular to a round section along its length also appears to be in the course of manufacture. Four manufacturing offcuts of copper alloy were also identified

Debris from the working of copper alloy included a quantity of offcut sheet (twenty-five pieces) with all edges tool cut, sheet fragments which had been deliberately folded (thirty-six pieces) probably to fit into the small crucibles in which they were to be melted down for re-use, and fragments of round-sectioned wire (eleven lengths). The folded sheet was found scattered over the site with no obvious concentration, while approximately half of the sheet offcuts came from Area 4. While some of the fragments of copper alloy wire found may be broken from single strand bracelets, one at least (295) has pointed terminals and appears complete.

There is also a significant amount of indirect evidence for non-ferrous metal-working. Many of the iron objects could be seen in radiograph to have radio-opaque specks likely to be of non-ferrous metal within the corrosion products. A sample of objects with these specks were investigated by an archaeological conservator and were found to be of copper alloy and occasionally also small blobs of lead alloy and it is assumed that this is also the case for the other examples.

The iron objects with radio-opaque specks of non-ferrous metal present had been in close proximity to non-ferrous smithing activities or, more likely, were dumped along with sweepings from the clearing of debris on the floor of the metalsmith's workshop.

Radio-opaque specks were noted on 15 per cent of the iron objects (excluding the timber nails) from Ickham, occurring principally in Area 4 (30 per cent), Area 4 extension (26 per cent), Channel C (15 per cent) and Pit 115, in Area 1 (6 per cent). Not all the timber nails were radiographed so that estimation of the quantity of nails with radio-opaque specks in the corrosion products is not possible. However, Pit 115 was notable in having large amounts, while they were also present in smaller amounts elsewhere. Few timber nails from Area 10 were radiographed.

Evidence for lead alloy working *Rebecca Sutton*

The following text is adapted from the Ancient Monuments Laboratory Report 32/1998 (Sutton 1998).

Approximately 39kg of lead alloy was recovered from the excavations at Ickham, much appears to have been collected for scrap. Five hundred and seventy samples of this material were analysed by XRF to look for evidence of recycling and manufacturing of lead alloy objects on site. A calibration curve was calculated from known standards so that the percentage of tin in each sample could be estimated and the results compared with the small number of other analyses of Roman pewter which have been published to date (summarised by Beagrie 1989).

The material was divided into seven categories: tableware, other lead alloy artefacts, fragments, offcuts, spillages and undiagnostic waste. Analysis was used to identify any correlations between composition and the different categories of material recognised. The XRF analysis of the tin content of each sample within each category was then plotted and the results described below. A full description of the method employed is appended to the laboratory report (Sutton 1998).

Tableware (3.75kg). The analysis of the tableware is discussed above (pp 242–3).

Other lead alloy artefacts (5.8kg). This category contained lead alloy objects other than tableware. The ferrules, many of the weights and some of the caulking were found to be made of lead or high-lead alloys. Other items such as some caulking and pot patches were found to be of pewter.

Fragments (4.42kg). Broken sheet fragments with no cut edges which could not be positively identified as coming from tableware were found to be principally of high-lead alloys. Some fragments in the high-tin range are likely to derive from broken pewter vessels.

Offcuts (4.8kg). Pieces of offcut sheet were of lead or high-lead alloy. A small number of fragments of higher-tin composition may derive from cut up pewter vessels.

Spillages (12.59kg). Spillages, that is fused masses which have formed during uncontrolled solidification, were found to be chiefly of lead or high-lead alloys, although a small number of spillages of other compositions did occur.

Undiagnostic waste (7.71kg). Waste material was present but whether deriving from a deliberate manufacturing

process or the result of an unintentional fire is uncertain. Like the spillages, most of this undiagnostic waste material was found to be lead or high-lead alloys, with a small amount having other compositions.

Pewter-working at Ickham

There is a variety of evidence for pewter-working at Ickham. A small amount of evidence of melting and casting exists, with much evidence for the collection of metal for recycling. A casting head or sprue (1336) with a 20 per cent tin content was found with eight small runners which would have fed molten metal down into the mould. A plano-convex lump of pewter (1337), with a tin content of 72 per cent, was of a shape suggesting it was melted and allowed to solidify in an enclosed environment, perhaps a crucible. Their presence gives clear evidence that casting took place on more than one occasion on the site. There is no evidence of exactly what was being made. A small 'golf-ball' sized lump of galena (80g), a lead ore, was found on the surface. This may indicate an input of raw material into the site, and perhaps trade, however, it is only one small piece, and if smelting was taking place in the vicinity much greater quantities might be expected. There is no clear indication of how much material of this type was found but not retained. The nearest sources of galena are the Mendips and Derbyshire.

A large amount of lead alloy artefacts in a range of functional categories were found on the site; but that alone does not provide evidence for manufacture. The amount of debris, especially that which shows signs of having once been molten, such as the spillages and undiagnostic waste, may be taken as a possible indication of manufacturing, however, some of the material could have formed during a fire, accidental, votive or otherwise.

There is evidence for the re-use of pewter and lead on the site. This is provided by offcuts with clear tool-cut edges and pieces of tableware with cut marks present. Other items had been folded. Three pewter plates (767–9, Area 7, context 802) found together, the most complete vessels found at Ickham, had been deliberately folded, two had been partially melted along one edge, possibly due to a fire or intentional melting for recycling. While plates may have been folded at the end of a ritual meal, one of the plates had been deliberately cut as well as folded suggesting it to be scrap. Other cut-up vessels also indicate the recycling of pewter.

The occurrence of apparently well-defined groups in the tin content of the pewter tableware suggests that the alloying of the metal was carefully considered, taking into account the properties of the metal. One reason for the differences in the lead-tin ratios may be cost, as lead was a considerably cheaper metal than tin in the Roman period. This idea is given weight by Beagrie (1989) who also sees the casting properties and the increase in hardness from the alloying of these two relatively soft metals as a reason. Pliny describes an alloy known as *argentarium,* which is composed of 'pale [tin] and dark lead in equal amounts' (Bailey 1932, Book 34, 160), and an alloy called *tertiarium*, which is 'an alloy of two parts dark lead with one of pale [tin]' (*ibid*). This suggests that the Roman pewterers had alloy recipes for lead-tin alloys, and it is possible that the pewterers at Ickham were also following set recipes to get the desired results.

Bone and antler waste

Ian Riddler

A small quantity of bone and antler waste came from two locations on the site. Two fragments can be provenanced merely to Area 4, and two further pieces came from contexts within Area 6.

Three of the four pieces of waste stem from red deer antler. The various sizes of the material allow a minimum number of two antlers to be given for the assemblage. The waste includes a naturally-shed burr which has been shaved along one side of the beam, as well as two sections of tines. One of these has also been extensively pared. This technique of antler-working is visible also on the late Roman material from Portchester (Webster 1975, 224–5 and fig 120.124). It may relate to the facetting of tines to form handles of square or octagonal section.

The bone waste is limited to a single modified fragment of a cattle-sized midshaft, as well as a cattle-sized rib with a diagonal pattern cut out of the distal end of the bone, a sheep metacarpal with a bevelled proximal end, a sheep-sized long bone fragment which had been longitudinally split in half and sawn, and two cattle-sized long bone fragments which had bevelled ends and score marks on both sides where the bone had been smoothed.

PART 5: THE SMALL FINDS
SPATIAL DISTRIBUTION AND CHRONOLOGY

Ian Riddler and Quita Mould

The nature of the archaeological investigations and artefact retrieval at Ickham, described above, has resulted in the collection of a large metalwork assemblage most of which, unfortunately is of imprecise provenance. The general area of recovery (amidst the sixteen areas of the site) is known for 33.5 per cent, and for a further 49.9 per cent some stratigraphic relationship can be established. However, 17.6 per cent of the metal objects can only be regarded as unstratified.

A small number of Anglo-Saxon, medieval and post-medieval finds were recovered, along with fragments of cast iron likely to be associated with recent activity on the site. Allowing for these few exceptions, however, there is no reason to think that the vast majority of the objects found are not of Roman origin. In most cases, objects of post-medieval date can be readily identified and distinguished from those belonging to the Roman period. The exceptionally well-preserved condition of much of the material has allowed a high percentage of the metalwork to be identified and, consequently, a wide range of items has been recognised.

The publication of Brown's catalogue of late Roman metalwork, appended to Christopher Young's description of the watermills (Brown 1981, 37–8 and figs 4–5), highlighted the occurrence of a military or 'official government' presence at Ickham during the late fourth and early fifth century. It was not until the recent analysis of the large collection of metalwork began that the possibility of the presence of the military during the later second and third centuries (and indeed during the first century also) came to be recognised. The indication provided by the small finds needs to be seen in a broader context, however. Although there are military objects of early Roman date, neither the coins nor the ceramics support the idea of an early military presence at the site itself. There is little pottery of first-century date and hardly any samian, and coins of this period are under-represented in comparison with Canterbury and Richborough. There may have been a fort in the vicinity, but it was not close to this site.

The study of the small finds has also suggested that there was early Anglo-Saxon activity in the area, although the evidence is insufficient to allow the complete nature or the full extent of that activity to be judged (*see* pp 307–9).

In the following text the small finds assemblage is assessed principally in terms of its distribution, particularly for each of the areas of the site. The chronology of the objects has been highlighted above in Parts 3 and 4 in relation to the Ceramic Assemblages. These assemblages form the basis for the following text, which is supplemented by a brief consideration of the material which is provenanced only to areas or to a small number of contexts within those areas. Although much of this material was recovered from metal-detecting and salvage work, it is clear nonetheless that it adds to the overall impression of the spatial distribution of the material culture across the Roman and post-Roman periods.

Early Roman small finds

None of the small finds correspond with any of the ceramic assemblages of Phases 1 or 2. The only exception is a single type 1b nail from Assemblage 2. There are, however, objects of early Roman date from the site, extending to *c* AD 175. Those that can be securely dated are summarised below.

No	Object	Type	Category	Context
176	copper alloy brooch	Colchester	dress	Area 1,105
184	copper alloy brooch	Alesia Hod Hill	dress	Area 1,105
197	copper alloy brooch	Nauheim	dress	Area 1,105
936	stone quern	oscillatory	household	Area 1. 105/1
937	stone quern	oscillatory	household	Area 1, 107
4	iron projectile	Manning Iia	military	Area 1, Channel C
5	iron projectile	Manning Iia	military	Area 1, Channel C
815	glass bowl		household	Area 1, base of Channel C
1197	iron chain		miscellaneous	Area 3, 302
177	copper alloy brooch	Colchester	dress	Area 4, 406
182	copper alloy brooch	Late La Tene	dress	Area 4, extension
185	copper alloy brooch	Alesia Hod Hill	dress	Area 4, extension
198	iron brooch	Colchester type	dress	Area 4
818	glass urn	Isings 63–5	household	Area 4
819	glass bath flask	Isings 61	household	Area 4
867	glass beaker or bowl	Isings 34 or 44	household	Area 4
45	copper alloy phalera?	Bishop 16b	military	Area 5
47	copper alloy box hasp		military	Area 6, 610.2
860	glass jug or flagon	Isings 52	household	Area 6,610.5
178	copper alloy brooch	Colchester Derivative	dress	Area 7, 712
44	copper alloy phalera?		military	Area 7, 712
183	copper alloy brooch	Late La Tene	dress	Area 10, 1001
215	copper alloy pin	Type 1	dress	Area 10, 1001
181	iron brooch	Late La Tene	dress	Area 10, 1002
217	copper alloy pin	Type 3	dress	Area 10, 1004
1218	copper alloy pin	Type 3	dress	Area 10, 1005
180	copper alloy brooch	Late La Tene	dress	Area 10, 1008
280	glass bead	melon	dress	Area 12
1	iron spearhead		military	Area 14
41	copper alloy harness fitting		military	Area 14
517	leather shoe	openwork upper	personalia	'ditches'
216	silver pin	Type 2	dress	'unstratified'
179	copper alloy brooch	Late La Tene	dress	'unstratified'

Table 69. Early Roman objects from Ickham.

They indicate that this material is spread across most of the site, with concentrations in Areas 1, 4 and 10. Elements of the copper alloy material in context 105 may, however, have been gathered as scrap. It is notable that many of these objects occur in late Roman contexts.

Material ascribed to areas of the site

As noted above, many of the finds from the site are assigned only to area, rather than to specific contexts. With a number of the areas, including 2, 3, 5, 8, 9, 10 and 14, very few contexts can be identified. There is some interest, however, in examining the distribution of small finds across these areas, because this brings out broad patterns of activity.

Area 2

There are 118 coins from this area, all of which are late Roman issues (Fig 38). All of the small finds from this area are unstratified, with the exception of two fragments of lead, which may have come from a drain. There are twenty-seven metal objects (excluding nails), along with a quantity of lead alloy waste and four fragments from glass vessels. The datable material is all late Roman although the glass, which includes fragments of a bottle and a bowl, has been placed broadly between the first and third centuries. Three late Roman belt fittings (**97**, 136 and **147**) can be dated to the mid or late fourth century. A fragment of appliqué from a leather helmet is comparable with that decorating another of fifth-century date from Richborough, while a shell-shaped mount is comparable with others of third- or fourth-century date from the same site. A pewter flagon handle (**795**) and a fragment probably from the neck of a vessel (801) were found along with a quantity (470g) of offcut sheet and 17 per cent of the solidified molten lead alloy (2,470g) recorded from the excavations, suggesting that lead and probably pewter-working were being undertaken here. The possible doming punch (1258, *see* p 291) with a domed copper alloy head on an iron shank and fragment of offcut copper alloy also indicate the working of copper alloy in this area.

Area 3

The seventy coins from this area reflect the pattern seen in Area 2; all are late Roman issues (Fig 39). Ninety-one objects of metal, a small quantity of timber nails and lead alloy waste, a small fragment from a glass vessel and part of a triangular comb were retrieved from Area 3. All of the objects are unstratified within the area, with the exception of several from the 'stone floor', which are described below. A small group of late Roman belt fittings is represented, including a copper alloy buckle (**120**), a lozenge-shaped mount (132) and a heart-shaped strap-end (**143**). The D-shaped buckle (**120**) can be dated to the last three decades of the fourth century. A fragment of copper alloy sheet appliqué from a leather helmet (**32**) is similar to others of early fifth-century date from Richborough. The bracelets (332 and 353) and knives (628 and 637) are also of late Roman types. An ear-ring (**205**) is of a style frequently found in contexts of third-century date. The latest object may be the comb fragment (**556**), which is of fifth-century date, and is likely to date to after AD 450.

A small range of tools, domestic items and structural fittings also came from this area. A small quantity of items deriving from the working of iron, copper alloy and lead alloy are also represented; hammerscale was noted within the corrosion products of a small quantity of the iron items. The only context noted within Area 3 was the 'stone floor' which produced a small range of lead alloy items: a weight (572), a box fitting (932), caulking (1203), lead alloy sheet offcuts (265g) and solidified molten lead alloy (425g). They were accompanied by an iron latch-lifter (**672**).

Area 4

The coins from Area 4 again reflect the pattern seen in Areas 2 and 3, albeit with a greater sample of 1,782 coins. The earliest coins are from Issue Period 14 but there is little before Issue period 17 (Fig 35). There are a few early coins from contexts 407 and 408 (Fig 37) but too few to alter the general pattern. The majority of the metalwork and other small finds came from Area 4, chiefly as surface finds labelled as 'Area 4' or from the Area 4 extension (Ceramic Assemblages 11, 18 and 21). A discrepancy between those recorded as coming from the extension and labelled as such was noted, and has been described above (pp 114–5). A smaller quantity of material was recovered from pit 407 (context 407.2) (Ceramic Assemblage 19, p 110), and an occupation deposit (context 407.1 and 408) (Ceramic Assemblage 20, pp 110–12). In addition, a small quantity was found in ditch and pit fills: ditch fill 401. U contained an iron flax heckle tooth (1318) and a type 1b nail, ditch fill 411 contained a copper alloy key handle (702) and a type 1b nail. A pit (412) contained a type 3 nail, while pit (414) contained an iron ribbed strip possibly from a helmet or a simple handle, a type 1b nail and four shanks.

The small finds from the Area 4 'floor' represent a group of particular interest. A small but prestigious group of copper

alloy comprising the 'Celtic' pin (**247**), a military mount (51) likely to date to the second to third century, a buckle (**19**) and a single strand bracelet (**291**) of type 1 were recovered from this context, along with an iron finger-ring key (**706**) and a small quantity of lead alloy waste. Only the mount can be dated with any precision and although there is a likelihood that the pin is of late Roman date, it is unfortunate that there is no secure dating here.

Area 5

There are seventy-three coins from Area 5 and they include a small number belonging to Issue Period 3, with the remainder stemming from Issue Period 18 or later (Fig 40). The eighty-three objects (excluding nails) from Area 5 are mostly copper alloy and iron and there is also a quantity of lead alloy waste, including approximately 9 per cent of the total amount of spilt molten lead alloy to be recovered from the site as a whole. A small assemblage of copper alloy fittings from military horse harness and belt fittings includes a leaf-shaped pendant (**46**) and a circular mount (45), possibly a *phalera*, which may come from first-century cavalry harness, although a later date could also be argued. One of the glass beads (**264**) can also be placed in the first or second century, whilst another (**265**) cannot be closely dated. A fragment of a glass jug or flagon (862) is of first- or second-century date and there is also a part of a glass bottle (829). The general image therefore is that early Roman material is slightly better represented here than in Areas 2–4, but at the same time it represents a very small percentage of the overall assemblage.

The remaining objects can all be dated to the third century or later. A stud (80) and a heart-shaped pendant (**60**) are third-century types. An amphora-shaped strap-end (**153**), and a heart-shaped strap-end (**145**) are distinctly late Roman and the D-shaped buckle loop (**118**) can be more precisely dated to the last three decades of the fourth century. The crenellated (379), single strand (297) and serrated (382) bracelets are also of third- or fourth-century date, while a pewter spoon (**751**) is also a late type. Several of the glass beads (**273**, **275** and **278**) are of late fourth- or early fifth-century types. An iron penannular brooch (193) is one of the few items that can be placed into the very late Roman or sub-Roman period.

When taken altogether, there is a likelihood of occupation here in the early Roman period. Equally, the balance of material is heavily weighted towards the late Roman period, and fifth-century objects may also be represented.

Craftwork tools are limited to a spoon drill bit (1262). A partly-made needle of copper alloy (1297) and a piece of scrap iron with a possible handling rod attached, along with a very small quantity of offcut sheets of copper alloy and lead alloy, some folded (indicating deliberate scrap collection) represent metal-working.

Twenty-two of the objects are stratified and they occur in a small number of contexts, which include 'Ditch 2' (which, in strict terms, is adjacent to Area 5), a roadway or ditch and 'drainage gullies 1 and 3'. Most of these objects, unfortunately, are iron nails, although a hinge, a stylus and a fragment of a glass bottle are also represented. A pair of shears with a wide strap spring (**996**) and a large iron handle mount came from the roadway or ditch.

Area 7

The twenty-one coins from Area 7 include two of second-century date; the remainder are all late Roman issues. Ninety-two objects (excluding nails) and a quantity of lead alloy waste came from Area 7. A small number of finds occurred in individual ditches (702, 706 and 709). A slide key (690) was found in a depression (705). The timber-lined well (701), backfilled at the end of the fourth century or later (Ceramic Assemblage 23, p 117) contained a fragment of bar iron and a small quantity of spilt molten lead alloy (120g). The majority of the material, however, came from machine-disturbed contexts (710 and 712).

The small range of datable metalwork found indicates that the contexts have been mixed and, indeed, contaminated by later material. A rectangular buckle plate with repoussé dot decoration (105) can be dated to the second half of the fourth century. A ring (**423**) with a glass setting is a third-century type and a vulvate stud (**57**) is probably of third-century date, whilst a possible *phalera* (44) belongs to the early Roman period. A Colchester Derivative brooch (**178**) dates to no later than AD 60/65. A knife (**643**) is of a type found in Anglo-Saxon and Saxo-Norman contexts and a small number of items of later date were also noted.

Craft tools (a chisel, a wedge and a spatula), domestic items and structural metalwork were also found. A lead masonry cramp (1183) came from a stone-built structure not identified on the site, and probably located beyond it, perhaps in the vicinity of the villa. Commerce is indicated by two lead weights (**567** and 574) and three styli (593, 595 and 597). An entry in the original finds note book records that 'a bronze weight - as a human bust (1337)' was also found (context 712); this object has not been seen subsequently but is likely to be a steelyard weight in the form of a bust of Minerva (cf the two examples from the Roman fort at South Shields: Allason-Jones and Miket 1984, 174, 3.4723

for comparanda). Transport and animal husbandry are represented by a hipposandal (1043), a linchpin (1075) and a socket broken from a hooked blade (1015). A ditch (context 702) contained a multiple unit strip bracelet (362) and the handle of an iron ladle (**729**).

Area 8

No coins are recorded from Area 8. Only twenty-one objects were retrieved from the area and a significant number of these are of post-medieval or modern date. There are, however, several items which can be placed in the Roman period. Two separate contexts were identified and numbered 801 and 802; most of the objects come from the former context, which refers to the topsoil in this area.

A small hooked blade (599) with spirally-twisted handle with a ring terminal, probably used as a razor, was found in context 802. A shallow, oval frying pan (**723**) was recovered from the same context. The pan may have contained the remains of three pewter dishes (767–9), all of which were folded and are likely to be scrap awaiting melting down for re-use. The majority of these frying pans have been found as a component of late Roman hoards, along with a range of other vessels, including pewter (Manning 1985, 104) as, possibly, may have been the case here. A possible smithing hearth bottom (1332) was found in context 801.

Area 10

It is uncertain exactly what the divisions 1001–1006 actually represent but it would seem by the occurrence of 1002 layer 2, 3 and 4 that they were various subdivisions within Area 10. As a quantity of modern metalwork could be recognised within each context this supports the idea that they represent separate subdivisions rather than layers within the area. The various subdivisions are considered in turn.

Area 10 Surface. A small group of ironwork including the handle of a pair of blacksmith's tongs (**1239**), a thick awl probably used as a drift or punch in metal-working (1291) and iron scrap were found on the surface of Area 10. A small amount of post-Roman/modern material could also be identified.

Context 1001. The forty-nine coins from 1001 are centred on the early Roman period, as indicated in Fig 31, with just two fourth-century issues. Objects from this context include a pin (**215**) of early type, a boss (48) which may be a *phalera* of first-century date, an openwork mount (55) probably dating to the second or third century and a post-medieval candle snuffer (1338).

Context 1002. There are just four Roman coins from this context, all of second-century date. The context provided a spoon-probe (**548**) of copper alloy and a small quantity of ironwork, principally domestic and structural with iron-working debris, most notably slag, from the bottom of a smithing hearth (1330). The knife (**642**) although found in Roman contexts is of a type commonly found on Anglo-Saxon and early medieval sites.

Roman coins are recorded in small numbers also from contexts 1003, 1004, 1005 and 1006 and here again early issues dominate, with the clear exception of 1006, where fourteen of the twenty-two coins are of fourth-century date.

Area 12

No Roman coins are noted from this area and the copper alloy arm of an equipoise balance (**565**) and a melon bead (**280**) were the only items to be recovered here.

Area 14

The twenty-five coins from Area 14 are mostly of early Roman date, with just two fourth-century issues. Eighty-seven objects can be assigned to Area 14. None of them came from any specific contexts within the area. Objects of copper alloy include a brooch (**188**), two buckles (**53** and 107), two finger-rings (**424** and 434), a mount (52), a nail cleaner pendant (333) and a further pendant (**49**). Military items consist of two spearheads (**1** and 2), an artillery bolt head (9) and a harness fitting (41). As noted above, a number of these items are of early Roman date, and comparatively few are late Roman, echoing the distribution provided by the coins. A fragment of a glass vessel (824) comes from an early Roman bottle of Isings type 50–1. In contrast, the lower bow and foot of a crossbow brooch (**188**) dates to the fourth century and a rectangular belt plate (107) can be placed in the second half of the fourth century. A knife (609) is of a type unlikely to date later than the end of the second century, whilst a copper alloy spoon (**760**) is not an early type. A small quantity of modern iron was also noted.

A range of craft tools were found, including a wide chisel (1248), a drill bit (**1261**) and a heavy awl or punch (**1287**). A small blade from a possible pair of metal snips (1259) was also recovered. Transport is indicated by the recovery of a hipposandal fragment (1049) and a bridle bit link (1060). A small quantity of lead alloy waste and iron slag was also recovered and a small quantity of iron appears to be associated with smithing activity, including bar iron, iron

rod, and a fragment of scrap iron with a handling rod. Two bars of iron set in burnt clay were also found in Area 14.

A few of the other items reflect the presence of a mill. They include two hinges and three keys (**688** and 700 and 701) as well as one of the angular collars (1087). It has been suggested above that these relate in some way to the working mechanism of Mill 1. The remaining seven collars (**1079**, 1080–5) came from the adjacent Area 10 although, intriguingly, there is also a single example from context 710 in Area 7 (1086).

Area 16

Only a few objects can be placed with certainty in Area 16, although it is possible that the original number was somewhat higher. No coins are recorded from this area. The assemblage is limited to a copper alloy handle (1339), an iron buckle loop (20), two keys (685 and 692), a chisel (1253) and a small quantity of lead alloy offcuts and sheet.

The chisel and some of the lead alloy waste are described on their original labels as coming from '16/Ditches'. The nature and precise location of these ditches is not known. It has already been noted that many of the leather shoes come from the 'Ditches'. The only ditches known on the site are those which accompany the road, the set to the east which form part of the field system to the north of the road, and those from Area 16. We have no records of objects from the ditch system of Area 3, much of which was not excavated. The leather shoes may, therefore, have come from the ditches of Area 16.

Early Anglo-Saxon settlement

The majority of the ceramics and small finds from Ickham are of late Roman date. The ceramics extend into the fifth century, if not appreciably beyond. Of particular note in respect of the post-Roman pottery are Ceramic Assemblages 18 and 26. Assemblage 18 provided a single sherd of a cooking pot in an early Anglo-Saxon fabric (pp 109–10). Assemblage 26, a dark grey silt lying over 610.3 and 610.4, included three sherds of a hand-made cooking pot in a fabric which is also thought to be early Anglo-Saxon in date (*see* p 118).

In addition, a hand-made jar from Area 4 'Section 5' resembles so-called 'Jutish' pottery of the type recovered from east of the Marlowe Theatre in Canterbury. The term 'Jutish' is no longer an appropriate description and it is better defined as an early Anglo-Saxon fabric with applied decoration (Blockley *et al* 1995, 824). It occurs in small quantities in Canterbury and some of those sherds utilise linear decorative schemes similar to that seen here (Blockley *et al* 1995, 864 and fig 372). Decorated sherds of this type have also been found outside Canterbury at Bifrons and Wingham, and they are likely to span a reasonable part of the early Anglo-Saxon period. It would be unwise to date them too early on the basis of very little evidence, and a fifth- to mid sixth-century date is preferred here (Blockley *et al* 1995, 869–70). The sherds from Wingham have been briefly noted, although they have yet to be published (Hawkes 1969, 187; Jenkins 1965, lix; 1967, lx).

Five sherds of early Anglo-Saxon pottery may not amount to a great deal but they do at least signify later, post-Roman occupation on this site. Each of the sherds stems from a cooking pot or a jar and is domestic in origin. There is no suggestion that any of the ceramics stem from a cemetery context. The likelihood of early Anglo-Saxon settlement on the site is strengthened by a consideration of the post-Roman objects. They are largely of a domestic nature and they include keys, knives and a fragmentary comb.

The comb (**556**) can be assigned to Böhme's type C and it is a form that belongs essentially to the fifth century (Riddler forthcoming a). Triangular combs have rarely been found in east Kent and they are much more common north of the Thames. Examples of Böhme type D combs, most of which probably belong to the later fourth century, are known from St Mary Cray and Eccles, but not from any sites further to the east. A case for a triangular comb has, however, come from Stour Street, Canterbury (unpublished).

The three keys are all made of iron, with suspension loops at one end and bits of an L or T shape. One example of a lift key (**684**) has a simple L-shaped bit running in a perpendicular plane to the suspension loop. It is a small key, extending to just 63mm in length. Within east Kent cemeteries, keys with simple L-shaped bits tend to be large and the wards are usually turned back towards the suspension loop (Evison 1987, 116; Hawkes 1973, fig 56). Smaller fragments have also been found, however. The Ickham example may be incomplete and its size suggests that it is likely to have been used to lock a casket, rather than a door. It seems to be too slender to be of Roman date.

A simple, L-shaped key from context 408 (**699**) is 125mm in length and lies within the range established for the Buckland cemetery of 100–140mm (Evison 1987, 116). It is similar to examples from that cemetery and is certainly of early Anglo-Saxon date (*ibid*, figs 32 and 44). A further key (**678**) has a T-shaped bit of a recognisable Anglo-Saxon form.

The knife of type 3.4 (**641**) has a curved back with a distinct shoulder above the tang and a straight blade edge, which is worn from use. It corresponds with Evison's type 4, which echoes Böhner's type C and is essentially a form of seventh-century and later date, extending to the Conquest (Evison 1987, 115; Goodall 1990, 850–1; Ottaway 1992, 572; Riddler 2001, 232). Type 4 knives are very similar in form to those of Type 1, the essential difference lying in the presence either of a straight blade edge, or a blade that curves towards the point. The point is missing on this knife but it is assumed that the blade edge was straight. The reconstructed length of the knife blade is 103mm, which places it within Härke's type 2, the middle group of knife sizes (Härke 1992, tab 5). Its tang is of almost the same length as the blade.

A second knife (638) is also likely to be of seventh-century or later date. It has an angled back, allowing it to be assigned to Evison type 5 (Evison 1987, 115). Two incised lines run parallel with the back of the blade, towards its defining angle. The blade was originally 85mm in length, allowing it to be placed within Härke's type 1. Knives of this type are common in Kent from the seventh century onwards, and they continue in use up to the Norman Conquest (Riddler 2001, 232). Over half of the knives from Middle Saxon Canterbury are of this form, and the type was also the most numerous at the Buckland Anglo-Saxon cemetery in Dover (Blockley *et al* 1995, 1077; Evison 1987, 115).

A third knife (643) belongs to Evison's type 1, for which both the back and the cutting edge curve towards the point. The type cannot be closely dated, although this example undoubtedly belongs to the Anglo-Saxon period.

No	Object	Type	Context
556	antler comb	Bohme C	Area 3
638	iron knife	Mould 3.3	Area 1, Channel C
641	iron knife	Mould 3.4	Area 1, 115
643	iron knife	Mould 3.5	Area 7, 712
678	iron key	T-shaped	Area 4, extension
684	iron key	L-shaped	Area 4
699	iron key	H-shaped	Area 4, 408

Table 70. Early Anglo-Saxon objects from Ickham.

The major early Anglo-Saxon sites of southern and eastern England are notable for the presence of considerable numbers of objects, many of which come from the backfills of sunken-featured buildings (West 1985; Hamerow 1993). This is not generally the case in rural east Kent however, where traces of early Anglo-Saxon settlement are now emerging to complement discoveries made both within Canterbury itself and to the west of the Medway (Blockley *et al* 1995, 280–334; Tyler 1992, 7981). Reasonable quantities of objects have come from some of the early Anglo-Saxon structures in Canterbury and from Manston Road at Ramsgate (Hutchinson and Andrews forthcoming). Elsewhere, however, at Harrietsham, Wainscott and Whitfield, few objects of early Anglo-Saxon date were recovered, even from the sunken-featured buildings. Moreover, settlement features of this date can be widely dispersed across a landscape.

This raises the distinct possibility that early Anglo-Saxon settlement succeeded the late Roman landscape at Ickham. The nature of that settlement is unclear, given that there are no structures of this date with which to associate the objects. The objects themselves are well-dispersed across the site, occurring in association with Mills 2, 3 and 4 as well as in Area 4 (where all of the post-Roman keys were found) and further to the east in context 712. There is an interesting reflection of the range of objects discovered at the nearby villa at Wingham, most of which were also of a domestic nature (Jenkins 1967).

Early Anglo-Saxon settlements lie near to cemeteries and stray finds of brooches from both the villa at Ickham and at Preston (the latter unpublished), as well as a burial at Stodmarsh, hint at the presence of cemeteries in this area (Hawkes 1982, fig 28; 1987, 3–6; Leigh 1984, 35). A cemetery at Wingham lies within this area, as do discoveries at Wickhambreux (Coyningham 1844). In general terms, this area is richly endowed with early Anglo-Saxon remains. A contrast can be drawn between the presence of domestic implements on this site and that of two brooches from the villa, one of which has been published. It may well be, therefore, that an early Anglo-Saxon settlement lay within the general area of the mills, close to the river, and an accompanying cemetery was located on higher ground at the villa, possibly echoing the situation to be seen at Eccles, where the cemetery has been found, but not the nearby settlement, and also the arrangement at Wingham, where traces of both a settlement and a cemetery are known (Shaw 1994).

PART 6: THE ENVIRONMENTAL MATERIAL

Animal bone

Maeve Palmer and Adrienne Powell

Animal bone was recovered from Areas 1, 4, 6 and 7. Almost half of the recorded assemblage came from contexts of late Roman date (Table 71), with 45 per cent identifiable to species. A further, similar, proportion came from immediately post-Roman contexts, primarily gravels sealing the late Roman fills of the mill channels, with 42 per cent identifiable to species. Pottery from these gravels is Roman in date. These contexts are likely to be flooding deposits and hence the pottery is probably redeposited material (*see* p 119). The animal bone may also be reworked Roman material, with the slightly greater proportion of horse and cattle in this group (78 per cent of the major species, compared with 65 per cent in the Roman) possibly reflecting post-depositional sorting and preferential removal of bones of the smaller animals. However, given the presence of Anglo-Saxon finds in the artefact assemblage it cannot be assumed that later material is absent, therefore the post-Roman material is not discussed beyond quantification in Tables 71 and 74.

Material without a feature description or context number was treated as unstratified and excluded from the assemblage. This included eighty-one bones from 'Area 4', possibly incorporating material from the timber-lined pit (feature 335) formerly labelled as a 'shrine', where there may have been a partial cattle skeleton. However, on examination none of the cattle elements were found to articulate. Only seven fragments of bone were labelled as from the 'shrine', two are sheep and five are unidentifiable.

The bone was generally in good condition, although a number of the waterlogged contexts produced bone with recent breakages and in a fragile condition. Most bones display scratch marks on the cortex which have been interpreted as marks caused by gravel, as they are not from butchery. The bone was hand retrieved, and there is a bias in favour of long bones. There were large numbers of loose horse and cattle teeth and very few loose teeth of smaller animals such as sheep and pig. Table 74 shows loose teeth as a percentage of loose teeth plus jaws: the greater proportion of loose teeth in the post-Roman material is consistent with attrition from water movement. Bones from smaller animals and birds are present in low numbers only. This bias also has

Species	Roman		Post-Roman		Total	
	no	%	no	%	no	%
Horse	44	15.60	59	22.78	103	19.04
Cattle	133	47.16	140	54.05	273	50.46
Sheep	82	29.08	38	14.67	120	22.18
Pig	14	4.96	19	7.34	33	6.10
Dog	5	1.77	1	0.39	6	1.11
Red deer	0		1	0.39	1	0.18
Other	4	1.42	1	0.39	5	0.92
Cattle-sized	86		119		205	
Sheep-sized	44		71		115	
Unidentified	215		168		383	
Total	627		617		1244	

Other:

Whale: 1

Fox: 1

Domestic fowl: 2 (1 Roman, 1 Post-Roman)

Goose: 1

Table 71. Number of identified specimens (NISP).

Species	Gnawed	Surface	Heavy	Rodent	Total
Cattle	4	2	6	1	13
Sheep	8		4		12
Pig					0
Horse	2		1		3
Unidentified	8		2		10
Total	22	2	13	1	38

Table 72. Distribution of gnawing damage.

Species	Chop	Knife	Both	Worked	Sawn	Total
Cattle	32	2	2			36
Sheep	16	3	2	1		22
Pig	5		1			6
Horse	2					2
Whale	1					1
Unidentified	70	6	7	4	3	90
Total	126	11	12	5	3	157

Table 73. Distribution of butchery marks.

Species	Roman	Post-Roman	Total (no)
Horse	88.89	97.44	48
Cattle	42.86	75.00	76
Sheep	50.00	50.00	28
Pig	33.33	100.00	9
Dog			3
Total	49.21	83.17	164

Table 74. Loose teeth as a percentage of loose teeth and jaws.

Element	Horse	Cattle	Sheep	Pig	Total
Horn core		2			2
Skull	2	2		1	5
Mandible	1	7	10	1	19
Atlas	1	1	1		3
Axis		1			1
Scapula	2	8	4	2	16
Humerus	1	8	4	2	15
Radius	2	11	8		21
Ulna	1	2	1		4
Pelvis	4	5	3	1	13
Femur	1	4	2		7
Tibia	4	4	11	3	22
Astragalus		4			4
Calcaneus		4	3	1	8
Tarsals		1			1
Metacarpal	1	16	11		28
Metatarsal	1	9	6		16
Phalanx I	2	3	1		6
Phalanx II	2	4			6
Phalanx III	1	1			2
Total	26	97	65	11	199
%	13.07	48.74	32.66	5.53	
MNI	2	9	10	2	23
%	8.70	39.13	43.48	8.70	

Table 75. Minimum number of elements for the main species.

Period	Context	R/L	Measurement	mm
Late fourth century	407	L	Thickness below M1	11.2
			Height behind M1	23.1
	107/2	L	Length P1 to P4	40.1
			Length P2 to P4	35.5
			Length carnassial	23.4
			Thickness below M1	12.6
			Height behind M1	26.0
			Height between P2 & P3	18.6

Table 76. Dog measurements: mandibular.

to be taken into account when discussing the significance of animals at the site.

There is only one instance of burnt bone in the assemblage. The majority of gnawing (Table 72) is canid and was only visible on 6 per cent of the bone. In terms of distribution by species, cattle bones were gnawed the most and horse bones the least. The type of gnawing varied from surface gnawing to heavy gnawing which resulted in chewed-off epiphyses. There is one example of rodent gnawing on a cattle bone. There is a high incidence of butchery (25 per cent) in the assemblage and it was seen on all the main species, mostly in the form of chop marks (Table 73).

Representation of the main domestic mammals

Sheep/goat bones have been classed as sheep for the purposes of this report. Although the presence of goat cannot be ruled out, no bones were identified (Boessneck 1969). Ribs and

Species	P4	M1	M2	M3	Age
Cattle				d	30–36 months
				g	adult
	f	l	k	g	adult
			k		adult
	k		j	g	adult
Sheep	(g)				2–24 months
	(h)				2–24 months
	(g)	e	c	C	12–24 months
		f	c	C	12–24 months
	g	h	f	e	36–48 months
	g	h	g	e	36–48 months
		j	g	f	36–48 months

Table 77. Tooth wear in cattle and sheep.

Age at fusion	Element	Fused	Unfused	Total
3–4 months	Humerus d	1		1
3–4 months	Radius p	2		2
5 months	Scapula	2		2
7–10 months	Phalanx 1	1		1
15–20 months	Tibia d	5	2	7
20–24 months	Metacarpal d	4	1	5
36 months	Calcaneus	3		3
36 months	Femur p			0
42 months	Humerus p			0
42 months	Femur d		1	1
	Total	18	4	22

Table 79. Sheep fusion data.

Age at Fusion	Element	Fused	Unfused	Total
7–10 months	Scapula	8		8
12–15 months	Radius p	9	1	10
15–20 months	Humerus d	4	1	5
15–20 months	Phalanx II	4		4
20–24 months	Phalanx I	3		3
24–30 months	Tibia d	2		2
24–30 months	Metapodial d	14	6	20
36 months	Femur p		1	1
36 months	Calcaneus	2		2
42 months	Femur d		1	1
42 months	Ulna p	1		1
42–48 months	Radius d	4	3	7
42–48 months	Humerus p	2		2
48 months	Tibia p		1	1
	Total	53	14	67

Table 78. Cattle fusion data.

Age at fusion	Element	Fused	Unfused	Total
9–12 months	Scapula	2		2
10–12 months	Phalanx II	2		2
12–15 months	Phalanx I	2		2
15 months	Metacarpal d	1		1
15 months	Metatarsal d	1		1
15–18 months	Humerus d	1		1
15–18 months	Radius p	2		2
24 months	Tibia d	3		3
36–42 months	Femur p	1		1
42 months	Radius d	2		2
42 months	Ulna p	1		1
42 months	Femur d	1		1
42 months	Tibia p	2		2
	Total	21	0	21

Table 80. Horse fusion data.

vertebrae were identified to species where possible and all unidentified long bone fragments were classed as cattle- or sheep-sized.

The minimum number of elements (MNE) was calculated for the main domesticates (Table 75) following the zone method of Serjeantson (1991). The minimum number of individuals (MNI) for each species was derived from the sum of the most frequently occurring zone, taking symmetry into account.

The MNE results for the four main species show that cattle bones are the most common (49 per cent). Sheep (33 per cent) and horse (13 per cent) remains are present in smaller numbers and pig remains comprise only 6 per cent of the main species. The decrease in the frequency of horse, compared with the number of identified specimens (NISP), reflects the exclusion of loose teeth from the MNE figures.

In terms of MNIs, sheep and pig increase in relative frequency, particularly the former which match cattle using this method. This is partially a result of the retrieval bias against small bones (carpals, tarsals and phalanges) which affects sheep and pigs more than horse and cattle and causes a misleading under-representation of these species in both the NISP and MNI figures.

Bone	Measurement	Ickham	ABMAP		
			Range	Mean	No
Scapula	GLP	61.8, 75.9	54.9–82.3	66.4	28
	BG	45.9, 50.7	37.6–56	44.9	47
	LG	53.9, 59.3	49.3–69.4	56.5	27
Humerus	GLC	255.1	226.3–300	257.2	7
	Bd	65.6, 81.3, 85.4	61–94.7	78.4	18
	BT	63.6, 76.1	50.6–86.1	70.9	24
	HT	37.1, 41.3, 46.1	37.5–55.5	44.2	6
Radius	GL	246	236–298	266.3	16
	BFp	62.1, 64.7, 76.1	59.7–83	69.4	38
Tibia	Dd	46.8	39–56	46.1	29
	Bd	60.2	43.3–71.8	58.8	88
Metacarpal	GL	180.0, 180.3, 186.0, 186.0, 194.0, 200.0	175.2–228	192.01	61
	Dp	29.2, 29.5, 29.6, 30.3, 31.6, 32.2, 35.3			
	Bp	50.0, 50.2, 50.4, 53.6, 56.6, 56.7, 59.3	45.3–65.1	54.4	105
	SD	27.1, 28.4, 30.0, 33.0, 34.0, 34.5			
	Dd	24.5, 25.4, 27.5, 27.6, 27.6, 28.3, 29.2, 31.3			
	Bd	50.1, 51.0, 51.7, 53.6, 53.7, 55.9, 56.3, 59.3, 61.8,	46–70.3	56.5	108
Metatarsal	GL	199.0, 210.5, 222.9	198–245	217.2	60
	Dp	35.5, 40.1, 40.3, 44.3, 48.3			
	Bp	42.8, 43.3, 44.3, 44.5, 49.0	36.5–52.5	44	77
	SD	24.8, 24.8, 29.9			
	Dd	27.6, 27.8, 42.2			
	Bd	41.6, 49.2, 50.3, 58.0	43.6–69	52.2	98
Calcaneum	GL	138.12	113.8–140.4	123.81	11

Table 81. Measurements of cattle bones.

The frequency of skeletal elements suggests that entire carcasses were present originally for all four main species. The body part distribution for the two best represented species, cattle and sheep, are similar, allowing for normal taphonomic effects of preservation and recovery. Skull fragments are poorly represented, although there are two partial horse skulls (Mill 4 channel and occupation silts) and a partial cattle skull ('wood-lined pit'). Vertebrae also are not represented in large numbers.

Other species

The other species occur in much smaller numbers, mostly less than 1 per cent of the total identifiable fragment count. All of the canine material is from the late Roman period, with the exception of an unfused proximal femur of an animal less than about 18 months, from context 128 (Ceramic Assemblage 4, pp 95–6). Also, this earlier specimen is the only example of post-cranial material, all the later remains being mandibular, with a single maxillary fragment with worn teeth from context 610.4 (Ceramic Assemblage 25, p 118).

The measurements from the late fourth-century dog mandibles are given in Table 76. The dog represented in context 407 (Ceramic Assemblage 19, p 110) is probably of labrador build and has dental infection in the alveoli of the third premolar and first molar. The mandible from context 107.2 (Ceramic Assemblage 13, pp 107–9) is of a heavily-built dog, the size and shape of the jaw being similar to that of a modern Rotweiller.

An almost complete skull was recovered from context 709, provisionally dated to the third to fourth century. The skull is very similar to that of a medium-sized modern Jack Russell terrier.

Other species present are fox (*Vulpes vulpes*), domestic fowl (*Gallus gallus*) and goose (*Anser* sp), with one bone occurring from each species. All are commonly recorded from other contemporary sites.

The most unusual bone in the assemblage was a piece of rib from a large whale from context 129, an irregular cut to

Species	Element	Height (mm)
Cattle	Humerus	1216.8
	Radius	1057.8
	Metacarpal	1114.2, 1116.1, 1151.3, 1151.3, 1200.9, 1238
	Metatarsal	1084.6, 1147.2, 1214.8
Sheep	Metacarpal	600.3, 621.5
	Calcaneus	592.8, 612.2

Table 82. Withers heights.

the east of Mill 1. The rib is broken at both ends but measures 560mm along the outer curve, with a greatest breadth of 82mm and a greatest thickness of 55mm. There is a small area of charring at one end, and a shallow slice 83.6mm in length chopped along one edge. It is probable that this bone was from a beached whale but this is an unusual find for south-eastern Britain, as the larger cetaceans do not normally travel this far south along the east coast (Evans 1991). The rib may have been brought from the Kentish coast several kilometres away, but could have come from even further afield. It was most likely intended for artefact manufacture, and the slice may be evidence of an early stage of this or of filleting meat from a stranded carcass. Smaller fragments of a contemporary whale are known from Capel-le-Ferne, near Dover, and there are several other recorded instances of whale bone in Roman contexts from Sussex and East Anglia (Riddler 2006, 258).

Ageing and sexing

Tooth wear was recorded after Grant (1982) and wear stages and respective ages were applied using Halstead (1985) for cattle, Payne (1973) for sheep and O'Connor (1988) for pig. The horse teeth were aged using Levine's (1982) measurements of crown heights for adult cheek teeth. Timing for epiphyseal closure was taken from Getty (1975). There were no sexed pelves.

There is little dental information for cattle. Table 77 shows the presence of adult but not elderly animals, with only one mandible from a younger animal of 2½ to 3 years in age. Most of the ageable bones were fused including some late-fusing elements, indicating animals reaching full adulthood (Table 78). However, the fusion evidence also suggests that more sub-adults were slaughtered than the dental evidence indicates, and that at least some younger juveniles were killed, although not in sufficient numbers to indicate stock breeding at the site. The overall pattern suggested is one where animals were brought in for consumption either as sub-adult culls or adults which had served as dairy or traction animals.

The aged sheep mandibles show the presence of animals between 1 and 4 years of age. Two loose deciduous premolars probably fall within the lower end of this range. The fusion data corroborate the dental ageing insofar as the few unfused bones suggest the same range in ages at slaughter and there is no evidence for animals older than four years (Table 79).

Bone	Measurement	Ickham	ABMAP		
			Range	Mean	No
Scapula	GLP	25.5, 33.4	25.8–34	30.2	20
	BG	14.9, 21.7	16.2–21.4	18.9	24
	LG	29.1	20.9–25.3	23.9	12
Radius	BFp	25.18	23.6–30.1	27.3	38
Tibia	Dd	17.0, 17.1, 19.8			
	Bd	21.4, 23.9, 24.9	23.8–25.7	24.7	3
Metacarpal	GL	123.4, 127.1	108.3–128.3	118.3	10
	Dp	12.3, 14.3, 14.8, 15.2, 16.3			
	Bp	20.3, 20.6, 21.0, 21.1, 21.4, 21.7	17.8–25.3	21.5	61
	SD	11.2, 12.9			
	Dd	13.7, 13.8, 15.3, 16.0			
	Bd	23.0, 23.2, 23.4, 24.2	22.4–27.8	23.9	16
Metatarsal	Dp	18.5, 18.9, 22.0			
	Bp	18.0, 19.0, 23.9	16.9–22.5	19	49
Calcaneum	GL	52.0, 53.7	49.3–59.4	54.2	12

Table 83. Measurements of sheep bones.

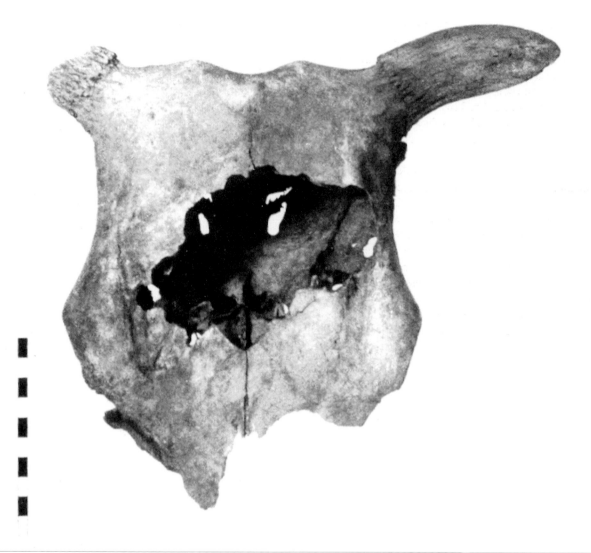

Pl XXV. Detail of pole-axed ox skull. Scale 20cm.

Ageing evidence for pigs was restricted to one complete mandible from an adult female (Schmid 1972), and a fused distal humerus.

There is no evidence in the Roman material for the presence of juvenile horses at Ickham. Crown height measurements taken on loose maxillary teeth produced six age estimates: two of 5½ to 8 years in age, one of 6 to 7¾ years, which may be from the same individual as one of the 5½ to 8 years teeth, one 17 to 18 years old, one greater than 14 years old and one greater than 15 years old. All ageable bones were fused (Table 80). Hence the evidence points to animals of working age, although the three older crown height estimates may have come from individuals at or near the end of their useful working lives.

Butchery

The butchery at Ickham is characterised by the use of heavy chopping implements, with the occasional use of a knife. The presence of large numbers of both cattle- and sheep-sized long bone fragments with chop marks could indicate that the bones were being split for marrow.

The long bones of cattle showed evidence of heavy butchery: epiphyses had been chopped off, probably from the cutting up of limbs into joints of meat, and a number of bones were split lengthways, which could indicate either the removal of marrow or an early stage of bone-working. The former option is the more likely. Mandibles also show evidence of butchery, including both disarticulation from the skull and filleting. The low number of vertebrae present means that there is no evidence of how the trunk was divided. The partial cattle skull had been pole-axed (Pl XXV).

Most of the butchery evidence on sheep bones suggests jointing and division of the carcass, although a few midshaft chop marks on long bones could also indicate marrow extraction and a knife mark on a calcaneus could be evidence of skinning. The only worked piece identified to species was a sheep metacarpal, from the timber-lined pit 335, with the proximal articulation removed, possibly by sawing, although the cut end may have been polished, and there are two small areas of polish on the dorsal and lateral surfaces, possibly through use.

The small number of pig bones means that there is not much evidence for the butchery of pig. A scapula had the epiphysis chopped off and another had cut marks around the glenoid. The butchery on long bones was similar to that

seen in sheep; they were either chopped mid-shaft or an epiphysis was removed.

The Roman contexts produced two butchered horse bones: a cranially chopped atlas, from removal of the head at an early stage of carcass treatment, and a pelvis chopped at the acetabulum. The latter, although indicating jointing of a carcass, should not necessarily be interpreted as evidence for human consumption of horses.

Pathology

A horse M^1 or M^2 displayed uneven wear with the distal margin of the crown worn down almost to the root, 13.7 mm less than the mesial crown height. The tooth lies too far back in the jaw for the unevenness to be related to bit wear and is most likely to be age related since irregular tooth wear is commonly seen in old horses (Miles and Grigson 1990) and the crown height suggests an age greater than 14 years. No corresponding lower teeth were observed.

There are several examples of pathological sheep mandibles. In one mandible the P_3 was displaced laterally in the tooth row. This may have caused problems for

Bone	Measurement	Ickham	ABMAP		
			Range	Mean	No
Scapula	BG	43.2, 46.8	46.6–59.4	54.3	6
	LG	52.9	38.3–48.5	44.6	7
Radius	GL	302.0, 341.0	298–439	333.9	10
	BFp	67.6, 79.6	64.6–75.5	70.55	8
Femur	GLC	331			
Tibia	GL	331.5, 348.0	306–355	331.8	5
	Dd	39.7, 43.0, 43.2	35–48.1	41.4	16
	Bd	65.2, 68.7, 71.4	57.7–77	65.7	16
Metacarpal	GL	202.9	204–250	221.63	6
	GLl	197.8			
	Bp	46.2	43.4–52.3	46.9	12
	SD	31.3	29.5–33.1	31.62	5
	Dd	36.8			
	Bd	46.7	28–51.1	45.8	11
Metatarsal	GL	263.3	232.3–294	263.2	16
	GLl	257			
	Dp	41.8			
	Bp	48.1	41.8–49	46.5	5
	SD	29.8			
	Dd	36.9			
	Bd	48.8	40.5–53.8	47.3	17

Table 84. Measurements of horse bones.

the animal when eating as the tooth would not provide a grinding surface for the occluding upper teeth. Another mandible had a congenital absence of the second premolar. The M_3 in a third mandible was rotated slightly buccally in the socket, and this mandible also exhibited an accessory foramen externally below the P_2, a congenital trait observed occasionally in archaeological material. A further mandible had an abscess below M_3.

There are two cattle lower third molars in which the distal column of the tooth is absent or reduced. This has been noted frequently in cattle, particularly at Iron Age and Roman sites (for example, Maltby 1979) and is regarded as an inherited trait. As a consequence the occluding upper third molar will be unevenly worn with the distal portion forming a downward-projecting hook, seen in one example from Ickham.

Two traumatic lesions were seen in sheep remains: an ossified haematoma on the anterior face of a metatarsal is quite probably the result of a blow, and a sheep-sized rib exhibited a healed fracture. Arthropathic conditions were noted in one specimen only, a cattle first phalanx with articular extension of the proximal surface and early periarticular exostosis.

Measurements

Measurements were taken following Driesch (1976) and are compared to material from contemporary sites in southern England contained in the Animal Bone Metrical Archive Project (ABMAP http:\ads.ahds.ac.uk/catalogue/specColl/abmap/index.cfm).

Although the assemblage is small a large number of cattle measurements were taken (Table 81). The cattle fall within the range of animals from contemporary sites, although largely grouping around the mean and smaller end of the distributions for various elements, and there are few large animals. Withers heights, calculated using the factors of Matolcsi (Driesch and Boessneck 1974) are shown in Table 82.

There were fewer measurements for sheep than cattle, but it seems they were more variable in size when compared with contemporary livestock (Table 83) since there are a few bones outside the range of the ABMAP data at both extremes.

The Roman assemblage produced just two measurable pig bones, the M_3s from the adult mandible, which were smaller (left: L = 28.5mm, Br = 14.9mm; right: L = 28.9mm, Br = 14.3mm) than the few comparative specimens available.

There were a large number of measurements on the horse bones (Table 84) and variation in size was obvious prior to measurement. There were two relatively large bones in comparison with the contemporary data, but most of the measurements group around the mean and the lower end of the range, and the greatest lengths of the long bones fall into Vitt's (Driesch and Boessneck 1974) average, small average and small groups. Some of the small material could have come from donkeys, but where Davis' criteria could be applied (Davis 1987) all the teeth were identified as horse.

Discussion

Caution must be used in interpreting an assemblage of this size. However, the remains are consistent with the industrial nature of the site suggested by the structural evidence insofar as there is no evidence for the breeding of any of the main domesticates on site. The horses were adults, animals of working age as well as animals at the end of their useful lives. The age profiles of the sheep and cattle, with no very young or old individuals, suggest animals brought in to supply meat, possibly from nearby rural communities or the villas at Wingham and Ickham. Some of the older ones could have provided a season or two of work (traction or dairying or wool production) before being culled and the presence of most parts of the skeleton from the main species indicates that the animals were brought to the site on the hoof.

Human bone

Ian Riddler [41]

At least six human burials were recorded at Ickham, though sadly it has proved extremely difficult to locate them in relationship to other features on the site.

One was a crouched inhumation (Burial A), of which only a crude plan of the skeleton *in situ* survives (Fig 28). This appeared to be largely intact, lying on its left side with its knees drawn up to its chest. No record of the grave cut or its location on the site exists in the archive, and the skeleton itself is lost.

Burial 903 was of a female, probably in her thirties. The bones were poorly preserved, soft, wet and very fragmentary. No measurements could be taken of either skull or long bones. Another skeleton was recorded (Burial 905), a male

---

41. Compiled from the archive reports of Justine Bayley, Carole Keepax and John Eley.

aged between 30 and 40 years. This specimen was quite well preserved, but the skull was warped and broken. There was slight to medium calculus deposit on most of the teeth. Some also showed very slight hypoplasia and there were signs of slight peridontal disease. There were also signs of degenerative joint disease (osteo-arthritis), especially in the lumbar and cervical regions of the spine. There are no plans of these two skeletons in the archive, nor is their location on site known. They were examined by Justine Bayley and Carole Keepax of the Ancient Monuments Laboratory (Bayley and Keepax 1974).

A further burial, labelled Burial B, was examined by John Eley in 1975. Its skull had been damaged *post mortem*; the right zygomatic arch, malar bone and superior maxillary area were removed, probably by site machinery. However, enough remained to calculate age by cranial sutures to about 45/50 years. The rest of the skeleton seems well preserved, with signs of osteo-arthritis on the vertebrae, becoming more pronounced in the lumbar area. Only a crude plan of the skeleton *in situ* survives, and there is no plan of the grave or its location on site. A photograph shows the skeleton lying partially on its right side, slightly flexed at the waist, with both hands on the right hand side of the body (Fig 27, Pl XIX, p 68).

One more burial is recorded, Burial C, a supine inhumation aligned east–west with its head removed by machine disturbance of the western end of the grave. Its hands were crossed at the waist, the legs straight. A sketch of this grave is in the archive, which shows the grave truncated to west and north by quarrying. John Eley was of the opinion that the body was that of an elderly male in an advanced arthritic state. Unfortunately this grave cannot be located on the site plan.

Found with this skeleton, but probably not from the same grave were six fragments of an infant's skull, a left femur without epiphysis about 77mm long, a left tibia 64mm long and a left fibula 60mm long. It was not possible to estimate the sex of this infant as there was so little remaining, but the lengths of the long bones are consistent with its being newborn.

PART 7: ICKHAM AND EAST KENT IN THE LATE ROMAN PERIOD

Paul Bennett [42]

Introduction

In an interim report on the site Christopher Young put forward an interesting hypothesis for the existence of an official depot at Ickham supplying flour and metalwork to local units of the Saxon Shore (Young 1981). His case was based on the close proximity of a building producing fourth-century official lead seals (Hassall and Tomlin 1979, 350–3), the quantity of military fittings identified amongst the finds, the presence of at least two mills (then a type of structure rarely identified in Roman Britain) and the substantial collection of metal artefacts which suggested that metal-working was taking place at the site. Although the official seals remain an unusual and enigmatic discovery (Still 1994), the other elements of the hypothesis are not as compelling as they were when the article was first published. The mills (re-analysis now suggests up to five mills may have occupied the site, *see* p 338), though rare and important, may now be viewed as ubiquitous late Roman industrial structures owing more to local design and craftsmanship than the workmanship we tend to associate with the Roman military. The military objects identified by Young constitute a relatively small proportion of the metal assemblage and these may now be viewed in context with a much larger and more varied collection of finds that are representative of numerous sections of east Kent society. The range of finds represented in the collection include military fittings but the majority is jewellery, industrial and agricultural equipment and domestic paraphernalia. Manufactured goods (wasters) were rare, but the working of pewter for the table and for jewellery is likely. Taken as a whole, the evidence appears to suggest that the principal activity may have been the repair of household, industrial, agricultural and military gear.

Although the proposition that Ickham may have been a military *officina* can no longer be sustained, the settlement was established against a major arterial road approximately mid way between the town and port of Richborough and the *civitas* capital at Canterbury. The settlement therefore enjoyed not only the passing trade of long distance travellers, but also that of a local population living and working in the central part of east Kent. The status of the site may now be best viewed as either an independent or estate-based quasi-industrial settlement which milled flour, collected scrap metal, manufactured metalwork, repaired metal goods and possibly processed flax and worked bone and leather for an extended community which included the military.

The settlement appears to have been abandoned in the early fifth century, coinciding with the break from the Western Empire, but Anglo-Saxon material in the latest deposits may indicate some later activity. The recovery of early Anglo-Saxon material suggests continuing use of the old Roman road and perhaps the waterways while the presence of medieval and later metalwork in the fills of a number of features also suggests that some contexts may have been disturbed in a later period.

This chapter provides an appreciation of the Ickham site, beginning with a summary history of the settlement. There follows an overview of the principal river and road systems of Roman east Kent, together with a more detailed discussion of the Richborough to Canterbury road and settlement in the Little Stour valley. The chapter concludes with a discussion setting the site in a local and regional context.

42. I am grateful to Christopher Sparey-Green, Keith Parfitt and Ian Riddler for their comments and contributions to this chapter.

The evolution of the Ickham settlement

Pre-Roman occupation

There is some slight evidence to suggest prehistoric occupation at the site, mainly in the form of worked flints found to the north of the main quarry. A crouched inhumation (Burial A) in association with a curving ditch perhaps marked the location of a small barrow of prehistoric date. A few residual sherds of late 'Belgic' pottery suggest a low level of late Iron Age occupation in the vicinity.

Early Roman occupation

A small amount of material, principally pottery recovered from Areas 10 and 14 (Assemblage 6) indicated activity in the late first century AD. At least two features may be dated to this period. A pit containing a cordoned necked jar, dated *c* AD 75–85 was recovered from beneath the road (Assemblage 1) and a ditch south of the road in Area 1, at the western end of the quarry (context 111) provided material dating up to *c* AD 80 (Assemblage 2). A number of undated features identified beneath the road in trial sections 2, 3 and 4 (Figs 8–9), a group of four linear ditches (331, 330, 305B and 305) to the north of the road, at the eastern end of the quarry and four ditches, south of the road (332, 311, 312 and P15), may also be related to an early phase of agricultural occupation. None of the features provided datable finds, but all appeared to have been cut by later features; two ditches located at the western end of the quarry, south of the road (111 and P15) may have formed part of an enclosure or field, set parallel to the line of the road and perhaps associated with it. The remaining ditches north and south of the road (save for 332) were set close together, appear to have been unrelated to the road and may represent early enclosures or fields.

The road and side drains

On the basis of the very few dated features sealed beneath metalling, the road can have been established no earlier than the late first century AD. Whilst the report of a mid second-century coin from 'beneath the road' suggests that the street may have been established on this line at a later date, the thickness and extent of laid gravel north and south of the road suggests that the road may have received at least one major resurfacing and the coin could therefore have been lost during an episode of road repair. A well-defined road drain to the south of the road did not appear to precisely follow the line of the metalling. Ditch and road were adjacent to one another at the eastern end of the quarry (Ditch 309), but diverged progressively to the west (P6). At the western edge of the quarry the possible continuation of the road ditch (cut by Channel A) lay approximately 8m from the road verge. To the north of the metalling, a wide gap separated road and ditch; to the west the gap was 13m, narrowing to 10m to the east. Gravel surfacing was present between the two ditches and overall, a shifting road line and perhaps road width was indicated. The northern ditch appears to have been maintained, with the final fills containing material dating well into the fourth century. To the south, recutting of the ditch was not so well marked and recovered finds suggest a closing date in the late third century.

The artificial channels

Four man-made channels were identified during the excavations. The earliest, Channel A, may have been constructed to power a mill down-stream of Mill 1 (perhaps in Area 15 and 16), not located during quarrying. Channel B, immediately south of Channel A, was the race for Mill 1, in use by *c* AD 220 and perhaps operated until *c* AD 270. The south-west end of Channel B was rebuilt to form Channel C, perhaps after *c* AD 320–2 to function as a race for Mill 2. At the end of the fourth century Mill 2 was replaced by Mill 3 up-stream but in the same channel. A fourth watercourse, Channel D, was located to the south-east of Channel C. This wide earthwork contained two substantial but enigmatic timbers that may constitute parts of a sluice, built perhaps in the early fifth century after Mill 3 had gone into disuse.

Air photographs indicated the presence of a palaeochannel south of the road (Pl I). The relict watercourse, largely in-filled with peat and organic silt, was clearly visible during the salvage excavation. The feature was present in Area 1 at the south-west end of the site where it extended roughly parallel to the road, tapering and then broadening to the north-east, where it appeared to bifurcate as it turned to the north, approaching the line of the road. In the absence of palaeoenvironmental or geomorphological study, it is difficult to be prescriptive about the nature of the watercourse or its relationship to the site, but it did appear to represent a low-lying depression through which water from the tail-races of Channels C and D ran during the life of the settlement. Even after the last mill ceased operating and with a rising water-table, it is possible that the waters of the Little Stour continued to flow, eroding the remains of the settlement, depositing alluvium and, as the rate of flow diminished, encouraging the development of a layer of peat to form across parts of the site.

The earliest watercourse

The earliest watercourse was probably Channel A. Although the position of Mill 1 cannot be positively proven, it is likely that Channel A did not act as a head-race for Mill 1, but may have channelled water to an earlier unlocated structure further east, perhaps in Areas 15 and 16. Construction of the watercourse is undated, but it appears to have cut an early road drain in Area 1 and possible early road ditches in Areas 1, 2 and 3 (111, P15, 311, 312 and 332). A small amount of second- to early third-century material, including pottery and tile fragments, recovered from Areas 3, 5 and 15 may derive from a related activity area. The watercourse remained open for a considerable period, with the top fills containing a number of fourth-century coins, waste metal finds, a wooden votive figurine (pp 215–17) and pottery (Assemblage 8, p 99) indicating that it was not completely infilled until after *c* AD 350.

The third-century settlement

The earliest excavated mill was Mill 1, fed perhaps by Channel B (P14 and 314). The western extremity of the channel was not located but is thought to follow the line of Channel C. Although the precise location of the mill cannot be proven, it must lie within Areas 10 and 14. A significant collection of third-century material (Assemblage 6, pp 96–9), together with coins dating to *c* AD 220–70, recovered from the area, perhaps confirms the mill's approximate position and date. The presence of metal-working waste, including furnace lining and a number of craft and agricultural tools recovered in this area, strongly suggests that the mill formed part of an industrial settlement, providing a range of services to the local community from the second quarter of the third century onwards.

Pre-dating the mill was a system of ditched enclosures located on the opposite side of the road (307, P11, P7, 303, 302 and P16). Few of the ditches were excavated, but the largest (307) recut on more than one occasion, may have functioned as both a principal boundary and a road drain. The ditch fills provided mainly third- to early fourth-century pottery (Assemblage 7, p 99), but this date probably relates to final infilling of the boundary. A north-west to south-east aligned ditch (Context 302), forming part of the enclosure system, provided pottery dating from the mid second century, including a significant quantity of bowls, dishes and beakers clearly indicating the presence of some form of domestic occupation, or perhaps, in line with the nature of the settlement, premises selling a limited range of domestic

vessels or even a catering establishment providing cooked food. The same context provided material dating into the mid fourth century. Overall, the enclosure ditches may have remained in use for a considerable period (perhaps two or more sub-phases: phase 1, P11, P7, 304; phase 2, 307, 303), with the complex finally being filled in the mid fourth century when a new system of ditches was cut. In addition to the range of domestic wares, ditch 302 provided a metal-working chisel, offcuts of lead alloy and a wood-working adze suggesting that metal-working and wood-working craftsmen may have been active nearby.

The fourth-century settlement

Mill 1 went out of use in the late third century and was replaced up-stream in a refurbished Channel C in Area 1. Although Mill 2 may have rapidly replaced Mill 1, a single coin of *c* AD 320–2 reported to have been found 'beneath the mill floor', may suggest that there was a gap between the two events. Whilst the head-race and the mill housing could have been rebuilt at this time, it is likely that Channel B (the former head-race for Mill 1) was used as a tail-race for Mill 2, channelling stream water into a developing palaeochannel to the east of the site.

A number of features excavated or recorded in Areas 4, 8 and 9 may broadly date to the period when Mill 2 was operating (*c* AD 270/322–390). Within Area 9 were a number of shallow, linear cuts, broadly set at right angles to the road. One feature (context 328) was set parallel to the street. None of the features provided datable finds, but it is tempting to interpret the linear features as beam-slots forming the foundations for timber-framed buildings constructed to the south of Channel B. As a number of the linear features were intercutting, more than one phase of building or structure is inferred.

An isolated gully, perhaps a beam-slot (Context 401) associated with two substantial post-holes, was located in the south-east corner of Area 4. The feature may tentatively indicate the gable end of a timber-framed building with two posts perhaps representing parts of the frame. One post was packed with animal bones and fragments of a leather shoe. The slot provided the spike of a flax heckle. A similar slot (context 317) and an associated post-hole recorded in the north-west corner of Area 4 may represent the east gable of an adjacent building.

Between the possible buildings was a curving gully (Context 409/411), perhaps for an eaves-drip feeding rainwater from adjacent buildings or for a boundary defining a property division. To the north of the boundary was a gravel-paved area, perhaps a courtyard between buildings (Context 413). Cutting the paving was a group of four pits (Contexts 407, 414, 410 and 335). Pit 407 contained twelve coins dated *c* AD 364–78, a large quantity of pottery (Assemblage 19, p 110) dated to the late fourth century and metalwork, mainly iron objects, some of which had hammerscale adhering to them. The lower fill of pit 414 contained pottery of the mid fourth century (Assemblage 10, pp 100–1); the upper fill (Assemblage 11, pp 101–3) contained fourth-century pottery together with iron objects with hammerscale adhering, including a broken pair of blacksmith's tongs and an iron lock. A third pit contained no datable finds but the fourth, (the furthest north, Context 335), cut close to the line of Channel B, was originally timber-lined and contained pottery of mid to late fourth-century date (Assemblage 18, pp 109–10) and a wide range of iron finds, some with adhering hammerscale residue.

Although the excavated and observed evidence is exceptionally difficult to interpret, one can tentatively speculate that a row of timber buildings may have existed south of Channel C. The first is represented by the group of linear slots in Area 6, cut by Channel D; a second is represented by a group of linear slots in Area 3; a third may be suggested by a dense group of linear slots in Areas 8 and 9 with a possible eastern gable for one phase of building represented by a slot in the north-east corner of Area 4. A slot and two post-holes in the south-east corner of Area 4 suggest a fourth building. The gravel area between buildings 3 and 4 may have been for a courtyard. The pits adjoining the buildings to the north contained pottery and coins dating into the mid to late fourth century, together with a significant collection of discarded metalwork. The presence of quantities of hammerscale and individual items such as blacksmith's tongs strongly suggests than one or more of these buildings may have been a metalworker's workshop, perhaps a smithy. Other commercial activity, principally more delicate metal-working, (perhaps the repair of military equipment, the production of pewter vessels and the manufacture of jewellery), but also the working of wood, leather, textiles and flax may have been taking place both here and on the opposite side of the road (see Context 302 above).

Some time in the mid to late fourth century Mill 2 was rebuilt only a few metres up-stream within Channel C. The rebuilding does not appear to have required a drastic modification of the mill-race, but an area of burnt clay beneath the race at the south-west end of the channel may have been associated with the rebuilding. The burnt soils contained pottery (Assemblage 12) dated *c* AD 340–400, suggesting that Mill 3 cannot have been constructed before

the mid fourth century. All the remaining material associated with mills 3 and 4 was recovered from infill deposits in the mill-race, or from features cutting the fabric of the race. Analysis of the pottery and coins recovered from Channel C (Assemblage 13, pp 105–7) suggests that Mill 3 was in use until *c* AD 390–400. A similar picture is reflected in the large collection of coins, pottery and finds recovered from two pits (107 and 115, pp 107–9) found cutting (and therefore post-dating) the fabric of the mill-race and tail either side of Mill 3.

A wide road ditch flanking the south side of the street (context 309) was probably in use throughout the second half of the fourth century (Assemblage 17, p 109). The finds, mainly recovered from the upper fills of the ditch, included a face flagon of a type known from Richborough dating into the late fourth century. The road drain was undoubtedly a multi-phase affair and the dating evidence recovered from it almost certainly relates to the final closing fills. During the working life of Mill 3, Channel B (the tail-race for Mill 2) may have finally gone out of use. Although good dating evidence is not available, if this is a correct assumption then formation of an unconstrained palaeochannel may have begun at this time.

Occupation appears to have continued north of the road well into the second half of the fourth century. Although the evidence is difficult to interpret, the ditches forming an early system of enclosures may have been filled by the mid fourth century and replaced by a new arrangement of ditches perhaps for a rectangular enclosure. The west and north sides of the enclosure may be represented by ditches P17 and P16; the southern side, adjoining the street, by a cluster of short lengths of intercutting ditches incorporating a possible narrow entrance (308, 329, 306). None of the ditches provided datable finds, but two late timber-lined features (333 and 701) may be associated with activity taking place within the enclosure in the later fourth century and possibly into the early fifth. Four other undated cut features, possibly unlined tanks (P25, P18, P10 and P9) may also be associated with use of the late enclosure.

The fill of tank 333 provided pottery dating into the late fourth and possibly the early fifth century (Assemblage 22, pp 115–17). Tank 701 provided a coin of Arcadius (*c* AD 388–95) and a similar range of pottery to that found in tank 333. A number of metal objects including molten lead alloy was recovered from tank 701, tentatively suggesting nearby metal-working activity. Although the timber-lined tanks may have been animal troughs, given the presence of running water east, west and south of the site, a more likely use for them is for some kind of industry, possibly for the processing of leather or for cloth production. In view of the presence of flax- and linen-working tools it seems plausible that flax may have been processed on or near the site, so the timber-lined pits or the unlined tanks located elsewhere in the enclosure, may have been part of a cloth production works, perhaps retting pits for making linen. In addition, reports of a ditch containing an unusual quantity of animal bones (that were not retained) may suggest the nearby presence of a nearby abattoir. Metal-working slag was also reported (Jim Bradshaw, pers comm) but none survives in the finds collections. The drag-line operators reported the discovery of quantities of building debris, including *tegulae*, *imbrex* and box-flue tiles associated with spreads of mortar, flints, pottery and burning, at two separate locations within the area, suggesting that some masonry-built structures may have existed nearby. No such materials were seen or recorded by those maintaining the intermittent watching brief and the reports remain unproven.

Of six inhumation burials recorded from the site, five may have come from within the enclosure. Two burials (Burials A and B) were lost to quarrying before they could be fully recorded. One of these (B) contained a complete pottery vessel of fourth-century date and hobnailed footwear. Of the three remaining burials, one (902) may have been buried with grave goods comprising a group of folded pewter plates laid within an iron frying pan, also of fourth-century date (but see p 42). Burial C was recorded in Areas 8–14, south of the road. A coin of Faustina the Younger (*c* AD 161–75) was found in the grave fill and fragments of a neonate infant were found nearby.

The trussed Burial A may have been prehistoric although such graves also occur in the early post-Roman period. Of the others Burial B and C are likely to be later Roman extended burials with typical grave goods of the period. If the folded pewter vessels were associated with Burial 902, this would be an unusual form of grave good, perhaps ritually 'killed' before interment. Burials within late enclosures such as this are not uncommon (Dolland's Moor, Folkestone: Rady 1989; Highstead: Bennett *et al* 2007), and scattered burials on the perimeter of enclosure systems in rural Roman contexts are common (Saltwood: Willson 2002, 37; Hersden: Barrett 2006; Crundale Limeworks: Bennett forthcoming). In view of the identification of multi-period barrow and grave-like cropmarks close to the road line, south-west of Wickhambreaux, then perhaps more than one group of burials may be associated with the settlement and they mark the potential east and west limits of settlement against the road.

The post-Roman settlement

At the end of the fifth century and during the life of the late northern enclosure, Mill 3 appears to have gone out of use and was superseded by another channel (D) to the south of the previous arrangement. Although evidence for a mill structure is enigmatic, the construction of the channel and surviving timbers (the most substantial recorded), strongly imply the existence of a mill. The mill tail-race was short and stream water from the race would have flowed across the land to the east, suggesting that by the time the channel was cut, industrial activity had ceased and the adjacent area was no longer occupied by buildings.

It is likely that Channel C was infilled at this time. Given that a new channel was cut for Mill 4, Channel C must have no longer been serviceable. The new channel was formed some way to the south of Channel C, suggesting perhaps an alteration in the line of the Little Stour may have also contributed to the cutting of a new channel. Whatever the case, it would seem unlikely that the redundant channel would have remained open for reasons of working access and of safety alone. The fills of the channel contained significant quantities of rubbish, particularly debris associated with metal-working and with fittings probably from a mill structure. Amongst the pottery in Assemblage 13 (pp 103–9) was material dating later than *c* AD 370, a significant quantity of metal scrap including broken metal-working tools, a fragment of crucible, hammerscale and 450 coins. Whilst the coins may have formed part of a hoard (perhaps derived from payments made to the miller during the working life of the mill) hidden prior to abandonment, overall the collection of finds indicates that rubbish may have been thrown into the mill channel from one or more nearby metal-working establishments producing objects in lead alloy, pewter and iron. Although the material may have derived from operating businesses, it is more likely that the infilling of the channel occurred at a time of major change, when the area east of Channel D was cleared of buildings, the old channel infilled and a new channel formed.

The lower fill of Channel D provided pottery and glass of later fourth-century date and a coin of *c* AD 388–402 (Assemblages 14–16, p 109). It is also significant to mention that Channel D did not contain the quantities of metal-working debris found in Channel C. This suggests that Mill 4 replaced Mill 3 very late in the fourth century or early in the fifth after clearance of the metal-working buildings had taken place. Some modification to Channel D may have occurred during use in the early fifth century. Associated deposits provided pottery and glass of late fourth- to early fifth-century date (Assemblage 24, pp 117–18) together with a few nails and a fragment of millstone. Early silt accumulations in the channel contained a few pottery sherds including part of a handled jug of North Gaulish origin paralleled at Tournai and dated *c* AD 350–420.

During the life of Channel D, waters from the tail-race would have poured across Areas 2, 3 and 4 and beyond. Material from the silts and clays capping the areas (Assemblages 20 and 21, pp 110–15) provided coins of Constantinian and Valentianic date, together with late pottery suggesting that occupation in the immediate vicinity of Mill 4 had ceased by the time the mill was operating and that a watercourse flowed over an area that once contained buildings from that time onward.

Abandonment deposits

Quite when occupation ceased on the site is difficult to determine. Mill 4 may have been the last surviving building against the south side of the street at the eastern end of the settlement. On the opposite side of the street, within the enclosure, some activity may have continued into the early fifth century, but quite how far into the century cannot be determined.

Even after the abandonment of Mill 4 it is likely that water still flowed through Channel D and that at times the entire site was subject to flooding. Deposits of silt and alluvium capping the latest archaeological features were probably deposited at this time and some scouring of the archaeological deposits may have taken place. As the rate of flow decreased, so the fluvial deposits gave way to the formation of peat. These later deposits were mainly removed by the drag-line during the stripping of topsoil prior to quarrying, but in Areas 1 and 6 the mantle of silt and peat deposits was removed by hand. The deposits provided nearly 500 sherds of pottery, all of fourth-century date (Assemblage 27, pp 118–19) and a small collection of metal objects, some containing hammerscale within their corrosion products.

Anglo-Saxon activity

Anglo-Saxon activity is indicated by a modest collection of objects, mainly pottery, but also keys and knives, recovered from the uppermost fills of late Roman features, principally Channel C and Channel D. No single feature could be identified as Anglo-Saxon and overall much of the identified material may have been mixed with abandonment or fluvial deposits capping the later Roman levels.

Later intrusive features

Several late pits were reported across the site of which Pit 412 in Area 4 is one. The most significant intrusive features, possibly of post-medieval date were found cutting Channel C (pits 107 and 115). Originally interpreted as 'scour' pits formed by the operating of the mill at a time of poor or no maintenance, the pits fall either side of the location of Mill 3. Although Pit 115 was located close to a wheel position, the size and shape of the pit, offset from the centre of the channel cutting race fabric, does not conform to the interpretation and some other formation process must be sought. Pit 107, located up-stream of a wheel position, also cut race fabric and this feature may not have been formed by scouring. In both cases the features may have been pits formed perhaps in the post-Roman period to dispose of stone and debris from the surface of the meadow (p 70). The backfill of both pits contained considerable quantities of late Roman pottery, metalwork and millstones. Some 448 coins, the latest dating up to *c* AD 402 were recovered from both pits (Assemblage 13) and these finds must have been associated with the mill or mill-race infill, but displaced during the cutting and backfilling of the pit. Many of the coins recovered from Pit 107 were corroded together suggesting that they may have been contained in a bag or box originally hidden or stored in the mill, but displaced when the pit was cut. A number of items of metalwork, most notably horseshoes, may also be of late Roman or post-Roman origin.

Other late features found cutting post-Roman deposits included an undated north–south ditch (P23) found cutting the east end of Channel D, and a north-west to south-east aligned gravel-filled ditch (P21) found cutting across the line of the palaeochannel between Channels C and D. A final ditch (109) located in the north-west corner of Area 1, may follow the line of a field boundary shown on the tithe apportionment plan of 1838. Most of this boundary was removed during topsoil clearance at an early stage of the quarrying operations.

East Kent rivers

Two freshwater rivers and two saltwater channels dominate the topography of east Kent. The rivers are the Great Stour and the Nailbourne, which in its lower reaches is called the Little Stour; the saltwater channels are the Wantsum and the Swale.

The source of both rivers lies in the south-western part of east Kent, on the North Downs escarpment west and north of Hythe near Aldington and Lyminge. For the greater part of its course, the Stour follows a south-west to north-east line linking Ashford and Canterbury to the Wantsum sea channel. The Nailborne strikes a more direct northerly course, along the Elham valley to Bridge, before trending north-east to meet the Great Stour and the Wantsum at Stourmouth. These river valley routes were major arteries of communication linking the southern and south-western parts of east Kent to the centre and to the south-east.

The Wantsum sea channel separated the Isle of Thanet from the mainland and formed both a haven for shipping and a safe-water passage for vessels rounding the north-east corner of Kent (Fig 2). The sea channel was approximately 2km wide at its greatest extent, but perhaps not particularly deep. At low water the width of the navigable channel may have reduced dramatically with extensive mud flats on either side, but it is unlikely that the channel would have been fordable in the Roman period and a ferry would have been required for the crossing, even during periods of very low tide. Given the tidal regime, the ferry landings at either side of the crossing point would probably have required durable and well-made linear 'hards' or pontoons to allow safe and reasonably dry loading and unloading for passengers and freight.

From late prehistoric times and throughout the Roman period the Wantsum represented a sheltered harbour for seagoing vessels and a possible short cut for shipping travelling to or from London and the Thames estuary, eliminating the need to round the potentially dangerous headland at North Foreland (Grainge 2002). Port facilities at Richborough were protected by a 4km long shingle spit formed by longshore drift (the Stonar Bank) creating a peninsular of land extending south from Thanet, now Ebbsfleet hill. Richborough, located on an island (an outcrop of tertiary rocks) to the west of the breakwater was connected to the mainland by a road and causeway (possibly 1.70km long) extending across salt marshes west of the island (Ogilvie 1968). A second as yet unproven southern causeway may have carried the Dover road, to the island. A settlement of later fourth-century date has recently been located on the island at Lowton, close to the predicted landfall of the putative southern causeway. The settlement, found during trenching for a pipeline, comprised a number of pits and post-holes, a possible building and metalling for a yard surface or road, sealed beneath a thick band of colluviated silt containing redeposited occupation material. The features and silt yielded fourth-century pottery together with coins dated *c* 330–78 (Parfitt 2008).

The north end of the Deal Spit flanked the southern side of the eastern channel. This broad sand spit bounded in part by a shingle bank on its seaward side (Robinson and Cloet 1953; Hawkes 1968) and by a zone of windblown sand on the landward side (Shephard-Thorn 1988, 36–70) known locally as the Tenant's Hills was also formed by longshore drift. A third shingle and sand spit, the Sand Downs existed to the east of Sandwich, extending for at least 1km to adjoin the present

day Sandwich Bay Estate. The presence of this and other banks and spits must have made the eastern channel mouth a difficult entry and the passage through the waterway probably required extreme caution, particularly on a falling tide or during adverse weather conditions. The mouth of the southern channel may have been less than 1km wide by the first century AD and the presence of the spits suggests that the southern edge of the channel did not extend beyond Sandwich, with much of the ground further south in the Lydden valley being perhaps largely salt marsh (Fuller 2006). The narrowness of the south-eastern channel mouth and spits may, in part, explain why Caesar chose to draw his fleet of 800 ships on the Deal spit, rather than risk a difficult entry into the haven in 55 and 54 BC (Frere 1999, 20). It was perhaps only possible for the greater number of vessels involved in the Claudian invasion (1,000 ships) to use Richborough port because they were organised in three divisions, to avoid difficulties of entry and internal navigational hazards (Grainge 2002, 61).

The spits were sufficiently well developed by the late Iron Age to have accommodated settlement. A substantial pre-Roman and Roman period site has been identified on the Sand Downs at Archer's Low (Frere 1988, 484; Frere and Tomlin 1991, 292). Significant quantities of high status Gallo-Belgic and Augustan-Tiberian imports are attested from the site, together with over fifty Celtic coins. Roman coins, pottery and building debris suggest continuity of settlement into the fourth century when a complex of buildings existed there, perhaps a villa. Although the Stonar Bank has yet to provide evidence of settlement, a few sherds of early Roman pottery are known from salvage excavations conducted there during gravel extraction in the early 1970s (Macpherson-Grant 1991). The Deal Spit has provided evidence for a small Romano-British fishing settlement on the Sand Hills at Dixon's Corner (Parfitt 2000). Established just before the conquest, the settlement, covering approximately one hectare was abandoned in *c* AD 225. A late third-century coin hoard is also known from Sand Hills, opposite Blackhorse Wall (Roach Smith 1882). These discoveries together with other reported finds suggest that the area was attractive for settlement from at least the late Iron Age.

A secondary haven for shipping may have existed at Stourmouth, or in the lower reaches of the Little Stour. Although goods could possibly have been transhipped there, it is more likely that the location would only have been suitable as a temporary anchorage for shipping waiting for the rising tide to assist passage up the Great Stour to perhaps a port facility near Sturry (Jenkins 1949).

Rather more peripheral to this study, the Swale separates the Isle of Sheppey from mainland Kent, providing even today, a protected 'inside' passage for shipping heading towards the Medway and the Thames estuary. Tidal creeks opening onto the channel connected mainland settlements (Faversham, Oare, Conyer, Milton Regis and Sittingbourne) and Watling Street to the waterway through a wide belt of marshland. A number of similar creeks subdivided Sheppey into islands whose southern reaches were also mainly of salt marsh. The marshes, mud flats, creeks and waters of the Wantsum and Swale would have been valuable assets not just as routes of communication by boat, but for rich marine and intertidal resources; fish, shellfish, water fowl, salt, reeds and quality clay for pottery, tile and brick manufacture.

A significant number of minor rivers and streams in east Kent were probably capable of driving mills in the Roman period and a few of these are worthy of review.

The Wingham river, closely tied to the history of the Ickham site, is a short, sinuous watercourse with a source (the Durlock stream) east of Woodnesborough at Ringleton Manor. The stream follows a westerly course to Wingham turning north-west to link with the Little Stour close to the Ickham site. A separate stream rises at Wingham Well to flow northwards to join the Wingham river. The route of this spring passes the Wingham Roman villa. A millstone re-used in a late level within the building is likely to have been an upper stone from a mechanical mill, suggesting the existence of a mill at the villa or nearby (Dowker 1882, 137; Jenkins 1984) or signalling a relationship between the villa and the mills on the Ickham site.

The Sarre Penn rises high in the contours at Dunkirk, and follows a course through Blean and Tyler Hill, collecting water from subsidiary springs at the western head of the Sarre Penn valley, to vigorously flow through Calcott and Hersden, broadly parallel to and north of the Great Stour, joining the Wantsum south-east of Chislet and north of the Upstreet–Sarre crossing to the Isle of Thanet. Although the upper reaches of the Sarre Penn may not have generated a sufficiently generous and seasonally guaranteed flow to drive an early mill, and the lower reaches too affected by tides, the mid range of the river, near a crossing of the Roman road to Reculver, is one possible location where a Roman watermill could perhaps have functioned successfully.

A series of small but fairly fast-flowing streams existed at the southern end of the Lydden valley, north-west of Deal. Here springs issue from Eastry, West Street, Northbourne Court and Sholden Downs to Hacklinge where they combine to form the North Stream which once flowed into an extensive salt marsh, (protected from the sea by the Deal Bank) to eventually merge with the eastern arm of the Wantsum channel (Fuller 2006).

The River Dour at Dover had sources south-east of Lydden where the end of the ridgeway of the Barham Downs meets the head of the steep Dour valley and at the north-east end of the Alkham valley near Chilton Farm. The streams combine at Kearsney to flow south-eastwards into a wide shallow bay with chalk cliffs on either side creating the Dour Gap and a haven for shipping (Philp 1981, 7–9). Mills on the Dour were numerous in the early medieval period and together with the Great Stour at Ashford (Westhawk Farm) and Canterbury, the Dour close to Dover is one of the most likely rivers and locations for a Roman period mill to have been built.

The Roman port at Lympne stood where a tidal lagoon was formed by the confluence of the rivers Brede, Tillingham and Rother flowing eastwards from East Sussex. A shingle spit backed by alluvium formed a natural breakwater with the sea and an anchorage for shipping protected from bad weather from every direction except the east (Cunliffe 1980, 258). Up-stream of the haven any one of these three rivers had the capacity and regularity of water to drive a mill.

All of these rivers possessed rates of water flow capable of driving a mill; most of them adjoined major arterial roads or passed through settlements and farmland capable of producing grain on an enormous scale and yet other than the Ickham discovery there is little to suggest that mills were constructed elsewhere. The rivers and streams of east Kent were almost certainly used as routes of communication (by following the course of the waterway on foot or by boat), as a resource for fresh water, foodstuffs or raw materials, or as a means of irrigation. Most of the rivers cited were free flowing all year, with the flow varying with the seasons and a changing pattern of rainfall. All of the rivers were used to drive mills from at least the early medieval period onwards and as milling technology was commonplace elsewhere in the Roman world, it is all the more surprising that in an area so rich in rivers, only at Ickham has evidence for a Roman mill been found.

The Roman road system of east Kent

One of the most important factors leading to the construction of a sequence of mills at Ickham was the line of the Roman road between Richborough and Canterbury. In light of this key relationship, our discussion now turns to the Roman road network of east Kent.

An extensive pre-Roman communication network, formed over millennia to link disparate settlements within a managed landscape almost certainly existed at the time of the Roman conquest. A number of major routeways may be deduced in the present landscape of east Kent, including, for example, long lengths of the North Downs (Margary 1955), a route crossing the Kingston and Barham Downs (Macpherson-Grant 1980b) and a route extending from Canterbury to Grove Ferry (Barrett 2006). The development of the Roman road system, beginning with the construction of Watling Street,[43] effectively created a new topography for east Kent, connecting old and new communities and linking the new collective to other parts of the Roman world. Whilst the new and principal corridors of the communication network were imposed on the geography of east Kent at, or shortly after, the conquest, at a local level most of the traditional trackways and routeways almost certainly continued in use, to create a layered system of communication that allowed easier access to every settlement and laid every resource open to exploitation.

Roman east Kent was dominated by a series of coastal settlements. Richborough (*Rutupiae*), located on an island close to the east mouth of the Wantsum channel, Reculver (*Regulbium*) against the north mouth of the Wantsum, Dover (*Portus Dubris*) at the mouth of the River Dour and Lympne (*Portus Lemanis*), against the south coast, close to the mouth of the Rother, all constituted nodal points within the geography of east Kent. Even the *civitas* capital at Canterbury (*Durovernum Cantiacorum*) was established up-stream of a navigable stretch of the Great Stour, close to the coast. Whilst the road network connected each of these centres to each other and to neighbouring settlements, it must not be overlooked that their importance probably owed as much to water-based transport as to a well-developed road system.

The Roman road system in the eastern part of the county is remarkably well preserved with many of the original (very straight) alignments still forming major arteries (Margary 1973). Viewed in totality there appears to be a discernible regularity and geometry to the arrangement. Canterbury, located against a ford of the River Stour, is placed centrally, with roads radiating like the spokes of a wheel to the nodal settlements, to London and to the south-west. The north–south line of the road linking Lympne and Canterbury is mirrored to the east by a road joining Richborough and Dover. An east–west road connecting Richborough and Canterbury, and westward to London, provides the third side of a square and a poorly understood route between Lympne and Dover, the fourth. The route linking Canterbury and Dover provides a north-west to south-east diagonal. A road extending from the Northgate of Canterbury north-eastwards

connects Thanet to the network and a spur of that road projects northwards to Reculver. Another main road extends south-west of the town to connect to Ashford, Westhawk Farm and the Weald of Kent.

Notwithstanding the recent debate about a possible landing base in Sussex (Manley 2002; Frere and Fulford 2001; Grainge 2002), the line of Roman Watling Street from a landing base at Richborough to Canterbury and westward to London was almost certainly the earliest in the east Kent network, being constructed at the conquest in support of front-line troops. It has been suggested, but has yet to be proven, that landings also may have taken place at Dover and Lympne and that the routes from individual harbours may have been constructed at or shortly after the conquest (Tatton-Brown 2001). A conquest period fortlet is proposed for the headland at Reculver (Philp 2005, 192–3); but whether this led to the building of an early road is not known. The route of Watling Street immediately west of the landing base and the west gate of the later Saxon Shore fort is well known to Fleet Farm (Ogilvie 1968, 37–40, plan p 230), but beyond this point to Wickhambreaux, where a well-defined cropmark for a road extending to Pine Wood can be seen (Fig 3), the primary line of the street has been lost. Although many have proposed a direct route from Fleet Farm to Pine Wood (see Panton 1994, 1–15) few are believable and none has been based on good evidence, including the route proposed by Margary (1973, 369) and much more detailed fieldwork is needed to rediscover the route (or more likely, routes) connecting Richborough and Pine Wood (*see* below p 331). From Pine Wood the road appears to run straight to Canterbury entering the town at Burgate and it is suggested (though again unproven) that this section of the route follows a primary line.

The road extending north-east from the Northgate of Canterbury crosses the Great Stour at a point between Sturry and Fordwich where a small early Roman villa or farm, the closest known to Canterbury, lies to the north-east of Sturry at Shelford (Boden 2004). The main villa has not been found but a small bath-house containing an apsidal *caldarium*, three unheated rooms and a *portico* may represent an attempt by a local landowner to adopt Roman values soon after the conquest. The Roman ford between Fordwich and Sturry may mark the furthest limit of tidal influence in the Roman period and the possible location of a port facility, tentatively identified during gravel extraction near the Island Road Estate at Sturry (Jenkins 1949).

43. The name 'Watling Street' is Anglo-Saxon (*Waeclinga straete*) and refers only to the name of the Roman road near St Albans. Only later did the name come to be used for the whole route to London and on through Kent to Dover, not Richborough (Cameron 1977, 134).

Crossing to the northern bank of the Stour the road continues to a point midway between Sturry and Westbere where the route intersects with the Reculver road. The south-west to north-east road continues past a prehistoric and Roman roadside settlement at Hersden (Barrett 2004) to the mouth of the Stour at Grove Ferry or Wall End where it meets the tidal waters of the Wantsum channel. Here it is presumed a ferry would have connected the road terminus to a facility some 2km distant on the Isle of Thanet at or near Sarre (above, p 327).

On the island, a major east–west artery (Gore Street, formerly Dunstrete), aligned approximately parallel to the Canterbury–Richborough road, extended from Sarre, through Monkton and Mount Pleasant following the 50m contour. A length of the road, including a major junction with a road aligned north-east to south-west was exposed during road improvements between the Monkton and Mount Pleasant roundabouts in 1994. East of the junction between the Roman roads was a major roadside agricultural settlement of mid second- to early third-century date (Hicks 2008, 101–278). The north-east to south-west aligned road appeared to be aligned to approach a Roman villa at Tivoli Park Avenue, Margate (Rowe 1923). A second Roman villa is known at Abbey Farm, Minster (Parfitt 2006, 115–33) approximately 1.5km south of the projected line of the east–west Roman street. At Minnis Bay, near Birchington a powered millstone was found covering a Roman cremation burial, one of eight burials discovered on the foreshore in 1938 (Powell-Cotton and Pinfold 1939, 191–4 and plates I and II), clearly suggesting the presence of a nearby settlement. Although the stone does not imply the presence of a mill (there are no rivers on the island capable of powering a mill), it does suggest perhaps that the object may have once been part of a cargo or ballast from a vessel destined for elsewhere that arrived on the island accidentally, or that it was a curiosity taken to Thanet.

The Reculver road follows a relatively straight north-east course crossing the Sarre Penn at Tile Lodge Farm, a tributary of the Sarre Penn (feeding down from the Blean uplands) at Rushbourne Manor and a third stream at Ford before approaching close to a major agricultural hilltop settlement at Highstead (Bennett *et al* 2007). Here, a near continuously occupied settlement has been attested from 300 BC to the second half of the third century AD. An extensive complex of enclosures, field systems and paddocks was traced by excavation and air photography during gravel extraction. The site also provided a well-preserved, two cell corn-drier or hypocaust dating up to the fourth century. At Hillborough the road changes alignment towards the fort at Reculver, located

against the northern mouth of the Wantsum, close to the site of a major Iron Age settlement (Philp 2005, 66).

Two Roman roads approach Canterbury from the south-east, meeting at a junction in the suburb of Wincheap (Hicks and Shand forthcoming). The line of Stone Street branches off the Canterbury–Wye–Ashford road, just west of Worthgate and Wincheap Green, but has only been traced for a short distance into the modern suburbs (Rady 1999, 9). The road can be identified at Street End near Lower Hardres (3 miles south of Canterbury) where it follows a straight north–south track across the high downs almost to the coast. Here the road changes alignment close to Newingreen before dropping down steep contours to *Portus Lemanis*. This entire area has been badly affected by landslips and the road connections to the fort and port have been lost. To the west of Lympne however, at Aldington another Roman road extending parallel to and south of the East Stour can be determined in the landscape following a north-west to south-east line to the site of a small Roman town at Westhawk Farm, Ashford (Booth *et al* 2008).

From the Wincheap intersection, the Wye–Ashford road extends along the valley of the Great Stour, initially following the east bank, but probably crossing to the west at Shalmsford Street. The course of the road cannot be determined between Horton, where a hollow way, possibly the course of the road has been identified (Sparey-Green 2005) and Boughton Corner on the shoulder of the Great Stour valley west of Wye. From Boughton and Kemp's Corner however, the road can be traced to approach Westhawk Farm.

A major road connected Lympne and Dover. Though not precisely known, the route probably followed the foot of the North Downs linking an agricultural settlement at Saltwood (Willson 2002), an important villa at Folkestone (Winbolt 1925; 1926) and a settlement at Farthingloe Farm (Bennett 1989, 46) to Dover.

The road connecting Dover and Canterbury climbs the north-east side of the Dour valley from the Roman port to Lydden. The route then follows an ancient ridgeway across the Barham and Kingston Downs, dropping into the Elham valley at Bridge (2.5 miles south of Canterbury) where as the place name suggests, a Roman bridge may have been sited to carry the road over the River Nailbourne before continuing on a slightly adjusted line to enter Canterbury at Ridingate (*see* below, p 339).

The Dover–Richborough road (the east side of the square) projects on a single alignment almost due north past a roadside settlement or farmstead at Maydensole Farm (Cross and Redding 2000) to Eastry, where a short branch road to the east may have given access to an important ritual centre at

Worth (Holman 2005, 8–10). From Eastry the accepted route (Detsicas 1983, 36) takes the road to Woodnesborough where a possible branch road extended north-eastwards to a small villa or farm south-west of Sandwich (Bennett 1978; Parfitt 1980). The road continued from Woodnesborough to Each End, east of Ash (Hicks 1998) where a Roman settlement was located against the southern edge of the Wantsum channel. An expanse of metalling uncovered here, together with a later timber building (perhaps a warehouse or granary) and a number of burials, may suggest the presence of a minor port facility or fishing settlement, not unlike the site at Dixon's Corner on the Deal Bank. Each End may have been a 'dead-end' junction, where the Dover road and an extension of Watling Street, east of Ash adjoined the channel.

Recent work on Richborough island for a mains sewer diversion has revealed traces of a later fourth-century settlement against the south-west edge of the island at Lowton, on land thought to have been close to the high water mark of the Wantsum (Parfitt 2007a). One possible explanation for the existence of a settlement in this position, set apart from the late Roman port facilities, Shore fort and town, may be that a southern causeway may have connected the island to the mainland at that time. Geological maps show a tongue of gravel and clay projecting from the mainland like a finger towards the location of the new settlement and this may have encouraged Roman engineers to utilise the feature and bridge any gaps to provide a connection to the island. Whilst the newly discovered settlement may simply mirror that at Each End, positioned against the edge of the Wansum, it is just possible that the Lowton settlement flanked a road and causeway connecting the island to the mainland, with the road continuing to the south-west to intersect with the Ash–Each End road at Goss Hall. Much more work requires to be done before the theory can be substantiated, but the presence of a hitherto unknown settlement in that position and the apparent late date of occupation are clearly significant factors in their own right. The Each End settlement flourished until well into the fourth century AD (indeed there is evidence of sixth-century occupation), but was perhaps 'by-passed' at an early date by a new route extending north-west from Woodnesborough to Ash. From Ash a south-west to north-east aligned section of Watling Street is assumed to have approached Fleet Farm and a causeway linking the mainland to Richborough. The early by-passing of Each End may suggest that safe use of the southern causeway (if one existed) may have depended upon the state of the tide or the season of the year.

When viewed in totality the road network of east Kent is remarkably regular. A number of the surviving routes appear to indicate that alignments owed perhaps more to map-based design than consideration of the topography (Davies 1998) and this perhaps reflects the hand of the official surveyor. The network must be viewed as part of a planned system linking the cantonal capital to the ports and principal settlements of the canton. Part of the network was probably established soon after Roman annexation, with other roads rapidly added to link newly developed sites and to supplement rather than supersede established native routes.

The Canterbury to Richborough road, then, was the first major Roman road to be constructed, together with its continuation to the west of Canterbury; its primacy linked with military strategy and the establishment of London as a provincial centre shortly after the mid first century AD. All other roads effectively connected east Kent to the line of Watling Street and to Canterbury.

The Richborough to Canterbury road and settlement in the Little Stour valley

The eastern and western extremities of the Richborough to Canterbury road have been described above and the discussion now turns to the central part of the route, from Ash westwards, to where the road crossed low-lying marshy ground at the confluence of the Little Stour and the Wingham river. This section of road to Pine Wood on the heights to the west of the Little Stour valley has effectively been lost. The accepted view is that to avoid boggy ground, an Iron Age trackway running from Pine Wood through Littlebourne, Bramling and Wingham, was incorporated into the line of the Roman road (Margary 1973, 36–9; Detsicas 1983, 33–5; Panton 1994, 1–15), the route returning north-east to climb steep contours to Broomhill and along the existing highway to Ash. The section of the route linking Ash and Broomhill was almost certainly late or post-Roman in date, formed perhaps when the original road had been submerged by a rising water-table. Given the date and importance of Watling Street, laid as it must have been to the dictates of military surveyors, it seems unlikely that this circuitous route would have been the original alignment. Early Watling Street is likely to have followed a more direct route and if the southern deviation existed at all in the Roman period, it is likely to have been a late development, perhaps designed to give access to a villa at Wingham (Smith 1978; Jenkins 1984) and an enigmatic building to the west of Britton Farm (*see* below, p 337).

The line of Watling Street from Canterbury's Burgate extends as a single alignment due east from the city and can be seen as an earthwork in Pine Wood. A kink in the earthwork close to the western edge of the Little Stour valley indicates an adjustment in road line to the north-east.

Pl XXVI. Slight earthworks of Roman road, boundary ditches and enclosures north-west of road, east of Wickhambreaux, looking west. Photograph: Jim Bradshaw, June 1974.

On the valley floor, air photographs taken prior to gravel extraction show a pattern of plant growth indicating the presence of a north-east to south-west aligned road (Pls 1 and II), extending approximately 1km across the valley from the north-eastern edge of Wickhambreaux to cross the excavated site. At ground level close to Wickhambreaux the road was identified as a slightly raised agger flanked by narrow ditches with low external banks (Pls II and XXVI). Other air photographs show ephemeral traces of ditches north of the road defining a system of enclosures on the flood plain. A similar system of enclosures has also been identified during ditch cutting nearer Littlebourne (Sparey-Green 2005).

Immediately south-west of Wickhambreaux the line of the road has been identified in a satellite photograph taken in April 2008. Earlier cropmark photographs and the satellite image show a row of at least eight ring-ditches aligned parallel to and on the north side of the projected road line (Fig 3 and 123). The two largest are double concentric ring-ditches up to 30m in diameter and almost certainly of prehistoric origin. The remainder are much smaller but are also likely to be prehistoric. There are additionally a number of rather more ephemeral cropmarks closer to the road and the edge of the village which may indicate the presence of Roman or Anglo-Saxon burials and perhaps boundary ditches. If these non-prehistoric features are contemporary with the road, it is conceivable that they may represent field divisions and perhaps a multi-period cemetery. If this is the case, then a significant part of the Ickham roadside Roman settlement may yet exist between the possible cemetery and

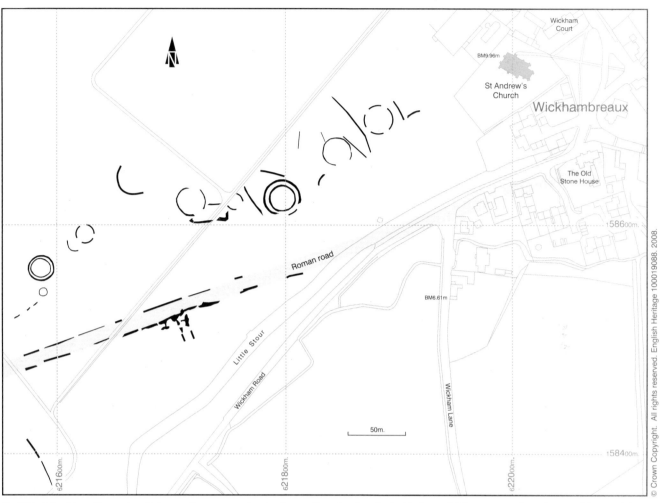

Fig 123. Extract from the modern Ordnance Survey map showing the position of archaeological features visible as cropmarks and mapped from aerial photographs by English Heritage.

the edge of the quarry. The presence of the row of burial mounds might also betray the existence of a track, pre-dating the Roman road and following a near identical line.

Fig 123 shows the line of the road and a possible building adjoining it to the south. Metal detection and fieldwalking in the area by a joint team of detectorists and archaeologists in November 2008 produced forty-seven Roman coins broadly dating from the early second to the later fourth century, (two fourth-century coin hoards are also known from this general area), 260 sherds of pottery (including coarseware, samian ware and amphora) and 140 fragments of roofing tile, brick and box-flue tile, all from a zone south of the road (Keith Parfitt, pers comm). These discoveries clearly suggest a possible continuation of the roadside settlement west of Wickambreaux. Whether the settlement formed a continuous strip or discontinuous groupings of buildings and land division has yet to be established. Taken as a whole, however, there is good reason to believe that the Ickham settlement in some form, extended from south-west of Wickambreaux, to the line of the Wingham river and perhaps as far as Wenderton to the north-east.

To the north-west of the site, midway between it and Stourmouth, on high ground between the converging valleys of the Little Stour and Wantsum, are cropmarks for a promontory site with at least two enclosures and other features (Pl XXVII). The settlement was undoubtedly located to take advantage of the topographical position between two waterways, but its date and function remain unknown.

Within the quarry the road has been shown to be substantial and well metalled, being between 7–10m wide.

Pl XXVII. Promontory site with at least two enclosures and other features visible, to the north-west of Ickham. Looking north-east. Photograph: Paul Bennett.

A total length of 400m of road was exposed during gravel quarrying. The pre quarry photographs also show the course of a palaeochannel extending parallel and south of the road (Pl I). At a point roughly co-incident with the north-eastern end of the quarry, the two marks converge and the road cannot be traced in photographs beyond this point. Casual records of observed road metalling during quarrying near the Wingham river to the north-east in 1972 (Jim Bradshaw and James Ogilvie, pers comm), showed the road line continued with sightings of pointed stakes and horizontal timbers, faggots and brushwood, indicating at least the substructure of the road where it crossed soft ground (between TR 2341 5915 and TR2342 5916). On the opposite north bank of the river, the road has not been located, but settlement remains at Wenderton (Tomlinson 1961; James Ogilvie, pers comm) and a pottery kiln at Preston (Dowker 1878, 47–8) suggest perhaps that having crossed the river, the northerly route would have climbed the contours to a point north of Little

Wenderton Farm to follow the natural line of the ridge now marked by noteworthy tracks (the Preston/Wingham parish boundary) linking Perry, Nash and Ash. From Ash the road changed angle again to the north-east to reach Fleet Farm and the mainland end of the causeway to Richborough.

A number of features including ditches associated with a field system were located beneath the road, suggesting some form of settlement activity prior to road construction. The features have been tentatively dated to *c* AD 70–80 and suggest that the road cannot have been constructed until the late first century at the earliest. The discovery of a mid second-century coin from 'beneath the road metalling' (above, p 24) may even suggest that the road was not laid out until that time or later. The presence of the coin might equally indicate that a major resurfacing of the street took place at the time the coin was lost. Although the precise dating of the road cannot be established, on available evidence one can be sure that it was not on a primary (conquest period) line.

In summary then, although the excavated and observed sections of road may not have followed the precise line of early Watling Street, they do represent a version of the route, perhaps established at some time between the later first and the later second century. This section of Watling Street from perhaps that time onward appears to have been built in a series of straight but staggered lengths of road beginning at the mainland end of the causeway with a 3km length of straight road to Ash. It is interesting and perhaps significant to note that each of the three remaining sections (Ash to Wenderton, Wenderton to Pine Wood and Pine Wood to Burgate) were of near identical length, measuring approximately 4.7km. The total route from Richborough to Canterbury measured some 17.10km.

Accepting that the Ash–Little Wenderton–Pine Wood route is a version of Watling Street, then what of the southern route proposed by Margary? Whilst it is now possible to dismiss the route entirely, there may yet be evidence to suggest that the modern highway (a turnpike road of late eighteenth- or early nineteenth-century date) follows at least in part, a later Roman branch road, constructed perhaps to give access to the Wingham villa and to the Britton Farm Roman building. Allowing that the present road from Broomhill to Ash is probably post-Roman in origin, from Wingham, the branch road would perhaps have climbed the steep contours of Broomhill northward following an ancient hollow way to intersect with Watling Street above Little Wenderton Farm. This route would have benefited from straightforward crossings of the Little Stour and the Wingham river and provided an otherwise dry route across the upper reaches of the Little Stour valley. An existing track through Pine Wood and Oldridge Wood to Fordwich may also follow a prehistoric track or a Roman branch road.

The Little Stour

Although it is difficult to determine on the basis of excavated features and material evidence, which came first, the road or the settlement, there can be no doubt that the settlement would not have existed without the Little Stour. The source of the Nailbourne (a perennial stream) rises at the southern end of Elham valley, at Lyminge and drops over 100m in elevation through 20km of rolling chalk downland before meeting a spring at Well Chapel, south-west of Littlebourne. Below this point the river is known as the 'Little Stour' and it was the combined waters of the Nailbourne and Well Chapel spring that, in conjunction with the road, provided the stimulus for settlement.

The precise location of the Roman stream bed is difficult to determine on the basis of existing evidence (although shadowy traces of a possible palaeochannel can be seen on air photographs north-west of the quarry) but one can assume that Watling Street would have crossed the river close to the western edge of the quarry. It has been assumed that a bend or ox-bow in the river existed at this point, allowing the natural stream to pass north of the road (by bridge or ford) whilst man-made channels served the mills on the south.

Discussion: the Ickham site in its wider context

The line of Roman Watling Street from Richborough through Canterbury to London was not only the earliest Roman road in Kent, but also during the period of the conquest and until the early second century, the most important. It is perhaps ironic that the opening section of this arterial route from the Claudian landing base, early supply depot, principal port of entry and the site of a monumental arch proclaiming *perdomita Britannia,* should still be shrouded in doubt and uncertainty.

A case has been made above (p 331) for a later (late first century) version of the route and it is hoped that the proposal will gain a measure of acceptance. Although no trace of an early road was found on the Ickham site, there can be little doubt that for a period of about fifty years following the conquest, the route from Richborough across the valley of the Little Stour would have been very busy indeed. Given the location, approximately mid way between Richborough and Canterbury, it is an ideal situation for an early (and late) posting station and it is therefore curious that no trace of an early road or occupation has been found. The development of one of the canton's earliest villas at Wingham (Dowker 1882; 1883) by a member of the local élite presumably owed something to the proximity of Watling Street and it is not impossible that the villa was connected to the street by a purpose-built spur road or by a pre-existing track. In the early second century when Richborough was perhaps superceded by Dover in importance as the principal port to the province, the site remained a significant port of entry and an important settlement. Richborough and Dover then were the first ports and Canterbury the first new town and cantonal capital to be encountered when entering the province. Much of the traffic from the continent to Canterbury and places west would have followed the route, initially in the wake of the Roman army, including a short period when a military detachment was based at Canterbury (Bennett *et al* 1982, 28–30), but soon after by Roman traders and others seeking to do business in this opening new market. From earliest days, the route from Richborough to Canterbury, aligned perhaps to cross the Little Stour valley to the north of the Ickham site, would have been well-used. Perhaps repeated flooding below the junction of the Little Stour and Wingham river brought about by a rising tidal regime in the lower reaches of the Little Stour made the original line of the road difficult to maintain. Whatever the case, on the basis of excavated evidence, the road found on the Ickham site is unlikely to pre-date the late first century, a period when Richborough was still the port of entry and Canterbury was beginning to see the construction of its first Roman buildings, including an early theatre-temple complex (Frere 1970; Bennett 1980; Blagg 1995).

By the early second century Dover became the dominant port and as Wacher (1995, 191) has noted it was the road from Dover to Canterbury rather than that from Richborough that determined a major element of Canterbury's grid. Interestingly, the longer north-east to south-west axis of the town follows the line of a pre-Roman track running along the Stour valley. Although the Richborough road approaches the town heading straight towards an early crossing of the Stour, the alignment makes for an awkward intersection with the later grid. It is also the case that the line of the Dover road achieves an uncomfortable angle with the temple-theatre complex. These inconsistencies in the Richborough and Dover alignments and the grid suggest that the early road may have owed its line not just to the ford, but also to a more complex pre-Roman topography that at present cannot be understood. One possibility is that a major cult centre or sanctuary site may have existed in this location and that one of the first steps in establishing the town was the construction of a new religious complex following a Gallic model of a combined theatre and temple precinct. The size and scale of the complex, built in *c* AD 80–90 (Frere 1970, 83–5; Bennett 1980; Blagg 1995) represents both a huge investment in resources and a key cultural symbol signalling acceptance of *Romanitas* by local élite. Construction of a Roman state sponsored monumental quadrifrons arch, built at this time at Richborough (Strong 1968), also appears to represent a celebration of conquest. The construction of twin lighthouses on the heights east and west above Dover, perhaps in the early second century, may also be seen as not just a practical aid to navigation but a state funded symbol of conquest (Haverfield and Wheeler 1934, 47–50; Philp 1981, 99–100).

The road grid for east Kent was probably fully established by the early second century and a number of 'native' settlements encouraged by improved routes of communication were beginning to adopt the Latin language, Roman styles of dress and buildings. In addition to the Roman villa at Wingham, a bath-house presumably attached to a native farmstead was constructed just outside Canterbury at Shelford (Boden 2004) and a substantial villa at Folkestone (Winbolt 1925). A large agricultural settlement is attested at Highstead (see p 330), with perhaps the development of masonry buildings in the early second century, stimulated by the construction of the Canterbury–Reculver road (Bennett *et al* 2007). A string of settlements on the south-eastern edge of the Lydden valley, most of them superseding late Iron Age settlement, appear to have been linked to the construction of the Dover–Richborough road. These include a villa at Cottington lakes (Fuller 2006, 48); a roadside settlement at Maydensole (Cross and Redding 2000); a temple complex at Worth (Parfitt forthcoming a); a settlement at Foxborough Hill, Eastry (Esmond-Cleary 1999, 374); a settlement, possibly a minor port, at Archer's Low (Parfitt forthcoming b); a small villa at Sandwich (Bennett 1978; Parfitt 1980), a settlement at Each End, Ash (Hicks 1998) and on the foreshore, a possible fishing settlement at Dixon's Corner (Parfitt 2000). A number of more extensive roadside settlements broadly comparable with Ickham may also be dated to this period: at Saltwood (Willson 2002), Hersden (Barrett 2004), Monkton, on the Isle of Thanet (Hicks 2008) and more distantly, at Westhawk Farm, Ashford (Booth *et al* 2008).

Perhaps the best understood roadside settlement is at the latter site. Westhawk Farm lies at a major junction of the Stour valley road (Canterbury–Ashford) and a route extending west from Lympne and Aldington. Covering more than 20 hectares, the settlement comprises a series of regular house plots on one side of the principal road and an open area with a probable shrine on the other. Its growth begins in the later first century and continues into the fourth, following a period of decline from *c* AD 250. A variety of industries are attested, including iron-working and a possible powered watermill. Less fully understood is the short-lived roadside settlement at Monkton (Hicks 2008). Here, an unusual number of sunken-featured buildings were uncovered, set against a well-developed hollow way. At least two substantial deep cellars were located, together with a large six-poster granary, a well cut to an extraordinary depth of 34m and two beam-in-slot buildings, including a small shrine on the outskirts of the settlement. The settlement of late first- or early second-century date was probably abandoned in the early third century. Although this was almost certainly an agricultural settlement, some industrial activities perhaps associated with fulling may have been taking place. At Hersden, a palimpsest site of prehistoric and Roman date overlooking the valley of the Great Stour, remarkable continuity of alignment in enclosure and field boundaries was attested, clearly indicating the antiquity of an adjoining trackway pre-dating a Roman road. Located mid way between Canterbury and Grove Ferry, the settlement may have acted as both a posting station, gaining sustenance from those using the highway and as a base for a farming community working the fertile brickearth soils.

At Richborough, although military occupation appears to have come to an end by *c* AD 80–90, the site develops into a civilian settlement complete with a possible *mansio* to cater for those waiting for passage across the channel or preparing for a journey inland (Cunliffe 1968). The development of the port and facilities at Dover, including twin lighthouses heralded a shift in emphasis away from Richborough and one can assume that traffic on the Richborough–Canterbury road was affected by its loss of status.

Settlement activity at Ickham appears to begin in earnest in the second century with the foundation of an enclosure system of ditches north of the road and a water channel (Channel A) to the south. The channel, cut too far from the road to be a road drain, may have been the head-race for a mill pre-dating Mill 1. The quarry cut across the settlement at an acute angle and the continuation of the channel north-westwards and the possible site of an early mill was either lost to quarrying or lay outside the quarry to the north-east.

From just a few sherds of first- to early second-century date, pottery from the site increases significantly in quantity from the mid second century onwards suggesting that Channel A and the putative predecessor to Mill 1 functioned from that time onwards. The precise position of Mill 1 could not be fixed on the evidence available, but we can be sure that Channel A did not service the mill. As Mill 1 has been dated on coin and pottery evidence to *c* AD 220–70 then the earlier dated material in this location may derive from an earlier occupation focus, perhaps a mill. Notwithstanding the presence of the channel and the earlier dated material, the existence of an early mill can only be speculated upon.

We can however be sure that during the third century a significant sized settlement had begun to develop on the Ickham site. Combined evidence from the excavation, air photographs and observations during quarrying in the area between 1972 and 1974, suggest that the settlement may have extended for almost a kilometre from close to the line of the Wingham river to the south-western suburbs of Wickhambreaux (*see* above p 333).

There has been some speculation as to whether the Little Stour would have been navigable in the Roman period, giving those using the site direct access to the Wantsum and the sea. Although the Little Stour would have provided an ample perennial flow to drive mill machinery, it is most unlikely that the stream was of sufficient size to have been navigable even by small boats up-stream of the mill. Even down-stream of the mill, had tidal surges flooded the valley to any degree, it is inconceivable that mills would have been built on the site, since their capability to function would have been compromised. The Little Stour joins the Great Stour and the estuary approximately 4km down-stream of the settlement and once spent water from the mill joined the main stream of the Little Stour and combined with the waters of the Wingham river, it is just possible that the stream thereby formed would have allowed a small boat to follow the flow to the estuary; it would have been far more difficult to row or punt against the current to get back. The tidal regime would have influenced the amount of water collecting at the mouth of the Little Stour and for a kilometre or so inland and one could make a case for this area being used as a temporary anchorage for shipping waiting for the tide to take them up the Great Stour to Fordwich or Sturry. Whatever the case, there can be little doubt that those living and working at the Ickham settlement would have enjoyed ample supplies of clean, running water and the seasonal benefits of the estuary, the sea and all the associated resources.

The Ickham settlement can presently be recognised as one of at least five major sites within a 3km radius (Fig 3). At Wingham a substantial bath-house formed part of a larger site that comprised an aisled barn and another building probably of villa status (Dowker 1882; 1883; Jenkins 1984). The second site, near Britton Farm, east of Ickham, is notable for the recovery of stamped lead seals and building debris sufficient to indicate the existence of a substantial building with an official status (Dowker 1883, 355; Taylor 1932, 119; Still 1994). This, the nearest major building, lies approximately a kilometre south of the present site. A third building of unknown character adjoins Littlebourne, on the west bank of the Little Stour, some 2km. South-west of the gravel pit site. To the north, another little known site consists of unspecified building remains near Wenderton House, on the eastern bank of the Wingham river, close to the presumed route of the Ickham road heading east or north-east. A substantial collection of pottery from the Wenderton site collected during fieldwalking and the monitoring of service trenching by James Ogilvie, includes an extraordinary range of material dating from the first to the later fourth century. Whilst the finds may derive from a single long-lived building complex, yet to be discovered, the material gathered from a wide area is more likely to be associated with a roadside settlement, similar to Ickham but occupying a hilltop position on the edge of the escarpment and a steep climb up from the valley floor. Of the remainder, a series of early Roman cremation burials and one or more late Roman pottery kilns (Jessup and Taylor 1932, 163) are known in the area south of Preston. The kilns and their products are important locally and are well represented at Ickham, Richborough, Wenderton and Canterbury. Other kilns producing grog-tempered grey wares may exist in the area around Richborough or Canterbury (p 85). These products, terminologically called Richborough wares first appear in east Kent in the mid fourth century and continue in use into the early fifth century.

A second channel (Channel B) was constructed late in the first quarter of the third century and it is proposed that this was the head-race for Mill 1. The presence of Mill 1, dated by coins to *c* AD 220–70, together with the successor mills (Mill 2 built *c* AD 270–90; Mill 3 built *c* AD 390–400 and Mill 4, built AD 400+) taken together with the speculation for a fifth mill predating Mill 1 (p 337 above), constitute an outstanding contribution to the study of Roman watermills in Britain. Within the context of the settlement the presence of the mills provides evidence for the near continuous production of milled grain for over 200 years and perhaps as long as 250 years. This clearly indicates that from the first the construction of a mill in this location was seminal and perhaps the catalyst around which the settlement with attendant industries both formed and developed. Andrew Wilson has argued above (pp 62–3) that such mills were probably commonplace in the Roman landscape, having spread widely through the Roman world by the first century AD. The record of a millstone from a powered mill, found nearby at the Wingham villa, gives local credence to this statement. However, no powered millstones of Roman date have been recovered from a location in east Kent associated with a watercourse, the nearest being from Westhawk Farm. At Canterbury although numerous querns have been recovered and at least one animal-powered mill attested (Frere and Stow 1983, 53), there is no evidence for a water-powered mill, despite the presence of the River Stour. As we have seen above, there are a number of watercourses in east Kent that could have driven a mill, but traces of Roman mills have not, to date been found.

By the early third century Canterbury was a flourishing place with a fully developed civic centre, a regular grid of streets, numerous town-houses (Bennett 1980) and a rebuilt theatre (Frere 1970). An industrial suburb to the west of the town, active from the late first century onwards, producing mainly ceramic building materials and pottery, but also metalwork, was in serious decline. Overall there is little evidence for shops and only modest evidence for craft industries (Blockley *et al* 1995). In contrast, Richborough in the early third century, whilst still retaining its status as a port and town (probably of much diminished size) saw the return of the military and the construction of a signalling station, using the quadrifrons arch as the base of the timber signalling tower (Detsicas 1983, 25). A significant number of brooches of this period recovered from the site can be paralleled in the German frontier forts (Bayley and Butcher 2004, 2), perhaps suggesting that the troops manning the stations were from that area. The size of the detachment of naval or land army personnel is likely to have been small and would have had an insignificant impact on the economy of the area. Also at this time and perhaps as early as the second decade of the third century a new fort was constructed on a spur of land facing north into the Thames estuary and east across the Wantsum channel towards the Isle of Thanet at Reculver, in this case the fist cohort of a Batavian regiment (Philp 2005, 216). At the same time, at Dover, a fort built in *c* AD 117–38 went into disuse (Philp 1981). Martin Millett has made a case for this fort being used not as a naval base for the *Classis Britannica*, as has previously been suggested, but rather as part of a range of facilities, including port (for use by military and civilian shipping) and lighthouses, establishing Dover as a new key port of entry into the province, opposite Boulogne where a more regular fort is a better candidate for a *Classis Britannica* base (Millet 2007). Whilst analysis of the excavated and postulated facilities suggests that some of the buildings may have functioned as warehouses (perhaps replacements for the recently abandoned Richborough supply depot), others are clearly barrack blocks, not unlike those at Boulogne. Whilst the presence of warehouses may explain some of the irregularities within the layout of the Dover fort, there are also clear indications of a regular military establishment, including a possible Headquarters building, set centrally but close to a minor northern gate giving access to the western *pharos* and traces of a possible commanding officer's quarters nearby. The Dover facility on the basis of the known and postulated layout, though much smaller and subordinate to the base across the channel, is likely to have been a military facility providing permanent facilities for a garrison as well as accommodation for naval personnel or soldiers in transit across the Channel or passing around the coast. Whatever the function of the Dover facility, its role appears to have ceased by *c* AD 208.

That Dover even without a military base continued to be recognised as the dominant port well into the third century is indicated by the status of Canterbury's Ridingate, when the circuit of walls was constructed *c* AD 270–90. Ridingate appears to have been the only double-carriageway gate in the circuit and was clearly designed to act as the town main gate. It is interesting to note that not long after the gate was built, the double doors of the south-west carriageway were closed and never re-opened, the space being used as a workshop (Blockley 1989). This perhaps indicates that the importance of the Dover road had diminished and may suggest that Richborough succeeded Dover as the dominant port of the fourth century, thereby increasing the volume of traffic along the Richborough–Canterbury road.

At Canterbury despite huge investment in providing the city with a defensive circuit, town-houses established in the early second century were going into disuse and many of the public buildings were in decline (Blagg 1995, 17–18). Streets were reduced in size or went out of use, a number of public utilities notably drains were in disrepair and sections of the town appear to have been abandoned. In the countryside there is evidence for the growth of villa estates, indicating perhaps a movement of urban élite and investment away from administrative centres into rural areas. The stimulus for this may have been the development of forts, posting stations and beacons for the Saxon Shore fort system and the enhanced network of communication that formed part of that system. An equally convincing case however, can be made for the non-sustainability of urban life; maintenance of civic buildings, highways and public utilities could no longer be supported by the urban élite that in response, retrenched to the source of their wealth and status – their agricultural estates.

At Ickham, Mill 1 went out of use at this time and a new mill was constructed up-stream, re-using but rebuilding a section of the earlier head-race (Channel C). Mill 2 may have been built soon after *c* AD 270, but a coin found 'under the mill floor' may date construction after *c* AD 322. Whatever the construction date, Mill 3 eventually replaced Mill 2 in the same channel, perhaps some time after *c* AD 390 and a final mill channel was cut to the south of Mill 3 in the early fifth century. Overall, activity at Ickham appears to intensify from the early fourth century onwards. At a time when other settlements are in decline, Ickham appears to have been a thriving place.

Whilst the discovery of a series of later Roman mills on the Ickham site marks the place to be of exceptional importance, the salvage excavation also produced 4,610 coins, 205kg of pottery and over 3,000 objects classified as small finds and this too is remarkable. Given the circumstances of the salvage excavation, the methods of recovery of the artefacts and the partial 'weeding' of many of the contexts to reduce the bulk of the pottery or finds that were considered to be of lesser value (body sherds, animal bone, shell and metal-working slag appear to have been largely discarded), there is reasonable congruence between the dating of contexts by pottery and coins, but not by small finds which by and large dated earlier. Where non-congruity occurs it is usually a disparity between the dating of small finds with each other and in comparison with coins and pottery. The explanation rests with the industrial nature of the settlement and in particular the working of metals. Much of the small find assemblage comprises deliberately broken or folded items, cut sheets and fragments of metals broken deliberately small, all presumably collected for recycling. Many of the contexts in later third- and fourth-century contexts contain this material, with the metalwork having originally been made in a much earlier period and mixed in a way that one would rarely encounter on other archaeological sites. It is likely that material recovered during the salvage excavation represents a small proportion that was actually on the site, and a minute proportion of the mass collected for recycling that may have been on the site at one time. The material that found its way into rubbish pits or field ditches was probably surface waste; the larger collections of material found infilling channels or included in the flood silts in Area 4 is perhaps the product of wholesale clearances of the site late in the occupation sequence. On this basis any of the late contexts may have contained residual metalwork often in considerable quantity.

Coin and pottery dates broadly agree for most assemblages. In the early period there are few coins predating AD 260 and save for a few sherds of first- and second-century date, very little pottery that predates the early third century. Although much of the Ickham ceramic material comes from poorly recorded contexts, there are a number of well-stratified groups including large assemblages from the third-century Mill 1 and the post AD 270 Mills 2 and 3. Areas 4 and 5 provided mid to late fourth-century pottery and coin assemblages and late features at the north-east end of the site contained key late groups of material dated by coins and pottery. A very late date was also mirrored by coins and pottery in Channel D at the polar opposite end of the site. Overall there is good congruity between coin and pottery dates for most of the contexts.

Although there is ample evidence from earlier contexts to suggest that metal-working and other craft practices were taking place at Ickham throughout the third century, it is in the fourth century that the level of activity increases, particularly south of the road near the operating mill. Here, a range of gully-like features perhaps beam-slots, indicated the presence of buildings, principally in Area 4. A number of pits associated with the putative buildings contained a significant group of pottery, metal and other finds which together with material recovered from demolition and abandonment deposits clearly reflected a dynamic industry providing a range of services for a broad but locally based clientele. Metal-working in iron, copper alloy, lead, lead alloy and pewter were represented, together with evidence for leather-working, wood-working, textile production in linen (flax processing) and in wool, bone- and antler-working and agricultural practices.

Alongside the mills, metal-working appears to have been the dominant industry. Hammers used for planishing and as an anvil, together with evidence for blacksmith's tongs and other equipment indicate that at least one workshop may have been that of a blacksmith making and repairing tools and providing a wide range of fittings for equally diverse purposes. Agricultural implements included shears, hook blades, a spud, scythes, a hay rake and a hayfork. Traditionally the blacksmith provides horseshoes and hipposandals for those using the road and these are represented together with bridle bits, curb bits and cart fittings. A wide range of nails, straps and bindings are also amongst the finds suggesting that a variety of structural fittings were being produced both for those working the mill and for the community at large.

More specialist craftsmen were also in evidence through the wide range of objects in copper alloy and lead alloy recovered from the site. The pewter pendants are rare objects for which there are, at present, few parallels. The presence of another example from nearby at Wickhambreux and the fact that two of the pendants were made from the same mould suggest that they were made at Ickham and can be viewed alongside the hairpins with 'pewter' heads, perhaps another rare locally produced accessory. The quantity of lead alloy waste and scrap also suggests on-site manufacture of a range of rather more utilitarian pots, pans and drinking vessels. It is possible that the scrap was not only collected to be recast into other lead alloy items but also formed a constituent of other non-ferrous metal mixes.

In contrast, within the copper alloy assemblage, the evidence for manufacture is slight. There are single examples of unfinished needles (one copper alloy, one iron), as well as slight indications of an unfinished bracelet, one bent and cracked buckle, and an apparently unfinished belt fastener. In terms of the belt fittings, however, there are also slender indications of regional east Kent styles and this does suggest that they were made on site, as does comparison with the growing number of such fittings from east Kent, exemplified by examples from Canterbury, Each End Ash and Saltwood,

as well as Ickham. Beyond the belt fittings, it is clear that there is evidence of the collection of scrap metal for recycling, but few good indications of manufacture.

A large number of metal objects had radio-opaque specks visible within the corrosion products. On investigation of a sample, they were found to be minute specks of copper alloy and sometimes lead alloy and they have been interpreted as produced, in all probability, during metal-working processes and accumulated in the immediate area where this was taking place. It is suggested that they may have become incorporated into a deposit, along with sweepings from the workshop floor. These specks have also been found in the corrosion products of iron objects from Mill 2 (Assemblage 11), late features in Area 4 (Assemblage 18) and in fifth-century abandonment deposits (Assemblage 27) in Areas 1 and 4. It is likely that they all derive from one source, ie one episode of clearance, although they cover a wide area. As we have seen above, metal-working appears to have been focused around Area 4 in the late Roman period and it is here that the possible workshops may have been originally sited.

By what agency the scrap material was collected is difficult to say, but the waste metalwork appears to represent a wide chronological range, with every section of east Kent society represented. Whether scrap metal was exchanged in part payment for goods or that a late Roman 'Steptoe and Son' were doing the rounds of farms, villages, villas and military bases, paying for or collecting scrap for free, is impossible to say. Whilst most of the material collected was clearly destined for recycling, there can be no doubt that a small but significant number of pieces and debris represent manufacturing on the site.

Other materials were also present, including glass. The quantities of glass from Ickham are considerable for an east Kent rural site, if unexceptional for other locations. They also seem a little disproportionate, with the noticeable presence of early Roman bottles on a site principally of late Roman date. The presence of the number, range and date of the glass vessels represented is difficult to explain, but some form of storage of goods for retailing purposes might be one of a number of possibilities.

Other worked materials and tools suggest other forms of manufacturing or rural industries. Bone- and antler-working appears to have taken place and this industry may have extended to the opportunist exploitation of cetacean remains, a circumstance paralleled by unpublished material from Richborough and seen elsewhere in east Kent at this time (Riddler 2006). Leather-working may also have taken place on the site with surviving leather scraps concentrated in enclosure ditches north of the road, in Area 16. The remains comprise mostly of shoes, together with a few scraps of offcuts, which are not sufficient to allow anything to be said about on-site manufacture. Various tools suggest that wood-working took place on the site and the structural evidence for this activity, in the form of shaped timbers for the mills, is augmented by a wooden figurine of late Roman date. Textile production is indicated by both metal and ceramic objects, including the processing of wool, (both carding and spinning is in evidence) and with tentative evidence for retting pits and the recovery of parts of a flax heckle, the growing of flax and the manufacture of linen is suggested.

Agricultural equipment was also in evidence and there can be little doubt that a significant section of the community here may have tended fields and animals in the vicinity. The discovery of fishing weights and a boat hook also indicate exploitation of the local freshwater and marine resources. Exploitation of local oyster beds is also indicated by reports of oyster shells at the site, although none were collected for study.

In the absence of any other environmental material, beyond a small quantity of animal remains, and of any structures (outside of the mills), little can be said of any further activities, although the high quantity of mortaria does indicate food production on some scale. Circumstance may imply that a roadside market lay in the vicinity of the site, depending of course on whether the food was produced for local consumption, or whether it was destined for Canterbury, Richborough or more distant markets. A proportion of the metalwork suggests that Canterbury and Richborough were important markets for those working at Ickham and the quantities of jewellery and official items that dominate the object assemblage, may have been intended for those destinations. In the event, they were discarded.

Statistically, the recovered coins from Ickham dating from *c* AD 260 until AD 388 more or less follow a regional pattern and can be favourably compared with Canterbury and Richborough. Between *c* AD 388 and 402 however, a marked contrast can be drawn between the three centres, in that Ickham has notably fewer coins of this period than its neighbours or indeed other very late Roman sites in Kent. Whilst the lack of coins of the period may be a consequence of the nature of the excavation, it may reflect a tailing-off in industrial occupation on the site or a shift in retail focus to another part of the settlement. There are sufficient numbers of coins and pottery from the polar ends of the site and from either side of the road to indicate that the settlement was still functioning in the fifth century, but perhaps the nature of the settlement had changed before *c* AD 388, leading to a severe decline in trade and therefore in coin loss on the site.

The number of coins recovered from the site and particularly from within Channel C is redolent of 'retail' occupations. It can be argued that at least a proportion of the assemblage may have derived from fees paid by local farmers for the processing of grain. Interestingly, as noted above, there is another case for a mill producing large quantities of coins, the Agora mill in Athens (Parsons 1936, 88). Here the coin derived from the interior of a much more complete structure, the excavator postulating the one time presence of an internal timber floor through which the coins had dropped. In the case of Ickham, the greatest quantity of coins (some 450) was recovered from a pit cutting the head-race of Mill 3 in Channel C, the coins reportedly occurring in rows where they had presumably lodged between rotted boards of the mill structure or perhaps hidden in a bag or a box, and then been redeposited in a fused state in the pit fill. By contrast, a second pit, cut on the site of the Mill 3 wheel position, produced far fewer coins.

The significance of the quantity of coinage needs to be examined since the obvious explanation of trade is not the only possible interpretation. As noted above, the number of coins associated with the mills, especially Channel C is paralleled in at least one mill, albeit somewhat later in date and at the other end of the late Roman world. This could suggest transactions took place within the building, the most obvious being the payment for the grinding of corn. However, there are also other possibilities for the presence of coins, including the scattering of hoard(s) secreted within the building or in open ground within the settlement, the donation of offerings to a sacred spot or even the disposal of scrap metal. Of these possibilities the first is indeed credible during the late Roman period, even if it appears to pre-figure arrangements more familiar in medieval times. A derivation from the scattering of hoarded coin is not suggested by statistical analysis, while the ritual explanation is scarcely satisfactory. The last pre-supposes a fifth-century and post-Roman date of deposition, after the token coin has been effectively demonetised with the break from the money economy of the Empire. But it is, strangely, not so unlikely in view of the documentary evidence in the 'life' of St John the Almsgiver that a ship in this period returned from Britain half laden with coins, half with tin, the context suggesting that in this case the coins were hardly legal tender in payment but being transported as scrap (Baines 1948; Dark 1994; Penhallurick 1986, 245). The large quantities of coins here and, for that matter, at Richborough. might have been collected for re-use after melting down, but then discarded as unsuitable or unwanted. Although it is tempting to interpret the quantity of coins from the Ickham site as the debris of metal-working, the general distribution of the material (the record does not include detailed findspot information) and the presence of significant numbers of coins in stratified, pre fifth-century contexts, is not consistent with the interpretation and we return again to the view that coin numbers reflect a vibrant retail trade in the second half of the fourth century.

Although the evidence is far from clear, by the mid fourth century Canterbury may have become an administrative centre for the protection of east Kent and a resurgence of occupation within the town may have resulted. Timber buildings were constructed within the shells of abandoned and derelict masonry town-houses at this time. Sites never developed were developed for the first time and there is a marked increase in pottery and coinage (Blagg 1995), but as yet only small quantities of military gear and trappings (Ager 1987, 31). The Roman temple precinct appears to have been cleared of surrounding portico and perhaps internal buildings in the mid fourth century and there appears to be an increase in prosperity, perhaps related to the town's geographical location (and perhaps administrative role) at the 'hub of the wheel' of the east Kent road system.

There is a mixed picture elsewhere. The agricultural settlements at Highstead and Shelford had been abandoned by this time and a number of the settlements adjoining the Lydden valley also appear to have been vacated. Overall it would appear that there is increasing evidence for the decline of rural settlement, but perhaps not for villas. One unusual new foundation was at Worth. Here a Romano-Celtic temple was built on the site of an earlier shrine in the mid fourth century, dated by a coin of Constantine II (*c* AD 337–40). The site, poorly excavated in the 1920s, provided two buried fragments of a monumental statue (Klein 1928).

The Ickham settlement may have been at its zenith during the fourth century. Whether this was wholly a result of the status of the port of Richborough and of late Roman Canterbury is difficult to say, but developments at Ickham must have been stimulated to some degree by the militarisation of east Kent from the early fourth century onwards and increased traffic along the Richborough–Canterbury road. East Kent in the late fourth century may well have been a military zone, but as Millett has pointed out, troops on the ground may not have been that numerous and the effect of an enhanced military presence on the economy of east Kent may not have been that great. The forts at Reculver, Richbrough, Dover and Lympne and the defences of Canterbury were all manned, but the strength of the garrison overall may not have exceeded perhaps 2,000 men (Millett 2007). The forts were not designed as a response to a single set of events, rather to perhaps maintain

the security of the ports and the shipping of military supplies. Only after AD 367 can the fortifications be directly associated with a barbarian threat (Jones and Mattingly 1990, 140). The fourth-century garrison of the Shore forts are supposed to have been manned by *limitanei,* settled frontier troops, with other high grade mobile units, *comitatenses,* based in walled towns like Canterbury. It is exceptionally difficult to identify the presence of particularly the latter as many of the buckle and belt fittings connected with the army were in common use by other sections of the local population, particularly the civil service (*see* above pp 157–9) Indeed, the identification of Ickham as a production centre for such dress items and the speculated link with the military must be reviewed in light of this. Further still, despite the size of the fortifications, the complexes themselves appear to lack the service buildings one would expect to see in facilities with a large garrison, again suggesting that the military were just not that numerous and are therefore unlikely to have been a dominant force in the local economy.

Whilst military personnel mainly defended the ports, towns like Canterbury and Rochester may have acted as focal points for both the military and a local militia. A broad parallel for east Kent in the late fourth century might perhaps be made with Cyrenaica in the fifth century. At that time Bishop Synesius of Ptolemais records in a series of letters, the existence of a local militia comprising army, navy and civilian personnel forming a tactical force, based on towns, to defend against increasing raids by Libyan tribes (Reynolds 1976, 239–53). Like Cyrenaica, the defence of east Kent from increasing 'pirate' raiding may have owed more to a local militia, drawn from the young men of Canterbury and from wealthy, landholding families occupying villaestates in the Stour valley and elsewhere and older members of east Kent community with past military experience, than to regular troops drawn from the army and navy. That a local militia would have also required military-type trappings, may have acted as a further stimulus for the sustained occupation of metalworkers on the site and account for the numbers of such fittings recovered during the salvage excavation.

Certainly by the end of the fifth century there were very few military centres remaining in east Kent. On coin evidence Lympne was largely abandoned by *c* AD 350 (Reece 1989) and Reculver shows an absence of coins after AD 378 (Philp 1981, 120). Only Richborough, Canterbury, Rochester and perhaps Dover (Keith Parfitt and John Willson, pers comm) have produced large numbers of coins from the period *c* AD 388–402 (in the case of Richborough some 22,000 coins, perhaps pay for the troops that was never put in circulation). That Ickham has also produced a few late issues and late pottery clearly indicates continuing occupation and an operating mill into at least the opening decade of the fifth century.

The masonry building at Ickham, 1km south of the site, relocated by Jim Bradshaw in 1974 and the several lead sealings of the period AD 317–37 and 361–3 (Hassall and Tomlin 1979, 350–3) come into sharp focus in this period. The sealings derive from the breaking open of sacks or bales where materials were being processed on behalf of the state. The seals were discovered away from the Ickham site, but in literature have been erroneously connected with it (Detsicas 1983). One can only speculate about the nature of the building, but the finds clearly suggest some kind of official presence within a kilometre of the Ickham site, but not on the site itself, where if there were state or military control, one would expect other examples to have been found. The presence of the seals should rather be taken to demonstrate that the local garrisons (at Canterbury and Richborough) required to be supplied, mainly from local sources and this discovery therefore represents perhaps, at best, a collection centre for the military, or more likely evidence for one or two transactions by a local farmer with the military.

Malcolm Lyne has argued above (pp 135–8) that the wide variety of imported pottery present on the site and dated to the period *c* AD 370–400 and later, particularly that from Pevensey in Sussex and Burgh Castle in Norfolk, may indicate a close relationship with the military. This may be so in part, but surely the presence of this material is more a reflection of the proximity of the port at Richborough, not the military. After all, one third of all the late pottery (one half of all coarsewares) was of Richborough grog-tempered pottery and some material was from the local Preston kilns (in severe decline at that time). The presence of the material and the sheer variety of sources of supply for this late period is perhaps the most interesting aspect of the pottery collection as a whole. The list of continental sources represented includes Mayen ware from Eifel in Germany, late *bandes-lustrée* wares from Amiens, north-east Gaul, Argonne wares from north-east Gaul, late *terra nigra* from Arras and German marbled ware. These imports together with Harrold shell-tempered ware from Bedfordshire, Hadham ware from Hertfordshire and a wide range of Oxfordshire wares indicate good routes of communication (despite pirates) and a surprisingly vibrant local market, well into the late fourth century and possibly into the fifth.

The final phase of activity at Ickham may have occurred some time after *c* AD 390 when Mill 3 went into disuse and a fourth channel was cut (Channel D). Massive timbers located at the base of the channel have been interpreted as a mill base

by Robert Spain (pp 59–62), but the evidence for type of mill cannot be proven. Construction of Channel D appears to have coincided with a wholesale clearance of buildings east of the new mill and south of the road. Substantial quantities of metalwork, pottery and coins were deposited in Channel C. On the opposite side of the road two timber-lined tanks and a series of substantial unlined pits may have been used as retting pits for processing flax and making linen. The timber-lined pits contained pottery and coins dating to AD 388–402 (Assemblage 22). Channel D (Mill 4) contained a small but interesting collection of late or sub Roman pottery and coins dating into the fifth century (Assemblages 26).

A number of burials were recorded during gravel extraction north of the road at the eastern end of the site, though their precise location is unknown. An isolated burial was recorded to the south of the road. A crouched inhumation and reports of two cremation burials being destroyed by the drag-line (above, p 16) indicate earlier episodes of burial. Of the six or seven burials recovered from the site, none may be considered to be unusual and most probably represent individuals working and living at the Ickham settlement. The presence of the burials, together with numerous domestic items recovered from the site, clearly indicates that the make-up of the settlement was both commercial and domestic. The identification of grave-like cropmarks close to the road line south-west of Wickhambreaux, perhaps indicates the presence of another cemetery in that location (p 333).

At Canterbury there is evidence for burial within the town walls (possibly the result of epidemics and a breakdown of civic discipline: Bennett 1980; Hicks and Houliston forthcoming) and for late shops built over a street line (Blockley *et al* 1995). Coins recovered from the building, possibly a cobbler's workshop, included issues dating up to AD 402. A collection of late Roman silver deposited in the second decade of the fifth century (Johns and Potter 1985, 312–52) containing a series of silver spoons including one with a chi-rho symbol on the bowl and another with the inscription VIRIBONISM, 'I belong to a good man' may perhaps have been a Christian hoard. The hoard, which also contained four silver ingots of a type issued by emperors as donatives for troops or officials, may suggest that this material, together with another hoard from Richborough (RIB 2402.6), and evidence for the very late abandonment of both sites, were the property of officials gathering with the last remaining troops in this part of Kent in the early fifth century prior to departure.

Occupation of the Ickham site appears to have been near continuous from the mid second century onwards with the quantity of dated features and finds indicating increased commercial activity from the mid third into the mid fourth century. The site appears to have been most active in the second half of the fourth century and it is clear that a low level of commercial activity continued into the early fifth century. There can be little doubt that the nature and longevity of the settlement owed much to the status of the road and to road traffic between the port and provincial centre and it is likely that the presence of a mill in this location also acted as a catalyst to draw other industries or trades to the site. Few rural sites in east Kent display such extraordinary longevity and no other rural site has provided evidence for industrial and commercial activity extending into the early fifth century. It is worth mentioning at this point that the extent of the settlement was not established during the watching brief or the excavation and it is possible that the elements recorded may constitute only the north-eastern part of a larger 'ribbon' development that may extend up-stream of the quarry into undisturbed ground between the south-western edge of the quarry and the hamlet of Wickhambreaux.

Some assessment of the economic basis of the site should be attempted. The longevity of the settlement and the wide variety of trades represented and the significant number of coins recovered from mills 2 and 3 suggest a close trading relationship with the local community. Throughout the life of the settlement there were a number of major reorganisations (field systems, mill leats, mill structures, possible workshops), culminating perhaps in the early fifth century with the demolition of Mill 3 and possible workshops to the south, the infilling of the mill leat with resultant debris from the demolitions and the construction of Mill 4 to the south of the previous arrangement. Whilst it is possible that the settlement was run by a group of independent traders and craftsmen, including a miller, such an arrangement of individual independent entrepreneurs is unlikely to have continued in business for so long. The construction and maintenance of mills and mill-races alone would have required a consistent skills base and above all finance that is unlikely to have been available to an independent milling family over a number of generations. On the basis of existing evidence it is impossible to determine what that consistent guiding interest might have been, but one possibility is that the roadside settlement, comprising a mixture of domestic, agricultural, industrial and commercial elements (and cemeteries) may have formed part of a much larger estate, centred perhaps on a nearby villa, but with the landowning family holding a portfolio of other commercial interests in the locality (farms, woodland, fisheries, salt production, potteries, boat building, transport, etc) in common with the palimpsest commercial interests of powerful landowning

families in other parts of the Roman Empire (Heather 2006, 16).

It is tempting to compare this hypothetical estate, with the assessment of the adjoining Manor of Wickambreaux given in Domesday Book. In 1086, in addition to a settlement with thirty-six villagers, a church, a priest and thirty-two cottars (presumably living outside the settlement), the manor contained meadow, pasture, a considerable tract of woodland (pannage for eighty pigs) and a substantial expanse of arable worked by eleven ploughs (assessed at 4 sulungs). In addition, the manor contained two mills, which may well have exploited the same waterway as the Roman mill and on the extremities of the manor, presumably against the Wantsum, were two salthouses and three fisheries. Ickham, by comparison (which is arguably at too great a distance from the Roman settlement to be a natural successor to it) may not have been in existence much before *c* 742 (Wallenberg 1934, 521), and has a church, four mills, 35 acres of meadow and woodland sufficient for thirty pigs (Domesday, Kent (Morgan 1983) 3, 8). The hamlet of Seaton, arguably closest to the Roman settlement, cannot be dated by documentary evidence much before *c* 1292 (Wallenberg 1934, 523).

If the excavated site formed only part of a larger settlement, then the area up-stream, between the quarry and Wickhambreaux, may yet contain vital evidence of a successor Anglo-Saxon settlement. The place-name of Wickhambreaux is listed by Gelling as an example of a '*wickham*' name (Gelling 1978, 67–74). The meaning of such early Anglo-Saxon names has been well discussed and it would seem that they frequently occur on the line of a Roman road, often close to former Roman habitation sites. Quite probably the name derives from an Old English term for Romano-British settlement that survived into the early Anglo-Saxon period. The description would appear to fit the circumstances perfectly.

The presence of early Anglo-Saxon pottery and metalwork (principally keys and knives) in a very few of the latest contexts is interesting and has given rise to the speculation that a final clearance of the site may have occurred in the early Anglo-Saxon period. Whilst it is now accepted that the type of horseshoe found at Ickham can be dated to the late Roman period and need not be of early medieval origin (Reddé and Schnurbein 2001, 320–1, pl 108), the finds clearly indicate a level of post-Roman occupation on the site which conceivably may have been no more than the occasional episode of scavenging for metals or other re-usable remains, but equally may suggest that an early Anglo-Saxon settlement exists nearby. Although it cannot be proven, it is tempting to interpret the evidence as indicating a continuance of occupation at or near the site, into the period of the establishment of the earliest Anglo-Saxon settlements in Kent.

Several early Anglo-Saxon burials have been recorded in close proximity to Wickhambreaux, the most significant being at Supperton Farm on the 10m contour north-east of the village (Meaney 1964, 140–1; Richardson 2005, 82–3). A group of three Anglo-Saxon pottery vessels, possibly associated with a burial were recorded in the cemetery of Wickhambreaux church and a late sixth- or early seventh-century pottery bowl, perhaps from a burial is recorded from the village but without an exact find-spot. Cropmarks indicating prehistoric ring-ditches and more ephemeral markings perhaps indicative of later graves exist immediately south-west of the village, north of the Roman road and close to Wickhambreaux church (above, p 332) A significant number of early Anglo-Saxon cemeteries are known in association with prehistoric burial mounds (for example at nearby Ringlemere Farm (Parfitt 2007b), St Margaret's at Cliff (Parfitt 2004) and at Saltwood (Glass 1999, 210) and an Anglo-Saxon cemetery in association with prehistoric barrows south-west of the village is considered a strong possibility.

A postulated continued use of the Roman road linking the old Roman port and early Anglo-Saxon Canterbury, place-name evidence for Wickhambreaux, three or more early Anglo-Saxon burials near the village and the evidence for early Anglo-Saxon pottery and metalwork from the quarry site, all combine to support the supposition that the present village may be the successor roadside settlement and that continuity of occupation from sub-Roman to Anglo-Saxon could be indicated. Over two centuries of Roman milling at the site saw the replacement of mills up-stream of their predecessor and it is not inconceivable that in continuance of the tradition, an Anglo-Saxon mill may yet exist up-steam of the latest of the Roman mills. Far more speculative, is the proposition that the description of the Manor of Wickhambreaux recorded in Domesday Book may mirror the constituent parts of a surviving Roman estate centre perhaps originally run from the Wingham or Ickham villas.

In later periods milling remained an important feature of the landscape around Ickham. In the eighteenth century flour mills were built on the Little Stour, two at Littlebourne, one at Wickhambreaux and another at Seaton. The course of the river was diverted from Littlebourne Bridge for two miles to Seaton and was banked to help provide a head of water for the mills. Traces of these banks can still be seen in the fields west of Seaton. It seems likely that in post-Roman times the river system was somewhat smaller than in the previous period. Nevertheless it was still used for water transport until relatively recently. In 1801 the river was canalized moving it away from its old course (now known as the 'Blackhole Dyke'), which forms part of the parish boundary and barges plied between Seaton and Sandwich, importing Russian wheat for milling. The passing of the Corn Laws saw the decline of flour milling in the area and the last barge was finally laid up against Seaton quay in 1870.

PART 8: SUMMARY

Christopher Sparey-Green

The site at Ickham, on the flood plain of the Little Stour, east of Canterbury, Kent was investigated as a 'rescue excavation' following its discovery during gravel quarrying between 1972 and 1974. The work was carried out by a local amateur group directed by Jim Bradshaw with a final season under Christopher Young, funded by the then Department of the Environment (now English Heritage).

Slight evidence for prehistoric occupation on the valley gravels and peats comprised a scatter of worked flints, a crouched inhumation, a ring-ditch and residual sherds of 'Belgic' pottery from the late Iron Age.

The earliest Roman activity dated from the late first century AD and comprised pits and linear ditches, possibly part of an enclosure system. These were overlain by a gravel road with flanking ditches which crossed the site from south-west to north-east and was possibly the main route from Richborough to Canterbury. To the north-east the road crossed an ancient channel of the river, visible on air photographs taken prior to the quarrying. The road line was flanked by ditched enclosures which contained a well and several timber-lined tanks possibly for processing leather or cloth. At least six inhumation burials were also noted. Reports of building debris associated with pottery and burning suggest that more substantial buildings may have existed to the north-east, the present site being a roadside extension peripheral to a settlement destroyed during quarrying closer to the river.

Four linear channels flanking the road line appear to have channelled water from the river to power at least four mills recorded during quarrying. The earliest mill was in use in the early third century AD, the other channels in operation during the fourth and early fifth century. The timber mill buildings and channels were associated with fourth-century pottery, coins, quernstone fragments and a wooden votive figurine. Metal-working waste, furnace debris and tools suggest the mills formed part of an industrial settlement dating from the third century. Other metal objects include parts of pewter dishes, fragments of a lead tank and unusual decorative pendants which may have been made on site in the late fourth or fifth century. Large quantities of late Roman pottery, glass and leather were also recovered.

The latest mill channel may have continued in use into the fifth century but much of the site was eroded by a later palaeochannel which contained derived late Roman material and peat deposits. A scatter of Anglo-Saxon finds suggests some activity in the vicinity but the site appears to have reverted to meadowland adjoining the later river channel. A field boundary identified crossing the site is shown on the tithe apportionment plan of 1838, the land continuing as unimproved meadow until the commencement of quarrying in 1972.

Résumé

Le site d'Ickham, dans la zone d'inondation de la rivière Little Stour, à l'Est de Canterbury dans le comté du Kent, a été fouillé dans le cadre d'une opération de sauvetage archéologique pendant l'exploitation d'une carrière entre 1972 et 1974. Les fouilles ont été réalisées par un groupe d'amateurs locaux sous la supervision de Jim Bradshaw. La dernière période de fouille a été dirigée par Christopher Young, avec un financement du ministère de l'Environnement (depuis devenu English Heritage).

Les quelques traces d'occupation préhistorique se composent de silex travaillés dispersés dans les tourbes et les graviers de la vallée, d'une sépulture en position accroupie, d'une fosse circulaire, de débris de poterie belge datant la fin de l'âge du fer.

La plus ancienne activité romaine remonte au début du 1er siècle av. J-C, avec des fosses linéaires et des trous appartenant probablement à un système d'enceinte. Ces éléments sont traversés par un chemin de cailloux flanqué de fossés. Son orientation sud-ouest nord-est laisse penser qu'il pourrait s'agir de la route principale reliant Richborough à Canterbury. Au nord-est du site, la route passait sur un ancien bras de la rivière, visible sur les photos aériennes prises avant l'exploitation de la carrière. De chaque côté de la route, des enceintes définies par des fossés contenaient un puits et plusieurs réservoirs en bois, probablement pour la préparation de peaux ou de tissus. Au moins six sépultures ont été trouvées. Des débris de construction associés à de la poterie et à des feux suggèrent que les habitations les plus importantes étaient situées au nord-est du site. Le site actuel se présente comme une extension en bordure de route avoisinant un établissement détruit par l'exploitation de la carrière à proximité de la rivière.

Quatre canaux linéaires parallèles à l'axe de la route ont pu servir à apporter de l'eau de la rivière à quatre moulins (ou plus) dont les emplacements ont été identifiés pendant l'exploitation de la carrière. Le plus ancien moulin était utilisé au début du 3ème siècle av. J-C, alors que les autres canaux étaient opérationnels au 4ème siècle et au début du 5ème siècle. Les canaux et les bâtiments en bois des moulins contenaient divers éléments du 4ème siècle, tels que restes de poterie, pièces de monnaie, fragments de meules en pierre, et une figurine votive en bois. Des déchets de travail du métal, des débris de chauffe, et des outils permettent de penser que les moulins faisaient partie d'un établissement industriel datant du 3ème siècle. D'autres objets métalliques incluaient des plats en étain, des fragments d'une cuve en plomb, et des pendentifs décoratifs très particuliers qui peuvent avoir été fabriqués sur ce site à la fin du 4ème ou au début du 5ème siècle. Les fouilles ont aussi mis à jour de grandes quantités de poterie, de verrerie et de cuir de la fin de l'empire romain.

Le plus récent des canaux d'alimentation des moulins peut avoir fonctionné jusque pendant le 5ème siècle. Mais la plus grande partie du site a été érodée par un ancien canal qui contenait des dépôts de tourbes et des matériaux dérivés de la fin de l'époque romaine. La dispersion des trouvailles anglo-saxonnes suggère des possibilités d'activité à proximité, mais le site semble être retourné au stade de prairie jouxtant le bras le plus récent de la rivière. Une délimitation de terrain recoupant le site est présente sur le plan de répartition fiscale de 1838, et indique que le statut de prairie non travaillée a perduré jusqu'au début de l'exploitation de la carrière en 1972.

Zusammenfassung

Die Fundstätte von Ickham in der Aue des Flusses Little Stour östlich von Canterbury (Grafschaft Kent) wurde im Rahmen einer ‚Rettungsgrabung' untersucht, nachdem sie in einem von 1972 bis 1974 betriebenen Kiestagebau entdeckt worden war. Die Grabungsarbeiten oblagen einer örtlichen Amateurgruppe unter der Leitung von Jim Bradshaw sowie in der letzten Saison unter Christopher Young. Die Finanzierung übernahm das damalige Department of the Environment (Umweltministerium, heute: English Heritage).

Leichte Anhaltspunkte für eine prähistorische Besiedlung der tälernen Kies- und Torflandschaften ergaben sich aus dem verstreuten Fund bearbeiteter Feuersteine, einer Hockerbestattung, einem Kreisgraben sowie Scherbenrückständen „belgischer" Keramik aus der späten Eisenzeit.

Früheste römische Aktivitäten aus dem späten 1. Jh. beziehen sich auf Gruben und lineare Gräben, die Teil einer Umfriedung darstellen könnten. Darüber lag eine von Südwesten nach Nordosten über den Fundort führende Schotterstraße mit beidseitigen Gräben – vermutlich die Hauptverbindung zwischen Richborough und Canterbury. Im Nordosten führte diese Straße über ein altes Flussbett. Auf Luftfotos, die vor Beginn des Kiestagebaus aufgenommen wurden, ist dieses Flussbett zu erkennen. Am Straßenrand befanden sich Grabeneinfriedungen mit einem Brunnen und mehreren holzverkleideten Becken, die wohl für die Leder- oder Stoffverarbeitung eingesetzt wurden. Außerdem wurden mindestens sechs Grabstätten vermerkt. Berichte über Bautrümmer mit Keramik- und Brandfunden lassen darauf schließen, dass im Nordosten umfangreichere Bauten existierten. Bei der derzeitigen Grabungsstätte handelt es sich um einen Verlängerungsarm an der Peripherie einer Siedlung, die durch den Kiesabbau nahe des Flusses zerstört wurde.

Vier gradlinige Kanäle entlang der Straßenlinie deuten auf Wasserumleitungen vom Fluss hin, die mindestens vier (während des Kiesabbaus erfasste) Wassermühlen antrieben. Die erste Wassermühle war Anfang des 3. Jh. in Betrieb, die anderen Kanäle wurden im 4. und frühen 5. Jh. genutzt. Die hölzernen Mühlenbauten und Kanäle stehen im Zusammenhang mit Keramik, Münzen, Drehsteinfragmenten und einer hölzernen Weihefigur aus dem 4. Jh.. Metallabfälle, Schmelzofentrümmer und Werkzeuge lassen darauf schließen, dass die Werke zu einer Industrieansiedlung aus dem 3. Jh. gehörten. Zu den weiteren Metallfunden zählen Zinntellerteile, Fragmente eines Bleibehälters sowie ungewöhnlich dekorative Anhänger, die hier Ende des 4. oder im 5. Jh. entstanden sein könnten. Darüber hinaus wurden große Mengen Keramik-, Glas- und Lederfundstücke aus der späten Römerzeit ausgegraben.

Es ist möglich, dass die ältesten Kanäle bis ins 5. Jh. in Betrieb waren, wobei ein großer Teil des Standortes jedoch von einem späteren Paläo-Kanal abgetragen wurde, in dem sich Werkmaterialien spätrömischen Ursprungs und Torfablagerungen befanden. Verstreute Fundstücke angelsächsischer Herkunft weisen möglicherweise auf Aktivitäten in der Umgebung hin, obwohl der Standort am späteren Flussbett wohl wieder zu Wiesen umfunktioniert wurde. Eine über den Standort verlaufende, identifizierte Feldgrenze ist auf dem „Tithe Apportionment Plan" (Abgabenverteilungsplan) von 1838 eingezeichnet, wobei das Land bis zum Beginn des Kiestagebaus im Jahre 1972 als unberührte Wiese geführt wurde.

APPENDIX I: LEATHER OBJECTS AND SCRAP Quita Mould

No	Element	Attribute	Context
459	bottom unit		Area 4, extension Extension 'layer 3'
460	bottom unit	insole	'ditches'
461	bottom unit		Area 1, Channel C
462	bottom unit		'ditches'
463	bottom unit		'ditches'
464	bottom unit	heavily nailed	'ditches'
465	bottom unit	seat area	'ditches'
466	bottom unit		'ditches'
467	bottom unit		'ditches'
468	bottom unit	insole and upper	'ditches'
469	bottom unit		'ditches'
470	bottom unit	insole	'ditches'
471	bottom unit		'ditches'
472	bottom unit		'ditches'
473	bottom unit		'ditches'
474	bottom unit		'ditches'
475	bottom unit		Area 4, 408
476	bottom unit		Area 4, 408
477	bottom unit	middle lamina	'ditches'
478	bottom unit	heel stiffener	'ditches'
479	bottom unit		'ditches'
480	bottom unit		'ditches'
481	bottom unit	middle lamina	'ditches'
482	bottom unit	middle lamina	Area 4
483	bottom unit		Area 7, 701
484	bottom unit		Area 7, 712
485	bottom unit		Area 7, 712
486	upper, nailed construction	seam	'ditches'
487	upper, nailed construction	seam	Area 1, Channel C
488	upper, nailed construction	seam	Area 1, Channel C
489	upper, nailed construction	?fastening loop fragment	Area 1, Channel C
490	upper, nailed construction		'ditches'
491	upper, nailed construction		'ditches'
492	upper, nailed construction		'ditches'
493	upper, nailed construction		'ditches'
494	upper, nailed construction	heel stiffener fragment	'ditches'
495	upper, nailed construction	seam	'ditches'
496	upper, nailed construction	heel stiffener	'ditches'
497	upper, nailed construction		'ditches'
498	upper, nailed construction	heel stiffener and quarters	Area 4, 406
499	upper, nailed construction		Area 7, 701
500	thonging		'ditches'
501	thonging		'ditches'
502	thonging		'ditches'
503	broken fastening loop		Area 1, Channel C
504	upper seam fragment, possibly one-piece upper seat seam		'ditches'
505	seat and waste area of sole of unnailed shoe, one-piece or sewn		'ditches'
506	rectangular fragment with widely-spaced thonging		'ditches'
507	intersectional cutting piece		'ditches'
508	trimmings x 4		'ditches'
509	scrap		'ditches'
510	scrap		'ditches'
511	scrap		'ditches'
512	scrap		'ditches'
513	scrap		'ditches'
514	small delaminated fragment	?insole fragment	'ditches'
515	small delaminated fragment		'ditches'
516	small delaminated fragment		'ditches'
517	internal shoe lining and upper		'ditches'
518	upper lasting margin	?same shoe as 515	Area 1, Channel C
519	bottom unit, middle or insole and upper lasting margin		Area 1, Channel C
521	bottom unit, nailed construction		unstratified
522	bottom unit, nailed construction		unstratified
523	bottom unit, nailed construction		unstratified
532	bottom unit		unstratified
541	intersectional cutting piece		unstratified

Appendix 1. Leather objects and scrap.

APPENDIX II: ROMAN HAMMER HEAD   Robert Spain

Plates XXVIII and XXIX show an iron artefact found in Area 4 with other finds identified as Roman. Its size, 208 x 79 x 67mm max, and rectilinear shape, of forged solid iron with a central hole, weighing 3.93kg (8.67lbs) suggests a hammer-head. When it was found in 1974, the central cavity contained the remains of a wooden shaft that was cut through close to both faces of the iron (*see* p 289). No wedges, iron or wood, could be discerned in the shaft remains that might have indicated which side of the head the shaft existed. The shaft hole appears to be a nearly perfect cylindrical cavity 31mm diameter. Although the surfaces are corroded the diameter of the hole at each end appears to be the same. No tapering of the bore can be discerned that might have indicated which side of the head the wooden shaft extended.

Both ends of the hammer-head, one larger face and one small, display swelling or deformation indicative of repeated impact. This 'mushrooming' of the ends is a phenomenon that occurs with modern-day forging tools and chisels and bolsters, whose struck ends are not hardened and change shape in time. The surfaces of both faces are of similar shape, being slightly domed and noticeably curved at the outer edges, but they both display an unusual feature. The general plane of the faces is not parallel to the axis of the central hole or shaft as is usually found in the majority of hammers. The larger working face is inclined approximately 17 degrees to the axis, and the smaller face is obviously less, but more difficult to place a meaningful value to it due to the surface being more prominently curved.

It is unfortunate that the hammer-head was photographed some thirty-two years after its discovery. Shortly after the artefact came to light, an examination of its surfaces[44] revealed a feature that is now absent, completely removed by corrosion. On the inclined surface of the larger working face was a series of shallow, parallel concave corrugations. The axes of these corrugations were parallel to the axis of the shaft cavity.

Pl XXVIII. Hammer no 1233.

Pl XXIX. Hammer no 1233, detail.

---

44. Inspected by the author at Fortress House, London in August 1977.

353

The initial thoughts on the original use of this hammer-head were influenced by the general shape of the working faces and the assumption that their inclination ruled out the possibility of being a hand tool, because of the uncomfortable jarring action to the hands, arms and shoulders of the workman. It was first thought that the shape was probably generated by repeated mechanical action, and used as part of a mechanism or machine. Having regard to it being found in the environs of a watermill, the favoured function was that it could have been a component of a water-powered forge – a trip hammer. As the functional analysis progressed, alternative proposals were made for its function, but none of them could be satisfactorily sustained with the unusual evidence of deformation and wear displayed on the head.

Fortunate for this enquiry, modern day experiences of forge-work and smithing have been explored and contributed to the resolution of this fascinating artefact. The first practical observation was that the weight of the head is considered far too light to act as a forge hammer and the relatively small section of the wooden handle shows that it would not have endured the forces met with in striking. It is also thought that the inclined mushroom shape of the heads could have been produced by muscle power, and parallel examples are known to have occurred in some stone-masons' tools. The conclusion is therefore drawn that this hammer was used as a hand tool, and the most likely function of the corrugations seen originally on the larger working face is that they were intended for stone-dressing.

The favoured millstone dressing tool during the nineteenth and twentieth centuries was a *mill bill* – a tempered chisel, but lighter than this 3.93kg head. They were designed to dress the near-flat faces of French-burrs, the very hard stone commonly used for wheat-milling. The different styles of modern dressing involved creating furrows and usually between them, finer parallel grooves called '*stitching*'. Many Roman millstones have been found having furrows but not the finer grooves. A dominant physical feature of Roman millstones is the inclination of their grinding faces, which in the Ickham extant specimens varies from between 6 and 12.5 degrees from the horizontal. Although a few of the Ickham stones have traces of furrows, we do not know if it was common practice in Roman milling to dress new millstones and continually maintain the furrows. Our modern experience tells us that to do so creates a more efficient grinding process, a finer product and a greater throughput. Whether or not Roman millers adopted such standards is debatable. The majority of extant Roman millstones in *Britannia* do not have evidence of furrows, but this incidence may be affected by the high proportion of stones abandoned and degraded towards the end of their working life.

The other dominant feature of Roman millstones and certainly present in the Ickham collection is the distinct shape of the grinding surfaces. A radial section of a bottom stone from the eye of the stone to the rim is typically convex/concavo with the top stone having an identical mirrored shape to fit. With the millstones having these shapes, especially the top stone with its deep concave grinding face, we can imagine that the dressing and maintenance of the surfaces could have been facilitated by a hammer of the size and shape as the one under discussion. It is now considered entirely possible that the inclined faces of the hammer could have evolved from repeated working on the curved faces of the millstones, whilst the corrugations could have been created to provide a more delicate and accurate reduction of the surface.

If this proposed function for the hammer-head – a millstone dressing tool – is accepted, it is the first example of such a tool to be published. Its existence amongst the remains of numerous millstones tells us that it would have been in use during the working life of these late Roman watermills, either belonging to a particular miller or, perhaps belonging to journeyman millstone-dresser who served several mills in the area.

BIBLIOGRAPHY

Adams, N 1977, 'Leather shoes' in A Rogerson, 207–9

Ager, B 1985, 'The smaller variants of the Anglo-Saxon quoit brooch', *Anglo-Saxon Studies in Archaeology and History* 4, 1–58

Ager, B 1987, 'Late-Roman belt-fittings from Canterbury', *Archaeologia Cantiana* civ, 25–31

Ager, B 1990, 'The alternative quoit brooch: an update'in E Southworth (ed), *Anglo-Saxon Cemeteries. A Re-appraisal,* Gloucester, 153–61

Alföldi, A and Alföldi, E 1976, *Die Kontorniat Medaillons,* Berlin

Allason-Jones, L 1985, 'Bell-shaped studs?' in M Bishop (ed), *The Production and Distribution of Roman Military Equipment: Proceedings of the Second Military Equipment Research Seminar,* British Archaeological Reports (International Series) 275, 95–108

Allason-Jones, L 1989, *Ear-rings in Roman Britain*, British Archaeological Reports (British Series) 201, Oxford

Allason-Jones, L and Bishop, M 1988, *Excavations at Roman Corbridge: The Hoard*, English Heritage Archaeological Report 7, London

Allason-Jones, L and Miket, R 1984, *The catalogue of small finds from South Shields Roman fort*, The Society of Antiquaries of Newcastle upon Tyne monograph 2, Newcastle

Allen, D 1986, 'The glass vessels' in J Zienkiewicz (ed), 98–116

Allen, D 1992, 'The glass' in D Evans and V Metcalf (eds), 179–85

Allen, D 1993, 'Roman glass' in P Casey *et al*, 219–28

Allen, D 1997, 'The glass' in M Fulford, S Rippon, S Ford, J Timby and B Williams (eds), 'Silchester: excavation at the north gate, on the north walls, and in the northern suburbs 1988 and 1991–3', *Britannia* xxviii, 110–15

Amory, P 1997, *People and identity in Ostrogothic Italy, 489–554,* Cambridge Studies in Medieval Life and Thought: fourth series, Cambridge

Amouric, H, Thernot, R, Vacca-Goutouli, M and Bruneton, H 2000, 'Un moulin à turbine de la fin de l'Antiquité, – La Calade du Castellet (Fontvieille)' in P Leveau and J-P Saquet (eds), *Milieu et sociétés dans la vallée des Baux. Études présentées au colloque de Mouriès*, Montpellier, 261–73

Appels, A and Laycock, S 2007, *Roman Buckles and Military Fittings*, Witham

Arora, S K and Franzen, J 1990, 'Fundbericht Grevenbroich-Elfgen, Kr Neuss', *Bonner Jahrbücher* 190, 521

Arveiller-Dulong, V and Arveiller, J 1985, *Le verre d'epoque romaine au Musée Archéologique de Strasbourg*, Notes et Documents des Musées de France, 10, Paris

Aurrecoechea, J 1995–96, 'Las guarniciones de cinturón y atalaje de tipología militar en la Hispania Romana, a tenor de los bronces hallados en la Meseta Sur', *Estudios de Prehistoria y Arqueología Madrileñas* 10, 49–99

Bailey, K 1932, *The Elder Pliny's Chapters on Chemical Subjects*, London

Barker, P, White, R, Pretty, K, Bird, H and Corbishley, M 1997, *The Baths Basilica Wroxeter. Excavations 1966–90*, London

Barrett, D 2004, 'Island Road, Hersden', *Canterbury's Archaeology 2002–2003*, 25–7

Barrett, D 2006, 'Island Road, Hersden', *Canterbury's Archaeology 2004–2005*, 17–20

Bayley, J and Keepax, C 1974, *Ickham: human bone report*, Ancient Monuments Laboratory Report 1663, London

Bayley, J and Butcher, S 2004, *Roman Brooches in Britain*, Reports of the Research Committee of the Society of Antiquaries of London 68, London

Beagrie, N 1989, 'The Romano-British pewter industry', *Britannia* xx, 169–91

Béal, J 1983, *Catalogue des objects de tabletterie du Musée de la Civilisation Gallo-Romaine de Lyon*, Lyon

Bell, M 1994, 'An imperial flour mill on the Janiculum', *Le ravitaillement en blé de Rome et des centres urbains des débuts de la République jusqu'au Haut Empire.* Actes du colloque international organisé par le Centre Jean Bérard et l'URA 994 du CNRS. Naples, 14–16ᵣfévrier 1991 (Naples-Rome), 73–89

Bemmann, H 1984, 'Terra-Sigillata aus Abfallschichten des Bonner Legionslagers' in D Haupt (ed), *Beiträge zur Archäologie des römischen Rheinlands 4*, Rheinische Ausgrabungen, 23 (1984), 109–62, Bonn

Bennett, P 1978, 'A Roman building near Sandwich', *Archaeologia Cantiana* xciv, 191–4

Bennett, P 1980, '68–69A Stour Street' in 'Researches and Discoveries', *Archaeologia Cantiana* xcvi, 406–10

Bennett, P 1989, 'Channel Tunnel Excavations', *Canterbury's Archaeology 1987–1988*, 46–69

Bennett, P forthcoming, 'Excavations at Crundale Limeworks'

Bennett, P, Clark, P, Hicks, A, Rady, J and Riddler, I 2008, *At the Great Crossroads: prehistoric, Roman and medieval discoveries on the Isle of Thanet 1994–95*, Canterbury Archaeological Trust Occasional Paper 4, Canterbury

Bennett, P, Couldrey, P and Macpherson-Grant, N 2007, *Highstead near Chislet, Kent. Excavations 1975–1977*, The Archaeology of Canterbury (New Series) IV, Canterbury

Bennett, P, Frere, S and Stow, S 1982, *Excavations at Canterbury Castle,* The Archaeology of Canterbury I, Maidstone

Bennett, P, Macpherson-Grant, N and Blockley, P 1980, 'Four minor sites excavated by the Canterbury Archaeological Trust 1978–1979', *Archaeologia Cantiana* xcvi, 267–302

Benoît, F 1940 'L'usine de meunerie hydraulique de Barbegal (Arles)', *Revue Archéologique* 15.1, 19–80

Bernhard, H 1978, 'Zwei spätrömische Grabfunde aus Speyer', *Bonner Jahrbücher* 178, 259–79

Betts, I 1992, 'Roman tile from Eccles, Kent found at Colchester', in P Crummy (ed), 259–60

Biddle, M (ed) 1990, *Object and Economy in Medieval Winchester*, Winchester Studies 7, Artefacts from medieval Winchester, Part ii, Oxford

Bilkei, I 1980, 'Römische Schreibgeräte aus Pannonien', *Alba Regia* 18, 61–86

Bird, J and Williams, D 1983, 'German marbled flagons in Roman Britain', *Britannia* xiv, 247–52

Bíró, M 1987, 'Gorsium bone carvings', *Alba Regia* 23, 25–63

Bíró, M 1994, *The Bone Objects of the Roman Collection*, Catalogi Musei Nationalis Hungarici, Series Archaeologica II, Budapest

Bischoff, B 1979, 'Paläographie des römischen Altertums und des abendlandischen Mittelalters', *Grundlagen der Germanistik* 24, Berlin

Bishop, M 1988, 'Cavalry equipment of the Roman army in the first century AD' in J C Coulston (ed), 67–196

Bishop, M 1996, *Finds from Roman Aldborough. A Catalogue of Small Finds from the Romano-British Town of Isurium Brigantium*, Oxbow Monograph 65, Oxford

Bishop, M and Coulston, J 1993, *Roman Military Equipment from the Punic Wars to the Fall of Rome*, London

Bishop, M and Dore, J 1989, *Corbridge: Excavations of the Roman Fort and Town 1947–80*, Historic Buildings and Monuments Commission Archaeological Report 8, London

Black, E 1987, *The Roman villas of south-east England*, Oxford

Black, E 1994, 'Villa-owners: Romano-British Gentlemen and Officers', *Britannia* xxv, 99–110

Blagg, T 1995, 'The Marlowe Excavations: an Overview' in K Blockley *et al* 7–26

Blockley, K, Blockley, M, Blockley, P, Frere, S. and Stow, S 1995, *Excavations in the Marlowe Car Park and surrounding areas*, The Archaeology of Canterbury V, Whitstable

Blockley, P 1989, 'Excavations at Riding Gate, Canterbury, 1986–87', *Archaeologia Cantiana* cvii, 117–54

Boden, D 2004, 'Shelford Quarry, Broad Oak', *Canterbury's Archaeology 2002–2003*, 20–2

Boeles, P 1951, *Friesland tot de elfde eeuw*, S-Gravenhage

Boessneck, J 1969, 'Osteological differences between sheep (*Ovis aries Linne*) and goat *(Capra hircus Linne)*' in D Brothwell and E Higgs (eds), *Science in Archaeology*, London, 331–85

Böhme, H 1972, *Die Fibeln der Kastelle Saalburg und Zugmantel*, Saalburg Jahrbuch, Bericht des Saalburg Museums, xxix

Böhme, H 1974, *Germanische Grabfunde des 4. bis 5. Jahrhunderts zwischen unterer Elbe und Loire*, Münchner Beiträge zur Vor- und Frühgeschichte 19, Munich

Böhme, H 1985, 'Les découvertes du Bas-Empire à Vireux-Molhain. Considérations générales' in J-P Lemant (ed), Le Cimetière et la Fortification du Bas-Empire Vireux-Molhain, dép Ardennes, Römisch-Germanisches Zentralmuseum monograph 7, Mainz, 76–88

Böhme, H 1986, 'Das Ende der Römerherrschaft in Britannien und die angelsächsische Besiedlung Englands im 5. Jahrhundert', *Jahrbüch des Römisch-Germanischen Zentralmuseums Mainz*, 33, 469–574

Boon, G C 1959, 'The latest objects from Silchester, Hants', *Medieval Archaeology* iii, 79–88

Boon, G C 1974, *Silchester. The Roman Town of Calleva*, Newton Abbot

Boon, G C 1975, 'Two Celtic pins from Margam Beach, West Glamorgan', *Antiquaries Journal* lv, 400–4

Boon, G and Williams, C 1966, 'The Dolaucothi Drainage Wheel', *Journal of Roman Studies* lvi, 122–7

Booth, P (ed) 1997, *Asthall, Oxfordshire: Excavations in a Roman 'Small Town'*, Thames Valley Landscapes Monograph, 9, Oxford

Booth, P, Bingham, A-M and Lawrence, S forthcoming, *The Roman Roadside Settlement at Westhawk Farm, Ashford, Kent: Excavations 1998–99*, Oxford Monographs 2, Oxford

Bouquillon, A, Querre, G, Leclaire, A and Tuffreau-Libre, M 1994, 'La terra nigra tardive à Arras (Pas-de-Calais): études en laboratoire' in M Tuffreau-Libre and A Jacques (eds) 1994a, 213–24

Bourke, C and Close-Brooks, J 1989, 'Five insular enamelled ornaments', *Proceedings of the Society of Antiquaries of Scotland* 119, 227–37

Brailsford, J W 1962, *Hod Hill, Volume one, Antiquities from Hod Hill in the Durden Collection*, London

Branigan, K and Bayley, J 1989, 'The Romano-British Metalwork from Poole's Cavern, Buxton', *Derbyshire Archaeological Journal* 109, 34–50

Brent, J 1879, *Canterbury in Olden Times*, London

Brewer, R J 1986a, 'Other objects of bronze' in J D Zienkiewicz, 172–89

Brewer, R J 1986b, 'The beads and glass counters' in J D Zienkiewicz, 146–56

Brickstock, R J 2004, *The Production, analysis and Standardisation of Romano-British Coin Reports*, London

Brickstock, R J 2007, 'The coins' 79–94 in P R Wilson *et al*, 'Catterick metal-detecting project 1997–1999', *Yorkshire Archaeological Journal* 79, 65–153

Brodribb, A C C, Hands, A R and Walker, D 1973, *Excavations at Shakenoak farm, near Wilcote, Oxfordshire, Part IV*, Oxford

Brown, A 1994, 'A Romano-British shell-gritted pottery and tile manufacturing site at Harrold, Beds', *Bedfordshire Archaeology* 21, 19–107

Brown, A E, Woodfield, C and Mynard, D C 1983, 'Excavations at Towcester, Northamptonshire: The Alcester Road Suburb', *Northamptonshire Archaeology* 18, 43–140

Brown, D 1976, 'Fourth-century bronzework' in M G Jarrett, *Maryport, Cumbria: a Roman Fort and its Garrison*, Cumberland and Westmorland Antiquarian and Archaeological Society, Extra Series, 22, 76–82

Brown, D 1981, 'Appendix 1: some late Roman metalwork from Ickham' in C J Young, 37–8

Brown, P D C 1972, 'The ironwork' in A C C Brodribb, A R Hands and D R Walker, *Excavations at Shakenoak Farm, near Wilcote, Oxfordshire. Part III: Site F*, Oxford, 86–117

Brown, P D C 1976 'Archaeological evidence for the Anglo-Saxon period' in A McWhirr (ed), *Studies in the Archaeology and History of Cirencester*, British Archaeological Reports (British Series) 30, Oxford, 19–45

Brown, R A 1986, 'The Iron Age and Romano-British Settlement at Woodcock Hall, Saham Toney, Norfolk', *Britannia* xvii, 1–58

Brulet, R 1994, 'La céramique du Bas-Empire à Tournai: importations et vaisselle locale' in M Tuffreau-Libre and A Jacques 1994a, 81–94

Brun, J-P and Borréani, M 1998, 'Deux moulins hydrauliques du Haut Empire romain en Narbonnaise. Villae des Mesclans à La Crau et de Saint-Pierre/Les Laurons aux Arcs', *Gallia* 55, 279–326

Buchanan, J and Davis, H 1967, *Zosimus' Historia Nova*, San Antonio, Texas

Bucur, C 1978, 'Die Wassermühle aus Römische-Dazien im lichte Archäeologischer Funde', *Cibinium* (1974–8), Muzeul Brukenthal, Sibui, 183–98

Bullinger, H 1969, '*Spätantike Gürtelbeschläge*', Dissertationes Archaeologicae Gandenses 12, Bruges

Burley, E 1955, 'A catalogue and survey of the metal-work from Traprain Law', *Proceedings of the Society of Antiquaries of Scotland* lxxxix, 118–226

Burns, T S 1994, *Barbarians within the Gates of Rome: A Study of Roman Military Policy c 375–425 AD*, Indiana University Press

Bushe-Fox, J P 1925, *Excavation of the Late Celtic Urnfield at Swarling, Kent*, Reports of the Research Committee of the Society of Antiquaries of London V, Oxford

Bushe-Fox, J P 1928, *Second Report on the excavation of the Roman Fort at Richborough, Kent*, Reports of the Research Committee of the Society of Antiquaries of London VII, Oxford

Bushe-Fox, J P 1932, *Third report on the excavations of the Roman fort at Richborough*, Reports of the Research Committee of the Society of Antiquaries of London X, Oxford

Bushe-Fox, J P 1949, *Fourth report on the excavations of the Roman fort at Richborough*, Reports of the Research Committee of the Society of Antiquaries of London XVI, Oxford

Buteux, S 1997, *Settlements at Skaill, Deerness, Orkney*, British Archaeological Reports (British Series) 260, Oxford

Callender, M 1965, *Roman Amphorae*, London

Cameron, K 1977, *English Place Names*, London

Caple, C 1986, 'An analytical appraisal of copper alloy pin production: 400 to 1600 AD', unpublished University of Bradford PhD thesis

Caple, C 1990, 'The detection and definition of an industry: the English medieval and post-medieval pin industry', *Archaeological Journal* 148, 241–55

Carreras, C and Williams, D F 2002, 'Carrot amphorae: a Syrian or Palestinian connection?' in J H Humphrey (ed), *The Roman and Byzantine Near East*, Vol 3, 133–44

Casey, P J 1994a, *Roman Coinage in Britain*, Shire Archaeology, second edition

Casey, P J 1994b, *Carausius and Allectus: the British usurpers*, London

Casey, P, Davies, J and Evans, J 1993, *Excavations at Segontium (Caernarfon) Roman Fort, 1975–1979*, Council for British Archaeology Research Report 90, York

Castella, D (ed) 1994, *Le moulin hydraulique gallo-romain d'Avenches en Chaplix*, Lausanne

Chadour, A B 1994, *Rings. The Alice and Louis Koch Collection*, Leeds

Chambers, R A 1987, 'The Late- and Sub-Roman Cemetery at Queenford Farm, Dorchester-on-Thames, Oxon', *Oxoniensia* 52, 35–69

Charlesworth, D 1974, 'Glass vessels' in M Hassall and J Rhodes, 'Excavations at the New Market Hall, Gloucester 1966–7', *Transactions of the Bristol and Gloucestershire Archaeological Society* 93, 15–100

Charlesworth, D 1984, 'The glass' in S S Frere, 146–73

Chenet, G 1941, *La Céramique Gallo-Romaine d'Argonne du IVᵉ siècle et la Terre Sigillée décorée à la Molette*, Mâcon

Chenet, G and Gaudron, G 1955, *La céramique sigillée d'Argonne des IIme et IIIme siecles*, Gallia Supplément 6, Paris

Childe, V G 1943, 'Rotary querns on the Continent and in the Mediterranean Basin', *Antiquity* 17, 19–26

Clairmont, C W 1963, *The Excavations at Dura-Europos, Final Report IV, Part V: Glass vessels*, New Haven

Clark, J 1995, *The Medieval Horse and its Equipment c 1150–c 1450*, Medieval Finds from Excavations in London, 5, London

Clark, P 1995, 'The Romano-British site at Ickham, Kent: an assessment of the excavations 1973–1975', unpublished report.

Clark, P 1997, 'The Roman settlement at Ickham, near Canterbury: an assessment and updated research design', unpublished Canterbury Archaeological Trust report

Clarke, G 1979, *Pre-Roman and Roman Winchester: part II. The Roman cemetery at Lankhills*, Winchester Studies 3, Oxford

Clarke, G 1982, 'The Roman villa at Woodchester', *Britannia* xiii, 197–228

Clogg, P W and Haselgrove, C C 1995, 'The composition of Iron Age struck 'bronze' coinage in eastern England', *Oxford Journal of Archaeology* 14, 41–62

Coles, B 1990, 'Anthropomorphic wooden figurines from Britain and Ireland', *Proceedings of the Prehistoric Society* 56, 315–33.

Coles, B 1993, 'Roos Carr and Company' in J Coles, V Fenwick and G Hutchinson (eds), *A Spirit of Enquiry – Essays for Ted Wright*, Exeter, 17–22

Cool, H E M 1983, 'A study of the Roman personal ornaments made of metal, excluding brooches, from southern Britain' unpublished PhD thesis, University of Wales

Cool, H E M 1990a, 'Roman metal hair pins from southern Britain', *Archaeologia* 147, 148–82

Cool, H E M 1990b, 'Silver and copper alloy objects (other than brooches)' in S Wrathmell and A Nicholson (eds), 79–92

Cool, H E M 1993, 'The copper alloy' in M J Darling with D Gurney, *Caister-on-Sea Excavations by Charles Green, 1951–55*, East Anglian Archaeology 60, Gressenhall

Cool, H E M 2000, 'The parts left over: material culture into the fifth century' in T Wilmott and P Wilson (eds), *The late Roman transition in the North: Papers from the Roman Archaeology Conference, Durham*, British Archaeological Reports (British Series) 299, 47–65

Cool, H E M 2004, *The Roman Cemetery at Brougham, Cumbria. Excavations 1966–67*, Britannia Monograph Series 21, London

Cool, H E M, Lloyd-Morgan, G and Hooley, A D 1995, *Finds from the Fortress*, The Archaeology of York 17/10, York

Cool, H E M and Philo, C (eds) 1998, *Roman Castleford Excavations 1974–85. Volume I: the Small Finds*, Yorkshire Archaeology 4, Wakefield

Cool, H E M and Price, J 1987, 'The glass' in G W Meates, 110–42

Cool, H E M and Price, J 1993, 'Roman glass' in P J Woodward, S M Davies and A H Graham (eds), *Excavations at the Old Methodist Chapel and Greyhound Yard, Dorchester, 1981–1984*, Dorset Natural History and Archaeological Society Monograph Series 12, Dorchester, 150–67

Cool, H E M and Price, J 1995, *Roman vessel glass from excavations in Colchester, 1971–85*, Colchester Archaeological Report 8, Colchester

Cool, H E M and Price, J 1998, 'The vessels and objects of glass' in H E M Cool and C Philo (eds), 141–94

Corder, P 1943, 'A decorated lava quern from *Verulamium*', *Antiquaries Journal* xxiii, 158

Cotton, M A 1947, 'Excavations at Silchester 1938–9', *Archaeologia* xcii, 121–67

Coulston, J C (ed) 1988, *Military Equipment and the Identity of Roman Soldiers. Proceedings of the Fourth Roman Military Equipment Conference*, British Archaeological Reports (International Series) 394, Oxford

Coulston, J C 1990, 'Later Roman armour, 3rd–6th centuries AD', *Journal of Roman Military Equipment Studies* 1, 139–60

Coyningham, A 1844, 'Account of the opening of some Anglo-Saxon graves at Wingham, in Kent', *Archaeologia* xxx, 550–1

Cross, R and Redding, T 2000, 'Archaeological investigations at Maydensole, near Dover 1996–1999', *Kent Archaeological Society Newsletter* 46, 5

Crouch, K 1976, 'The Archaeology of Staines and the excavation of Elmsleigh House', *Transactions of the London and Middlesex Archaeology Society* 27, 71–134

Crummy, N 1979, 'A chronology of Romano-British bone pins', *Britannia* 10, 157–64

Crummy, N 1983, *The Roman small finds from excavations in Colchester 1971–9*, Colchester Archaeological Report 2, Colchester

Crummy, N forthcoming, 'Personalised plates: a construct for the finishing and marketing of late Roman antler combs' in I D Riddler, N I A Trzaska-Nartowski and A MacGregor (eds), Council for British Archaeology Research Report, London

Crummy, P 1981, *Aspects of Anglo-Saxon and Norman Colchester*, Council for British Archaeology Research Report 39, London

Crummy, P 1992, *Excavations at Culver Street, The Gilberd School and other sites in Colchester 1971–85*, Colchester

Cunliffe, B W 1968, *Fifth Report on the Excavations of the Roman Fort at Richborough, Kent*, Reports of the Research Committee of the Society of Antiquaries of London XXIII, London

Cunliffe, B W 1971, *Excavations at Fishbourne 1961–69, Vol. II. The finds*, Reports of the Research Committee of the Society of Antiquaries of London XXVII, Leeds

Cunliffe, B W 1975, *Excavations at Portchester Castle. Volume 1: Roman*, Reports of the Research Committee of the Society of Antiquaries of London XXXII, London

Cunliffe, B W 1980, 'Excavations at the Roman fort at Lympne, Kent 1976–78', *Britannia* xi, 227–88

Cunliffe, B W and Poole, C 2008, *The Danebury Environs Roman Programme. A Wessex landscape during the Roman era, Volume 4, Part 4: the Roman Villa and Water Mills at Fullerton, Wherwell*, Oxford

Cunliffe, B W and Spain, R J 2008, 'The canal and the mills' in B W Cunliffe and C Poole, *Part 4: the Roman Villa and Watermills at Fullerton, Wherwell*, Oxford, 73–100

Cüppers, H 1984, *Trier. Augustusstadt der Treverer. Stadt und Land in vor- und frührömischer Zeit*, Mainz

Curle, J 1911, *A Roman frontier post and its people. The fort of Newstead in the Parish of Melrose*, Glasgow

Curwen, E C 1937, 'Querns', *Antiquity* 11.42, June, 133–51

Czysz, W 1994, 'Eine baujuwarische Wassermühle im Paartal bei Dasing' *Antike Welt* 25, 152–4

Dannell, G B, Hartley, B R and Wild, J R 1993, 'Excavations on a Romano-British site at Park Farm, Stanground, Peterborough 1965–1967', *Journal of Roman Pottery Studies* 6, 51–93

Dark, K 1994, *Civitas to Kingdom: British political continuity 300–800*, Leicester

Davies, B, Richardson, B and Tomber, R 1994, *A dated corpus of early Roman pottery from the City of London*, The Archaeology of Roman London, Volume 5, Council for British Archaeology Research Report 98, London

Davies, H E H 1998, 'Designing Roman roads' *Britannia* xxix, 1–16

Davis, S J M 1987, *The Archaeology of Animals*, London

Dawson, M 1989, 'A review of the equipment of the Roman army of Dacia', in C van Driel-Murray (ed) *Roman Military Equipment: the Sources of Evidence. Proceedings of the Fifth Roman Military Equipment Conference*, British Archaeological Reports (International Series) 476, Oxford, 337–66

Dawson, M 1990, 'Roman military equipment on civil sites in Roman Dacia', *Journal of Roman Military Equipment Studies* 1, 7–15

Dawson, M 1994, *A Late Roman Cemetery at Bletsoe*, Bedfordshire Archaeology Monograph 1, Bedford

de Boisvillette, M 1840, 'Notice sur les substructions antiques de la ville de Gannes (Loiret)', *Mémoires et dissertations sur les antiquités nationales et étrangères*, ns 5, 212–31

Delacampagne, F. 1997, 'Les thermes de la rue Laitière à Bayeux (Calvados). Reflections sur la topographie antique et médiévale d'un quartier de la ville', *Revue archéologique de l'ouest* 14, 125–74

Deschler-Erb, S 1998, *Römische Beinartefakte aus Augusta Raurica. Rohmaterial, Technologie, Typologie und Chronologie*, Forschungen in August 27, Augst

Detsicas, A 1983, *The Cantiaci*, Gloucester

Devenish, D C 1979, 'Excavations in Winding Street, Hastings, 1974', *Sussex Archaeological Collections* 117, 125–34

de Hoog, V 1984, 'The Finds' in D Miles (ed), *Archaeology at Barton Court Farm, Abingdon, Oxon*, Council for British Archaeology Research Report 50, London, microfiche 5

Deyts, S 1983, *Les Bois Sculptés des Source de la Seine*, XLII supplément à Gallia, Paris, Editions du CNRS

Dickinson, B 1986, 'Potters' stamps and signatures on the samian' in L Miller, J Schofield and M Rhodes (eds), *The Roman Quay at St Magnus House, London*, London and Middlesex Archaeological Society Special Paper 8, 186–98

Dickinson, T 1982, 'Fowler's Type G penannular brooches reconsidered', *Medieval Archaeology* xxvi, 41–68

Dix, B 1980, 'Excavations at Harrold Pit, Odell, 1974–78', *Bedfordshire Archaeological Journal* 14, 15–18

Dixon, P 1976, *Barbarian Europe*, Oxford

Dowker, G 1878, 'Roman remains at Preston, near Wingham', *Archaeologia Cantiana* xii, 47–8

Dowker, G 1882, 'The Roman Villa at Wingham Part I', *Archaeologia Cantiana* xiv, 351–7

Dowker, G 1883, 'The Roman Villa at Wingham Part II', *Archaeologia Cantiana* xv, 136–42

Dowker, G 1887, 'A Saxon cemetery at Wickhambreaux', *Archaeologia Cantiana* xvii, 6–9

Down, A 1978, *Chichester Excavations* III, Chichester

Down, A 1981, *Chichester Excavations* V, Chichester

Down, A 1989, *Chichester Excavations* VI, Chichester

Driesch, A von den 1976, 'A Guide to the Measurement of Animal Bones from Archaeological Sites', *Peabody Museum Bulletins* 1, Harvard

Driesch, A von den and Boessneck, J A 1974, 'Kritische Anmerkungen zur Widerristhöherberechnung aus Längenmassen vor- und frühgeschichtlicher Tierknochen', *Säugertierkundliche Mitteilungen* 22, 325–48

Dudley, D 1967, 'Excavations on Nor'Nour in the Isles of Scilly, 1962–6', *Archaeological Journal* cxxiv, 1–64

Dumontet, M and Romeuf, A-M 1980, *Ex-voto gallo-romains de la Sources des Roches á Chamelières*, Musée Bargoin, Clermont-Ferrand

Durand-Lefebvre, M 1963, *Marques de potiers gallo-romains trouvées à Paris*, Paris

Duval, A 1974, 'Un type particulier de fibule gallo-romaine précoce: la fibule 'd'Alesia'', *Antiquités Nationales* 6, 67–76

Engelhardt, C 1866, *Denmark in the Early Iron Age, illustrated by recent discoveries in the peat mosses of Slesvig*, London

Evans, D R and Metcalf, V M 1992, *Roman Gates Caerleon*, Oxbow Monograph 15, Oxford

Evans, P G H 1991, 'Whales, dolphins and porpoises: Order Cetacea' in G B Corbet and S Harris (eds), *The Handbook of British Mammals*, Oxford, 299–350

Evison, V I 1965, *The Fifth-Century Invasions South of the Thames*, London

Evison, V I 1981, 'Distribution maps and England in the first two phases' in V I Evison (ed), *Angles, Saxons and Jutes. Essays presented to J N L Myres*, Oxford

Evison, V I 1987, *Dover: Buckland Anglo-Saxon Cemetery*, HBMC(E), Archaeological Report 3, London

Farrar, R A H 1973, 'The techniques and sources of Romano-British black-burnished ware' in A P Detsicas (ed), *Current Research in Romano-British Coarse Pottery*, Council for British Archaeology Research Report 10, London, 67–103

Faulkner, N 1996 'Verulamium: interpreting decline', *Archaeological Journal* 153, 79–103

Fowler, E 1963, 'Celtic metalwork of the fifth and sixth centuries AD', *Archaeological Journal* cxx, 98–160

France, N E and Gobel, B M 1985, *The Romano-British temple at Harlow*, West Essex Archaeological Group

Frere, S S 1957, 'Late Roman objects from Chalton, Hants', *Antiquaries Journal* 37, 218–20

Frere, S S 1970, 'The Roman Theatre at Canterbury', *Britannia* i, 83–113

Frere, S S 1972, *Verulamium Excavations, Volume I*, Reports of the Research Committee of the Society of Antiquaries of London XXVII, Oxford

Frere, S S 1984, *Verulamium Excavations. Volume III*, Oxford University Committee for Archaeology Monograph 1, Oxford

Frere, S S 1988, 'Roman Britain in 1987', *Britannia* xix, 416–84

Frere, S S 1999, *Britannia. A History of Roman Britain*, (fourth edition), London

Frere, S S, Bennett, P, Rady, J and Stow, S 1987, *Canterbury Excavations: Intra- and Extra-Mural sites, 1949–55 and 1980–84*, The Archaeology of Canterbury VIII, Maidstone

Frere, S S and Fulford, M 2001, 'The Roman invasion of AD 43', *Britannia* xxxii, 45–55

Frere, S S and Stow, S 1983, *Excavations in St George's Street and Burgate Street Areas*, The Archaeology of Canterbury VII, Maidstone

Frere, S S and Tomlin, R S O 1991, 'Roman Britain in 1990', *Britannia* xxii, 221–92

Frere, S S and Wilkes, J J 1989, *Strageath*, Britannia Monograph Series 9, London

Friendship-Taylor, D 1997, 'Roman/Saxon Mongrels part 2', *Archaeological Leather Group Newsletter* 5 (Spring), 2

Fulford, M G 1973, 'A fourth-century colour-coated fabric and its types in south-east England', *Sussex Archaeological Collections* 109, 41–4

Fulford, M G 1975a, 'The pottery' in B W Cunliffe, 270–367

Fulford, M G 1975b, *New Forest Roman Pottery*, British Archaeological Reports (British Series) 17, Oxford

Fulford, M G 1977, 'Pottery and Britain's foreign trade in the later Roman period' in D P S Peacock (ed), *Pottery and early commerce. Characterisation and trade in Roman and later ceramics*, London, 35–84

Fulford, M G and Bird, J 1975, 'Imported pottery from Germany in late Roman Britain', *Britannia* vi, 171–81

Fulford, M G and Huddleston, K 1991, *The Current State of Romano-British Pottery Studies*, English Heritage Occasional Paper 1, London

Fuller, S (ed) 2006, *The Geology, Archaeology and History of the Lydden Valley and Sandwich Bay*, Lydden Valley Research Group, Deal

Gähwiler, A 1984, 'Römische Wasserräder aus Hagendorn', *Helvetia archaeologica* 15, 145–68

Gähwiler, A and Speck, J 1991, 'Die römische Wassermühle von Hagendorn bei Cham ZG: Versuch einer Rekonstruktion', *Helvetia Archaeologica* 22, 33–75

Gaitzsch, W 1980, *Eiserne romische Werkzeuge*, British Archaeological Reports (International Series) 171, Oxford

Galloway, P 1979, 'Combs' in G Clarke, 246–8

Gardner, A 2008, *An Archaeology of Identity: Soldiers and Society in Late Roman Britain*, Walnut Creek

Garmier, J-F and Bouthier, A 1996, *30 Ans d'Archéologie dans la Nièvre*, Coulanges-les-Nevers

Garrett, C S 1938, 'Chesters Roman villa, Woolaston, Gloucestershire', *Archaeologia Cambrensis* 93, 93–125

Garrett, C S and Harris, F H 1938, 'Chesters Roman villa, Woolaston, Gloucestershire', *Archaeologia Cambrensis* 93, 93–125

Garrard, P 1988, 'The small finds' in A Hicks, 152–61

Gelling, M 1978, *Signposts to the Past: Place-names and the History of England*, London

Gentry, A, Ivens, J and McClean, H 1977, 'Excavations at Lincoln Road, London Borough of Enfield, November 1974–March 1976', *Transactions of the London and Middlesex Archaeological Society* 28, 101–89

Getty, R 1975, *Sisson and Grossman's The Anatomy of Domestic Animals*, fifth edition, Philadelphia

Gilkes, O J 1993, 'Iron Age and Roman Littlehampton' *Sussex Archaeological Collections* 131, 1–20

Gilles, K-J 1981, 'Germanische Fibeln und Kämme des Trierer Landes', *Archäologisches Korrespondenzblatt* 11, 333–9

Glass, F J 1927, *Pewter Craft*. The Artistic, Practical Handicraft Series, London

Glass, H 1999, 'Archaeology of the Channel Tunnel rail link', *Archaeologia Cantiana* xix, 189–220

Glob, P V 1971, *The Bog People*, London

Godwin, H and Willis, E H 1960, 'Cambridge University natural radiocarbon measurements II', *American Journal of Science Radiocarbon Supplement* 2, 62–72

Goethert-Polaschek, K 1977, *Katalog der Römischen Gläser der Rheinischen Landesmuseums*, Trier, Mainz

Going, C J 1987a, *The Mansio and other sites in the south-eastern sector of Caesaromagus: the Roman pottery*, Chelmsford Archaeological Trust Report 3.2/Council for British Archaeology Research Report 62, London

Going, C 1987b, 'A Middle Saxon buckle from Lincoln Road, Enfield', *London Archaeologist*, 5.11, 301–2

Goodall, I 1984, 'Iron objects' in A Rogerson and C Dallas (eds), 77–106

Goodall, I 1990, 'Knives' in 'Equipment and furnishings' in M Biddle (ed), 804–1005

Goodburn, R and Grew, F 1984, 'Objects of bone' in S S Frere, 69–75

Goodburn, R and Bartholomew, P (eds) 1976, *Aspects of the Notitia Dignitatum*, British Archaeological Reports (Supp Series) 15, Oxford

Gostenčnik, K 1996, 'Die Kleinfunde aus Bein vom Magdalensberg', *Carinthia* I 186, 105–37

Graham, A H 1986, 'The Old Malthouse, Abbotsbury, Dorset: The Medieval Watermill of the Benedictine Abbey', *Dorset Natural History and Archeaological Society Proceedings* 108, 103–25

Graham-Campbell, J A 1991, 'Dinas Powys metalwork and the dating of enamelled zoomorphic penannular brooches', *Bulletin of the Board of Celtic Studies* 38, 220–32

Grainge, G 2002, *The Roman Channel Crossing of AD 43: the constraints on Claudius's naval strategy*, British Archaeological Reports (British Series) 332, Oxford

Grant, A 1982, 'The use of tooth wear as a guide to the age of domestic ungulates' in B Wilson *et al*, 91–108

Green, C M 1980a, 'Hand-made pottery and society in Late Iron Age and Roman East Sussex', *Sussex Archaeological Collections* 118, 69–86

Green, C M 1980b, 'The Roman pottery' in D M Jones (ed), 39–79

Green, B, Rogerson, A and White, S G 1987, *The Anglo-Saxon Cemetery at Morning Thorpe, Norfolk,* East Anglian Archaeology 36, Gressenhall

Greene, K 1986, *The Archaeology of the Roman Economy*, London

Greenfield, E 1960, 'A Neolithic pit and other finds from Wingham, East Kent', *Archaeologia Cantiana* lxxiv, 58–72

Greep, S 1993, 'The bone objects' in D E Farwell and T L Molleson (eds), *Excavations at Poundbury 1966–80. Volume II: The Cemeteries*, Dorset Natural History and Archaeological Society Monograph Series, 11, Dorchester, 105–10

Greep, S 1995, 'Objects of bone, antler and ivory' in K Blockley *et al*, 1112–52

Gregory, A 1991, *Excavations in Thetford 1980–1982, Fison Way. Vol I*, East Anglian Archaeology 53, Gressenhall

Guido, M 1978, *The Glass Beads of the Prehistoric and Roman Periods in Britain and Ireland*, Reports of the Research Committee of the Society of Antiquaries of London XXXV, London

Guido, M 1999, *The glass beads of Anglo-Saxon England c AD 400–700*, Reports of the Research Committee of the Society of Antiquaries of London LVI, Woodbridge

Gurney, D 1986, *Settlement, Religion and Industry on the Roman Fen-Edge, Norfolk*, East Anglian Archaeology 31, Gressenhall

Gurney, D 2001, 'Archaeological finds in Norfolk 2000', *Norfolk Archaeology* 43.4, 694–707

Guy, C J 1981, 'Roman lead circular tanks in Britain', *Britannia* xii, 271–6

Haberey, W 1942, 'Spätantike Gläser aus Gräbern von Mayen', *Bonner Jahrbücher* 147, 249–84

Halsall, G 2000, 'Archaeology and the Late Roman frontier: the so-called *Foederatengräber* reconsidered' in W Pohl and H Reimitz, *Grenze und Differenz im frühen Mittelalter,* Vienna, 167–80

Halstead, P 1985, 'A study of the mandibular teeth from Romano-British contexts at Maxey' in F Pryor, C French, D Crowther, D Gurney, G Simpson and M Taylor (eds), *Archaeology and Environment of the Lower Welland Valley. Vol 1*, East Anglian Archaeology 27, Gressenhall, 219–24

Hamerow, H 1993, *Excavations at Mucking 2: The Anglo-Saxon Settlement*, English Heritage Report 21, London

Harden, D B 1962, 'Glass in Roman York' in *An inventory of the historical monuments in the City of York: vol 1:* Eburacum, Roman York, London, 136–41

Harden, D B 1973, 'Glass' in A C C Brodribb *et al*, 98–107

Harden, D B 1975, 'Glass vessels' in B Cunliffe, 368–74

Harden, D B 1977, 'Roman glass' in P A Rahtz and E Greenfield, 287–90

Harden, D B 1979, 'Glass vessels' in G Clarke, 209–20

Harden, D B and Green, C M 1978, 'A late Roman grave-group from the Minories, Aldgate' in J Bird, H Chapman and J Clark (eds), *Collectanea Londiniensia*, London and Middlesex Archaeological Society Special Paper 2, London, 163–75

Härke, H 1992, *Angelsächsische Waffengräber des 5 bis 7 jahrhunderts*, Zeitschrift für Archäologie Mittelalters, Beiheft 6, Cologne

Hart, F A 1984, 'Excavation of a Saxon Grubenhaus and Roman ditch at Kent Road, St Mary Cray', *Archaeologia Cantiana* ci, 187–216

Hartley, B R 1972, 'The samian ware' in S S Frere, 216–62

Hartley, B R and Dickinson, B M 2000, 'The samian' in P Rush, B Dickinson, B Hartley and K F Hartley, *Roman Castleford Excavations 1974–85. Volume III: the Pottery*, Yorkshire Archaeology 6, Wakefield, 5–88

Hartley, B R and Dickinson, B M 2008–, *Names on terra sigillata: an index of makers' stamps on Gallo-Roman terra sigillata (samian ware)*, 1–4, Bulletin of the Institute of Classical Studies Supplements 102-01–102-04, London

Haselgrove, C 1993, 'The development of British Iron Age coinage', *Numismatic Chronicle* 153, 31–63

Haselgrove, C 1995, 'Potin coinage in Iron Age Britain, Archaeology and Chronology', *Gallia* 52, 117–27

Haselgrove, C 2005, 'Early potin coinage in Britain: an update' in P de Jersey (ed), *Celtic Coinage: New Discoveries, New Discussion,* British Archaeological Reports (International Series) 1532, 17–27

Hassall, M W C 1976, 'Britain in the Notitia' in R Goodburn and P Bartholomew (eds), 103–17

Hassall, M W C and Tomlin, R O 1979, 'Roman Britain in 1978', *Britannia* x, 339–56

Haverfield, F J and Wheeler, R E M 1932, 'Military elements of Roman Kent' in *Victoria History of the Counties of England: Kent, Vol III*, (reprinted 1974), Folkestone and London, 13–59

Hawkes, C F C and Hull, M R 1947, *Camulodunum, First Report on the excavations at Colchester, 1930–1939*, Reports of the Research Committee of the Society of Antiquaries of London XIV, Oxford

Hawkes, S C 1961, 'The Jutish Style A. A study of Germanic animal art in southern England in the fifth century', *Archaeologia* xcviii, 29–74

Hawkes, S C 1968, 'The physical geography of Richborough' in B W Cunliffe, 224–31

Hawkes, S C 1969, 'Early Anglo-Saxon Kent', *Archaeological Journal* cxxvi, 186–92

Hawkes, S C 1973, 'The dating and social significance of the burials in the Polhill cemetery' in B Philp, 186–214

Hawkes, S C 1974, 'Some recent finds of Late Roman buckles', *Britannia* v, 386–93

Hawkes, S C 1982, 'Anglo-Saxon Kent *c* 425–725' in P E Leach (ed), *Archaeology in Kent to AD 1500*, Council for British Archaeology Research Report 48, London, 64–78

Hawkes, S C 1987, 'Some early Anglo-Saxon objects from east Kent', *Archaeologia Cantiana* cv, 1–8

Hawkes, S C and Dunning, G C 1961, 'Soldiers and settlers in Britain, fourth to fifth century', *Medieval Archaeology* 5, 1–70

Hawkes, S C and Dunning, G C 1962–3, 'Krieger und Siedler in Britannien Während des 4. und 5. Jahrhunderts', *Bericht der Römisch-Germanischen Kommission* 43–4, 155–231

Hayes, J W 1997, *Handbook of Mediterranean Roman Pottery*, British Museum Press

Heather, P 2006, *The Fall of the Roman Empire: A New History of Rome and the Barbarians,* Oxford

Heighway, C 1987, *Anglo-Saxon Gloucestershire*, Gloucestershire County Library

Heinrich, L 1992, *The Magic of Linen: Flax Seed to Woven Cloth,* Victoria, Canada

Henig, M 1977, 'A cube from Kingscote, Gloucestershire', *Antiquaries Journal* lvii, 320–1

Henig, M 1978, *A corpus of Roman engraved gemstones from British sites*, British Archaeological Reports (British Series) 8, second edition, Oxford

Henig, M 1994, *Classical gems. Ancient and modern intaglios and cameos in the Fitzwilliam Museum, Cambridge*, Cambridge

Henig, M 1995a, *The Art of Roman Britain*, London

Henig, M 1995b, 'The Roman finger rings' in K Blockley *et al*, 1000–5

Henig, M 2002, *The Heirs of King Verica. Culture and Politics in Roman Britain*, Stroud

Henig, M 2004, 'Remaining Roman in Britain AD 300–700: The evidence of portable art' in R Collins and J Gerrard, *Debating Late Antiquity in Britain AD 300–700*, British Archaeological Reports (British Series) 365, Oxford, 13–23

Henig, M and Morris, E 2002, 'Pendant' in S Davies, P Bellamy, M Heaton and P Woodward, *Excavations at Alington Avenue, Fordington, Dorchester, Dorset, 1984–87,* Dorset Natural History and Archaeological Society Monograph 15, Dorchester, 180–1

Henkel, F 1913, *Die römischen fingerringe der Rheinlande*, Berlin

Hermann, J (ed) 1985, *Die Slawen in Deutschland,* Berlin

Hermet, F 1934, *La Graufesenque (Condatomago)*, Paris, reprint Marseille 1979

Hicks, A 1998, 'Excavations at Each End, Ash, 1992', *Archaeologia Cantiana* cxviii, 91–172

Hicks, A 2008, 'The Roman settlement' in P Bennett *et al*, 101–278

Hicks, A and Houliston, M forthcoming, 'Excavations at Whitefriars, Canterbury, 1999–2003'

Hicks, A and Shand, G forthcoming, 'Excavations at Wincheap Roundabout, Canterbury'

Higgins, D A 1997, 'A possible Roman buckle plate from Betchworth', *Surrey Archaeological Collections* 84, 190–1

Hills, C 1981, 'Barred zoomorphic combs of the Migration period' in V I Evison (ed), 96–125

Hills, C and Penn, K 1981, *The Anglo-Saxon Cemetery at Spong Hill, North Elmham. Part 2*, East Anglian Archaeology 11, Gressenhall

Hills, C, Penn, K and Rickett, R 1987, *The Anglo-Saxon Cemetery at Spong Hill, North Elmham. Part 4*, East Anglian Archaeology 34, Gressenhall

Hirst, S M 1985, *An Anglo-Saxon Inhumation Cemetery at Sewerby, East Yorkshire,* York University Archaeological Publications 4, York

Hobbs, R 1996, *British Iron Age Coins in the British Museum*, London

Holbrook, N and Bidwell, P T 1991, *Roman Finds from Exeter*, Exeter Archaeological Reports 4, Exeter

Holbrook, N and Thomas, A 1996, 'The Roman and Early Anglo-Saxon settlement at Wantage, Oxfordshire. Excavations at Mill Street, 1993–4', *Oxoniensia* 61, 109–79

Holman, D 2005, 'Iron Age coinage and settlement in East Kent', *Britannia* xxxvi, 1–54

Holt, R 1988, *The Mills of Medieval England*, Oxford

Howe, M, Perrin, J and Mackreth, D 1980, *Roman Pottery from the Nene Valley: A Guide*, Peterborough City Museum Occasional Paper 2, Peterborough

Hughes, M 1980, 'The analysis of Roman tin and pewter ingots' in W Oddy (ed), *Aspects of Early Metallurgy,* British Museum Occasional Paper 17, London, 41–50

Hull, M R and Hawkes, C F C 1987, *Corpus of ancient brooches in Britain: Pre-Roman bow brooches*, British Archaeological Reports (British Series) 169, Oxford

Hunter, J 1997, *A Persona for the Northern Picts*, Inverness

Hunter, L 1967, 'The living past in the Appalachias of Europe: watermills in Southern Europe', *Technology and Culture* 8, 446–66

Hutchinson, A and Andrews, P forthcoming, 'Excavations on a Late Bronze Age, Anglo-Saxon and medieval settlement site at Manston Road, Ramsgate, 1995–1997' in P Andrews, K Egging Dinwiddy, C Ellis, A Hutchinson, C Philpotts, A B Powell and J Schuster, *Kentish sites and sites of Kent. A miscellany of four archaeological excavations*, Wessex Archaeology Report 24, Salisbury

Iles, R 1997, 'Roman finds from the Winchester district', *Winchester Museum Service Newsletter* 27, 5

Isings, C 1957, *Roman Glass from Dated Finds*, Groningen

Jackson, D and Ambrose, T 1978, 'Excavations at Wakerley, Northants', *Britannia* ix, 115–242

Jackson, D and Dix, B 1987, 'Late Iron Age and Roman settlement at Weekley, Northants', *Northamptonshire Archaeology* 21, 41–93

Jackson, R and Potter, T 1996, *Excavations at Stonea, Cambridgeshire 1980–85*, London

Jacobi, H 1912, 'Römische Cetreidemuhlen', *Saalburg Jahrbücher* 3, 75–95

Jacobi, L 1897, *Das Romerkastell Saalburg bei Homburg Vor der Hohe*, Saalburg

Jacono, L 1938, 'La ruota idraulica di Venafro', *L'ingegnere* 12, 850–3

James, S 1984, 'Britain and the late Roman army' in T Blagg and A King (eds), *Military and Civilian in Roman Britain. Cultural Relationships in a Frontier Province*, British Archaeological Reports (British Series) 136, Oxford, 161–86

James, S 1988, 'The *fabricae*: state arms factories of the Late Roman Empire' in J C Coulston (ed), 257–331

Jarrett, M and Wrathmell, S 1981, *Whitton: An Iron Age and Roman Farmstead in South Glamorgan*, Cardiff

Jenkins, F 1949, 'Miscellaneous notes: recent excavations in the Canterbury district: Sturry', *Archaeologia Cantiana* lxii, 145–6

Jenkins, F 1956, 'A Roman tilery and two pottery kilns at *Durovernum*, (Canterbury)', *Antiquaries Journal* 36, 40–56

Jenkins, F 1960, 'Two pottery kilns and a tilery of the Roman period at Canterbury (*Durovernum Cantiacorum*)', *Archaeologia Cantiana* lxxiv, 151–61

Jenkins, F 1965, 'Wingham' (p lvii) in 'Annual Report for the Year 1965', *Archaeologia Cantiana* lxxx, xlii–lxii

Jenkins, F 1966, 'Wingham' (p lxvi) in 'Annual Report for the Year 1966', *Archaeologia Cantiana* lxxxi, xlii–lxvi

Jenkins, F 1967, 'Wingham – the Roman villa' in 'Annual Report for the year 1967', *Archaeologia Cantiana* lxxxii, xlii–lxii

Jenkins, F 1968, 'Roman Britain in 1967', *Journal of Roman Studies* lviii, 205–6

Jenkins, F 1984, 'The re-excavation of the Roman 'villa' at Wingham', *Archaeologia Cantiana* c, 87–99

Jessup, R F and Taylor, M V 1932, 'Topographical Index' in W Page (ed), *A History of Kent, III*, Victoria History of the Counties of England (reprinted 1974), Folkestone and London, (reprinted 1974), Folkestone and London, 144–75

Johansen, Ø 1980, 'En rundskulptur av tre fras Skjeberg I Ostfold', *Viking* 44, 69–90

Johns, C 1996, *The Jewellery of Roman Britain. Celtic and Classical Traditions*, London

Johns, C forthcoming, 'The small finds from the burials' in *Excavations in the Castle Street and Stour Street Areas*, The Archaeology of Canterbury VI, forthcoming

Johns, C and Potter, T 1983, *The Thetford Treasure. Roman Jewellery and Silver*, London

Johnson, S 1983, *Burgh Castle: Excavations by Charles Green, 1958–61*, East Anglian Archaeology 20, Gressenhall

Jones, B and Mattingly, D 1990, *An Atlas of Roman Britain*, Oxford

Jones, C and Sherlock, D 1996, 'Early decorated Roman spoons from London', in J Bird, M Hassall and H Sheldon (eds), *Interpreting Roman London. Papers in memory of Hugh Chapman*, Oxford, 165–76

Jones, D M (ed) 1980, *Excavations at Billingsgate Buildings 'Triangle', Lower Thames Street, 1974*, London and Middlesex Archaeological Society Special Paper 4, London

Jones, M and Rodwell, W 1973, 'The Romano-British pottery kilns at Mucking', *Essex Archaeology and History* (3rd series) V, 13–47

Jones, R 1975, 'The Romano-British farmstead and its cemetery at Lynch Farm, near Peterborough', *Northhamptonshire Archaeology* 10, 94–137

Keller, E 1971, *Die Spätrömischen Grabfunde in Südbayern*, Münchener Beiträge zur Vor- und Frühgeschichte 14, Munich

Keller, P T 1989, 'Quern production at Folkestone, South-East Kent: an interim note', *Britannia* xx, 193–200

Kent, J P C 1978, *Roman Coins*, London

Kilbride-Jones, H 1980, *Zoomorphic Penannular Brooches*, Reports of the Research Committee of the Society of Antiquaries of London XXXIX, London

King, D 1986, 'Petrology, dating and distribution of querns and millstones. The results of research in Bedfordshire, Buckinghamshire, Hertfordshire and Middlesex', *Bulletin of the Institute of Archaeology of the University of London* 23, 65–126

Kinsley, A G 1989, *The Anglo-Saxon Cemetery at Millgate, Newark-on-Trent, Nottinghamshire*, Nottingham Archaeology Monograph 2, Nottingham

Kinsley, A G 1993, *Broughton Lodge: excavations on the Romano-British settlement and Anglo-Saxon cemetery at Broughton Lodge, Willoughby-on-the-Wolds, Nottinghamshire 1964–8*, Nottingham Archaeology Monograph 4, Long Eaton

Kirk, J R 1949, 'Bronzes from Woodeaton, Oxon', *Oxoniensia* xiv, 1–45

Klein, W G 1928, 'Roman temple at Worth, Kent', *Antiquaries Journal* viii, 76–86

Knight, J K 1996, 'Late Roman and post-Roman Caerwent. Some evidence from metalwork', *Archaeologia Cambrensis* 145, 35–66

Kruger, B (ed) 1978, *Die Germanen*, Berlin

Langouet, L and Meury, J L 1976, 'Les éléments de la machinerie gallo-romaine d'Alet', *Les Dossier du Centre Regional Archéoligique d'Alet,* 113–25

Leach, P 1982, *Ilchester vol I: excavations 1974–1975*, Western Archaeological Trust Monograph 3, Bristol

Leahy, K A 1984, 'Late Roman and early Germanic metalwork from Lincolnshire' in N Field and A White (eds), *A Prospect of Lincolnshire*, Lincoln

Lee, J E 1862, *Isca Silurum: or, an illustrated catalogue of the Museum of Antiquities at Caerleon*, London

Leeds, E T and Riley, M 1942, 'Two early Saxon cemeteries at Cassington, Oxon', *Oxoniensia* 7, 61–70

Leigh, D 1984, 'Ambiguity in Anglo-Saxon Style I art', *Antiquaries Journal* lxiv, 34–42

Levine, M 1982, 'The use of crown height measurements and eruption-wear sequences to age horse teeth' in B Wilson *et al*, 223–50

Lewis, M J T 1997, *Millstone and hammer: the origins of water power*, Hull

Lewis, P and Jones, G 1971, 'The Dolaucothi Gold Mines', *Bonner Jahrbücher* 171, 288–300

Linklater, A and Sparey-Green, C 2004, 'Ickham Court Farm, Ickham', *Canterbury's Archaeology 2002–2003*, 22–4

Lloyd-Morgan, G 1994, 'Worked bone' in S Cracknell and C Mahany, *Roman Alchester: Southern extramural area 1964–1966 excavations. Part 2: Finds and Discussion*, Roman Alchester Series I, Council for British Archaeology Research Report 97, 211–16

Lucas, A T 1953, 'The horizontal mill in Ireland', *Journal of the Royal Society of Antiquaries of Ireland* lxxxiii, 1–36

Lucas, A T 1969, 'A horizontal mill at Knocknagranshy, Co Limerick', *North Munster Archaeological Journal* xii, 12–22

Lucas, A T 1986, 'A two-chute horizontal mill at Newtown, Co Tipperary', *North Munster Archaeological Journal* xxviii, 16–27

Ludowici, W 1927, *Stempel-Namen und Bilder Römischer Topfer Legions Ziegel-Stempel Formen von Sigillata-und anderen Gefassen aus meinen Ausgrabungen in Rheinzabern, 1901–1914*, Munchen

Lyne, M A B 1994a, 'Late Roman hand-made wares in South-east Britain', unpublished doctoral thesis, University of Reading

Lyne, M A B 1994b, 'Late Roman helmet fragments from Richborough', *Journal of the Roman Military Equipment Studies* 5, 97–105

Lyne, M A B forthcoming a, 'The pottery from 2–8 High Street, Staines'

Lyne, M A B forthcoming b, 'The Iron Age and Roman pottery' in D J Tomalin (ed), *The Wootton-Quarr Survey*

Lyne, M A B and Jefferies, R S 1979, *The Alice Holt/Farnham Roman Pottery Industry*, Council for British Archaeology Research Report 30, London

MacAdam, R 1856, 'Ancient Water-Mills', *Ulster Journal of Archaeology*, iv, 6–15

Macdonald, P, Manning, W and Riddler, I 2008, 'The small finds' in A Hicks, 190–233

MacGregor, A 1978, *Roman Finds from Skeldergate and Bishophill*, The Archaeology of York 17/2, York

MacGregor, A 1985, *Bone, Antler, Ivory and Horn. The Technology of Skeletal Materials since the Roman Period*, London

MacGregor, A 1995, 'Roman and Early Medieval Bone and Antler Objects' in D Phillips and B Heywood (eds), *Excavations at York Minster. Volume 1. From Roman Fortress to Norman Cathedral*, London, 414–27

MacGregor, A and Bollick, E 1993, *A Summary Catalogue of the Anglo-Saxon Collections (non-ferrous) in the Ashmolean Museum*, British Archaeological Reports (British Series) 230, Oxford

Mackreth, D F 1988, 'Excavation of an Iron Age and Roman enclosure at Werrington, Cambridgeshire', *Britannia* xix, 59–151

Mackreth, D 1996, *Orton Hall Farm: A Roman and Early Anglo-Saxon Farmstead*, East Anglian Archaeology 76, Gressenhall

Macpherson-Grant, N 1980a, 'The Pottery' in P Bennett *et al*, 274–89

Macpherson-Grant, N 1980b, 'Archaeological work along the A2: 1966–1974', *Archaeologia Cantiana* xcvi, 133–83

Macpherson-Grant, N 1991, 'Excavations at Stonar, near Sandwich', *Canterbury's Archaeology 1989–1990*, 46–8

Magnus, B 1997, 'The firebed of the serpent: myth and religion in the Migration period mirrored through some golden objects' in L Webster and M Brown, 194–207

Maltby, M 1979, *The animal bones from Exeter 1971–1975*, Sheffield

Manby, T G 1966, 'Anglian objects from Wensleydale', *Yorkshire Archaeological Journal* 41, 340–4

Manley, J 2002, *AD 43: The Roman Invasion of Britain*, Stroud

Manning, W 1964, 'A mill pivot from Silchester', *Antiquaries Journal* xliv, 1, 38–40

Manning, W 1972, 'The iron objects' in S S Frere, 163–95

Manning, W 1976, *Catalogue of Romano-British Ironwork in the Museum of Antiquities Newcastle upon Tyne*, Newcastle upon Tyne

Manning, W 1985, *Catalogue of the Romano-British Iron Tools, Fittings and Weapons in the British Museum*, London

Manning, W and Painter, K S 1967, 'A Roman iron window-grille from Hinton St Mary, Dorset', *British Museum Quarterly* 31, 122–30

Manning, W, Price, J and Webster, J 1995, *Report on the Excavations at Usk 1965-1976. The Small Finds*, Cardiff

Marchant, D 1990, 'Roman weapons in Great Britain, a case study: spearheads, problems in dating and typology', *Journal of Roman Military Equipment Studies* 1, 1–6

Margary, I D 1955, *Roman Roads in Britain: 1*, London

Margary, I D 1967, *Roman Roads in Britain*, (revised edition), London

Margary I D 1973, *Roman Roads in Britain*, (third edition), London

Margeson, S 1993, *Norwich Households: The Medieval and Post-Medieval Finds from Norwich Survey Excavations 1971–1978*, East Anglian Archaeology 58, Gressenhall

Marsden, P R V 1967, *A ship of the Roman period, from Blackfriars, in the City of London*, London

Marsh, G 1981, 'London's samian supply and its relationship to the development of the Gallic samian industry' in A S Anderson and A C Anderson (eds), *Roman pottery research in Britain and north–west Europe. Papers presented to Graham Webster*, British Archaeological Reports (International Series) 13, Oxford, 173–238

Martin, R 1965, 'Wooden figures from the source of the Seine', *Antiquity* xxxix, 156, 247–52

Martin, E 2000, 'Archaeology in Suffolk 1999', *Proceedings of the Suffolk Institute of Archaeology and History* 39, 495–531

Martin, E 2001, 'Archaeology in Suffolk 2000', *Proceedings of the Suffolk Institute of Archaeology and History* 40, 65–108

Marzinzik, S 2003, *Early Anglo–Saxon belt buckles (late 5th to early 8th centuries AD)*, British Archaeological Reports (British Series) 357, Oxford

McIwain, A 1980, 'Quernstones' in D M Jones (ed), 132–3

McWhirr, A D 1981, *Roman Gloucestershire*, Gloucester

McWhirr, A, Viner, L and Wells, C 1982, *Romano–British Cemeteries at Cirencester*, Cirencester

Meadows, I 1992, 'Three Roman sites in Northamptonshire: excavations by E Greenfield at Bozeat, Higham Ferrers and Great Oakley between 1961 and 1966', *Northamptonshire Archaeology* 24, 77–94

Meaney, A 1964, *A Gazetteer of early Anglo–Saxon Burial Sites*, London

Meates, G W 1987, *Lullingstone Roman Villa. Vol II. The wall paintings and finds*, Maidstone

Merten, J 1987, 'Die Esra–Miniatur des Codex Amiatinus. Zu Autorenbild und Schreibgerät', *Trierer Zeitschrift* 50, 301–19

Miles, A E W and Grigson, C 1990, *Colyer's Variation and Diseases of the Teeth of Animals*, Cambridge

Millett, M 2007, 'Roman Kent' in J H Williams (ed), 135–84

Milne, G 1985, *The Port of London* 7, 79–86

Monaghan, J 1987, *Upchurch and Thameside Roman Pottery: A ceramic Typology, first to third centuries A D*, British Archaeological Reports (British Series) 173, Oxford

Moore, J W 1975, 'Hastings town and parks: new archaeological finds', *Sussex Archaeological Collections* 112, 167–72

Morgan, P 1983, *Domesday Book 1, Kent*, Chichester

Morin-Jean, J 1913, *La verrerie en Gaule sous l'empire Romain*, Paris

Moritz, L A 1958, *Grain mills and flour in Classical Antiquity*, Oxford

Mould, Q 1990, 'The leather objects' in S Wrathmell and A Nicholson (eds), 231–5

Mould, Q 1991, 'Metalwork' in P S Austen, *Bewcastle and Old Penrith. A Roman Outpost Fort and a Frontier Vicus Excavations, 1977-78*, Cumberland and Westmorland Antiquarian and Archaeological Society Research Series, 6, 185–212

Mould, Q 1997a, 'Leather' in T Wilmott, 326–41

Mould, Q 1997b, 'Ironwork' in P Booth (ed), 82–9

Neal, D S 1974, *The Excavation of the Roman Villa in Gadebridge Park, Hemel Hempstead 1963–8*, London

Neal, D S 1989, 'The Stanwick Villa, Northants: an interim report on the excavations of 1984–88', *Britannia* xx, 149–68

Neal, D S, Wardle, A and Hunn, J 1990, *Excavation of the Iron Age, Roman and medieval settlement at Gorehambury, St Albans*, English Heritage Archaeological Report No 14, London

Neville, R C 1856, 'Description of a remarkable deposit of Roman antiquities of iron, discovered at Great Chesterford, Essex in 1854', *Archaeological Journal* xiii, 1–13

Niblett, R 1985, *Sheepen: an early Roman industrial site at Camulodunum*, Council for British Archaeology Research Report 57, London

Nielsen, L C 1986, 'Omgård. The Viking Age water-mill complex. A provisional report on the 1986 excavations', *Acta Archaeologica* 57, 177–210

Northover, P 1992, 'Material issues in the Celtic coinage' in M Mays (ed), *Celtic Coinage: Britain and Beyond. The Eleventh Oxford Symposium on Coinage and Monetary History*, British Archaeologcal Reports (British Series) 222, Oxford, 235–99

Oldenstein, J 1976, 'Zur Austustung römischer Auxiliareinheiten Studien zu Veschlagen und Sieral an der Austrung der römischen Auxiliareinheiten des Obergermanisch-Raetischen Limesgebietes aus dem zweiten und dritter Jahrhundert n.Chr', *Bericht der Römischen Germanischen Kommision* 57, 49–284

Ogilvie, J D 1968, 'The Fleet Causeway' in B W Cunliffe, 37–40

Ogilvie, J D 1977, 'The Stourmouth-Adisham water-main trench', *Archaeologia Cantiana* xciii, 91–124

O'Connor, T P 1988, *Bones from the General Accident Site, Tanner Row*, The Archaeology of York 15/2, London

Ó Floinn, R 2001, 'Patrons and politics: art, artefact and methodology' in M Redknap, N Edwards, S Youngs, A Lane and J Knight (eds), *Pattern and Purpose in Insular Art*, Oxford, 1–14

O'Reilly, J P 1902-4, 'Some further notes on ancient horizontal water-mills, native and foreign', *Proceedings of the Royal Irish Academy* 24, 55–84

Ó Ríordáin, S P 1941, 'The excavation of a large earthen ringfort at Garranes, Co Cork', *Proceedings of the Royal Irish Academy* 47c, 77–150

Orton, C R 1975, 'Quantitative pottery studies: some progress, problems and prospects', *Science and Archaeology* 16, 30–5

Oswald, F 1936–7, *Index of figure-types on terra sigillata ('samian ware')*, Annals Archaeology and Anthropology 23.1–4, 24.1–4, University of Liverpool

Ottaway, P 1992, *Anglo-Scandinavian Ironwork from 16–22 Coppergate*, The Archaeology of York 17/6, York

Ottaway, P 1993, *English Heritage Book of Roman York*, London

Owles, E and Smedley, N 1967, 'Two Belgic cemeteries at Boxford', *Proceedings of the Suffolk Institute of Archaeology* xxxi, 88–107

Painter, K S 1977, *The Mildenhall Treasure*, London

Palmer, R E 1926/7, 'Notes on Some Ancient Mine Equipment and Systems', *Institution of Mining and Metallurgy Transactions* 36, 299–310

Panton, F H 1994, 'The Canterbury–Richborough Roman road: a review', *Archaeologia Cantiana* cxiv, 1–16

Parfitt, K 1980, 'A probable Roman villa on the Sandwich by-pass', *Kent Archaeological Review* 60, 232–48

Parfitt, K 1999, 'Two La Tène brooches: Waldershare and Preston-by-Wingham' in 'Researches and Discoveries', *Archaeologia Cantiana* cxix, 376–8

Parfitt, K 2000, 'A Roman occupation site at Dixon's Corner, Worth', *Archaeologia Cantiana* cxx, 107–48

Parfitt, K 2004, 'Assessment of Excavations at 'Eden Roc', Bay Hill, St Margaret's at Cliffe', unpublished CAT archive report, November

Parfitt, K 2006, 'The Roman Villa at Minster-in-Thanet, Part 3: The Corridor House, Building 4', *Archaeologia Cantiana* cxxvi, 115–33

Parfitt, K 2007a, 'Report on Evaluation Trenching near Castle Farm, Richborough, June and September 2007', unpublished CAT Archive Report, November

Parfitt, K 2007b, 'Excavations at Ringlemere Farm, Woodnesborough, 2002–2006', *Archaeologia Cantiana* cxxvii, 39–55

Parfitt, K 2008, 'Report on discoveries by the Canterbury Archaeological Trust, at Lowton, Richborough (Trench 11)', unpublished archive report, January

Parfitt forthcoming a, 'A temple complex at Worth, Kent'

Parfitt forthcoming b, 'Report on Test-Pitting across the Sandown Area, 2005–2006', unpublished CAT Sandwich Survey Report 10

Parsons, A W 1936, 'A Roman water-mill in the Athenian Agora', *Hesperia* 5, 70–90

Partridge, C 1981, *Skeleton Green. A late Iron Age and Romano-British site*, Britannnia Monograph Series 2, London

Payne, G 1897, 'The Roman villa at Darenth', *Archaeologia Cantiana* xxii, 49–84

Payne, S 1973, 'Kill off patterns in sheep and goats: the mandibles from Asvan Kale', *Anatolian Studies* 23, 281–303

Peacock, D P S 1980, 'The Roman millstone trade: a petrological sketch', *World Archaeology* 12, 43–53

Peacock, D P S 1987, 'Iron Age and Roman quern production at Lodsworth, West Sussex', *Antiquaries Journal* 67, 61–85

Peacock, D P S and Williams, D F 1986, *Amphorae and the Roman Economy*, London

Peal, C 1967, 'Romano-British plates and dishes', *Proceedings of the Cambridge Antiquarian Society* lx, 19–37

Pearce, J W E 1929, 'Roman coins from Icklingham', *Numismatic Chronicle* 5th series 9, 319–27

Penhallurick, R D 1986, *Tin in Antiquity*, London

Pescheck, C 1978, *Die Germanischen Bodenfunde der römischen Kaiserzeit in Mainfranken*, Münchener Beiträge zur Vor- und Frühgeschichte 27, Munich

Philp, B 1973, *Excavations in West Kent, 1960–1970*, Kent Archaeology Research Reports 2, Dover

Philp, B 1981, *The Excavation of the Roman Forts of the Classis Britannica at Dover, 1970–1977*, Third Research Report in the Kent Monograph Series, Dover

Philp, B 1989, *The Roman House with Bacchic Murals at Dover*, Gloucester

Philp, B 2005, *The Excavation of the Roman Fort at Reculver, Kent*, Tenth Report in the Kent Monograph Series, Dover

Pirling, R 1974, 'Das Römische-fränkische Gräberfeld von Krefeld Gellep 1960–63', *Germanische Denkmäler der Völkerwanderungszeit Ser B Die fränkischen Alterümer des Rheinlandes* 8, Berlin

Pitt-Rivers, A H L-F 1887, *Excavations in Cranborne Chase, near Rushmore*, Vol I, London

Pitt-Rivers, A H L-F 1892, *Excavations in Cranborne Chase, near Rushmore*, Vol III, London

Pollard, A M 1983, 'X-ray fluorescence analysis of the Appleford hoard of Romano-British pewter', *Journal of the Historical Metallurgy Society* 17/2, 83–90

Pollard, R J 1987, 'The pottery' in S S Frere *et al*, 284–98

Pollard, R J 1988, *The Roman Pottery of Kent*, Kent Archaeological Society Monograph Series 5, Maidstone

Pollard, R J 1995, 'Mid and Late Roman Pottery' in K Blockley *et al*, 690–736

Porter, S 1997, 'Small finds' in S Buteux, 96–132

Potter, T W and Trow, S D 1988, 'Puckeridge-Braughing, Hertfordshire. The Ermine Street Excavations 1971–72. The Late Iron Age and Roman Settlement', *Hertfordshire Archaeology* 10, 1–191

Powell Cotton, P H G and Pinfold, G F 1939, 'The Beck Find. Prehistoric and Roman site on the foreshore at Minnis Bay', *Archaeologia Cantiana* li, 194–203

Price, J 1979, 'The glass' in H S Gracie and E G Price, 'Frocester Court Roman villa: second report 1968–77: the courtyard', *Transactions of the Bristol and Gloucestershire Archaeological Society* 97, 37–46

Price, J 1982, 'The glass' in G Webster and L Smith, 'The excavation of a Romano-British rural establishment at Barnsley Park, Gloucestershire, 1961–1979: part II: c AD 360–400', *Transactions of the Bristol and Gloucestershire Archaeological Society* 100, 174–85

Price, J and Cool, H E M 1983, 'Glass from the excavations of 1974–6' in A E Brown *et al*, 115–24

Pröttel, P M 1988, 'Zur Chronologie der Zwiebelknopffibeln', *Jahrbuch des Römisch-Germanischen Zentralmuseums Mainz*, 35.1, 347–72

Rady, J 1989, 'The Roman countryside' in 'Channel Tunnel Excavations', *Canterbury's Archaeology 1987–1988*, 45–69

Rady, J 1999, 'Nos 7–8 Gordon Road', *Canterbury's Archaeology 1996–1997*, 9

Rahtz, P A 1981 'Medieval milling' in D W Crossley (ed), *Medieval Industry*, Council for British Archaeology Research Report 40, 1–15

Rahtz, P A and Bullough, D 1977, 'The parts of an Anglo-Saxon mill', *Anglo-Saxon England* 6, 15–37

Rahtz, P A and Greenfield, E 1977, *Excavations at Chew Valley Lake, Somerset*, London

Rahtz, P A and Meeson, R 1992, *An Anglo-Saxon Watermill at Tamworth. Excavations in the Boleridge Street area of Tamworth, Staffordshire in 1971 and 1978,* Council for British Archaeology Research Report, 83, London

RCHM 1928, *An Inventory of the Historical Monuments in London 3: Roman London,* London

Reddé, M and Schnurbein, S von (eds) 2001, *Alésia. Fouilles et recherches Franco-Allemandes sur les travaux militaires Romains autour du Mont-Auxois (1991–1997), Vol 2, le Matériel*, Paris

Redknap, M 1995, 'Mayen ware from Canterbury' in K Blockley *et al*, 737–40

Reece, R 1989, 'Lympne' in V A Maxfield (ed), *The Saxon Shore A Handbook*, Exeter

Reece, R 1991, *Roman Coins from 140 Sites in Britain*, Cotswold Studies, Vol 4, London

Rees, S E 1979, *Agricultural Implements in Prehistoric and Roman Britain*, British Archaeological Reports (British Series) 69, Oxford

Reusch, W I 1970, 'Kleine, spitzkonische amphoren', *Saalburg Jahrbücher* 27, 54–62

Reynolds, J (ed) 1976, *Libyan Studies: Select papers of the late R G Goodchild*, London

Reynolds, P 2005, 'Levantine amphorae from Cilicia to Gaza: a typology and analysis of regional production trends from the 1st to 7th centuries' in J M Esparraquera, J B Garrigos and M A Ontiveros (eds), *LRCW 1. Late Roman Coarse Wares, Cooking Wares and Amphorae in the Mediterranean: Archaeology and Archaeometry*, British Archaeological Reports (International Series) 1340, 563–612

Richardson, A 2005, *The Anglo-Saxon Cemeteries of Kent*, British Archaeological Reports (British Series) 391, Oxford

Riddler, I 1988, 'Late Saxon or Late Roman? A comb from Pudding Lane', *London Archaeologist* 5, 372–4

Riddler, I 2001, 'The small finds' in M Gardiner, R Cross, N Macpherson-Grant and I Riddler, 'Continental trade and non-urban ports in mid Anglo-Saxon England: Excavations at *Sandtun*, West Hythe, Kent', *Archaeological Journal* clviii, 228–52

Riddler, I 2006, 'Worked whale bone' in K Parfitt, B Corke and J Cotter, *Excavations at Townwall Street, Dover: Excavations 1996*, The Archaeology of Canterbury (New Series) 258

Riddler, I 2008, 'Querns' in P Macdonald *et al*, 203–11

Riddler, I forthcoming a, 'Early and Middle Saxon comb design: the settlement evidence' in I Riddler, N Trzaska-Nartowski and A MacGregor (eds), *Combs and Comb Making*, Council for British Archaeology Research Report, London

Riddler, I forthcoming b, 'Querns' in J Rady (ed), *The Archaeology of the Channel Tunnel UK Terminal Cheriton, near Folkestone, Kent and its environs*, The Archaeology of Canterbury New Series

Riddler, I and Vince, A 2005, 'Late Iron Age Small Finds' in B Bishop and M Bagwell, *Iwade. Occupation of a North Kent Village from the Mesolithic to the Medieval Period*, PCA Monograph 3, London, 80–1

Roach Smith C 1882, 'Retrospective observations respecting a hoard of Roman coins found in the sand hills, near Deal', *Archaeologia Cantiana* xiv, 368–9

Robinson, A H W and Cloet, R L 1953, 'Coastal evolution in Sandwich Bay', *Proceedings of the Geological Society* 64 (Part 2), 69–81

Röder, J 1953, 'Zur Lavaindustrie von Mayen und Volvic (Auvergne)', *Germania* 31, 24–7

Roe, F 1997, 'Worked stone (except flint)' in P Booth (ed), 100–1

Roe, F 2001, 'Worked stone' in P Booth (ed) *Westhawk Farm, Kingsnorth, Ashford, Kent - Archaeological post-excavation assessment report*, Oxford, 55

Roes, A 1958, 'The toothed blades from Chalton', *Antiquaries Journal* 38, 244–5

Roes, A 1963, *Bone and Antler Objects from the Frisian Terp Mounds*, Haarlem

Rogers, G B 1974, *Poteries sigillées de la Gaule Centrale, I: les motifs non figurés*, Gallia Supplément 28, Paris

Rogers, N S H 1993, *Anglian and other finds from Fishergate*, The Archaeology of York 17/9, London

Rogerson, A 1977, *Excavations at Scole 1973*, East Anglian Archaeology 5, Norwich

Rogerson, A and Dallas, C (eds) 1984, *Excavations in Thetford 1948–59 and 1973–80*, East Anglian Archaeology 22, Gressenhall

Romeuf, A M 1978, 'Un Moulin à eau gallo-romain aux Martres-de-Veyre (Puy-de-Dome)', *Revue d'Auvergne* 92, 23–41

Rudling, D and Gilkes, O J 2000, 'Important archaeological discoveries made during the construction of the A259 Rustington Bypass, 1990', *Sussex Archaeological Collections* 138, 15–28 and microfiche

Ruprectsberger, E M 1978–9, *Die römischen Bein- und Bronzenadeln aus den Museen Enns und Linz*, Linzer Archäologische Forschungen 8–9, Linz

Rynne, C 1988, 'The archaeology and technology of the horizontal-wheeled watermill, with special reference to Ireland', unpublished doctoral thesis, University College, Cork

Rynne, C 1989, 'The introduction of the vertical watermill into Ireland. Some recent archaeological evidence', *Medieval Archaeology* 33, 21–31

Rynne, C 1992a, 'Milling in the 7th century: Europe's earliest tide mills', *Archaeology Ireland* 6, no 2, 22–4

Rynne, C 1992b, 'The early Irish watermill and its continental affinities', *Medieval Europe 1992, Pre-printed papers* 3, York, 21–5

Schiøler, T and Wikander, Ö 1983, 'A Roman water-mill in the Baths of Caracalla', *Opuscula Romana* xiv, 47–64

Schmid, E 1972, *Atlas for the Identification of Animal Bones*, Amsterdam

Scott, I R 1990, 'Ironwork from Well 1' in S Wrathmell and A Nicholson (eds), 197–206

Serjeantson, D 1991, 'Rid Grasse of Bones: a taphonomic study of the bones from midden deposits at the Neolithic and Bronze Age site of Runnymede, Surrey', *International Journal of Osteoarchaeology* 1, 73–89

Shaw, R 1994, 'The Anglo-Saxon cemetery at Eccles: a preliminary report', *Archaeologia Cantiana* cxii, 165–88

Shephard-Thorn, E R 1988, *Geology of the County around Ramsgate and Dover*, Memoir Geological Survey, London

Shepherd, J D 1978, 'A preliminary study of the base designs of mould-blown glass bottles', unpublished dissertation, University of London

Shepherd, J D 1985, 'Roman Glass' in B Cunliffe and P Davenport, *The Temple of Sulis Minerva at Bath*, Oxford University Committee for Archaeology, Monograph 7, Oxford, 161–4

Shepherd, J D 1986, 'The glass' in A McWhirr (ed), *Houses in Roman Cirencester*, Cirencester, 117–21

Shepherd, J D 1995, 'The glass vessels' in K Blockley *et al*, 1227–59

Sherlock, D 1982, 'The spoons' in W J Wedlake, 201–4

Sherlock, D 1987, 'The silver spoons' in G W Meates, 61–2

Sherlock, D 2000, 'The backs of Roman spoons in Britain', *Britannia* xxxi, 365–70

Shortt, H de S 1959, 'A provincial Roman spur from Longstock, Hants, and other spurs from Roman Britain', *Antiquaries Journal* 39, 61–77

Sim, D 1997, 'Roman chain-mail: experiments to reproduce the techniques of manufacture', *Britannia* xxviii, 359–71

Simpson, C J 1976, 'Belt-buckles and strap-ends of the Later Roman Empire: a preliminary survey of several new groups', *Britannia* vii, 192–223

Simpson, F G 1976, *Watermills and military works on Hadrian's Wall: Excavations in Northumberland, 1907–1913*, Kendal

Small, A and Buck, R 1994, *The Excavations of San Giovanni di Ruoti. Vol I: the villas and their environment*, Toronto

Smith, D J 1960, 'A Roman silver pin from Halton Chester', *Archaeologia Aeliena* xxxviii, 231

Smith, D J 1978, 'Regional aspects of the winged-corridor villa in Britain' in M Todd (ed), *Studies in the Romano-British Villa*, Leicester, 117–47

Sommer, M 1984, *Die Gürtel und Gürtelbeschläge des 4. und 5. Jahrhunderts im römischen Reich*, Bonner Hefte zur Vorgeschichte, Nr 22, Rheinische Friedrich-Wilhelms-Universität, Bonn

Spain, R J 1977, 'Millstones and querns from Ickham, Kent', unpublished archive report

Spain, R J 1984a, 'The second-century Romano-British mill at Ickham, Kent', *History of Technology* 9, 143–80

Spain, R J 1984b, 'Romano-British watermills', *Archaeologia Cantiana* c, 101–28

Spain, R J 1984c, 'Millstones from Barton Court Farm' in D Miles (ed), *Archaeology at Barton Court Farm, Abingdon, Oxford*, Council for British Archaeology Research Report 50, London, microfiche 5, A13–5: B5

Spain, R J 1992, 'Roman water-power: a new look at old problems', Imperial College of Science and Technology, unpublished doctoral thesis

Spain, R J 1996, 'The millstones' in D F Mackreth, 105–13

Spain, R J 2004, *A Possible Roman Tide-Mill*, http://www.kentarchaeology. ac/authors/rspain.html

Sparey-Green, C 1984, 'A Late Roman buckle from Dorchester, Dorset', *Britannia* xv, 260–4

Sparey-Green, C 1987, *Excavations at Poundbury, Volume I: The Settlements*, Dorset Natural History and Archaeological Society Monograph Series 7, Dorchester

Sparey-Green, C 2005, 'Roman enclosures in the Little Stour Valley at Ickham and Well', *Archaeologia Cantiana* cxxv, 243–57

St John Hope, W H and Fox, G E 1898, 'Excavations on the site of the Roman city at Silchester, Hants, in 1897', *Archaeologia* lvi, 103–26

Stanfield, J A and Simpson, G 1958, *Central Gaulish Potters*, London

Stead, I M 1976, 'The earliest burials of the Aylesford Culture' in G de G Sieveking, I H Longworth and K E Wilson (eds), *Problems in Economic and Social Archaeology*, London, 401–16

Stead, I M 1980, *Rudston Roman Villa*, Yorkshire Archaeological Society

Stead, I M and Rigby, V 1986, *Baldock, the excavation of a Roman and Pre-Roman settlement 1968–72*, Britannia Monograph Series 7, London

Stead, I M and Rigby, V 1989, *Verulamium: the King Harry Lane site*, English Heritage Archaeological Report 12, London

Steensberg, A 1952, *Bondehuse og vandmøller i Danmark gennem 2000 år. (Farms and water-mills in Denmark during 2000 years)*, Copenhagen

Steensberg, A 1978, 'The horizontal water mill: a contribution to its early history', *Prace i Materiały Muzeum Archeologicznego i Etnograficznego w Łodzi, Seria Archeologiczna* 25, 345–56

Still, M 1994, 'Parallels for the Roman lead sealing from Smyrna found at Ickham, Kent', *Archaeologia Cantiana* cxiv, 347–56

Stow, S 1995, 'The Jutish Pottery from East of the Marlowe Theatre' in K Blockley *et al*, 825–7

Strong, D 1966, *Greek and Roman Gold and Silver Plate*, London

Strong, D 1968, 'The Monument' in B W Cunliffe, 40–73

Struve, K W 1975, *Germanen Machen Sich Bilder Von Göttern, Notice du Catalogue - Historiche Museen der Stadt Köln, Römer-Illustrierte Köner, das Neu Bild Der Alten Welt (1945–75)*, Köln

Stuiver, M and Reimer, P 1986, 'A computer program for radiocarbon age calculation', *Radiocarbon* 28, 1022–30

Stuiver, M, Reimer, P J, Bard, E, Beck, J W, Burr, G S, Hughen, K A, Kromer, B, McCormac, F G, van der Plicht, J and Spurk, M 1998, 'INTCAL98 radiocarbon age calibration, 24,000-0 cal BP', *Radiocarbon* 40, 1041–84

Summerfield, J 1997, 'The small finds' in T Wilmott, 269–361

Sumpter, A B 1990, 'Pottery from Well 1' in S Wrathmell and A Nicholson (eds), 235–45

Sutherland, C H V 1974, *Roman Coins*, London

Sutton, R 1998, *Analysis of Roman pewter tableware and debris from Ickham, Kent*, Ancient Monuments Laboratory Report 32/1998, London

Swift, E 2000, *Regionality in Dress Accessories in the Late Roman West*, Monographies Instrumentum 11, Millau

Symonds, R P 1992, *Rhenish Wares, Fine Dark Coloured Pottery from Gaul and Germany*, Oxford University Committee Archaeological Monograph 23, Oxford

Symonds, R P 1999, 'Pottery and Small Finds' in D Lakin, 'A Romano-British Site at Summertown Way, Thamesmead, London Borough of Bexley', *Archaeologia Cantiana* cxix, 325–30

Syson, L 1965, *British Water-Mills*, London

Tatton-Brown, T 2001, 'The evolution of 'Watling Street' in Kent', *Archaeologia Cantiana* cxxi, 121–33

Taylor, M 1932, 'Country houses and other buildings' in W Page (ed), *A History of Kent, III*, Victoria History of the Countries of England (reprinted 1974), Folkestone and London, 102–26

Thomas, S 1960, 'Studien zu den germanischen Kämmen der römischen Kaiserzeit', *Arbeits- und Forschungsberichte zur Sächsischen Bodendenkmalpflege*, 8, 54–215

Tildesley, J 1971, 'Roman pottery kilns at Rettendon', *Essex Journal* 6, 35–50

Tilson, P 1973, 'A Belgic and Romano-British site at Bromham', *Bedfordshire Archaeological Journal* 8, 23–66

Tomalin, D J 1987, *Roman Wight. A guide catalogue*, Newport, Isle of Wight

Tomlin, R S O 1976, '*Notitia Dignitatum omnium, tam civilium quam militarium*' in R Goodburn and P Bartholomew, 189–209

Tomlin, R S O 1992, 'The Roman carrot amphora and its Egyptian provenance', *Journal of Egyptian Archaeology* 78, 307–12

Tomlinson, F W 1961, 'Sandwich' (p liii) in 'Annual Reports for the years 1960 and 1961', *Archaeologia Cantiana* lxxvi, xlii–lxxvi

Trent, E M 1975, 'Examination of bearing from Saxon watermill', *Historical Metallurgy* 9, 1, 19–25

Trett, R 1983, 'Roman bronze 'grooved pendants' from East Anglia, Norfolk', *Archaeology* xxxviii, part III, 219–34

Trovò, R 1996, 'Canalizzazioni lignee e ruota idraulica di età romana ad Oderzo (Treviso)', *Quaderni di archeologia del Veneto* 12, 119–34

Tuffreau-Libre, M and Jacques, A (eds) 1994a, *La Ceramique du Bas-Empire en Gaule Belgique et dans les regions voisines*, Lille

Tuffreau-Libre, M and Jacques, A 1994b, 'La ceramique du Bas-Empire à Arras (Pas-de-Calais)' in M Tuffreau-Libre and A Jacques 1994a, 9–20

Tylecote, R F 1962, *Metallurgy in Archaeology*, London

Tyler, S 1992, 'Anglo-Saxon settlement in the Darent valley and environs', *Archaeologia Cantiana* cx, 71–81

Valentin, J and Robinson, S 2002, 'Excavations in 1999 on land adjacent to Wayside Farm, Nursteed Road, Devizes', *Wiltshire Archaeological and Natural History Magazine* 95, 147–213

van Arsdell, R D 1989, *Celtic Coinage of Britain*, London

van Driel-Murray, C 1987, 'Roman footwear: a mirror of fashion and society' in D E Friendship-Taylor, J M Swann and S Thomas, *Recent Research in Archaeological Footwear*, Association of Archaeological Illustrators and Surveyors Technical Paper 8, 32–42

van Driel-Murray, C 1993, 'The leatherwork' in C van Driel-Murray, J P Wild, M Seaward and J Hillam, *Preliminary reports on the Leather, Textiles, Environmental Evidence and Dendrochronology*, Vindolanda Research Reports New Series, Volume III, Hexham, 1–75

van Driel-Murray, C 1995a, 'Nailing Roman shoes', *Archaeological Leather Group Newsletter* 1, 6–7

van Driel-Murray, C 1995b, 'Leather shoes and sandals' in W Manning *et al*, 114–21

van Driel-Murray, C 2001, 'Footwear in the north-western provinces of the Roman Empire' in O Goubitz, C van Driel-Murray and W Groenman-van Waateringe, *Stepping through Time*, Westchester (CA), 337–76

van Es, W A and Verwers, W J H 1980, *Excavations at Dorestad 1. The Harbour: Hoogstraat I*, Nederlandse Oudheden 9, Amersfoort

Vatin, C 1972, 'Wooden sculpture from Gallo-Roman Auvergne', *Antiquity* xlvi, 181, 39–42

Volpert, H-P 1997, 'Die römischer Wassermühle einer villa rustica in München-Perlach', *Bayerische Vorgeschichtsblatter* 62, 243–78

Wacher, J 1995, *The Towns of Roman Britain*, second edition, London

Wainwright, G J 1979, *Gussage All Saints: an Iron Age Settlement in Dorset*, Department of the Environment Archaeological Reports 10, London

Wallenberg, J K 1934, *The Place-names of Kent*, Uppsala

Walton Rogers, P 1997, *Textile Production at 16–22 Coppergate*, The Archaeology of York 17/11, London

Wardle, A 1990, 'The artefacts other than coins, pottery and glass vessels' in D S Neal *et al*, 113–68

Watson, J 2000, 'Organic material associated with metalwork from Ickham, Kent', English Heritage Ancient Monuments Laboratory Report 78/2000

Watts, D J 1988, 'Circular lead tanks and their significance for Romano-British Christianity', *Antiquaries Journal* 68, 210–22

Watts, M 2002, *The Archaeology of Mills and Milling*, Stroud

Webster, G 1958, 'The Roman military advance under Ostorius Scapula', *Archaeological Journal* cxv, 49–98

Webster, G 1981, 'The excavation of a Romano-British rural establishment at Barnsley Park, Gloucestershire, 1961–1979. Part I: AD 140–360', *Transactions of the Bristol and Gloucestershire Archaeological Society* 99, 21–77

Webster, J 1975, 'Bone and antler' in B W Cunliffe, 215–25

Webster, J 1992, 'The objects of bronze' in D R Evans and V M Metcalf (eds), 103–63

Webster, J 1995, 'Surveying and measuring equipment' in W Manning *et al*, 243–5

Webster, L and Backhouse, J 1991, *The Making of England. Anglo-Saxon art and culture AD 600–900*, London

Webster, L and Brown, M 1997, *The Transformation of the Roman World*, London

Wedlake, W J 1982, *The excavation of the shrine of Apollo at Nettleton Wilts (1956–71)*, Reports of the Research Committee of the Society of Antiquaries of London XI, London

Weeks, J 1982, 'Roman carpentry joints: adoption and adaptation' in S McGrail (ed), *Woodworking techniques before AD 1500*, British Archaeological Reports (British Series) 129, Oxford, 157–68

Weitzmann, K 1979, *Age of Spirituality. Late Antique and Early Christian Art. Third to Seventh Century*, New York, Metropolitan Museum

Welsby, D A 1982, *The Roman Military Defence of the British Provinces*, British Archaeological Reports (British Series) 101, Oxford

West, S E 1985, *West Stow: the Anglo-Saxon village*, East Anglian Archaeology 24, Gressenhall

West, S E 1990, *West Stow, Suffolk: the prehistoric and Romano-British occupations*, East Anglian Archaeology 48, Gressenhall

Wheeler, R E M (Mrs) 1931, 'The preliminary excavations of Verulamium, 1930, *St Albans and Hertfordshire Architectural and Archaeological Society Transactions*, 15–24

Wheeler, R E M 1943, *Maiden Castle, Dorset*, Reports of the Research Committee of the Society of Antiquaries of London XII, Oxford

Wheeler, R E M 1946, *London in Roman Times*, London Museum Catalogues 3, London

Wheeler, R E M and Wheeler, T V 1932, *Report on the Excavation of the prehistoric, Roman and post-Roman Site in Lydney Park, Gloucestershire*, Reports of the Research Committee of the Society of Antiquaries of London IX, Oxford

White, R H 1988, *Roman and Celtic Objects from Anglo-Saxon Graves*, British Archaeological Reports (British Series) 191, Oxford

Whiting, W, Hawley, W and May, T 1931, *Report on the excavation of the Roman cemetery at Ospringe, Kent*, Reports of the Research Committee of the Society of Antiquaries of London VIII, Oxford

Wickenden, N P 1988, 'Some military bronzes from the Trinovantian civitas' in J C Coulston (ed), 234–56

Wikander, Ö 1985a, 'Mill-channels, weirs and ponds. The environment of ancient watermills', *Opuscula Romana* 15, 149–54

Wikander, Ö 1985b, 'Archaeological evidence for early water-mills, an interim report', *History of Technology* 11, 151–79

Wikander, Ö (ed) 2000a, *Ancient Water Technology*, Technology and Change in History 2, Leiden

Wikander, Ö 2000b, 'The water-mill' in Ö Wikander (ed), 371–400

Wild, J P 1970, *Textile Production in the Northern Roman Provinces*, Cambridge

Williams, D F and Tomber, R 2007, 'Egyptian amphorae in Britain' in S Marchand and A Marangou (eds), *Amphores D'Egypte: de la casse époque à l'époque Arabe*, Cahiers de la Céramique Egyptienne 8, Vol II, 643–50

Williams, J H (ed) 2007, *The Archaeology of Kent to AD 800*, Kent History Project 8, Woodbridge

Williams, W J 1933, 'The Roman ditch at Heronbridge', *Journal of the Chester Archaeological Society* 30, 111–7

Wilmott, A and Rahtz, S P Q 1985, 'An Iron Age and Roman settlement outside Kenchester (*Magnis*), Herefordshire. Excavations 1977–1979', *Transactions of the Woolhope Naturalists' Field Club*, 45.1: 36–185 and microfiche, with a report on the pottery by R S Tomber

Wilmott, T 1997, *Birdoswald. Excavations of a Roman Fort on Hadrian's Wall and its Successor Settlements: 1987–92*, English Heritage Archaeological Report 14, London

Willson, J 1989, 'The coarse pottery' in B Philp, 76–98

Willson, J 2002, 'Land north of Saltwood Tunnel', *Canterbury's Archaeology 1999–2000*, 35–8

Wilson, A I 2000, 'Drainage and sanitation' in Ö Wikander (2000a), 151–79

Wilson, A I 2001a, 'The water-mills on the Janiculum', *Memoirs of the American Academy at Rome* 45, 219–46.

Wilson, A I 2001b, 'Water-mills at Amida: Ammianus Marcellinus 18.8.11', *Classical Quarterly* ns 51.1, 231–6

Wilson, A I 2002, 'Machines, power and the ancient economy', *Journal of Roman Studies* xcii, 1–32

Wilson, A I 2003, 'Late antique water-mills on the Palatine', *Papers of the British School at Rome* 71, 85–109

Wilson, B, Grigson, C and Payne, S 1982, *Ageing and Sexing Animal Bones from Archaeological Sites*, British Archaeological Reports (British Series) 109, Oxford

Wilson, D M 1976, *The Archaeology of Anglo-Saxon England*, London

Wilson, M 1968, 'Other objects of bronze, silver, lead, iron, bone and stone' in B W Cunliffe, 93–109

Wilson, M 1983, 'The Pottery' in S S Frere and S Stow, 192–309

Wilson, M 1984, 'Amphorae' in S S Frere, 201–66

Wilson, M 1995, 'Pottery from Canterbury Excavation Committee Sites', in K Blockley *et al*, 682–9

Wilson, P R 1989, 'Aspects of the Yorkshire signal stations' in V A Maxfield and M J Dobson (eds), *Roman frontier studies 1989 Proceedings of the XVth international congress of Roman frontier studies,* Exeter, 142–7

Wilson, P R 2002, *Cataractonium: Roman Catterick and its Hinterland. Excavations and Research 1958–1997*, Council for British Archaeology Research Report 129, York

Winbolt, S E 1925, 'Roman Villa, Folkestone', *Archaeologia Cantiana* xxxvii, 209–10

Winbolt, S E 1926, 'The Roman Villa at Folkestone', *Archaeologia Cantiana* xxxviii, 45–50

Windell, D, Chapman, A and Woodiwiss, J 1990, *From Barrows to Bypass: Excavations at West Cotton, Raunds, Northamptonshire, 1985–1989*, Northampton

Wrathmell, S and Nicholson, A (eds) 1990, *Dalton Parlours: Iron Age Settlement and Roman Villa*, Yorkshire Archaeology 3, Wakefield

Young, C J 1975, 'Excavations at Ickham', *Archaeologia Cantiana* xci, 190–1

Young, C J 1977, *Oxfordshire Roman Pottery*, British Archaeological Reports (British Series) 43, Oxford

Young, C J 1980, The pottery' in B W Cunliffe, 275–83

Young, C J 1981, 'The Late Roman water-mill at Ickham, Kent, and the Saxon Shore' in A Detsicas (ed), *Collectanea Historica. Essays in memory of Stuart Rigold*, Maidstone, 32–40

Youngs, S M (ed) 1989, *The Work of Angels: Masterpieces of Celtic Metalwork, 6th–9th centuries*, London

Youngs, S M 1995, 'A penannular brooch from near Calne, Wiltshire', *Wiltshire Archaeology and Natural History Magazine* 88, 127–30

Youngs, S M 2007, 'Britain, Wales and Ireland: holding things together' in K Jankulak and J M Wooding (eds), *Ireland and Wales in the Middle Ages*, Dublin, 80–101

Ypey, J 1969, 'Zur Tragweise frühfränkischer Gürtelgarnituren auf Grund niederlandischer Befunde', *Berichten van de Rijksdienst voor het Oudheidkundig Bodemonderzoek* 19, 89–117

Zienkiewicz, J D (ed) 1986, *The Legionary Fortress Baths at Caerleon. Volume Two: The Finds*, Cardiff

Zurowski, K 1973, Methoden zum Weichmachen von Geweih und Knochen in frühslawischen Werkstätten, *Berichten über den II Internationalen Kongress für Slawische Archäologie*, Berlin, 483–90

Zurowski, K 1974, Zmiekczanie porozy i kosci stosowane przez wytworcow w starozytnosci i we wczesnym sredniowiecze, *Acta Universitatis Nicolai Copernici, Archaeologi*, 4, 3–23

INDEX

Abingdon, Oxfordshire
  Barton Court Farm 214
    millstones 283
air photographs 8, 20, 29, 34, 41, 71, 322, 330, 332, 335, 337, 347
Aisne valley, France 154
Alcester, Warwickshire 177
Alchester, Oxfordshire 227
Aldborough, Norfolk 151
Aldington, Kent 326, 330, 336
Alfriston, Sussex 193
Alkham valley 328
Alt Friesack, Germany 217
Amiens, France
  Roman pottery 135, 343
Andernach, Germany 248
Anglo-Saxon 13, 70, 71, 107, 109, 309
  cemeteries 9, 309, 332, 345
  finds 142, 152, 157, 158, 176, 183, 186, 206, 214, 215, 228, 231, 232, 303, 306, 307, 308, 311, 321, 326, 344, 347
  millstones 283
  watermills 67, 68, 289, 345
animal bone
  bird 311
  dog 314
  cattle 33, 301, 311–318
  donkey 318
  fox 314
  goat 312
  goose 314
  horse 311–318
  pig 311–313, 315, 317
  sheep 301, 311–318
  whale 314, 315, 340
antler, antler-working 70, 115, 178, 187, 188, 196, 201, 203, 213, 225, 301, 340
Anton, river, Hampshire 63
anvil 289, 340
Apulum, Dacia 159
Arras, France 93, 111, 112, 135, 190, 343
Ashford and District Archaeological Society 3
Assemblage 1 16, 95, 100, 322
Assemblage 2 24, 95, 303, 322

Assemblage 3 29, 95
Assemblage 4 95–96, 122, 314
Assemblage 5 96, 145
Assemblage 6 96–99, 122, 138, 265, 322, 323
Assemblage 7 26, 99, 323
Assemblage 8 28, 99, 323
Assemblage 9 25, 99–100, 100, 122
Assemblage 10 41, 95, 100–101, 324
Assemblage 11 41, 92, 100–102, 101, 126, 134, 212, 324, 340
Assemblage 12 103, 324
Assemblage 13 70, 103–108, 122, 126, 211, 217, 235, 265, 314, 324, 325, 326
Assemblage 14 29, 109
Assemblage 15 29, 109
Assemblage 16 29, 109
Assemblage 17 24, 109, 324
Assemblage 18 33, 109–110, 122, 126, 128, 307, 324, 340
Assemblage 19 40, 110, 122, 127, 305, 314, 324
Assemblage 20 39, 110–112, 122, 127, 193, 212, 305
Assemblage 21 112–115, 122, 127, 128, 129
Assemblage 22 32, 115–117, 115–118, 128, 138, 324, 343
Assemblage 23 33, 117, 122, 211, 306
Assemblage 24 31, 117–118, 325
Assemblage 25 31, 118, 314
Assemblage 26 31, 118, 148, 307
Assemblage 27 118–119
Asthall, Oxfordshire 299
Athens, Greece
  Agora mill 60, 62, 277, 283, 341
  bearing block 67, 287

Baldock, Hertfordshire 142, 171, 175, 176
Ballachulish, Argyll 215
Barbegal, France
  watermill 63, 279
Barham Downs, Kent 328, 329
Barnsley Park, Gloucestershire 176, 245, 248
Barrington, Cambridgeshire 175, 176
barrow (see also ring-ditch) 322, 325, 345
Barton on Humber, Lincolnshire 152
Bath, Somerset 239, 248
bath building 8, 20, 336, 337
Bayeux, France 203

bearings, bearing blocks (*see* mills)
Benwell, Tyne and Wear 132, 262
Betchworth, Surrey 154
Bifrons, Kent 193, 308
Birchington, Kent
  millstone 330
Birdlip, Gloucestershire 172
Bishops Stortford, Hertfordshire 135
Blackhole Dyke 6, 71, 345
Blean, Kent 328, 330
Bletsoe, Bedfordshire 152
Bokerley Dyke, Dorset 201, 206
bone-working 142, 317
Bonn, Germany 156
Borough Hill, Northamptonshire 257
Boulonnais, France 245
Boxford, Suffolk 171
Braak, Germany 217
Brading, Isle of Wight
  Roman pottery 135
Bradwell, Buckinghamshire 155
Brancaster, Norfolk 205
Brede, river 328
brewing 218
Bridge, Kent 326, 330
Britton Farm, Ickham
  Roman building 8, 275, 331, 335, 337
Broddenbjerg, Denmark 217
Bronze Age 15
Brougham, Cumbria 189
Burgheim, Germany 156
Burgh Castle, Norfolk
  Roman pottery 104, 135, 137, 343
burials 13, 68–70, 318–319, 347
  Burial A 16, 69, 318, 322, 325, 343
  Burial B 16, 69, 119, 206, 207, 211, 325
  Burial C 70, 319, 325
  Burial 902 42, 69, 325
  Burial 903 42, 69, 318
  Burial 905 70, 318
  cremation 16, 338, 343
butchery 311, 312, 316–317

Caerleon, Gwent 148, 149, 151, 152, 183, 188, 189, 205, 228,
    245
Caerwent, Monmouthshire 152, 155, 283
Caesar, landing 54 BC 327
Caister-on-Sea, Norfolk 197, 297
Calcott, Kent 328
Camerton, Somerset 240
Canterbury (*Durovernum Cantiacorum*), Kent 303, 321, 326,
    328, 329, 336, 342, 343
  brooches 171, 176
  Burgate 331
  combs 213
  defences 342
  glass 245, 248
  manufacturing centre 240, 268, 272, 275, 338
  Marlowe excavations 142, 196

military equipment 154, 158, 159
  pins 187
  querns 223, 251, 255
  Ridingate 330, 339
  St Martin's hoard 193
  St Stephen's kiln 268
  Worthgate 330
Canterbury Archaeological Society 2
Capel-le-Ferne, Dover, Kent 315
Carlisle, Cumbria
  carrot amphorae 121
Carnuntum, Austria 245
Cassington, Oxfordshire 184, 185
Castleford, West Yorkshire 132, 175, 189
Ceramic Assemblages, *see* Assemblage
Chalton, Hampshire 297
Chamalières, France 217
Chartham, Kent 262
Chedworth, Gloucestershire 297
Chelmsford, Essex 91, 111, 135, 148
Chester, Cheshire 149
Chesters, Northumberland 63, 65, 66, 132, 183, 184
Chew Park, Somerset 248, 282
Chichester, West Sussex 112, 171, 175, 176, 248
Childeric 119
Chislet, Kent 328
Christianity 203, 217, 218, 343
Cirencester, Gloucestershire 185, 248
Classis Britannica 338
Claudian invasion 43 327
Cloontycarthy, County Cork 283
coins 24, 25, 73–84, 190, 193, 195, 215, 218, 303, 322, 323,
    324, 325, 326, 334, 337, 341, 343
  Area 2 304
  Area 3 304
  Area 4 305
  Area 5 305
  Area 7 306
  Area 8 306
  Area 10 306
  Area 12 307
  Area 14 307
  Area 16 307
  hoard 62, 74, 78, 79, 80, 83, 325, 333, 341
  Mill 1 338, 339
  Mills 2 and 3 3
  Mill 4 343
Colchester, Essex 148, 151, 154, 155, 156, 157, 158, 165, 171,
    173, 175, 176, 177, 181, 187, 189, 197, 199, 201, 215,
    218, 220, 245, 248, 249, 255, 295, 304, 306
Coldham Common, Cambridgeshire 291
Cologne, Germany 92, 132
comitatenses 159, 342
Corbridge, Northumberland 165
Cottington lakes 336
cremation cemetery 8, 9
Crickley Hill, Gloucestershire 155
cropmark 2, 9, 329, 332
Croydon, Surrey 152

Crumlin, County Dublin 183
Culpho, Suffolk 157
Cyrenaica, Libya 342

Dacia (Romania) 151, 283
　Dobeta, Dacia 151
Dagenham, Essex 215
Dalheim, Luxembourg 157
Dalton Parlours, West Yorkshire 209, 210, 212, 228
Dasing, Bavaria 65
daub 31, 35, 38, 117
Deal, Kent 119, 138, 328
　Deal spit (Tenant's Hills) 327
　Dixon's Corner 327, 331, 336
　Sand Hills 327
Dolaucothi, Carmarthenshire 287
Domesday survey 71, 344, 345
Dorchester, Dorset 155, 193
Dorchester-on-Thames, Oxfordshire 92, 157, 214
Dorestad, Netherlands 258
Dour, river 328, 329, 330
Dover (*Portus Dubris*), Kent 87, 138, 220, 228, 328, 329, 330,
　　335, 336, 337, 338
　Buckland Anglo-Saxon cemetery 308
　Shore fort 87, 138, 342
Droxford, Hampshire 176
Dunkirk, Kent 328
Dunstrete 330
Dura-Europos, Syria 244
dyeing 218

Each End, Ash, Kent 158, 331, 336, 340
Ebbsfleet hill 327
Eccles, Kent 268, 275, 308, 309
Eifel, Germany 91, 135, 343
Elfgen, Kreis Neuss, Germany
　watermill 59
Elham valley 326, 330, 335
enclosures 1, 9, 12, 15, 16, 21, 24, 25–26, 28, 32, 33, 39, 42,
　　72, 99, 322, 323, 324, 325, 326, 330, 332, 333, 334, 337,
　　340, 347
environmental remains 258, 322, 341
En Chaplix, Avenches, Switzerland 61, 63, 65, 66
Exeter, South Devon 173

fabrica xii, 159
Fairford, Gloucestershire 176
farming 322, 337, 341, 344
Faversham, Kent 193, 328
ferry 327, 330
Fimber, Yorkshire 176
fish 34, 142, 328
Fishbourne, West Sussex 121, 175, 228
flax (*Linum usitatissimum L*) 298, 341
　flax processing 33, 276, 297, 297–298, 305, 321, 324, 325,
　　340, 343
Fleet Farm, near Richborough, Kent 329, 331, 334
Folkestone, Kent
　Dolland's Moor, burial 325

East Wear Bay quarries 251, 254
　Greensand quarry 251
　St Eanswythe shrine 218
　villa 330, 336
Frocester, Gloucestershire 156, 248
Fullerton, Wherwell, Hampshire 279
　bearing block 287
　watermill 50, 55, 59, 63, 282, 283
fulling 218, 337
Furfooz, Belgium 152

Gadebridge, Hertfordshire 165, 181
galena 213, 300
Garranes, County Cork 185
Gorehambury, St Albans, Hertfordshire 151
Goss Hall, Ash, Kent 331
Great Chesterford, Essex 63, 176, 283
Great Oakley, Northamptonshire 172
Great Stour 6, 326, 327, 328, 329, 330, 337
Grovely Wood, Wiltshire 203
Grove Ferry, Kent 329, 330, 337
Guadalquivir valley, Baetica 120
Gussage All Saints, Dorset 175
gynaecea 159

Hadrian's Wall 44, 62, 63, 65, 131, 183, 221, 287
Hagendorn, Switzerland
　watermill 59, 60, 65, 66, 67
Halton Chesters, Northumberland 184
Haltwhistle Burn Head, Hadrian's Wall
　watermill 44, 60, 63, 65, 66, 68, 282, 287
Harrietsham, Kent 251, 309
Harwell, Berkshire 156
Hastings, East Sussex 135
Hauxton Mill, Cambridge 248
hearth (*see also* metal-working) 16, 21, 103, 228
Hersden, Kent 325, 328, 330, 336, 337
Hethersett, Norfolk 173
Higham marshes, Kent 88
Highstead, Kent 325, 330, 336, 342
High Down, Sussex 144
Hod Hill, Dorset 144, 145
Holstein, Switzerland 264
Howletts, Kent 193
Hoxne, Suffolk 190, 193
human bone (*see also* burials) 42
hut (*see also* sunken-featured building) 12, 13, 78, 79, 83, 103

Icklingham, Suffolk 189, 190, 218
Ilchester, Somerset 175
Inworth, Essex 91
Ipswich 193
Ireland
　early medieval mills 66, 67, 283
　medieval millstones 289
　pins 183, 184, 185
Iron Age
　occupation 8, 74, 322
　trackway 331

Isle of Wight 87, 96, 135
Ivy Chimneys, Essex 297

Janiculum Hill, Rome
  watermill 55, 57, 59, 62, 67, 279
jewellery manufacture 321, 324

Kenninghall, Norfolk 176
Kingscote, Gloucestershire 190
Kingsholm, Gloucestershire 142
Kingsteignton, Devon 215
Kingston, Surrey 112
Kingston Down, Kent 193, 329, 330
Kingsworthy, Hampshire 176

Lackford, Suffolk 215
Lagore, County Meath 215
Lankhills, Winchester, Hampshire 107, 119, 145, 154, 155, 156,
      157, 177, 178, 181, 189, 190, 199, 201, 203, 206, 225,
      248
leather-working 107, 142, 212, 293, 294, 340
Les Allieux, France 130
Les Martres de Veyre, Auvergne, France 59, 91, 121, 128
Lezoux, France 91, 122, 127, 129, 131, 132
limitanei 342
Littlebourne, Kent 9, 71, 331, 332, 335, 337, 345
Little Island, Cork 67
Little Stour river x, 1, 2, 4, 5, 6, 7, 8, 9, 10, 18, 20, 21, 26, 42,
      43, 57, 71, 72, 321, 322, 325, 326, 327, 328, 331, 333,
      335, 336, 337, 345, 347, 348
Londesborough pin 185
London 88, 89, 152, 213, 220, 225, 232, 239, 254, 260, 268,
      298, 327, 331
  Bishopsgate 244
  Blackfriar's wreck 63
  Moorfields 245
  Roman pottery 88, 89, 135
  Roman tile 275, 268
  Shadwell 92
Long Wittenham, Oxfordshire 176
Lösnich, Germany 60
Loveden Hill, Lincolnshire 215
Lowton, Thanet, Kent 327, 331
Lullingstone, Kent 176, 228, 239, 248
Lydden valley 327, 328, 330, 336, 342
Lydney, Gloucestershire 176, 203
Lyminge, Kent 326, 335
Lympne (*Portus Lemanis*), Kent 87, 134, 135, 137, 328, 329,
      330, 336, 342
Lyons, France 82, 188

Magdalensberg, Austria 220, 221
Maiden Castle, Dorset 157, 175
Maidstone, Kent
  Maidstone Museum 89, 91, 218
  Mount Roman villa 270
Margam, West Glamorgan 183, 184
Margate, Kent
  Roman pottery 138
  Tivoli Park Avenue 330

Margidunum, Nottinghamshire 148
Maryport, Cumbria 156
Maydensole Farm, Dover 330
Medway, river 91, 218, 309, 328
metal-detecting 3, 4, 8, 73, 76, 77, 78, 178, 207
metal-working 33, 41, 45, 71, 159, 220, 240, 289, 291, 293,
      298–301, 321, 323, 325, 339, 340, 342, 347
  blacksmith, smithing 41, 42, 103, 227, 289, 291, 306, 307,
      324, 340, 354
  bloom 298
  bronze casting 159, 164
  copper-working 40
  crucible 104, 300, 325
  hammerscale 33, 41, 71, 103, 107, 109, 110, 119, 305, 324,
      325, 326
  hearth 42, 97, 99, 264, 298, 306, 307
  iron-working 142
  lead-working 40, 142, 195, 242, 300–301, 325
  pewter-working 324
  scrap bronze 241
  slag 325, 339
midden 39, 89, 101, 135
Mildenhall, Suffolk 175, 176, 193
military
  presence 137, 138–140, 141, 209, 223, 249, 251, 254, 303,
      305, 321, 342–343
  equipment 142–168, 305, 307
mills
  Mill 1 45–47
  Mill 2 47–54, 55–57
  Mill 3 47–49, 54–57
  Mill 4 58–62
  bearings 47, 50, 55, 57, 59, 63, 283, 285–289
  mill-race 43, 47, 48, 49, 50, 52, 54, 55, 56, 57, 58, 59, 60, 61,
      62, 65, 66, 95, 96, 103, 138, 285, 324, 326
    head-race 43, 44, 45, 48, 55, 58, 60, 61, 65, 323, 337, 338,
      339, 341
    tail-race 29, 44, 45, 47, 48, 57, 65, 66, 67, 71, 283, 323, 324,
      325, 326
  penstock 55, 60
  scour pit 29, 55, 70, 83, 103
  sluice gate 4, 54, 58, 59, 61, 62, 63, 322
  tide mill 45–47
  water-wheel 47, 54, 55, 57, 58, 59, 60, 61, 62, 66, 279, 283
mill pond 62, 71
Milton-next-Sittingbourne, Kent 193, 328
Minster, Kent
  Abbey Farm 330
Minster Lovell, Oxfordshire 156
Monkton, Kent 201, 218, 223, 251, 255, 330, 336
Morett, County Laois 68
Morning Thorpe, Norfolk 176
Mucking, Essex 111, 157, 176
München-Perlach, Bavaria 65

Nailbourne, river 326, 330, 335
Nassington, Cambridgeshire 176
Neolithic occupation 8
Nettleton, Lincolnshire 63, 65, 175, 223, 239, 240
Neuss, Germany 59, 149

Newstead, Roxboroughshire 183, 184, 185
Nor'Nour, Isles of Scilly 173
North Foreland, Thanet 327
North Stream 328
Norwich, Norfolk 248
Notitia Dignitatum 158, 159
Nydam, Denmark 165

Oberdorla, Kr Muhlhausen, Germany 217
Oderzo, Italy
   watermill 65, 66
Omgard, Jutland, Denmark
   early medieval mill 67
Orton Hall Farm, Cambridgeshire 201, 287
Orton Waterville, Cambridgeshire 213
Ospringe, Kent 248
Oudenburg, Netherlands 154
Oxborough, Norfolk 152

palaeochannel 11, 41, 322, 323, 324, 326, 334, 335, 347
peat 8, 15, 20, 39, 41, 42, 44, 70, 71, 72, 322, 326, 347
pendants, lead alloy 40, 107, 111, 141, 167, 190–196, 239, 340, 347
penstock (*see* mills)
Peterborough, Cambridgeshire 175
Pevensey, Sussex 135, 137, 343
Pictish pins 183
Piddington, Northamptonshire 210
Pine Wood, Littlebourne, Kent 329, 331, 335
Pompeii, Italy 245, 293, 294
Poole's Cavern, Buxton, Derbyshire 291, 293
ports 136
   Archer's Low 336
   Dover (*Dubris*) 330, 335, 336, 337, 338
   Each End, Ash 331
   Lympne (*Portus Lemanis*) 330
   Richborough (*Rutupiae*) 6, 321, 327, 331, 335, 336, 338, 339, 342, 343, 344
   Sturry 327, 329
Portchester, Hampshire 89, 96, 116, 117, 137, 159, 176, 177, 203, 248, 297, 301
pottery
   prehistoric
      Iron Age/'Belgic' 24, 95, 347
   Roman
      'Castor box' 103, 110, 113, 119
      Alice Holt ware 88, 89, 96, 100, 101, 110, 112, 116, 135, 137
      amphorae 97, 120–121, 132, 133, 138, 333
      Argonne 84, 89, 91, 103, 105, 109, 110, 111, 114, 117, 121–132, 135, 136, 343
      Cologne white ware 92
      East Sussex Ware 87, 135, 137
      German Marbled Ware 92, 93, 136, 343
      Hadham 89, 92, 95, 110, 135, 343
      Hampshire grog-tempered 87, 96, 135, 137
      Harrold shell-tempered ware 89, 96, 135, 343
      Hoo/North Kent 91
      Mayen ware 85, 91, 112, 135, 343
      mortaria 84, 93, 105, 109, 111, 112, 114, 117, 120, 132, 135, 136, 138, 341
      Moselkeramik 92, 100, 103, 132
      Native Coarse Ware 85, 91, 95, 96, 99, 132
      Nene Valley 92, 93, 96, 101, 114, 135
      New Forest 92, 135
      Overwey/Portchester 89, 96, 116, 117, 137
      Oxfordshire 92, 93, 96, 97, 99, 100, 102, 103, 105, 109, 110, 111, 112, 114, 117, 120, 132, 135, 343
      Pevensey ware 93, 135
      Rettendon 89, 91, 135
      Richborough grog-tempered 85, 96, 99, 112, 117, 135
      samian 84, 91, 93, 95, 96, 97, 100, 103, 105, 109, 111, 114, 117, 119, 121–132, 303, 333
      terra nigra tardive 93
      Thameside 88, 91, 101, 132, 133
      Upchurch ware 91, 97, 100, 132, 133
   Anglo-Saxon 31, 33, 39, 73, 109, 110, 118, 307, 308, 326, 344, 345
      Frisian 101
      Jutish 119, 307
Poundbury, Dorchester, Dorset 175, 188, 201
Preston, Kent 6, 8, 309
   Dearston Farm kiln 8, 9, 18, 88, 89, 91, 116, 135, 334, 338, 343
Pudding Pan Rock, Kent
   samian pottery 132
Pulborough, East Sussex
   lead tank 218

querns 8, 35, 70, 107, 112, 142, 223, 232, 251–255, 277, 279, 281, 283, 285, 338, 347

radiocarbon dating 8, 215, 217
Radlett, Hertfordshire 268
Ralaghan, County Cork 215
Ramsgate, Kent
   Manston Road, sunken-featured building 309
Reculver (*Regulbium*), Kent 328, 329, 330, 338
   Shore fort 159, 342
recycling 339, 340
   amphorae 121
   glass 245
   iron 264
   pewter 218, 242, 300
Reigate, Surrey 268, 275
religious objects (*see also* ritual, shrine, votive) 141, 148, 181, 213, 215–218
Remagen, Germany 245
Richborough (*Rutupiae*), Kent 1, 6, 7, 9, 43, 71, 85, 136, 138, 145, 146, 151, 155, 157, 171, 181, 187, 193, 205, 240, 304, 305, 321, 324, 327, 328, 329, 331, 334, 335, 336, 338, 340, 341, 342, 343, 347
   coinage 73, 74, 82, 303
   pottery 87, 95, 99, 109, 116, 119, 276
   Shore fort 159
ring-ditch 69, 347
Rio Tinto mines, Spain 289
ritual (*see also* votive, religious objects, shrine) 110, 167, 213, 215, 217, 300, 325, 341

Rochester, Kent 138, 342
Rome 62, 82, 83, 158, 193
   Baths of Caracalla 67
   see also Janiculum Hill
Romney Marsh 134
Roos Carr, East Yorkshire 215
Rother, river 328, 329
Rotherley, Wiltshire 206
Rudston, Yorkshire 175
Rushall, Wiltshire 183, 185
Rushbourne Manor, Hoath 330
Ruskington, Lincolnshire 176

Saalburg, Germany 132, 151, 152, 173, 299
Saepinum, Italy
   watermill 67
Saham Toney, Norfolk 148
salt 87, 88, 134, 328, 344
Saltwood, Kent 157, 325, 330, 336, 340, 345
Sandwich, Kent 6, 345
   Archer's Low 327, 336
   Sand Downs 327
   Stonar Bank 327
   villa 331, 336
San Giovanni, Italy
   watermill 59
Sarre Penn, river 328, 330
Scarborough, Yorkshire 188
Scole, Norfolk 175, 211
Seaton, Kent 1, 5, 72, 344, 345
Segontium, Gwynedd 188
Selsey, West Sussex 283
Sewerby, Yorkshire 176
Shakenoak Farm, Oxfordshire 232, 248
Shelford, Broadoak, Canterbury 329, 336, 342
shellfish 328
shoemaking 207, 211
Shore fort 72, 87, 99, 119, 134, 135, 137, 138, 140, 159, 329,
     331, 339, 342
shrine 32, 33, 93, 110, 122, 151, 158, 179, 215, 217, 240, 311,
     336, 342
Silchester, Hampshire 63, 155, 171, 189, 201, 205, 239, 283
Skeleton Green, Puckeridge, Hertfordshire 171, 172, 228
skins, skinning 317
Skjeberg, Ostfold, Norway 217
Sleaford, Lincolnshire 176
sluice gate (*see* mills)
Sources de la Seine, France 217
South Shields, Tyne and Wear 151, 205, 232, 276, 306
Spong Hill, Norfolk 214, 215
Spring Valley, Essex
   watermill 63
Staines, Surrey 88, 133
Stanwick, Northamptonshire 297
Stodmarsh, Kent
   Anglo-Saxon burial 309
Stonea, Cambridgeshire 155
Stone Street 330
Stonham Aspal, Suffolk 155
Stourmouth, Kent 327, 333

Strasbourg-Koenigshoffen, France 248
Street End, Lower Hardres, Kent 330
Sturry, Kent 327, 329, 330, 337
St James de Compostela, Spain 151
St Malo, France 66
St Margaret's at Cliff, Kent
   Anglo-Saxon cemetery 345
St Mary Cray, Kent 214, 308
St Paul's Cray, Kent 119
St Petersburg, Russia
   gold pendants 193
sunken-featured building 3, 28, 308, 309, 336
supply depot 137, 159
Sutton Scotney, Hampshire 137, 159, 335, 338
Swale channel 326, 327
Swarling, Kent 171

Tamworth, Staffordshire
   Anglo-Saxon watermill 68, 289
tank
   lead 215, 217, 218, 347
   wood-lined 32, 33, 73, 324
Thetford, Suffolk 175, 193, 232, 258
tide mill (*see* mills)
tides 6, 8, 9, 45, 47, 327, 328, 329, 336, 337
tile 20, 33, 45, 69, 265–274, 323, 333
Tile Lodge Farm, Sturry, Kent 330
Tillingham, river 328
timbers 3, 18, 20, 26, 29, 45, 47, 54, 60, 62, 66, 67, 95, 103,
     262, 281, 322, 325, 334, 341, 343
   boat timbers 265
   planks 29, 32, 33, 45, 48, 49, 50, 54, 60, 66
   posts 26, 29, 32, 33, 43, 45, 47, 48, 49, 50, 52, 53, 54, 55, 56,
     59, 65, 66, 323
   see also wood, wood-working
Tournai, Belgium
   Roman pottery 118, 326
Towcester, Northamptonshire 176, 189
trade 136, 300, 321, 341, 342
Traprain Law, East Lothian 183
Treignes, Belgium 156
Trier, Germany 82, 91, 122, 127, 128, 129, 156, 205, 215, 244
Tyler Hill, Canterbury, Kent 328

Usk, Monmouthshire 100, 220, 232, 262, 276, 283

Vellaquie, North Uist 184
Venafro, Italy
   watermill 59, 60
Verulamium, Hertfordshire 103, 121, 132, 158, 171, 176, 189,
     227, 228, 248, 297
Vichy, France
   Terre-Franche samian kiln 132
Viken, Norway 193
Villimpenta, Italy 217
Vindolanda, Hadrian's Wall 64, 151, 209
Vindonissa, Switzerland 227
votive (*see also* religious objects, ritual, shrine) 79, 84, 300, 323,
     347

Kent
atured building 309
Northamptonshire 175
rdshire 264
ne and Wear 132
hislet 330
bey, Essex 298
annel 6, 8, 45, 47, 136, 142, 326, 327, 328, 329,
30, 331, 333, 337, 338, 344
Street 328, 329, 331, 335
ield, Suffolk 104
31, 33, 55, 58, 59, 60, 61, 66, 117
32, 33
Chapel, Littlebourne 335
enderton, Kent 3, 8, 18, 275, 333, 334, 335, 337, 338
Horse Marsh 18
Westhawk Farm, Ashford, Kent 328, 329, 330, 336, 338
West Stow, Suffolk 175
Whitfield, Kent
  sunken-featured building 309
Wickhambreaux, Kent 1, 2, 7, 9, 20, 71, 72, 325, 329, 332, 337,
  343, 344, 345
  Supperton Farm 345
Willoughby on the Wolds, Nottinghamshire 176
Willowford, Hadrian's Wall
  watermill 63
Winchester, Hampshire (*see also* Lankhills) 159, 173, 297

Wingham, Kent 8, 308, 309
  Anglo-Saxon cemetery 9
  Roman villa 8, 63, 275, 309, 318, 331, 335, 336, 337, 338,
    345
Wingham, river 2, 5, 6, 8, 10, 15, 16, 18, 20, 72, 328, 331, 333,
    334, 335, 336, 337
Wingham Well, Kent 328
wood, wood-working (*see also* timbers) 20, 26, 28, 29, 41, 66,
    100, 142, 293, 323, 340, 341
  ash (*Fraxinus* sp) 225, 276
  box (*Buxus* sp) 289
  hazel (*Corylus* sp) 258
  maple (*Acer* sp) 217
  oak (*Quercus* sp) 257
Woodchester, Gloucestershire 155
Woodeaton, Oxfordshire 181, 201
Woodhall, Suffolk 213
Woodnesborough, Kent 328, 331
wool 298, 318, 340, 341
Woolaston, Gloucestershire 282
Worth, Kent 138, 139, 331, 336, 342
  temple 138
Wroxeter, Shropshire 131, 148, 173, 183, 184, 185
Wye, Kent 87, 138, 139, 330

York 107, 145, 187, 201, 210, 213, 232, 248

Zugmantel, Germany 151, 173, 175